ANATOMY OF SCOTLAND

ANATOMY
of
SCOTLAND

Editors
Magnus Linklater and Robin Denniston

Chambers

EDINBURGH   NEW YORK

Published 1992 by W & R Chambers Limited
43–45 Annandale Street, Edinburgh EH7 4AZ

British Library Cataloguing in Publication Data

A catalogue record for this book is
available from the British Library

ISBN 0-550-21300-7

Editorial Manager Min Lee
Cover design by Art and Graphics Ltd
Typeset by Hewer Text Composition Services, Edinburgh
Printed in England by Clays Ltd, St Ives plc

CONTRIBUTORS

KEITH AITKEN	Industrial Editor of *The Scotsman*
BRYAN CHRISTIE	Health Correspondent of *The Scotsman*
TORCUIL CRICHTON	a reporter for the *West Highland Free Press* and *Scotland on Sunday*
ROBIN DENNISTON	a former publisher, and a Minister of the Scottish Episcopal Church in Fife
RODDY FORSYTH	a writer, and football correspondent for *BBC Radio Scotland*
PETER JONES	Scottish Political Editor of *The Scotsman*
MAGNUS LINKLATER	Editor of *The Scotsman*
GEORGE ROSIE	a playwright and historian who writes on Scottish affairs for newspapers and television
TREVOR ROYLE	an author and Defence Correspondent for *Scotland on Sunday*
RUTH WISHART	a columnist and feature writer for *The Scotsman*, who broadcasts for the BBC
ALF YOUNG	Economics Editor of *The Herald*

CONTENTS

Foreword

by
Magnus Linklater

This is a book about how Scotland works. It is about who runs it, where power lies, and the way in which that power is exercised. It seeks to define the nature of Scotland's separate character and institutions and to establish the extent to which, in the late 20th century, this diverse and complex place is still a nation apart. At the same time, it confronts some of the myths that go to make up the image that Scotland presents to the world and questions the extent to which they are still valid today.

It does not lay any claim to being a definitive or comprehensive guide to modern Scotland. It is neither intended as a Who's Who nor a learned work of reference. It is, rather, the result of an investigation by a team of writers which has been kept deliberately small, and while our conclusions may not be as personal as those contained in that famous volume, Anthony Sampson's *Anatomy of Britain*, it nevertheless presents a particular view of the country and its institutions.

The members of the team are all journalists who live and work in Scotland and they have approached the task of seeking to understand it in the way they know best – by talking to people. Hundreds of interviews have been conducted, and hours of patient inquiry carried out amongst Scots of all kind, whether in positions of power and influence, or on the receiving end of authority, amongst the professions, in politics, the civil service, the boardroom, the courts, at schools and universities, on the stage and behind the camera.

Throughout these interviews the broad themes we have addressed have been largely the same: how far has the Scotland of today maintained its individuality? Are the decisions which shape our lives made in Scotland or elsewhere? To what extent have the power bases in Westminster and, increasingly, Brussels, eroded the nation state? And how much does all of that still matter to ordinary Scots?

Inevitably, history has played its part in our inquiries, if only to help measure the extent to which the old myths about Scotland's past still colour perceptions today: 'For that', as Robert Louis Stevenson said, 'is the mark of the Scot of all classes; that he stands in an attitude towards the past unthinkable to Englishmen, and remembers and cherishes the memory of his forebears, good or bad; and there burns alive in him a sense of identity with the dead even to the twentieth generation.' That, we rapidly found, is as true today as it was in *Weir of Hermiston*, 100 years ago.

It may help to explain why a majority of Scots still feel as strongly about the issue of self-determination as it apparently ever did. But it may also go some way to explaining why the separate identities of Scotland's politics, education, law, medicine, financial institutions, arts and media have been maintained and sometimes even reinforced in the face of steady pressure from the south. The defence of that separate identity is a matter about which those who administer Scottish institutions feel keenly, but it is also, surprisingly, respected and even encouraged by English politicians and administrators who, far from resenting it, often seem positively to envy it. Indeed, many of the southern incomers who have been given top jobs in Scotland have become the most passionate defenders of the very Scottishness they were suspected of eroding.

Certain broad issues emerge. Politically, Scotland remains a 'restless nation', as dissatisfied with its present constitutional arrangements as it has been so often many times since the late 19th century, yet apparently unable or unwilling to take steps forceful enough to effect dramatic change. This book was conceived before the general election of 1992, but completed in its wake, thus allowing us to analyse the reasons for the electorate's apparent reluctance to seize greater political power for Scotland. Economically and industrially the country has changed dramatically in the post-war years, establishing ever stronger links with Europe, but vulnerable to the vagaries of the world economy as well as to decisions taken outwith the country, and to its dependence on multinational companies whose loyalty may lie elsewhere. That there are dangers ahead for a country whose traditional industrial base has all but vanished is undeniable, but throughout our inquiries we discovered confidence and even optimism, often in the most unexpected places. Culturally, Scotland demonstrates an individuality as assertive as ever, drawing from a strong sense of what it means to be Scottish without descending into some of the more mawkish parochialism of the past.

Scotland is a small country, and in finding out who runs it, we came, time and again, across some familiar figures. Their lines of influence cross and criss-cross, and they are represented at many different levels in Scottish life. It would, on the other hand, be very hard to talk about a Scottish 'establishment'. That small group of powerful men and women is more striking for the variety of their attitudes, and for their individuality, than for their common perceptions. In this they are markedly different from their counterparts in the south, where shared backgrounds, and, perhaps, proximity to the centre of government, forges a far clearer definition of what is meant by the ruling class. The Scottish top brass can be as intransigent as the average citizen, and at least as questioning about the status quo. The notion of clubland, it seems, is alien to the Scottish character save in so far as it may be a guarantee of a decent dram.

In dividing the book into its component parts we have laid ourselves open to inevitable criticism. Some of the subject headings may seem to have been arbitrarily chosen, others to be simply perverse. Why, for instance, separate chapters on the Highlands and Glasgow, but none on the Lowlands or Edinburgh? The answer is that we have looked at those aspects of Scottish life we regarded as interesting and important in forging its modern character. Edinburgh as the capital city, and the central belt as the industrial heartland, inevitably run through the whole book. The Highlands, on the other hand, so important to Scotland, yet so distinctive a part of it, merited, we felt, special examination. Equally, the resurrection of Glasgow from a point where it faced industrial extinction to its present eminence was, in our view, a phenomenon that required detailed analysis. There will, inevitably, be gaps; there will be people and places unfairly omitted; there are others whose inclusion may be questioned; but this is not, we repeat, an encyclopaedia, a Who's Who, an academic monograph or a textbook. It is meant to be enjoyed as well as to inform.

In compiling the book we have received help from many quarters and many people. Most of the latter are to be found here between its covers. Some preferred not to be named, but most were happy to be quoted. They gave us much time and help and for that we are thoroughly grateful. Talking to them was a richly rewarding experience. If Scotland's best resource is its people, then this country has much to be proud of and much to feel encouraged about.

Anatomy of Scotland

Introduction

The political aide to the British Chancellor of the Exchequer surveyed the milling scene in the foyer of an Edinburgh hotel with some exasperation. Watching the reporters, photographers and television crews, all from the Scottish media, as they badgered his political master with merciless questions, he remarked: 'We never have this problem when we go to the West Country.'

In that comment lies much of the mystification with which English politicians still contemplate their northern neighbour, and though they tend, on their visits to Scotland, to be polite and sympathetic as they listen to expressions of Scottish individuality, they may, in moments of private irritation, echo Dr Johnson: 'Seeing Scotland, Madam, is only seeing a worse England.'

Surmounting that first hurdle of understanding—that Scotland is not simply an extension of England but is a nation with its own history and institutions—is demanding enough. Grasping that this translates into a different environment with a wholly different set of attitudes and perceptions can be simply baffling.

The Chancellor in question was John Major, later Prime Minister. Unlike his predecessor Margaret Thatcher, he had come first to Scotland determined to listen rather than to lecture. But he too found it hard to understand that Scottish politics might present any more special a case than, say, Yorkshire.

And who indeed can blame him? Scotland, after all, shares with every part of the United Kingdom the same Prime Minister, the same Houses of Parliament, the same Monarch, the same language, the same money, the same taxation system, the same framework of local government, industrial development, training and police, to say nothing of much of its history and the steady impact of government policies formulated at Westminster over the past 285 years. It can even be argued that the problems of which it regularly complains have not been markedly different from those in other areas of high unemployment and relative deprivation, such as the north-east of England.

But despite these commonalities, Scotland remains inherently different. Gradually over the last few decades awareness has grown of a set of myths and assumptions about the nature of Scotland and Scottishness that have, over the years, with peculiar obstinacy and persistence, coalesced to form the

1

character of the nation as it sees itself today. What they emphasize is not the similarities and shared experiences that Scotland and England have enjoyed over the centuries, but the distinctions.

A popular assumption is that the separate history of Scotland effectively came to an end in 1707 with the abolition of both the English and the Scottish parliaments and the creation of a new parliament of the United Kingdom. Thereafter, it is said, history was British. To an extent this was, for most Scots, true. In building empires abroad and fighting foreign wars, Scottish identity was submerged in that of a greater Britain. The Scots were enthusiastic colonizers and saw no difficulty in helping to raise the Union flag wherever British imperial ambitions lay. Scottish regiments provided the backbone of British armies from Ticonderoga in the 18th century to Tobruk in the 20th. But as empires and the memories of war fade, so the sense of Britishness begins to dissipate, and the Scottish element reasserts itself, sustained by a set of myths and legends which have never quite been extinguished.

The definition of myth here has been set out by three researchers at Edinburgh University's Centre for Educational Sociology, John Gray, Andrew McPherson and David Raafe. In their book – *Reconstructions of Secondary Education; Theory, Myth and Practice Since the War* – they put it as follows:

'We do not mean by myth things that are thought to be true, but that are, in fact, always false; nor do we mean things that are valuable but that are, in fact, beyond human attainment or consent. Instead we use the term myth to refer to a story that people tell about themselves, and tell for two purposes. These purposes are, first to explain the world, and second, to celebrate identity and to express values.'

Thus, while one of the myths particularly important to the English is that they are a great sea-faring nation, a myth sustained in 1982 by the sea-borne assault to recapture the Falklands, the Scots, who are no strangers to the sea, regard themselves rather as a nation of shipbuilders or fishermen. And while England, since the days of the empire, has seen itself as a civilizing nation, spreading enlightenment and democracy in the wake of conquest, the Scots have contented themselves with the export of manpower, skills and enterprise. Their one isolated attempt at an imperial venture, the Darien colonization scheme in central America in 1695, was such an unmitigated disaster and cost so much in terms of capital and lives that it almost broke the nation's spirit and is still cited as one of the factors which hastened the Union of the Parliaments in 1707.

That Act too carries its myths, since one of the keener debates in Scotland today concerns the effect of the Union on the development of the nation, one view contending that the Union was a civilizing influence on a backward Scotland, the other that it tore the heart out of the country. The former view was backed by the historian Hugh Trevor-Roper in an article in *The Times* in 1976 where he wrote that the pre-1707 system in Scotland was one of 'political banditry run by force and corruption'. This attitude has been fiercely contested by Gordon Donaldson, Historiographer Royal to the Queen in Scotland. In a lecture during the Edinburgh Festival of 1989, he maintained that while England was under the despotic rule of the Tudors, 'in Scotland men were at liberty to form political parties to put pressure on the Government'. Through reference to records of executions, he maintains that 16th-century Scotland was a safer and more kindly country than 16th-century England.

Arcane as these arguments may appear to be, they are all part of a powerful mythology in Scotland. The emblems of its history—Bannockburn, Flodden, Mary Queen of Scots, Glencoe, Culloden, and many others—are called in aid by politicians and commentators today to an extent inconceivable in England, and the merits or demerits of the Union are very much part of the current debate. Unionists argue that it is only by maintaining the link with England that stability and prosperity can be maintained, while nationalists argue with equal fervour that only by breaking it can Scottish energies be properly utilized and prosperity realized.

Indeed the myth itself has taken on modern garb. One keenly argued contention is that since Scotland enjoys 20 per cent more spending per head on public services like education and health from central government than England and Wales, to break with Westminster would put this cash pipeline at risk and send Scotland back to a deprived pre-1707 state. Nationalists, on the other hand, cite arguments raised in a celebrated television programme, *Scotching the Myth*, which maintained that if government spending on such items as defence procurement or the subsidy on mortgage tax relief or transport was taken into account, then it was the south-east of England and not Scotland which was the true 'subsidy junkie'.

There are deeper myths, however, cited by three academic writers, Arthur Midwinter, Michael Keating and James Mitchell in their book *Politics and Public Policy in Scotland*, which provide a distinct dynamic in forming Scottish social and economic attitudes today. They are the Highland Clearances, Red Clydeside and the so-called democratic intellect.

Accounts of the notorious 19th-century clearances have been greatly exaggerated. The number of violent incidents, burning of cottages and enforced transportations was relatively small, and in examining the statistics it emerges that during the relevant period in the early 19th century, the population in the Highlands where the clearances took place actually fell to a lesser extent than in the Lowlands where there were no clearances. Nevertheless the story of the Highland Clearances has left a legacy of collective guilt which affects successive governments and which may even have helped contribute to the establishment of such bodies as the Highlands and Islands Development Board. In a modern echo, the decline of heavy industry in Scotland, the de-industrialization of its central belt, and in particular the closing-down of its steel industry, have been likened in their time to the industrial equivalent of the clearances in the north.

Just as persuasive a demonology is that of the Red Clydesiders, the revolutionary trade unionists who fomented the industrial unrest of the 1920s which led to government tanks and troops on the streets of Glasgow. A modern Scottish Tory minister can still warn of nationalist dangers by citing the nascent socialism of the west of Scotland, while the Scottish National Party has called in aid the heroic memory of the Red Clydesiders to boost its cause amongst the young.

The third myth cited by Midwinter and his colleagues is perhaps the most powerful of them all. That is the so-called 'democratic intellect', a national perception that all Scots share skills and opportunities to an extent not widely echoed elsewhere. It is perhaps part of a wider myth, that of egalitarian Scotland, which has its clearest expression in the Presbyterian church and the Scottish education system. The democracy of the Kirk, governed not by bishops but by locally chosen kirk sessions, presbyteries, synods and the General Assembly, contributes strongly to the idea of an egalitarian state, while the tradition that Scottish education offers every pupil, irrespective of class or wealth, the potential to attain the highest of academic standards, informs policy-making right across the political spectrum and is widely accepted south as well as north of the border.

The egalitarian myth permeates political debate and underpins much of Scotland's institutional structures. The Scottish Nationalist leader, Alex Salmond, put it thus in September 1990: 'I think that people are looking for a political party which is collectivist in terms of its view of social provision. In terms of how society looks after the disadvantaged, people want to see a collective ethos. That has a very keen response in Scottish society. [There is] great resonance and support for the health services, and a state-led comprehensive education system.'

And from the opposite side, a Conservative politician, Malcolm Rifkind, a former Secretary of State for Scotland, put exactly the same point, albeit differently framed, in the course of a speech in 1987: 'The attitudes and policies which have dominated Scottish life have been essentially paternalist. It has been assumed by the Labour Party, by the trade unions, and even by a significant proportion of Scots who do not ascribe to socialist values, that only Government, central or local, is capable of providing the resources, the initiative and the leadership that can provide our people with their social and economic requirements. A paternalist, well-meaning bureaucracy has been the desired framework for generations of Scots.'

That speech was one of a number made by Rifkind in the wake of one of the Conservatives' great electoral disasters in Scotland when, in the general election of 1987, they lost 11 out of their 21 parliamentary seats. Even constituencies in areas of relative prosperity swung against the party, reducing its representation in the country to its lowest post-war level. Rarely has the distinction between Scottish political attitudes and those in England been so marked. As Rifkind and his colleagues surveyed the wreckage of Tory hopes, they determined that only by changing basic attitudes and levering Scotland free of its apparent reliance on central decision-making, could they release the creative and entrepreneurial energy they felt sure was lurking below the surface. This, they argued, would allow the Scottish people to achieve their potential, and the Conservatives to recoup their support. As Rifkind said: 'Quite consciously and deliberately, we are determined to change many of the attitudes and policies that have dominated Scotland for years and which are responsible for many of Scotland's social, economic and industrial problems. Such an objective is bound to be highly controversial and full of political risk, but it is essential, if Scots and Scotland are to realize their full potential.'

Rifkind's analysis confirms the existence of something that remains a puzzle to many of his English colleagues—the existence of a Scottish identity which transcends the mere fact of its geographical position and its separate institutions. This cannot simply be ignored nor, apparently, can it be easily changed. Whether, as a result, Scotland is a prisoner of its own mythology is a matter for the keenest discussion. On the other hand, perhaps it can only progress if that mythology is given free rein and the country is allowed to develop its own distinct character unfettered by Westminster control.

These fundamental matters confronting the nation and its people were resolved not one whit by the general election of April 1992. It produced, against most expectations it must be said, the first improvement in Conservative fortunes in Scotland since 1979 which helped to ensure John Major's return to power in a fourth Conservative term. But it also produced enormous frustration amongst those who had expectations that the election would restore some degree of self-government to Scotland. It not only under-lined the duality of Scottish Society—that it is both British and Scottish, but also that this duality is inadequately expressed in the British political system which many feel is dominated by English politics and values.

How Scotland will progress from here on is not simply a question of how Mr Major or any subsequent prime minister responds to this matter, but is also very much in the hands of Scotland's institutions and the people who run them. Their power to shape events in social, economic and political arenas should not be underestimated.

What is contained here does not pretend to be in any sense prescriptive, nor does it deal in political analysis. It is, rather, an exploration of power and responsibility in Scotland, where it lies and who controls it. It seeks to answer the question of how far Scottish institutions are indeed separate in character, and in doing so it identifies those who run them and gives them their current dynamic.

1

Law and Order

George Rosie

Scots law is Scotland at its most intractably different. By guaranteeing the existence of Scots law, the Treaty of Union of 1707 created a constitutional anomaly which is unique in Europe and probably the world; a distinctive legal system without a legislature. But a legal system which Professor Levy Ullmann of Paris claims is an historic achievement. 'Scots Law as it stands', he has declared, 'gives us a picture of what will some day be the law of the civilised nations—namely a combination between the Anglo-Saxon system and the Continental system.'

Not all legal experts agree with Ullmann. Some see Scots law as a hopeless legal backwater, shot through with anomalies and anachronisms restricting its practitioners to a career within the confines of Scotland. Others, with Ullmann, cherish Scots law for being a synthesis of the precedent-based Anglo-American system and the codified Franco-German system. Scots law, they argue, is beautifully poised between the two great legal philosophies of the western world. The reasons for the unique position of Scots law are not hard to find. The 'Auld Alliance' with France grafted layers of Roman law on to Scotland's medieval Norman feudal system, a process which was enhanced by the enthusiasm of the Scots intelligentsia for the universities of Paris, Leyden, Utrecht and Bologna. Even after the Union of 1707 enterprising Scots preferred Europe to England, which has led one eminent Scots jurist, Lord President Hope, to write, 'In the eighteenth century Scots Law came within an ace of sinking its identity in the Franco-German school . . .' But as England loomed larger through the 18th and 19th centuries, Scots law began to be shaped by English procedures and, above all, by the statutes passed by the British parliament in Westminster. After the Jacobite rebellion of 1745/6 the ancient Barony Courts (which were run by clan chiefs, aristocrats and lairds) were scrapped by parliament. As Westminster extended its grip throughout the 19th and 20th centuries, Scots law grew steadily closer to the English model.

Akin but far from identical. Differences remain. There is, for example, no appeal to the House of Lords from criminal cases heard in the High Court of Justiciary. In Scotland the appeal judges are the final court. A Scots jury consists of 15 people and not 12, and a simple 8–7 majority is enough to convict. A Scots jury can return a verdict of 'Not Proven', which usually means 'we think you did it but the prosecution cannot prove it'. There are no preliminary public hearings such as the English 'magistrates hearings' and, after a private 'judicial examination', accused people go straight to trial. But that trial must be held within 110 days of the committal. No one languishes for years on bail in Scotland as they do in England. And, except for minor traffic offences, evidence must be corroborated by at least two witnesses. The word of one policeman is never enough. Also, a Scottish sheriff is a working judge and not the ceremonial figure he is in England. Nor are differences confined to criminal law. Normally the level of damages for defamation (libel) in Scotland is set by the judge. But a defamatory statement is actionable in Scotland even if it is made only to the person defamed, and no third party is involved. Minors of 16 can marry without the permission of their parents. There are no coroners in Scotland, and deaths are investigated by the public prosecutor—the Procurator Fiscal—who presents his evidence to a sheriff. And all crimes in Scotland are prosecuted by the procurators fiscal and never by the police themselves, a system the English have recently put in place and called the Crown Prosecution Service. But where the English system appears to be running into all kinds of problems (partly due to underfunding) the Scottish system seems to be working well.

The highest civil court in the land is the Court of Session, which consists of 25 judges divided into an Inner House of 9, and an Outer House of 16. The Court of Session always sits in Parliament House in Edinburgh. The same judges hear criminal cases as the High Court of Justiciary, in which capacity they go on 'circuit' around Scotland. Scotland's top judge has two titles: Lord President of the Council as head of the civil court, and Lord Justice General as head of the criminal courts. Number two in the judicial pecking order is the Lord Justice Clerk who is traditionally responsible for shaping sentencing policy in the criminal courts.

The workhorses of the Scottish judiciary are the 220 or so sheriffs and temporary sheriffs (roughly the equivalent of the county court judges in England and Wales). Scotland is divided into six sheriffdoms, each of which is run by a sheriff principal who presides over the sheriffs on his patch. In civil cases decisions made by the sheriffs can be appealed to the sheriff principal. Sheriffs can hand down sentences of up to three years and unlimited fines (or both). The lowest courts in the land are the district courts where the lay magistrates are limited to imposing fines of up to £1000 and gaol sentences of 60 days (which some legal experts argue is too high for lay judges).

Scotland's prosecution services are headed by the British Government's two law officers, the Lord Advocate and the Solicitor General in Scotland. They operate through the Crown Office which runs the Procurator Fiscal Service. Theoretically at least, the Scottish police answer to the procurators fiscal. Procurators fiscal can only appear in the sheriff and district courts; pleading in the higher courts is restricted to advocates (barristers in English parlance).

That monopoly will end in 1992 when solicitors will be allowed to appear before the Court of Session.

The Scottish Bar is regulated by the Faculty of Advocates, whose head (the Dean) is elected by the membership. Solicitors are more loosely organized. Some are members of the ancient Society of Writers to Her Majesty's Signet (the WS) or the Solicitors in the Supreme Court (the SSC). All solicitors must be members of the Law Society of Scotland. A large and growing proportion of the Scottish legal profession is female, but, at the end of 1991, no woman has climbed to the High Court bench.

The Law Commission for Scotland reviews the workings of the law, recommending changes where it thinks they are necessary. Its chairman is usually one of the Lords of Session, ie a High Court judge.

The bench

It could be argued that Scotland is the most judge-haunted land in Europe. Scots law is one of the residues of pre-Union Scotland, and part of it (the High Court of Justiciary) pays no tribute to Westminster. One result is that Scots judges fill something of the role of statesmen. Their decisions loom disproportionately large. And the fact that they traditionally lived check-by-jowl with the hoi polloi in the tenements and lands of Edinburgh in a way that the legal magnates of England never did, gave Scots a peculiar intimacy with their jurists. There is an offence in Scots law of 'murmuring' (ie traducing) the judges of the High Court. Not that it ever seems to have done much good. In the 18th century it was not uncommon for a judge to be pelted with mud and rubbish on his way across the High Street of Edinburgh if the citizenry did not approve of his decisions. Nor was the dignity of the bench enhanced by the regular sight of the judges reeling down the road, extremely drunk courtesy of the claret shippers of Leith or the illegal *uisquebeath* distillers of the Old Town.

Many Scots judges, real and imaginary, have passed into the folklore of Scotland. They are certainly a kenspeckle bunch: Lord Kames, the great reformer; Lord Gardenstone who is reputed to have slept in the same room as his beloved pigs; Lord Monboddo who, many years before Darwin, concluded that men and primates were somehow related; Lord Braxfield, the brutal, good-natured, hanging judge, upon whom Robert Louis Stevenson modelled his Weir of Hermiston; Duncan Forbes of Culloden, the staunch Whig who did his best to soften the blow of Culloden. Nowadays the Scottish bench is distinctly less colourful. The 24 descendants of Kames, Gardenstone, Monboddo etc, are serious, respectable, middle-class, middle-aged men, whose pursuits are mainly hillwalking, sailing, fishing or golf (although Lord Cowie once played rugby for Scotland and Lord Osborne confesses to an enthusiasm for cooking and for playing the drums). As yet there are no women in their ranks, and only one identifiable Catholic (Lord McCluskey) and one Jew (Lord Caplan). Most of them are the product of some of the best of the Scottish day schools (Edinburgh

Academy, Glasgow Academy, Greenock Academy) with a leavening of public schoolboys (Fettes, Loretto, Gordonstoun). An extraordinary proportion (70 per cent) are members of the New Club, an exclusive convocation which inhabits the upper floors of an undistinguished block on Princes Street. A few judges are members of the smaller and slightly more raffish Scottish Arts Club in Rutland Square at the west end of Edinburgh. But there is a consensus among law watchers that Scots judges show less of the renowned ignorance of everyday life of their English counterparts. 'Scotland is a small place', says one advocate. 'It's pretty hard for our judges *not* to know that Hearts are called the Jambos, or that Donnie Munro sings with "Runrig" as well as being the rector of Edinburgh University. They're bright and well informed people, for the most part.'

Most of Scotland's judges are appointed by the Prime Minister at the recommendation of the Lord Advocate of the day, and with the approval of the Lord President of the Council, Scotland's top judge. The Lord President's approval is not always forthcoming; when Lord Stott was Lord Advocate in the 1960s he had serious problems steering one of his appointments, James Leechman, past Lord President Clyde (father of the present Lord Clyde). The Lord President himself finds his way to the job via the good offices of the Secretary of State for Scotland and the Prime Minister. It is all done discreetly, and not everyone is happy with the way it works. 'I'd like to see a more open system of judicial appointments,' says Alan Johnston, Dean of the Faculty of Advocates. 'I think it's time we reduced the mystery and appointed our judges through some kind of commission.' But there is little sign that the 'mystery' Johnston says surrounds Scottish judges is about to be lifted. Lord Hope, the current Lord President, declined to be interviewed for this book, preferring simply to offer a few references to the standard texts on the role of the Scottish judges.

Some lawyers feel that the time has come to instigate a proper, European-style judicial career structure, whereby judges learn their trade in the lower courts and tribunals and proceed up the ladder to become Lords of Session. At the moment our High Court judges are selected almost exclusively from the Faculty of Advocates, 'Which effectively rules out some of the ablest legal minds in Scotland,' says Doctor Robert Macreadie of Edinburgh University. 'People like Sheriff Gerald Gordon, for instance, who wrote the text books on criminal law, are not very likely to become High Court judges. And that is a great pity. The only High Court judge we have who served some time on the lower benches as a sheriff and a sheriff principal is Lord Caplan.'

The current Lord President of the Council and Lord Justice General is David Hope, who made his reputation as a brilliant tax and commercial lawyer. At 53, Hope is the youngest Lord President for many years. Many eyebrows were raised when he was appointed straight into the top job without any previous judicial experience. There is a theory that Hope's appointment was pushed through by the Conservatives to avoid any future Labour Government giving the job to the left-inclined Lord McCluskey. 'But David Hope was a good choice,' according to Robert Black, Professor of Scots Law at Edinburgh University. 'He's a very able judge. And while he's conservative, it's with a small "c", and not overtly political. He's been trying to get the judges to be more efficient, by insisting that they get their judgements out within a reasonable time. And that has caused quite a lot of grumbling on the bench.'

Number two in the judicial pecking order is the Lord Justice Clerk, Donald Ross. Ross, a Dundonian and a former Dean of the Faculty of Advocates, is more than a decade older than Hope. As Lord Justice Clerk he is responsible for shaping court policy over criminal law, while Lord President Hope looks after the civil law of Scotland. Ross too was something of a surprise appointment when he was 'made up' in 1985; the man most widely tipped for the job was the popular Lord Clyde (whose father and grandfather were also High Court judges).

The Court of Session is divided into the 'Inner House' and the 'Outer House'. The Inner House consists of two 'Divisions', first and second, with Lord Hope at the head of the first and Lord Ross at the head of the second. Civil case decisions made by any of the 15 judges of the Outer House can be appealed to three of the nine judges of the Inner House, and/or to the Judicial Committee of the House of Lords in London. That latter move is never popular with Scots lawyers, as the majority of judges on the Judicial Committee are English.

The supreme criminal court in Scotland is the High Court of Justiciary, an institution which is one of the last bastions of an independent Scotland. The decisions of its appeal court—which normally consists of three judges—are final. There is no appeal to the House of Lords in London. The English law lords have no say in Scotland's criminal proceedings.

Proportionally, Scotland is well represented on the Judicial Committee of the House of Lords, with three judges out of 11. The Lord High Chancellor, James Mackay, is a Scots judge. His two compatriots are Lord Keith of Kinkell and Lord Jauncey of Tullichettle. 'But it's getting quite hard to fill the Scottish billets in the House of Lords,' says Professor Robert Black. 'It's not a very popular job and the Government sometimes has to twist an arm or two. The salary [£85 000 a year in 1991] is about the same as it is in Scotland, and it means a great upheaval shifting from Edinburgh to London. And who wants that?'

The international reputation of Scots law received something of a boost at the end of 1991 when David Edward, Professor of European Law at Edinburgh University, and Director of the Europa Institute, was appointed to the bench of the European Court. Before his elevation Judge Edward served for two years on the bench of the Court of First Instance of the European Communities. The Scottish bench is now preening itself on the fact that two of the British jurists in Europe are Scots (the other is Lord Mackenzie Stewart).

The shrieval bench

Ninety-three sheriffs preside over the courts of the six ancient sheriffdoms (now Grampian, Highlands and Islands; Tayside Central and Fife; Lothian and Borders; North Strathclyde; Glasgow and Strathkelvin; South Strathclyde, Dumfries and Galloway). The boundaries of the sheriffdoms bear hardly any resemblance to any of the existing local authority boundaries. (One Scots historian has remarked on the fact that the 'Briton's Stone' near Loch Lomond, which once marked the limit of the ancient Kingdom of Strathclyde, also marked the boundary between the sheriffdoms of Perth and Dumbarton. Shrieval boundary lines, in other words, are very ancient.) While the high courts of Scotland have unlimited powers of sentence, the sheriff courts are strictly circumscribed. They can only hear cases where the penalty is less than three years in gaol. Some insiders suggest that the backlog of work in the high courts would be unjammed by allowing the sheriff courts to sentence up to five years in gaol. Others say that would simply put more pressure on the sheriff courts which are already struggling to cope with a rising crime rate, and a soaring number of small debt claims.

In 'summary' cases a sheriff sits alone, and makes his own judgements. In 'solemn' cases he sits with a 15-strong jury which decides the verdict, leaving the sheriff to pass sentence. Some sheriffs—such as Sheriff Nigel Thomson of Edinburgh and Lothian—are famous (some would say notorious) for their 'creative' sentencing. A young man who raided a music shop, for example, was sentenced to learn to play an instrument and report to Sheriff Thomson at regular intervals to demonstrate his progress. Others have been sentenced to write essays which explain their crimes.

Any social profile of Scotland's sheriffs would show a distinct resemblance to that of the High Court judges: white, male, middle-aged and middle class. The same backgrounds, the same schools, the same universities, the same clubs. More Roman Catholics, perhaps, and a few more Jews. But so far no Moslems, and still a tiny proportion of women: Hazel Aronson and Isobel Poole of Lothian and Borders, Laura Duncan and Daphne Robinson of Glasgow and Strathkelvin and Gail Patrick at Kirkcaldy. Five out of 93, or just over 5 per cent of the bench. Traditionally, Scotland's sheriffs were seasoned advocates, but that is changing. For some years the bench has been filling up with men (and the occasional woman) who were once solicitors. 'Which makes eminent sense,' says one newish sheriff. 'Many solicitors are well used to pleading in the sheriff court, and to handling sheriff court procedures.'

There is also a corps of 120 or so temporary sheriffs who sit on the shrieval bench for four or five days a month. Most of the 'temps' are court solicitors with at least five years experience, and are well used to sheriff court procedures. A few are legal academics. In 1991 they were paid at the rate of £200 a day plus fairly generous expenses, a rate that one describes as 'not bad' but hardly up to the kind of money that can be earned by a hard-charging advocate.

Each sheriffdom is administered by a sheriff principal, five of whom are Queen's Counsel. The exception is Robert Hay, Sheriff Principal of North Strathclyde, who is the first ever solicitor-sheriff to be appointed to a principal's job. 'And not before time,' according to Professor Robert Black, who disapproves of the traditional grip that senior advocates have had over the position. In civil cases, a sheriff principal can act as a one-man court of appeal. Judgements made by sheriffs can be referred to the sheriff principal for reconsideration and, if that fails, to the Court of Session. But in criminal cases the sheriff principal is bypassed and appeals go straight to the appeal judges of the High Court of Justiciary.

District courts

The bottom end of the Scottish judicial ladder rests on the network of district courts created by the District Courts (Scotland) Act of 1975. These deal exclusively with minor criminal matters: petty vandalism, breach of peace offences, urinating in the street, drunk and disorderly, bar-room scuffles, minor traffic offences. No young person under the age of 16 can appear, and no civil cases are referred to the district courts.

Almost all the men and women who preside over the district courts are lay magistrates, unqualified in the law, but regarded as reliable and responsible citizens. They are appointed by the Secretary of State for Scotland on the recommendation of the local Justice's Committee, and are kept on track by their legally qualified court clerks. Unsurprisingly, many advocates, solicitors and procurators fiscal regard the lay judges of the district courts with suspicion. 'Many of them do their best,' says one Edinburgh solicitor 'but lay magistrates know very little law, so everything depends on the quality of advice they get from their clerks, and that can be very patchy. And they can be too easily led by their clerks. Some of their verdicts seem to contain neither legal rhyme nor legal reason.'

The advocates

Alan Johnston, the Dean of the Faculty of Advocates in Scotland is a large, burly, red-faced man with an engaging grin and a garrulous manner. He operates from an elegant office off the Advocates Library in Parliament House, in Edinburgh. The walls are lined, floor to ceiling, with a dazzling variety of legal tomes. Over the fireplace is a portrait of his predecessor Henry Erskine, the last incumbent dean to be toppled by a challenger. 'Pure politics,' Johnston explains, 'Erskine was a Whig who did not approve of the way the Tories ran the war with France. So Dundas went after him, with the support of his cousin Henry Dundas, Viscount Melville.'

Nowadays, voting for the Dean of Faculty is a much more decorous affair. The election takes place at the Anniversary Meeting of the Faculty in January, and is carried out on a system of proportional representation devised by James Mackay, now Lord Chancellor of Great Britain. Once voted in, the Dean is there for three years, after which he is normally (although not by right) elevated to the bench as a High Court judge. For three years the Dean presides over a faculty which is is one of Scotland's more venerable institutions. Part of the College of Justice which was founded by King James V in 1532 (in exchange for a loan from the Vatican), the Faculty is responsible for the education and practice of Scotland's senior courtroom lawyers. Along with the judges of the inner and outer house, and the solicitors of the Writers to her Majesty's Signet and the Solicitors in the Supreme Court, it is one of the props of the legal establishment.

The main office bearers are the Dean of Faculty, the Vice-Dean, the Treasurer, the Clerk, and the Keeper of the Library. The library is one of the Faculty's most priceless assets. Open 24 hours a day to members of the Faculty, it is a historic collection which formed the basis of the National Library of Scotland (one of the copyright libraries in Britain which are legally entitled to receive a copy of every new book published). Dean Johnston is now constitutionally responsible for around 1 000 members of the Faculty of Advocates of whom 320 or so practise in Scotland. Between 40 and 50 of them are Queen's Counsel (QC), and the remainder 'juniors'. Advocates 'take the silk', or are promoted to QC, after about 12–15 years of reputable work. 'And anybody who has been a junior for 25 years gets made up,' Johnston says. 'But that rarely happens. They've either made it long before then, or have fallen by the wayside.' Entry is open to anyone with a reputable degree and the ability to pass the faculty's rigorous exams. 'But the quickest and most usual way to the bar is to take a law degree at a Scottish university and do two years' traineeship with a firm of solicitors.' After that, the aspiring advocate has to spend a year 'devilling' (working for nothing) for a practising advocate, known as the 'devilmaster'. 'The fact that they don't get paid is becoming something of a problem,' Johnston says. 'Some of them do other things, mainly university teaching. But devilling is demanding and time consuming and there's not much time for anything else. Some people have great difficulty supporting themselves. The Faculty is trying to find ways of offering bursaries and scholarships, but it's not easy.'

Not that the months spent devilling seem to deter aspiring advocates. In recent years the faculty has grown at an extraordinary rate. Numbers have doubled over the past 10 years, and the 1991 intake of 26 is the biggest ever. 'I'm not quite sure why,' Johnston says. 'Maybe because it is an interesting, worthwhile and reasonably well-paid job.' A problem is the level of fees the Government pays for legal aid work. 'That works out at £320 a day for a QC and two-thirds of that for a junior,' Johnston says. 'Which may sound like a lot of money, but it is not when you take into account the amount of research and preparation that has to be done. We're arguing that the level needs to be doubled, just to keep up with the expenses.'

Since he was called to the bar in 1967, Johnston has seen a distinct tendency for advocates to specialize, a process which he regrets but thinks inevitable. 'Theoretically all advocates can argue any case,' he says. 'But that is not the way of the world. People specialize. We now have a criminal bar where the members are so busy they find it very difficult to do any other kind of work. The people who specialize in planning spend most of their time outside of Edinburgh.' And, Johnston says, company and tax law is so specialized and intricate that the advocates who make it their speciality have little prospect of doing anything else. 'Most of their work is preparing written opinions,' he says. 'They only appear in court for the occasional revenue case.'

Many advocates making their way up the legal ladder spend two or three years acting as advocates depute for the Crown Office. Their job is to prosecute serious cases on behalf of the crown in the High Court of Justiciary. At the sheriff court the job is done by the Procurator Fiscal. 'That's usually seen as an important stage in an advocate's career,' Johnston says. 'And when a job is offered, they are well advised to take it.'

The unsung heroes of the Faculty of Advocates are the seven clerks—four men and three women—each of whom look after their own 'stable' of advocates. The clerks are employed by a faculty-owned firm called Faculty Services Ltd which runs a computerized billing system. The clerks act as brokers, administrators, organizers and marketing experts for the stable of men and women they serve. If a solicitor cannot instruct the advocate he wants, the clerk will shunt him in the direction of another in the stable who, he believes, is just as proficient.

Dean Johnston believes that while the Faculty of Advocates works well, some improvements could be made, both for the practitioners and for the public. 'One thing we are thinking about is producing a faculty directory which would give more details about the skills of individual advocates,' he says. Such a catalogue of talent would be aimed at solicitors looking for an advocate who specialized in, for example, shipping, oil-industry law, planning, or medical matters. As Johnston sees it, the biggest cloud on the horizon is the steadily increasing importance of European law which threatens gradually to erode Scots law. The problem is constitutional. Scotland is one of the stateless nations of Europe, and is unique in having a legal system without a legislature. As such it has to rely on the good offices of a political establishment which knows little about it. 'I'm afraid that most Europeans, and the English, see us as the northern circuit of the English legal system,' Johnston says. 'At some European conferences the Dean of Faculty has to go in on the coat tails of a junior Home Office minister who knows nothing about Scots law.

Our own minister—the Secretary of State for Scotland—has no European status.'

The solicitors

If Scotland has a 'Mister Fixit' it is Sir Charles Annand Fraser, KCVO, DL, one-time Purse Bearer to the Lord High Commissioner to the General Assembly of the Church of Scotland, and trustee to the Scottish Civic Trust. Not only is he the Chairman of Adam & Co, the top people's private bank, but he is also a director of British Assets Trust PLC, Grosvenor Developments, Scottish Widows Fund and Life Assurance Society, Scottish Business in the Community, United Biscuits (Holdings) PLC, Lothian & Edinburgh Enterprise Ltd, and Scottish Television PLC.

However, the intriguing thing about Sir Charles Fraser is not his long string of directorships, but the fact that he is a lawyer, a solicitor. He has been a partner in the old-established Edinburgh legal firm of W & J Burness, Writers to Her Majesty's Signet, since 1956, and between 1966 and 1972 served on the Council of the Law Society of Scotland. He is firmly in a Scottish tradition: the lawyer as 'man of business'. That is the man who looks after his client's interests by dodging malodorous deals and increasing his client's wealth by advising him where to invest his money.

Corporate law it is now called, and Fraser is one of Scotland's best exponents of the art. But as a partner in one of the biggest general practices in Scotland he has a good overall view of the profession. 'It's changed a lot since I came into it,' he says. 'There is much more specialization now. Some people deplore this, but I would argue it has been a good thing for the Scottish public. It is very presumptuous of any lawyer to believe he can operate in the whole ambit of the law.' There is, he believes, a disturbing measure of complacency in the legal profession in Scotland. 'Of course there's a proud history in the Faculty of Advocates, and the Society of Writers to Her Majesty's Signet and all the other bodies. But we must be careful not to dwell too much on our Glorious Past. We must be willing to adapt—and adapt quickly—to changes. Otherwise we'll be left behind. Chasing crumbs.' And crumb-chasing is what many Scots solicitors fear that they are doing already. With so many Scottish companies being snapped up by London-based corporations, rates of legal aid being squeezed by the government, rents and overheads soaring and property buying and selling being done by estate agents and unqualified 'licensed conveyancers', many of Scotland's solicitors are looking into the future with unease.

Solicitors are by far the biggest component of the Scottish legal profession. At the last count (which was the end of 1990) there were 7 922 of them, of which just over 7 000 held practising certificates. While the huge majority worked in Scotland, a few hundred were scattered around the English-speaking world: 390 in England and Wales, 18 in Australia, 24 in Canada, 45 in Hong Kong and 18 in the USA. Another few dozen were plying their trade in foreign parts ranging from the Solomon Islands and Bahrain to Zimbabwe. The 7 000 or so solicitors working inside Scotland were organized into around 1 000 private practices, with 594 working for local authorities, 385 working for central government, 101 in assorted public bodies (such as Scottish Homes, the new town development corporations) and 210 in commerce and industry. Another 65 were on the dole, 4 were on maternity leave and 4 were working freelance.

Far from being a profession of creaking greybeards, the age profile shows that the great majority of Scots solicitors—around 60 per cent—are under 40 years old. While the trade is still male dominated, there are proportionally more women in it than than there are in most professions or in other parts of the law. More than 2 400 solicitors on the roll (28 per cent) are now women, and of the recent intakes almost half have been female. The law faculties of the Scottish universities are showing the same trend. Whether this will change the nature of the profession remains to be seen. However, most of the big legal firms in Scotland now list women among their partners, and more are coming up through the ranks as senior assistants and associates. 'The presence of female lawyers certainly benefits female members of the public,' says one Edinburgh solicitor. 'Many women find it much easier to recount their problems—which are often very personal—to another woman. But it's hard to generalize. There are plenty of women working as commercial lawyers who are just as aggressive as any male.'

Constitutionally, the solicitors of Scotland—like the rest of the legal profession—are answerable to the Lord President of the Court of Session, Lord Hope, the country's top High Court judge. Lawyers are admitted into the profession by petitioning the Court of Session. If the Law Society of Scotland wants to change the rules governing the way that solicitors work, it has to be done via the Lord President, and Lord President Hope takes a lively interest in the way solicitors carry out their business.

Although the profession is now effectively regulated by the Law Society of Scotland, that body was only established in 1949. Before then several venerable societies did the job. The oldest, and still the most prestigious, is the Society of Writers to Her Majesty's Signet which for centuries had the exclusive right to stamp the Royal Signet on legal documents. The Signet Library (designed by Robert Reid and William Stark in 1813) in Parliament Square is one of the glories of neo-classical Edinburgh. On the other side of Parliament House are the premises of the Solicitors in the Supreme Court, another society of Edinburgh lawyers which runs its own library. In Glasgow the Royal Faculty of Procurators of Glasgow looks after the interests of the city's solicitors (and does its best to check the influence of legal Edinburgh). The solicitors of Aberdeen confused things further in 1685 when they formed the Society of Advocates, and began calling its members advocates. However, it is the Law Society of Scotland which now has responsibility for the day-to-day running of the profession. Operating under a council of senior solicitors (plus a full-time staff), from an Edwardian terrace at the west end of Edinburgh, the Society simultaneously looks after the solicitors' interests, regulates their goings on, and, when necessary, disciplines the wayward. The waywardness of lawyers can be spectacular. At the end of 1991 an Edinburgh solicitor was gaoled for defrauding his clients, building societies and banks of more than £4 million. Most of this bill will be picked up by the rest of the profession through the Scottish Solicitors Guarantee Fund. The Law Society of Scotland claims that no other profession or commercial organization operates such an 'open-ended guarantee' against dishonesty or incompetence. 'If a chartered accountant runs away with the money from his client's till,' says Scott Galt of the Law Society of Scotland, 'all that his client can do is join the creditors in the queue. The rest of the accountancy profession is not going to find the money. But we do.'

That is only one of the ways that Scottish solicitors feel themselves under unfair pressure. As they see it the Government are allowing their bread and butter, the buying and selling of property, to be snatched from the table by the new breed of licensed conveyancers, while at the same time refusing to allow legal aid—especially civil legal aid—to keep up with soaring costs. The result has been that many firms, particularly the ones with expensive city-centre premises to keep up, have stopped doing civil legal aid work altogether.

The Law Society have been arguing for some years that there is a real crisis over civil legal aid which is now threatening justice in Scotland. It estimates that to pay a senior lawyer plus his office overheads and other expenses costs around £68 per hour (at 1990 prices). But the going rate for civil legal aid is £37 an hour 'which means that the profession has to subsidize the system to the tune of £30 an hour,' says Scott Galt, 'which is absurd'. To add insult to the financial injury the Law Society have discovered that the rate for their counterparts in England in 1990 was £83 per hour, and accountants handling small-scale bankruptcies in Scotland are paid £62 an hour by the British government, £25 an hour more than the lawyers. 'Respect for the law,' the Law Society of Scotland argues 'is dependent not only on the quality of that law, but also access to justice in terms of the law.'

However after years of strenuous lobbying (mainly by the Glasgow Bar Association via the Law Society) Scottish solicitors will be allowed, from 1992, to argue their clients' cases in the Court of Session. This privilege has traditionally been reserved for members of the Faculty of Advocates. Hitherto solicitors have been restricted to defending in the sheriff and district courts. Some lawyers, solicitors as well as advocates, see this as the first alarming step towards a US-style, all-purpose profession. Sir Charles Fraser is far from sanguine about the profession's prospects, even for the dozen or so big firms who undertake corporate law. 'Our client base, the sources of our instructions, are slipping away,' he says. 'More and more of the decisions are taken elsewhere. Who is responsible for running British Steel in Scotland? Nobody knows. Who runs British Airways up here? I don't know. And the reason I don't know is because no decisions are taken here. They are all taken at company headquarters in London.' A few Scottish solicitors have been trying to offset this effect by opening offices in London, something Fraser views with mixed feelings. 'I certainly think it's a good idea to have a listening post or a marketing operation in London,' he says. 'But I doubt if many—or indeed if any—Scottish practices have the resources to compete with the huge London firms who can throw 15 or 20 lawyers at any problem.'

For all that, he believes that Scots solicitors have one great asset they can exploit, 'and that's a reputation for integrity and rectitude. That is a very valuable commodity in this time of Maxwell, Polly Pecks, BCCI and the Guinness affair. The amount of dishonesty in the corporate world is truly frightening.'

The prosecutors

In the Great British Pecking Order the Lord Advocate comes fairly low. In the Order of Precedence of Scotland he comes a long way down the list, well behind the dukes' younger sons and the Keepers of the Great Seal and the Lord Justice General. And while he is the Government's senior law officer for Scotland he is not entitled to a seat in the Cabinet like the Lord High Chancellor (who also outranks him in the House of Lords). But there was a time when the Lord Advocate was the most powerful, and therefore most feared, figure in Scotland. When the post of Scottish Secretary was scrapped between 1746 and 1882 the Lord Advocate became the British government's viceroy in Scotland. In the absence of any real politics, he became the man responsible for ensuring that Westminster's writ ran north of the border.

Although 'The Advocate' no longer has the power to chill Scots to the bone (at least not the law-abiding ones) he is still responsible for prosecuting the law in Scotland. The current incumbent is Alan Rodger, QC and he acts in tandem with his Solicitor General, Thomas Dawson, QC. Both are political appointees. Both advise the government on Scottish legal matters and help draft Scottish legislation. And when their political luck runs out, the Lord Advocate is normally elevated to the bench, and the Solicitor General usually returns to the bar to make more money than he ever did as a government minister. (Unusually, the previous Lord Advocate, Lord Fraser of Carmyllie accepted the job of Minister of State at the Scottish Office.) The law officers have an office in London (where the parliamentary draftsmen lurk) but the heart of their fiefdom is the Crown Office in Edinburgh. This now occupies most of the old Royal High School, the building earmarked as a home for the Scottish Assembly. From there, the 100 or so lawyers and administrators of the Crown Office preside over the Procurator Fiscal Service, a venerable prosecution system described by its admirers as the finest in Europe (and which the English have only just got round to emulating). Like much of the Scots legal establishment, the prosecution system can be traced back into late medieval times. The Procurator Fiscal was originally an agent (procurator) who collected fines from offenders which were paid into the Sheriff's treasury (fisc).

The legal functionary responsible for the running of the Crown Office and its prosecution service is the Crown Agent. The present holder of that post is John Duncan Lowe, a Glasgow-educated lawyer who joined the Fiscal Service in 1974 and has been in and out of the Crown Office ever since. From his roost on the south flank of the Calton Hill he wields considerable influence. One of Lowe's predecessors startled Scotland's high street newsagents in the 1970s by pursuing them for displaying popular magazines like *Playfair* and *Penthouse*. These, he argued at the time, were liable to 'corrupt the morals of the lieges'.

The men and women at the sharp end of the system are the procurators fiscal and their assistants and deputes whose job is to prosecute the criminal classes through the country's sheriff courts and district courts. They are not, however, allowed to pursue their quarry in the High Court of Justiciary. They are all fully-fledged, quite senior civil servants, paid for by the taxpayer. Until recently the Procurator Fiscal Service had difficulty recruiting young lawyers of the right calibre, but hard times have made it easier. The service is organized on the six sheriffdoms of Scotland. For every sheriffdom there is a Regional Procurator Fiscal (RPF), essentially a policy-maker and administrator, whose staff varies in size depending on population and geography. The RPF for Glasgow and Strathkelvin, for example, has 65 fiscals, assistant fiscals and depute fiscals under him. The RPF for South Strathclyde, Dumfries and Galloway has six. 'The Regional PFs are very much their own bosses,' says a Crown Office spokeswoman. 'There's no question of anyone here at the Crown Office telling them what to do. Nor do they have operational control over the fiscals in their regions. The local fiscals are the master of the instance in deciding whether or not to prosecute.'

Constitutionally at least, the fiscals have also responsibility for investigating the crime. 'Of course, the fiscals leave most of that to the police,' she explains. 'But there are certain crimes in which they do get involved: when a murder is committed the duty fiscal attends the scene of the crime to safeguard the evidence. He or she also attends the post mortem examination, too. It's unpleasant, but you get used to it. The fiscal usually keeps in close touch with the police officer in charge of the case, usually a detective chief superintendent or chief inspector.'

Having supervised the investigation of the murder, the fiscal cannot prosecute. Murder (along with treason, rape and incest) is regarded as a 'Plea of the Crown' and is automatically dealt with by the High Court of Justiciary. Only advocates are allowed to plead at the bar of the High Court, which is why the Crown Office keeps its own stable of 11 advocates, known as advocates depute (they deputize for the Lord Advocate). In these serious cases it is the advocates depute of the Crown Office who decide whether the police and the Procurator Fiscal have gleaned enough hard evidence to take the case to the High Court. If not, the case papers are marked 'No Pro', meaning 'No Proceedings'. Usually that is the end of the matter. The Crown cannot—or at least does not—change its mind. But in the early 1980s the Crown Office was seriously embarrassed when three Glasgow youths were gaoled for rape and serious assault after the case had been abandoned by the Crown Office. It was taken up as a rare private prosecution. The debacle led to the resignation of the then Solicitor General Nicholas Fairbairn. And since the 'Glasgow Rape Case' (as it became widely known) no serious rape has been marked 'No Pro' without being referred to the Lord Advocate himself.

Scotland has proved no more immune to white collar crime than any other corner of the western world. To handle it the Crown Office set up a special Fraud Unit comprising one assistant solicitor and three legal assistants. 'The idea is to handle major frauds,' says the spokeswoman, 'the kind of crime that local procurators fiscal may not have the expertise or manpower to cope with. The Fraud Unit also deals with the business of confiscating any gains made from drug-related crimes.' Some of the Crown Office lawyers have also been investigating alleged war crimes among a few east European emigrés living in Scotland.

As there is no such functionary as a coroner in Scotland, the Crown Office and the Procurator Fiscal Service fulfill the role of investigating certain categories of death. Under the Fatal Accident Inquiries (Scotland) Act of 1976 there are three categories of death which must be inquired into: deaths at work, deaths in custody, and deaths which it might be 'in the public interest' to investigate. The latter category is at the discretion of the Lord Advocate, and the decision to go ahead with a Fatal Accident Inquiry (FAI) is sometimes made after pleas by a family, or pressure from the media (or both). FAIs are held before a sheriff, who listens to the evidence presented by the fiscal and makes a 'determination' at the end of it. Some FAIs, such as those emanating from diving accidents, helicopter crashes or equipment failures on oil platforms, involve much complex and highly technical evidence. 'If there is to be a prosecution—let's say under the Safety at Work Act—we like to get that out of the way first,' she explains. 'An FAI could prejudice any criminal proceedings if it were held before the trial.'

The worst single crime that the Crown Office has ever been obliged to investigate happened in December 1988 when Pan Am Flight 103 was destroyed by a bomb over the town of Lockerbie. The burden of assembling the evidence of the crime fell on James T Macdougall, the Procurator Fiscal for Dumfries and Kirkcudbright. Macdougall was made a Commander of the British Empire (CBE) in the 1992 New Year's Honours List. And if the perpetrators of the bombing are ever brought to trial before the High Court of Justiciary in Edinburgh (or possibly Dumfries) the Crown's prosecution will certainly be led by the Lord Advocate of the day.

The police

There is no better insight into some of Scotland's more acute problems than to talk to Detective Chief Superintendent Jim Fleming of the Strathclyde Police. He is responsible for the Criminal Investigation Department's Specialist Services over a force area which stretches from the wilds of Argyll to inner-city Glasgow: 'Which means the drugs squad, the serious crime squad, the fraud squad and the stolen vehicles squad,' he says. 'Along with criminal intelligence, the identification branch, handwriting and ballistics, and technical support, such as tape recording and so on. Everything except Special Branch.'

And DCS Fleming has never been busier. 'Some crimes seem to be going through the roof,' he says. 'Not so many murders, although we have had a few gangland killings recently. But the drugs problem goes on getting worse. Stealing vehicles is reaching epidemic proportions, and where they used to turn up a few days later, now they are vanishing. They are being ringed—sold outside of Scotland or being cannibalized for the parts. And fraud—especially mortgage fraud—is another problem. My fraud squad have got something like £5 million worth of work on their desks right now.' Most alarming of all, he says, is the penchant Scottish villains are showing for carrying firearms. 'There are a lot of guns out there. Up to the end of 1991 we had 252 robberies with firearms. Some of those might have been replicas, but others were real enough, and people were hurt. Some weapons seem to have found their way back from the Persian Gulf. Only 10 per cent of the troops coming back into Britain were searched for weapons, so we're beginning to pick up the Gulf War souvenirs. We've already had one murder done by a Kalashnikov assault rifle which was taken from the Iraqis.'

However, as DCS Fleming and every other policeman is at pains to point out, seeing Scotland through the crime figures is seeing it through a distorting glass. High crime figures can simply mean that the police are operating more efficiently, or that crimes which traditionally went unreported (like wife beating) now go on the book. Despite the lurid headlines, victims of violence are few and far between and most are young males. Statistically, Scotland is as safe as any other part of Britain. According to Government figures, 'violence against the person' is worse in most parts of England than it is in Scotland. While many of Scotland's outer-city housing estates have their problems, they do not appear to be haunted by the profound alienation that erupts into the kind of mass violence that England has seen.

Policing Scotland has never been easy. The country has always had a distinct tendency to split into warring factions, as Robert the Bruce recognized when he appointed Gilbert Hay, the Earl of Errol, the High Constable of Scotland; or, 400 years later, when the Black Watch regiment was raised to police the disaffected Highlands. Much of Scots history has been a murky and depressing tale of clan against clan, Lowlands against Highlands, Presbyterian against Episcopalian, one border dynasty against another. Central authority (ie the Crown) always had problems setting its stamp on Scotland, despite the early introduction of the sheriff as the king's representative in the country. For centuries peacekeeping was a hit-and-miss business, and most communities relied on 'town guards'. The most notorious was the Edinburgh guard, an ineffective squad of ageing, red-coated Highlanders who carried muskets during the day

Law and Order

and Lochaber axes at night. They could do nothing when the Edinburgh mob decided to lynch John Porteous, Captain of the Town Guard (the equivalent of the Chief Constable) in 1736. By the turn of the 19th century various City and Burgh Police Forces began to spring up: Glasgow (1800), Edinburgh (1805), Paisley (1806), Perth (1811), Aberdeen (1818), Airdrie (1822), Dundee (1824). But police forces were not made compulsory in Scotland until the Police (Scotland) Act of 1857, which also created the positions of Chief Constable and Her Majesty's Inspectorate of Constabulary. Informal arrangements continued well into the 20th century. Female prisoners were looked after by the wives of policemen until women constables were appointed in 1924.

The distinctive diced cap band of the Scottish police dates from 1932. With the reorganization of local government in 1974 the number of police forces in Scotland was reduced from 22 to eight. They have 'authorized establishments' (ie numbers of officers allowed by the government) which vary enormously. In order of size they are: Strathclyde (6 954); Lothian & Borders (2 439); Grampian (1 116); Tayside (1 001); Fife (754); Central (638); Northern (631); Dumfries and Galloway (333). As most forces are manned to a level slightly below their establishment, there are around 13 500 police in Scotland, 300 short of the government approved level. Another 1 800 men and women serve as 'special' (ie part time auxiliary) constables. The ratio of policemen to population is slightly better in Scotland than it is in England: one to 377 compared to one to 402 south of the border.

Together the eight police forces cost the Scottish taxpayer around £400 million a year (at 1991 prices) which works out at just under £80 for every man, woman and child in Scotland. The Secretary of State for Scotland pays 51 per cent of the cost, while the appropriate local authorities pay 49 per cent. This reflects the constitutional arrangement whereby the Scottish police are answerable to both central government *and* their local councils. Like every other publicly-funded body in Britain, the Scottish police forces are strapped for cash. The situation is acute in Strathclyde where the establishment has remained the same since 1975 despite 16 years of steadily rising crime, and a growing sickness rate among officers. Some detective work by Superintendent David Smith of the Management Services division has revealed that the Strathclyde Police's annual capital budget (to pay for new police stations, equipment, new cars, computers, motorcycles etc) is about one-third that of the English forces of the same size: £3.4 million compared to Manchester's £15 million or the West Midlands' £14 million.

Scotland's eight chief constables now include at least two Englishmen, the outspoken Dr Ian Oliver of Grampian (and formerly of Central) and Leslie Sharp, the recently appointed Chief Constable of Strathclyde. Sharp was something of a surprise. His previous charge was the Cumbria Police, a north of England force which is less than one-fifth of the size of Strathclyde, and which contains no city approaching the dimensions of the Glasgow conurbation (or which has anything like Glasgow's problems). And all the Scottish police forces are supervised by another Englishman who is new to Scotland. He is Colin Sampson, Her Majesty's Chief Inspector of Constabulary (HMCIC) for Scotland (who as Chief Constable of West Yorkshire was given the job of reporting on John Stalker's investigations into the Royal Ulster Constabulary). Colin Sampson operates with a small staff out of New St Andrew's House in Edinburgh, and HMCIC's annual report to the Secretary of State for Scotland is one of the best available insights into the operation of the Scottish police. (One of the things that it reveals is that the crime 'clear-up' rate varies from force to force. In the Northern Police area—which is peppered with small communities where everyone knows one another—61 per cent of all crimes are cleared up. In the sprawling conurbations of Strathclyde the clear-up rate is only 28 per cent. The Scottish average is 33 per cent, although about 70 per cent of serious violence is cleared up, while the majority of housebreakers get away with its villainy.)

Three organizations have been formed to represent the interests of serving police officers: the Association of Chief Police Officers (Scotland) which represents chief constables, deputy chief constables and assistant chief constables; The Association of Scottish Police Superintendents for the ranks of chief superintendent and superintendent; and the Scottish Police Federation for police up to the rank of chief inspector.

Every recruit entering the Scottish police goes through two eight-week courses at the Scottish Police College at Tulliallan Castle in Alloa. With its expensively modernized Italian/Gothic premises, excellent new library and 90 handsome acres of wooded parkland, Tulliallan is one of the most agreeable campuses in Scotland. In a normal year around 1 000 students—5 per cent of them graduates, 25 per cent of them women—pass through the 'Junior Division' which trains the new recruits. Tulliallan's Senior Division specializes in 'command' courses for senior officers, some of whom come from as far afield as Hong Kong. The Traffic Division helps traffic police brush up their particular skills, while the Detective Division is designed to enhance the expertise of the officers trying to contain the booming criminal industries in fraud and drugs.

Another, less well-known, all-force institution is the Scottish Crime Squad (SCS). Headquartered at Stuart Street in Glasgow, and concerned mainly with serious crime, the SCS is made up of detectives from all eight Scottish police forces. A recent count showed 82 of them, plus 13 civilians, operating from offices in Glasgow, Edinburgh and Stonehaven, with a technical unit at Dunfermline. Normally the squad's Commander is a detective superintendent from Strathclyde; 'That's because we put up most of the manpower,' says DCS Fleming. 'His second-in-command usually comes from the Lothian and Borders Police. Most officers are seconded for three—occasionally four—years to the Scottish Crime Squad. They do a lot of cross-force investigations, mostly for the Scottish forces, sometimes for the English. They have their own surveillance teams and drug units.'

Fleming does not share the view that the SCS has outlived its purpose, which

24

was to provide a flying squad to the dozens of small police forces that existed before the great reorganization of 1975. 'Some forces, like ourselves and Lothian and Borders, have their own serious crime squads,' he says. 'But not all of them. Some are still too small.' Most Scottish policemen regard drug-dealing as the most serious and most intractable problem facing the police. 'Drug peddling has all kinds of consequences,' says Chief Superintendent Willie Rae of Strathclyde Police. 'It can develop into organized crime and the kind of gang warfare that leads to killings. It creates all kinds of petty crime among the users, who'll mug anybody and steal just about anything to get their drugs. And it makes life a misery for all the decent folk that the dealers live among. It's pretty hard bringing up kids in a place where the back green and the stair are littered with used heroin needles, and where the dealers keep two Rottweilers.'

The eight regular forces do not have a monopoly on policing Scotland. The British Transport Police have a 'Scotland Division' which looks after the land, premises and rolling stock owned by the British Railways Board. The Ministry of Defence Police are responsible for policing the network of military and intelligence-gathering installations. At certain crucial points, such as the nuclear submarine base at Faslane on the Clyde, they are backed by Royal Marines from the specially trained Commaccio Company. The United Kingdom Atomic Energy Authority (UKAEA) Constabulary are also present north of the border, at the Dounreay nuclear facility in Caithness and the Chapelcross nuclear power station near Lockerbie. Heavily armed UKAEA police also guard the shipments of nuclear waste and fuel as they are shunted around the country. The two Royal parks in Edinburgh, Holyrood Park and the Royal Botanic Gardens, are both patrolled by men from the Royal Parks Constabulary.

But nothing agitates Scotland's civil libertarians more than the policing we never see, particularly telephone tapping. The police forces, the UKAEA police, the Customs and Excise and the Security Service (MI5) all have powers to 'intercept communications' on the strength of a warrant issued by Her Majesty's Government. North of the border that means the Secretary of State for Scotland, or, in his absence, the Secretary of the Scottish Home and Health Department. Complaints of unjustifiable tapping go to the Interception of Communications Tribunal, one member of which is Ivor Reginald Guild, LLB, WS, partner in the Edinburgh law firm of Shepherd & Wedderburn, Procurator Fiscal to the Court of the Lord Lyon, and Baillie of the Abbey Court of Holyroodhouse who is also head of the Constables of Holyroodhouse, one of the oldest continuing police forces in the world.

Tradition, whether in upholding the law or in maintaining order, is central to the separate nature of the Scottish judicial system. The fact that so much importance attaches to it, lies not just in a respect for the past as in a belief that its individuality has virtues that render it superior to most of its rivals. From office junior to senior judge or chief constable that belief is more or less unshakeable, and though there is no lack of criticism of the way the system works, there are few indeed who would challenge its right to exist. That confidence alone guarantees its survival.

2

The Establishment and the Aristocracy

George Rosie

Some pillars of the establishment carry a bigger load than others. Take, for example, David George Coke Patrick Ogilvy the 13th Earl of Airlie. He is hardly a household name, but he is certainly influential: Lord Chamberlain to Her Majesty the Queen and in charge of the Royal Household; Chancellor of the Royal Victorian Order of which he is a knight; Knight of the Most Ancient and Noble Order of the Thistle; Lieutenant in the Royal Company of Archers; Lord Lieutenant of the County of Angus. His connections are more than ceremonial. He is currently a director of the Royal Bank of Scotland, the biggest bank north of the border, the Perth-based insurance giant General Accident, and the Stratton Investment Trust. In the past he has been a director of J Henry Schroder Wagg, Schroder's PLC, the Ashdown Investment Trust and Scottish and Newcastle Breweries.

His family networks are equally impressive. His brother Angus Ogilvy is a City of London businessman who joined the royal family by marrying HRH Princess Alexandra of Kent (the Queen's niece). The Earl of Airlie's wife Virginia (née Ryan) comes from a wealthy US family and is one of the Queen's Ladies of the Bedchamber, as well as being a trustee of the Tate Gallery and the National Gallery. Airlie's son and heir David John Ogilvy is managing director of the London art dealer Richard L Feigen Ltd and is married to Geraldine Harmsworth, daughter of the press baron Lord Rothermere, while his eldest daughter, Lady Doune, is wife of the colourful Northamptonshire landowner Sir Hereward Wake who once owned the Amhuinnsuidhe Estate in the Outer Hebrides.

The Earl of Airlie is reputed to own more than 12 000 hectares of land north of Kirriemuir in Angus. His principal residence, Cortachy Castle, is set in heavily wooded land beside the River South Esk. He also has a house in Chelsea, a short taxi-ride from the House of Lords where he sits as a cross bencher. Like his brother Angus (and many of their ilk) he was educated at Eton. His military service was with the Scots Guards, a regiment much favoured by Scotland's

26

dukes, marquesses, earls and viscounts. He now sits at the centre of a network of contacts and influence which extends from Angus through Edinburgh to the City of London and on into Buckingham Palace and the Palace of Westminster.

But despite his obvious importance in Scotland the Earl of Airlie refused (or was not allowed) to be interviewed for this book. Requests via his estate office in Angus produced only a polite letter from Buckingham Palace which explained that, as the Earl of Airlie was Lord Chamberlain of the Queen's Household, and therefore in a position of extreme confidence, he could not be interviewed. Under any circumstances.

In many respects he is the quintessential Scottish aristocrat. English educated, well-connected with the ceremonial establishment, discreet, covered with honours, and with powerful ties in the south of England. What is more, he is one of many. For a country with a population of only 5 million, Scotland fairly bristles with dukes and marquesses, earls and viscounts, lords and knights. It was ever thus. At the time of the Treaty of Union with England in 1707 Scotland had a population of 1.25 million and 154 peers, that is, one peer to 8 000 people. The English, on the other hand had to make do with 164 peers for 5.5 million people, or one peer to 32 000. When the clan chiefs and 'bonnet lairds' (minor gentry) were included, one Scot in every 45 regarded himself as above the common herd; all of which may seem at odds with the country's democratic (and radical) aspirations, but which goes some way to explaining the historic European epithet 'Proud as a Scot'.

Scotland's landed class has survived to an astonishing extent. Despite the cost of maintaining huge estates and crumbling castles, despite inheritance taxes and hostile governments, despite pressure for land reform and access to the public, the great names which are studded thorough Scottish history remain, often still living on the same tracts of land they held through the religious wars of the 17th century and the Jacobite rebellions. Diminished and thinned in rank they may be, but they are still largely in place, and showing every sign of hanging on. They have done so by adapting to circumstances, marrying into 'new' money, setting up trusts, carving out a niche in the City, letting out the sporting rights on their heather-clad hills, opening up the family home to the public, or selling off parcels of land here and there to keep going. Their tenacity is remarkable.

The peerage and the gentry

Not all peers conform. A notable exception to the aristocratic rule is Angus Alan Douglas Douglas-Hamilton, 15th Duke of Hamilton, 12th Duke of Brandon and Scotland's premier peer. Where many of his contemporaries in the upper aristocracy still own large swathes of Scotland (the Duke of Buccleuch is reputed to be the biggest private landowner in Europe), the Duke of Hamilton runs an arable farm in East Lothian. Nor does he share the aristocracy's enthusiasm for blood sports: 'I hate the idea of killing living creatures for fun,' he says. True, he was educated at Eton, but he describes his schooldays there as 'a total disaster'.

27

His own four children are being educated at Scottish schools. And while most of Scotland's aristocracy and gentry are Episcopalian or Roman Catholic, Angus Douglas-Hamilton is a dyed-in-the-wool member of the Church of Scotland. 'Because that is the church of the Scottish people,' he says. 'I may not be much of a Christian but I'm a good Protestant.'

Nor was his military career spent with a fashionable regiment like the Scots Guards or the Household Cavalry, but in 81 Squadron of the Royal Air Force. 'I flew photo-reconnaissance Canberras in the Far East,' he recalls. 'The Vietnam war was just getting under way so we did a lot of work for the Americans. They had great equipment but for some reason they couldn't take a decent photograph. I was invalided out with an ulcer, and had a war pension before I was 30. I got as far as flight lieutenant, which ain't very far.' A regret he shared with his father, the 14th Duke, was that he never got to fly Spitfires. 'He was too old,' he says, 'and I was too young.' When he attends the House of Lords (which is not very often) he sits on the cross benches because 'the company is better'. Although his younger brother Lord James serves as a minister in the Tory Government, the Duke of Hamilton does not toe that line. The idea of political power devolved to a Scottish Assembly does not send chills up his spine. And his business career does not consist of gentle merchant banking lunches interspersed with periods of estate management. Instead he runs Ibex Vehicles, a small engineering company which makes diesel-fuelled cars and trucks which he says 'will go places that Land Rovers will never go'. One of his ambitions is to break the world speed records for diesel-fuelled vehicles, to which end he has been touting around the oil companies for cash support. 'But I never use my title for that,' he says. 'They just wouldn't take me seriously.'

Not many of Angus Douglas-Hamilton's counterparts share his view of the world. The striking thing about the Scottish aristocracy is the extent to which they have become anglicized, educated at English public school and Oxbridge, high church rather than Church of Scotland, increasingly detached from Scottish political life.

At the top of the aristocratic ladder are Britain's 24 dukes, and no fewer than eight of them (33 per cent) are Scots. They are the Dukes of Hamilton, Argyll (who is also chief of Clan Campbell), Atholl, Buccleuch and Queensberry, Fife, Montrose, Roxburghe and Sutherland. Some of their titles predate the Union of 1707. Next rung down are the marquesses. Again the proportion of Scots is very high. Scotland may only have 9 per cent of Britain's population, but it has more than 25 per cent of Britain's marquesses. There are nine in all: the marquesses of Aberdeen and Temair, Ailsa, Bute, Huntly, Linlithgow, Lothian, Queensberry, Tweeddale and Zetland. When we get to earls the proportion of Scots dwindles rapidly, but there are still enough to go around. There are 27 of the pre-Union variety, plus a handful of the later creations, such as the Earl of Cromartie (created 1861), the Earl of Gowrie (1945), Earl Haig (1919) and the Earl of Mansfield (1776). Of the five women who are countesses in their own right, four are Scots: the Countess of Dysart, the Countess of Loudoun, the Countess of Mar and the Countess of Sutherland. There are, however, very few Scottish viscounts, either of pre-or post-Union creation. The Viscounts of Arbuthnott, Falkland and Oxfuird account for the former, and Muirshiel, Stuart of Findhorn, Thurso and Younger of Leckie for the latter. And Scots peers with the pre-Union rank of baron number only 15 or so out of a UK total of more than 400, although some of the titles are ancient. Lord Forbes, who is Scotland's premier baron, can date his back to 1445, as can Lord Gray. Of the 16 women who are baronesses in their own right, five hold Scots titles.

However ancient their claims on Scotland may be, the Scottish aristocracy and gentry have become steadily more dislocated from the rest of the country. For many generations they have looked to England for their social (and political) cues. 'There's no denying we've become deplorably anglicized in the last few hundred years,' says the Duke of Hamilton. While middle-class Scotland appears to have lost its taste for anglicizing its children, the aristocracy and the gentry have not. The educational background of the nine Scottish dukes is revealing in this respect. The Dukes of Atholl, Buccleuch, Hamilton and Montrose all went to Eton and Oxford. Both the Duke of Roxburghe and the Duke of Sutherland attended Eton and Cambridge. Only the Dukes of Argyll and Fife went to school in Scotland—Glenalmond and Gordonstoun respectively—and both of those are modelled on English public school systems. One consequence of the Englishing of the Scottish upper classes has been their steady conversion from Presbyterianism to the Anglicanism of their southern counterparts. With many exceptions, such as the Presbyterian Dukes of Argyll and Hamilton and the Roman Catholic Earl of Perth, upper-class Scotland favours the Scottish Episcopal Church, a denomination still known in some rural parts as 'the laird's kirk'. (Or, because the Episcopalians were the first to introduce the pipe organ, 'the whistling kirk'.) An intriguing manifestation of aristocratic Episcopalianism is the 'Cathedral of the Isles' at Millport on the little island of Cumbrae. This tiny piece of Victorian Gothic designed by George Butterfield was funded by George Boyle, the 6th Earl of Glasgow, who pumped huge sums of money into the Scottish Episcopal Church. So much so, in fact, that the Earl went spectacularly bankrupt in 1885, leaving the diocese to find the money for the upkeep of the building. It is now used as a retreat house and study centre.

But such zealotry is rare. 'My grandfather, my father and myself were all brought up as Episcopalians,' says the Earl of Elgin, 'but the family used to attend all the churches on our estates. In the morning we would go to the "Piskie" church, then for the evening service we might go to the Church of Scotland or the Free Church. But in the 1970s my wife and I decided to settle down and become full members of the Church of Scotland.'

Military service in certain regiments is an important component in most aristocratic backgrounds. A large number of Scots peers carried a musket in the Scots Guards. Ex-Scots guardsmen include the Duke of Fife and the marquesses of Aberdeen and Temair, Ailsa, Linlithgow and Lothian. The Duke of Roxburghe and the Marquess of Queensberry rode tanks and armoured cars in the Royal Horse Guards. As Chief of the Clan Gordon, the Marquess of Huntly served in the Gordon Highlanders, and the Duke of Argyll in the Argyll and Sutherland Highlanders.

For all their numbers and grandeur the Scottish peerage cannot be said to figure amongst the movers and shakers of the House of Lords. According to *Dod's Parliamentary Companion* no Scots peers are listed for the session 1991–2 in the panel of deputy speakers. None appear on the panel of deputy chairmen. No Scottish peer acts as chairman for one of the many House of Lords committees or subcommittees, with the exception of Lord Jauncey of Tullichettle who chairs the Consolidation Bills, Joint Committee. And Lord Jauncey is one of the law lords.

Although Conservatives predominate amongst Scotland's peers there is a wide spread of opinion, even among the upper ranks. Like the Duke of Hamilton and the Earl of Airlie, the Countess of Mar, Scotland's premier countess, sits as a cross bencher. Viscount Falkland, who is Scotland's premier viscount, votes with the Liberal Democrats. Only the premier marquess (Huntly) and the premier baron (Forbes) accept the Conservative whip.

The pages on 'Peers Political Interests' in *Dod's* make uninspiring reading. Only three Scots peers—Lord Forbes, the Earl of Haddington and the Countess of Sutherland—appear to be interested in agriculture, and only Lord Sanderson and the Earl of Selkirk have a declared interest in housing. Lord Sanderson is also interested in trade and industry, along with Lord Goold (one-time Conservative Party chairman in Scotland) and Lord Campbell of Alloway. Remarkably few of the Scots peers list Scottish affairs as one of their interests. Those who do are Baroness Carnegie of Lour, Lord Forbes, Lord Fraser of Kilmorack, Lord Macaulay of Bragar, Lord Polwarth, Lady Saltoun of Abernethy, the Earl of Selkirk and the young Earl of Cromartie (who is specifically interested in land use in the Highlands). And three of those (Carnegy, Fraser and Macaulay) are life rather than hereditary peers. There are, of course, others who speak frequently, and with some expertise on their chosen subjects: Viscount Thurso comes down from Caithness to speak on salmon and nuclear waste; the newly ennobled Lord Macfarlane of Bearsden speaks up for Glasgow. But the picture is not that of a notably energetic political sector.

'I suppose you could say we are keeping our heads down politically,' says one viscount. 'In these democratic days, we're well aware of the fact that nobody elects us to the House of Lords. We'd get nothing but stick if we opened our mouths too much. But if we say nothing at all, we get accused of being a bunch of Tory backwoodsmen with nothing in our pates but huntin' shootin' and fishin'. There's a sense in which we cannot win.'

Certainly the days when the peerage and the gentry dominated the rural councils seem to be over. The lists of convenors and committee chairmen published in the municipal yearbooks contain few traces of blue blood. In

1991 Mackintosh of Mackintosh was chairman of the Highland Regional Council's Roads and Transport Committee, while Alistair Forsyth of that Ilk was convenor of the Industrial Development Commitee of the Angus District Council. But the gentry-count remains fairly high in quangos like the Historic Buildings Council, Scottish Natural Heritage and in voluntary bodies like the National Trust for Scotland; the president of the National Trust for Scotland is the Marquess of Bute who succeeded the Earl of Wemyss and March in 1991. The Trust's Curatorial Committee has tended in the past to be particularly high-toned, counting among its number the Marquess of Bute, the Hon R C Corbett, Mrs Eleanor Munro of Foulis, Lady Shaw Stewart and the Duchess of Sutherland. The Duke of Atholl is on the Investment Committee. Like a small number of the Scottish aristocracy, the Duke is a seasoned business-man, chairman of the Westminster Press, and one-time director of BPM Holdings and Pearson Longman Ltd. The Marquess of Queensberry was a founding member of the Queensberry Hunt design group. The Duke of Argyll's business interests are steeped in whisky. He is a director of Aberlour Glenlivet Distillery Co, S Campbell & Son, White Heather Distillers and Muir Mackenzie & Co. The Earl of Airlie is one of the *éminences gris* of the City of London.

Among the upper aristocracy such commercialism is still exceptional. Public life remains the order of the day. The Marquess of Bute is particularly active in this respect. The list of organizations with which he has been involved includes the National Fund for Research into Crippling Diseases, the Historic Buildings Council for Scotland, the Design Council, the Oil Development Council for Scotland, the National Galleries of Scotland and the National Museums of Scotland. But far more of the country's dukes, marquesses, earls, viscounts and lords are inclined to stay home on their estates. For all the recent fuss about Scottish land being snapped up by Dutchmen, Germans, Arabs and others, vast stretches of it remain in the hands of the Scottish aristocracy. The Duke of Buccleuch, for example, owns around 270 000 hectares of southern Scotland, with stately homes at Dalkeith, Bowhill and Drumlanrig. Until recently the Earl of Seafield's lands (around Cullen on the Moray Firth coast, and Aviemore in Strathspey) amounted to more than 70 000 hectares, although that has been dwindling fast. The Countess of Sutherland's landholdings in the far north are now a fraction of what they used to be but still account for more than 60 000 hectares. Precise figures are hard to come by, but best estimates are that eight of the 10 biggest private landowners in Scotland are from the aristocracy and the gentry. They are the Duke of Buccleuch (number 1), the Earl of Seafield (3), the Countess of Sutherland (4), the Duke of Atholl (5), Farquharson of Invercauld (6), the Earl of Stair (9), and Cameron of Lochiel (10). The Duke of Argyll and Lord Lovat are not far behind. The Queen's landholdings around Deeside are relatively modest. An estimated 14 000 hectares; not even in the top 50 estate owners.

Many of Scotland's landowners acquire legal powers when they inherit their land. An archaic form of feudalism—a system of law that England dispensed with in medieval times and the French swept away during the Revolution—still prevails in Scotland. Feu duties have been abolished, but feudal tenure, the holding of land from a feudal 'superior', still exists. And feudal tenure gives many landowners legal powers over properties they do not own. They can, for example, act as a de facto planning authority by insisting on slates instead of tiles, stone instead of brick, white paint instead of blue, and forbidding the use of a garden for any kind of business. If a property owner wants to build a garage, kitchen extension or pigeon shed his feudal superior can charge him for issuing a 'Minute of Waiver' allowing it to happen. The vassal can appeal to the land court in Edinburgh, but that procedure can be time-consuming and costly. Most vassals just stump up. One Deeside landowner was recently charging up to £1 000 for a Minute of Waiver.

Even more threatening is the 'right of preemption' which many feudal superiors retain. This gives them the right to step in and buy, at the best price, any property which comes on the market and over which they have feudal superiority. Thus if a father wants to sell a house to his son, and the local feudal superior is prepared to match the son's price, the superior must have the house. Legally there is nothing the family can do about it. It is a device which a minor landowner called Michael Nightingale has used to build up his property portfolio in the town of Cromarty, and one which the Earl of Seafield used on his estates around Aviemore and Cullen. Feudal tenure is an archaic system, and the Law Commission for Scotland is currently working out ways to consign it to the legal dustbin.

Her Majesty's Household in Scotland

The central prop of the establishment is 'Her Majesty's Household in Scotland'. This residue of the ancient Scottish court is organized into four component parts: the heraldic or ceremonial household (which is peppered with dukes, earls and knights plus a few academics and artists), the ecclesiastical household (senior Church of Scotland ministers), the medical household (physicians, surgeons and apothecaries) and the Royal Company of Archers (a peculiarly Scottish admixture of the aristocracy, landed gentry, and the industrial top brass). The Royal Company of Archers is probably the most exclusive club in the land, with a waiting list which is described as 'very, very long'.

The Queen's Household is supposed to attend to the Monarch when she is in residence in Scotland (which is usually every summer). It is all that is left of the ancient Scottish court which packed its bags and stole away to London with James VI in 1603. And like most corners of the British establishment, Her Majesty's Household in Scotland is overwhelmingly male, middle-aged and upper class. How its members are selected is a mystery known only to Buckingham Palace. 'Some are hereditary, of course,' says Sir Malcolm Innes of Edingight, the Lord Lyon King of Arms, and one of the Household's most influential members. 'The Lord High Constable is always the Earl of Errol. And the Duke of Argyll is the Hereditary Master of the Household in Scotland. But as for the others? Well, certain names just *emerge*. To suggest names to the palace would be something of an impertinence.' Most of the appointments are purely ceremonial and/or honorary, and some have a resounding medieval resonance. Traditionally, the Lord High Constable of Scotland was responsible for maintaining law and order. The current incumbent, the Earl of Errol, might be hard put to keep Scotland free of brigandage and turbulence from his farmhouse near Basingstoke in Hampshire. Nor are too many practical demands put on the Earl of Dundee, the Hereditary Bearer of the Royal Banner of Scotland (the Lion Rampant), or the Earl of Lauderdale, the Hereditary Bearer of the Scottish National Flag (the Saltire), or, for that matter, the Hereditary Carver (currently Sir Ralph Anstruther of that Ilk) whose job it was to slice the monarch's suckling pig or goose.

Four of the royal castles and palaces in Scotland have hereditary keepers. The Duke of Hamilton is responsible for looking after Holyrood Palace, N J Crichton-Stuart has the stewardship of Falkland Palace in Fife, the Duke of Argyll tends to Dunstaffnage Castle near Oban (once the power base of the great Clan MacDougall) while the Earl of Mar and Kellie oversees Stirling Castle. The recently installed military governor of Edinburgh Castle, Lieutenant-General Sir Peter Graham, is also a member of the Queen's Household. 'My family have been keepers of Stirling Castle since the 1500s,' the Earl of Mar says, 'although it was taken away from us because one of my ancestors led the Jacobite rebellion of 1715. In fact, the keepership wasn't restored to the family until 1923, when my grandfather got it back, probably because my grandmother was a great friend of King George V. My job is to meet the Queen when she visits Stirling Castle. That's been four or five times since I became keeper. I used to wear one of my Scots Guards uniforms, but now I wear my tartans. I also happen to be chief of the name Erskine'. The Duke of Hamilton performs the same role at the Palace of Holyroodhouse. 'When the Queen is there I see her in and I see her out,' he says. 'I could wear my RAF uniform—I'm an Honorary Air Commodore—but usually I wear civvies, which means my kilt. Theoretically I'm responsible for what goes on in the Palace, but the Lord Chamberlain's department takes care of all that. But I've also got to be on call during the General Assembly of the Church of Scotland when the Lord High Commissioner is holding court at the Palace.'

The Scottish intelligentsia does have something—although not much—of a presence in the Queen's Household. Professor Douglas Henderson, administrator of the beautiful Inverewe Gardens in Wester Ross acts as the Queen's Botanist in Scotland. The post of Astronomer Royal for Scotland is currently empty, having been recently vacated by Professor Malcolm Longair, a world-class cosmologist and astrophysicist. The portrait painter David Donaldson and Sir Eduardo Paolozzi are the Royal Painter and Limner, and Sculptor in Ordinary respectively. These last two are interesting choices. While no

33

Picasso, David Donaldson has an irreverent eye. His recent portrait of Margaret Thatcher scandalized the establishment, and was exiled for some time to the storeroom of the Scottish National Portrait Gallery in Edinburgh until press inquiries embarrassed the gallery authorities into hanging it. Eduardo Paolozzi, a first generation Italian-Scot from Edinburgh, is one of the most original artists Scotland has produced for generations.

'No emoluments and purely honorific,' is how Professor Gordon Donaldson, the Historiographer Royal in Scotland describes his role. 'I do *not* advise the royal family on Scottish history. Maybe I should. They make some howlers, like the time when Prince Charles described himself as being descended from Henry VIII. He's not. He's descended from Henry's *sister* Margaret who married James IV of Scotland. And why did Charles and Di go to Normandy to commemorate the death of William the Conqueror, but didn't come to Scotland to mark the death of Mary Queen of Scots? Answer me that?'

Her Majesty's spiritual welfare in Scotland is looked after by the large battery of Presbyterian ministers who form the Ecclesiastical Household. There are 20 in all, headed by the Dean of the Chapel Royal, the Reverend William Morris (minister at Glasgow Cathedral), and the Dean of the Order of the Thistle, the Very Reverend Gillesbuiag Macmillan (minister at the High Kirk of St Giles). The Queen's Domestic Chaplain in Scotland is the Reverend Keith Angus. Nine of the Household are described as 'Chaplains in Ordinary' and eight are 'Extra Chaplains'. In June 1991 Buckingham Palace appointed a woman as one of the Chaplains in Ordinary. She is the Reverend Mary Levison (née Mary Lusk) an Oxford-born Presbyterian who campaigned successfully throughout the 1960s to have women ordained in the Church of Scotland. Mrs Levison herself was ordained in 1978, and retired as a working minister in 1983. In 1988 she was the first ever woman to act as Moderator of the Glasgow Presbytery.

Surprisingly perhaps, this quiet corner of Her Majesty's Household has its critics. All the ministers in the Ecclesiastical Household are drawn from the established Church of Scotland. 'Maybe the time has come to revise that arrangement,' says one senior Church of Scotland minister. 'The days when the Kirk had almost total control over the religious life of Scotland are long gone.'

The Queen's physical health appears to be rated less highly than her spiritual wellbeing. The Medical Household consists of two Physicians, two Surgeons and two Extra Surgeons, plus an Apothecary to the Household at Balmoral and an Apothecary to the Household at the Palace of Holyroodhouse. All of them are drawn from the upper ranks of the Scottish medical (and pharmaceutical) professions.

The most important ceremonial functionary in the Queen's Household is Sir Malcolm Innes of Edingight, the tall, portly, sandy-haired lawyer who as the Lord Lyon King of Arms is responsible for enforcing heraldic law and order north of the border. 'And as the Monarch's herald, I also announce the dissolution of parliament from the Mercat Cross in Edinburgh,' he says, 'And inaugurate the governor of Edinburgh Castle. And attend the opening of the General Assembly of the Church of Scotland.' But such ceremonial goings on are the exception. Most of the Lord Lyon's day is taken up considering requests for a 'Grant of Arms' from individuals and companies. Any suburban golfclub looking for a coat of arms to sport on their blazers, or whisky blender hoping to use a crest to add some 'tone' to packaging, have to run their heraldic plans past the Lord Lyon for his approval. And that approval is not always granted. Every one that is approved is entered into a carefully kept (and beautifully illustrated) register which is held in Edinburgh. 'That's the bread and butter of the job,' he says. 'You'd be surprised at the number of companies, institutions and societies etc who want a Grant of Arms to trade under, or just to pin over their door. I'd say that 75 per cent of our work is handling applications for private arms, and the other 25 per cent is corporate work. Having your own coat of arms seems to be as popular now as it has ever been.' The Lord Lyon describes his role as an arbiter. 'I'm the judge of all heraldic matters in Scotland. I must decide whether a company or an individual has a right to a Grant of Arms. Or who is to own a baronetcy, or a clan chieftainship, or be the head of a family name. Sometimes these things can be quite hotly contested. It's up to me to decide which way it goes.'

However, there is more to the Lord Lyon and his court than this. He and it have a recognized constitutional position. The Lyon Court is a full-blown (if minor) court of law. He is both an Officer of the Crown and Officer of the Kingdom. He is automatically knighted on his appointment, and since the year 1554 to 'strike or deforce' the Lord Lyon has been regarded as an act of high treason. He is also responsible for the behaviour of the Messengers at Arms who carry out the bidding of the Court of Session and the High Court of Justiciary. These days he must be a (Scots) lawyer of three years' standing, he has his own procurator fiscal (prosecutor) and his own courtroom. And under acts of parliament dating back to 1592, 1672 and 1669 he has considerable power: 'unwarrantable' arms and crests can be forcibly erased, goods seized, and in extreme cases, offenders gaoled. If an issue—such as the recent claim for the chieftainship of the Keppoch Macdonalds—is contested, then the Lyon Court is held in public, usually in the Lyon's headquarters in the Register Office at the east end of Princes Street. On those occasions, all the trappings and paraphernalia of the law are invoked, and the court assembles under the portraits of the former Lords Lyon. 'But any decision I make can be appealed—first to the Court of Session and then to the House of Lords.'

The Lord Lyon rules over the heraldic landscape with the assistance of three heralds, Albany, Ross and Rothesay, and two pursuivants, Kintyre and Unicorn. 'There is a vacancy for a herald at the moment,' Innes says. 'And I'm not surprised. They haven't had a pay rise since 1694. They still get £200 Scots, which is the equivalent of about £8 sterling. A year, that is. But two of the heralds, John Spens and Crispin Agnew, are lawyers, so that helps.' Malcolm Innes wears his considerable powers lightly. He is an amiable, talkative man, well used to briefing quizzical foreign and English journalists in the arcane mysteries of Scottish heraldry and clanship. And he is only too aware of the disdain with which London traditionally regards Scottish heraldry. In the hallway to his office there is a glass case in which hangs an elaborate, gold-embroidered 'tabard' worn by many of his predecessors. 'That tabard has the English form of arms, with the three Leopards,' he says. 'Now, successive Lords Lyon asked for it to be changed to the proper, Scottish form, the Lion Rampant. But the Treasury always refused to put up the money. Too expensive, they said. Eventually the proprietor of MacGowan's Toffee—quite a famous brand at the time—came to the rescue and paid for a new tabard. Otherwise we'd still be wearing the English form of arms.'

Sir Malcolm Innes is also a member of yet another branch of Her Majesty's Household: the Royal Company of Archers, the Queen's Bodyguard for Scotland, the most exclusive pseudo-military force in Britain. Its slightly odd hierarchy (in which lieutenants outrank brigadiers) embraces dukes, earls, marquesses, knights, retired cabinet ministers, naval officers, generals, captains of industry, clan chiefs, plus well-heeled businessmen and Edinburgh lawyers by the score. It is the point at which the Scottish establishment dovetails into Her Majesty's Household. Lord Clydesmuir is the company's leader, with the rank of Captain-General and Gold Stick for Scotland. His immediate subordinates (ie captains) are Lord Home of the Hirsel (one-time prime minister), the Duke of Buccleuch, Sir John Gilmour Bart, and Sir Hew Hamilton-Dalrymple, the Royal Company's Silver Stick. Lesser mortals include the Earl of Wemyss and March, the Earl of Dalhousie, the Marquess of Lothian, Lord Younger of Prestwick, the Marquess of Graham, Sir David Nickson (late of the Confederation of British Industry) and the ubiquitous Earl of Elgin. 'I've been an archer since 1951,' Sir Hugh Hamilton-Dalrymple says, 'and I suppose the biggest change I've seen over the years is the military experience of the intake. In the years after the war just about every man coming into the company had some kind of military experience. Nowadays, hardly any of the new people have. Not that they are worse archers for that, but they are slightly different.' The total membership is confined to around 400, the waiting time is five or six years, and according to the Earl of Elgin 'quite a few applicants pop off before their name comes up'. Just about every High Court Judge, industrialist and senior civil servant in Scotland longs to don the finery, and march about Edinburgh, defending the Monarch. Archery goes on too. 'We have about 50 members who shoot regularly,' Hamilton-Dalrymple says. 'In the winter they practise at the indoor butts at the back of the Archers Hall, and in the summer the Queen gives us permission to shoot in the grounds of Holyrood Palace. But I'm not a shooting archer myself. Never have been.' Neither is the Duke of Hamilton. 'I only went down to the butts once,' he says. 'I was hopeless. My first shot landed on the roof, and my second succeeded in smashing a big ashtray that was nowhere near the target. I knew that I was never going to be any good at it, so I never went back. In fact I've only ever paraded once, and that was in 1977 at the Queen's jubilee.'

There are probably more archery prizes now than there have ever been: the Edinburgh Arrow, the Musselburgh Arrow, the Peebles Arrow, the Montrose Arrow and the Selkirk Arrow. The Royal Company like to claim that the competition for the Musselburgh Arrow is the oldest in the archery world, dating back to at least 1603. The winner has the right to graze his goose on Musselburgh links. The Royal Company also run a three-yearly shoot-out at Holyrood Palace with the Woodmen of Arden, an upmarket archery society from the depths of gentrified England. The Woodmen's uniform of green tailcoats, white trousers and slouch hats is almost (but not quite) as fancy as the Royal Company's. 'That's a very sociable occasion,' says Hamilton-Dalrymple. 'They bring their wives when they come and we take our wives when we go down to the Forest of Arden.' A full turnout of the Royal Company is quite an impressive sight. What they lack in military bearing (not to say youth) they make up for in sartorial splendour. Middle-aged paunches are tucked behind tunics of Lincoln Green. Bald pates are covered by dark bonnets crowned with eagle's feathers. Liver-spotted hands are hidden by white gloves. Backsides softened by many a business lunch are squeezed into tight green trousers. But the campaign medals that many of the Royal Company wear are real enough, and many of them were hard won; DSOs, MCs and DSCs are plentiful. The Royal Company of Archers may not be able to claim the ancient lineage of, say, the Court of the Lord Lyon, but it has been around since 1676 when a handful of prominent Edinburgh gents decided to revive '. . . the noble and useful recreation of archery . . .' Charles Erskine, the Lord Lyon of his day, was among their number, and their very first captain-general was the 2nd Earl of Atholl. After being granted a Royal Charter by Queen Anne in 1704, the company kept a low profile for most of the 18th century due to the Jacobite tendencies of some (although not all) its members.

However, by the end of the century the Royal Company of Archers had climbed back into favour and respectability. The Archers Hall, the company's premises on the south side of Edinburgh, were built in 1776. At one stage they were used as a hostelry and dance hall to raise some money for the hard-pressed organization. The Royal Company has had some unlikely members: the poet Allan Ramsay, the painter Henry Raeburn, the novelist Sir Walter Scott. On one famous occasion in October 1818 the company entertained a party of American Indians who were appearing in a show at the Theatre Royal. An impromptu archery competition was arranged at which the startled redskins were completely outshot by the Edinburgh toffs. At the ensuing festivities ('beef, bread and strong ale') the Indian spokesman, one Long Horns, sheepishly explained that his people's archery was so dismal because they had long ago switched to muskets and rifles. But it was not until George IV's famous tartan-decked visit to Edinburgh in 1822 that the Royal Company was granted the additional title of 'King's Bodyguard in Scotland', probably due to the lobbying of Sir Walter Scott. Since then, every time a British monarch has descended on Edinburgh, the warriors have dusted down their Lincoln-green uniforms, straightened their eagle feathers, twanged their bowstrings and marched out to guard the monarch's body.

The Thistle Knights

Every year, on the Sunday closest to Saint Andrew's Day, the flower of Scottish chivalry, the Most Ancient and Most Noble Order of the Thistle, make their appearance. A dozen or so elderly gentlemen, togged out in long dark-green robes and sporting black velvet caps sprouting imitation osprey feathers, troop across Parliament Square in Edinburgh from the Signet Library and into the Thistle Chapel at the east end of the High Kirk of St Giles. They are preceded by the Lord Lyon King of Arms and his heralds and pursuivants. After a 20-minute service presided over by the Reverend Gillesbuiag Macmillan, the Dean of the Thistle (during which they pray for the Queen and the Queen Mother) the Knights of the Thistle process into St Giles to take part in the morning service. They occupy the royal pews, and their Chancellor, Lord Home of the Hirsel, takes the Queen's seat. 'We get a very large and distinguished congregation on these occasions,' Macmillan says. 'The Lord Provost is always there, the senior councillors, the Lord President and the judges.'

Such goings on at the High Kirk of St Giles—the centre of world Presbyterianism—are not universally popular. To some of the sterner members of the Church of Scotland the whole colourful panoply reeks of hierarchical Episcopalianism if not outright popery. 'There are those who would say that it is neither conventional nor Presbyterian,' says Gillesbuiag Macmillan, 'but most people seem to enjoy it.' The proceedings invariably attract a crowd of curious onlookers. 'If you're going to have a ceremony it is as well to do it properly,' says the Earl of Elgin, who was made a Knight of the Thistle in November 1982. 'Scotland has a great and honoured past. We must not forget the past for the convenience of the present. There may only be a few people involved in it, but everybody in Scotland is touched by it.'

This may be true, but does not answer the question: What is the Order of the Thistle (motto 'Nemo Me Impune Lacessit') *for*? One explanation is that it continues to provide a unique link between the crown and the ancient kingdom. Another, displayed in the Thistle Chapel itself, is that the Order is 'Scotland's proudest accolade'; a way of rewarding the brightest and the best for their services to Scotland. But that particular claim is dubious. For one thing, at least half of the Thistle Knights are hereditary gentry, worthy and hard-working men, no doubt, but not exactly key figures in national life: The Earl of Wemyss and March, Sir Donald Cameron of Lochiel, the Earl of Selkirk, the Duke of Buccleuch, the Earl of Elgin, the Earl of Dalhousie, the Earl of Airlie, Lord MacLehose of Beoch. There are three retired politicians: Lord Home of the Hirsel, Lord Whitelaw (the most recent member) and Lord

Thomson of Monifieth (one time EEC commissioner). Workaday Scotland (ie the law, commerce and industry) is represented only by Lord Clydesmuir, Viscount Muirshiel, Sir Iain Tennant, and Lord Cameron, the retired high court judge.

The fact is that Buckingham Palace seems to draw the Thistle Knights from a very small pool. Heredity is synonymous with distinction. When it comes to dishing out chivalric honours, the Palace does not appear to favour Scotland's working businessmen, academics, trade union leaders, medical men, writers, painters, scientists, sportsmen, government administrators, or media barons. Bloodlines are almost everything. No fewer than nine dukes of Buccleuch, eight dukes of Atholl and six dukes of Hamilton have been Thistle Knights. Seven marquesses of Lothian have sported the dark green robe. The first 'commoner' to be appointed to the Order was Sir William Stirling Maxwell of Keir, Bart, and that was as late as 1876. Since then only 14 non-peers have made it. Malcolm Innes of Edingight, who as Lord Lyon King of Arms is secretary to the order, is at a loss to explain exactly how people are invested as Thistle Knights. 'A name just emerges,' he says, 'and it is passed on to Buckingham Palace. But it is the palace which decides.' Although heraldry buffs like to claim that the Order of the Thistle dates back to the days of James III, there is very little evidence to support this. The order was, in fact, the brainchild of King James VII (and II of England) who cooked it up in 1687 in an attempt to restore some kind of Roman Catholic splendour to Presbyterian Scotland. The first recipients were James's placemen, Catholics like the Earl of Perth, his brother the Earl of Melfort and the Duke of Gordon. The most fitting home for the new Thistle Knights was thought to be the abbey church beside Holyrood Palace. The Presbyterians were cleared out to make way for the King's new order of chivalry.

The Queen's lieutenants

Every time a member of the royal family swoops on any part of Scotland, waiting to greet him or her is a figure of a middle-aged or elderly personage in a dark blue military uniform, usually wearing a sword. He is also there when a local factory wins the Queen's Award for Industry and/or Export, or when it comes to dishing out minor gongs, such as British Empire Medals, and he is there at the graveside when a local notable is Promoted to Glory. He is, of course, the Lord Lieutenant of the County, the Queen's local representative. The fact that the counties no longer exist in Scotland seems neither here nor there. Scotland is graced with no fewer than 31 of these figures, all of them men, most of them middle-aged, many of them ex-military, and quite a few of them from the aristocracy or the landed gentry. At the last count (late 1991) there was one duke, five earls, two viscounts, a marquess and seven knights. No fewer than 16 of them—more than half—sport military titles, ranging from humble captain to major-general. The only trace of democracy in their ranks are the four Lord Provosts of Edinburgh,

Glasgow, Aberdeen and Dundee (elected councillors to a man and woman) all of whom are lords lieutenant ex officio.

But it is a role that the Earl of Elgin, the Lord Lieutenant of Fife since 1982, takes seriously. 'I'm very conscious of the fact that I am the Queen's representative,' he says. 'And if there is a royal visit going on anywhere on my patch I try to make sure that everything is well organized. And *that* can be quite time consuming. Sometimes with the younger royals you get only a few weeks warning. They flash around the country quite a lot, you see.' One of the lord lieutenant's more ticklish social chores is to recommend to Buckingham Palace which locals should be invited to the Lord High Commissioner's garden party in May and/or the Queen's garden party in July. 'Can be a bit tricky that one,' says one lord lieutenant who asked to remain anonymous. 'Awfully hard to know who to put on the list and who to leave off. Especially in a small community. The word soon gets around. And competition for invitations can be pretty fierce. A chap can get himself into all kinds of trouble if he's not careful.'

Once appointed to the job, the lords lieutenant are in place until they are 75, unless they die before. 'So my regime runs out in 1999,' the Earl of Elgin says. 'If I last that long. I quite enjoy the work, to tell the truth, although there is no money involved. All you get is your expenses, but that hardly covers things.' Not that he is agitating for a daily wage. The men who stand in for the Queen do not, by the look of them, need the money. The Lord Lieutenant of the Stewartry of Kirkudbright, for example, is Sir Michael Herries, former chairman of the Royal Bank of Scotland. Roxburgh, Ettrick and Lauderdale can call on the services of the Duke of Buccleuch while Lanarkshire has the Lord Clydesmuir, one-time steel magnate. And the Queen's man in Morayshire is Captain Sir Iain Tennant, director of the Clydesdale Bank, Grampian Television and much else besides. It is a humdrum job which has its moments. The Earl of Elgin startled a delegation of Soviet military men who were visiting Maritime Headquarters at Pitreavie near Dunfermline by inviting them to dine with him at his huge ancestral home at Broomhall. 'They were a bit taken aback at first,' he says. 'And wanted to know: Why the invitation? But I explained that I was the Queen's representative in Fife and they were delighted. They amazed me by turning up at my door with an oil painting of my ancestor James Bruce who'd been a field marshal in the Russian army in the 18th century. He'd helped them develop their artillery. We all had rather a jolly evening.'

Clans and clandom

One of the more colourful corners of the Scottish establishment is the clan system (or at least what remains of it). Although the real thing was brutally destroyed at (and after) the Battle of Culloden in 1746 its phantom has continued to haunt Scotland. Since the 19th century every major Scottish family, not just the Highland ones, has been regarded as a 'clan'. Even the fearsome border tribes like the Johnstones, Kerrs, Elliots and Scotts (who would have gutted a Highlandman on sight) have been assigned clan crests and tartans. There are now 120 officially constituted Clans or Names in Scotland, many of them with an attached train of septs and sub-septs. Regulating this whole prickly constitutional/sentimental tangle is the job of the Lord Lyon, who tries to ensure that the right man or woman is made chief, and that their armorial bearings are not abused. 'There is a view that in Scotland the monarch is the chief of chiefs,' the Lord Lyon says. 'The *ard righ*, high king, in Celtic custom. And if you see someone like Cameron of Lochiel at a Highland gathering, he is a bit like royalty. Like the Queen at a garden party. I've seen hard-nosed Australian businessmen reduced almost to tears when they meet their clan chief.'

He regards the growth of the 'clan centres' around Scotland as a 'very interesting' phenomenon. Most have been built with small sums of money raised by clan or family members, although the lavish Clan Donald Centre at Armadale in Skye owes a lot to the US money of Ellice Macdonald. 'There is a danger of these things turning into a bit of Disney World,' the Lord Lyon says. 'But everyone is aware of the danger'. However, clandom has a way of trying to entice tourists with the worst kind of gush. 'A fortress stronghold in an idyllic loch-side setting,' states the brochure for Dunvegan Castle on Skye, ancestral home of the Macleods, 'surrounded by dramatic scenery, where seals play and eagles soar.' This castle, 'steeped in history', provides the visitor with a glimpse into 'great Clan Battles; legends; tragedies; murders most foul and great loves and romances'.

Once again, layers of the Scottish establishment overlap. Many of the clan chiefs and heads of families are major Scottish aristocrats: the Duke of Argyll (Campbells), the Duke of Buccleuch and Queensberry (Scotts), the Marquess of Ailsa (Kennedys), the Marquess of Lothian (Kerrs), and the Marquess of Huntly (Gordons). Among the earls who are also family heads are the Earl of Errol (Hays), the Earl of Southesk (Carnegies), the Earl of Perth (Drummonds), the Earl of Mar and Kellie (Erskines), the Earl of Cromartie (Mackenzies), the Earl of Airlie (Ogilvys), and the Earl of Caithness (Sinclairs). 'It's fair to say that clans and clan chiefs are not so warmly regarded in Scotland as they are abroad,' says the Earl of Elgin, head of the Bruce family. 'At the big clan gatherings they have in the USA clan chiefs are treated like kings. They're put on a pedestal. Their clansfolk come for miles to meet them. But not here. I don't know why that should be.'

Despite this, Elgin takes his Bruce family duties seriously. He is a long-time member of the Standing Council of Scottish Chiefs which, he says, his father helped set up 'to protect or safeguard against the misuse of the chiefs' armorial bearings: the Lord Lyon cannot do too much to protect the chiefs' interests, so we try to do it ourselves.' The Council tries to enforce a system of royalties on the manufacturers and retailers of clan crests, badges, brooches and other souvenirs which are widely sold in the tourist industry. 'Money from the royalties goes to the Council who uses it for charities or bursaries,' he says. 'It's only a few thousand a year, but it's useful. And the principal has to be maintained.' Elgin says that in addition the Council gives advice to the various Highland games and clan gatherings which are now popular worldwide, particularly in the USA and Canada. 'We also lunch together annually,' he says, 'which is a reasonably jolly occasion.'

Of the 120 'Chiefs of Clans and Names' (as the directories describe them) 44 live outside Scotland. Most extra-Scottish family heads are comfortably esconced in the south of England, but a good number are scattered around the world: the head of the Boyds lives in Malaga, Spain; the Clan Chattan is led from Gwelo, Zimbabwe; Sir Jean Dunbar of Mochrum presides over his family from Long Island City, New York; the Dundas of Dundas can be found in South Africa; Neil Hunter of Hunterston has made his eyrie in La Massanna, in the Principality of Andorra; Peter Lamont of that ilk makes his home in Manley, New South Wales; and the officially recognized chief of the Clan Urquhart is contactable at 4713 Orleans Boulevard, Jefferson, Louisiana, USA.

All of this raises the question: Does it matter? Apologists for the colourful Anglo-Scottish status quo argue that it exerts a benign influence on the land, that it attracts foreigners to Scotland to visit, angle, shoot, stalk and, hopefully, invest. They also argue that, above all, the panoply of dukes, marquesses, viscounts and knights represents a historical continuity that is politically stabilizing. We tamper with it, they say, at our peril.

On the other hand its critics argue that the whole thing is an anachronism. They can see no reason why the Duke of Argyll, for example, should sit in parliament simply because he is his father's eldest son. All countries, they say, have a de facto class system and pecking order. But only in Britain are differences of class and heredity built into the law and constitution of the land.

3

Doctors, Medicine and Health

Bryan Christie

Medical research

Around 40 years ago, Sunday was quite literally a day of rest for many people
in Scotland as they took to their beds on doctors' orders. The best that could
be recommended then for a patient with high blood pressure was rest and
plenty of it. The eighth edition of Frederick W Price's *Textbook of the Practice
of Medicine*, published in 1950, which was the standard textbook of the time,
puts great store by the patient's 'manner of life'. A stay in bed on at least
one day a week is a central part of the proposed treatment, although cold
and hot baths are best avoided. 'I have been disappointed with the results of
the administration of mistletoe and liver extract', adds Dr Price. Today, by
contrast, an extensive range of drugs is available to treat a condition which,
Dr Price would be surprised to discover, has also been shown to respond quite
positively to increased levels of exercise.

The advance of medical science has been so rapid that it is easy to overlook just
how basic some things were when the NHS was established in 1948. The drugs
available today to control high blood pressure provide just one example of the
type of progress which would have been unthinkable by previous generations.
Who could have imagined in the 1940s that one day people would be walking
around with someone else's heart beating in their body; that elderly people
could be fitted with new hips and knees; that a gall bladder could be surgically
removed using keyhole techniques which avoid the need to cut open the patient;
that sophisticated tests would be available to screen the unborn for congenital
defects?

Scotland has played a major part in this revolution. Nineteenth-century
medicine owed much to pioneers like Sir James Simpson who discovered
chloroform and Joseph Lister who developed antiseptics. These landmarks
have been followed in more recent times by advances such as the first
kidney transplant, carried out in Britain in 1960 by Sir Michael Woodruff
at Edinburgh's Western General Hospital; the development of ultrasound
scanning by Professor Ian Donald in Glasgow; Sir Dugald Baird's pioneering

work in reducing infant mortality in Aberdeen; and the establishment of the first coronary care unit in Europe by Professors Michael Oliver and Desmond Julian at the Edinburgh Royal Infirmary, which led the world in the immediate treatment of acute heart attacks.

Scotland is also home to a successful research community which attracts millions of pounds in grants every year from medical charities, pharmaceutical companies and other sources. Edinburgh and Glasgow are among the top five universities in Britain in generating research income from outside sources, much of it medically related. The Medical Research Council has seven research units in Scotland and provides grant aid to a large number of associated scientists who are involved in a wide variety of projects. Such scientific inquiry has already paid dividends. Two notable achievements have been the development of the world's first artificial vaccine against hepatitis B infection, by Professor Ken Murray of Edinburgh University's Department of Microbiology, and the development of a simple blood test to detect spina bifida in unborn children by his university colleague Professor David Brock of the Department of Genetics. The 1988 Nobel prize winner for medicine was a Scots-born researcher, Sir James Black, who developed betablocker drugs for the treatment of heart disorders, including high blood pressure, and another family of drugs which block the production of acid in the stomach, preventing ulcers. These drugs are in extensive use around the world and Sir James has been credited with helping more people in his laboratory than thousands of doctors at the bedside.

Health and wealth

This record of achievement suggests some inevitability about medical progress and appears to offer the tantalizing prospect of doctors being able to find an answer for most human ailments. In reality, medicine is largely ineffective in the face of many modern ills. In Scotland that reality is only too apparent; the country's rich medical tradition stands in stark contrast to its poor medical record. In the 18th century, medical teaching in Scotland led the world, and through its three royal medical colleges it continues to have an international influence which belies its small size. In the late 20th century, however, death rates from heart disease, cancer and strokes are among the worst in the developed world, while life expectancy for both men and women is amongst the lowest (see Figs 1–5). Two out of three people who die in Scotland every year do so from heart disease or cancer, chronic conditions which are strongly related to the way we live.

While there have been signs in recent years of a welcome fall in death rates particularly among middle-aged men in Scotland, it is acknowledged that too many Scots are still indulging in a trinity of unhealthy habits. They eat badly, smoke too much and drink to excess. The British Regional Heart Study which analysed the medical history of 7 000 middle-aged men throughout Britain, suggested that it is the particular conditions which exist in Scotland which lie

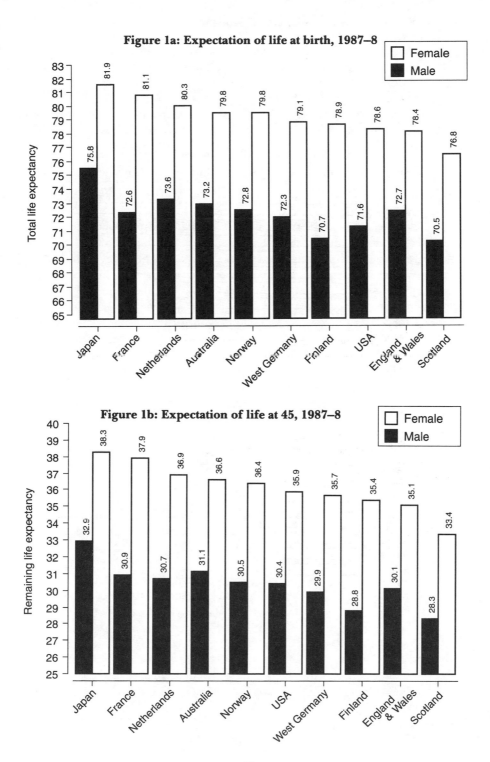

Figure 1a: Expectation of life at birth, 1987–8

Female
Male

Total life expectancy

Japan 75.8 / 81.9
France 72.6 / 81.1
Netherlands 73.6 / 80.3
Australia 73.2 / 79.8
Norway 72.8 / 79.8
West Germany 72.3 / 79.1
Finland 70.7 / 78.9
USA 71.6 / 78.6
England & Wales 72.7 / 78.4
Scotland 70.5 / 76.8

Figure 1b: Expectation of life at 45, 1987–8

Female
Male

Remaining life expectancy

Japan 32.9 / 38.3
France 30.9 / 37.9
Netherlands 30.7 / 36.9
Australia 31.1 / 36.6
Norway 30.5 / 36.4
USA 30.4 / 35.9
West Germany 29.9 / 35.7
Finland 28.8 / 35.4
England & Wales 30.1 / 35.1
Scotland 28.3 / 33.4

Figure 2: Age-standardized mortality rates

Malignant neoplasm of trachea, bronchus and lung in males

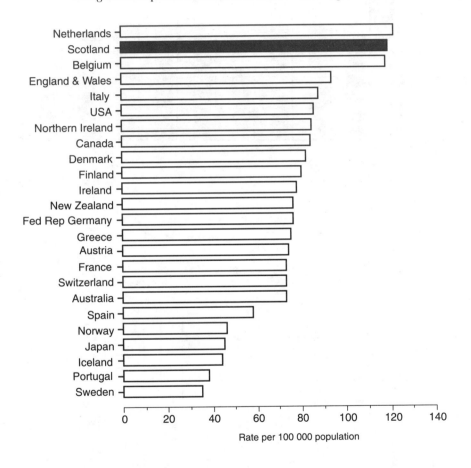

Figure 3: Age-standardized mortality rates

Malignant neoplasm of trachea, bronchus and lung in females

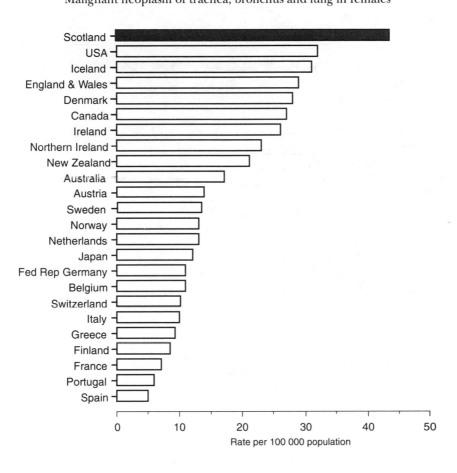

Figure 4: Age-standardized mortality rates

Diseases of the circulatory system in males

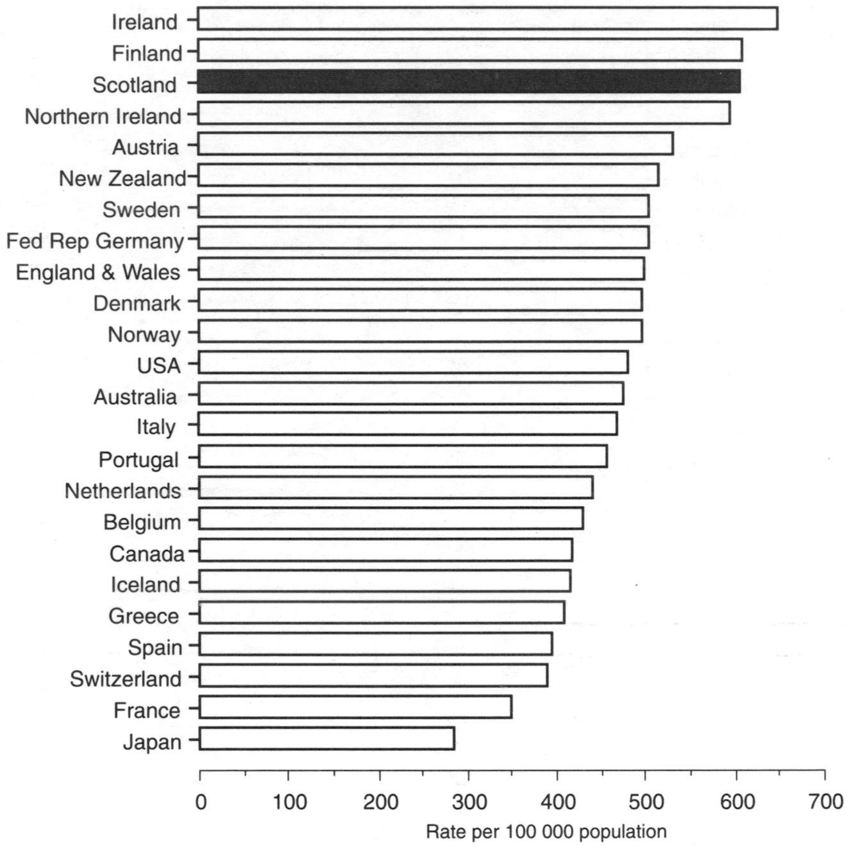

Rate per 100 000 population

Figure 5: Age-standardized mortality rates

Diseases of the circulatory system in females

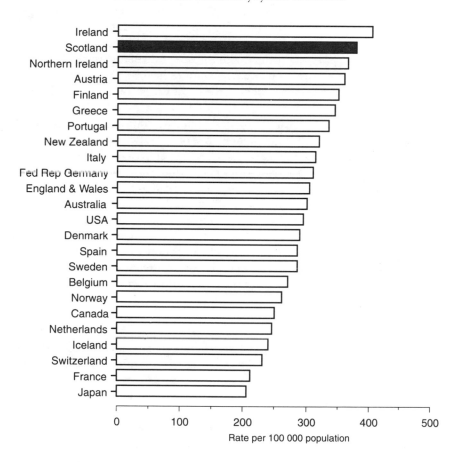

behind this phenomenon. The study found that men living in Scotland were twice as likely as those living in the south-east of England to develop heart trouble. But when they looked at what happened to people who left Scotland to live in the south, they found that the rate of heart attacks and heart disease among this group fell compared with the people who remained in Scotland. Similarly, people who moved from the south to Scotland were found as a group to have increased their risk of heart trouble. The prevailing habits of a particular area seem to be adopted by incomers. In the south-east where the diet is more varied and smoking rates are lower, this can be good news for the migrating Scot; for incomers to Scotland, it can have the opposite effect. The environment people live in plays an important part in their state of health as the widening differences in the position of the relatively rich and poor indicates.

Although the NHS was established with the intention of divorcing health care from personal finance or other factors irrelevant to health, on average the child of a manual labourer today can expect to die eight years younger than the child of a lawyer. Health is still very much wedded to wealth. This is particularly marked in Greater Glasgow where the neighbouring communities of Bearsden and Drumchapel contrast strongly. Bearsden is one of Glasgow's most attractive and prosperous suburbs; Drumchapel one of its most deprived housing estates. Bearsden has one of the lowest death rates in the whole of Scotland; Drumchapel one of the highest. Residents of Drumchapel are twice as likely to die before the age of 65 than their counterparts in Bearsden. Vera Carstairs, a researcher with the Department of Community Medicine at Edinburgh University, has compared levels of deprivation and disease throughout Scotland and analysed these with similar data from England. She has found that more people are living in deprived conditions in Scotland and has concluded that these adverse conditions may explain some of Scotland's health problems.

AIDS

AIDS (Acquired Immune Deficiency Syndrome) has become the latest disease to locate itself in such communities. The sharing of contaminated drug injecting equipment in rundown housing estates in the early 1980s has left Scotland with some of the highest rates of infection among drug-users in the world. The virus spread in what became known as shooting galleries. Young people, who claimed unemployment and boredom led them to take drugs, had little difficulty obtaining supplies of heroin, which flooded into Scotland at the beginning of the 1980s. Police action in confiscating needles and syringes and blocking their supply to users meant that clean equipment was harder to get hold of. As a result, groups of up to 20 gathered to share equipment. The circumstances combined to advance the spread of HIV, the virus that leads to AIDS. It was introduced into this scene in Edinburgh sometime in 1983 and by the time the problem was identified in late 1985, hundreds of people had become infected. Dundee experienced a similar explosion of infection among its drug community. The response by the Government, health professionals and community groups was rapid and effective. Drug-users were supplied with clean injecting equipment through needle exchange schemes and a series of publicity campaigns was mounted which helped control the spread of the virus. Today in Scotland few new cases of drug-related infection are being recorded but the wave of infection in the early 1980s has left around 5 000 people HIV-positive. In Edinburgh it is estimated that in the 15–44 age group, one man in 100 and one woman in 250 is infected. The fear for the future is that Scotland could experience a second wave of heterosexual infection.

The country's well-integrated health service has helped maintain close contact with those infected, allowing the progress of the disease to be tracked. This is just one of the many ways Scotland is adding to the international understanding of the disease. Worldwide interest has also been generated in the way Scotland is caring for people with HIV and AIDS, whether they be children needing foster care, infected prisoners serving gaol sentences, or those in the last days of their lives being looked after in Edinburgh's Milestone House, Britain's first purpose-built AIDS hospice.

But why does Scotland have such poor health when it benefits from first-class health services? The simple answer is that health services make a minimal contribution to health. The National Health Service is in many respects a National Sickness Service, extremely well equipped to treat people when things go wrong but largely ineffective in preventing the problems occurring in the first place. Scotland's former chief medical officer, Dr Kenneth Calman, who now holds the same post in England and Wales, explained that five factors have an impact on health: genetic inheritance, socio-economic status, environment, personal lifestyle and health services. Of these, health services have the least effect 'yet that is where all the money goes'. On top of this, 90 per cent of the health service's resources go into the expensive hospital sector which treats only 10 per cent of patients. All the others are seen in the community by family doctors, community nurses, health visitors, pharmacists and other professionals.

Dr John Marks, who graduated from Edinburgh University on the day the NHS was established in June 1948 and is a former chairman of the British Medical Association, made a similar point to Dr Calman's but in a different way. 'If all doctors stopped working tomorrow and all we had instead was good water, clean air, reasonable housing and food for everybody, that would do more for the people's health than we doctors do in all our lifetime.'

Right-wing politicians have traditionally been unwilling to accept this argument, preferring to blame individuals for their own ill health. However, in a health education strategy document published in 1991, Scotland's Health Minister Michael Forsyth emphasized that the Government is committed to the promotion of health in its widest sense: 'Developments in community care, housing and environmental improvements and urban renewal are all part of the total effort the Government is making to improve the quality of life and thereby the health of the Scottish population.' The statement did not signal the end to damp council housing but at least the connection between living conditions and ill health appeared to have been recognized.

Prevention is the goal because it should lead to the avoidance of so much costly subsequent treatment, but it is notoriously difficult to change individual behaviour. No one knows for instance if the fall in premature heart disease deaths among middle-aged men is due to acceptance of messages about cutting out smoking and improving eating habits or if such people simply belong to a generation that wants to stay slim enough to get into a pair of jeans. Meanwhile, the scale of Scotland's present problems means that resources remain anchored in the hospital service to provide the patch-and-mend service that so many require. In 1990/91 a record 1.15 million people were treated in the Scottish hospitals but the demands were such that just over 60 000 people were on the waiting list for treatment, a slight increase on the previous year.

The NHS in Scotland

Crisis is a word used frequently in the health service and, at times, appears to be its natural condition. Although many individuals remain impressed with the local service they receive, at a national level complaints are as common as praise. When the health service came into being in Scotland on 5 July 1948, it took responsibility for some 64 000 beds from the former voluntary and local authority hospitals. The specialist services that existed then were concentrated mainly in the teaching hospitals of the main cities. Developments to provide communities with access to hospitals nearer their homes progressed slowly. Only one new hospital, the Vale of Leven, was built in the period between 1948–58 but the building programme took off in the 1960s and has continued right up to the present day. Dumfries and Galloway Royal Infirmary was little more than a cottage hospital in the 1960s with wood-built wards being added to cope with increasing numbers of patients. There was a drastic shortage of toilets and it was difficult to keep the wards cool in the summer and warm in the winter. In 1975, it was replaced by a new 450-bed hospital, which provides good local care and has close links with specialist centres elsewhere. This pattern has been repeated throughout Scotland with new hospitals being built in recent years at Melrose, Livingston and Ayr. The health service today has fewer beds—just over 52 000—than it did in 1948. Then, it was common to spend weeks in hospital. The advent of day surgery and improved treatment have cut the time people are spending in hospitals, leading justifiably to cuts in the number of beds that are needed. However, complaints have followed that in some hospitals the cuts have gone too far and people have been discharged prematurely, to vacate beds for other patients.

The NHS is the biggest employer by far in Western Europe. It has 150 000 staff in Scotland alone, 1 in 15 of the Scottish working population. In many towns the local hospital will be the biggest employer. In 1948, at a time when the health service cost £28 million to run, there were only some 900 senior medical hospital staff in Scotland. By 1990 when costs had risen to £3.4 billion that number had quadrupled and the total number of doctors employed in all parts of the service stood at almost 11 000. Nursing staff numbered nearly 75 000.

The Scottish health service has always been more generously funded than its equivalent in England and Wales. There are more doctors and nurses per head of population, more hospital beds and a general higher level of service (see Fig. 6). In the specialty of obstetrics, for instance, there is one consultant to 416 births in Scotland compared with a ratio of 1 to 697 in London and 1 to 1 005 births in Yorkshire. Higher standards of care can be given by Scottish general practitioners who have, on average, 1 600 patients on their lists compared with an average of some 2 000 in England. But although Scotland compares well with England, the international position looks less impressive. Many other developed countries spend more on health, have more doctors and nurses and more hospital beds (see Fig. 7). Despite sizeable increases in expenditure in recent years, the health service has found itself running harder to stay still. The NHS, now well into its forties, is facing something of a mid-life crisis. It has become more capable, but pressure has now been exerted on what is affordable.

Conflict has followed between the political, emotional and logical components of the NHS. Logical attempts to organize the service in the best possible way are too often diverted by political considerations and emotional attachments. Dr Mac Armstrong, a general practitioner in Argyll and chairman of the Scottish Committee of GPs, said: 'Health is a great political football. Sometimes the moves made with that football are not particularly helpful. We need to get the debate about health out of this facile area.'

The NHS was created by politicians and they continue to control its destiny. They decide how much money is to be spent and issue guidance on which services should be developed. The Secretary of State for Scotland is ultimately in charge of the Scottish health service and he delegates responsibility for planning, organizing and providing health care to the country's 15 health

Figure 6: NHS provision in Scotland

		Scotland	UK
1989–90	Doctors per 10 000 population	19	14
1989–90	Hospital in-patient beds per 1 000 population	11	7
1987–8	Health spending as proportion of GDP	7.5%	6.1%
1990–1	Health spending per head of population	£609	£511

Figure 7: Health indicators, 1989

	Life expectancy at birth (years)		Infant mortality (per 1 000 live births)	Health spending as % of GDP	Doctors per 10 000 population
	Male	Female			
Japan	75.9	81.8	4.6	6.7	16
Germany	71.8*	78.4*	7.5	8.2	30
USA	71.5	78.5	9.7	11.8	23
UK	72.4*	78.1*	8.4	5.8	14
France	72.4	80.6	7.5	8.7	30
Canada	73.0*	79.8*	7.2*	8.7	22
Netherlands	73.7	80.0	6.8	8.3	24
Scotland	70.5	76.5	8.7	7.5	19

* 1988 and 1986 source: OECD

boards. Decisions taken by boards are then implemented in the part of the service the patients see—the hospitals wards and family doctor surgeries.

Health boards have limited freedom. They work within the limits of the money given to them and have to submit plans for major service changes to ministers for approval. Their long-term plans can end up being opposed by politicians with short-term aims. The closure of Edinburgh's Bruntsfield Hospital illustrates this point. In 1985 Lothian Health Board sought the Secretary of State's approval to close the hospital as part of a wider plan to rationalize hospital services in the city. However, the Bruntsfield was a popular hospital in a marginal constituency at that time held by the Earl of Ancram, a Conservative MP and Scottish Office minister. Permission was refused. In the event, the minister lost his seat. The plan was resubmitted shortly afterwards and approved.

Politicians also exercise an influence on what the health service's priorities should be. An examination of important policy documents like SHAPE (Scottish Health Authorities Priorities for the Eighties) and SHARPEN (Scottish Health Authorities Review of Priorities for the Eighties and Nineties) shows how this system works, or fails to work, depending on differing points of view. Both these documents were published after long consultative exercises and embodied government policy. Both accorded the highest priority to the needs of the elderly, the mentally handicapped and the mentally ill, but in the years immediately after the SHAPE report was published, spending on these groups actually fell in parts of the country. Elderly people with dementia were identified in the SHARPEN report as needing the top priority for service development, yet Scottish Action on Dementia is still trying to get these words translated into action for the 80 000 people in Scotland suffering from dementia and the many thousands more who care for them. Its chairman Angus Mitchell said: 'Policies look fine on paper, but with little cash to support them, we are sceptical as to whether the Government has its heart in the right place.'

One reason given for the lack of action is that politicians have to get elected and although, logically, the documents indicate where money should be spent, practically, there are other priorities. Dr Vivienne Nathanson, Scottish secretary of the British Medical Association, said the public and media focus of the health service is on general hospitals. 'The public gets concerned about campaigns for children's hospitals but not for the care of the elderly. Politicians do not not push through SHAPE and SHARPEN because there are more votes in the sick child. In the trade-off between the elderly and the young, the young always win.'

The relationship between politicians and doctors has never been an easy one. The creation of the NHS was something of an arranged marriage between two unloving partners. In the 1980s they came closer than ever before to filing divorce papers. The British Medical Association spent £1 million on a publicity campaign opposing the Government's health service reforms. It included billboard advertising which asked the public, 'What do you call a person who doesn't accept medical advice?' The answer was the Conservative Health Minister of the time.

The doctors had responded aggressively, in a manner that did not win universal approval in their ranks, to an unprecedented attack on their power. The confrontational Conservative Government had already undermined the power of health unions through the introduction of the system of competitive tendering which saw private companies moving in to take over cleaning and catering contracts in hospitals. Other contracts were won by in-house teams of health service workers but often at the price of reduced hours and wages for those involved. Now attention was on the doctors. While they had shown themselves prepared to change—some had become more aware of costs and others were active in analysing their own performance to ensure the most efficient and effective results—the pace of change was slow. The Government speeded it up.

The health service they set out to change is a curious enterprise. Which factory boss, for instance would allow his production managers to spend whatever they wanted irrespective of the plant's overall targets? But consultants have just such autonomy. They can admit whomever they want, treat them in whichever way they want and discharge them whenever they want, and someone else has to deal with the financial consequences of their actions. This freedom led to wide variations in practice across the country and increased the need for a better system of control.

Although doctors make up only a small percentage of the total NHS staff, they are the most powerful group within the service. Dr Helen Zealley, the Director of Public Health in Lothian believes doctors' power has its roots in the doctor–patient relationship. 'Most patients come to them as supplicants. Repeating that over and over again produces almost a parent–child relationship and the doctor is constantly being reinforced in the parent's role. They then get confidence from that and tend to determine what will happen and how resources will be used. By having that confidence they expect their views to be regarded as something important, often to the exclusion of other relevant viewpoints.'

Doctors can save lives, eradicate disease and restore ailing faculties to people who are usually impressed and extremely grateful. But they can exercise an equally powerful negative force, resisting change if they find it unacceptable. One example of this has been evident in Edinburgh over the past 40 years in plans to restore or rebuild the city's famous Royal Infirmary. As long ago as 1960, a report on the then 90-year-old building concluded it had reached crisis point, but a lack of agreement in the medical profession meant that no positive action was taken. Thirty years later, economic realities concentrated minds and the first moves were made which are expected to lead to the Infirmary's main services moving into a new hospital to be built on a greenfield site.

Any change in the health service is judged on whether or not it is in the interests of patient care. While doctors have usually been justified in protesting at moves detrimental to patient care, at times they are prone to emotional over-exaggeration. A phrase has been coined for such activities. It is called 'shroud waving'. One example of this was the introduction in 1985 of the limited list of drugs to be available on prescription for non-life-threatening conditions. This was opposed as a threat to doctors' clinical freedom which would harm patients. However, when adjustments were made to the list, it was seen by others as a sensible attempt to make the most effective use of medicines. There is no doubt doctors lost respect over their resistance to this change and left themselves open to further attack. This came in the form of general managers.

Consensus management and general managers

For more than 30 years the health service was run on consensus, with doctors at the heart of decision making. The NHS was created in the image doctors wanted. The postwar Labour Party's aim of creating an integrated, locally controlled national service with a salaried medical staff had to be abandoned in face of medical opposition and what came about in 1948 was a tripartite structure of hospital, general practitioner and local authority services with a large element of centralized control. Family doctors also retained their status as independent contractors. Senior consultants ran the medical side of hospitals, matron was responsible for nursing activities and a hospital secretary saw to the fabric of the building and general administration. When the service became more integrated under the responsibility of health boards in 1974, the system of consensus management was retained, with boards being run by a team of chief medical officer, chief nursing officer, board secretary and finance officer. David Peters, the general manager of the Borders Health Board, who has worked in the health service since 1963, described the management system of four equals as self-defeating. 'There was no consistency in management, it was very, very easy to stall and delay things and getting change achieved was very difficult. There were horrendous rows all over the place.'

Some consensus teams did manage to work together but the difficulty in identifying who was in overall control was something commented on forcibly by the NHS management inquiry which recommended that the system be changed, 'If Florence Nightingale were carrying her lamp through the corridors of the NHS today she would almost certainly be looking for the person in charge.'

Consensus management was scrapped in 1985 when the Government appointed general managers to have the lead role in directing health boards. In place of a consensus was a manager described in one Scottish Office circular as a 'driving force, seeking and accepting direct and personal responsibility for developing management plans, securing their implementation and monitoring their achievement'. But a consensus system that was based on trust had been replaced with one founded on distrust, and suspicion grew that ministers were increasing their power over the service. Managers were appointed on short-term contracts and could be dismissed if their performance did not measure up to what was expected of them.

While most managers have sought to work in partnership with health professionals, others have gone their own way. This has been particularly evident in Glasgow where Laurence Peterken has been in charge since 1986. Peterken, a former managing director of the fashions division of Debenhams, was controller of operational services for the Greater London Council before moving to Glasgow. The medical profession and other health service staff soon became concerned at his lack of respect for their views. This was most noticeable when an advertisement was placed in a European Community journal inviting tenders for the supply of laboratory services to Glasgow hospitals. The people running the existing service were never consulted nor were the statutory medical advisory bodies. The tendering idea was dropped after protests but Peterken remains unrepentant about his status as the manager most health service staff love to hate. 'One always gets painted with a black brush if you're changing anything in the NHS in Glasgow and perhaps in Scotland generally, where there tends to be a fairly left-of-centre, trade union oriented attitude to life.'

The reduced influence of doctors at local level has been mirrored at the centre where the Chief Medical Officer for Scotland, the senior medical man working in the civil service department which runs the health service, is now answerable to a chief executive, Don Cruickshank, who has been recruited from private industry. Professor Geoffrey Chisholm, past president of the Royal College of Surgeons of Edinburgh said: 'Many of us would say the CMO's job had been, for want of a better word, downgraded by the appointment of Don Cruickshank'. Professor Chisholm is also concerned that the managerial system introduced on the advice of the former Sainsbury supermarket executive Sir Roy Griffiths poses a great threat to teaching and research. 'The whole concept of teaching, training and research is in jeopardy from the Sainsbury approach, which would say that the priority for a surgeon should be to do more and more operating and therefore leave less time for teaching, training and research.'

But management is not all bad news for doctors. Dr Nathanson said: 'There is a tendency to blame managers for laying down limits of what you can do but most doctors would feel that management has been able to help them deliver care. Most general managers have contributed enormously in trying to get rid of wastage—but there is a feeling now that managers are not just managing, but changing the direction of the organization, regardless of the will of the people within it.' Equally, general management has been credited with helping provide the NHS with the components essential to any successful organization and which it previously lacked: direction, leadership, good communications, cost-effective information systems and targets that are monitored, for example.

However, the editor of the *British Medical Journal*, Dr Richard Smith, who trained in Edinburgh, believes there is a deep cultural divide between doctors and managers. 'The language of managers is incomprehensible to doctors and sounds to them wildly inflated, even surreal. Doctors are also concerned about the shift of power to managers. A decade ago no hospital administrator would have stood in the way of eminent consultants, but now they are chided for being late for their outpatient clinic and told they cannot operate on Thursdays.' Professor Michael Oliver, a world-renowned cardiologist and past president of the Royal College of Physicians of Edinburgh is worried that managers are taking decisions about the care of patients without having the expertise to do so. 'During the last 25 years or so, there has been an explosion of medical and scientific knowledge which provides clear-cut facts concerning the benefits, or otherwise, of new procedures and treatments for patients. At the moment many managers are unaware of these and they are taking decisions of considerable importance on the basis of expediency.'

Divided loyalties within the health service are something that concern its chief executive in Scotland, Don Cruickshank. He has a wide experience of business and commerce having been general manager of Times Newspapers and managing director of Richard Branson's Virgin communications group. He was also chairman of Wandsworth Health Authority in London before returning to his native Scotland. He says the NHS is not a single organization. At one level, it is a loose federation of health boards, at another it is a series of hospital units but most importantly it is seen as hospital wards, GP practices, independent practitioners and professional groups. Staff identify with the ward, practice or hospital within which they work. 'Their loyalty tends to be to that team and the patient it cares for. Not to the wider organization.' Cruickshank said any successful enterprise needs shared values and common goals. One of his first tasks on taking over as chief executive was to define what the NHS is there to provide. He described the subsequent report which was produced, *Framework for Action*, as the toolkit which staff could use to improve the service. It set out the purpose and values of the health service and encouraged staff to contribute in the fullest possible way to agreed goals to deliver the best possible care for patients. However, while the centre encouraged togetherness, divisions split the service locally. The first applications to create self-governing hospital trusts in Scotland (see below) faced massive opposition from both health service staff and the public. Despite this, the applications from the Royal Scottish National Hospital for the mentally handicapped at Larbert, the Foresterhill group of hospitals in Aberdeen and a group in South Ayrshire were approved by the Secretary of State.

The Government's White Paper *Working for Patients*, published in 1989, provided the clearest sign of who was in control. It was drawn up without consulting the profession, and proposed a number of untested structural changes, which did not address the central problem facing the service which—according to the profession—was a lack of adequate resources. The reforms introduced a market philosophy to health care, with health boards established as purchasers of services and hospitals as providers. Hospitals could become self-governing and family doctors could operate their own budgets. The changes were aimed at getting the service to compete for patients. The logic was that the best hospitals would attract the most patients, allowing them to prosper and expand and the others would be forced to improve their performance to keep up. But it was seen in Scotland as a solution to a problem affecting the south-east of England. How could competition be promoted in Scotland where large parts of the country are served by only one local hospital?

There is an old joke about Scotland's relationship with England. Two Scottish soldiers are rowing across the channel after the retreat from Dunkirk in World War II. One turns to the other and says, 'If the English surrender now, it's going to be a long war.' That reflects the majority feeling of health service staff in Scotland about the reforms. In England, the war against the market system of health care ended in early defeat with large numbers taking up the idea of trusts and GP budgets. In Scotland by comparison there has been some managerial enthusiasm but overwhelming professional and trade union opposition.

Cultural differences between Scotland and England are reflected in the health service. Scotland is generally recognized to have a greater public service ethos, a greater sense of community, and this has produced marked differences from England. Private medicine has never established much of a foothold in Scotland and community involvement has helped the country become self-sufficient in blood supplies, something England and Wales have yet to achieve. Dislike of market-orientated reforms illustrates this difference. Drummond Hunter, a former secretary to the Scottish Health Service Planning Council which was set up in 1974 to co-ordinate planning in the service said: 'Scottish democratic humanism has produced a marked emphasis in the Scottish health service on collective, public sector provision as against individualistic or private provision. It has also led to a participatory planning ethos rather than a managerialist one.'

Anyone who thinks medicine is an exact science which cannot be influenced by external cultural considerations should ask why the Germans have 85 drugs for low blood pressure, a condition which is not even medically recognized in the USA and Britain; why the aggressive, can-do approach of US surgeons results in twice as many women's breasts being surgically removed compared to Britain and Sweden where breast cancer rates are roughly similar; why British doctors are much less likely than their international colleagues to show interest in unorthodox medicine.

Public participation

Although the health service exists for the benefit of the patient, there has been a marked reluctance to involve the public in its operation. The struggles of the 1980s paid remarkably little attention to the views of patients or the public. Penny Richardson, director of the Association of Scottish Local Health Councils, said the reforms were effectively about three groups in the health service—politicians, doctors and other staff—battling it out for supremacy. The public, a little confused at times, looked on from the sidelines. At the same time, the representative nature of health boards was reduced further and the public's statutory voice within the service—health councils—cut in number.

The backbone of that opposition was broken by the Conservative victory in the 1992 general election which made it inevitable that the reforms would advance. Within days of the election result, managerial teams in Grampian, with some medical support, submitted plans to turn their hospital units into self-governing trusts and the idea was under active consideration in many other hospitals across the country. The politicians were firmly in the driving seat and many professionals found themselves unwilling passengers on a journey not of their choosing.

Making the service accountable to the public has been a problem since the NHS began. The individuals appointed to serve on the first overseeing committees were nominated by the Secretary of State. Andrew Eunson, honorary secretary of the board of management of the Edinburgh Royal Infirmary, was one of those who objected at the time. He said it 'showed a surprising distrust of the people and of popular representation'. It was hospital management by the officially approved. Forty years later, the same complaints are still made. The establishment from 1991 of smaller, executive-style health boards was attacked as marking a further decline in community participation. Local authority and trade union representatives used to occupy places on most boards in Scotland. In 1979, the Scottish Trades Union Congress (STUC) had 36 serving representatives. By 1990 that figure had shrunk to seven and no trade union representative was appointed in April 1991 when new criteria for eligibility were introduced, based on business acumen and the level of personal contribution a member could make. From 1991 health boards had adopted a business model, being run like company boards of directors rather than the participatory committees envisaged in 1974. Grahame Smith, assistant general secretary of the STUC said: 'The voice of the wider community, as expressed through representatives of organizations such as the STUC, has been systematically eliminated from Scottish health boards.' He described them as 'worthless empty shells with no relevance to the population they are supposed to serve'.

At the same time that boards were being remodelled, the number of health councils in Scotland was reduced from 44 to 18 and their members cut from 900 to 280. Health councils are made up of community representatives who monitor services on behalf of the public. Further changes meant that members could be sacked by the health board for misconduct such as disclosing confidential information. Such strictures do not apply to representatives of user consultative committees which oversee the operation of such utilities as the Post Office or Scottish Gas. 'What power do people have if their statutory representatives can be sacked by the organization they are supposed to be monitoring?' asked Penny Richardson. While formal channels have been narrowed, patients have been making their views known through other routes and exercising some influence on the service. Self-help groups like the cancer support organization Tak Tent whose name is taken from the old Scots phrase for take care have helped foster a climate in which patients are treated as people and not labelled as being just a set of symptoms. 'Politicians of all political parties have claimed they are putting patients first by issuing charters detailing how the service will be changed to make it more patient sensitive.' But Ms Richardson remained sceptical. 'There is a culture shift at an individual level but it has not gone far enough. All the political parties now have patients' charters but no one wants the lay view in at the beginning of planning the health service.'

Health care in the future

The Labour Government which established the NHS believed it would create a healthier nation and as people became healthier they would have less and less need for its services. Their optimism was misplaced and within four years of its creation, the financial reality of providing a free service had become so apparent that prescription charges had to be introduced. These charges have increased and have been extended in recent years as health service costs continue to spiral. Ritual complaints from unions, politicians and professional staff about financial stringency have obscured the real benefits that the service has brought over the years. The infectious diseases which were once mass killers, such as tuberculosis, diptheria and typhoid, have been conquered, the death rate at childbirth has fallen to its lowest ever level, and extra years of life at a higher quality have been given to thousands of Scots. Health services, whether they be provided by health visitor, ambulance paramedic, family doctor or leading consultant, are more fully integrated and more evenly distributed.

However, there remains an enormous burden of disease and disability which the present system has proved incapable of preventing. A medical model of care which looks on individuals as objects of treatment is partly to blame.

61

The ideal expression of that system is the highly trained doctor working in a modern hospital, pushing back the frontiers of knowledge. While important advances have been secured from that system, it does nothing to address the real reasons why problems occur in the first place. Community-based initiatives like the Healthy Cities project, which Glasgow is taking part in, offer a more radical approach. These are collaborative efforts involving a wide range of professionals aimed at encouraging local communities to define their own health needs and devise ways of addressing them. Edinburgh University's Research Unit in Health and Behavioural Change is thinking along the same lines: 'In the last analysis a generally healthy public requires fundamental change in political and professional behaviours, change that is much more likely to influence the public health than giving up butter or taking up jogging.'

Better coordination is also needed across government departments to ensure that agricultural, energy, transport, housing and other policies take full account of their impact on health. The promotion of health could even be separated from the provision of health services by making the Scottish Office Environment Minister responsible for promoting health in its widest sense. Scotland's problems merit such new approaches, but they will only become possible if politicians are prepared to surrender their own short-term aims in favour of longer-term solutions.

Historically, the main solution favoured by politicians has been to change the structures within the health service. A dose of more effective management has been the Conservatives' recommended cure but this brings with it the prospect of increased administrative costs at questionable value to the patients. Moreover, the distinctive nature of the Scottish service may not survive the advance of market forces. It has developed along different lines to the system in the rest of the UK, but it is under threat from a Westminister-based model of health care which sees hospital provision in Aberdeen as no different from that in Acton. Scotland is not just another region of the UK with its health service on par with that of an English regional authority. It has developed a system of health care which has been admired all over the world. The close links between academic and clinical medicine, between the administrative centre and the regions, the integration of general practice and the hospital sector, and the overall high level of expertise, are all special characteristics which have helped make the Scottish health service unique. Doctors and other health service staff have made it clear in recent years what they are against—what has been less evident is the existence of positive thinking about how the rest of the Scottish health service can be preserved within the structures being drawn up by politicians. The current management solution may seem perverse when most other countries look to Britain as a model of effectiveness, with a health care system which is unmatched for the value for money it provides. Curiously, while Britain is borrowing ideas from the incentive-driven Americans, the USA is looking to see if it can learn anything from the British system of budgetary controls. Other countries are trying to reshape their systems to cope with ever-rising costs. In

New Zealand, there are plans to end free hospital care for those earning more than £10 000, health professionals in France have gone on strike over proposals to cut medical spending and in Italy nearly half of all patients have had to take their own pillows and sheets into hospital and 1 in 7 their own food. Every developed nation is experiencing the same squeeze, having an abundance of possible services but a limit of available money. Already infertility treatment is only being offered in some parts of Scotland on payment and in some cases patients have had to wait for new drugs because no funds have been allocated to buy them. The rationing of medical services will be a major issue for the health service in the next 20 years. Dr John Richmond, president of the Royal College of Physicians of Edinburgh says it is already with us. 'One of the great ethical difficulties now is how best to make clinical decisions with finite financial and other resources. For example, for every heart transplant, it might be possible to do 10–12 coronary by-pass operations. Who is going to decide which of these to promote? If resources are scarce should there be a selection of patients, for example on the basis of age?' One alternative to limiting services is to raise money from other sources. In Sweden patients are charged for every day spent in hospital, and a flat rate charge for food and accommodation costs in Scottish hospitals for those who could afford to pay would go far to helping raise extra income. Most school children have to pay for their own meals. Is it reasonable any longer to provide free food for people in hospital?

The changes imposed on the medical professionals in the 1980s have made them look more critically at themselves. In the last century Robert Louis Stevenson felt able to describe the physician as 'the flower of our civilisation'. In the late 20th century that flower has faded. Although surveys show the public continue to hold doctors in high regard, there is more recourse to law when things go wrong and greater demands to involve patients in what, after all, is their own treatment. The doctor-knows-best attitude is under challenge. Dr Richmond said: 'The medical profession has had a position of privilege; we have not been exposed to a lot of questioning by our patients, the public, or by politicians. Sometimes we have been viewed as an autonomous, perhaps arrogant, lot. It is no bad thing that we should be openly accountable and accept an efficient management structure in the health service—that is, provided managerial considerations never override what is in the best interest of the patient.'

Doctors responded to their exclusion from the corridors of power by embarking on their own attempt to map out the way the health service should develop into the 21st century. The British Medical Association produced a report, *Leading for Health*, which sought to rescue the debate from a narrow political focus and open it out to examine taboo subjects like patient charges and rationing. It raised the questions of whether health care could continue to be funded exclusively from taxation or if charges should be introduced; if rationing is inevitable and if so if it should be done openly, rather than covertly as at the moment; and it examined whether the balance was right between spending on treatment and prevention. The eventual aim of the exercise is to provide answers to these and many other questions but, significantly, it opened by just asking the questions. These are to be presented to politicians. 'Mostly they will not have ready answers', concluded the report, 'nobody does.'

4

Scotland and Defence

Trevor Royle

From the military point of view Scotland has always provided the strategist or defence planner with a number of challenges. First, the land mass sprawls over a large area, just over 7.5 million hectares. One-third the size of the UK, it consists largely of high land and rough grazing; less than 2 million hectares provide pasture or arable land. Some idea of the size of the area can be gauged by superimposing Scotland upon England: Scotland then stretches from Aldershot in the south to the borders in the north, and from Liverpool in the west to Scarborough in the east, even before the western and northern isles have been taken into account.

Second, physical barriers like the Mounth (the mountain massif which includes the Cairngorms) and the Southern Uplands make communications difficult. Historically, the high lands provided a refuge in time of war and helped, therefore, to preserve Scotland's independence. Invaders from the south were forced to use the eastern coastal route to bypass the Cheviots or the difficult upland terrain in the west between Annandale and the central belt.

Other problems are posed by the length of the coastline, which is the longest in the UK—over 0.4 million hectares of foreshore—much of which consists of long sea lochs and broad open firths. Most of the high lands are sparsely populated or uninhabited and the weather conditions are harsh and unpredictable. Rivers and inland lochs also provide barriers, and the pattern of north–south roads was determined by the presence of glens and mountain passes, some of which, like the Pass of Drumochter on the main road between Perth and Inverness, rise up to over 450 metres.

The role of the military in Scotland

Although modern communications, improved roads and air transport make light of the physical distances, Scotland still provides a challenging yet rewarding environment for the estimated 22 000 servicemen and women (over 30 000 including the reserve forces) who are based in the country. In UK defence terms Scotland is an important part of the integrated national defence structure and has played an influential role in NATO's forward defence strategy. However, the Scottish Office has no responsibility for defence matters and there is no separate or identifiable 'Scottish' defence organization, although soldiers in Scotland's seven infantry regiments, two foot guards battalions and one armoured regiment would insist that their history, traditions and uniforms give them an individual identity which sets them apart from their English colleagues. The formulation and execution of defence policy is the responsibility of the Ministry of Defence in London and the three services in Scotland are under the operational command of headquarters in England: the Royal Navy at Fleet Headquarters at Northwood near London, the Army at United Kingdom Land Forces Headquarters at Wilton in Wiltshire and the Royal Air Force at Strike Command Headquarters at High Wycombe in Buckinghamshire.

Each of the three services is headed by a senior officer: the Flag Officer (senior naval officer) and the Air Officer (senior RAF officer) also include Northern Ireland within their bailiwicks, while the General Officer Commanding Scotland (GOC Scotland, senior Army officer) is responsible for Scotland only. As the representatives of the armed forces in Scotland they all play an important representative role in Scottish life and take an interest in furthering the services' image in Scotland, but they do not possess any formal day-to-day links with the Scottish Office. (As a matter of courtesy, all three meet the Secretary of State for Scotland and maintain contact with his office throughout their periods of command.) The most obvious point of connection is disaster relief, a field in which the three services have made valuable contributions in recent years. After the Lockerbie air disaster in 1988, for example, men of the 1st Royal Highland Fusiliers and RAF search and rescue helicopters and mountain rescue teams assisted the emergency services, although the operation remained under the control of the Chief Constable of Dumfries and Galloway.

Under the terms of Military Aid to the Civil Community (MACC) any chief constable can request assistance from the armed forces and, when it is given, this comes free of charge provided that lives are theatened during the emergency. Theoretically, when there is no obvious threat to human life, a charge is made by the armed forces: this was the case at Lockerbie, which was a non-survivable accident, and the cost of employing servicemen was eventually met by the Scottish Office. By their very nature, though, most emergencies involve some threat to human life, as in February 1989 when, during the floods in Inverness, troops were used to help in the operation to prevent the River Ness from breaching its banks.

The next levels of assistance are Military Aid to the Civil Ministries (the use of military personnel and equipment during the firemen's strike of 1978 was one example), and Military Aid to the Civil Authorities (the period of transition to major war). Although requests for servicemen are readily met by senior officers, who believe that it helps with training, any operation involving the use of the armed forces with the emergency services always comes under the ultimate control of a chief constable.

Civil and home defence in time of war, or during the transition to war, also provides an interface between the Scottish Office and the armed forces in Scotland. In such an eventuality the GOC Scotland would become Regional Military Commander of No.1 Home Defence Region (ie Scotland) and the Secretary of State would become its Controller. Twice a year, therefore, the GOC Scotland chairs a meeting of the Joint Services Planning Committee—made up of representatives of the armed forces, the emergency services and the Scottish Office—in order to clarify each organization's role in time of war. While the military would be responsible for safeguarding 'key points' (main bases, supply routes, power stations etc), the emergency services would deal with civilian matters, again under the direction of the police forces. Zone Police Commanders Designate, North and South, and Zone Fire Commanders Designate, North and South, would be appointed to match the division of the Army's Scottish Command into 51 (Highland) and 52 (Lowland) brigade areas. Thankfully, the twice-yearly meetings of this committee have been purely theoretical, but they do give an indication of the close links which still exist between the armed forces and the community in terms of home and civil defence.

Otherwise, the forces in Scotland are very much integrated commands, each with their own structures which have been determined not just by Britain's defence needs but also by Scotland's geographical location.

Areas of responsibility

The Royal Navy

Responsibility for naval affairs in Scotland is vested in the position of Flag Officer Scotland and Northern Ireland (FOSNI). The first holder of the post was Admiral Sir Robert Swinburne Lowry KCB who was appointed on 1 July 1913 with the sonorous title of 'Admiral Commanding the Coast of Scotland'. The holder in 1992 is Vice-Admiral Sir Hugo White, a sailor with a wide range of experience including sea command as an admiral of surface flotillas, command of surface ships (HMS *Bristol* as a flagship and HMS *Avenger* during the Falklands conflict of 1982) and submarines (he commanded the conventional patrol submarine HMS *Oracle* and was the first commander of the Submarine Sea Training organization at the Clyde Submarine Base). He has also held several staff appointments including Assistant Chief of Naval Staff at the Ministry of Defence, the post he held before coming to Scotland.

In its time the Royal Navy has used the Firth of Clyde, the Moray Firth and the Firth of Forth as safe havens for its warships, the latter being a vital base during the two world wars. Loch Ewe in the north-west and Scapa Flow in the Orkney Islands have offered similar facilities during the wartime years. Today, the Royal Navy's presence is centred in Rosyth on the Forth and Coulport and Faslane on the Clyde although FOSNI is also responsible for 36 other shore establishments. (45 Commando at Arbroath comes under the direction of the Commandant General Royal Marines.) In 1992 there were 10 000 personnel and 52 warships based in Scotland. These included four Type 42 destroyers and 35 minor war vessels (minehunters, minesweepers and patrol ships of the Fisheries Protection Squadron) at Rosyth, and four Resolution class Polaris boats of the 10th Submarine Squadron and nine fleet and patrol submarines of the 3rd Submarine Squadron on the Clyde.

Although born an Englishman at Torquay in 1939, Admiral White admits to a strong affinity with Scotland—years on the west coast with the submarine service saw to that—and he is quick to point out that sailors always produce a fierce loyalty for the ships in which they serve. 'Unlike the Army we haven't got individual regimental links,' he admits, 'but there are living within the Navy large numbers of Scots and they very much want to be based up here and work up here.' As well as taking pride in the Navy's high recruitment figures in Scotland, some 10 per cent of the UK total, like other holders of his post, White is much impressed by the so-called 'Scottish Navy', the Rosyth-based minor war vessels which operate in coastal waters. Because some, like the Island class patrol vessels, are not much bigger than deep-sea trawlers and because they operate in all weathers, the personnel get on well with the local fishermen and many of them have remained in the squadron for nine years or more. 'They have a strong Scottish bias in these ships' companies,' says White, whose own career has kept him in larger ships.

While FOSNI does not command the Clyde submarine base—it is under the command of a commodore who reports to Flag Officer Submarines at Northwood—White admits that he is interested in the performance of the two resident squadrons and would obviously become involved if there were any major change of policy regarding their future. Under the terms of the 1991 *Statement on the Defence Estimates* the Government confirmed that an 'independent strategic nuclear force remains the cornerstone of our defence capability' and that from the mid-1990s onwards a force of four Vanguard class Trident carrying boats would replace the ageing and troubled Polaris boats. Despite its £9 billion price tag—the 1991 estimate—and despite the possibility that the number of each missile's warheads might have to be downloaded in future strategic arms reduction talks, the government has maintained its faith in Britain's independent nuclear deterrent based in Scottish waters. 'We still haven't got all the decisions falling out from the peace dividend,' says White, who concedes that the possibility of global war is remote. 'I think the focus will shift away from preparing for World War III and looking north-east. The focus will now move on to our capabilities required to meet a more generalized defence policy.'

To emphasize the role played by Scotland in NATO's forward defence strategy, the post of FOSNI is double-hatted, having both UK and NATO responsibilities. On the home front, Admiral White is the sea area commander for the waters around the UK from Morecambe to the Wash and the Atlantic westward out to Greenland and north up to the high Arctic. His second national task is that of naval land area commander for the whole of Scotland and Northern Ireland, where he takes an interest in the integrated security policy for the province. The NATO commands are equally challenging. He is a subordinate commander for two of the three NATO commands—Atlantic and Channel (the third being Europe)—which would put him, and Scotland, at the forefront of any conflict in Europe.

FOSNI's headquarters are at Pitreavie Castle near Dunfermline in Fife, the home of Scotland's maritime headquarters, with a command bunker which would become Britain's strategic fleet headquarters should Fleet Headquarters at Northwood outside London ever be destroyed in the event of a major war. White shares this with the Air Office Scotland and Northern Ireland, for it is an axiom of maritime tactics that there can be few surface operations at sea without an air element.

The Royal Air Force

The present Air Officer Scotland and Northern Ireland (AOSNI) is a Scot, Air Vice-Marshal Allan Blackley, who was educated at Perth Academy and Glasgow University where he took a degree in aeronautical engineering. His career has taken him from Cranwell to Deputy Chief of Staff (Operations) at Headquarters Allied Air Force Central Europe at Ramstein in Germany—the post he held before coming to Scotland—by way of operational postings in Cyprus and Germany and staff posts at the Ministry of Defence, but like other former fighter pilots his passion remains fast jets. A portrait of a gas-guzzling Lightning interceptor at the point of take-off hangs in his office and any reference to this undoubtedly graceful aircraft is met with a wry smile: 'That was one of the noisiest planes we ever had, the dear old Lightning. But when they were phased out of service four or five years ago we found that the locals complained that they were no longer there, after years of complaining about the noise!'

Although only founded in 1918—before that it had been the Royal Flying Corps—the Royal Air Force has been responsible for the establishment of 93 operational locations in Scotland, many of them wartime bases or dispersal fields which have long since been made redundant. In 1992 the RAF's main stations were at Leuchars in Fife (two squadrons of Tornado F3 air defence fighters), Lossiemouth in Grampian (two squadrons of Tornado GR1 maritime strike aircraft planned to replace the obsolescent Buccaneers in 1993, and the Jaguar Operational Conversion Unit) and Kinloss, also in Grampian, which houses the Nimrod maritime patrol aircraft. Also in AOSNI's parish are the early warning and communications facilities at RAF Buchan in Grampian and RAF Saxa Vord in the Shetland Islands.

Not every RAF facility in Scotland is concerned with strategic defence. Pitreavie Castle also houses the headquarters of the Royal Air Force's Search and Rescue (SAR) organization, and its yellow Sea King and Wessex SAR helicopters are a familiar sight in Scottish skies, especially along the coastline and in the upland areas. Responsible for providing SAR cover for millions of square kilometres of ocean, and for the whole of the UK land area, Pitreavie's Rescue Co-ordination Centre and its southern counterpart at Plymouth, are on permanent alert to assist aircraft and shipping in distress. To meet this need Nimrods and helicopters of the RAF and SAR helicopters of the Royal Navy and HM Coastguard are strategically located around Britain's coastline, while RAF Mountain Rescue teams at Leuchars and Kinloss are immediately available to assist at major incidents. Although their primary task is to assist at aircraft and ship-related accidents, some 95 per cent of their work is generated by civilians who find themselves in trouble. The RAF has around 10 000 personnel based in Scotland.

Like his near-neighbour at Pitreavie, Blackley sees the Royal Air Force in Scotland in a UK and NATO context. Although he has fond memories of learning to fly in gliders at Edzell while he was an air cadet, Blackley realizes that the Scottish air bases are only one part of the jigsaw that makes up the doctrine of air power. 'In the old aeroplanes like Meteors or Hunters, by the time you got to the end of the runway, it was time to come back,' he says. 'You couldn't go anywhere and people thought locally. The young modern airman isn't like that. Although they're based in Scotland they do see the world; they see a great deal of it and they think like that. On any particular day you might get a chap out of Leuchars and he might fly off to the north of England and land at a base in Lincolnshire . . . or he might go off and take a tanker and five hours later they're flying in Mediterranean skies. So their minds are being stretched: they don't just think of their backyards.'

Briefly stated, the ultimate purpose of the doctrine of air power, as interpreted by Blackley and his colleagues, is to use the flexibility, reach and timeliness of air power to support national or multinational defence. In Scottish terms it means using the bases for the maintenance of the instruments of that policy—the aircraft, air and ground crews—but the application of air power can be exercised anywhere in the world, as was seen during the war in the Gulf when the RAF, including Tornados, Buccaneers and Nimrods from Scottish air stations, put theory into practice in the UN coalition's battle to oust Iraqi forces from Kuwait in January and February 1991. The ability of air power to react quickly to such circumstances was highlighted by the fact that one squadron of RAF fighters was in place and operational within 48 hours of the Government's decision to send forces to Saudi Arabia, and that a second squadron was operational within a further 48 hours.

The Army

If the Royal Navy and the Royal Air Force see their presence in Scotland in UK or NATO terms the same can hardly be said of the Army which is perhaps the most visible of the services in Scotland. Indeed, in some minds the figure of the kilted Jock says 'Scotland' in a way that few other advertising symbols can, and the idea persists that the Scottish Tourist Board would be hard pushed to find a substitute if he did not exist. Even the post of GOC Scotland is different. Unlike FOSNI or AOSNI he does not possess a NATO role but he is the Governor of Edinburgh Castle and Colonel Commandant of the Scottish Division, the administrative grouping for the seven Scottish infantry regiments: The Royal Scots, The Royal Highland Fusiliers, The King's Own Scottish Borderers, The Black Watch, Queen's Own Highlanders, The Gordon Highlanders and The Argyll and Sutherland Highlanders. (As part of the Options for Change defence review the number will be reduced to five in 1994 following the amalgamations of The Gordon Highlanders with the Queen's Own Highlanders, and the Royal Scots with the King's Own Scottish Borderers.)

Invariably the post of GOC Scotland is held by a senior officer from one of the Scottish regiments and the incumbent in 1992 was no exception. Indeed, Lieutenant-General Sir Peter Graham displays many of the criteria which the civilian public expect of a Highland officer. Brought up in Scotland, though educated mainly in England, he is a Gordon Highlander with a keen interest in piping and military history and he is a firm supporter of the virtues which the Scottish soldier brings to the British Army. 'There is much pride in what we as a small nation have achieved in feats of arms, in the wars, serving the British Army and the Crown over many years,' he says. 'Here am I, Colonel of a regiment [The Gordon Highlanders] which is 197 years old. We have 28 battle honours on one colour, 12 on the other. We have 19 Victoria Crosses, which along with the Grenadiers is the largest of the 1881 amalgamated regiments. We have a good deal to be proud about. It goes right the way through to the junior soldier. People are proud that you have a son in the Army, serving in a Scottish regiment. It is an honourable profession.'

Like others who have held the post of GOC Scotland Graham also approves of the concept of the regiment as a family with strong links into the local communities from which they recruit. His predecessor, Lieutenant–General Sir John Macmillan, reinforced the idea that there are strong emotional links between the Scots and their tartan-clad regiments when he said in 1989: 'I think that the advantage we have in Scotland is that there is a Scottish identity, even if it's only manifested by a feeling that those so-and-sos down in England don't understand us. At least it helps to keep us together.' In the autumn of 1991 Macmillan and a group of former GOCs Scotland formed a committee to campaign against the proposed amalgamations of the Scottish regiments.

During the nineteenth century the army maintained 19 garrisons, forts or barracks in Scotland, including the highland forts—William, Augustus and George—which had been built in the wake of the previous century's Jacobite rebellions. Today, the major centres are Army Headquarters Scotland at Craigiehall outside Edinburgh, the Scottish Division Depot at Penicuik, the Royal Artillery missile range at Benbecula in the Western Isles, the Regional Depot and District Workshops at Stirling, Redford and Dreghorn Barracks in

Edinburgh and the barracks at Fort George outside Inverness. All told the GOC Scotland is responsible for overseeing 92 separate military locations; he also has full command of all Regular and Territorial Army personnel, cadets and Army Department civilians. In the chain of command he is accountable to the Commander-in-Chief United Kingdom Land Forces and under the functional command of the Commander, United Kingdom Field Army. For administrative purposes, and reflecting the size of Scotland, there are two brigade areas, Highland and Lowland, with their headquarters at Perth and Edinburgh Castle. There are 2 500 regular servicemen and women in Scotland while the Territorial Army numbers 8 800, 14 per cent of the UK total.

Training and recruitment

Although all three service chiefs fulfil different operational roles in Scotland, one aspect of the country is common to all of them. The terrain, especially in the more remote and sparsely habited areas, provides excellent facilities for military training. In 1991 Scotland provided the army with 208 000 man-training days, not just for troops based north of Hadrian's Wall, but also for those from English-based formations. The Army maintains major training areas or ranges at Garelochhead in Strathclyde, Barry Buddon and Cultybraggan in Tayside and Castlelaw in Lothian. 'We do offer a great deal of training in different types of country,' explains General Graham. 'You can get anything from the peaceful to the barren, to the rugged, to the down-right hostile.'

Low-flying training is carried out by the RAF in parts of the Borders, Dumfries and Galloway and Highlands, although fast-jet training at low level will reduce by 30 per cent from 1992. There are also bombing ranges at Tain and Cape Wrath which are used not just by the Royal Air Force but also by aircraft from other NATO countries. The Royal Aircraft Establishment at West Freugh near Stranraer operates a weapons development facility, mainly for missile testing, and it was there that the GEC Ferranti Tiald laser-guidance system was tested before being rushed into service for use in the Gulf War.

The waters off Scotland's coast provide ideal sea conditions for training for minehunting and minesweeping and major NATO exercises are carried out in the northern Atlantic waters for which FOSNI has responsibility. By their nature naval exercises rarely interfere with civilian life, but there is one area of naval operations which can bring the Royal Navy into contact with other ships going about their normal business: the waters of the Firth of Clyde, which provide an ideal environment for testing and training officers who seek promotion to command submarines. Known as 'perisher' courses, the testing has to be carried out under realistic wartime operational conditions, a difficult procedure when the waters are also used by fishing boats. In November 1990 the submarine HMS *Trenchant* snagged the nets of the fishing boat *Antares* which capsized and sank with the loss of all four hands. Following the official inquiry, which blamed operational procedures during training, the Clyde Submarine

Base agreed to provide fuller information to local fishermen when exercises were taking place. Previously this was kept secret for reasons of national security.

In addition to providing the three services with physical conditions which help their training, Scotland is also a ready source of manpower. The Royal Navy estimates that at least 10 per cent of their recruits come from Scotland with a further 20 per cent from the north of England and Northern Ireland who join the service because it gives them the opportunity of working in Scotland as opposed to the Channel coast. RAF figures are similar, but it is the Army which has benefited most from a regular supply of recruits from Scotland, not just for the Scottish regiments but also for other formations. In the five-year period between 1986 and 1991 Scotland provided 11.86 per cent of the total while in the year 1 April 1990 to 31 March 1991, 1 787 men and women enlisted in the Army from Scotland. Of these, 555 went into the seven infantry regiments of the Scottish Division and 122 into the Scots Guards, helping to make them the best recruited infantry regiments in the British Army. 'Those are impressive figures,' says General Graham. 'We're providing 11.8 per cent of the Army from 9 per cent of the United Kingdom population.'

The changing defence environment

Until the end of the 1980s the defence pattern in western Europe was relatively clear. Confrontation with the USSR was an everyday reality and as part of NATO's response Scotland was called upon to play a role in the forward maritime defence strategy which was aimed at containing the Soviet threat from naval and air forces based in Murmansk and the Kola peninsula. Perceived by some strategists as a well-equipped, though land-locked aircraft carrier, Scotland had two major roles: to guard the north Atlantic approaches in time of war and to provide the forward base for prosecuting any naval war which might have broken out in the Norwegian Sea as Soviet naval and air forces attempted to win control of the vital Iceland–Greenland gap. The 7.5 million hectares of the Scottish land mass would have been the first obstacle any advancing Soviet forces would meet in a break-out to the north Atlantic and it would have been over the northern seas and the Scottish skies that the main air battle would have been fought. 'Scotland is very much the forward base in the UK for maritime operations as we perceive them, with NATO's forward strategy of prosecuting any war which might occur in the Norwegian Sea,' explained Air Vice-Marshal David Brook, AOSNI, in the spring of 1989, just months before the collapse of the Warsaw Pact and the USSR's willingness to negotiate with the west a significant cutback in nuclear and conventional forces in Europe.

To meet the challenge as Brook and his NATO colleagues envisaged it, some 10 per cent of the country's naval and air forces were deployed in Scotland, in addition to a substantial US presence, the most obvious being the 14 Poseidon-carrying submarines which had been based at the Holy Loch since the 1960s. Other US facilities included the satellite communications and command stations at Forss and West Murkle in Caithness and Mormond Hill in Grampian, the Naval Security Group surveillance centre at Edzell in Angus, reserve air bases at Stornoway in the Western Isles and Machrihanish in Kintyre, and the Military Airlift Command staging post at Prestwick. All told, the US forces numbered 2 800 military personnel and 300 civilians, although these figures will be reduced when the US Navy closes its submarine base at the Holy Loch. The last of the Poseidon boats was withdrawn in October 1991 because the longer-range Trident missile does not require a forward operating base.

Then, in 1990, the Cold War came to an end with the collapse of the Warsaw Pact, a fact acknowledged at the NATO summit held in London on 5 and 6 July 1990 when members agreed to pursue a new strategy, moving away from 'forward defence and flexible response' towards 'flexible presence'. However, NATO remains a defensive alliance which will 'never in any circumstances be the first to use force'. It has reduced its reliance on nuclear weapons, but some weapons remain to fulfil an essential role in the overall deterrent strategy of the alliance. This was confirmed in November 1991 after President Bush and President Gorbachev agreed to make substantial reductions to their countries' holdings of tactical nuclear and conventional weapons. Finally, it was proposed that both NATO and the former Warsaw Pact countries should make a declaration that they were no longer adversaries and that they should reaffirm an intention to refrain from the threat of force against the territorial integrity or political independence of any state.

Set against the Strategic Arms Reduction Treaty (START) of 31 July 1991 which placed limitations on strategic nuclear weapons, and the Conventional Armed Forces in Europe Treaty (CFE) which reduced force holdings in Europe, the unification of Germany within NATO and the reduction of the Soviet threat, there are now solid grounds for supposing that the defence task in Scotland has become less urgent. Some changes have already taken place. Air Vice-Marshal Blackley admits that there is a more 'relaxed' atmosphere at RAF Leuchars, Strike Command's premier air defence base in the UK, and that the days are past when, for training purposes, the station was put on an emergency war-footing without any prior warning, but he cautions against any undue optimism that the armed forces can be cut back to the bone. 'Instead of the immediacy of countering the Soviet bear,' he says, 'we're now providing an insurance policy against brush fire wars—anything happening anywhere.' This is known as 'crisis management'—the use of all available resources to deter aggression, to provide support, to sustain life and observe intentions and, should those fail, to respond to escalation. In other words, to meet the changing needs of the 1990s and beyond, the UK will need balanced armed forces which, according to Tom King, Secretary for Defence in 1991, should be 'flexible and mobile and able to contribute—both in NATO and, if needed, elsewhere'.

The British response to the changing defence environment came in the

Conservative Government's *Options for Change* in the summer of 1990. It was then set aside until after the Gulf War had come to an end and fuller details of the changes were revealed in, and prior to the publication of, the Defence Estimates in July 1991. As these affected Scotland, Rosyth could have been the biggest loser. The Navy Board, which advises on naval matters, considered the closure to be one of the options open to them, although the privately owned Babcock Thorn Royal Dockyard facilities would have been retained. However, the documents relating to the closure were leaked to the local MP, Gordon Brown, and following a well-orchestrated campaign to save Rosyth, a compromise was reached whereby the base would be reduced in size, with the loss of 2 000 naval and civilian jobs, but most of the minor war vessels would be retained. The four Type 42 destroyers and one squadron of minehunters will be transferred to Portsmouth, leaving Rosyth with a smaller number of home-based vessels. The move will result in savings of £70 million over a five-year period.

While the partial reprieve of the Rosyth naval base was welcomed locally, it raised a number of awkward questions about the conduct of the review and about the relationship between the Scottish Office and the Ministry of Defence. Leaked documents about the proposed closure revealed that Scottish ministers had not been consulted by the Ministry of Defence, who clearly intended to present the decision as a fait accompli under *Options for Change*. A ministerial row in Whitehall was then averted by the intervention of Prime Minister John Major, after Tom King acknowledged that Rosyth alone of Britain's main naval bases had been the subject of a detailed closure study. Political rather than strategic imperatives appear to have been behind the ensuing compromise which allowed Rosyth to continue in being, albeit at a reduced level. The Navy Board undoubtedly had sound reasons for considering the closure of the Rosyth naval base, because it seemed to offer substantial savings—estimated at £140 million a year—while preserving the Royal Navy's ability to contribute to maritime operations in the eastern Atlantic; but, for political reasons, this view was over-ruled by the Prime Minister.

Although the RAF suffered major reductions under *Options for Change*, the units in Scotland did relatively well. Leuchars moved over entirely to Tornados and the elderly Phantom F4 was phased out of service. Lossiemouth will receive maritime strike aircraft equipped with Sea Eagle missiles and Kinloss will become the main base for the Nimrod maritime patrol aircraft. The largest cuts were reserved for the Army, which saw its manpower cut from roughly 156 000 to 116 000 and its infantry battalions reduced from 55 to 38 by a process of amalgamations and disbandments. The Scottish regiments took their share of the cuts: in addition to the four infantry battalions chosen for amalgamation, one foot guards battalion, the 2nd battalion Scots Guards, will go into 'suspended animation' in 1993. Because these cuts affected regiments with traditions and histories which go back to the 17th century, and because the Scottish regiments have close affiliations with their recruiting areas, the cuts were met with anger and dismay at all levels of Scottish life. True, some sections of the community welcomed the changes, mainly due to a belief that the Scottish soldiers' cherished history had been gained in bloody wars or in subjugating innocent people and that such totems no longer had any place in the late 20th century, but the consensus view in Scotland was that the cuts to the infantry were unwise in view of Britain's continuing global commitments.

The services were not the only losers. Scotland has a well-established defence industry and there are real fears that the peace dividend will bring unemployment to it. The loss of the Merlin anti-submarine warfare helicopter contract to the Westland consortium cost GEC Marconi 150 jobs. GEC Ferranti in Edinburgh plan to lay off 700 workers due to the decline in demand for specialized avionics. Barr and Stroud, the Glasgow-based optics firm which is part of the Pilkington group has also been forced to make workers redundant due to a reduction in orders for thermal-imaging devices in the Army's armoured vehicles. There are continuing doubts whether the contract to refit the Royal Navy's nuclear submarines will go to Rosyth and the future of the Yarrow shipyards in Glasgow continues to depend on new frigate orders from the Royal Navy. The importance of the defence community to the Scottish economy was underlined by a report published by Fife Regional Council in October 1991 which showed that 30 per cent of Fife's GDP was related to business in the defence field. Air Vice-Marshal Blackley estimates that Leuchars alone contributes £20 million a year to the local community. And it should not be forgotten that the services employ large numbers of civilians: the Army 1 500 and the Royal Navy 1 200 through its contracted-out supply and transport services. Some of those jobs could still be at risk if there are further cuts to the UK defence budget.

In common with other major changes in national life, the lesson of the new strategic situation and the political response to it will take a long time to sink in and the learning process is certain to be slow. 'I think there is more pain to come in defence terms,' says Admiral White. 'There will be continuing pressure to reduce defence. What I'm looking at doesn't look rosy in defence terms. We haven't yet got out of the wood of the last round of defence decisions. I know that in the Navy there's still enormous pressure to rationalize the support area so it's absolutely streamlined to support our new mean, lean front line.'

As the century draws to a close the relationship between Scotland and the services which defend the UK will change. Unless eastern Europe or the former USSR poses a military threat—an unlikely outcome—it is doubtful if Scotland will remain a 'fortress', or more properly a 'land-locked aircraft carrier' bristling with weapons. However, although the collapse of the Cold War and the lessening of east–west tensions have been widely welcomed, only a fool would say that the UK and her NATO allies should reduce their defences to the point where they are no longer effective. If Britain wants to retain lean, mobile and highly professional forces they will have to be properly trained, and with facilities disappearing in Germany, it is hard to avoid the impression that Scotland, with its rugged terrain and sparsely populated areas, could provide the means. Already in 1992 there are signs that the Army in Scotland intends to increase its provision of barracks, and the naval facilities on the Clyde and the three major air stations show little sign of contracting.

When the century began, Scotland had a substantial military population and the Navy was looking northwards for a secure anchorage for its capital ships which were so vital for Britain's defences. And when the fledgling Royal Naval Air Service and Royal Flying Corps came into being it did not take them long to make inroads into Scotland; the first military airfield was built at Montrose in 1913, the same year in which a naval seaplane base opened at Cromarty. Given the strength of the history and traditions which have woven the armed forces into the fabric of Scottish life, it is safe to say that, despite the defence reforms of the 1990s, the relationship will continue unchallenged well into the 21st century.

5

Religion

George Rosie

There is a theory—and it is a fairly plausible one—that it is impossible to understand Scotland without understanding Scotland's religious history. Certainly the Christian religion seems to have played a more central role in Scottish life than elsewhere in the UK (with the exception of Northern Ireland). The General Assembly of the Church of Scotland is listened to in a way that the General Synod of the Church of England is not. The system of state-funded Roman Catholic schools is envied by Catholics elsewhere in the UK. The sensitivies of Free Churchmen over the running of ferries on Sundays generates genuine concern and debate. Religious broadcasting takes a slice of the budgets that puzzles the programme-makers south of the border.

For all that, only 10 per cent of the Scottish population now attend church regularly, although that compares well with 2 per cent in England and Wales. In England 87 per cent of the population regard themselves as 'unchurched'. In Wales it is 77 per cent. In Scotland the figure is 62 per cent, which suggests that 38 per cent regard themselves as church members. The Scots may be more religious than the English or the Welsh, but the difference is marginal. The days when every pew in the land was filled have gone probably for good. The two main denominations—the Church of Scotland and the Roman Catholic Church—do their sums very differently, and other denominations are reluctant to talk numbers, but the most recent figures show 770 217 members of the Church of Scotland, 774 550 Roman Catholics (this includes everyone baptised in the church), 35 000 Episcopalians and around the same number of Methodists, Congregationalists, Baptists, Salvationists, Quakers etc. There are probably another 25 000 Muslims, Hindus, Sikhs and Buddhists.

But none of this should obscure the part played by religion in shaping Scottish society. Scotland's preoccupation with God has a long and turbulent history. Ever since the ancient Celtic Church of St Columba gave way (albeit reluctantly) to mainstream Roman Catholicism, the Scots have been squabbling with one another over the best way to worship. It is a process which has engaged some of Scotland's best brains and most energetic talents. And they are still at it. Religious fractiousness is still on the agenda. It was only a few years ago that the Free Presbyterian Church of Scotland split in two, because one of its prominent members, Lord Mackay, attended the funeral of a Roman Catholic colleague. This simple act of respect was regarded by many zealots within the Free Presbyterian Church as a dangerous flirtation with the 'whore of Rome'.

There is a paradox here. For all the noise and aggravation which has resounded in Scotland, the country's religious history is *relatively* benign. The rise of Protestantism in 16th-century Scotland was never accompanied by the kind of gruesome turbulence that haunted, say, Germany. The Reformation itself was carried through with a remarkable lack of bloodshed. There were far fewer martyrs (of either stripe) in Scotland than there were in England. Even the casualties of the 'killing times' of the 1680s were relatively minor. The traditional figure of 18 000 Presbyterian 'martyrs' is a wild exaggeration.

Nevertheless, the central role of religion in Scottish life and politics cannot be denied. One of the fatal mistakes the Stuart kings made was to try to ram Episcopalianism down the throat of Presbyterian Scotland. It was a high-handed strategy which resulted in the defeat of the Jacobite rebellions of 1690, 1709, 1715, 1719 and 1745 when the Stuart cause was resolutely ignored or resisted by Protestant Scotland. With many exceptions, the clansmen who rallied to the Stuart banner were Episcopalian and Roman Catholic.

In the 19th century religion in Scotland was marked by two great events or, to be more accurate, processes. One was the Disruption of the Church of Scotland in 1843 when the established Church split almost in two. The other was the great immigration of Irish Catholics around the middle of the century. The former eventually restored the ancient democracy of the Kirk while the latter reinstated the ancient Roman Catholic hierarchy to Rome's 'special daughter', as Scotland was known to the medieval Popes. Irish immigration also brought with it the kind of Orange/Green sectarianism which still disfigures Scottish life.

The Church of Scotland

As Principal Clerk to the General Assembly of the Church of Scotland, James Weatherhead must have one of the finest offices in Edinburgh. It is a big airy room situated on the fourth floor of the Church's headquarters in George Street, Edinburgh, with a view out over the northern reaches of the city to the hills of Fife. The only thing in the room that looks at all out of place is a handsome 19th-century engraving of the first General Assembly of the Free Church of Scotland in May 1843. It is taken from an oil painting by David Octavius Hill, and it is a superb record of all the Presbyterian zealots who followed Thomas Chalmers out of the Church of Scotland in the historic Disruption of the Church.

It raises an interesting question. Why should the man who is effectively the Kirk's chief executive officer want to remind himself of the fateful day the Church of Scotland split down the middle? 'Independence from the state,' Weatherhead says firmly. 'That's what the Disruption of 1843 was all about. It was an important battle in a long war that finally guaranteed the independence of the Church of Scotland from state interference. And that's something that any British government—Tory or Labour—would tamper with at their peril.' James Weatherhead's pride in the political and spiritual independence of the Church of Scotland is shared by most of the church's ministers and elders. What they know—albeit imperfectly—is that the struggle for that independence was long, arduous, and occasionally bloody. In the 'killing times' of the 1680s many decent Presbyterians were sent to 'glorify God' from a gallows in the Grassmarket, or were shot to death by British dragoons on the upland moors.

The final victory was not won until 1921 when parliament passed the Church of Scotland Act which agreed that the Church, and the Church alone, could adjudicate finally 'in all matters of doctrine, worship, government and discipline in the Church'. In all internal matters the Church of Scotland's courts were '*subject to no civil authority*'. This makes the constitutional position of the Church of Scotland unique in Britain. By the 1921 Act the British parliament relinquished all power over the internal affairs of the Kirk, an abrogation of parliamentary sovereignty which has never been repeated, except at the point of a gun. At a stroke, the Church of Scotland finally won what they had sought for more than 360 years: a legally established Church totally independent of the state.

Britain's other established Church, the Church of England, has the Queen at its head, its archbishops and senior bishops are appointed by the Prime Minister, and 29 of them sit in the House of Lords, as of right. The Monarch has no role in the Church of Scotland. All she can do is appoint a Lord High Commissioner to observe the proceedings of the annual General Assembly, and report back to her. The Commissioner has no part in the proceedings other than to pass on the Monarch's good wishes and hold a few soirées at Holyrood House.

For the most part the Lord High Commissioners are drawn from the list of the great and the good. The appointment is one of the Scottish establishment's little perks and treats, and the gentry and aristocracy loom large. Recent appointments include the Earl of Elgin, Sir John Gilmour, Baron Maclean of Duart and Morven, Viscount Arbuthnott, Sir Iain Tennant and the Right Honourable Donald Ross, the Lord Justice Clerk. In 1969 the Queen attended in person. One young minister is (anonymously) scathing about the kind of people selected to be Lord High Commissioner. 'It's always some toff with a title or a double-barrelled name,' he says. 'Baron this, Lord that, Sir something or other. The only exception that I can think of was Willie Ross after he'd stopped being Secretary of State for Scotland.'

However, the Monarch and her Commissioners are kept at arms length, which is the way the great Reformers intended it to be. John Knox made it very plain to Mary Stuart, Queen of Scots, that her Scotland and God's Scotland were different. The structure of the Church of Scotland was hammered out in the 16th century by John Knox and, more thoroughly, by his successor Andrew Melville. It is was—and remains—extraordinarily democratic.

The basic building block of Kirk democracy is the right of every congregation to elect their own minister. That right was laid out in Knox's *First Book of Discipline* (1560), reinforced in Melville's *Second Book of Discipline* 1578, constitutionally enshrined in 1690, removed by the British Parliament in 1712, restored in 1874 and held ever since. The elected minister then 'moderates' the 'kirk session' which runs the congregation's affairs. Every congregation elects members to attend the presbyteries and synods. Nowadays there is no discrimination on grounds of sex. Women have been ordained in the Church of Scotland—as ministers and elders—since 1966.

Beyond the congregations lie three layers of church courts: the presbyteries (of which there are 49); the synods (of which there are 12) and the annual General Assembly which is the Church's highest court. The Church is now planning to dispense with the 12 Synods. 'There were some congregations who wanted to hang on to them,' says James Weatherhead. 'But most thought they'd served their purpose. They were very badly attended and expensive to run. They'll be gone in a couple of years.'

Weatherhead has no doubt that the essential plank in the Presbyterian system is the presbytery. There are now 49 of them in the Church of Scotland, geographically organized from Shetland down to Galloway, each with its own (strictly temporary) moderator and presbytery clerk. Most presbyteries meet monthly. The biggest presbytery in Scotland is Presbytery Number 16, Glasgow. Presbytery Number 47 takes in the whole of England, from Newcastle-on-Tyne to Guernsey and Jersey plus all the Church of Scotland's military chaplains. The town of Corby in Northamptonshire has three Church of Scotland parishes, set up to minister to the Scots who followed the steel industry south. Nor are the presbyteries confined to Britain. Number 48 is a 16-congregation presbytery of Europe which stretches from Brussels to Malta, taking in the ancient Church of Scotland congregation at L'Auditoire in Geneva. It is administered by the Reverend Roy Hill from Cascais in Portugal. Presbytery Number 49 is the Kirk's presence in Jerusalem.

The Church's supreme court is the General Assembly of the Church of Scotland, which meets in Edinburgh every May, and is now the nearest thing Scotland has to an elected parliament. Like every kirk session, presbytery and synod in the land, the General Assembly is moderated by a senior minister who is elected by his peers. Once elected, he becomes *for one year only*, the Church of Scotland's representative. 'Not the head of the church,' says Dr William MacMillan, the minister of St Mary's Church in Dundee, who was Moderator for 1991–2. 'The Church of Scotland has only one head, and that is Jesus Christ himself.' This is an old certainty, and one that Scots Protestants have been hurling at the state since 1561 and which the state, from time to time has regarded as subversive. In fact, the history of Presbyterianism in Scotland is essentially an account of the long confrontation between God's Scotland and the King's Scotland. Ever since John Knox reduced Mary Queen of Scots to tears by rubbishing her 'divine right' to rule, and his successor Andrew Melville called James

VI 'God's silly vassal' Scots Presbyterianism has been at odds with the Anglo-British state.

The Kirk's cherished right of every congregation to *elect* its ministers was abhorred by the Stuart monarchs, and for most of the 17th century the Stuarts did their best to force the more hierarchical system of Episcopalianism on Lowland Scotland. They were resisted (fitfully) until the inept James VII and II was run out of Britain in 1688. Two years later the Scottish Church returned to the Presbyterian form of government of Knox and Melville.

But the triumph of Presbyterianism was undermined by the Patronage Act of 1712 which gave the Scots lairds the same right English squires had to appoint, or 'intrude' ministers on local congregations. The Patronage Act was a flagrant and illegal violation of the Revolution Settlement of 1690 and the Treaty of Union of 1707, both of which guaranteed the independence of the Scottish Church. Although the Kirk complained bitterly, their pleas fell on deaf ears. The English-dominated parliament of Britain could see no fault in a system which enabled anglicized landowners to appoint like-minded clergymen. Patronage was seen by the establishment as a useful instrument of political control and social progress. The issue rumbled on inside the Kirk for more than 130 years, as the 'moderate' faction clashed with the 'evangelicals' until, in the words of Lord Palmerston, 'Scotland was aflame about the church question'. Finally, in May 1843, Dr Thomas Chalmers led 400 or so ministers out of the Church of Scotland to form the Free Church of Scotland.

The Presbyterian rebellion of 1843 was brilliantly planned, well funded and took the British establishment by surprise. The government's information was that no more than a handful of ministers would risk their livelihoods. Instead, around 40 per cent marched out into the wilderness, abandoning churches, homes, stipends, social standing, security. The Disruption of 1843 was an act of genuine heroism that reverberated around Scotland, and within 10 years the fledgling Free Church of Scotland had built more than 800 churches, 700 manses, 3 theological colleges and 600 schools—in the teeth of vicious opposition from some of the most powerful men in Britain. It could be argued that the Disruption was the only rebellion in 19th century Britain that actually succeeded.

The rift in the church inflicted by the Disruption began to heal towards the end of the 19th century. The Patronage Act of 1712 was finally repealed in 1874, the secession churches merged with the Free Church in 1900 to form the United Free Church of Scotland, and in 1929 the United Frees were reunited with the established Church of Scotland, minus, of course, the many Presbyterian congregations who preferred to remain outside the establishment.

The latter half of the 20th century has been relatively trouble free, although Presbyterian sensitivities were outraged by the small part the Moderator of the General Assembly, Dr Pitt-Watson, was allowed to play in the Coronation in 1953. And the fact that he was photographed on his knees in front of a British monarch, just like any deferential Anglican, was widely muttered over. More than one Scottish churchman saw the posture as a historic humiliation. Much more serious was the blazing row which erupted in the late 1950s over the 'Bishops in the Kirk' report. This was a tentative plan to unite the Church of Scotland with the Episcopal Church in Scotland by making bishops into permanent moderators of the presbyteries. The idea was greeted with howls of outrage, and claims that the Episcopalian tail would end up wagging the Presbyterian dog. A vigorous press campaign was drummed up by the *Scottish Daily Express*, whose editor Ian MacColl was a Kirk elder, session clerk and member of the Glasgow presbytery. The plan foundered (although there was an attempt to revive it in the mid 1960s).

Although the latter half of the 19th century is usually regarded as the golden age of British churchgoing, in fact membership of the Church of Scotland peaked as late as 1961 when there were 1.29 million people on the congregational rolls. Since then it has been all downhill: 887 000 in 1984; 854 000 in 1986; 838 000 in 1987; 823 000 in 1988; 804 000 in 1989; 787 000 for 1990 (the last year for which figures are available). The decline in numbers attending Communion services is even more marked. James Weatherhead concedes that there is 'no reason' to think that the 1990s will see the downward run reversed. 'The paradox is that financially, we're doing surprisingly well,' he says. 'And I'm not just talking about the return on our investments. The income we receive from offerings is holding up, even though the membership itself is declining. What it means, I suppose, is that we have got fewer people donating more, which says something about the level of commitment among our members.' The figures certainly bear Weatherhead out. Per capita offerings jumped from £30.23 in 1984 to £44.81 in 1989. The Kirk's total income in 1989 (the last year for which figures are available) was £66.3 million, of which £36.2 million came out of the collection plates.

Despite this, the Kirk's 1 250 or so ministers are not living in anything approaching luxury. In 1991 the basic stipend for a Church of Scotland minister was £12,107, plus a manse. 'But the government have complicated things by making the manse an item that can be taxed as a benefit in kind,' James Weatherhead says. 'So that's come as a bit of a blow to us. We're still trying to sort it out.'

Some of the Church's money is spent fulfilling a role on the world stage by pump-priming missions abroad and paying for the Moderator's flag-flying trips to (in 1991–92) Lisbon, Brussels, London, Strasbourg, Geneva, Lausanne, Moscow and St Petersburg. One of the interesting things about the Kirk is that it is the *only* inst; that it is the *only* institition which pre-dates the Union of 1707 and still has an international persona. Scots law and the Scottish educational system are confined north of the border, but the Kirk spans the continents. Through its established church, Scotland is the heart of world Presbyterianism.

Responsibility for the education and training of the Kirk's ministers lies with the General Assembly's Education Board and its Education for the Ministry Committee. The latter is 'charged with the recruitment, selection and education of candidates for the ministry' (*Church of Scotland Year-Book*). All four of Scotland's 'old' universities, Edinburgh, Saint Andrew's, Glasgow and Aberdeen, have faculties of divinity which turn out students with the appropriate degrees. But New College in Edinburgh (which was built by the old Free Church in 1846) is the most important source of aspiring Church of Scotland ministers.

Although the modern Kirk shows no sign of succumbing to the kind of schisms that plagued it in the 18th and 19th centuries, (when Auld Licht Burghers and New Licht Burghers jockeyed for souls with Auld Licht Anti-Burghers and New Licht Anti-Burghers and Cameronians denounced them all) it is not without its internal tensions. One of them is a nagging, and occasionally quite heated, argument over the ordination of women, something that the Church of Scotland introduced in 1966. 'What has happened is that a number of younger, fundamentalist ministers have come into the church since then,' says Dr William MacMillan. 'And they believe that the Bible expressly forbids women from being ordained as ministers. My view is that these men knew what the policy of the Church was before they became ministers. If they did not approve, then they should have joined another Church. However, I don't think they have very much support.'

But one of the young fundamentalists, the Reverend Andrew McGowan, the minister at Trinity Possil and Henry Drummond Church in Glasgow disagrees. 'I reckon there are at least 75 ministers who would not ordain women under any circumstances, and I'm one of them. There are another couple of hundred who would be very reluctant indeed. The whole of Christendom is split on this issue, and the number of Christian Churches which allow the ordination of women is very small indeed.' The Biblical justification for his position he says, is very strong and he cites as an example 1 Timothy, Chapter 2, Verse 12: 'But I suffer not a woman to teach, nor to usurp authority over the man, but to be in silence.' 'I believe that the Bible is God's word,' MacGowan says simply. 'So I would never participate in the ordination of a woman, whatever the consequences for myself.' He is fearful that the Kirk could be in for a bout of self-inflicted damage if it tries to discipline ministers like himself who are flatly opposed to the ordination of women. 'If a Church of Scotland congregation wants to ordain a woman that's fine by me,' he says. 'But if it does *not*, then the General Assembly should not force it on them. That would be a very big mistake.'

This enthusiasm for democracy is an ancient strand in Scottish Presbyterianism. Taken to extremes it can lead to the kind of fractiousness which bedevilled the 18th-century Kirk, when congregation after congregation 'seceded' from the Church of Scotland to join the many Secession churches which did not return to the establishment fold until 1929. But it also makes Scotland a more democratic country than England. Kirk ministers are expected to say what they think. No one in Scotland raises an eyebrow when, say, the influential Church and Nation Committee of the General Assembly mauls the Government for its policies on housing, the poll tax, the NHS or education. The Bishop of Durham's 'radical' utterances are milk and water compared to the tongue-lashing the Very

Reverend James Whyte gave Margaret Thatcher when she made her famous appearance at the General Assembly of 1989. She accepted the dressing down with considerable grace.

The fact is the Kirk and the British state are still at odds, particularly over the issue of an elected assembly for Scotland. Ever since 1948 the Church of Scotland has supported the idea of a directly elected parliament for Scotland (20 years before the Labour Party were converted to the idea). In 1989 the General Assembly accepted a closely argued 'deliverance' (resolution) from the Church and Nation Committee that sovereignty lay with the people of Scotland, not with the British parliament, and that it should be expressed through a directly elected Scottish parliament.

Such a constitutional notion is anathema to the Kirk's many Conservatives. During the debate on the Scottish Assembly a heated row broke out with theologians like Professor Tom Torrance claiming that the General Assembly had been hijacked by the political nationalists. But the Devolutionists held firm, and won the day. The Church of Scotland is now behind the *Claim of Right* as drafted by the Campaign for a Scottish Assembly, and pushing hard.

The Reverend Will Storrar, who wrote the paper on which the 1989 deliverance was based, regards the Kirk's support for home rule as crucial to the political health of Scotland. The lack of it in March 1979, he argues, helped reduce the vote for an assembly in the referendum. 'A letter had gone out to every minister in Scotland to be read from the pulpit on the Sunday before the referendum,' he says. 'It was written to remind congregations that the Church of Scotland had supported the idea of an elected assembly since 1948, and still did. But a nifty piece of footwork by Andrew Heron (a seasoned theologian)—who argued that it was interference in party politics—got the letter withdrawn. So it was never read out. If it had been, it might have made a difference. There are almost 1 700 congregations in Scotland. That's a lot of voters.'

Not that all the Kirk's members are as enthusiastic about home rule for Scotland as Will Storrar and his colleagues. Many feel that it is a mistake for the Church of Scotland to be so vocal on this and other politically charged subjects. Experienced churchmen like Robert Kernohan, one-time editor of the Church's magazine *Life and Work*, and Andrew Heron argue that the Kirk is fast becoming a creature of the liberal left and in danger of alienating many of its more conservative members. This point of view is shared by some of the younger Biblical fundamentalists like the Reverend Andrew McGowan. 'It's a sign of the times,' he says, 'a symptom of the Church's own lack of confidence. Society sets the agenda and the Church follows, instead of the other way around. We've got people who have an opinion on everything from Ravenscraig to the need for an assembly, but who don't believe in the resurrection of Christ. There are people walking around in the Church of Scotland who are no more than atheists in ecclesiastical clothes.'

The liberal-inclined ministers and elders who dominate the Church and Nation Committee seem undeterred. At the General Assembly of 1991 they promoted deliverances arguing that Scottish interests such as fishing, conservation, transport, the steel industry and homelessness 'have received inadequate attention at Westminster' and urged the Kirk to press the government for 'the early establishment of a Scottish parliament within the UK'. Their deliverances were debated. The General Assembly voted overwhelmingly in favour. The long confrontation between the Church of Scotland and the British state continues.

Other Presbyterians

The Kirk has no monopoly on Presbyterianism in Scotland. In the 400 or so years since it first evolved, Scottish Presbyterianism has shown a remarkable tendency to split and then split again. Mercifully, the 'reunifications' of the late 19th and early 20th century relieved Scotland of the bizarre fragmentation of the late 18th century, but there are still more than enough Presbyterian churches to go around. At the last count there were no fewer than six churches organizing themselves along Presbyterian lines: the Church of Scotland, the Free Presbyterian Church of Scotland, the Associated Presbyterian Congregations, the Free Church of Scotland, the Reformed Presbyterian Church of Scotland, and the United Free Presbyterian Church of Scotland. Most of them have their roots in the ecclesiastical tangles of the 19th century when the Disruption of 1843 split the Church of Scotland more or less down the middle. In the latter half of the century the Free Church began to fall apart as many of its sterner members felt it was backsliding into the arms of a corrupt and essentially ungodly establishment.

In 1892, in response to a Declaratory Act designed to make the regime less harsh, 4 000 people (mainly Highlanders) walked out of the Free Church to form the Free Presbyterian Church of Scotland. Eight years later, in 1900, another 27 congregations refused to join in the union with the secession churches, and hijacked the name of the Free Church of Scotland (now usually known as the 'Wee Frees'). And when the United Free Presbyterian Church fell back into the arms of the established Church of Scotland in 1929 another 114 or so congregations stayed out to carry on the name.

This tendency for Presbyterian congregations to go their own way on a point of principle still exists. In 1989 the Free Presbyterian Church fell into two parts when its most prominent member, Lord Mackay of Clashfern, the Lord Chancellor of Britain, attended the funeral of a Roman Catholic colleague. Half the church rallied to his support, while half denounced him bitterly. The result was that Mackay's supporters marched off to found the Associated Presbyterian Congregations (APC), which now has 26 congregations, stretching from Aberdeen to Vancouver (although most of them are to be found in the Highlands).

The Free Church of Scotland has a higher profile. From its headquarters-cum-theological college at the top of The Mound in Edinburgh the Church runs its congregations through nine presbyteries and three synods. Its General

Assembly is held on the same week as the Kirk's, which is suicidal in terms of publicity. However, its publication the *Monthly Record* goes some way to redressing the balance: for years it was edited by Professor Donald Macleod, an erudite and witty Hebridean whose monthly column was required reading among Scottish literati.

Although its headquarters are in Edinburgh, and it has congregations all over Scotland (plus a two-presbytery synod in North America), seven of the Free Church's nine presbyteries—Argyll and Lochaber, Caithness and Sutherland, Inverness, Lewis, Lochcarron, Ross, Skye and Uist—are in the Highlands and Islands. In some areas the Free Church remains strong; the church at Kenneth Street, Stornoway, for example, boasts the biggest Presbyterian congregation in Britain—more than 2 000 people—which in the first six months of 1991 collected a whopping £90 000 for the Church's coffers. The minister, the assistant minister, the lay preacher, and the session clerk are all called MacLeod (as are 22 other Free Church ministers). For its size the Free Church of Scotland also has a remarkably large world presence. There are missionaries in South Africa, the Transkei, and India, and in Peru where it runs the Collegio San Andres in Lima. It is also an enthusiastic supporter of the Christian Witness to Israel which, from an office in Chislehurst in Kent, seeks to convert Jews to Christianity—a practice now widely criticized.

The headquarters of the Free Church of Scotland is worth a visit, if only for the original version of the painting by David Octavius Hill of the church's first General Assembly in 1843. Hill and his partner Robert Adamson took calotypes (an early kind of photograph) of everyone involved in the great event (and some who were not), then Hill spent more than 20 years putting them on to canvas. It is a remarkable record of the evangelical Presbyterians of the period: Thomas Chalmers, Hugh Miller, Thomas Guthrie, Robert Candlish, David Brewster, even the young Parsee convert Dhanjibhai Nauroji.

One of the smallest of the Presbyterian churches, the Reformed Presbyterian Church of Scotland also owns an historic artefact. This is the Magdalen Chapel in the Cowgate, a grubby little building with a beautiful interior which contains the only pre-Reformation stained glass left in Scotland. If the High Kirk of Saint Giles was the focus of the Reformation in Scotland, the Magdalen Chapel was its workplace. Here Knox, Melville and their colleagues hammered out the ideas of the Reformation. Here, too, the bodies of the 17th century Covenanters hanged in the Grassmarket were prepared for burial. The plain table where the strangled corpses were dressed is still there.

The United Free Presbyterian (UFP) Church (ie the descendants of the congregations who refused to join the union with the Kirk in 1929) continues. It has 8 300 members divided among 72 congregations which are organized into five presbyteries. The UFP is not in the best of health; according to a spokesman it has been losing members at the rate of around 300–400 a year, 'which is the same kind of decline that other churches are showing'.

Other Protestants

Presbyterianism may be the dominant form of Protestantism in Scotland, but it is not the only one. There are also around 6 000 Methodists, 5 000 members of the Salvation Army, 16 000 Baptists, 14 000 Congregationalists and a 'few hundred' members of the Society of Friends (Quakers). None of these churches are indigenous to Scotland. Most are imports from south of the border, the northern branches of organizations which have their headquarters elsewhere in Britain (and usually London).

The Baptists are the biggest group of non-Presbyterian Protestants in Scotland. There are 166 churches in the Baptist Union of Scotland and another five 'independent' congregations. The biggest of the Baptist churches in Scotland, the 800-strong Charlotte Baptist Chapel in Rose Street in Edinburgh, is outside the union. Although Baptists first appeared in Scotland in the 1650s along with Cromwell's troopers, the first 'home grown' congregation emerged at Keiss in Caithness in 1750. 'That was because the Laird of Keiss Castle was converted to Baptism on a visit to the south,' says Robert Armstrong of the Baptist Union for Scotland. 'He went home and built a small church, which is still there.' Scotland's Baptists retain a powerful suspicion of the Roman Catholic church. According to Armstrong the Baptist Union of Scotland withdrew from the ecumenically disposed Action of Churches Together in Scotland (ACTS) in 1989 because the Roman Catholic hierarchy was involved.

The Congregational Union of Scotland is more ecumenical. Its 14 000 or so adherents are organized into 97 congregations stretching in a 'long S-shape' from Annan in Dumfrieshire to Lerwick in Shetland. The Congregationalists have stronger roots in Scotland than the other Protestant minorities. They are descendants of the 'Old Scotch Independents' who date back to 1768. 'Congregationalism in Scotland is very different from the English variety,' says a spokesman. 'Ever since 1897 when the Congregational Union merged with the Evangelical Union it has been a strange mixture of Scots Presbyterianism and classical Congregationalism. That's something unique to Scotland.' The Congregationalists also have fairly close ties to the Kirk and there are a number of joint Congregational/Church of Scotland ventures throughout Scotland. The 1991 General Assembly of the Church of Scotland passed an act uniting three congregations in Paisley: the High Church, St John's Church and the Paisley Congregational Church.

The Synod of the Methodist Church in Scotland has 6 000 full members in 50 congregations sited mainly in Scotland's bigger communities. Synod secretary Walter Attwood says that while the Church in Scotland is 'very much part of the British Methodist Church', and there are no high-profile Scots Methodists to compare with, say, Lord Soper, the Church has a long history north of the border. 'John Wesley himself made more than 20 visits to Scotland,' he says, 'and what a reception he got. But he made relatively few converts. It was the immigrants from the south who came to work in the iron foundries and industries of the Central Belt who really brought Methodism to Scotland.'

The 5 000 or so 'soldiers and adherents' of the Salvation Army in Scotland are organized into three 'divisions' based in Edinburgh, Aberdeen and Glasgow with their headquarters at Buchanan Park in Glasgow. Colonel David Napier, head of the organization's Scottish Command, says that the majority of Scotland's Salvationists are women, and that there is a strong family tradition in the Salvation Army. He also says that the Salvation Army continues its tradition of fending for some of the poorest of Scots by running hostels and 'day centres' in the Pleasance and Grassmarket in Edinburgh, and Oxford Street, Campbell Street and Clyde Street in Glasgow. 'We do get help from local authorities,' he says, 'But it is a fairly expensive business. And not just in terms of money.'

Scottish members of the society of friends are few and far between. Marian Morton, clerk to the General Meeting for Scotland, says there are Quaker meeting houses in Edinburgh, Dundee, Aberdeen and Perth and that in Edinburgh 'there is a majority of English voices'. There are very few Quakers in Glasgow and the west. She admits candidly that the overwhelming majority of Scotland's Quakers are 'well educated and middle class, somewhat to our regret'.

The Episcopalians

The Primate of the Church of England lives in a Jacobean wonderland set in 4.5 hectares of well-kept gardens on the banks of the Thames, but his Scottish counterpart lives in a recently built bungalow called 'Benvoulin' on the outskirts of North Ballachulish in Argyll. And while the Archbishop of Canterbury's private office is well staffed, the Primus of the Episcopal Church in Scotland runs his church from a makeshift office in his garage. 'Ah, but what the Archbishop *doesn't* have,' says Bishop George Henderson, pointing to the high peaks of the Beinn Bheithir range on the other side of Loch Leven, 'is a view like that.' Bishop Henderson's way of life says a lot about the position of the Episcopal (ie Anglican) Church in Scotland. It is small, disestablished, relatively hard up, and spreads its clergy fairly thin. For a variety of historical reasons, many of its adherents are in the more remote parts of northern Scotland. As Bishop of the United Diocese of Argyll and the Isles—and formerly, for 22 years, a Labour Party councillor—George Henderson ministers to a flock of a few thousand scattered over 3 000 square miles of some of the roughest coastline in Europe. He presides over 25 Episcopal churches from St Moluag's at Eorrapaidh on the northern tip of Lewis, to St Kiaran's at Campbeltown at the south end of the Mull of Kintyre. He was elected 'Primus Inter Pares' by the seven Episcopal bishops in 1990, and one of his first jobs as Primus was to represent the Church at the Anglican Consultative Council, a gathering of the world's Anglican primates. 'Usually it is held somewhere warm and exotic like the Caribbean, but when I got to go they held it at Newcastle near Belfast,' he says ruefully. Bishop Henderson admits that his Church does not rank high on the Anglican pecking order. 'We must be very near the bottom of the Anglican league,' he says. 'Maybe the Anglican Church in the Indian Ocean is smaller. Maybe.'

But for all its size—in 1992 it had less than 35 000 members—the Episcopal Church in Scotland is influential, and highly vocal. Bishops like Michael Hare Duke (St Andrews and Dunblane) and Richard Holloway (Edinburgh) are favourites of the media, and much quoted on controversial topics. Richard Holloway, indeed, irritated Her Majesty's Government at the time of the Gulf War by pointing out that 'the closer you got to London the more vocal was the support from Christian leaders'. The war, Bishop Holloway argued, revealed significant differences of attitude north and south of the border. 'The bishops of the Church of England, with a few exceptions, were strong in their support for Government policy,' he declared, 'while Church leaders in Scotland were almost totally united in their opposition to it.' There is a feeling in Church circles that Holloway's candour was one of the reasons that the Scottish Episcopal Church was allowed no official role in the post-war ceremonies at Glasgow Cathedral, and why he was not considered a possible archbishop of Canterbury when Lord Runcie retired recently.

The Scottish Episcopal Church is no stranger to contention. It has a long and intriguing history. Nothing irritates Episcopalians more than to be regarded as members of the 'English' church. Episcopalian historians like to remind Scots that for much of the 16th and 17th centuries Episcopalianism was the established system of government in the Church of Scotland, and that Presbyterianism did not finally come into its own until after the 'Glorious Revolution' of 1688. In the 1690s Episcopalians felt the sting of repression, when hundreds of worthy ministers and their families were 'rabbled' out of their churches (and homes) by Presbyterian mobs, and ragged bishops rode the countryside struggling to keep their flocks together. The Jacobite rebellions of 1715, 1719 and 1745 did not help. It was mainly the Episcopalian clans which supported the Stuarts, and thus gave a stigma to the Church which Hanoverian Britain took a long time to forgive. But as the Scottish aristocracy and gentry became almost totally anglicized in the course of the 19th century, Anglican forms of worship became the norm among Scotland's élites. By the middle of the century the Scottish Episcopal Church had become the 'Laird's Kirk', a label it has never quite shrugged off. And while the 17th and 18th century forms of worhsip in Scots Episcopalianism were 'low' to the point of being almost indistinguishable from Presbyterianism, the Church became distinctly 'high' under the influence of the Tractarian and Catholic movements of the 19th century.

There are some important differences between the Scottish Episcopal Church and its big sister south of the border. 'For one thing the Government has no say in our affairs,' says the Church's spokesman Aeneas Mackintosh. 'There are no archbishops, our Primus is elected by his fellow bishops, and all our bishops are elected by the clergy and the laity.' Mackintosh explains that every Episcopalian congregation has an annual general meeting at which a Vestry Committee is elected which in turn elects a lay representative to the diocesan synod and the governing General Synod. The Church has its administrative headquarters at the west end of Edinburgh's New Town, next door to the theological college, which educates 25–30 students at any one time. The Church's 35 000 communicant members are shepherded by 7 bishops, 200 full-time rectors, and around 100 non-stipendiary ministers.

Like Anglican churches everywhere, the Scottish Episcopal Church operates through a system of dioceses. There are seven: Aberdeen and Orkney; Argyll and the Isles; Brechin; Edinburgh; Glasgow and Galloway; Moray, Ross and Caithness; and St Andrews, Dunkeld and Dunblane. There are Episcopalian cathedral churches in Inverness, Aberdeen, Dundee, Perth, Edinburgh, Glasgow, and Oban, plus the extraordinary little 'Cathedral of the Isles' on the island of Cumbrae.

While clergy and laymen alike bristle at the 'English' epithet, a large number of the Church's members do hail from south of the border. However, Bishop Henderson says that it is wrong to assume that all English immigrants join the Scottish Episcopal Church. 'Many of them are so accustomed to being members of a church by law established,' he says, 'that they join the Church of Scotland. Even if it is Presbyterian.'

An even greater proportion of the Church's bishops and clergy are English. The 'clerical biographies' in the Church's year-book reveal dozens of rectors who were born and educated in England, ordained in the Church of England, and then given charges in the Scottish Episcopal Church. 'There is complete mutuality between the two churches,' Mackintosh says. 'And there is no doubt that most of the traffic is from the south to the north.'

But not all. Patrick Rodger, recently retired as the Bishop of Oxford and now living in Edinburgh, describes the contrast between the Anglican communions of Scotland and England. 'The big difference is money,' he says. 'The Church commissioners of the Church of England handle many millions. In my diocese of Oxford—which covered Oxfordshire, Buckinghamshire and Berkshire—I had 832 churches, and 800 clergy under me. That's four times the size of the Episcopal Church in the whole of Scotland.' In Scotland, Rodger says, Episcopalian congregations tend to be small, but 'the level of committment is very high. They are there because they want to be. They know that they must give—and give generously—to keep their church going. There is no Church Commission standing in the background waiting to dole out huge sums of money. We are entirely self-supporting. And some of our churches are little more than glorified huts.'

One striking exception is St Mary's Cathedral (1879–1917) in Edinburgh by Sir George Gilbert Scott, probably the finest large-scale Victorian Gothic building in the city. The money for it came from the Coates Estate, given to the Church by the Misses Walker. 'That's why the two great spires are called Barbara and Mary,' Rodger explains. While acknowledging the Church's debt to its wealthy donors, Rodger is uneasy about its social composition. There is no doubt that in some parts of Scotland, and particularly around Edinburgh, the Scottish Episcopal Church comprises the affluent classes at prayer. And in the rural stretches of Angus, Perthshire and Aberdeenshire, the congregations are well laced with double-barrelled names and military titles. 'I'm afraid there is still a trace of the "Laird's Kirk" about us,' Rodger admits. 'You see exactly the same thing in the United States. And that is unfortunate, because the idea of a Church divided, or organized, along social lines is a denial of the gospel.'

Predictably perhaps, the Scottish Episcopal Church showed little enthusiasm for the campaign against the Conservative government's poll tax, although Bishop Henderson did make his distaste well known. But the Church has joined with the Catholics and Presbyterians in pressing for a measure of Home Rule for Scotland, and one of its clergy, Canon Kenyon Wright, is a vociferous spokesman for the Campaign for a Scottish Assembly. As a one-time Labour councillor, Bishop George Henderson is well aware of the conservatism of Scottish Episcopalianism. He suggests that it may well have contributed to the Church's steady decline. Gordon Donaldson, the Queen's Historiographer in Scotland, and a life-long Episcopalian, takes the view that it is the 'absurdly high' nature of the Scottish Episcopal Church which has alienated many Scots. Patrick Rodger suggests that Scottish Episcopalianism is 'high' as a reaction to Scotland's Presbyterian establishment. Whatever the reason, the decline in membership has been serious. In 1982 there were 40 000 communicants; in 1989 there were 35 000, a drop of 12.5 per cent in less than a decade. 'People keep telling me that we have reached the bottom now,' says Bishop Henderson, 'but I can see little evidence of that. These are difficult times for all the churches in Scotland.'

(In June 1992 Bishop Henderson was succeeded as Primus by the Right Reverend Richard Holloway, Bishop of Edinburgh. Although well known for his outspoken views, Bishop Holloway is a clergyman in the traditional Episcopalian mould; from 1968 to 1980 he was Rector of Old St Paul's in Edinburgh, one of the 'highest' Episcopalian congregations in Scotland.)

The Roman Catholics

The Roman Catholics are, of course, the oldest religious community in Scotland. There has been a Roman Church in Scotland ever since the Synod of Whitby in 664 where it was decided that the tribes of north Britain should follow the path of Rome rather than of the ancient Culdee (Celtic) church. 'Even if your fathers were true saints,' Rome's high-handed advocate told the Celtic delegation, 'surely a small company on a corner of a remote island is not to be preferred to the universal Church of Christ which is found throughout the whole world.'

The Scottish version of the Roman Church was always rough around the edges. In the 11th century Queen (and later Saint) Margaret imported Dominican monks from England to help smooth them off, a process which was continued by her pious son David. In 1216 the Scottish Church became the Holy See's 'special daughter', a position that was to prove useful in the

14th century for fending off English claims to Scotland. By the 15th century the Roman Church in Scotland was sliding into an apathy and venality which became common throughout Europe, and mutterings of protest began to be heard, probably in response to the writings of the English heretic, John Wyclif. Although Martin Luther's books were banned in the early 16th century, the Scottish Church's enthusiasm for France and things French (and a tendency to burn intellectuals like Patrick Hamilton and George Wishart) did not help the cause of Christ.

The long reign of the Roman Church came to an abrupt end in 1559 when a powerful group of aristocrats known as 'the Lords of the Congregation' sided with the Reformers, purged Scotland of French influence (with English help), denied the authority of the pope, banned the Latin mass, and began dismantling the Church. Officially, the ancient hierarchy ended with the death of the Archbishop of Glasgow in Paris in 1603. While Jesuit, Dominican and Franciscan missionaries managed to keep the flame guttering in some corners of Scotland, the enthusiasm of Scottish Catholics for the doomed Jacobite cause covered them in odium. Things began to improve with the Catholic Relief Act (1793), the Catholic Emancipation Act (1829) and in 1878 the Roman Catholic Hierarchy in Scotland was reinstated, thanks to the huge immigration of Irish workers in the middle of the 19th century. The Irish origins of modern Scottish Catholicism can be seen from the names listed in the *Catholic Directory for Scotland*; Kellys, Gallaghers, Murphys, Quinns and O'Kanes abound.

In modern Scotland, the Roman Catholic Church has established itself as the second largest Christian community in the land, with more than 787 000 members. 'Some Catholics say we are about to become the biggest church in the land,' says the Church's information officer Father Tom Connelly. 'That's a nonsense. Our membership figures are calculated differently from the Church of Scotland's. We count as a member every Catholic who has been baptized. The Church of Scotland only counts its adult communicants . So, in fact, we've a long way to go before we catch up with the Kirk.'

The Roman Catholic Church in Scotland is organized into eight dioceses and archdioceses: Glasgow, St Andrews and Edinburgh, Motherwell, Paisley, Aberdeen, Galloway, Dunkeld, Argyll and the Isles. The biggest of them is Glasgow, with a membership of 281 000, followed by Motherwell with 175 000. Surprisingly perhaps, the Archdiocese of St Andrews and Edinburgh is third, with 120 000 Roman Catholics. The Church has around 1 000 priests in Scotland, 464 parishes, and there are about 12 000 baptisms a year.

There are eight Roman Catholic cathedrals: St Mary's in Edinburgh; St Mary's in Aberdeen; St Columba's in Oban; St Andrew's in Dundee; the Good Shepherd Cathedral in Ayr; St Andrew's Cathedral in Glasgow; Our Lady of Good Aid Cathedral in Motherwell; and St Mirin's Cathedral in Paisley. The only one of outstanding architectural merit is St Andrew's in Glasgow which is an 'A'-listed building, designed by James Gillespie Graham in 1816, and extended by Pugin in 1892. There are major 'religious houses' at Nunraw Abbey near Haddington, at Pluscarden near Elgin and at Fort Augustus at the south end of Loch Ness. Central Scotland is well endowed with nunneries: Carmelites, Poor Clares, the Little Sisters of the Poor, and the Daughters of Charity of Saint Vincent de Paul. In recent years Scottish nuns have moved away from teaching into social work, and running homes for the elderly and the disabled.

There are seminaries at Cardross, Aberdeen, Edinburgh and Glasgow. A remarkable proportion of Scottish priests study at the ancient Scots colleges in Rome and Salamanca in Spain. 'There used to be a Scots College in Paris,' says Father Connelly. 'That was very ancient. Founded in 1325. But after the Scots students got mixed up in the student unrest of 1968 the Church authorities and the French government closed it down.' Connelly argues that this tradition of studying in Europe gives the Scottish priesthood an internationalist outlook. 'Most of the bishops and senior clergy were educated at the Scots colleges abroad. They've built up an old boys' network which keeps them in touch with one another. They're all well organized, and raise money for their old colleges.' Five of the eight bishops—Winning, Conti, Renfrew, Devine and Taylor—studied at the Scots College in Rome.

Like all the Christian Churches in Britain, the Roman Catholic Church in Scotland is a dwindling community. 'That's reflected in all sorts of ways,' says Connelly. 'Fewer and fewer people at mass. Fewer and fewer Catholic weddings and communions. And a marked decline in the number of young people coming forward with a vocation. We've even made a careers video called *Think Again* in an attempt to interest youngsters in the religious life. Nowadays we set up our stall at the careers exhibitions along with engineers, accountants and lawyers. That would have been unthinkable 20 years ago.'

If the Roman Catholic Church in Scotland has a titular head it is His Eminence Cardinal Gordon Joseph Gray. Gray is a genuinely historic figure. Born in Leith in 1910 he became Archbishop of St Andrews and Edinburgh in 1951 and was made Cardinal in 1969. As such, he was the first Scot to be awarded the Red Hat since 1546 (14 years before the Scottish Reformation). He is also the only Scot to have taken part in two conclaves to elect a pope, and in the summer of 1982, at his residence of St Bennet's in Edinburgh, he played host to Pope John Paul II. However, Gray has been in poor health for some years, and in 1984 resigned as Archbishop. He now lives quietly at St Bennet's.

The most obvious candidate to succeed him would be the Most Reverend Thomas Joseph Winning, the Archbishop of Glasgow. Known to most of his clergy and laity as 'TJ', Winning is by far the most important Catholic churchman in Scotland. As president of the Bishops' Conference, the body which runs the Church in Scotland, and head of the biggest archdiocese in Scotland, Winning wields a great deal of power and influence. A handsome, amiable, and persuasive man of 62, Winning is much respected (some would say feared) as an advocate and politician. The son of a west of Scotland railway worker, he studied at the Scots College in Rome, acted as its Spiritual Director from 1966 to 1970, became a parish priest in Motherwell and Glasgow, bishop-auxiliary in

Glasgow in 1971 and was 'translated' as Archbishop of Glasgow in 1974. In 1976 he launched a monthly tabloid newspaper called *Flourish*, which is now run with verve by a young Irish priest called Noel Barry. The success of *Flourish* (there are 280 000 Catholics in the archdiocese) did not endear Winning to the *Scottish Catholic Observer* which regards the diocesan tabloid as unfair competition. Nor is Winning a man to duck controversy. In fact, he seems to thrive on it. During the Gulf War ceremonies in Glasgow Cathedral, Winning went into the pulpit and made it plain that he took a very dim view of the conduct of the war. In 1978 he raised many hackles by accusing the British of becoming a nation of 'spiritual dwarves', and later that year denounced the 'grave and heart-rending violation of human rights' in Catholic Argentina. He also challenged Prince Charles to justify the Law of Succession which keeps Roman Catholics off the British throne. So far, Prince Charles has let the gauntlet lie.

Practically, Winning's most important job is as president of the Bishops' Conference, which steers the Church through the reefs and shallows of Scottish life. The Bishops' Conference operates via a series of eight commissions (working committees) each of which is presided over by one of the diocesan bishops. The Commission on Christian Doctrine and Unity, for example, is supervised by Mario Conti, Bishop of Aberdeen. Joseph Devine, the Bishop of Motherwell looks after the Commission for Communications. The crucially important Commission for Education is presided over by Winning himself. There is no doubt that one of his main aims in life is to defend Scotland's system of state-funded Roman Catholic schools, a system that its many critics say perpetuates the religious bigotry and sectarianism that still haunts the country. It is regulated under the Education (Scotland) Act of 1918, which was regarded at the time as a great step forward. But Winning has a fight on his hands. The Catholic school system has powerful opponents. The population of the Catholic schools has been dwindling rapidly. The Strathclyde Regional Council, which runs most of Scotland's Catholic schools, is determined to rationalize a system that makes little economic sense. St Gregory's Secondary in Cranhill, for example, was built for 1 682 pupils and in May 1991 had 366. St Pius Secondary in Drumchapel had 345 children rattling about in a school designed for 1 700. The Sacred Heart Secondary at Girvan had only 80 pupils and so could offer them only a very limited choice of courses. The debate over the Roman Catholic schools is fraught with politics. When Jim Sillars of the SNP then MP for Govan, told a meeting of Catholic head teachers that he (and his party) supported the idea of Catholic schools, Archbishop Winning was fulsome in his praise for the nationalist MP. 'It was refreshing,' the Archbishop said 'to find a capable politician, particularly one who is not a Catholic, with the honesty, courage and integrity to come into the open to defend the interests of Catholic parents and children.' As Sillars's Labour Party opponent was Ian Davidson, chairman of the region's education committee, this was a telling statement. The Archbishop was inviting—without saying so—the Catholics of Govan to support the man who supported their schools.

This amalgam of religion and politics is one of the facts of Scottish life. To a large extent (and with plenty of exceptions) Catholic Scotland expresses itself politically through the Scottish Labour Party. There is nothing mysterious about this; well into the 20th century Irish Catholics formed one of the poorest communities in Scotland. It was natural that the Catholics should invest their loyalty in the Labour Party. The SNP are now trying without much success to prise that loyalty loose.

The non-Christian faiths

Like every other pluralistic society Scotland has its share of non-Christian religions. For its size Scotland's Jewish community has produced a remarkable amount of talent: David Daiches the writer, Lionel Daiches his advocate brother, Muriel Spark the novelist, Chaim Bermant the journalist, Malcolm Rifkind, one-time Secretary of State for Scotland and now Secretary of State for Defence. There are four Jewish congregations in Glasgow, one in Edinburgh and a small one in Dundee. But we're getting smaller by the year,' says a spokesman for the Edinburgh Hebrew Congregation. 'Our young people tend to drift off to the bigger Jewish communities in places like Leeds, or Manchester and London, and then never come back.'

Islam, on the other hand, seems to be doing well. There are an estimated 15 000–20 000 Muslims in Scotland, most of them in the four cities, particularly Glasgow. But there is also a sturdy community of Muslim Pakistanis in Stornoway, some of whom speak Gaelic. There is a large, richly ornamental mosque in the Gorbals district of Glasgow, and a more subdued building under construction on the south side of Edinburgh. A converted church in Leith serves as a temple for Edinburgh's Hindu community.

But perhaps the most exotic and surprising religious community in the whole of Scotland is the Kagyu Samye Ling Tibetan Monastery in Eskdalemuir near Langholm. It was founded in 1967 by Tibetan monks as a retreat and a centre for study and meditation and welcomes visitors of every faith or none. The vivid, pagoda-like buildings sit quite happily in the dark conifers and rolling green hills of Eskdalemuir. In 1992 the monks acquired the aptly named Holy Island off Arran and promised to make it accessible to people of 'all religions'.

But for all the richness and diversity of Scottish religious life, God's Scotland is a shadow of its former self. Churches of all denominations and faiths are faced with shrinking congregations, many struggling to survive. The country is now littered with redundant church buildings many of which are private homes, retirement flats, discotheques or even casinos. As the second millenium closes, the ancient conceit that the Scots are among God's 'elect' peoples is very hard to maintain.

6

Education

Peter Jones

Scottish education in all its elements—the institutions, the examinations, the curriculum, its ethos—has become one of the jewels in the crown of Scottish identity. Indeed, a distinctive education system is one of the primary features that distinguish the Scots from the English. It is part of the folklore of Scotland, and England for that matter, that the Scottish education system is superior to that of England. Scots who reach positions of British prominence routinely refer to the benefits of their education. A profile in the *Independent on Sunday* in May 1991 of John Smith, the Labour MP and foremost Scottish politician of his generation, noted: 'Smith insists on the superiority of Scottish education.' Non-Scottish politicians, when they travel north, dutifully acknowledge that traditional perception.

Whether that view is justified, either when comparing Scottish education to the English system or to that of western Europe, is a subject of increasing debate. Politicians argue about crumbling buildings, inadequate equipment and falling academic standards; the damage done to extra-mural activities by teachers' strikes just as fiercely in Scotland as in England. Nevertheless, if Scottish education is examined in crude import/export accounting terms it suggests a success story. While Scotland has about 9 per cent of the UK population, Scottish universities have about 15 per cent of the UK student population. But, because Scotland is removed from centres of power and influence, the proportion of young Scots graduates who find their careers elsewhere is extremely high. The sociologist Isobel Lindsay, also a nationalist politician, in a migration study published in the 1991 *Scottish Government Yearbook*, reported: 'Of Glasgow University's Scottish-domiciled 1988 graduates, 33 per cent left Scotland for their first job. The 1988 figure for Strathclyde University was over 40 per cent. In a historical study of Aberdeen graduate migration from 1860–1960, more graduates were found to be working outside Scotland in their last reported job than in their first; particularly, the number overseas was higher'. The expatriate Scot has been a familiar figure throughout the world since the days of the British Empire, and contributes to the image at home and abroad of a superior Scottish education system.

A different ethos

What makes Scottish education different? At seven years, primary education lasts a year longer than in England. Teaching methods vary: in Scotland they tend to be more traditional, for example, more inclined to whole-class teaching from the blackboard than group or child-centred learning. Sharp variations arise in the secondary school system, particularly after the end of compulsory schooling in the fourth year. The post-16 curriculum in Scotland is historically broader in scope: academically able pupils will generally take three to five Higher (H-grade) courses, compared to two to three Advanced (A-level) courses in England. The H-grade is a one-year course whereas A-levels take two years. As H-grades are the main qualification for higher education entry, Scots can qualify for university or college a year earlier than in England. The sixth year at secondary school is regarded as an optional extra or a second chance at gaining entry to higher education rather than the crowning year of achievement.

Researchers credit the H-grades as the reason why, at the start of the 1990s, nearly 25 per cent of young Scots were qualified (three or more H-Grades) for higher education compared to the 17 per cent so qualified (two or more A-levels) south of the border; and that in turn explains why a greater proportion of Scottish school-leavers went on to higher education: about 24 per cent compared to about 15 per cent in England and Wales.

In higher education, the structure is again different. The Honours degree course is four years rather than three as in England, a length which is consistent with the earlier entry. The Scottish universities in particular offer the distinctive Ordinary degree, based on passes in a range of subjects at first-and second-year levels and achievable in three years.

Other features which make Scottish education different are the relatively small independent fee-paying schools sector, a state sector which is more thoroughly comprehensive, a binary higher education divide which has been more complementary than competitive, and a more centralized administrative structure. All this has arisen because of a separate history, which in turn has been underpinned by a distinctive ethos to which policy-makers, teachers and parents alike subscribe. Some think this ethos is summed up by the breadth of education offered. Ronald Crawford, of the Universities of Scotland Standing Conference in the October 1990 *Scotland on Sunday* Student Guide, said: 'To put it at its most basic, the whole ethos of education in Scotland is in breadth of knowledge. That doesn't necessarily mean quantity taking precedence over quality of education. It simply gives students more opportunity to vary their options in terms of what further education courses to take, because they have a much broader grounding.'

But Andrew McPherson, director of Edinburgh University's Centre for Educational Sociology has argued that the mythology is more complex, a point accepted by Peter Scott, editor of *The Times Higher Education Supplement*. He wrote in *The Scotsman* in November 1990: 'The debate about the future of Scotland's universities and schools still has to take place in the shadow of two grand over-arching beliefs, powerful myths that shape the possibilities of that debate even in the last decade of the 20th century.' As with McPherson, Scott's two myths are those of the 'lad o' pairts' and the 'democratic intellect'. It can be argued that there is a third, that of the 'dominie' which has had a direct influence on the governing institutions of Scottish education, particularly those pertaining to teachers.

Most historians root the distinctiveness of Scottish society in the Reformation, especially John Knox's famous *First Book of Discipline*, published in 1560 when there was a substantial education system in place already. By Knox's time, Scotland had universities in Aberdeen, Glasgow and St Andrews while England only had Oxford and Cambridge. In 1496, James IV had ordered compulsory education from the ages of six to nine for the sons of barons and freeholders. But Knox's plan was a breathtaking vision, probably the first of its kind in Europe, for a national system of education. Under the control of the Reformed Church, as the historian May Mackintosh has described in her book *Education in Scotland, Yesterday and Today* (1962), there was to be 'a ladder of education, reaching from the parish school to the university. Every town church was to appoint a schoolmaster who was to teach Latin and grammar. The larger towns were to have colleges where languages, rhetoric and logic would be taught by schoolmasters paid "honest stipends". Children whose parents were poor, but who were "apt for learning" were not to be deprived of their chance.' Knox's plan was blocked by the Crown and nobles, but as the Reformation proceeded, much of it trickled into operation, with acts placing schools under the control of the Kirk (1567 and 1693) and establishing them in every parish (1616, 1646, 1696).

By the 19th century, Scottish education was well-established, relatively socially open and with virtual universal literacy. In 1868, the landmark reports of the Royal Commission on Schools in Scotland (Argyll Commission) set the tone for much subsequent debate. In an oft-quoted paragraph, the Commissioners said: 'It cannot be too often repeated, that the theory of our school system, as originally conceived, was to supply every member of the community with the means of obtaining for his children not only the elements of education, but such instruction as would fit him to pass to the burgh school, and thence to the university, or directly to the University from the parish school.'

The comment encapsulates the myth of the 'lad o' pairts', a phrase popularized by the pseudonymous Ian Maclaren's classic of Scottish kailyard literature *Beside the Bonnie Brier Bush*. The character is so solidly embedded in the Scottish pysche, that as critics Isobel Murray and Bob Tait remark in *Ten Modern Scottish*

Novels (1984): 'No Scottish novel with a background of poverty would be quite complete without its "lad o' pairts", the bright boy who is chosen as a member of a secular elect to rise in the world through education.' But in order to rise, the 'lad o' pairts' needed the 'dominie', an interesting survival of a Latin word into Scots. *Dominie* means not just teacher, but also a person of standing and respect in the community, in whose hands the bright child's future will be assured, and from whom everyone else will receive a basic grounding in the three Rs: reading, writing and arithmetic.

Originally, parish teachers were examined and appointed by the presbytery, in much the same way as ministers were by their kirk sessions, an essentially democratic process. The 'dominie' in charge of the little school was, however, essentially a rural phenomenon, a model which could not cope with the urban expansion brought on by the Industrial Revolution. In Glasgow in 1834, by no means the worst area, only one-fourteenth of school-age children were reported to be at school, historian Christopher Smout observes in *A Century of the Scottish People 1830–1950* (1986). After the Argyll Commission reports, a Scottish Education Act was passed in 1872 which laid the basis for a state-run education service. The establishment of the Scottish Office in 1885 provided the necessary state administrative framework for just such a service, and power over schooling began to pass from the Kirk.

At least as important in defining Scottish education was a distinctive ethos called the 'democratic intellect', after a book of that name published in 1961 by the Scottish philosopher George Davie. He himself adapted a phrase coined by the Scottish Conservative politician Walter Elliot, who wrote in 1932 of Scots having a heritage of 'democratic intellectualism'. The concept is wide, rooted in a philosophy which contends that reasoning, while it should be grounded in experience, ought to stem from principles and not simply from an assemblage of observed facts. It has a clear expression in the adage that Scots law is founded on principle and not on precedent. But the concept also involves the principle of generalism: that education should be a broad learning experience. Entry to education, it is argued, should be democratic or meritocratic, rather then being determined by social status or financial means, so that higher education is genuinely an intellectual commonwealth.

Whether Scottish education has always fully lived up to its own mythology is a matter of debate. George Davie's book is not a celebration, but an angry argument that a unique Scottish intellectual tradition has faded in the face of a relentless effort to fit Scottish higher education into English traditions. What remains, and clearly breadth of learning is still a characteristic, Davie contends to be a mere shell. His argument has been criticized, but the reputation of his book has become such as to make it a powerful totem.

All too often, the dominie, rather than being a benign talent scout, turned out to be a tyrannical disciplinarian. The late A S Neill described him as a 'dull devil fearful of compromising the little respectability he has and alarmed at anything that detracts from his petty dignity'. Neill in his autobiography *Neill! Neill! Orange Peel!* (1973) described his own conformity as 'a young dominie' around 1900 at a school near Bonnyrigg, Lothian run by an elderly disciplinarian called Miss MacKinley: 'I was ordered to thrash any child who even whispered, and did so because I was really scared of the old woman.'

Under this pre-war regime, learning was by rote, with the pupils chanting out multiplication tables or the Shorter Catechism. Understanding was not an objective. Like many others, Neill concluded that rote learning coupled with constant beatings simply bred into the pupil a sense of inferiority. Indeed it is amazing that anyone ever became a 'lad o' pairts' under the system he described in the 1920s. There were certainly few 'lasses o' pairts', though there was a growth in the number of women entering universities in the 1890s.

The three traditions of Scottish education need to be kept in perspective. Where the 18th and 19th century lad o'pairts survived beatings and rote learning to go to university, he tended to be the exception rather than the rule, the rule being that higher education was largely reserved for the middle classes. Talk, particularly in the 1980s, was of teachers suffering a declining social status and, becoming increasingly demoralized, a condition brutally summed up in the opening words of James Kelman's book *A Disaffection*: 'Patrick Doyle was a teacher. Gradually he had become sickened by it.'

Since the 1960s, school and higher education has undergone much change, suggestive of failure either to meet modern social demands, or to live up to the old mythology. Nevertheless, it is true that those who run the education system, especially the schools system, have continued to believe firmly in Scottish traditions and sought to make education live up to them. Andrew McPherson and Charles Raab interviewed most of those in the driving seats of the system 1945–75 for their massive work *Governing Education*. McPherson concluded: 'The majority of the 11 Scottish educationists whom we interviewed spontaneously identified their own origins with the "lad o' pairts", and, with differences of emphasis, virtually all described the post-war Scottish system as socially open. One ex-HMSCI (Her Majesty's Senior Chief Inspector) told us that many of the influential Association of Directors of Education shared this view, as did his colleagues in the SED [Scottish Education Department]. Both former Secretaries to the department confirmed this last judgement, one of them saying "it was something in our blood".' Even Michael Forsyth, who became a controversial Scottish Education Minister in 1987 and challenged many of the cherished symbols of the system, told his party conference in 1991: 'Children from the most humble of backgrounds have climbed the ladder of success, proud to proclaim the virtues of Scottish education and the skills it gave them, and the dreams it fulfilled.'

The system

Primary education

Primary education has moved a long way from the grim scenes described by A S Neill. Today's primary schools are places where play is mixed with pedagogy, and where group project work is more important than blackboard learning. The modern approach stems from the SED's 1965 *Memorandum on Primary Education in Scotland*. Frank McEnroe, of Glasgow University's Department of Education, while critical of some aspects of the document in an essay *Freudianism, Bureaucracy and Scottish Primary Education* (1983) states: 'The 1965 statement must be one of the most radical in the history of Scottish primary education, and A S Neill would have agreed whole-heartedly with its credo.' It sought to abolish disciplinarian traditions that demanded conformity to a known set of rules, and to introduce a system of child-centred learning, whose guiding principle is that education should be based on the needs and interests of the child.

In the 1990s, a further revolution commenced with the SED's *5–14 Development Programme*. It sprang from a conviction in Government circles, more sustained by evidence in England than in Scotland, that primary standards of attainments in literacy and numeracy had declined. Launched in 1988, the programme introduced a more standardized curriculum to primary schools, with teaching built around five main areas: language, mathematics, environmental studies, expressive arts, and religious and moral education. While guidelines set out the study aims in each area, how learning should proceed, the balance between the five subjects, and also levels of attainment, teachers are expected to be flexible in taking account of the particular circumstances of their class. But one element, the Government's move to create national tests of pupils' language and mathematics attainments in primaries four and seven, proved controversial. Opposition from the main teaching unions, parental organizations and some education authorities resulted in more than half of the pupils being withdrawn from the first round of tests in 1991 by their parents, and teachers' boycotts reduced the proportion who actually sat the tests to around a quarter.

Secondary education

Changes in secondary education from the 1960s have been just as dramatic. The pride of secondary education is the leaving examination system. The central feature is the 'Higher', originally the Higher Grade of the School Leaving Certificate when introduced in 1888. Its main function has been to act as a university entrance qualifying examination. In the 1950s moves were made to broaden out certification, and the Lower Grade of the Leaving Certificate was replaced in 1962 with the Ordinary Grade, aimed at 30 per cent of secondary pupils.

The 1965 revamping of exams into the Scottish Certificate of Education with its H- and O-Grades coincided with comprehensive reorganization, abolishing the distinction between junior (non-academic three- and four-year secondary schools) and senior (five- and six-year academically orientated) secondaries. The distinction applied more to urban than rural schools which, apart from internal selection and streaming, had by necessity been virtually comprehensive.

Selection through the Qualifying Examination or 'Quali' as it was known, was also abolished. Prior to the raising of the school leaving age from 15 to 16 in 1973, with pupils transferring to secondary school at age 12, it was possible for a child to leave school with just over two years secondary education. In 1952, only 21 per cent of school leavers stayed on after reaching 15 years. In 1990, 77 per cent of 16-year-olds were participating in education. In 1952, 8 per cent of pupils left school with a certificate qualification, but by 1964 the proportion was 27 per cent and by 1976 it was 65 per cent. The raising of the school leaving age increased the pressure on certification. In 1976, despite the original aims, 60 per cent of pupils were achieving one or more A–C grades (formerly the pass grades) in O-Grade exams. O-Grade was too demanding for a significant number of pupils who were leaving school with no recognized qualification, and not demanding enough for the most able pupils.

Reports from two committees set up by the SED, one chaired by Sir James Munn, then rector of Cathkin High School, Cambuslang, Glasgow, and the other by Dr Joseph Dunning, principal of Napier College, were published in 1977. For the 14–16 age group, the Munn report recommended a new flexible curriculum to meet the needs of pupils of all abilities, and the Dunning report called for all pupils to be able to take certificate courses with achievement being measured by exams and internal assessment by teachers. By 1992 the O-Grade will have more or less been replaced by the Standard Grade. It is more than just an exam, it is a two-year course of study for 14–16 years olds based around core subjects or 'modes' of language (English and a foreign language), mathematics and science, and five other modes: social and environmental studies, technology, creative and aesthetic studies, religious and moral education, and physical education. There is considerable emphasis on flexibility. The variety of courses on offer within each mode gives greater scope for meeting pupils' interests, and opportunity is given to teachers to make their own decisions over course content and methods. Examinations, again to cater for all abilities, are set at three levels: Credit, General, and Foundation. The emphasis of certification is less on how the pupil has performed in comparison to other pupils and more on performance against stated standards, hence the name Standard Grade.

The same worry about catering for a wide range of abilities led the SED in 1989 to set up a committee chaired by John Howie, Professor of Mathematics at St Andrews University to investigate the Higher. Originally designed for only 10 per cent of the age group, by 1990 Highers were being taken by 50 per cent of the age group. While 24 per cent of school leavers had the three Highers necessary to qualify for higher education, there were 33 per cent who had no Highers, and no certificate to show for their extra year at school. To try to offer vocational qualifications to non-academically orientated pupils (for whom the Highers were not designed), schools had begun at the start of the 1990s to offer some of the short National Certificate courses of the Scottish Vocational Education Council.

There was also a view that the Highers, because they did not encourage independent study and research, did not fully equip the academic pupil for higher, and particularly university, education. Partly for that reason the SED introduced in 1968 the Certificate of Sixth Year Studies (CSYS). But researchers have not found that students who did the CSYS did any better. The solution offered by Professor Howie's committee was radical, indeed brave, considering that it proposed abolishing a century of tradition behind the Highers. The central idea was to offer courses of study under the title Scottish Upper Secondary Award after Standard Grade which would be completed in the third rather than fourth year of secondary. Two types of certification were proposed. One was mainly vocational, based on the Scottish Certificate (Scotcert), on Scotvec's National Certificate awards. The other was mainly academic, the Scottish Baccalaureate (Scotbac), to be based on the Highers and CSYS, and aimed at preparation for higher education, not just in Scotland, but also in Europe. Opting for Scotcert or the Scotbac in fourth year would not necessarily be a final decision. Both would have the same core skills content—communication, numeracy, problem-solving, and core subject content—languages, mathematics, sciences and others—thus enabling a degree of switching for those studying both at school and further education college. Assessment, Howie proposed, should be more on the Scotvec model of cumulative achievement across the skills and subject areas, moving away from subject and examination orientation, although there would be examinations in the final Scotbac year.

Implementing the report, as Howie himself acknowledged, would have immense implications, not the least of which would be whether the traditional four-year Scottish university education would still remain necessary. Published in the heat of the run-up to the 1992 general election, it provoked many months of intense debate. Change had to come, for as the Howie report argued forcefully: 'when measured against the characteristics which high-quality upper secondary education should display, our system is seriously wanting in many respects'. It concluded: 'We commend our proposals as providing the possibility of a stable and unified system of academic and vocational education which can put Scotland near the top of the world educational league.'

Catholic schools

For one section of the Scottish population, 1918 is a landmark date. One provision of the 1918 Education Act, which abolished parochial school boards and established education authorities, allowed churches to transfer schools to the new authorities but to retain control over the appointment of teachers, particularly with regard to those teachers' religious beliefs and character. For the Roman Catholic Church, it was and has been ever since, a vital concession. But it aroused ferocious opposition from Orange Order Protestants who complained that (their) ratepayers were subsidizing Catholicism: 'Rome on the Rates'. Nevertheless since 1918 there has been a fairly extensive network of schools where the state pays the bills, the pupils follow the state curriculum, but the school as a whole follows the ethos of the Roman Catholic Church. Teachers in all subjects are expected, not just to teach their subject, but to 'reinforce a moral order' as a Catholic headmaster put it. In 1991, there were 370 primary and 67 secondary Roman Catholic schools teaching 79 000 primary and 48 000 secondary pupils throughout Scotland, three-quarters of them located in Glasgow and its hinterland. The position of the Labour Party is ambivalent, ideologically inclined against the Catholic intrusion into a comprehensive system yet electorally dependent on the Catholic vote. In a 1991 row over school closures, a Roman Catholic churchman reminded Charles Gray, the leader of Strathclyde Regional Council, of the power of the Catholic vote in a private note, which Councillor Gray promptly published. Closure rows arise because Glasgow's Catholic schools, mostly located in working-class housing estates, are acutely afflicted by problems of falling birth rates in, and population shifts away from, these areas. But merger with a non-denominational school is absolutely unacceptable to the Catholic Church, which regards Christian teaching in non-denominational schools as non-existent.

Parents, not without justification, regard Catholic schools as having a better than average academic record and a better disciplinary atmosphere. This is attractive to many non-Catholic parents. In Dumfries, despite the presence of three other secondaries, more than half of the children at St Joseph's College in 1990 were non-Catholic. The Schools are particularly appealing to Asian parents. In 1990, 40 per cent of the pupils at St Albert's Primary in Pollokshaws were Asian-Scottish. This presents an argument for pluralism within Scottish education, and although Catholic education is often held to contribute to religious bigotry, it can also be argued to have helped to defuse religious tension. In the home and the school, linked by the priest, the Catholic parent has a culturally secure environment in which to bring up children, and equip them with the skills they need for a secular world.

Private education

The small but thriving private sector educates only 1 in 40 primary, and 1 in 20 secondary pupils throughout Scotland, but its influence has been much greater than its size suggests. Educationally, the emphasis on sport, the house system, and systems of prefects has spread from the private to the state sector. Socially, private education has been responsible for educating much of Scotland's élite. The education researcher Geoffrey Walford, writing in 1987 in *Scottish Educational Review* found that about 4 in 10 of those listed in *Who's Who in Scotland* 1986 had been to private school, half of Scotland's judges had been to a Scottish private school, and that two-thirds of Scotland's sheriffs had been privately educated.

Nowhere is private education more thoroughly interwoven into social life than in Edinburgh, where 1 in 8 secondary pupils are at private schools. Edinburgh clearly displays the legacy of the great Victorian self-help and philanthropic educational drive. Much wealth generated by the industrial revolution and the empire went into founding schools, partly so the sons of industrialists and merchants were equipped, either to manage their inheritance, or to claim a place in the imperial civil service. In this latter regard, the grandest of the private schools, like Sir William Fettes's Fettes College in Edinburgh, were modelled along the lines of English public schools as entry to the Victorian civil service depended on an English public school-style education. Others like Edinburgh jeweller George Heriot, or money-lender and goldsmiths George and Thomas Hutcheson of Glasgow, or wealthy Aberdonian Robert Gordon, founded the schools which bear their names today with objectives of helping orphans or the children of bankrupted merchants.

Since the 1950s, the quality gap between the state and private sector has narrowed. The academic results record or equipment provision at a state school like James Gillespie's High in Edinburgh bears close comparison with that of the nearby private George Watson's College. But private education remains desirable for many parents. At an approximate average annual cost of £3 000 and in the middle of a recession, there was in 1991 little let-up in the competition for private school places. It is especially popular with parents who themselves went to a private school. Schools like Merchiston Castle in Edinburgh and Loretto School at Musselburgh have their traditional sources of pupils in Border and East Lothian landowning and farming families. Within the city of Edinburgh, the west end is where most of the pupils of Stewart's–Melville College are to be found. George Watson's pupils mostly come from the neighbouring suburbs of Colinton, Morningside, Merchiston, Grange and Marchmont. Unwritten folklore also maintains that certain schools are good for particular professions: the Edinburgh Academy, for example, is said to be the place from which to build a legal career. However these distinctions are slowly disappearing. In 1990, only four of the Edinburgh Academy's leavers intended to study law at university. The assisted places scheme, which, in 1990, amounted to a £6 million subsidy to private schools through the Scottish Office paying all or some of the fees of 2 700 children of low-income families, together with a similar number on bursaries, means that at least a quarter of all pupils come from families who could not otherwise afford the fees. While some private school heads will talk of pursuing excellence, others talk the language of the comprehensive head teacher, of seeking to produce well-rounded, self-confident individuals. Frank Gerstenberg, Principal of George Watson's College said: 'We would shudder at the word élite. How do you judge success—a great salary? Or because they are helping to contribute to society in their own way. I think that is terribly important.' Gerstenberg, whose teaching career has otherwise been entirely at English private schools, is enthusiastic about Scottish education: 'It's so flexible and it encourages tremendous breadth. If England wants to improve its system, it doesn't have to look very far.'

In the Scottish private sector, unlike the position in England, the majority of places (84 per cent) are non-boarding, which gives Scottish private education less of an exclusive tag. And the boarding schools excepted, Scottish private schools offer, and are enthusiastic about, the Scottish curriculum and examinations. The private school heads are also thoroughly involved in the institutions supervising exams and the curriculum. Thus, as with Catholic education, there is a good case for arguing that private education in Scotland is an additional and even enriching element in Scottish education, rather than an intrusion.

Figure 1: Scottish school and pupil statistics

	1979–80	1989–90
No. of education authority schools	3 788	3 778
No. of grant-aided schools	59	9
No. of independent schools	96	121
Pupils at education authority schools	998 900	786 300
Pupils at grant-aided schools	18 900	1 400
Pupils at independent schools	16 400	33 100
Adults in school	0	13 600

Source: Scottish Abstract of Statistics 1990, Scottish Office, April 1991

The institutional landscape

The Scottish Office Education Department

In the search for where power lies within the Scottish education system, all routes eventually lead to the Scottish Office Education Department; SOED for short since 1990, SED before that. Until 1992, only the universities were outwith the remit of the SOED, but one of the final acts of the 1987–92 Conservative government was to move financial control of Scotland's universities from the Department of Education and Science to the Scottish Office. Finance is only one of the levers of power available to the SOED. Scotland has had for most of the century a single examination system, and, since the 1960s and perhaps earlier, effectively a national curriculum. The Scottish Education Minister 1986–7, John (now Lord) MacKay, recalled being asked in 1987 by Kenneth Baker, Education Secretary for England and Wales, why more Scottish youngsters stayed on at school after age 16. MacKay told him: 'Simple—the Highers, and one examination board for the whole country.'

Until the 1950s, SOED administration was run by former HM Inspectors of Schools, but the increasing complexities of financing education and turning policy into legislation, required professional administrators to take charge. Though the SOED administrative work was traditionally routine, officials have had their moments. One teaching union official recalled that as the 1986 teachers' pay and conditions dispute neared an end, a sticking point was over holidays. The unions sought seven extra days holiday to give parity with the situation south of the border. Union leaders, who knew extra holidays were popular with their members but not with the public, were flabbergasted when the principal Scottish Office negotiator casually said: 'Well the Treasury doesn't believe you have less holidays, so you might as well have them.' A complete settlement duly followed, and the negotiator, Russell Hillhouse, went on to become permanent secretary in charge of the whole Scottish Office.

In the 1950s, there is little doubt that the Inspectorate in general, and John Brunton, Senior Chief Inspector 1955–66, in particular, controlled Scottish education. Inspectors marked the Higher exams, took a close interest in the curriculum, and ran the teacher training colleges. But the system was resistant to change. The 1947 Report of the Advisory Council on Education in Scotland, which offered a liberal and far-sighted view of secondary education (calling for comprehensive education and a national curriculum which is extraordinarily close to the Standard Grade programme) was largely ignored.

In 1964, towards the end of Brunton's career, in a move which emphasizes his power, the Scottish Certificate of Education Examination Board, now the Scottish Examination Board, was set up to run the examinations which had become too burdensome for the Inspectorate. Another Brunton-inspired move was the formation in 1965 of the Consultative Committee on the Curriculum, which now advises the department as an external public body, the Scottish Consultative Council on the Curriculum. This devolution of control over exams and the curriculum has diffused SOED power into what education insiders call the 'policy community'. It includes satellite organizations such as the Scottish Community Education Council, which promotes youth activities and adult education, the Scottish Council for Research in Education, and the Scottish Council for Educational Technology, which, among other things, acts as a focus for developing the use of micro-electronics and distance learning. Of growing power is the Scottish Vocational Educational Council or Scotvec, responsible for the job- and career-orientated courses centred on the increasingly important further education sector.

The Exam Board's initial authority lay in the rapid expansion of examinations with the introduction of O-Grade. Sitting examinations was the main goal teachers could offer pupils after the school leaving age was raised. But its identity and independence were firmly established under the chairmanship of Dr Farquhar Macintosh, whose considerable qualities were recognized by successive Scottish Office administrations. After a career of teaching in Glasgow, then promoted posts in Inverness, Portree and Oban and finally the rectorship of the Royal High School, Edinburgh, he became chairman of the Exam Board in 1977 and remained in that post for a further 13 years. In the 1970s, the Board was heavily inclined towards the pursuit of academic excellence, but under Dr Macintosh's chairmanship it moved towards the idea of certification for all.

The Curriculum Council has also grown in stature since its early days. It is the Scottish Secretary's principal advisory body on all matters relating to the primary and secondary curriculum. Initially chaired by the senior SOED civil servant, its authority was reinforced by Sir James Munn who chaired the Curriculum Committee from 1980 to 1987. He had already chaired the committee which produced the 1977 report on the curriculum bearing his name. The power of the Curriculum Council grew in the late 1980s after the dispute of 1985–7 when teachers refused to do the development work on Standard Grade, and much of the new curriculum had to be devised centrally.

Theoretically, local education authorities, who, rather than the SOED, are statutorily responsible for providing a curriculum and schools, could reject the SOED-inspired curriculum and implement one of their own, though they would have to satisfy the Inspectorate it was good enough. While some authorities like Lothian and Grampian experimented with English CSE (Certificate of Secondary Education) examinations, in practice, the local authorities by participating fully in the Exam Board and the Curriculum Council, have used the national system as their educational policy base. That does not expunge conflict from the system. The decision by the incoming education minister Michael Forsyth in 1987 to introduce elected school boards—parent power—was seen by local authorities as an attempt by central government to erode their local power.

The 12 local authorities have two main channels through which they can make collective efforts to resolve such conflicts. One is public, and goes through the education committee of the Convention of Scottish Local Authorities (COSLA), whose ability to change ministerial minds should not be underestimated. They succeeded, for example, in reducing the extent of the powers which were originally proposed for the school boards. Whoever chairs COSLA's education committee has a ready-made political platform; one which has been used effectively by two Strathclyde education conveners, Malcolm Green (1982–90) and Ian Davidson (1990–2), both astute politicians. The COSLA education convener also chairs the management side of the Scottish Joint Negotiating Committee on teachers' pay and staff.

A second less well-known channel of influence goes through the officials, the authorities' directors of education. The views of people like David Robertson, Tayside's director of education 1975–89, and David Semple, Lothian's director of education from 1975, carry weight in the SOED. Occasionally the directors see SOED papers in their draft form before they go in a more final form to their political masters on the education committee. Directors have high status within the 'policy community' since they have their own policy staff—the advisers—sometimes collectively known as the advisorate. They visit all the schools to advise teachers on new curricula and new methods, and in recent years to maintain classroom quality in a role akin to that of inspectors. If anything is likely to go wrong in the schools system, then the directors through their advisers are among the first to know about it.

Despite complaints by local authorities of increasing central control and financial restrictions, the power to innovate and experiment remains, especially if convener and director forge a partnership. Before becoming Labour MP for Carrick Cumnock and Doon Valley in 1979, George Foulkes was the Labour educational convener of Lothian Regional Council from 1974. He brought in a substantial innovation, the introduction of community high schools. As this involved substantial renegotiation of teachers' contracts, and the importation of experienced community school teachers from England, the political initiative needed much administrative support from David Semple. In Strathclyde, political backing for a strong administration headed by Frank Pignatelli, appointed director of education at the age of 41 in 1988, enabled an administrative experiment in delegating financial control to individual schools to succeed. Though Pignatelli is a high-profile official, and incidentally probably the first Catholic director of education, he needed strong political backing to overcome teachers' suspicions.

The teachers' unions

The teaching profession is also equipped with much institutional muscle. The General Teaching Council (GTC) is said to be unique in education throughout the world. It was set up in 1966 (one consequence of the 1961 teachers' strike) by the Scottish Secretary Willie Ross to take over certification of teachers. All teachers in state schools have to be registered with the GTC. Its elected council comprises teachers from schools and colleges, officials and councillors from local authorities, representatives of higher education, especially colleges of education, the churches, and nominees of the Scottish Secretary, a consensual structure typical of the main Scottish educational bodies. Its uniqueness lies in the self-regulation it affords the teaching profession, particularly over entry to the profession. The 1990 GTC handbook emphasizes that teaching in Scotland is a 'profession': 'An important hallmark of any profession is that control of entry is in the hands of its members.'

Although the GTC is responsible for disciplining teachers, it has failed to become the principal representative body for teachers in the way that, say, the Law Society is for lawyers. Aside from such bodies as the Association of Head Teachers in Scotland, Scotland's 57 000 teachers see their unions as the main guardians of their interests. The biggest, with 45 500 members in 1990, and the most powerful, is the Educational Institute of Scotland (EIS), founded in 1847. The Scottish Secondary Teachers Association (SSTA), formed in 1946 by secondary teachers who felt their views were gaining insufficient attention in the EIS, had 7 100 members in 1990. There are two other small unions, both UK-wide, the National Association of Schoolmasters/Union of Women Teachers and the small Professional Association of Teachers.

Both the EIS and the SSTA are perhaps best described as trade unions in professional clothing; officials of both wear academic robes at official occasions, but not at meetings of the Scottish Trades Union Congress, of which they are members. One man, John Pollock, an Ayrshire rector steeped in the Labour movement and who was EIS general secretary 1975–88, was responsible for turning the EIS from a staid no-strike professional body into a remarkably disciplined trade union, pulling the SSTA in a similar direction.

If the 'dominie' tradition survives among teachers, it does so collectively in the professional aspirations of the teachers' unions, and in the degree of self-regulation afforded by the GTC. Arguably, the history of social standing afforded by the 'dominie' tradition provided the base on which the GTC was built. If teachers enjoy a greater public standing in Scotland than do their counterparts in England and Wales, an impression for which there is some supporting evidence, a likely reason is the 'dominie' tradition. But as the unions gained negotiating power, they lost professional influence within the system, something which Pollock's successor, Jim Martin, who became EIS general secretary at the age of 34, sought to rectify. Though the EIS, the SSTA and the other unions compete for membership, Martin and particularly the SSTA general secretary since 1985, Alex Stanley, have cooperated, aware that disputes among the English teaching unions gave the government the opportunity to break up the Burnham pay negotiating committee, whereas in Scotland the joint national negotiating committee machinery survived.

Parent power

The remaining interest group is that of the consumer or parents. For many years, their voice was heard at a national level through the low profile Scottish Parent Teacher Council, or occasionally through the Scottish Consumer Council. At local level there were consultative schools councils which mainly discussed non-educational matters like evening use of games halls. But in 1987, the Conservatives made giving parents a stronger voice a manifesto priority. The result was the replacement of schools councils covering groups of schools by boards for individual schools, with powers to take decisions over the matters which the councils could only discuss. It was clear that the Conservatives saw the boards' decision-making role as an expanding one. By and large, the first elections in 1989 produced moderate-minded boards. But they also produced a new phenomenon, the parent activist. When the issue of testing primary four and seven children came to the fore in 1990, names like Judith Gillespie from Edinburgh, Ann Hill from Dumfries and Galloway, or Diana Daly from Aberdeen, featured regularly in the press. By 1991, regional groupings like Educational Alert in Grampian, had sprung up, and were coalescing into the

Parents Coalition, a Scotland-wide network of parent activism. If the Education Minister responsible for setting up the boards, Michael Forsyth, thought the parents would be a heavy counterweight to trendy educationalists, he was right, but only insofar as the parent activists cast him as the ideologist whose ideas had to be resisted. While this was gratifying to the local authorities and the teaching unions, both of which wooed the new parent activist groups, the lesson from the early days of parent power is that it is no certain ally of any particular section of the education community.

The question of centralization

A constant theme of the education debate throughout the 1980s was the extent to which power had become centralized in the hands of the Scottish Office as the arm of central government. For most of the 1987–92 Conservative Government the Scottish Education Minister was Michael Forsyth, a minister unusually determined to achieve a clear set of political goals. Forsyth challenged the system as never before, and that is at the root of the accusation of centralization by various interest groups. This argument has been put most forcefully by Walter Humes, an education lecturer at Glasgow University. In his book *The Leadership Class in Scottish Education* (1986), he argued that the professionals and bureaucrats within the SOED ran the system for their own benefit; and that since political input to the policy-making process was weak, the power of the SOED and local authority directors was strong. In June 1989, assessing his own argument in the light of Forsyth's impact, Humes contended in an article in *The Scotsman* that Forsyth had strengthened the political input and reduced the role of the professionals and bureaucrats by making populist appeals to parents. He continued: 'Most fundamentally of all, the agenda in Scottish education—school boards, opting out, national testing, teacher appraisal—are very much Forsyth's handiwork. It is unlikely that any of those would have featured had the professionals and bureaucrats been allowed to continue in their old ways. In a sense, the present minister has taken the system by the scruff of the neck and given it a good shake.'

But as Humes also noted, there has been a certain amount of continuity. The 5–14 programme, for example, derived from a political view, held north and south of the border, that the primary system was not working, that a better curriculum, better forms of assessment, and better forms of reporting were needed. But the primary four and seven testing element that eventually emerged—a fairly complicated form of skills assessment by class teachers—was a long way removed from Forsyth's original ideas of short simple pencil and paper tests taken under exam conditions. Forsyth's ideas underwent intense debate between the administration, Inspectorate and the Minister. The process, common to all policy innovations, is usually characterized by SOED officials as 'moving by a series of compromises' towards something which 'delivers the political imperative and is also educationally sensible'.

In England the comparable process required legislation. In Scotland, apart from the testing element, the programme was implemented by consensus, after consultation. The SOED regards the consultation element as vital if innovation is to gain acceptance. 'We are trying to create a kind of ownership of the whole thing,' a senior official said. The SOED is immensely skilled at that: when the 5–14 programme was first announced, there were fierce objections from nearly every quarter. By 1992, apart from the question of testing, which became a totemic focus of political opposition to Michael Forsyth, opposition had turned to acceptance and welcome.

The SOED is also skilled at using its satellites to further its own policy-making agenda. Opinion built up within the department from the early 1980s that curriculum in the fifth and sixth year of secondary school needed to be overhauled, especially as Standard Grade came on stream. But to take such a course of action would mean the Higher examination could be perceived to be under attack, and officials recognized that any minister might feel it was politically too dangerous to take any action. So external momentum from the Exam Board and other sources was created. Ministers were still reluctant, fearing 'Tories attack Highers' headlines, and insisted that if a committee was to examine the Highers, there should be no possibility that its chairman could be accused of being a 'Tory stooge', as one minister put it. Eventually Forsyth and Rifkind agreed that the Howie committee should be set up to investigate and report. That mobilization of opinion was a well-tried SOED technique: a letter from the department to the Exam Board suggesting they should ask ministers to take a look at O-Grade led to the setting up of the Munn and Dunning committees. These kinds of actions argue that Hume's accusations of a self-serving and complacent bureaucracy are overly savage. Determined politician though Michael Forsyth was as Education Minister, he found that his ability to bring about change was limited. The education system is an interconnected cat's cradle. Pull at any one point in one direction, and links in the other direction will prevent too much movement. But real power exists at the centre, and is just as much in the hands of officials as ministers.

Since 1984, the SOED has had three heads, James Scott 1984–7, Russell Hillhouse 1987–8, and since April 1988, Gerald Wilson. In civil service terms, that is a fairly rapid turnover, and could have reduced the effectiveness of the SOED were it not for the continuity to be found a little lower down the hierarchy. For example, on the administrative side in 1991 could be found as under-secretary in charge of schools Hamish Robertson whose civil service curriculum vitae includes 25 years work off and on in education. There was also the under-secretary responsible for further and higher education, Alastair Weatherston, with 16 years experience in the department. And there was Nisbet Gallacher, since 1987 HM Senior Chief Inspector, and a member of the Inspectorate since 1969.

They and their staff represent an enormous pool of knowledge about Scottish education, its weaknesses and strengths, its institutions and characters, its history and its possible future. Knowledge is power, and though that power is at the service of the minister, the minister can be carried along by it. Even Michael Forsyth would sometimes jocularly state that he had been 'programmed' by the department to say this or that. Other former education ministers can be less light-hearted about it. One, after talking angrily about a policy decision he believed had been ignored by the Inspectors, said: 'They thought they were that powerful, and the interesting thing was that from the Permanent Secretary down, they were considered to be that powerful.'

The higher education hotbed

If Scotland's international reputation in education rests on anything, it is on the universities. Much is usually and quite rightly made of the substantial contribution to European thought emanating from the 'hotbed of genius' that was Scotland and especially Edinburgh during the 'Enlightenment' of the 18th and early 19th centuries. The dazzling intellectual achievements of the political economist Adam Smith or the philosopher David Hume, to pick but two of the 50 men of genius that one could apparently encounter within half an hour in Edinburgh's High Street continue to reverberate 200 years later. Less is usually and perhaps wrongly made of the contribution of the emigrant graduates of Aberdeen who taught three of the first five presidents of the United States, men like Donald Robertson of whom James Madison said: 'All that I have been in life I owe largely to that one man.' Without these past glories, there would be little of the present strength of Scotland's higher education; the standing of modern science and technology faculties owes much to the work done by Enlightenment scientists like the chemist Joseph Black or the geologist James Hutton.

But in the contribution being made to the future brainpower of Scotland, the universities are only a part. For example, the unpretentious Jewel and Esk Valley College in Dalkeith, Midlothian, had by 1991 established strong links with the offshore oil industry in Aberdeen and a national reputation for

Figure 2: Higher education student numbers

Type of institution	Full-time		Part-time	
	1985–6	1988–9	1985–6	1988–9
University	46 209	48 859	5 618	6 274
Central Institution	22 131	23 704	9 169	8 871
Local Authority College	6 996	8 032	23 060	23 683
Colleges of Education	4 433	4 373	1 379	929
Total	79 769	84 968	39 226	39 757

Source: Scottish Abstract of Statistics 1990, Scottish Office, April 1991

Figure 3: Undergraduate entrants to
full-time higher education

Type of institution	1985–6		1988–9	
	Total	% Female	Total	% Female
Universities	12 070	43	12 868	44
SED Central Institutions	7 700	48	7 951	50
DAFS Central Institutions	140	23	116	29
Local Authority Colleges	4 150	45	5 133	50
Colleges of Education	1 160	75	1 090	48
Total	25 220	46	27 158	48

SED: Scottish Education Department; DAFS: Department of Agriculture and Fisheries for Scotland

Source: SED Statistical Bulletin No. 12/J2, Scottish Higher Education Statistics, August 1990

its oil-related engineering training courses. In between such further education colleges and the universities are places traditionally known, because their finances have been run centrally by the SOED, as the Central Institutions. They are the colleges of education, art, agriculture, and five big technological teaching institutions.

Altogether in 1988/89, some 335 000 people were taking a higher education course (Figs 2 & 3). Because of a declining birth rate, the numbers of Scottish school-leavers fell from a peak at the start of the 1980s of around 94 000, a decline which is expected to level out at just under 60 000 by the middle of the 1990s. However, the number of people, including 16–18-year-olds, participating in higher education has continued to grow. Whereas in 1979 about 18 per cent of young people went on into higher education, in 1989 the proportion was about 24 per cent. The number of older people, or mature students, taking up higher education has also increased. There is a general consensus that these trends must be continued as stated in a White Paper *Access and Opportunity* published by the Scottish Office in 1991: 'Continuing education and training is important if people are to be prepared for higher skilled and paid jobs. People of all ages need to be ready to adapt to new technologies and demands in the workplace.'

Further education colleges

Colleges like Jewel and Esk Valley form a network of 46 further education (FE) colleges throughout Scotland, including small colleges in each of the three main island authority areas. FE colleges have a Cinderella status within tertiary education which FE staff much resent. The sector educates and trains some 200 000 people a year (Fig. 4), though official statistics describe that work rather brutally as 'non-advanced higher education', ie less than Higher National

Certificate (HNC) standard. But, as one college principal remarked: 'FE is not just for hewers of wood and drawers of water and country dancers coming in the evening.' Apart from the general 1980s shift away from craft-based teaching towards business and computer system-based studies, there has been some outstanding industry–college development of highly specialized courses. Shell Expro/Aberdeen Technical College's engineering training centre, and Esso Chem/Kirkcaldy College of Technology's petro-chemical training programme are examples. Glenrothes and Buckhaven Technical College's broadcasting courses, and Perth College of Further Education's contemporary commercial music programmes have been successful innovations.

Most courses studied at FE colleges qualify for the National Certificate, now administered by the Scottish Vocational Educational Council (Scotvec), an amalgamation of the Scottish Technical Education Council and the Scottish Business Educational Council. Under the chairmanship of Dr Peter Clarke, formerly the Principal of the Robert Gordon Institute of Technology, Aberdeen, and stemming from the Government's 1983 *16-plus Action Plan*, Scotvec, which also administers the HNC and HND (Higher National Diploma) qualifications, has radically restructured vocational education for 16–18-year-olds not interested in academic Highers. A wide spectrum of modular 40-hour courses was devised from which students can 'pick and mix' according to their requirements, usually 20–22 modules for a full-time course, six or seven for day release. Continuous assessment of students' ability to perform tasks is the basis of certification, a method which though burdensome for teachers has proven popular with the students and those employers who understand the system.

At the start of the 1990s, the Conservative Government decided to take FE colleges out of local education authority administration and turn them into self-governing bodies financed directly from the SOED. Local authority representation on the governing college councils was severely reduced and local employers took at least half the seats. Generally, FE colleges were targeted

Figure 4: Students in non-advanced higher education

Type of institution	Full-time		Part-time	
	1985–6	1988–9	1985–6	1988–9
Central Institutions	484	678	18 541	23 720
LA Day Colleges	27 696	31 547	116 779	136 305
LA Evening Centres	141	540	12 275	9 424
Others	1 141	1 742	409	5 478
Total	29 464	34 507	148 004	174 927

LA: Local Authority

Source: Scottish Abstract of Statistics 1990, Scottish Office, April 1991

by the Government as an expanding sector taking a lead role in the drive to improve the workforce skills. College mergers are likely, such as that in 1986 between Dundee College of Commerce and the Kingsway Technical College to form Dundee College of Further Education. New colleges may even be founded, the general atmosphere of the sector being, in the 1990s, one of expansion.

The Central Institutions

Around 1900, a number of institutions sprang up to fill demands for courses not supplied by the universities, especially in technical education. Under the SED's central control, they remained primarily teaching institutions where any research has been of a strictly practical and teaching-related kind. Courses have been controlled by the SED to ensure the Central Institutions (CIs) complement rather than compete with the universities.

The list of CIs includes three art colleges, each with about 1 000 students:

Figure 5: Students at Scottish Central Institutions, 1989–90

Institution	Full-time equivalent nos
Dundee Institute of Technology	2 140
Glasgow Polytechnic	4 498
Napier Polytechnic	5 780
Paisley College of Technology	3 046
Robert Gordon Institute of Technology	3 549
Queen's College, Glasgow	959
Queen Margaret's College	1 473
Duncan of Jordanstoun College of Art	1 134
Edinburgh College of Art	1 100
Glasgow School of Art	999
Royal School of Art, Music, and Drama	399
Scottish College of Textiles	617
Craigie College of Education	312
Jordanhill College of Education	1 676
Moray House College of Education	1 356
Northern College of Education	1 002
St Andrew's College of Education	650

Note: Full-time equivalent figures for students attracting government funding.

Source: Turmeau, William, *Higher Education in Scotland*, unpublished paper, March 1991

Glasgow School of Art, Edinburgh College of Art (which like another CI, the Scottish College of Textiles, Galashiels, is an associate college of Heriot-Watt University), and Duncan of Jordanstone College of Art in Dundee (which has linked with the University of Dundee for degree-awarding purposes). There is also the Royal School of Art, Music and Drama. Their contribution to Scotland's international cultural reputation has been enormous; Glasgow's 1980s crop of artists included such internationally acclaimed names as Steven Campbell and Adrian Wisniewski. All the colleges can claim to have produced fine artists, but their students also study, for example at Dundee, computer-aided architectural design, town and regional planning, and hotel and catering management.

Until 1990, the CIs also included three agricultural colleges: the North (Aberdeen), East (Edinburgh) and West (Ayr). They still exist, but as the Scottish Agricultural College under a single principal and board of directors, and financed by the Scottish Office Agriculture and Fisheries Department, in 1990 to the tune of £18.5 million. Other CIs include Queen Margaret College, Edinburgh, and the Queen's College, Glasgow, both noted for specialisms in paramedical courses such as physiotherapy.

Apart from a small number of secondary teachers qualifying from Stirling University, the supply of Scottish schoolteachers comes through specialist colleges of education, to which university graduates must go to obtain a post-graduate teaching qualification. Since the mid-1980s, when there were seven colleges, there has been much reorganization. Dundee and Aberdeen Colleges have merged to form the Northern College, based in Aberdeen. Moray House, Edinburgh, which absorbed Dunfermline College of Physical Education, Edinburgh, linked in 1991 with Heriot-Watt University. Craigie College in Ayr, which trains only primary teachers, discussed linkage with Paisley College of Technology and Strathclyde University, which is also to absorb Jordanhill College of Education. The only Roman Catholic College of Education, St Andrew's College, Glasgow, held merger talks with Glasgow University.

The most glamorous and exciting group of CIs in the 1990s have been the five big technological institutions: Dundee Institute of Technology, Glasgow Polytechnic, Paisley College of Technology, the Robert Gordon Institute of Technology (RGIT) and Napier Polytechnic. Their teaching knowledge with practical applications and limited research geared mainly to the needs of industry, has been quite different from that of the universities with their liberal education values and heavier research programmes. But the CIs take great pride in their own ethos. A 1991 document produced by RGIT said: 'Scotland inititated a binary system 90 years ago to help Scottish industry. Intellectual snobbery and an anti-industry culture hampered, but failed to stop, its development.' In 1991, a White Paper *Higher Education, A new Framework*, announced the government's intention to end the binary divide, by allowing polytechnics to become universities. After RGIT's principal David Kennedy kicked up a fuss (RGIT had not bothered to seek polytechnic status) the Scottish

Office made it clear that university status would be considered (later granted) for the four largest technological institutes, Dundee being thought too small. Throughout the 1980s, the Government was sympathetic to the approach and aspirations of the CIs, which it regarded as more cost-effective and adaptable than those of the eight universities.

Napier's progress is a remarkable example of what can be achieved by vision and determination. Under Joseph Dunning, Principal 1963–81, and his successor William Turmeau, it has taken less than 30 years to move to university status. It was founded in 1964 as the Napier College of Science and Technology, named after the 16th century inventor of logarithms, John Napier. His birthplace, the Tower of Merchiston, is now incorporated in Napier's Merchiston campus, giving the institution an instant, if bogus, 400 years of history. Under Dunning, merger with the Edinburgh College of Commerce achieved CI status. Under Turmeau, relentless expansion on to six campuses brought it in 1991 to around 9 000 full- and part-time students, more than those attending Heriot-Watt. Turmeau's buccaneering outspokenness occasionally brought him into conflict with other principals, particularly when they found they were not included in Turmeau's periodically published visions of the future of Scottish education. In 1991, in comments on the government's plans to abolish the binary line, the Principal of Glasgow University, Sir William Kerr Fraser spoke of fears of levelling down, and the Principal of St Andrews University, Professor Struther Arnott, was concerned there would be a 'less discriminating, more parsimoniously funded system'. At Napier's graduation ceremony, Turmeau rounded on both men's views as 'totally wrong', and suggested their worries were 'more likely to be generated by fears of competition than of compromising quality'. He added, in a note of cheerful menace: 'And in that respect, they do have grounds to be worried.'

The universities

Worries that quality might be compromised have surfaced before, in the 1960s when Scotland's four ancient universities saw four new arrivals, following the Robbins report on higher education. Strathclyde University, whose Livingstone Tower rears up close to Glasgow's George Square, has its roots in Anderson's Institution of 1796, named after an eccentric professor known to his students as 'Jolly Jack Phosphorus'. In 1912, that became the Royal Technical College, then in 1956 the Royal College of Science and Technology, which merged with the Scottish College of Commerce and gained university status in 1964. Strathclyde remains based on science and technology. Professor Sir Graham Hills, Principal 1980–91, particularly pushed the theme of technology transfer between industry and university. This is achieved primarily through research institutes, set up where academic research interests coincide with commercial research and development interests. The economic forecasts of the Fraser of Allander Institute regularly contribute to public debate, while the Turing

Institute with a turnover of £1 million and a staff of 40 is one of the largest units working in artificial intelligence in Europe.

Heriot-Watt University, which received its Royal Charter in 1966, originated in 1821 with the foundation of the Edinburgh School of Arts, intended for ordinary working people to receive advanced technical education. In the 1850s the names Watt and Heriot were added, the first in homage to the Scots inventor, the second when the institution gained access to the endowments of educational benefactor George Heriot. Unlike Strathclyde University, which refused the offer of a green field site at East Kilbride, 'the Watt' as it is colloquially known, has gradually moved out to a campus at Riccarton on the west side of Edinburgh. Like Strathclyde, it is a technological university, and has also gone down the industry/university technology transfer road by establishing institutes. Two notable examples are in offshore engineering, where the university has an offshore equipment testing centre in Orkney, and in brewing and distilling, linking with an ancient Edinburgh industry. Heriot-Watt also has the advantage of having on campus the first university science park in the UK, originally 11 hectares when founded in 1972, expanded since to 20 hectares. By 1990 there were some 30 companies on it, one for example being Medical Laser Technologies Ltd, producing equipment at the forefront of medical technology and which was a spin-off from the university physics department.

Dundee University, founded in 1967, grew out of the Queen's College which was separated from its parent, St Andrews University, by the Tay estuary and 15 miles. It dates back to 1881 when Miss Mary Ann Baxter of a local jute dynasty endowed the college and decreed the professors be paid 10 per cent more than elsewhere. That history gives the university strengths in traditional areas like medicine, dentistry, and law. Since he became Principal in 1987, after cuts in government grant which saw departments closed or merged, Michael Hamlin, an engineer who spent eight years working in industry before moving to the academic world, has taken a firm budgetary line. Universities should not be run as businesses, but in a business-like fashion, he argued, as outside finance was sought, to the extent that the proportion of Dundee's income from the Government has been reduced from three-quarters to a half in 1980–90.

Of the four Robbins-inspired universities, Stirling has the most beautiful setting, tucked in a fold of hills round a loch on the outskirts of the town, but it went through a bleak period in the 1980s. It had few friends when it was founded in 1967. Some academics at the ancient universities thought it 'unnecessary', and some still insist that if a new university had to be founded at all, it should have been at Inverness. Happily, in Stirling's 21st year, Principal John Forty announced a degree-awarding link was being established with Inverness College of Further and Higher Education. Having emerged from the 1980s when student numbers were less than 3 000, a level dangerously close to not being viable, the 1990s are planned to be a period of expansion; indeed Stirling began the decade with a growing reputation for innovation. Its academic year structure of two 15-week semesters rather than three 10-week terms has proved to be a model likely to be followed by other universities. Its multidisciplinary Institute of Aquaculture, and its Centre for Japanese Studies have attracted a lot of interest.

Of the ancient universities, St Andrews is the oldest by virtue of a papal bull promulgated in 1414, though teaching had begun on that corner of the Fife coast, then an important ecclesiastical centre, in 1410. It is an intimate place to study, where 4 000 students make a big impact on a town of 12 000 people. When St Andrews lost Queen's College in 1967, it had hastily to expand its science faculty to avoid being left as a liberal arts college with a venerable divinity faculty. The arts image and its antiquity may be the reasons why St Andrews had in 1990 the highest proportion of English-domiciled students of all the Scottish universities. While its setting makes it tempting to apply the word 'sleepy' to St Andrews, Principal Struther Arnott, a Lanarkshire-born biophysicist made sure the academic community was going to be anything but that. After taking up post in 1986, he embarked football-manager style on an academic recruitment programme, his most spectacular coup being the transfer of media-star Paul Wilkinson, Professor of International Relations, from Aberdeen University.

Losing Professor Wilkinson was perhaps the least of the turmoil which afflicted Aberdeen in the 1980s. It had to suffer two rounds of cuts in funding, one causing 170 staff redundancies in 1971, and another more painful cut in 1986 which cost more than 200 redundancies and six arts faculty departments. It left the university, which is a 19th-century fusion of King's College (founded 1495) and Marischal College (founded 1593), without a classics department but with traditional strengths in law and medicine intact. Principal George McNicol, a distinguished doctor, had to preside over some radical surgery, but his bedside manner in peremptorily telling the patient it needed a 40-week academic year, and amputation of departments, won him few friends. But he retired in 1991 with student numbers 19 per cent up over the decade, and 11 new chairs established, mostly in science and medicine.

Along with Strathclyde, Glasgow can claim to have the most Scottish population of the universities with 85 per cent of its students coming from Scottish homes, many indeed staying in their parental home in Glasgow. It was founded in 1451, and moved to the Victorian Gothic building looming over the city's west end in 1870. Over half its students take science courses, and its medical faculty is the largest in the UK outside London. Some of the medical research is of world importance, particularly that into cancer. It was at the veterinary school that Sir James Black, eventually to win the Nobel Prize for Medicine in 1988, lectured in 1950–8. The university's move in 1988 to attract one of its graduates as Principal, Sir William Kerr Fraser, was shrewder than it knew at the time, for as financial control of the universities switched to the Scottish Office in the 1990s, no Scottish principal was better placed than a former Scottish Office permanent secretary.

Though Edinburgh is not the largest nor the most ancient of Scotland's universities, it is certainly the grandest. On hearing of a plan by Struther

Arnott of St Andrews that the eight universities ought to form a University of Scotland, a distinguished Edinburgh professor snorted: 'Rather like the corner shop telling Sainsbury's what to do.' The range of subjects taught and researched at Edinburgh is indeed vast, from the Faculty of Divinity where theology has been taught at the New College since 1583 to the more recent Centre for Speech Technology Research working on computers which respond to speech. None of that prevented the university from plunging into an unexpected financial crisis in 1990. Its Principal, Sir David Smith, formerly Professor of Rural Economy at Oxford, has had to defend difficult and unpopular decisions, such as the sale of assets and redundancies. A proposal to leave the Chair of Scottish History unfilled for two years after Professor Geoffrey Barrow retired caused public uproar which reduced the vacancy period to one year.

Though it has little visible presence, there is also the Open University, the idea of Fife-born Jennie Lee, Arts Minister in the 1964–70 Labour government. It had in 1990, 8 600 Scots enrolled on undergraduate courses, 10 800 taking short courses, and 940 students on Open Business School Courses.

The universities were badly squeezed by the 1980s Government spending clampdown, indeed the pips squeaked in Dundee, Aberdeen, and Stirling. The chairman of the University Grants Committee, Sir Peter Swinnerton-Dyer, became something of a hate figure, and there is still a legacy of bitterness. In his 1991 graduation speech, Dundee's principal Michael Hamlin said that since 1980 and excluding medicine and dentistry, the staff–student ratio at Dundee had deteriorated from 8:1 to 14:1. Yet there had been no recognition of that

Figure 6: University student numbers

| University | 1978–9 | | 1988–9 | |
	Total students	% of Scottish undergrads	Total students	% of Scottish undergrads
Aberdeen	5 606	80	6 251	71
Dundee	3 066	62	3 826	56
Edinburgh	10 799	74	11 325	56
Glasgow	10 655	94	13 146	85
Heriot-Watt	3 295	73	3 659	65
St Andrews	3 406	47	3 903	38
Stirling	2 807	63	3 732	49
Strathclyde	6 963	90	9 291	87
Total	46 597	78	55 133	68

Source: Scottish Abstract of Statistics 1990, Scottish Office, April 1991

increase in productivity, and he argued: 'Universities are still disparaged by Government as places unwilling or unable to change.'

The 1980s scares are one reason why the university principals, from being almost solidly against the devolution of financial control from London to the Scottish Office, swung round to being in favour when the change was announced in 1991, largely as a consequence of changed funding mechanisms in England. It was both a victory to SOED officials, who had great regrets that the Scottish Office had not managed to capture the universities in the 1970s, and a challenge to meet the target of having by the year 2000 over 40 per cent of school-leavers going into higher education. There is a challenge also of getting adults into higher education; at Stirling about 500 people attend access courses from which they can enter higher education, some travelling 50 miles for an evening class.

The 1990s are likely to be a decade of institutional mergers, not only in the name of efficiency, but also in pursuit of the aim of blurring the university/ Central Institution division. It is a task likely to appeal to the first chairman of the Scottish Higher Education Funding Council, Professor Jack Shaw, a popular appointment whose accounting expertise encompasses both academic and business experience. It is an environment also likely to appeal to William Turmeau, the Napier Principal who was laughed at when he forecast in 1989 that there would be Scottish Office control of funding, and much merger activity. Dr Turmeau expects to see in the 1990s all except the FE colleges merge into 12–13 universities, each with between 5 000 and 10 000 students. Struther Arnott of St Andrews has suggested a multi-campus University of Scotland, while Sir David Smith of Edinburgh has mooted federal links between all the higher education institutions, rather like the University of California.

Much attention should also be focused on the Ordinary or general degree which has gone out of fashion. Though Scottish academics like to defend its virtues, they will acknowledge privately that employers prefer Honours degrees. However, in the same way as universities have found their traditional faculty and subject department structure too rigid and some have reorganized into schools or multidisciplinary institutes, the redevelopment of the Ordinary degree into a multidisciplinary three-year qualification as is envisaged by a number of principals should ensure its revival.

The future

The Scottish education system is no different from that of any other country in the sense that it has been relentlessly pressured to adapt to changing economic and social demands. Education as a serious political issue in modern times dates from the 1964 general election when Labour leader Harold Wilson promised voters a better future via technological progress. Since then, notions that the country's economic condition is related to the health of the education system have taken root.

Scottish education undoubtedly responded by developing the Standard

Grade, the National Certificate, and bringing in the work-experience and work-related courses of the Technical and Vocational Initiative (TVEI) in schools. In so doing, educationalists were forced to examine closely the successes and failures of the system. Thereby the mythology of Scottish education was confronted.

This led to a quiet acknowledgement that education had been overly-thirled to the interests of the lad o' pairts, and had failed to do much for those who were not to be launched into the academic world. There is also a recognition that the system is not entirely democratic. The route into higher education is still much harder for pupils from working-class families. Glasgow and Strathclyde universities experimented in the housing schemes of Easterhouse and Drumchapel with a special entry scheme to try to overcome the problem.

The public was also brought into contact with the particular mythology of Scottish education quite sharply in the early 1980s, when the public spending disciplines of Margaret Thatcher's government extended to education, provoking widespread debate over the nature and value of Scottish education. This had particular significance in the late 1980s when substantial change was brought about by a Government whose mandate in Scotland was increasingly questioned. It made the public receptive to arguments presented by local authorities and the teaching unions, amongst others, that the Government's proposed reforms were unwanted and irrelevant importations from England. As Walter Humes argued in the 1984 *Scottish Government Yearbook*, such fears of anglicization 'are, of course, not always unjustified, but one effect of this mode of perception has been to make Scottish educationalists resistant to change; almost any proposal for reform can be interpreted as an assault on Scottish identity where a climate of touchy defensiveness prevails'. However, in the 1990s another mood change became apparent as the economic challenge of Europe loomed larger. Professor John Howie in a March 1991 interview in *The Scotsman* argued: 'One of the troubles of Scotland is that we can't see beyond England.' Professor Howie and others looked to Europe and discovered that in numbers of youngsters staying in education after 16 and going into higher education, Scotland has targets still to reach.

Generally, the more that is learned about European patterns of education, the less Scotland has been able to rely on comparisons with England for reassurance about the strength of Scottish education. It makes it easier to accept that the answers to some awkward questions might be found in Scotland: why in 1989 were only 20 per cent of school-leavers in Glasgow and Lanarkshire qualified for higher education, but 27 per cent were qualified in Central, Lothian and Tayside regions? Or why are women such an insignificant minority in positions of influence?

Though the days of the autocratic head teacher 'dominie' have gone, there remain outstanding administrators within both the SOED and the local authorities, and some sharp politicians. Different pressure groups have won roles in the system—parents and industrialists—and they can produce individuals who

make an outstanding contribution. Education also has some immensely perceptive researchers and commentators, such as Andrew McPherson of Edinburgh
University, Walter Humes of Glasgow University, and Willis Pickard, the editor
of *The Times Educational Supplement Scotland.*

The 1990s therefore offer the possibility, indeed the necessity, of abandoning
touchy defensiveness and ensuring that the egalitarian and meritocratic Scottish
educational ethos becomes a genuine reality. The progress of the universities
and the further education colleges to create an education system unified under
the ambit of the Scottish Office, plus an atmosphere in which all the political
parties agree on the need to nurture and expand education, presents those who
will be in charge for the next two decades with an unparallelled opportunity to
create a dynamic first-class education system.

Figure 7: Percentage of age group staying on in full-time education

Country	Year	Minimum leaving age	% age 16	% age 17
Australia	1986	15	71	50
Belgium	1986	14	89	77
Canada	1986	16–17	95	77
Denmark	1986	16	88	68
France	1986	16	78	68
Fed Rep Germany	1987	15–16	69	43
Italy	1982	14	54	47
Japan	1988	15	92	89
Netherlands	1986	16	92	77
Spain	1986	16	60	52
Sweden	1985	16	91	85
USA	1986	16–18	94	87
UK	1986	16	49	34
Scotland	1986	16	63 (53)	32

Notes: Figure in brackets for Scotland is the percentage of 16-year-olds who participate voluntarily; an additional
10 per cent have to stay on until Christmas of the fifth year as they are too young to leave voluntarily. Countries
with variable leaving ages have regional differences. For the Netherlands and Germany, compulsory part-time
education is included.

Source: Centre for Educational Sociology, University of Edinburgh

7

The Media

Magnus Linklater

The press

The Scots like their newspapers—and they like them to be Scottish. Not only do they read more per head of population than anywhere else in the UK, they have sustained a remarkably healthy indigenous press during a period when English regional morning titles have suffered a decline. In Scotland 66 per cent of the population reads a morning paper compared to a UK national average of 64 per cent; 83 per cent read a Sunday paper compared to a UK figure of 71 per cent; and while, over the past 10 years, sales of daily newspapers in England have declined by about 6 per cent, in Scotland they have remained relatively static. That state of affairs may not continue, however. More recently, there have been distinct signs that the Scottish market is beginning to shrink, thus following a trend in newspaper sales which can be discerned from the USA to Europe as reading habits decline amongst the young.

The longstanding enthusiasm shown by Scots for the printed word goes hand in hand with a radical streak in Scottish journalism which can be traced back to the 18th century. With a bit of romantic licence one can go further and see early signs of it in the robust polemics of the Jacobite pamphleteers which irritated and alarmed the court of William and Mary and continued thereafter to plague the Hanoverian kings. The rebellions of the 18th century and the religious upheavals of the 19th century provoked a tradition for passionate pamphleteering in which eloquence and outrage came together in a particularly Scottish manner. Some would say it continues right up to the present day in the letters columns of *The Scotsman* and the *Herald* or the campaigning zeal of the *West Highland Free Press*.

The first newspaper published in Scotland seems to have been an Edinburgh reprint of reports from London concerning the struggle between Charles I and parliament, published under the cumbersome title *Diurnal Occurrances, Touching the dailie proceedings in Parliament from the 27 of December to the third of Januarie, 1642.* Some years later, a newspaper called the *Mercurius Scoticus* surfaced in Leith in July 1651, only to be firmly suppressed under Cromwell. Following the Restoration, the *Mercurius Caledonius*, edited by a Scotsman, Thomas Sydserf, and published in Edinburgh, made its appearance in January 1661. It was banned by the Scottish Privy Council, and it was not until the relaxation of censorship in the early 18th century that regular newspapers like the *Edinburgh Evening Courant* and the *Caledonian Mercury* began to flourish. However, these were hardly vigorous publications. The news they purveyed was described by one commentator as 'meagre tidings of what had happened long ago, or never happened at all'. There were livelier stirrings in the university city of Aberdeen, where the *Aberdeen's Journal* was founded in 1747, to become, much later, the *Press and Journal*, a newspaper which continues to this day. The *Glasgow Advertiser*, founded in 1783, became the *Herald* in 1805, and elsewehere, small weekly papers like the *Kelso Chronicle*, then later the *Kelso Mail* (1797), established a reputation for uncomfortable radicalism.

The birth of *The Scotsman* in January 1817 as a journal devoted to liberal values, came about because its founders were convinced 'that nothing of a very spirited or liberal nature can find its way through the Edinburgh daily or weekly Press; that many political matters and transactions in Scotland are thus never generally known; and that the conductors of the Edinburgh prints act editorially as if they dreaded nothing so much as the idea of being thought independent.' The *Herald's* founder, John Mennons, an Edinburgh man, was equally keen to establish his paper's independence, informing his readers in the first issue that 'he engages in the task of informing and instructing his fellow citizens from the most disinterested motives'. This concern for honesty led a later editor, Samuel Hunter, to inform his readers in one issue, with a frankness rare in his profession: 'Our news tonight is altogether of a negative description. There are no further speculations respecting the intentions of the Continental Powers—there have been no disturbances in Paris—there are no new peers in the Gazette—and no new murders in Ireland.' Hunter's forthright opposition to the Reform Bill had him burnt in effigy at Glasgow Cross, but his newspaper flourished, its disarming straightforwardness in tune with the interests of the populace.

A marked concern for Scottish, as opposed to Union affairs, could be seen in other papers which date from this period—the *Stirling Journal*, the *Fife Herald*, and the *Elgin Courier* amongst others. In 1886 William Thomson, a Dundee shipowner, took control of the *Dundee Courier and Argus* and made his son, D C Thomson, a full partner, thus founding a newspaper group which is still a redoubtable family concern today. In the years that followed, several of D C's nephews joined the firm, including W Harold Thomson, whose sons are chairman and vice-chairman today. The present directors are all great grandsons of William Thomson.

Today, in what is by any standards a highly competitive market, the Scottish papers hold their own well against the London-based national press which regards Scotland as a potentially lucrative area, and which, from time to time, launches bids to wrest it from their grasp. With more than 160 paid-for titles in existence, the Scottish press does not lack for variety. But it has to work hard to hold on to its position. To do so, newspapers, the popular ones in particular, have moved steadily away from a parochial cultivation of things Scottish—what the writer William Ferguson caricatured as 'ben and glen romanticism'—into a harder-nosed brand of journalism which competes on a more even plain with its English competitors. But it is still aggressively Scottish, disposed to defend Scottish institutions, including several sacred cows, against attack from outside. Scottish universities, Scottish law, Scottish steelworks, Scottish sport, all of these and more can rely on unequivocal support from the press in Scotland. What that has meant in political terms is a press that has not been well-disposed towards a Government which, over the past 13 years, has been perceived as having contributed to the decline of some or all of these symbols of independence.

This relative uniformity of view presents the weaknesses as well as the strengths of Scottish journalism. It is undoubtedly a drawback that there is, save in the enclave of Dundee and amongst English-based papers, no widely-read right-wing press. That may partly reflect the mood of the times, but it means that far too many received ideas about the state of the nation go by unchallenged. Is Scottish education really so very much better than English? Is the law in Scotland demonstrably superior in every respect? Can one safely assume that hospitals are better-managed without any privatized element? Was the preservation of the Ravenscraig steelworks at all costs really such a worthwhile goal? The case for the opposition view on such issues does not have a notably strong and consistent platform. Writers with a right-wing perspective like Allan Massie, Michael Fry or Brian Meek are rarities, and there may be a risk that a substantial proportion of readers in Scotland feel themselves, so to speak, journalistically disenfranchised. It is perhaps significant that the largest-selling quality daily newspaper from outside the country is the *Daily Telegraph*.

Mirror Group Newspapers

The daily paper with the highest circulation in Scotland, the *Daily Record*, was launched in 1895, the first halfpenny morning paper in Britain, and the first in Scotland to use pictures. It was part of a company formed in Glasgow in 1847 by Lord Rothermere together with Lord Northcliffe, who provided capital to print and publish the *North British Daily Mail* from premises in Frederick Lane in Glasgow. That paper was incorporated with the *Daily Record* in 1901 to become the *Daily Record and Mail*. Today the *Record*, and its sister paper the *Sunday Mail* are part of the Mirror Group, but proud of their editorial independence from their English partners. Although the *Record* could be said to compete for Scottish readers with its sister paper from the south, the *Daily Mirror*, their circulations are sometimes amalgamated to demonstrate that they are level-pegging in the UK with their great rival, *The Sun*. This is probably counter-productive for the *Record*, since it disguises the fact that it outsells

The Sun by nearly 3 to 1 in Scotland (760 000 to 277 000), though the gap is closing.

The chairman of Mirror Group Newspapers and its subsidiary company the Daily Record and Sunday Mail Ltd, was, until his death in 1991, Robert Maxwell. A proprietor whose inclination to interfere with his newspapers was legendary, he was famous in Scotland as the man who stepped in to help the short-lived *Scottish Daily News* in Glasgow, only to preside over its closure. He nevertheless chose to leave the *Record* and *Mail* well alone, happy presumably that their circulations were healthy and their profits acceptable. That these continue to impress was shown by the 1990 figures demonstrating pre-tax profits of £19.3 million on a turnover of £43.9 million.

Endell Laird, the *Record*'s editor-in-chief, can remember only four occasions when his boss arrived in the office, and claims that his interference was minimal. Indeed, in some senses, Laird says, there is more autonomy now than ever. 'In the days of Pickering, Jacobson and Cudlipp [previous Mirror chiefs] the front page of the *Record* had to be the same as the *Mirror*,' he says. Nevertheless, no one working for Maxwell was permitted to step out of line for long and the political stance of the paper (pro-Labour), its backing for Maxwell-inspired projects (the saving of the Commonwealth Games for instance), and a general understanding of the Maxwell philosophy, were all ingredients which enabled Laird to stay on side with Maxwell, while at the same time quietly steering the *Record* into independent waters. Together with his chief executive, Victor Horwood, he sits on the main board of Mirror Group News as well as the Scottish company, while still editing the *Record* on a day-to-day basis. The future ownership of Mirror Group Newspapers, to which the *Record* and *Mail* are umbilically linked, will fundamentally affect the progress of two highly successful newspapers.

Laird's main task in recent years has been to fend off competition from Rupert Murdoch's *Sun*, which, with a Scottish edition printed in Glasgow and run in aggressive style from an office in Kinning Park, has increased its circulation by 60 per cent in the last 10 years. The effect of *The Sun*'s shrewd, if unexpected, decision early in 1992 to jump on the SNP bandwagon and urge support for the Nationalists, has faded following the 1992 election. So far, Laird has succeeded in holding off the challenge, partly by successfully expanding out of its western base, and taking readers and advertisers from the eastern seaboard. The *Record* also has a surprisingly high proportion of ABC readers (the top bracket) with a 55 per cent penetration of this highly lucrative sector.

Its sister paper, the *Sunday Mail*, has, since 1991, been edited by Jim Cassidy, who was also the launch editor of the biggest freesheet in Scotland, the *Glaswegian*. Like Laird, Cassidy had a battle on his hands when the *Mail* faced competition from the *Sunday Scot*, a new tabloid Sunday launched by the millionaire entrepreneur David Murray, with the help of two ex-*Sun* journalists, Jack Irvine and Steve Sampson. But the launch issue was a disappointment, and the paper never achieved its circulation targets. The *Sunday Mail*, forewarned and forearmed, mounted a spirited defence of its position and was never seriously troubled. The *Sunday Scot* folded after only four months in 1991.

D C Thomson Ltd

That left the *Sunday Mail* competing as before with its main rival for the popular Sunday readership in Scotland, the *Sunday Post*. In doing so it was challenging a peculiarly Scottish phenomenon. The *Sunday Post* could once lay claim to being the most popular newspaper in Scotland. It is still in the *Guinness Book of Records* as the world's 'most read' paper, with an estimated readership of 6 out of 10 of the entire population of Scotland aged 15 and over. Its cartoon strips, Oor Wullie and The Broons, are still national institutions, its couthy style and homespun philosophy have struck a chord with a whole generation of Scots for whom home, hearth and heartland were the bedrock of their beliefs. But it is an ageing generation. Over the past decade, the *Sunday Post*'s hold has been slipping, its circulation in Scotland down from just under 1 million to below 800 000. At the same time the *Mail*, with its brash streak of tabloid populism has overtaken it, and now threatens to reach the same kind of Scottish circulation that the *Post* enjoyed 10 years ago. However, the *Post* enjoys a significant circulation outside Scotland, and when this is added in, it still sells some 1.2 million copies. To some jaundiced commentators it represents a distinctly reactionary element. 'As far as I'm concerned,' wrote the historian and journalist Tom Nairn, 'Scotland will be reborn the day the last minister is strangled with the last copy of the *Sunday Post*.' He may have to wait a bit.

Its owner, D C Thomson, based solidly in Dundee, should never be underestimated. It remains a major newspaper company which is still Scottish-owned, and it is run on splendidly autocratic lines by the Thomson family, who believe in treating their staff as members of a large, if somewhat Victorian family. Strictly non-union, it hands out pay increases in the form of bonuses, trains its own journalists, and instils a proper regard for discretion about the company's affairs amongst its staff. Its offices, in a fine red sandstone building in the heart of the city, are still redolent of tradition, with brown corridors, linoleum and glazed partitions. The chairman, Brian Thomson, always referred to as 'Mr Brian', presides over a board which consists almost entirely of family members. The most powerful non-family director is the company's managing editor, Bill Anderson, who has worked for the *Sunday Post* for 35 of his 57 years.

But if this suggests an old-fashioned approach, it is belied by D C Thomson's development plans. The company has completed a £50 million investment in new press halls, which now allows it to use colour in all its titles, there are computers on the desks, the very latest in new technology, and plans for on-screen page make-up. The company's *Dundee Courier*, with a 117 000 circulation, is the largest-selling regional title in Scotland, with a lock-hold on readers in Tayside; it has broken with tradition by putting news instead of advertisements on its front page. Titles as diverse as the *Evening Telegraph*, the *Weekly News* and the *People's Friend* are complemented by the *Scots Magazine*, and a host of publications for women and teenagers, while comics such as the *Dandy* and the *Beano*, are not only institutions in themselves, but have given career starts to many journalists who went on to become lynchpins in the industry.

The 'quality' papers

The two major 'quality' papers, the *Herald* and *The Scotsman*, easily outperform their London broadsheet rivals, *The Times, The Guardian, The Independent* and the *Daily Telegraph* whose combined circulation in Scotland is some 75 000. This is 11 000 less than the total of *The Scotsman* alone.

With a circulation of more than 120 000, the *Herald* predominates in the west of Scotland, where its sale is concentrated in the Glasgow and Strathclyde area. It is, however, a national Scottish paper with a wide range of writers and columnists which gives it a strong sense of its own identity. Recently, it has dropped the word Glasgow from its main title, redesigned its pages and is concentrating on building its readership throughout Scotland, perhaps emulating one of its most illustrious editors, Charles Russell, who favoured large headlines, remarking, 'A glance at our old files and at some newspapers issued now, will show how really repellent a paper may be made to look by an excess of modesty.' The paper's owners, George Outram, whose name derives from an early editor, an Edinburgh advocate, found themselves in the autumn of 1964 locked in a titanic struggle for ownership of the paper. Two businessmen were involved: a Scot, Hugh Fraser, and a Canadian, Roy Thomson, owner of *The Scotsman*. It was won eventually by Fraser through the medium of his company, Scottish and Universal Investment Trust (SUIT), though Fraser did not live to see the day when he assumed full ownership; he died in November 1966, after being elevated to the peerage as Lord Fraser of Allander. In June 1979, SUITS was acquired by the multinational Lonrho company headed by 'Tiny' Rowland who also owns the *Observer*. Rowland never had to worry particularly about his Scottish papers (profits of £6 million on a turnover of £58 million), and played no direct part in running them. Then, in May 1992, Liam Kane, Outram's managing director, whose experience has included working for the *Record* and for Rupert Murdoch's News International, announced a successful management buyout from Lonrho, bringing the *Herald* back into Scottish hands for the first time since 1964. For a price of £74 million he and his team, which included the editors of the *Herald* and the *Evening Times*, acquired the two papers as well as Outram's profitable magazine division, with titles such as the *Scottish Farmer* and *Scottish Field*. The new company, called Caledonian Newspaper Publishing, has the backing of major Scottish financial institutions, and it is Kane's ambition to challenge *The Scotsman's* self-proclaimed position as Scotland's national newspaper.

Under its present editor, Arnold Kemp, formerly deputy editor of *The Scotsman*, the *Herald* has thrown itself behind the expansion and development of the City of Glasgow, while maintaining a strong romantic attachment to the grass-roots culture of the area it represents. It periodically castigates the City establishment for decisions which, in its view, fail to keep faith with the populist traditions held dear by Glasgow's citizens, and its most popular columnist, the sardonic Jack McLean, views the modern world with ill-concealed suspicion from the fastness of his favourite bar. Writers such as Alf Young on economics, Brian Meek on sport and politics, and Murray Ritchie in a wide-ranging weekly column, give the paper a broadly centrist political range. Under a Conservative administration it has won few friends in the Scottish Office, but has nevertheless a high reputation in the business community. And in a City where the religious divide is deep and abiding, it has managed to avoid falling foul of both Catholics and Protestants. Kemp is proud both of the paper's independence from outside influence (he can think of only one instance when Lonrho attempted to interfere with an editorial decision), and the investment in the paper's editorial team. Salaries are generally higher than elsewhere, there is still a four-day week, and staffing is generous. He describes his new managing director, Kane, as 'a risk-taker', and says that while he supports his goal of creating a national paper, his own ambition is to make the *Herald* 'a really good metropolitan paper, informed by where it is published, yet international in outlook. It should,' he adds, 'be self-confident about its identity like the *New York Times*.'

While the *Herald*, with its rich Glasgow advertising market, is extremely profitable, its sister paper, the *Evening Times*, has suffered, as all evening papers in Britain have, from the steady decline in this particular market. Assailed by the impact of television, it has dropped from a circulation of more than 200 000 10 years ago, to 160 000. A punchy, campaigning paper, headed by the phlegmatic George McKechnie, it is nevertheless struggling to hold on to its readership. Brand new presses, introduced to give the two papers colour printing, suffered from long-drawn-out teething troubles which hit the evening paper particularly hard.

Across the east–west divide, in Edinburgh, The Scotsman Publications, a subsidiary of Thomson Regional Newspapers, itself owned by the Thomson organization based in Toronto, field a group of paid-for and free newspapers, including *The Scotsman*, the *Evening News*, *Scotland on Sunday*, and the *Herald and Post* free papers. Its managing director, Joe Logan, an Aberdonian, runs the group on a tight fiscal rein and can claim significant gains recently, both in building circulation and profits. *The Scotsman*, which dropped some 8 000 copies in the decade between 1980 and 1990, a decline accelerated by bitter disputes between journalists and management in 1986 and 1987, has steadied on 86 000 and has begun to climb upwards again. It is a highly profitable publication. It stands marginally to the right of the *Herald*, has a slightly higher proportion of affluent 'AB' readers, is committed to devolution for Scotland, and has recently undergone an extensive redesign, aided by a £15 million investment in new colour presses. As a Scot myself, and an editor whose professional experience has been largely in Fleet Street, I believe in building on its reputation as a national paper for Scotland, and see the serious competition as coming not so much from the *Herald* as from the London-based national papers. There is a greater appetite for papers like *The Independent, The Times, The Guardian* or *Telegraph* in Edinburgh and the Lothians than there is in the west. It says something about the culture of the east; perhaps a more anglicized population, perhaps a more internationally minded business community. Whatever the reason, the 'English' press, with its greater resources, pose a threat to *The Scotsman*'s position, though a recent decision by *The Times* to cease printing a Scottish edition in Glasgow has somewhat blunted its impact.

The Scotsman's sister paper, the *Evening News* has launched a formidable drive against the circulation drift that has hit almost all evening papers. From a figure of more than 130 000 10 years ago, it has fallen to just over 100 000, but its tough Glasgow-born editor Terry Quinn, who came to Edinburgh via the *Bradford Telegraph*, has made full use of colour printing and new technology make-up to transform the look and feel of the paper. It is now determinedly aimed at building 'community' readership. 'The only antidote to the present doom and gloom is to produce newspapers that readers need and want,' says Quinn. 'Evening papers are uniquely placed to help people get more value out of their city and their daily lives.' In 1992 Quinn was succeeded as editor by Harry Roulston, editor of the *Press and Journal*.

The newest arrival in the *Scotsman* group is the Sunday paper *Scotland on Sunday*, a quality broadsheet paper which has been one of the success stories of the Scottish press. There had been a clear gap in the Scottish Sunday market ever since the death, in 1983, of the much-lamented *Sunday Standard*, published by Outram from Glasgow. It sank under the weight of high production and editorial costs, but it was nevertheless still selling over 100 000 at the end. With new technology and de-manning in the industry, the prospects for a new launch improved, and it became a question as to which of the rival groups would go first. The Scotsman Publications won, and, after a faltering start, *Scotland on Sunday* has reached a circulation of more than 80 000, which is rising rapidly. In 1991, under its editor Andrew Jaspan, who joined it from the *Sunday Times*, it became the fastest-growing paper published in Britain. Untainted by east–west rivalry, it is seen primarily as a Scottish paper, and, since it flies an early edition to the South, it enjoys a substantial English circulation.

It faces competition from the Scottish edition of the *Sunday Times*, and to a lesser extent the *Sunday Express* and *Mail on Sunday*. But these, as with the Scottish editions of daily papers like the *Express* and *Mail*, suffer from being adjuncts to the main paper rather than full-blown rivals. Though they have offices and staff in Glasgow and Edinburgh, the number of pages devoted to Scottish matters is inevitably limited.

Further north, Aberdeen Journals, also part of the Thomson regional group, dominates the Grampian area. The *Press and Journal*, one of Scotland's longest-established regional papers, is published from Aberdeen and circulates throughout the Grampians and the Highlands. With nine editions published every weekday, it manages to cover in detail local stories in every area it reaches, and is as a result required reading from Aberdeen to Fort William and beyond. A damaging strike by journalists in 1990 threatened to send its circulation, once around 115 000, plunging below 100 000, but the haemorrhage has been staunched by its editor, Harry Roulston, and his ebullient managing director, Alan Scott. Few of those who went on strike were allowed back on to the paper, which has recruited a whole new generation of young journalists. At the same time the introduction of new colour presses has given it and its sister evening paper, the *Evening Express*, edited by Dick Williamson, a new lease of life.

There is no doubt, however, that for a time evening papers in Scotland were beginning to look like an endangered species. Adding to the gloom was the fact that only 27 per cent of Scots read an evening paper compared to a national UK average of 29 per cent. Various options, including transforming them into morning papers, as has happened to a number of US publications, have been considered. Only in the more local sector was there greater cause for optimism. The *Greenock Telegraph*, selling some 21 000 copies, has only dropped 2 000 over the last 10 years.

The local press

It is not the only success story of its kind. The local press in Scotland is rich, varied and vigorous. Recent research shows that 60 per cent of Scottish adults read a paid-for weekly newspaper, more than any other UK region. By contrast, only 58 per cent read a free newspaper, compared to a UK average of 71 per cent. The main theory for this disparity is that free papers tend to flourish in urban areas, and since a significant proportion of Scotland's population still lives in outlying or rural areas, their allegiance to their local weekly paper tends to remain strong.

Freddie Johnston, who runs one of the most successful local newspaper groups in Scotland, indeed in the UK (its profits in 1990 were £7 million on a turnover of £63 million, the latter figure outstripping even the *Daily Record*) has a slightly different theory. 'Society is more static in Scotland,' he says. 'We are deeply resistant to change. People are more interested in their own communities, their neighbours, their near vicinity.' Since Johnston Press now owns more local papers in England than it does in Scotland (they include the *West Sussex County Times, Bury Times* and the Yorkshire Weekly Newspaper Group), he can make direct comparisons. He claims that, with a few exceptions, his newspapers in Scotland are enjoying record circulations, while in England this is by no means the case. He says too that the relative failure of free newspapers north of the border is a factor. 'The Scots are suspicious about getting something for nothing,' is his comment. But he is far from sanguine about the future. 'There is a rising tide of semi-literacy in Scotland as elsewhere,' he warns, 'and this is bad news for papers of whatever kind. At one time you were isolated in your community if you did not read and write. With television this is no longer the case.'

Other successful weekly newspaper groups include Trinity Holdings who own newspapers in Paisley, Stirling, Kilmarnock and Perth; West Independent Newspapers, run by David Campbell, whose territory in the West includes Ayrshire; the Tweedale Press Group in Berwick; the Dunfermline Press in Fife, whose chairman Norman Lessels is also chairman of Standard Life, and which has recently expanded out of Fife to acquire newspapers previously owned by United Provincial Newspapers. These include the *Greenock Telegraph* and other papers in Dumbarton, Paisley, Helensburgh, Barrhead and Clydebank. One newspaper which belongs to no group is the *West Highland Free Press*, edited by Ian McCormack, and founded by the Labour MP Brian Wilson. A radical, campaigning paper, run from Broadford on Skye, it is a thorn in the flesh of local landowners and a platform for old-fashioned polemical journalism.

Free newspapers in Scotland may not be as successful as their English equivalents, but they nevertheless inhabit a lively and highly competitive sector, often set up by paid-for newspaper groups to defend their own advertising market. Pushed through letter-boxes up and down the country, these papers, packed with advertising, are largely an urban phenomenon, and, perhaps inevitably, the largest of them is in Glasgow, the *Glaswegian*, with a distribution of nearly 300 000, owned by what was formerly the Maxwell group. Maxwell also competes in Edinburgh and Lothians with the *Herald and Post* series, published by the Scotsman group, which has recently expanded successfully into Dunfermline. Other big players, mainly in the central belt, are Trinity, Johnston Press and County Media.

Television

Scottish Television

In 1990, Scottish Television, which serves the central belt of Scotland, carried out a survey of viewers' interests. Nearly half of those polled said there were still too few Scottish programmes being shown, despite the fact that the company was already broadcasting more than its required minimum of 520 hours a year of regional programmes. Only 2 per cent said there were too many Scottish programmes and over a third said that they would watch more often if more Scottish programmes were scheduled. Not much sign there of a dilution of the national interest, despite the fact that a generation of viewers has grown up under the influence of a television schedule dominated by English and US programming.

In pitching for the licence to continue serving its region as required by the Broadcasting Act 1990, Scottish Television, like the smaller independent companies, Grampian and Borders, inevitably stressed its Scottish credentials. It promised 340 extra hours of programmes made in Scotland, which, together with Gaelic and Scottish productions made elsewhere, committed it to broadcasting 1 300 hours of Scottish television every year from 1993, a greater range of local programming than in any other ITV region.

Its results suggest that this will continue to be a successful formula. Scottish Television's profits in 1990 were £11.23 million on a turnover of £114 million. Profit, it seems, is linked with a growing awareness of television's Scottish credentials. 'The Scottish media used to be very un-Scottish,' says Gus Macdonald, the 52-year-old managing director of Scottish Television. 'That's no longer the case. Our research shows that the nation wants its own agenda, and as we approach the stage when you'll have 20-odd satellite channels, it's more important than ever to have one that is identifiably Scottish.' At the same time, however, if it is to grow, it needs to make programmes which it can sell to the Independent Television network; programmes like its very successful Glasgow detective series, *Taggart*. This means being British in outlook, while retaining its Scottish base and character.

Macdonald and his team, based at Scottish Television's headquarters in Cowcaddens, Glasgow, are now notorious for having won the coveted franchise for the lucrative central region of Scotland with a cheeky bid of only £2 000. So confident were they in the formula they were offering, in their own track record, and in the prediction that they would have no serious rivals, that they decided not to put their shareholders' money seriously at risk. As one commentator said afterwards: 'Macdonald should be given a massive bonus for carrying it off, and then immediately fired for taking such a liberty.'

Much has changed, however, since the late Lord Thomson who first bid for the franchise in 1954, famously remarked that independent television was 'a licence to print money'. (It was. Though Thomson found it hard to persuade Scottish institutions to back him, he made £1 million in the first year of operation, and thereafter enough to launch his future takeovers of the *Sunday Times* and *The Times*). Fighting for advertising revenue in a tough market and under changing government requirements, has meant selling programmes more aggressively to the UK network, reducing staff, and farming out more work to independent producers. Scottish have shed 250 jobs over the past five years, slimming down to just 600 employees, most of them based at Cowcaddens, but with around 6 per cent at the Gateway studio in Edinburgh. An estimated 35 per cent of local output is now made by independent producers.

The key to its financial future lies in the number of programmes it can sell to the ITV network. Alastair Moffat, director of programmes and a former administrator of the Edinburgh Festival Fringe, is in charge of network production, which currently occupies about half of the company's staff. He is looking to repeat the success of programmes like *Taggart*, the soap opera *Take the High Road*, and the more recent network drama, *The*

Advocates. A link-up with Hollywood is producing a 13-part animation series created by a Scot, Tony Collingwood, which has been pre-sold in various countries, covering its production costs. Selling productions like these is not only lucrative (the *Taggart* order has been worth £25 million), it has meant that Scottish Television is now amongst the top 10 UK producers. 'My secret weapon is England,' says Macdonald. 'They have 10 times our audience, they speak our language, and they help pay for our programmes.' (*Taggart*, for instance is entirely paid for now by the English network.) Despite these worthy ambitions, however, it remains the case that while 1 in 10 of the British population lives in Scotland, Scotland produces less than one-hundredth of the programme material shown in peak time throughout the UK.

Macdonald regards the company's chairman, Bill Brown, who spends approximately two days a week at Cowcaddens, as an essential sounding-board for ideas. Brown, apart from being chairman of the Scottish Amicable Life Assurance Society, was a founding director of Channel Four, and was awarded the Royal Television Society's gold medal for outstanding service to television in 1984. The board also numbers the ubiquitous Sir Charles Fraser, Angus Grossart and Gavin Laird amongst its members. Simon Forrest, controller of corporate affairs and formerly news editor on Channel Four News, is a key executive. David Scott, with a solid background in newspaper journalism, is head of programmes and runs the news and current affairs side, while Eileen Gallagher, controller of broadcasting, is a member of the Network Planners Group, and is therefore a vital link with the national network.

Grampian Television

Another Scottish television company which successfully retained its franchise was the smaller Grampian Television, based in Aberdeen, but covering a geographical area—from Tayside north to Shetland and west to the Hebrides—larger than Switzerland. One of the implications of this is the number of transmitters required to cover the area: between 70 and 80 masts, compared to just one to cover London.

Grampian, which celebrated its thirtieth birthday in September 1991, just a fortnight before learning whether it would survive to celebrate its thirty-first, bid £720 000 for its licence. This was heavily outbid (the counter-offers were £2.9 million and £1.2 million), but Grampian retained the franchise on the grounds that it was most likely to supply a quality service. It recorded a pre-tax profit in 1991 of £2.4 million on a turnover of £20.7 million. Its chief executive, Donald Waters, a local man from Nairn who has been with Grampian for 17 years, played on the quality of the station's local programmes, emphasizing the three targets Grampian had set itself from the beginning: 'To bring the area to itself, to bring the area to the outside world, and to bring the outside world to the area.' Covering such a vast and disparate part of the country is a challenge, and one that was met in the early years by a distinctly folksy output. Programmes like *Bothy Nights*, *Calum's Ceilidh*, and *Thingummyjig*, are still remembered with a mixture of affection and embarrassment. At the same time, however, the station discovered and launched the career of one of television's most glamorous presenters, Selina Scott, who still maintains her links with the company.

These days Grampian relies on well-made material such as its daily news show, *North Tonight*, a trial by television programme called *We the Jury*, successful documentaries, some of which it has made in combination with foreign television companies and sold on to Channel Four, children's series, sport, Gaelic programmes, and entertainment, notably in the shape of the *Art Sutter Show*. The only regret Waters has is that, on a revenue of £20 million, he cannot justify going heavily into drama, which can cost up to £500 000 an hour. Now that Waters has beaten off the opposition, the main risk is a takeover bid from one of the richer ITV companies. But in the current economic climate that looks less likely than it once did.

The man responsible for the creative side at Grampian is the programme director, George Mitchell, born in Edinburgh, who joined Grampian from Central Television, where his main experience was on documentaries. 'A company like Grampian has no aspirations to do primetime drama and sitcoms,' he says. 'It does, however, have a strong track record in documentaries . . . the fact that it's set in some of the most stunning scenery in the world makes it just the location for wildlife filming and endurance events.' Robert Christie is director of television, and Alistair Gracie heads news and current affairs.

Both Grampian and Scottish Television benefit from one of the more surprising Government handouts of recent years. In 1993, £9.5 million of Scottish Office funds channelled through a special committee of the Independent Television Commission will pay for 250 hours of Gaelic language programming each year. Since there are only about 80 000 Gaelic speakers in Scotland, this is generous funding for a minority. It has meant that a wide range of programmes, including children's television, documentaries, current affairs, cookery, DIY and fashion, as well as a remarkably popular drawing game, *De Tha Seo*, are now regularly screened, some of them at peak viewing times. Scottish Television has set up a Gaelic Advisory Committee under Sir Kenneth Alexander, and has started a training trust jointly with Grampian. The challenge facing both companies is to satisfy Gaelic viewers without alienating the others.

Border Television

Further south, Border Television does what its name suggests, and straddles the border area between England and Scotland, stretching south to Cumbria and the Isle of Man, north to Peebles and Berwick-on-Tweed. One of the smallest of the ITV companies, with little over 0.5 per cent of ITV's total income, it has always suffered from financial constraints, and the problem of serving its very different English and Scottish audiences. But by concentrating on making good programmes and cutting its overheads, it has survived, held on to its franchise, and is confident about its future. It currently has a turnover of some £10 million a year and pre-tax profits of around £800 000.

Border's chairman is Melvyn Bragg, the author and broadcaster, a native Cumbrian, who has helped raised its national profile in between his many other commitments further south; its managing director is another Cumbrian, James Graham, who has built the station's reputation for network children's programmes and local documentaries. Graham cites the description given to the company by Lord Whitelaw at its thirtieth anniversary celebrations in 1991: 'a force for unity' across both sides of the Borders. 'It is essentially a programme-driven company,' says Graham. 'It regularly achieves some of the highest audience ratings in the UK.' Muir Sutherland, a Scot, is director of programmes, and can point to Border's success in winning four gold medals in three years at the New York Film and Television Festival. Its news and current affair programme, *Look Around*, covers regional news from Carlisle, but it has offices in Galashiels to support the news service it provides on the Selkirk transmitter for viewers in the Borders.

BBC Scotland

Faced with the vigorous challenge of these independent television companies, BBC Scotland is uncompromising in its aim. 'We are the voice of the nation,' says Patrick Chalmers who was, until the end of 1991, its controller (he moved to Hong Kong to work for the BBC's new world service television station, and was succeeded by John McCormick, an Ayrshire-born graduate of Glasgow University). Chalmers's claim is based on the fact that BBC Scotland, unlike the regional independent companies, reaches every corner of the country. There are local stations in Aberdeen, Dundee, Inverness, Stornoway, Portree, Orkney, Shetland, Solway and Tweed, as well as Glasgow and Edinburgh. The national network is required by the BBC's charter to reflect the distinctive culture, language, interests and tastes of the Scottish people. But in doing so it faces a problem: funding, or rather the lack of it. The annual licence fee has, for some time, been fixed at a lower level than the cost of living, and the BBC has faced increasing costs with an effectively diminishing income. This has meant drastic cuts. The number of jobs, in television and radio, has been reduced by almost 200, about a fifth of the total employed in Scotland. At the same time, the BBC, like ITV, is required to take more programming from independent producers: its target is 25 per cent by 1993.

BBC Scotland's total annual operating budget is around £43 million, which pays not only for its staff, programmes, engineering costs, maintenance and administration, but also for the Scottish Symphony Orchestra. It produces around 650 hours of television programmes for Scottish audiences each year and some 200 hours for the BBC1 and BBC2 networks. But it cannot boast the same measure of independence that its more commercial rivals have. For one thing it is very much an adjunct of the BBC in London to which it is responsible, which determines its budget, and which exercises bureaucratic control. 'There is no sense in denying that we are part of an increasingly centrist system,' says Chalmers. 'We are a bit like Alsace-Lorraine.' Whether this has affected their television viewing figures is hard to say, but certainly in the Central Belt they have been losing out recently to Scottish Television whose own figures show a share of 43.5 per cent against the BBC's 34 per cent.

The BBC's controller in Scotland is part managing-director, part editor-in-chief, though he is not involved in details of programme content. He has direct access to the director-general in London, and through him to the BBC's Board of Governors. The controller is also responsible to the Broadcasting Council for Scotland, which is represented on the Board of Governors by the national governor. The current national governor and chairman of BBC Scotland is Professor Sir Graham Hills, former principal of Strathclyde University, who presides over the Broadcasting Council for Scotland. Though this post is said to be a political appointment, and is therefore viewed with some suspicion, he is chosen from a list supplied in the first place by the controller. The Scottish Office is involved in vetting the list, as is the director-general and the Home Office. The final choice is by the Queen in Council, but she will respond in most cases to the Home Secretary's recommendation. The Broadcasting Council is there to see that Scottish interests are being properly represented. In most cases this means backing the controller, but the council is equally responsible to the Board of Governors in London, so the controller will be well aware that he can only step so far out of line. During his time, however, Chalmers reports that relations between him and the Council were excellent. There has, however, been periodic friction between the BBC and Scottish Office ministers, particularly the abrasive Michael Forsyth who has complained about anti-government bias.

Nevertheless BBC Television, headed by Colin Cameron, has an impressive record in terms of programme production. Its news and current affairs department, under Ken Cargill, produces the highly successful *Reporting Scotland* programme, which is watched by 0.75 million people every day—about the same as the combined audiences for Scottish, Borders and Grampian news programmes. The department is also responsible for the documentary series *Focal Point*, and the political discussions of *Left, Right and Centre*. Sports coverage, through such programmes as *Sportscene*, is a high priority. Drama is equally strong, with network productions such as *Tutti Frutti*, its successor *Your Cheatin' Heart*, the adaptation of Melvyn Bragg's *A Time to Dance*, plays by writers as diverse as Tom Kempinski, Alan Plater, William McIlvanney,

Trevor Griffiths and David Mamet, and a brand new soap opera, *Strathblair*, set in the Perthshire village of Blair Atholl. The television drama department is headed by Bill Bryden, whose own experience in the theatre north and south of the border is wide-ranging. He was the first winner of the Gulliver Award for artistic excellence, set up by the industrialist Sir James Gulliver, and his massive production of *The Ship*, a spectacular evocation of Clydeside, first seen in Glasgow in 1990, was filmed in its entirety by BBC Scotland's Music and Arts Department. This department, headed by John Archer, has ambitions which lie beyond Scotland; when Vladimir Ashkenazy made his exile's return to Russia, he was filmed by BBC Scotland. 'Why not?' says Archer. 'If Russian television wasn't up to it, why not BBC Scotland, with its outstanding record in television music?' His department has also produced for television Judith Weir's new work for Scottish Opera, *The Vanishing Bridegroom*, and commissioned a series called *The Director's Place* in which international moviemakers film the places from which they derive their inspiration. In Rab C Nesbitt, BBC Scotland has created a Scottish comic character who is as universal as any on television today. It is for that reason that BBC 2 now produces it, and it is shown all over Britain. Pat Chalmers is also proud of BBC Scotland's record as a sponsor of the arts. He points out that the £15 million they have spent on arts projects makes them a greater patron than the Scottish Arts Council, while the Scottish Symphony Orchestra is of international standing.

BBC Scotland sometimes gives the impression of a television station fighting a commercial battle with one hand tied behind its back. It is certainly a more bureaucratic outfit than its rivals. But given what it does with these disadvantages, it is worth asking what it might do given a little more entrepreneurial leeway.

Performers and presenters

So far, television has been discussed purely in terms of who runs what. But for the viewer, the greatest impact comes from those who appear on the screen rather than those behind it. Scottish television in general has thrown up some highly professional performers and presenters who have set their own stamp on the media in Scotland. The women are particularly impressive. Kirsty Wark of the BBC is certainly the best political interviewer in the country, and her programme *Left, Right and Centre* is essential viewing for anyone interested in Scottish politics. Her handling of *The Scotsman* debate in early 1992 in front of an audience of 2 500 was a model of cool professionalism. Sheena Macdonald of Scottish Television is equally capable, and her show, *Scottish Women*, in which current affairs are debated by an all-women audience is unique in the UK. It is perhaps not surprising that both women have been in demand in London. Viv Lumsden of Scottish Television, Anne Mackenzie of Grampian and Jackie Bird of BBC Scotland share similar qualities in front of the cameras. And lest all this should sound discriminatory, it should be recorded that Eddie Mair of BBC Scotland not only fronts *Reporting Scotland* in the evening but is on the air at an unseemly hour of the morning on *Good Morning Scotland*, while John Duncanson, of Grampian's *North Tonight*, is something of an institution in the north-east.

Radio

BBC Radio Scotland

The BBC's *Good Morning Scotland* sets the nation's agenda every day. It also has a habit of irritating Conservative Scottish Office ministers who, when under pressure, detect bias in its reporting. They do not, however, tend to fare well in the argument, because political and industrial reporting is in the hands of Kenny McIntyre, who is not only one of the most experienced commentators on the air, but has an enviable reputation for breaking major political stories widely followed up elsewhere. There was a time when *Good Morning Scotland* was considered dull and parochial, but it has improved greatly in recent years, in tune with the livelier political scene in Scotland. Local BBC stations up and down the country break into the programme for half an hour every morning with their own news. Altogether BBC Radio Scotland, headed until 1992 by Neil Fraser, broadcasts over 35 hours of news and current affairs every week. Programmes like *Head On* with the combative Colin Bell, *Speaking Out* with Lesley Riddoch, and *Queen Street Garden*, an arts programme presented by Neville Garden, have become national institutions in Scotland, while the drama, documentaries and music which Radio Scotland regularly produces have won several international awards. Like BBC Scotland, Radio Scotland's headquarters are in Queen Margaret Drive in Glasgow, but the recently reopened and refurbished studios in Queen Street, Edinburgh, have given the corporation north of the border a much-needed boost.

Independent local radio

Scotland also has seven main independent local radio stations, five of which are owned by the rapidly expanding Radio Clyde Holdings which now runs Radio Clyde itself, Radio Forth in Edinburgh, Radio Tay, Radio Borders, and Northsound. In addition the group owns around 21 per cent of the Inverness-based Moray Firth Radio. This leaves West Sound, based in Ayr, as Scotland's only truly independent Scottish local radio station.

However, several franchises have been granted recently for small community radio stations and so far three have been launched: CentreSound in Stirling, East End Radio in Glasgow and Heartland Radio in Aberfeldy. It cannot be said that the prognosis is all that good. East End Radio has ceased transmission, and CentreSound has signed a management contract with Radio Forth. The group behind a fourth station in West Lothian abandoned the project before going on air.

Radio Clyde has been built up under the chairmanship of Ian Chapman, former head of Collins the publishers. His chief executive is James Gordon, and the board is particularly strong, with, amongst others, Bill Brown, chairman of Scottish Television, Richard Findlay, chairman of Radio Forth, and Sandy Orr of the Caledonian Bank. The station reaches the biggest audience by far of all the independents, broadcasting to a total of more than 0.5 million people, 60 per cent of its potential 'reach'. Radio Forth comes next with something over 100 000, but it is the lively station Max AM in Edinburgh that is becoming something of a cult amongst the young and the not so young, with a combination of sixties pop music and irreverent comment.

The greatest challenge facing the smaller independent stations will come in 1993, when, as a result of the new Broadcasting Act, they will face heavier transmission charges. At the moment, transmitter networks have a subsidy system whereby the larger stations cushion smaller companies. This, however, is due to stop under the Act, which will mean the smaller stations carrying the full brunt of the charges. West Sound alone estimates its costs could rise from £16 000 to £60 000.

The challenge which the Scottish media, whether press or television, faces in holding on to its market, is to balance a genuine appetite for news and comment on Scottish affairs with a growing awareness of what is available from the outside world. So far, while foreign and UK content has climbed steadily up the agenda, there has been no dilution of national character; if anything the reverse is the case. Those who claim that in consequence the media presents too narrow a view of the Scottish scene are merely confronting the reality of what is happening north of the border today. As interest in Scotland's politics and culture has increased, so has the coverage in newspapers, or television, and on radio. There is no conspiracy of interest, merely a confluence of opinion.

Writing more than 10 years ago, James Kellas defined the national consciousness as 'an assertion of Scottishness on the part of an amorphous group of interests and individuals, whose identity is caught up with that of Scotland'. That amorphous group is as strong an influence today within the media as it has ever been. Whether it has profoundly influenced public opinion, or whether newspapers and television are themselves simply the mirror of the society they represent can be endlessly debated. But they seem to be in tune with the mood of the nation today. For better or for worse, Scotland has the media it deserves.

Newspaper circulation in Scotland

Title	Jul/Dec 90	Jul/Dec 91	Variation
Daily Record	777 879	760 003	- 17 876
The Scottish Sun	278 666	289 700	+ 11 034
Scottish Daily Express	145 582	141 027	- 4 555
Herald	120 714	118 836	- 1 878
Dundee Courier	117 221	116 600	- 621
Press and Journal	103 810	105 800	+ 1 990
Evening Times	166 566	155 949	- 10 617
Evening News	101 770	99 346	- 2 424
The Scotsman	84 554	85 520	+ 966
Evening Express	73 332	71 624	- 1 708
Evening Telegraph	12 600	N/A	N/A
Greenock Telegraph	21 231	20 875	- 356
The Sunday Market			
Sunday Post	1 226 555	1 137 758	- 88 797
Sunday Mail	888 099	880 899	- 7 200
Sunday Express	90 027	90 669	+ 642
Sunday Times	69 831	70 163	+ 332
Scotland on Sunday	68 838	75 826	+ 6 988

Note: Based on ABC figures and trade estimates

ERRATUM

Page 144: **Newspaper circulation in Scotland**

Evening Telegraph *should read*

	Jul/Dec 90	Jul/Dec 91	Variation
	43 600	41 286	-2314

8

The Arts, Culture and Identity

Ruth Wishart

The last quarter of the 20th century in Scotland has seen an intensification of the debate about the political parameters of Scotland's nationhood. A loud bravado mingled with, or prompted by, an inferiority complex have been much in evidence since the referendum in 1979. That poll asked the electorate to accept the Scotland Act and the plans for what was then a relatively modest Assembly with limited powers, to be housed in the Royal High School in Edinburgh. Scotland, the nation which, uniquely, opted out of sovereignty in 1707, just managed to whisper yes to a pale imitation of that autonomy on 1 March 272 years later. Since 40 per cent of the entire electorate had to say yes regardless of what percentage actually chose to register an opinion at the polls, the provisions of the Act could not be implemented. The Callaghan government fell shortly afterwards. Since the SNP's Westminster numbers were reduced in the subsequent election from 11 to two, the desire to express our Scottishness seemed less than full-throated.

So it remained for the next few years but that situation has now been transformed once more as we go into the 1990s. A rising number of expatriate Scots are returning to pursue their careers. There is a greatly increased interest in the Scottish languages, most especially in Gaelic and more recently in Scots. Poetry and the visual arts are flourishing, and a recent report on the economic impact of the arts in the Highlands and Islands found a renewed cultural vigour and sense of identity. It also discovered that of 28 new arts initiatives, 24 had been set up by incomers and tended to involve classical music or drama rather than traditional arts. The presence of English immigrants, and their influence, is an important element in defining the current preoccupation with identity. A powerful factor in rekindling Scots' interest in their own cultural heritage in the mid-1980s was the suggestion that it was being eroded by widespread anglicization. There were fears that even to articulate such concerns would encourage a particularly unsavoury form of anti-English racism, yet clearly the involvement of 'the white settlers' need not be negative, as the evidence of the survey demonstrates.

But the roots of the uneasiness lie elsewhere. In recent years all Scotland's major cultural organizations and some of its other arts-related institutions have acquired English chief executives. And many Scots of all political persuasions now express concern that they bring to their tasks both a per- spective and cultural values which, although valid in their own right, do not rest easily upon Scottish attitudes and priorities which have been moulded from different experiences and traditions. Moreover, certain Scottish Office ministers seemed intent on fashioning a seamless policy robe throughout the UK in areas like health, education and the law. In the eyes of some observers this struck at the very heart of their sense of Scottishness, since the law and the education service seemed distinctly different. These politi- cal and cultural shifts to southern values, paradoxically, set in train a fresh appreciation of all things Scottish, and a fresh determination to pre- serve them.

Inevitably this has led to friction, not least in the corridors of Edinburgh power. Edinburgh has sometimes been regarded as an anglicized city. This can be traced back to the Union of 1707 and the subsequent removal of the Scottish court to London. It became fashionable to have children educated in England, or in Scottish schools modelled on the English public school system. Given that background the arrival in Edinburgh of the public school educated Englishman, Timothy Clifford, to be director of the National Galleries of Scotland should not have exposed him to cultural shock. Yet Clifford, with a particular passion for the classical Italian school, epitomizes the underlying tensions of the anglicization debate. When he and the chairman of his board of trustees, Angus Grossart, unveiled a plan to build a Gallery of Scottish Art the response was decidedly mixed; some critics suggesting the main effect would be to ghettoize Scottish art, reducing its status by not having it hung alongside European and international contemporaneous work. Others, including members of Mr Clifford's staff, thought he wished to get rid of the Scottish work from the main National Gallery thus leaving more space for the Italian masters. Duncan Macmillan, art historian and curator of Edinburgh University's Talbot Rice Gallery, suggested that the solution to the space problems which had led the board to seek ways of liberating two-thirds of their Scottish collection from the vaults would be to give indigenous work a higher priority and store other schools. Initially the favoured site for the new gallery was identified as a building adjacent to the current Scottish Gallery of Modern Art in Belford Road, and this was also seen in some quarters as a further centralization of what are deemed to be national assets. The results of an independent report, published in July 1992, favoured two sites in Glasgow (while suggesting repairs to the Royal Scottish Academy were a greater priority).

All this indicates how culture and nationalism interact in Scotland in the

1990s. A similar controversy followed the decision to build the new Museum of Scotland on a site adjoining the current Royal Scottish Museum in Chambers Street. A very public row broke out when, as the winning architect was chosen from over 400 submitted designs, Prince Charles resigned from the Board of Trustees. This was not, it emerged, because he feared the new building would represent a monstrous tartan carbuncle—it is an extension rather than a separate entity—but because he was unhappy about the consultation process and his comparative lack of involvement. The plans have also been under attack by more humble citizens including Duncan Macmillan and Julian Spalding, director of Glasgow Art Galleries and Museums. Spalding, like Clifford, is an Englishman who once ran Manchester's main gallery. Although a quite dissimilar personality he also found himself swiftly embroiled in a bitter war of words in 1990. He was cast as the villain of the decision not to appoint the then keeper of the People's Palace, Elspeth King, to a post as curator of social history. That decision was seen as part of the debate in Glasgow about the perceived imposition of 'alien' cultural values.

A third incident occurred in 1991 when Christopher Bishop, a Londoner appointed as chief executive of the Scottish National Orchestra, acquired a new chairman, Lord Goold, former chairman of the Tory Party in Scotland Their board proposed adding a royal prefix to the orchestra's name and thus it became first, the Royal Scottish National Orchestra, and, barely weeks later, the Royal Scottish Orchestra. This caused a furore, to which Bishop responded that the new name would give the orchestra an added cachet, particularly in respect of attracting touring work, while Goold suggested that the prefix 'national' smacked of the parochial. Both failed to understand that in many Scottish eyes there was a particular pride attached to having a Scottish *National* Orchestra, and that the adjective was regarded as enhancing rather than belittling. Scottish Opera also considered applying for royal status, and its board rejected the idea on the grounds that the existing name had widespread popular appeal.

There is of course a very strong tradition of Scottish paranoia at work here, ever ready to expose examples of English insensitivity. Many Scots resent the way in which London is deemed the centre of any meaningful universe; the way locations are described as being in the north-east or south-west without any qualification that the author means 'of England'. They resented too the yelps of well-bred disapproval to Scottish accents on *The World at One* and *Woman's Hour*. Individually such minor blips are hardly worth recording, but collectively, and seen against a background where Scottish values may be at risk, they have helped to politicize many hitherto unflappable citizens.

Some suppose that Scotland's current preoccupation with its identity would come to a natural end if there was a Scottish parliament, for then, so the theory runs, the Scots will have nobody to blame but themselves. The election result in April 1992 suggested it would be some little time before that theory could be put to the test.

The role of language

Professor Sandy Fenton, director of the School of Scottish Studies in Edinburgh reviewed the first three parts of the *Dictionary of the Older Scottish Tongue* in 1966 with these words: 'Language and culture cannot, of course, be equated, but one is a clear index to the other . . .'

The renewed interest in the languages and dialects of Scotland since then underline the preoccupation Scots now have with defining their culture, protecting it, and looking to its future development. The decision of the Scottish Office to put £9 million into an exercise to reinvigorate Gaelic principally through the medium of television has had a profound impact not just on the perceived status of that language, but the aspirations of those who speak it. At the moment some 80 000 people are thought to be able to use Gaelic as a working language with an extended Gaelic community of perhaps 250 000 who have some understanding of the language. The last decade of the 20th century has witnessed some remarkable broadcasting phenomena, not least the sight on Scottish Television of peak-hour slots being devoted to Gaelic quiz shows and cookery classes. That station's current director of programmes, Alastair Moffat, is a lowland Scot raised within a few miles of the Border, who decided that the Gaelic strand in the Scottish culture was crucial to an appreciation of our heritage, and an important building block for our future. Now, having learned the language himself, he presides over a schedule for the 1990s for which 250 hundred hours of Gaelic programming are already in the pipeline. Neither are these esoteric late night offerings aimed only at Scots with an intellectual interest in the history of Gaelic culture; tomorrow's Gaelic programmes will be contemporary, concentrating on mass market concerns such as the fashion and rock industries, whilst still affording space to traditional music and song. A Gaelic soap opera is also being made although a painful illustration of previous neglect is the fact that the station found plenty of Scots actors who don't have the Gaelic and plenty of Gaelic speakers who can't act, but relatively few with a facility for both. Rhoda McLeod, the station's head of Gaelic programming maintains that the fact that this has been integrated into mainstream viewing has helped the general upsurge in interest which, she says, has caused many Gaelic language classes to be over-subscribed. Now Scottish itself plans an on-screen Gaelic class based on a similar series devised by the Welsh Gaelic language channel SC4, to be presented by Rhoda McLeod herself and backed up by other mixed media material including a magazine.

That interest is mirrored if not quite duplicated by BBC Scotland who were early pioneers of successful modern television programmes in Gaelic including an award winning television programme for toddlers—*Dotaman*—which is now in its eighth year. Ken McQuarrie, head of BBC's Gaelic television department, is convinced that cultural and economic self confidence go hand in hand and that the re-emergence of Gaelic is important across all political, social, linguistic and geographical divides in Scotland. 'The fact that we have material going out in Gaelic for young children for 25 minutes every day is particularly important in as much as it gives them an early appreciation—wherever they live in Scotland—that they live in a society with three living languages.' His schedules have also gone into mainstream subject matter with a series of investigative documentaries in Gaelic, and another tracing the involvement of Gaeldom with sea-based economies. BBC's Gaelic output on radio is broadcast on FM under its own banner—Radio Nan Gaidheal—a deliberate tactic says Neil Fraser, former head of Radio Scotland, to give it a particular identity. Fraser's problem was that whilst the frequency operation allows the north and west of Scotland to enjoy 30 hours of Gaelic programming every week, it has only been possible to broadcast just over seven elsewhere, although 40 per cent of Gaelic speakers are in the central and southern catchment area. However those living west of a rough diagonal line from Elgin to Oban, but including Kintyre and Islay, will benefit from the split-off of Gaelic into another FM network served by an additional transmitter which allows the Gaelic service more room for expansion.

Whilst none of these programmes could hope to attract the mass audiences of a soap opera in English, there have been good responses from people not themselves part of the Gaelic tradition. Roderick MacKinnon's *Teach Yourself Gaelic* has gone through 17 reprints since it was part of the material for a televised course in the language in the early seventies and Gaelic music programmes have recorded viewing figures far in excess of the number of Gaelic speakers in Scotland. In a paper they prepared for the Scottish Arts Council's Charter for The Arts, Dr John Bryden and Dr Niall Mackinnon echo Ken McQuarrie's argument that these efforts to nourish and encourage the Gaelic tongue are crucial to the retention of Scottish culture as a whole: 'Many of the symbols of Scottish identity are drawn from the cultural resources of the Gaelic speech community, and although transformed and attenuated, have been adopted as key cultural markers of Scottish national identity by non-Gaelic Scots.'

They argue that the increased wearing of the kilt and interest in piping, however much they distort the origins they claim to celebrate, have become potent global symbols when adopted as commercial aids by Scots-based concerns. Others are less happy about the attachment of Scots to 'highland' dress, which is currently enjoying a social revival not least among the young, and are appalled at the vast quantities of kitsch. Yet Scottish football fans happily sport the tartan, fly the flag, and favour Scottish regalia abroad and in England that they would not wear at home.

More recently the phenomenal success of Gaelic rock bands such as Runrig has shown it is possible to marry tradition to popular entertainment in a way which has validity for all age groups. Runrig have become more than a symbol of the saving of Gaelic; their music has touched a chord in a nation looking for a new sense of itself. In 1991, in Edinburgh Castle, the band gave one of many sellout concerts. Hundreds who failed to get tickets gathered to listen in nearby Johnstone Terrace. As this group of young Gaels sang one of its many improbable anthems, a new arrangement of *Loch Lomond*, a small army of standing and excluded fans danced and sang, waving Scottish flags. Runrig has breached the Scottish north–south divide and its success has been built on a musical repertoire whose lyrics articulate its social concerns and celebrate its Scottishness. It is a band for a particular time and mood in Scotland. Its lead singer, Donnie Munro, now rector of Edinburgh University, has described the heartbeat of his band as 'the power and strength' of the Gaelic culture. But he wants the contribution of contemporary music to be determinedly forward looking: 'to create in new ways but with old passions; to get out from the gloomy shadows of the National Mod [the annual Gaelic festival]'.

It is now the Scots language which feels the poor relation in terms of linguistic renaissance. Scots, initially the northern branch of Anglo Saxon, has roots in the south of Scotland which stretch back to the seventh century. Five centuries later it began to replace Gaelic in the west and north. By the early 15th century it was the language automatically used to record Acts of Parliament in Scotland and had replaced Latin as the main literary and documentary language, although it was not given the name Scots until the end of that century. There are those who question its legitimacy as a language at all, considering it, at best, to be a loose federation of local dialects. That is a view robustly rejected by people like Billy Kay, the author and broadcaster, whose programmes and publications on The Mither Tongue have contributed to an upsurge of interest in Scottish words. It is Kay's contention that the failure to think of Scots automatically as a separate language like Gaelic is part of the reason for its decline, and explains why its recent popularity has not attracted the same funding and commitment as Gaelic. There are other reasons for the decline which have similarities with the Gaelic: Scots came to be viewed as a lower-class form of expression which would inhibit progress. And, as with Gaelic, children were routinely punished and ridiculed in school for using the speech they had learned at their mothers' knee. The hostility to spoken Scots, and indeed to English spoken with a discernibly Scots accent, was until recently quite widespread. Within the last few years outraged listeners to Radio 4 were inveighing against a continuity announcer and the presenter of the flagship *The World At One* addressing them in their native Scots accents. And more recently the Royal Scottish Academy of Music and Drama became embroiled in a row because some of its Scots students either couldn't or wouldn't accept a departmental demand to speak in 'received pronunciation'. The 'snob factor' should not be underestimated. The translation of the New Testament from Greek into Scots by the renowned classical scholar William Laughton Lorimer contains a foreword by his son Robin, who completed the work after his father's death. He recalls the paradox of his father's childhood which combined a thirst for linguistic knowledge with a contempt for the local tongue: 'When he was only nine years old, he responded to his mother's conflicting requirements that her children must all endeavour to learn as many languages as possible, but must not themselves speak Scotch, by beginning to keep a notebook in which he wrote down Scots words and phrases.' Robin Lorimer added: 'Although my father subsequently lost the notebook in which he recorded idiomatic Scots, he never forgot how much it differed from English spoken with a Scots accent.' Although the Scots language of Billy Kay's own native Ayrshire might offer a different vocabulary to that of a Scots speaker from Buchan, the differences, he believes, are merely those which evolved as descriptive terms for particular local customs or objects. Once your ear is in he suggests, Scots speakers from any Scottish region can perfectly well understand others from a different area because they are basically speaking a common language.

Sandy Fenton of the School of Scottish Studies looks at Scots from a slightly different perspective claiming that 'Lallans' was an artificial creation which attempted to create a national language by marrying different dialects, while Scots is essentially the language of the lowlander, derived from northern Anglo Saxon. Anglicization also badly affected Scots, says Fenton, so that by the 18th century very little written Scots remained outside personal diaries except the occasional legal text and some popular heroic and comic poems. These in turn led to the revival of Scots writing which was more colloquial 'with less of the formal style Scots had been capable of as a national language'. Spoken Scots survived longer, despite the growing influence of English literature, and increased contacts between Scotland and England. The Union produced a widespread use of standard English, as indeed did the Reformation and the import of prayer books and forms in English.

Yet the rearguard action which has been fought in the 20th century, particularly in the publication of reference and dictionary works, has been nothing short of heroic. The demand has been routinely underestimated by publishers who thought they would have only esoteric appeal. Warrack's *Scots Dialect Dictionary* 1911 was an early success and went into several reprints, and the 10-volume *Scottish National Dictionary*, 1929 dealing with modern Scots, represents a quite phenomenal commitment on the part of the editors and their dedicated band of supporters as does the more recent *Concise Scots Dictionary* 1985, which has since been followed by *The Scots Thesaurus* 1991. Still under construction are the final parts of the *Dictionary of the Older Scottish Tongue* 1937 with seven volumes already in print and which started publication over 50 years ago. Work on the final three has been consistently hampered by lack of funds. The Scottish Office Education Department was finally prevailed upon in 1991 to make a contribution of £18 000, a welcome input of course, but a tiny fraction of the £9 million pumped into Gaelic. The interest of the public in these literary celebrations of the Scots tongue has been remarkable, with books such as the *Concise Scots Dictionary* becoming instant successes. But the acid test of a living language of course lies in its commonplace usage. Billy Kay surmises that in present-day Scotland the vocabulary in Scots is wide and only a change in attitude towards Scots is required. He is confident that were Scots formally acknowledged as a separate language we would rapidly become, if not fluent Scots speakers, instinctively bilingual again. Scots, he argues, has actually fewer barriers to overcome given that most Scots people know a range of Scots words whereas few outside Gaeldom have even the most basic Gaelic vocabulary.

A J Aitken, in his introduction to the *Concise Scots Dictionary*, admits that since the law, the church, and the education system all use standard English 'it may therefore be reasonably asked if there is any sense in which Scots is entitled to the designation of a language any more than any of the regional dialects of English in England'. That question has been preoccupying Scots for three centuries, but he concludes that Scots possesses several attributes which raise it above dialect status. First he says it is more radically different from standard English than any English dialect is; it boasts a far wider vocabulary, and many of its pronunciations are 'strikingly different'. And although Scots shares some words with northern English dialects, 'easily the most definite dialects-boundary in the English speaking world is the Scottish English border'. In his conclusions he seems to harbour no doubts as to the status of Scots: 'The unique characteristics of Scots, its linguistic distinctiveness, its occupation of its own dialect island bounded by the border, its individual history, its own dialect variation, its varied use in a remarkable literature, the ancient loyalty of Scottish people to the notion of the Scots language, as well as the fact that since the 16th century Scots has adopted the nation's name, all of these are attributes of a language rather than a dialect.'

There is a widespread view that the Europeanization of the UK, will, paradoxically, benefit the case for full recognition of Scots. There already exists an EC bureau devoted to the protection and propagation of lesser-used languages which represents over 30 different communities and some 40 million electors. The very fact that children in Scotland at the end of the 20th century should still be found throughout the country speaking in distinctive dialects is some indication of the staying power of Scots. In the sheer breadth and variety of the vocabulary too there is a richness of expression and a considerable body of indigenous literature. There are now signs that the resurgence in Scots is not confined to academic institutions. An appeal launched for a new Scots Language Resource Centre in Perth was pitched at all those concerned with the need to preserve a distinctively Scottish manner of everyday speech. A fund has also been launched by the School of Scottish Studies to establish a research fellowship aimed at having young postgraduates spend two years at a time compiling handbooks on major themes of Scottish life. Earlier this year, a campaign was launched in Grampian Region to encourage Scots schoolchildren to be proud of the fact that the Doric essentially and naturally made them bilingual. Meanwhile the next project of the Scottish National Dictionary Association is a Scottish/English dictionary. That it will enjoy healthy sales north of the border is no longer in much doubt.

The impact of literature

Just as with the Scots tongue, rumours of the passing of Scots literature have often proved exaggerated. Cairns Craig, editor of the fourth volume of *The History of Scottish Literature*, reminds us that T S Eliot wrote in 1919: 'Was there a Scottish Literature'? As the Union of 1707 shifted the political emphasis southwards, so Scottish writing suffered from periodic bouts of introspective angst from the early 17th century onwards. But by the time T S Eliot's dismissive review appeared and Scottish publishing was at a low ebb, what came to be known as the Scottish Literary Renaissance of the 1920s was already under way, encouraged in part by the renewed vigour of Irish writing. However, the Scottish universities—which might in other societies have provided the creative heart of indigenous writing—only established departments concentrating on Scottish studies almost 20 years after World War II. The effect of this is depressingly apparent in the sketchy knowledge of most educated adult Scots concerning any Scottish writing beyond Burns and Scott. That indifference to our literary heritage has a long and ignoble tradition. In the 1920s, Hugh MacDiarmid—Christopher Grieve as he then was—wrote that 'Scottish literary criticism, as distinct from British (which really means English), scarcely exists at all'. Yet it is difficult to think of any other part of the English-speaking world which could offer scholars a richer variety than Scottish literature in terms of both quality and antiquity. The traditions on which modern Scots writers can draw include work in several distinctive dialect schools like that of the north-east Buchan countryside as well as in Scots, Gaelic and English.

Despite the lack of academic attention, Scottish writing this century has flourished. Cairns Craig suggests that we are caught between two cultures and this has proved a curious source of inspiration: the 'apparent lack of a coherent tradition, the lack of a coherent national culture, far from impeding development, have been major stimuli to creativity'. Scottish literature is part of the search for a new political identity, and after the failure of the 1979 referendum on a Scottish assembly, the relative apathy of the electorate was reflected in a further bout of soul searching in the literary community. One of the continuing inspirations, even during periods of political or social stagnation, has been Scotland's continuing relationship with European cultures, which has prevented Scottish writing from vanishing into English or US literary genres. However, a period of intense intellectual activity and creativity like the Scottish Enlightenment did not imbue the country with a sense of its national self because internationalism predominated. Neither has Scottish literature been immune from agonized debates over the significance of language, or the selection of source material. Muriel Spark, only one of whose novels is set in Scotland, is rarely thought of as a Scottish novelist. Allan Massie's considerable reputation has only the most peripheral connection with the fact that he lives and writes in the Scottish Borders. Other Scottish novelists make language central to their writing: James Kelman by writing in the first person and the Glaswegian vernacular, Alasdair Gray in modern classics such as *Lanark* by the inclusion of fantastical episodes and William McIlvanney by a highly individual tone of voice. MacDiarmid, in his early writing, thought it more likely that Scottish writers of significance would adopt standard English in order to give greater access to their work, and, rather more controversially, because 'the English language is an immensely superior medium of expression'. He was not suggesting that Scots writers attach themselves to the traditions of English literature, merely that what he then called the Doric was too limited. Even when he became wholly converted to the cause of reviving what he described as 'the vernacular', (and what others insisted was synthetic Scots), he warned enthusiasts: 'whatever the potentialities of the Doric may be, however, there cannot be a revival in the real sense of the word unless these potentialities are in accord with the newest and truest tendencies of human thought . . . If all that the movement is to achieve is to preserve specimens of Braid Scots, archaic, imitative, belonging to a type of life that has passed and cannot return, in a sort of museum department of our consciousness—set apart from our vital preoccupations—it is a movement which not only cannot claim our support, but compels our opposition.' But the more he wrote in Scots, and the more words he sought and uncovered, the more versatile MacDiarmid found that expanding vocabulary. Finally he came to the conclusion that Scots rather than English would be the linguistic engine driving a literary revival in Scotland. It was a language which catered for attitudes and observations which were radically different from English or anglicized perspectives. And, having once supposed it a limited tongue, he now credited it with more subtlety of expression: 'another feature of the Doric is the fashion in which diverse attitudes of mind or shades of temper are telescoped into single words or phrases, investing the whole speech with subtle flavours of irony, commiseration, realism and humour which cannot be reproduced in English. In onomatopoeic effect, too, the Doric has a wider range and infinitely richer resources than English.' By this time MacDiarmid thought of Scots as a living, growing language.

Location has also proved a potent source of inspiration for Scots writers, such as George Mackay Brown who writes as a native of Orkney. In contrast, the multifaceted Iain Crichton Smith left his native Lewis but remained ever conscious of the separation from his roots. The vibrant poetry of Norman MacCaig evokes many parts of Scotland, notably Edinburgh and Sutherland, whose backdrops have dominated his work for many years. Similarly Carradale on the mull of Kintyre proved the inspiration for the less well-known poetic works of novelist Naomi Mitchison, and acts for her, suggests Joy Hendry, editor of the Scottish literary magazine *Chapman*, as a microcosm of Scotland as a whole.

Whilst Scottish literature may have been undervalued from time to time, women's writing has been particularly invisible so far as the wider critical world has been concerned. This is especially true of poetry, Hendry says, whilst in fiction, apart from Spark and Mitchison, only Joan Lingard, Jessie Kesson, Janice Galloway and Elspeth Davie have attracted critical attention.

Poetry is the healthiest vein running through contemporary Scottish culture at the end of the 20th century, and not just because of major figures such as Sorley Maclean, whose bilingual anthologies have brought him richly deserved renown, Edwin Morgan, and Douglas Dunn. Younger talents such as Robert Crawford and Tom Powe have been widely noticed whilst the sharply observed social commentary of Liz Lochhead shows the vigour of younger female writing.

Whether the energy which infuses these talents is a reflection of a growing confidence in the existence of a distinctive Scottish culture and identity, or whether their work, conversely, is one of the elements which has helped to build that confidence is a matter for debate. Certainly an increasing number of young writers are finding inspiration and creativity from making the conscious decision to work from a Scottish base. Many of them have become engaged in the wider debates which have so enlivened the Scottish scene. One example was the long-running argument which surrounded the successful application by Glasgow to become Cultural Capital of Europe during 1990. Attitudes to this initiative polarized between those who thought that arts-based tourism was an important part of that city's future and a healthy way of attracting inward investment and relocated jobs, and those who thought Glasgow's social and socialist history were being sanitized and hijacked by 'cultural cowboys'. Alasdair Gray and Jim Kelman both opposed the 1990 celebrations, considering them an irrelevance to Glasgow's social problems. Yet other writers saw that year as a watershed, not just for Glasgow, but for Scotland. Before the 1992 election, Liz Lochhead, James Kelman, and the Gaelic poet Aonghas MacNeacail felt able to add their signatures to a group styling itself Artists for Independence.

The Scottish theatre

For much of its post-war existence the theatre in Scotland has agonized over the desirability of a national theatre company. Some people feel that another attempt to create such a body, whether or not with a specific theatrical base, would provide a valuable focus for Scottish writing and a seductive lure for some émigré Scottish talents. Others feel that the preoccupation with pursuing this Holy Grail has diverted too much attention already from existing companies. The company assembled by Tyrone Guthrie in 1948 for the first revival of Sir David Lindsay's *Ane Satyre of The Thrie Estates* was felt by many people to be the obvious basis for a national theatre, although it had come together specifically for the Edinburgh Festival. The Scottish National Players in the 1920s had had similar ambitions, as did James Bridie when he founded the Glasgow Citizens' company just before the end of World War II. The Lyceum in Edinburgh in the 1970s with Bill Bryden as artistic director acted in some senses as an unnofficial national theatre employing the services of some major Scottish talents such as Roddy MacMillan and Fulton Mackay. And with plays such as Bryden's own *Willie Rough*, set in the shipyards and MacMillan's *The Bevellers*, there was a genuine excitement not just about the ability to assemble and keep such indigenous acting talent, but about their performing work which addressed itself, albeit retrospectively, to Scottish social and political issues.

It was the Scottish Arts Council (SAC) which came up with the notion that one of the smaller Scottish theatres should become a specific home for Scottish drama. That was greeted more enthusiastically in the SAC's Edinburgh think tank than by the Perth citizenry, although it did lead, inadvertently, to a rich seam being mined in Perth theatre by the innovative Joan Knight. By far the most structured attempt to create and sustain a Scottish repertory company which would form the genesis of a national theatre began in 1981 with the formation of the Scottish Theatre Company, initially under the direction of Ewan Hooper, and latterly under Tom Fleming. Hooper's initial agenda was to produce new Scots plays, and to revive some neglected older ones. He also announced his intention of producing Scottish versions of European classics, a prospect viewed with some scepticism by *The Scotsman*'s arts editor Allen Wright: 'The package sounds promising,' he wrote at the time, 'as long as it does not rely too heavily on our playwrights' penchant for plucking great plays out of their original settings, and planting them in Scotland. From Aristophanes to Goldoni, and from Molière to Ibsen, the dramatists of the world have been subjected to this treatment which has only worked when the adaptation has matched the qualities possessed by certain actors—like Russell Hunter as *The Servant of Twa Maisters* and Duncan Macrae as *The Laird O'Grippy*.'

Wright believed few people understood that to project what he termed 'the spirit of the nation', it was not necessary to have 'tartan trappings . . . Most of our playwrights and their producers seem to be more concerned with manners of speech or historical traditions, than with the particular tensions within Scottish society.' In the event, the first full season of the new company produced a varied repertoire, the major success of which was a Scots translation of a European classic; Robert Kemp's *Let Wives Tak Tent* based on Molière's *L'Ecole des Femmes* starred Rikki Fulton whose own drawing power might have been largely responsible for its success. Less healthy were the company's other offerings in year one. A revival of Tom McGrath's *Animals* which had enjoyed great success at The Traverse played to poor houses despite being judged a critical success. An adaption of *Ghosts* found the audience rattling round Glasgow's Theatre Royal, and the much fancied *Civilians* written by Bill Bryden and starring Fulton Mackay and John Grieve, failed to fill the modest seating capacity of the Eden Court in Inverness. After its second season there were real fears that the fledgling venture would go under, despite a memorable revival by Tom Fleming of Robert McLellan's *Jamie the Saxt* which proved, among other things, that there were still plenty of actors around who could use the Scottish language vividly. Ewan Hooper, founder and chief inspiration, left the company in 1982 and Tom Fleming took over. It survived for another five years and the review committee appointed by the Scottish Arts Council concluded that its demise was occasioned by three main factors: consistent underfunding, leading in turn to a presence which became increasingly seasonal, and the lack of 'an adequate permanent space'. The Scottish public got one last glimpse of what might have been in the 1991 festival when, to fill a last minute gap in the programme for the Assembly Hall, the Scottish Theatre Company was hastily reassembled by Fleming to stage their revival of *The Thrie Estates* with which they had enjoyed such critical success not just in Scotland but, memorably, as the guests of a Polish festival five years before.

The demise of the Scottish Theatre Company in 1987 meant the loss of the sole national organization which had a mission to provide opportunities for Scottish actors and Scottish playwrights although companies such as Theatre Alba continue to present work performed in Scots and more radical spirits such as Communicado, Wildcat, and 7:84 regularly address Scottish issues. The Traverse continues to commission work from Scots-based playwrights like John Clifford and a new company, the Fifth Estate, based at Edinburgh's Netherbow Theatre, has made a considerable impact.

Yet there is something of a vacuum at the centre of Scottish drama. The drama department of the Scottish Arts Council took stock of the situation in an outline discussion paper prepared for the Charter for The Arts in Scotland discussions in 1991. They acknowledged the funding problems produced by a situation where 85 per cent of the SAC's drama budget was committed to revenue clients, leaving project-funded companies particularly vulnerable. Their analysis suggested that Scotland's nine permanent repertory companies and 30 non-producing theatres and arts centres have contributed to an 'increasing confidence in Scottish theatre practice which can be seen in the number of recent plays which have looked sharply at Scottish life and character, and in the vigorous reassertion of a Scottish acting tradition'.

In contrast, many younger playwrights feel their attempts to write work reflective of political and social undercurrents in contemporary Scotland go unheralded and unstaged unless they attract the attention of London-based directors. This indifference is particularly galling in a small country where some of the potential outlets for Scots writing, such as the Pitlochry Festival Theatre, have, until now, stuck doggedly to standard risk-free fare in order to maximize their audiences. Pitlochry's contribution from the Arts Council has now been made contingent on its staging one new work per season.

The frustrations of wanting to write in your own country and of your own country without adequate shop windows for your work is obviously painful. But perhaps, for Scots, it's not new. The journalist Jack House, witnessing the critical furore which greeted that first revival of *The Thrie Estates* in 1948, had his own explanation: 'It is difficult to say who were the most astonished—the Scots who thought nothing good could be done by people they knew personally, or the London critics who thought nothing good could be done by people they didn't know personally.'

'The Citz'

The theatre which commands the most international respect in Scotland, and perhaps in Britain, could not accurately be described as a Scottish Theatre; rather a theatre which is located in Scotland.

The Citizens theatre in the Gorbals area of Glasgow, 'The Citz' to its many admirers, has gained a considerable reputation over the last two decades. Its prestige has been won by rooting itself firmly and deliberately in a European tradition making only occasional, and even token forays into indigenous drama. The triumvirate who have fashioned this dramatic phenomenon celebrated 21 years of collaboration in the autumn of 1990, when Glasgow was European Capital of Culture. They saw their role in this celebration as providing typically Citizens rather than typically Glaswegian fare, and two of their most lauded productions were Pirandello's *Enrico Four* (minus the advertised Richard Harris, who pulled out), and a new production of *Mother Courage* with Glenda Jackson. Jackson is one of many who have a particular rapport with this company and the philosphy of artistic director Giles Havergal, and his long serving partners Philip Prowse and Robert David MacDonald. 'I admire the theatre's profound internationalism,' she says, 'its unique social policy, and not least the fact that it all happens in Glasgow. It's a very special theatre in a very special city.'

Some of the things which make that theatre special are small but significant, like the manner in which the programme notes are traditionally assembled with the Citizens' entire company credited in alphabetical order. If the bar staff in the weeks of Jackson's performances have surnames beginning with the letters A to I then they are listed before she is.

When the Citizens was remodelled the auditorium was revamped in traditional gilt-edged style. In startling contrast the new foyer and bar area were fashioned in high-tech metal and glass. The frontage of the upstairs bar looks on to an uncompromising block of high-rise flats. Havergal wanted it that way, so that the theatre would remember what it was about, and who it represented. Further redesign has created two small auditoria in addition to the main theatre. Its social policy includes a long-term commitment to offering the cheapest seats compatible with balancing the books and a range of concessions. That commitment not only makes the Citizens accessible for wage earners since the standard seat price is £5, but it also offers free seating to pensioners and the unemployed on the door, and, uniquely, in advance. In addition university and school students pay just £1. Yet despite this, the company has a hard-won reputation for fiscal prudence. Every department from carpentry to publicity has to make a solid case for even modest expenditure. The bonus for keeping an assiduous eye on the budget has been that both the district and regional authorities, and individual sponsors, know that an investment in the Citz will be properly utilized. The local authorities too have been impressed by the efforts made to integrate the company with the community. The Theatre Around Glasgow company, now virtually autonomous, but begun under the auspices of the Citizens, was one of the earliest theatre education projects and Havergal protected it and guaranteed its survival even during periods of unforeseen calamities. What the Citizens has come to stand for above all else is quality, of a kind not always appreciated on its own patch. Scottish critics are no longer outraged as they were at the beginning of Havergal's reign when he staged an all-male *Hamlet* in which black G strings featured prominently. But neither do they always give it the acclaim won elsewhere in Europe. Michael Coveney, the theatre critic of *The Guardian* wrote a history of the Citizens in celebration of Havergal's 21-year tenure in 1990. He says: 'Local commentators . . . are still liable to under-rate The Citizens perhaps because, while aware of the great civic struggle that has been endured, they do not see how brilliantly the Citizens has prospered in this respect through a combination of high cunning and tactical nous compared with other theatres in Britain. There is also a pervasive reluctance to admit that there is anything special about the Citizens, and all the more so if London critics keep saying there is.'

It is a steadfast principle at the Citz that it is never regarded, most certainly not by its core directors and designers, as a launch pad for something better elsewhere. The excellence they strive for, they believe, makes the Citizens a desirable destination in its own right. Many fine actors, some of them nurtured there, unhesitatingly agree. And although Philip Prowse, in particular, is much in demand as a guest director in London, the roots of his creativity, and his unquestioning commitment lie in the company. Sian Thomas who went on to work at the RSC and the National following her spell at the Citizens, told Michael Coveney that the atmosphere was at once intoxicating and frightening and suggested that it was 'the mood of sexuality that hovers in the air that makes you feel, as an actor, that you are in Europe, not in England or even Scotland'. In contrast David Hayman, who starred as that early Hamlet and also directed at the Citz before embarking on his screen career and taking over the Scottish 7:84 company, has the perspective of a locally born Scot who, for 10 years, acted with this exotic company: the perspective too of a man whose early directorial success (with John Byrne's *Slab Boys*) was actually at the Traverse in Edinburgh. Hayman feels that the Traverse, the Lyceum in Edinburgh, and the much acclaimed Communicado company all owe artistic debts to the Havergal/Prowse/MacDonald presence. Hayman was one of many young actors nurtured by the Citizens into subsequent star status. But the theatre also attracts established performers, and the production of *The Vortex* with Maria Aitken and Rupert Everett, which went on to London, combined sumptuous design with imported actors willingly immersed in the Citizens' style.

There are those who think that the Citizens itself owes a debt that has not been fully acknowledged. Although the last 22 years have seen it win recognition

159

for itself, and, vicariously, for the city and the region in which it operates, some argue it has jettisoned the heritage left by its founding father, the playwright James Bridie. Bridie saw the Citizens' company which he formed in 1943 as the nucleus of a Scottish National Theatre. The name came from an earlier venture in the city, the Glasgow Rep, which had been formed before World War I. The Rep's clarion call was bold: 'The repertory theatre is Glasgow's own theatre. It is a citizens' theatre in the fullest sense of the term. Established to make Glasgow independent of London for its dramatic supplies, it produces plays which the Glasgow playgoers would otherwise not have an opportunity of seeing.' Boldness did not make for longevity, and it was followed just four years later by the Scottish National Players. By the time Bridie's initiative came along a third company, Glasgow Unity, was reaching the end of its lifespan, and many of its actors were attracted to a formula which mixed the classics with a steady diet of new Scottish plays. Havergal set his face against that legacy when he arrived in 1970, forming a company which was young and overwhelmingly English. Michael Coveney notes: 'Today the Citizens has renounced Scottishness, but renounced Englishness too. A swaggering cultural crusade was designed to knock an audience out of its sense of composure, and into a forbidden garden of sensual, aesthetic, intellectual and moral riot.'

Not the perfect location for a Bridie revival during the 1990 celebrations, which many Scottish critics urged on Havergal. In rejecting what he would undoubtedly have seen as inappropriate tokenism, Giles Havergal stayed true to what has become a second Citizens' tradition, a tradition in which the company has gone on a voyage of exploration through some of the more esoteric corners of European writing, whilst balancing the books by including in the repertoire some extravagantly staged restoration comedies and a regular sprinkling of British and European classics. It has chosen to exclude itself from the debate about the role of the Scottish theatre in defining Scottish identity. But in the quality, and scope of its work, in its commitment to risk and its long standing flirtation with outrage, it has brought to Scottish theatre significant respect.

The Traverse

The Traverse Theatre has now moved to its third home in Edinburgh, yet artistically it shows no signs of abandoning the attachment to innovation and adventure which was the hallmark of its Lawnmarket birth in 1963.

The original premises had served variously as a roof for down-and-outs, and a brothel. Created from an apartment, the stage area was just 15 feet wide with a low ceiling which doubled as the floor of the cafe bar overhead. Its early years were a triumph of determination over environment.

Not that the early patrons—a capacity house was 60—resented the dimensions. That claustrophobia, later duplicated in the smallest auditorium of its second home in the Grassmarket, was used by successive directors as an atmospheric aid. As theatre critic Joyce McMillan notes in her history of the first 25 years, the Traverse was born because there came together a critical mass of people who wanted it to happen. Jim Haynes, an American who had begun Edinburgh's first and prodigiously successful paperback bookshop, and the arts impresario Richard Demarco, then a humble art teacher, saw it as both an extension to their rumbustious social life, and an antidote to the bungalow mentality which triumphed in Edinburgh for those weeks when the Festival was absent. Tom Mitchell, the self-styled Cumbrian 'designer' and the publisher John Calder were also present, as were friends of theirs including Sheila Colvin, now director of the Aldeburgh Festival, but formerly associate director of the Edinburgh Festival and the Traverse's first honorary secretary.

Although the Traverse's international reputation rests with its tireless commitment to new work, that first season under Terry Lane concentrated on already well-respected material, albeit little known in a British context. With eight British and one world premiere it was a daunting challenge, or, as one critic put it rather more succinctly 'suicidally ambitious'—a phrase which might equally well serve as a description of the rest of the Traverse's life. But the Traverse is still very much alive, and still kicking against the traces of conformity.

It has undergone several changes of style and approach as each artistic director has imposed a different presence, some exiting with noises off. The departure of the first incumbent, Terry Lane, now the proprietor of an extremely good bookshop, was of the more acrimonious variety, just one year into the the new venture. Filling the gap before Jim Haynes became artistic director was the much respected actor/director Callum Mill. By 1966 Haynes too was gone, his own committee having fallen out with the venture's inspirational co-founder. Problems included the appointment of a controversial deputy, a lack of information about budgets and forward planning and, crucially, a feeling that in his emphasis on importing luminaries from the London scene Haynes was perpetuating one of the prejudices the Traverse set out to dismantle: that a theatrical product could not be a dramatic and critical success without metropolitan connections. 'The Traverse isn't in Scotland it's in the world', was Haynes's battle cry. Few quibbled with determination to make a mark internationally. But many of the Traverse's early adherents wanted internationalism observed through Scottish eyes and often with a Scottish accent. Like so many Scottish theatrical ventures, the Traverse had to locate its work in a context which made it more than a peripheral contribution to the British theatrical tradition. The Haynes era was notable for the quality of unpredictable excitement which characterized his entire lifestyle. As former *Scotsman* critic Ronald Mavor, later of the Scottish Arts Council, once memorably observed: 'A great feature of those days was Jim, everybody's easy friend, and always on the verge of getting Orson Welles to play King Lear with music by either Lionel Bart or Stravinsky on a cart in James Court. Jim's greatest gift was to believe anything possible and, by gentle enthusiasm, to keep everybody's daft notions alive until as often as not, they took shape. Everybody went to the Traverse, and Jim would introduce you to Timothy Leary, the Lord Provost, and a man who was growing blue carrots in the interval between acts.'

There was little doubt about the quality of most of the work successive directors brought first to James Close in the Lawnmarket and subsequently to the Grassmarket home it has left in a controversial move to a purpose-built theatre within the office and hotel complex behind the Usher Hall. Gordon McDougall succeeded Haynes and his early work there was generally thought to err on the side of security. But then came a period where the more conventional McDougall worked in partnership with the resolutely risk-taking Max Stafford Clark, and, in tandem with Stafford Clark, became responsible for a period of controversial work, the sexual content and design of much of which worried the more staid leader writers. Whatever else the Traverse might have become in the late sixties, anonymity was thereafter not an option. When McDougall left to go into television, Max Stafford Clark began a new era with the emphasis still firmly on the experimental. Part of that policy involved a workshop company, the artistic director having told his committee that the Traverse had to stay at the cutting edge. His aim was to maintain an avant-garde theatre in Edinburgh, not just a small theatre with a new play policy. That commitment attracted some fine actors to the core company, and put the Traverse firmly on the international map. But Stafford Clark's programme attracted a mixed reaction from the critics, and also from within the Traverse itself. Rosalind Clark, who was involved at the same time in the Children's Theatre Workshop, was among many voices raised in favour of work which would be more generally accessible. However, in the midst of this controversy the James Court building was pronounced unsafe for further use, and the hunt for new premises became a more pressing concern. The building selected, in West Bow on the edge of the Grassmarket, needed extensive renovation, work which was only completed, and a building inspection carried out, less than an hour before the official opening by Arts Minister Jennie Lee. Stafford Clark remained throughout that removal, physically helping to shape the new theatre, and presented an autumn programme before resigning in December 1969, to the regret of those who admired his receptiveness to new ideas, and the relief of those who wondered if the Traverse could afford them.

Michael Rudman was the next occupant of one of the contemporary theatre's increasingly hot seats. Rudman, while continuing to ensure more than half of his schedule involved British or world premieres, was careful to tailor that schedule to cater for a variety of dramatic tastes. He also pioneered the famous Traverse Trials in which ambitious young lawyers such as John Smith and Malcolm Rifkind could hone their debating skills. What he did not do, however, was recognize the specifically Scottish dimension of the theatre, even when the occasional Scottish work evoked an enthusiastic response. But he left the Traverse not only in a healthy situation but with a financial surplus.

In 1973 Mike Ockrent took over, an Edinburgh graduate with a dramatic pedigree which included working with Joan Knight at Perth Theatre. Ockrent's remit was to shift the balance from British to international work, and to place more emphasis on design. While his two-year tenure found room for a more European programme, non-established playwrights in search of a stage had a fairly thin time of it. Ockrent's period also coincided with a particularly frutiful period at the neighbouring Lyceum, where Bill Bryden was producing some radical Scottish work.

In 1975 Ockrent was followed by Chris Parr who determined that the Traverse too would present more new Scottish work. His policy may have reflected the political mood of that moment, when the rise of the nationalist tide and the run-up to the Devolution referendum of 1979 both emphasized a new cultural identity. At this period, thanks to the generosity of outgoing chairman Lord Rosebery, the Traverse became the owner of its own site, a move which allowed expansion. Parr's decision to include much new Scottish writing led to plays by Hector MacMillan, Tom Gallacher, George Byatt and Tom McGrath. The latter's *The Hardman* written with Jimmy Boyle, was a major success as was John Byrne's *Slab Boys* trilogy directed by David Hayman. Parr left in 1981 falling out with his committee partly over the endlessly running sore of funding, and partly because he seemed relatively indifferent to raising the theatre's profile during the Festival.

After Parr came Peter Lichtenfels, who beat off an astonishing 81 candidates for a job which had not led hitherto to long-term employment, at least not at the Traverse. Lichtenfels shared the committee's view that the Festival afforded a very particular shop window for the work of the Traverse which was important not just in terms of international reputation, but as a means of continuing to attract funding and sponsorship. That year the productions, including *Trafford Tanzi*, helped gain Lichtenfels Festival audiences of over 90 per cent, a success he followed up in 1982 with the much acclaimed *Woza Albert* and Liz Lochhead's *Blood and Ice*. By 1984 his festival programme ran to 13 shows, seven of them Traverse productions, and almost 200 performances, and the programme itself won a special Fringe First award.

One of the young directors who came to work with Lichtenfels in the early 1980s was Jenny Killick, then just in her early twenties. Her own impressive work with new young writers culminated in collaborating with him and by 1985 the duo enjoyed considerable critical success including John Clifford's extraordinary *Losing Venice*. She took over as the theatre's first woman artistic director later that year. Jenny Killick's period continued the commitment to new writing, and to the international scene. But she found the adminstrative demands of the job increasingly interfering with her development as a director, and despite having built a considerable reputation, left to go south to take a course in television direction.

By then the theatre had voluntarily shed its club status in response to the suggestions of the Labour district council. So it was into a rather different atmosphere that Ian Brown arrived from his directorship of the Glasgow Citizen's exciting Theatre About Glasgow Group in October of that silver jubilee year. Public access gave an opportunity which matched Brown's enthusiasm for making drama accessible. Already with TAG and productions such as *Great Expectations* he had explored the possibilities inherent in cross-fertilizing drama, music and dance, and he repeated that formula in staging work such as the much acclaimed *Bondagers*. Brown is also committed to expanding the company's European horizons, preferably in tandem with like-minded companies. And so, in 1993, there will be a co-production with a Parisian theatre group which also has a considerable reputation for staging new work. The play will premiere at the Traverse before going to France. For the next collaboration, that chronology will be reversed. Thus, as the Traverse enters its third decade, and its third home, it continues to be predictable only in attempting the unexpected.

The Edinburgh Festival

The ravages of World War II were only two years behind them when the Edinburgh Festival was launched in 1947 by a group including local politicians and the Festival's first director Sir Rudolf Bing. They were clear from the outset that the event would never be labelled parochial. It would celebrate the arts in Scotland, and it would also bring to Scotland the most prestigious possible productions from abroad. What they sought, in the words of the founding document, was a festival which would 'enrich the cultural life of Europe, Britain and Scotland and provide a period of flowering of the human spirit'.

In the 45 years since that ringing declaration of intent there have been many glorious opportunities for such a flowering. No major orchestral talent is missing from the roll of Edinburgh Festival honours and many major soloists and conductors made debuts in the 'Athens of the North'. The great stars of drama and opera have all appeared at Edinburgh and over the years successive directors have brought differing personal strengths to the three-week programme, and stamped their personalities on the occasion.

The Earl of Harewood, Peter Diamand, John Drummond, Frank Dunlop and now Brian McMaster have all in turn been charged with fulfilling the annual and daunting requirement to ensure that Edinburgh remains the world's premiere festival of all the arts. That it still enjoys such pre-eminence is a triumph not just of organization, but over the political and financial obstacles which have punctuated its history. In recent times it has had to compete in a very much more crowded market place with festivals springing up in Avignon and New York, in addition to more established rivals such as Salzburg. And in its latter years it has faced criticism for failing to secure the services of the very top music performers. Some of that criticism is valid. Even at the beginning of Frank Dunlop's tenure in the early 1980s it was possible to envisage several of the world's leading orchestras having Edinburgh on their itinerary in the same year. But the spiralling costs of transportation and rising fees have all contributed to a music programme which, in the late 1980s and early 1990s, was certainly less glittering than a decade before. Yet Edinburgh has to be judged not just on the fluctuating merits of its component parts, but on the whole extraordinary, cultural confection, which is reckoned to pump between £50 and £80 million into the local economy. In contrast the overall budget for the three weeks is a little over £3 million which comes, in roughly equal parts, from public subsidy, box office and earned income, and business sponsorship. For that sum, modest in comparison to what is available for the much more limited programme in Salzburg, visitors to the festival have a full drama and music programme, and an increasingly broad dance programme. If there has been a long standing weakness it has been in trying to integrate the visual arts more comprehensively into the package. Even so there have been some quite stunning festival exhibitions over the last few years; the Cezanne/Poussin retrospective at the National Gallery, and *The Vigorous Imagination*, a celebration of contemporary Scottish art at the Scottish Gallery of Modern Art, were both extraordinary in their very different fashion. But both were essentially mounted by the National Galleries of Scotland themselves with generous private sponsorship. It is undoubtedly one of the tasks of the current festival director, Brian McMaster, the former director of the Welsh National Opera company, to find ways to incorporate the visual arts into Festival planning.

The ability to create strong drama and music programmes in the same year were often supposed to be mutually exclusive talents. John Drummond, who went on to become the controller of BBC Radio 3 and now runs the London Promenade season, is said to have had a significant impact on the musical side yet when he first came to the festival he had no particular pedigree in that domain. Similarly, his successor, Frank Dunlop was always more highly rated for his dramatic offerings. Both judgements were probably facile, but Dunlop, whatever subsequent battles he became embroiled in, will always be remembered for a truly Titanic world theatre season. A regular element of his programme was what began as the Toho company from Japan and metamorphosed into the Ninegawa. They took Edinburgh by storm with their Japanese language version of *Macbeth* and had several triumphs, most notably a production of *Medea* staged outdoors in the quadrangle of the University's Old College. To attempt any outdoor activity in an Edinburgh 'summer' requires directorial courage bordering on the foolhardy. Yet so mesmeric was the performance of this company that when, on a evening where the heavens had opened without respite, the audience, asked by the cast if they wanted to leave, stayed damply enchanted where they were. There have been musical triumphs over the years, and operatic watersheds such as the 1977 production of *Carmen* which starred both Placido Domingo and Teresa Berganza, the memorable visits of the Lyons and La Scala opera companies, Claudio Abbado's *Lohengrin* and Alexander Gibson's *Gurrelieder*. More recently were the appearance of the Shostakovich Quartet and the high emotion of the 1991 concerts of the Leningrad Philarmonic (now the St. Petersburg). That year they played to a packed Usher Hall when all the players knew that there had been a coup in their homeland. The tension of those evenings forged a bond between orchestra and audience that few present will ever forget.

Throughout the 1980s, the most regular dramatic offering in the Edinburgh Festival was an annual row between its director and the local authorities. There were two basic reasons for this conflict, which may now be over. One concerned the level of local authority funding, and the long-term commitment to its provision. The other was a more philosophical difference about whether or not the Edinburgh Festival had become too elitist. There was a particular irony in this row coming to a head under the stewardship of Frank Dunlop, a man whose career as a director and impresario had won him a reputation as a populist. His arrival coincided with a period of political instability. The Labour Group had recently won power in what had hitherto been a traditionally Tory town. Their earlier administrations were characterized by a basic insecurity which, in some councillors, manifested itself in a desire to be seen to be ideologically pure. In questioning the expenditure on the Festival at a time when the city had major social problems, particularly on its housing estates, that particular section of the Labour Group found themselves in improbable alliance with the philistine wing of the Conservative Group who couldn't see the point of a Festival in the first place. There was a period where some councillors appeared to attend events only in order to walk out.

While these battles raged, the Festival's identity became uncertain. Efforts were made to make it more accessible to local communities. The opening up of the old Leith Theatre and the staging there of the marvellous Swedish Folk Opera in successive years was a typical piece of Dunlop inspiration. In contrast the decision to erect a tent in Pilrig Park to house more 'accessible' events, proved an expensive disaster. Means may be found, as the second New York Festival did in 1991, of using sponsorship to buy and distribute festival tickets, as well as operating a concessionary ticketing policy. With the growing links between the Festival and community-based arts groups this would help to ease any lingering tensions. The identity of the prime movers in the ruling Labour Group has itself changed in the last decade.

Not the least of the debates over the years had concerned just who ran the Festival. The Labour administration saw the ruling Festival Council as a self-perpetuating oligarchy of the great and good, voting each other on to the council from membership of the wider Festival Society, and forming a permanent majority in alliance with Tory councillors. But the 'old guard' on the Festival Council had a different perspective, supposing that the built-in majority for the district councillors on the Council, who would now be Labour, would mean the Festival would be in the hands of what they doubtless saw as the forces of darkness. Until they were revised in 1986, the articles of association of the Festival Society meant that there was a restriction on new members who required to be selected by the existing membership. A survey of that membership, prepared in 1985, revealed that almost two-thirds were over 60. Over 87 per cent came from the professions, 20 per cent being financiers or lawyers, a further 20 per cent academics, 27 per cent professionals in the arts themselves, 6 per cent industrialists, 6 per cent MPs, 8 per cent lawyers, and 8 per cent from the aristocracy with—as the confidential research paper delicately had it—'no other apparent occupation'. It was also overwhelmingly male in composition. The members of the Festival Society had even more in common however. Over half had been educated privately, and over 40 per cent of them were Oxbridge graduates. Of those whose biographical details were available to the authors of the survey, 23 per cent belonged to Edinburgh's New Club. Of course all 62 district councillors had automatic membership of the Society as did 10 regional councillors. But there were at that time only 183 lay members and they did not constitute a broad cross-section of Scottish society. The revision of the rules regarding entry in 1986 broadened the base of the membership and caused considerable uproar. In effect the only future qualification for the Festival Society would be the £11 it cost to apply. By 1991 the membership had grown to 310, but the background and age profile of the new members did not seem significantly different and 150 of the total are still the original life members. At the AGM in 1992 there were just six people under the age of 40 and the average age was 60.

What has changed, is how the actual Festival Council operates. The composition still allows for seven members of the District Council, seven members of the Festival Society, and representatives from the Chamber of Commerce and the Trades Council in addition to two co-opted nominees. However the bulk of the Council's management role is now undertaken by a smaller executive committee chaired by the Lord Provost often under the direction of the deputy, Professor Jack Shaw. Also on that committee are George Younger, the Royal Bank chairman, and academic Nick Phillipson who chaired the committee which headhunted possible candidates to succeed Frank Dunlop. Donald MacDonald, chairman of the Scottish Chamber Orchestra is also on the executive, as is Councillor George Kerevan, chairman of the Council's Economic and Development Committee. So while the full 21-strong Council is technically the board to which the Festival management team and its director reports, the new streamlined committee wields considerable power.

The District Council decision to fund the Festival on a rolling three-year agreement—even if the overall sum is still inadequate—was also a major advance. Many of the councillors have become active in the promotion of the Arts and were instrumental, with local business interests, in launching the scheme to buy and refurbish the Empire Theatre with a view to staging full-scale opera and ballet. This project, initially worked on by Frank Dunlop and Edinburgh lawyer Sandy Orr, business partner of Donald MacDonald and the chairman of Scottish Opera, now has the backing of an influential board of Trustees including George Younger, and Lord Macfarlane, chairman of United Distillers. In tandem with a commercial advisory group, they intend that the Empire should attract sufficient funding to open in its new guise late in 1993, when Edinburgh's 40-year campaign for an opera house will finally be concluded. It is not a solution which has pleased everyone, and one of the original campaigning groups is still vocal in its criticism of this compromise option. Yet, realistically, the purchase of the Empire by the Council for less than £3 million, even if refurbishment eventually takes another £15 million at tomorrow's prices, still represents a significant bargain. It will provide Edinburgh with the kind of venue essential to maintain its festival prestige, given that many of the major opera and ballet companies in the world have either been unable to include Edinburgh in their itinerary, or have had to tailor their offerings to theatres inadequately suited for the purpose.

Another challenge for Brian McMaster is how to find a way of co-ordinating the interests of the many other events which now enhance Edinburgh in August, particularly the Festival's own flourishing Fringe which often administers almost 1 000 performances. Frank Dunlop, during his outgoing festival in 1991, criticized the quality of the Fringe, a charge robustly rejected by Fringe administrator Mhairi Mackenzie Robinson. It is almost impossible to see how this amazing annual adventure could ever be made subject to any form of quality control, or indeed who might impose it. The Fringe, which has over the years unveiled some fine talents and been responsible for significant dramatic premieres, is a marketplace where the consumers vote with their feet. Companies who arrive in the Scottish capital with ill-thought-out productions, poorly staged, or comedy which amuses only the would-be comedian usually find empty halls eloquent testimony to the need to try harder.

In addition to the Fringe, and the Military Tattoo, Edinburgh in August plays host to a Jazz Festival, a Television Festival and its own venerable Film Festival. Every two years a burgeoning Book Festival sets up a tented village in Charlotte Square. Over the years suggestions have been made as to whether these various attractions should have staggered starting dates, not just for the benefit of the event-weary consumer, but also to maximize their commercial impact. But many people are convinced that it is the very fact of Edinburgh, for one month at least, appearing to be the centre of the cultural universe, which gives that period its special charm and excitement.

Other Scottish festivals

Many other Scottish Festivals have become established cultural flagships for the areas they represent. In all there are now over 50 annual festivals throughout Scotland, the most pre-eminent of which include Orkney's St Magnus Festival, built largely round the composer Sir Peter Maxwell Davies; the Borders Festival begun and nourished by the original efforts of Judy Steel, and others of long standing in Perth, Stirling and Dunkeld. These, and others of their kind, have demonstrated not just the determination of smaller centres to mount annual celebrations of local culture, but of their ability to secure the services of considerable talents to enhance their programme. And, in the 10 years since the first Feis (Gaelic festival) was begun on Barra, 22 more Feiseian have blossomed. In 1993 the inaugural Fotofeis will celebrate both indigenous and international photographic talents all over Scotland.

Lying somewhere in between these events, and the juggernaut of Edinburgh, is Glasgow's Mayfest. Its task is at once to encourage community programming, whilst buying in international product with a populist appeal. The festival priorities are different from, and less ambitious than those of Edinburgh. But part of the legacy of Glasgow's year as cultural capital of Europe in 1990 was an ambition to be able to attract major talents such as Peter Brook to the city. It also became clear that Glasgow was enthusiastic about a partnership with Edinburgh and the first tentative steps were taken in 1992 to discuss joint Festival ventures.

The visual arts

In 1989 the Scottish Gallery of Modern Art presented an Edinburgh Festival exhibition which it titled *The Vigorous Imagination*. It was an acknowledgment of the energy which has infused Scottish art in the last quarter of the 20th century, and the increasing confidence of young contemporary painters who, unlike many of their celebrated predecessors, were to enjoy success and adulation at an early stage of their development. Prominent among these were the young men who studied together at the Glasgow School of Art in the late 1970s and early 1980s and who came to be dubbed 'the new Glasgow boys'. Some of their work was included in an exhibition at Glasgow's Third Eye Centre in 1985 when they were barely two years beyond graduation.

The most immediately successful were Steven Campbell, who went on to become a cult figure in fashionable New York galleries, Ken Currie, Pete Howson, and Adrian Wisniewski. Together with Stephen Conroy they were in the vanguard of a new self-confident group of young Scottish artists who have continued to paint for the most part in Scotland. Howson works from a studio in the Gallowgate area of the east end of Glasgow and his work chronicles the life and times of people whom the good ship Enterprise has clearly left on the pier. Ken Currie's work is also infused by a political awareness. The mural cycle he completed for the People's Palace in Glasgow in commemoration of the bicentenary of the massacre of Calton weavers, and his later depiction of unemployed and part-time workers, show his stated commitment 'to paint about the realities of the human condition as well as to depict the existing possibilities for world reconstruction'. Steven Campbell's odyssey has been rather different, using whimsy and surrealism and some surprising source material such as the profoundly un-Scottish world of P G Wodehouse, to which he brings an anarchic Scottish eye. There has been controversy over Campbell's work and over the extent to which his rise to fame and fortune has been governed by his adoption by the New York cultural establishment. It is too early to judge the lasting impact of the Glasgow boys. A very different style is adopted by Stephen Conroy, whose canvases are often reminiscent of other celebrated artists whom he admires such as Degas and Sickert. His technical skills and creative flair have already won him a considerable following. Adrian Wiszniewski, who studied architecture before continuing at the School of Art in Glasgow has also been the subject of considerable transatlantic attention, but chose in the late 1980s to work in Northumberland. His lament was the one familiar throughout every branch of the arts in Scotland, that so long as he was a local Scottish face he would not be accorded the respect given to incoming talent.

Graduates of Edinburgh College of Art from the same period were also enjoying critical success. Some of the artists who founded the 369 Gallery such as Caroline McNairn and Fionna Carlisle have produced colourful and vigorous work enhanced in McNairn's case by the opportunity to work in Moscow for a period. That particular gallery has had a track record of finding and encouraging female talent regularly showing, amongst others, artists such as Joyce Cairns who has been influenced by the potent work of John Bellany. All the current younger talents have been able to enjoy an environment where some major Scottish painters are still making a substantial contribution to contemporary styles. Sir Robin Philipson, who died in 1992, epitomized the courage of an artist who sought new adventures, and never allowed his celebrity to interfere with his experimental instincts. Bellany, who works in London and Scotland and who was the subject of a major retrospective in Glasgow in 1992, is as productive as ever following a major illness. His early work depicting the symbols of his fishing village childhood has given way to the searing series from his hospitalization. Now he has turned his considerable imagination and vivid use of colour to horticultural and landscape themes.

In Edinburgh the prolific duo of John Houston and Elizabeth Blackadder provide richly contrasting styles, whilst in Glasgow David Donaldson, his pupil Duncan Shanks and Barbara Rae all command increasing attention. Gwen Hardie continues to enjoy a considerable reputation in Europe. It would be almost impossible to attempt to categorize the eclectic output of Ian Hamilton Finlay whose work, frequently collaborative, spans many disciplines, but whose imagery, polemical style and witty commentary, have been an important catalyst for many of his contemporaries. The extraordinary sculpted images created from natural substances by Andy Goldsworthy have also been a vivid component of the artistic tapestry in Scotland in recent years; the patience of his construction matched only by the brevity of the life expectancy of many of his best creations. A more permanent monument to Scottish inventiveness is the extraordinary sculpture of Sir Eduardo Paolozzi.

Another comparatively recent phenomenon in the Scottish art world has been the increased interest both at home and abroad of earlier Scottish schools, principally the work of the colourists, F C B Cadell, S J Peploe, G L Hunter and J D Fergusson, and to a lesser but still enthusiastic extent, the original Glasgow Boys: James Guthrie, John Lavery, E A Walton, Arthur Melville, E A Hornel and George Henry.

It took a US scholar, Jude Burkhauser, to unearth some of the lesser-known talents of what she termed Glasgow Girls, the women who were also prominent in art and design around the turn of the century. Burkhauser was the moving spirit in assembling an exhibition in 1990 at Glasgow's Kelvingrove Art Gallery which rectified that silence by bringing together the work of painters like Bessie MacNicol, Norah Neilson Gray, and Stansmore Dean and designers including Jessie King, Annie French, and Margaret Macdonald and her sister Frances who had hithero been known through collaboration with their husbands, Charles Rennie Mackintosh and Herbert McNair. Mackintosh himself has become something of a late 20th-century icon, and so widespread is the imitation of his design in furniture and crafts that the minor industry it has spawned is known colloquially as 'Mockintosh'.

Like all other aspects of Scotland's cultural life, the visual arts have not been immune from the effects of recessions. Several major galleries have been in trouble, and are operating very much at the margins. The two Scottish branches of the Fine Arts Society were forced to close in 1992 leaving just the London parent gallery, although the Glasgow premises continue in a new guise under the director Roger Bilcliffe. But the growth of the printmakers workshops in Scotland has also proved an important source of additional exhibition space. In addition to the proposed Gallery of Scottish Art, yet to be sited, Glasgow has announced its intention to create a second major gallery of Modern Art in the West. So, if there are concerns on the commercial side, there are grounds to be optimistic that creatively the next turn of the century could prove as significant a milestone in Scottish painting as the last.

Music

The audiences for many different musical styles in Scotland are growing simultaneously. Two thriving international jazz festivals in Glasgow and Edinburgh and a smaller version in Dundee demonstrate that the country has produced significant artists and composers in the last decade. Similarly, in rock music, Scots bands have enjoyed unparalleled success in the wider world with groups like Runrig, Simple Minds, Hue and Cry and Deacon Blue building significant followings nationally, and sometimes internationally. There is however no major record label in Scotland, a problem the rock and traditional bands share with the country's classical musicians.

The Traditional Music and Song Association, despite pitiful funding (in 1992 given a modest boost), has a solid base in almost 30 branches in Scotland, and the increased interest in traditional music is underlined by many radio programmes featuring traditional bands and supported by over two dozen Strathspey and Reel societies. Piping too has enjoyed something of a revival and although there is only one formal teaching college, local pipe bands, the Royal Scottish Pipers Society, the Royal Scottish Pipe Band Association, the Piobaireachd Society, and the police and army all have active teaching units.

Fiddle music is also in a vibrant period and when a tour was undertaken by the Shetland fiddler Aly Bain specifically to encourage local participation each venue proved to be over-subscribed by young enthusiasts. Young folk singers are less ubiquitous according to the Traditional Music and Song Association's president Sheena Wellington, herself a distinguished performer. The problem lies with the relative failure to teach singing in schools, and the association now has a pilot schools project up and running in Grampian which it hopes to replicate elsewhere.

Classical music enjoys a period of creative renaissance coupled with financial instability. Scottish Opera, based in Glasgow, has acquired a substantial deficit and cancelled the latter half of an acclaimed Ring Cycle, yet, at the same time, in its home base, regularly plays to 90 per cent plus audiences. Curiously it has met with more consumer resistance in the capital city of Edinburgh, but this may be in part because the Edinburgh opera audience has never warmed to its touring base at the Playhouse, which was preferred to the Kings because of the larger stage and seating capacity. For some productions such as the new Judith Weir opera, *The Vanishing Bridegroom*, the Edinburgh audiences were poor and only reached acceptable levels when the company staged popular classics. In the 1992–3 season it returned to the Kings after which its Edinburgh touring season will be extended at the Empire. Other touring venues have been more supportive, in particular Newcastle where advance bookings are always healthy. Scottish Opera has long argued that it is being penalized for behaving like the national company it is, and complains it receives proportionally less from public funding than its counterpart in Wales. One of the remedies proposed is for the Arts Council of Great Britain to make additional touring grants available for its English touring programme. It has also successfully urged the Scottish Office to help clear its deficit, noting that the Welsh Office did so for Welsh National Opera early in 1991 when that company was threatened with closure. Scottish Opera's plight is less desperate, but it was true to assert, as the company did, that without some alteration to its funding structure its future as a full-time national company was uncertain. In the 1992 round of SAC revenue grants the company won a handsome £500 000 injection while the Scottish Office decided to make an exceptional payment of the same sum to help reduce the running deficit in the spring of this year. A third bonus came from another £500 000 injection from the new Sports and Arts Foundation, all of which put the national opera company on a much more secure footing.

The Royal Scottish Orchestra (RSO), is our only full-sized symphony orchestra, although full programmes are undertaken both by the BBC Scottish Symphony Orchestra and the Scottish Chamber Orchestra (SCO). The RSO appears at its Glasgow base, the new concert hall, at the Usher Hall in Edinburgh and, rather less frequently in Dundee and Aberdeen. 1991/2 is the RSO's centenary season and as part of its celebrations it took a scaled down version of the full orchestra to remoter regions including Lewis and Orkney. Every three years in association with Glasgow University and the BBC the RSO has a festival of contemporary music—Musica Nova. This enjoys critical success, but not large audiences. Recently a row between management and players caused the SAC to put its grant on ice until matters had been resolved.

The SCO, whose 37 players are hired on a contract basis, tours more extensively and has built up a reputation for its wide educational programme, and its commitment to new work. It also performs as what amounts to the orchestra-in-residence for part of the year at the Queens Hall in Edinburgh and the City Hall in Glasgow. Foreign tours have played an important part in raising its profile internationally. It has been a significant influence in nurturing young Scots composers and regularly uses Sir Peter Maxwell Davies and James MacMillan as tutors in its summer school. It won the prestigious Prudential Award in 1991.

The BBC Scottish Symphony Orchestra was selected by the new director of the Edinburgh Festival to perform at the 1992 opening concert. Normally it will give at least a dozen concerts in its own studio in Glasgow, as well as appearing at the concert hall there and in Stirling regularly and several other towns and cities intermittently. The BBC music department is an important influence and commissions new work regularly. Like the other BBC-based orchestras it is nervous about its future as the BBC trims its commitments in the runup to the new charter in 1996.

The fact that many of Scotland's communities are remote from Central Belt activity has not necessarily impeded their own musical development, and perhaps has led to greater local creativity. The touring policies of the major companies have also made much good music available. It may be that hearing *Tosca* in the village hall to the accompaniment of an upright of indeterminate vintage falls short of Callas, but companies like Scottish Opera's Opera Go Round maintain high standards in difficult circumstances.

Scottish Opera, the SCO, the RSO and the Scottish Ensemble collectively absorb 92 per cent of the SAC's music budget. It has become very difficult for young musicians and singers who are not attached to a major company to continue to work regularly in Scotland and many drift south. Yet there remains a vibrancy in the music scene in Scotland. It is wonderful to watch the impact of groups like Live Music Now as they work with autistic children, to witness Evelyn Glennie transfix a highland audience on an SCO tour, to hear a triumphant concert at the St Magnus Festival, to see Tommy Smith at his most inventive in the glorious claustrophobia of the Renfrew Ferry at Mayfest, young fiddlers at a local rally or thousands entranced by Runrig live on Edinburgh Castle esplanade. The musical spirit seems willing, even if the bank balance is weak.

Dance

Dance in Scotland is spread over a wide range of disciplines from the serious formality of small children involved in Highland and Scottish country dancing to the radical choreography of contemporary groups.

The Scottish Ballet was formed in the mid-1960s when Peter Darrell brought many of the former Western Ballet company to Glasgow. The company has grown significantly since those early years and now runs an educational arm, Steps Out, to which it recently added Scottish Ballet 2, a smallscale company with a remit to take high-standard performances to remoter rural communities. The main company undertakes its third Far Eastern tour in 1992 and performed earlier in Moscow, Kiev and St Petersburg. In essence Scottish Ballet faces the same financial difficulty as Scottish Opera in that it is required to function as a national organization on a level of grant which militates against introducing much new work. Scottish Ballet, like Opera, has used the precedent of Welsh National Opera receiving extra central government assistance in recognition of its role in helping government agencies achieve inward investment. Since Scottish Ballet's tours have also taken place with the active involvement of both regional and central government trade missions, they have argued for the Scottish Office to make other funds available outwith its SAC allocation. The SAC has discussed with its parent body a new payment structure for tours undertaken by the ballet company in the south. Scottish Ballet's other complaint has been that it has been successful in not exceeding its budget. Good housekeeping has meant some painful surgery on staffing levels and repertoire. And it concludes that it has fared no better than those companies, particularly English ones, who have been more profligate. But whether or not Scottish Ballet is funded adequately, it does take a very large share of the SAC's dance budget leaving small sums to nourish other dance initiatives. And its latest SAC grant was well in excess of inflation levels.

The only other Scottish company which has managed to sustain dance on a year-round basis is at Dundee Rep which concentrates on a contemporary programme. But there is a group of dancers and choreographers who work individually with smaller companies putting on occasional performances. Choreographers like Frank McConnell have built reputations for work with small dance theatre initiatives and also in collaboration. McConnell worked with Communicado on *Jock Tamson's Bairns* in the Tramway production which launched Glasgow's 1990 drama season. The cross fertilization of dance with mainstream theatre has resulted in productions like Theatre Around Glasgow's *Great Expectations*.

Dance has unfortunately been given an increasingly low profile within mainstream education, and has suffered disproportionately from local authority cuts in spending. The SAC now funds eight dancers in residence throughout Scotland, and the Dance School of Scotland trains young dancers at Knightswood in Glasgow whilst continuing their mainstream education. These courses still end at the age of 16, which encourages a drain of talent south and often results in the young dancers staying in England where there are greater employment opportunities.

Like indigenous music, traditional Scottish country dancing has enjoyed something of a revival of late. The Scottish Country Dance Association could always rely on a hard core of adherents here, and in those countries which exported enthusiasts to its annual summer school. But a recent phenomenon has been the huge popularity of dance-centred ceilidhs with a much younger audience in venues such as Glasgow's Riverside Club.

The Scottish Arts Council

The Scottish Arts Council is the body from which most financial cultural blessings flow in Scotland, though its relationship with its many and varied clients is often something less than cordial. Over the years it has attracted widespread criticism, usually targeted on the level of the sums it disburses, the criteria by which it decides who gets how much, and the alleged secrecy surrounding the decision-making process. However, in the early 1990s this body was the subject of a radical internal reorganization instigated by its new director Seona Reid, a Glaswegian who returned to Scotland to take up the post in September 1990 following the departure of Timothy Mason to administer English Regional Arts. The restructure follows a detailed internal review which suggested that strategic objectives tended to be hindered by the fact that individual departments within the SAC had become used both to running their own show and to fighting their own particular corner. This in turn led to policy being shaped by these departments and then rubber stamped by the Council. A secondary difficulty caused by the relative autonomy was that its methodology was often discernibly different. The previous management structure militated against effective directorship, given that almost everbody was in a position to report directly. The new structure which was put fully in place in 1992 retains the various art form departments, but is now grouped differently so a Performing Arts Department will now be the umbrella for drama, dance and music with a director for music and another for drama and dance. Combined arts and literature will also come under one division, though again with a director for each, and visual arts will be the third leg. Each of these three will take responsibility for funding, policy and development in their own field, as well as operating an advisory service to clients. In addition there is a new Policy and Development Department, a central division which will also embrace communications. This will now be the main policy making think tank especially in the fields of education, broadcasting and youth arts. Christine Hamilton, formerly the arts officer for the Scottish Trades Union Congress, was appointed deputy director to Seona Reid at the end of 1991, and she operates as director of this division with a senior development officer and a part time research assistant. Whilst the various art form directors continue to report to Reid, this department has responsibility for the coordination of the various art form departments and deals with day-to-day administration in an attempt to encourage more interdepartmental cooperation and more uniformity of approach.

This streamlining of the Scottish operation, important as it is, does not address the core debate about the relationship of the SAC not just to the bodies it funds, but to its own paymasters. The SAC is 25 years old this year and was the successor to a Scottish subcommittee of the Arts Council of Great Britain. The SAC still enjoys committee status, although, unlike the English Regional Arts Councils, reports directly to the main UK council, and not merely to its planning officers. The Scottish and Welsh Arts Councils consider this to be an important difference. The recent reorganization of the English regional structure which has led to greater central intervention in policy through demands for integrated planning and the identification of shared policy objectives, sent a chill down Scottish and Welsh spines. Metropolitan apathy towards Celtic arts has hitherto led to minimal interference from London.

It has always been the case that the SAC made its own decisions about how best to distribute its funds. When additional enhancement funding became available in 1991, the Council required applicants to put in detailed bids. In contrast in England an almost instant distribution to clients, created widespread antagonism. So now battle have been joined in earnest to protect that fiscal autonomy. The last chairman, Sir Alan Peacock, made a bid for a federalized arts council structure saying that: 'nothing less than a continuation of a system by which control of the allocation of funds rests firmly within Scotland is satisfactory'. The maintenance of that system is now the task of his successor Bill Brown, the much respected chairman of Scottish Television.

The SAC gets its global funding allocation from the Arts Council of Great Britain, which in turn is a subsidiary department of the Office of Arts and Libraries, and the Arts Minister, on behalf of this department, has to lobby the Treasury for his annual budget. There have been an unprecedented number of arts ministers over the last few years. Richard Luce, a Foreign Office casualty at the time of the Falklands, was given the post in the mid 1980s following Lord Gowrie, who indicated that the ministerial salary did not permit him to live in the manner to which he was accustomed. Luce, with no discernible track record in the Arts, was viewed with little enthusiasm, yet he managed to secure signficant funding increases, though he ran into problems with the customer demand for his Business Sponsorship Incentive Scheme outstripping the money supply available. He was briefly replaced in 1990 by David Mellor who showed signs of wishing to make the post significant when the change of leadership in the Conservative Party led to John Major rewarding him with the job of First Secretary to the Treasury. The man who took over at the end of that year was Tim Renton, former chief whip and a noted opera buff (though ministers who know a little of what they are talking about are often considered more dangerous!). In 1992 David Mellor took over an enlarged Ministry of Fun which included the Arts, Sport and Heritage. The SAC gets its own budget in the same way as the Scottish Office is dealt with by the Treasury. It is subject to what has become known as the Goschen formula, 10.45 per cent of the global Arts budget for Britain, outside of any hived off on ministerial whim for special projects. (The Scottish Office enjoys a slightly greater percentage.) It is a perennial source of irritation in SAC circles that the topslicing which occurs to fund these special projects before Goschen is applied invariably involves some specifically English initiative such as the cost of reorganizing the English regional structure in 1990. At the moment the arithmetic leaves the SAC with almost £23 million to spend and the six art form committees with a delegated responsibility from the 22-member Arts Council itself disburse the money. All funding allocations outside of annual revenue grants have to be referred back to the Council. Each committee has an average of 10 members chaired by a council member. Council members, who normally sit for three years but are eligible for a two-year extension, are selected in theory by the Arts Council of Great Britain, on which the chair and deputy chair of the SAC both sit. But new council members are generally recruited by the SAC itself who then submit two names for each vacancy for the approval of the Scottish Secretary. The private political views of some recruits would probably rather surprise the Scottish Secretary, and the members of the SAC are by no means as geriatric as is popularly supposed. They are required to attend six Council meetings a year, attend at least that number of committee meetings and be available to interview clients, and this means that the make-up of the committee has been traditionally skewed towards the leisured classes or those sufficiently senior to create time. Seventy per cent of the Council is male, though a new equal opportunities policy means that the gender balance should improve. That same bias is reflected within the committees whose members are selected by the Council. Until recently this process was something of a formality, with one name being offered to the Council for a committee vacancy. The application of the equal opportunities policy has led to more candidates being considered. As yet committees are still very much Central Belt orientated—which is also where most of the funding goes—and still meet principally in Edinburgh.

Although the details of all the decisions are made public, critics of the Council, not infrequently disenchanted clients or would-be clients, accuse the organization of secrecy, pointing out that all decisions are taken privately, behind closed doors. This remains a contentious area, particularly during intermittent crises such as the temporary closure of the Fruitmarket Gallery in Edinburgh and the demise of the original Third Eye Centre in Glasgow. A public row over the future of the 369 Gallery in Edinburgh caused its director to state he would continue without SAC funding which some thought foolhardy. The SAC feel that if its own meetings were made open to the public, decisions would be taken beforehand by sections of the committees forming caucuses. However, in 1991 it embarked on a massive public consultation exercise before publishing its new Charter for The Arts in Scotland. It was an ambitious attempt to gauge opinion. Discussion papers were prepared, some in-house, some commissioned from interested bodies across the cultural spectrum. These were used at public access meetings throughout Scotland where anyone was invited to comment on the strengths and weaknesses of the various activities and art forms, and to offer recommendations. The policy initiatives based on the charter are due to emerge in November 1922.

There are other funders in the Scottish game whose influence has increased over the last decade. Strathclyde Region, prior to its poll-tax collection problems, had become a major funder of the arts, commissioning its own series of concertos from Sir Peter Maxwell Davies and being heavily involved with Glasgow's 1990 programme. Glasgow District itself has spent huge sums on the arts. When the city bid for the cultural capital title it was able to identify £24 million spent in the city annually on the arts from various sources, and it guaranteed £15 million of the £40 million budget for its 1990 celebrations. Outwith the massively swollen contributions for 1990, the District Council was the moving spirit behind the annual Mayfest of which it is still the major supporter. The success of this led to the director of the Festivals Unit, Bob Palmer, becoming a fulltime director of performing arts in the city. Similarly Edinburgh District Council, after a period of uncertainty, has now committed funding to the International Festival, and Lothian Region also contributes. Local authorities now put £30 million into the arts in Scotland, and there have been discussions as to whether the Convention of Scottish Local Authorities ought now to become involved in helping to shape the policy of individual contributors. Meanwhile business sponsorship of the arts has risen steeply in Scotland and the Association of Business Sponsorship of the Arts has a Scottish office and a Scottish committee. With a contribution to the Edinburgh Festival which now equates with District Council input, and smaller but crucial sums going into fledgling festivals such as the Borders, business has become a major player in the funding game. But now able to write cheques for £22 million plus, and with access to further Enhancement Funding which in 1991 accounted for over £700 000, the SAC, now a proactive development agency, is still the most influential investor in Scottish arts.

Boardroom incest

Scotland, in some respects, is a village. Just as the people who are involved with the arts in areas like Wester Ross or Galloway are all familiar with each other, so too are there tight-knit and interlocking groups running the major national arts organizations in Glasgow and Edinburgh. For a nation which prides itself on its radical thinking, a remarkable number of the people who matter belong to the Scottish and the business aristocracy. The Marquess of Bute, for instance, is involved in many cultural organizations and chairs both the Scottish Advisory Committee to the British Council—with a seat on the main board of the latter body—and the Board of Trustees of the Royal Museums of Scotland. The Countess of Dalkeith, who became chair of Scottish Ballet in 1990, has a longstanding interest in the arts and her husband, the Earl of Dalkeith, was on the board of Scottish Opera and is now an honorary vice-president. Lord Goold, former chairman of the Scottish Tory Party, now chairs the board of the Royal Scottish Orchestra, while Lord Balfour of Burleigh, former chairman of the Edinburgh Book Festival and of the SAC, chairs the Scottish Committee of the Association for Business Sponsorship of the Arts. Angus Grossart is chairman of the Board of Trustees of the National Galleries of Scotland and lends his support to many other arts initiatives in addition to his membership of the Scottish Tory Business Group. Lord Macfarlane of Bearsden, former chair of Scottish Ballet, is also chair of the Fine Art Society among whose directors is Angus Grossart. Lord Macfarlane, in turn, is a trustee of the National Galleries and a fellow member of the Scottish Business Group. George Younger, former Scottish Secretary of State and now chairman of the Royal Bank, sits on the executive committee of the Edinburgh Festival Council, and is a trustee, as is Lord Macfarlane, of the project to turn the Empire Theatre in Edinburgh into an opera house. Earlier this year he also joined the Scottish Committee of the Association for Business Sponsorship of the Arts. Sandy Orr, a prominent Edinburgh lawyer, was the driving force behind the Empire project. He is now chairman of Scottish Opera and a former member of the SAC and chair of its music committee. The former chairman of Scottish Opera is Sir Gerald Elliot who was formerly chairman of the SAC. Sir Alan Peacock, who retired in April as SAC chairman is a director of one of Mr Orr's companies, MacDonald Orr. Donald MacDonald, Mr Orr's partner, is chair of the Scottish Chamber Orchestra board.

The argument generally advanced for this boardroom incest is that these people are senior enough to create space to do the job, and are well placed to approach their fellow chief executives for funding. The result, however, is that the people sitting on arts boards for the major institutions come from a narrow and rather incestuous section of Scottish society. But in a sense the cast list for all manner of cultural and political activities in Scotland is rather small and increasingly interacts.

The period following the 1992 election saw the emergence of various cross-party groupings campaigning for a referendum on the governance of Scotland. In every case there was a strong representation of writers, artists, and other performers. As Scotland struggles to re-define its identity and chart it political future, the demarcation lines between the arts, culture, and politics have become increasingly difficult to discern.

9

Local Government

Peter Jones

Scotland's local authorities range from the vast to the diminutive. Strathclyde Regional Council serves 2.3 million people and is the biggest local authority in Britain. Nairn District Council has just over 10 000 people. The largest and smallest local authorities are alike an important part of the political and institutional landscape. The 65 councils are responsible for spending just over half of the Scottish Office budget: in 1991/92 £5.7 billion on current spending (salaries and other running costs) and £501 million on capital spending (buildings, roads, etc), with another £991 million going on housing current spending and £564 million on housing capital spending.

But they have been through testing times in recent years. Regularly criticized for overspending by central government, shaken by the poll tax and a series of financial body-blows such as the BCCI scandal, they now face the possibility of wholesale reform. The question is whether their present structure can take them through into the 21st century.

Reorganization: the 1973 Local Government (Scotland) Act

Since 1974, arising from the 1973 Local Government (Scotland) Act, mainland Scotland has had a two-tier system of 53 district councils on the lower level, and nine regional councils on the upper level. The three island groupings of Orkney, Shetland, and Western Isles, have single-tier, multi purpose authorities. The system replaced a patchwork quilt of five types of councils which had endured since 1929 and for which there was apparently such fondness that by the 1980s there was a growing demand for a 'return' to single-tier councils. Such sentiment was mostly confined to the four big cities, Glasgow, Edinburgh, Dundee, and Aberdeen, where the post-1975 district councils were seen as poor beasts compared to the pre-1975 powerful city corporations. Outside areas with a strong local identity like Ayrshire where a revived county council would be popular, there was no noticeable nostalgia for the old 196 landward district councils, 176 small burghs, 21 large burghs, and 33 county councils, to which over 5 000 councillors were elected compared to 1 682 in 1990.

That was perhaps curious, given that local government has some 800 years of history. Evidence suggests that under David I (1124–53) Berwick, Edinburgh, Roxburgh, Aberdeen, Dunfermline, Crail, Elgin, Inverkeithing, Perth, Stirling, Linlithgow, and Haddington had burgh status and thus control of local and foreign trade and crafts. Royal authority enabled churchmen to found the burghs of St Andrews, Glasgow, Brechin, Dunblane, Kelso, Jedburgh, and Paisley; and for local lords to establish Renfrew and Lochmaben. By 1500 there were 150 burghs, and in about 50 royal burghs, burgesses were being entrusted with the collection of local taxes and supervision of local affairs. The burgh reform Act of 1833 enabled the middle classes to elect councils. Magistrates and police commissioners were empowered to tax property to pay for services like lighting and water supplies. Towards the end of the century, elected county councils based on sheriffdoms replaced the landowner committees responsible for administering taxes and roads.

The latter half of the 19th century was an age of tremendous municipal improvement, with Glasgow the pioneer. In 1859, Queen Victoria opened Britain's first planned municipal water supply scheme: 35 miles of tunnels and aqueducts bringing 50 million gallons of water a day from Loch Katrine. Municipal gas and electricity supplies, tramway systems and hospitals followed. What was not addressed, however, was housing.

By 1910, there were over 1 million people living in the Glasgow area, three times as many as in the 1830s. Most lived in the characteristic Scottish housing unit, the tenement. This three- or four-floor block with two flats on each floor on either side of the common stair was a product of the feu duty system where a title deeds holder paid a sum of money to the ground superior in perpetuity. It made land more costly, but Scots law also made multiple ownership in a block of flats easier than in England. However, the overcrowding in Scotland's tenemented cities was appalling. Though there was some slum clearance, there was little to no municipal building of houses. This was because the middle classes both believed in, and had a vested interest in, the housing market remaining in private hands. But in 1919, Lloyd George's government decided central government should subsidize house-building. In the next 20 years, 338 000 houses were built. Cost-cutting meant many were dreary boxes, row upon row of them, skimpily built on the outer fringes of cities. Some schemes, such as Ferguslie Park in Paisley, Craigmillar in Edinburgh and Raploch in Stirling, were built as slum clearance projects in the 1930s, only to become slums themselves 40 years later.

These were the schemes, with their hopelessly deficient social and shopping facilities, with all their problems of vandalism, which the *district* councils inherited on reorganization. Housing was the main district function, together with local planning and amenity services such as parks and libraries. The *regions'* main functions were education and social work, roads and water services, police and fire. The three islands authorities combine with Highland Regional Council for police and fire, but otherwise they are self-contained authorities.

In any regional authority, the powerful officials are the chief executive and his departmental heads, especially the heads of the finance department and major spending departments like education and social work. Officials in charge of lower-spending functions like strategic planning or economic development are also powerful. That rough hierarchy of power is broadly matched on the elected member side; the chairmanship of the finance or policy and/or resources, education, social work, transport, planning and economic development committees are sought-after posts for the ambitious councillor. In the district councils, housing and planning are usually the most important areas, both for officials and councillors, after finance.

In politically dominated councils, the political groups elect a leader. If the group controls the council, the group leader becomes the leader of the council. The trend throughout the 1980s was for the leader to become much more powerful than the titular head of the council—the convener, lord provost in the four cities, or provost in some districts—who was increasingly confined to an ambassadorial role on behalf of the authority. Only in a non-political council does the convener have real power, although if a council administration is divided between two political groups, the convener has a more important role. For example, in 1986, an independent Grampian regional councillor, Geoff Hadley, found himself unexpectedly the regional convener holding the ring between the Liberal Democrats and the SNP who formed a joint administration.

In Labour-controlled authorities, an important element in the power equation is the district party in the case of district councils, or the regional party in the case of regional councils. The district/regional party was a creation of the left-driven reforms in Labour structures in the early 1980s. It comprises elected delegates from the constituency Labour parties in the area covered by the council. Under party rules they supervise selection and deselection of councillors, write the manifesto for council elections, and also nominate elected councillors for particular civic posts. Its intervention can be decisive. In 1988, the Dundee district Labour party nominated 31-year-old teacher, Mary Ward, for the council leadership. Had the matter been left in the hands of the elected councillors, the previous leader, Tom McDonald, would probably have been re-elected, but they accepted the 'advice' of the district party.

For most conveners or lord provosts, the job is a political cul-de-sac, often a 'reward' for a long career as a councillor. Some find it difficult to adjust. In 1988, Aberdeen District Council's ruling Labour group elected as Lord Provost one of their longest-serving members, Robert A Robertson. He took exception to the Labour group policies, publicly criticized the group, and as a result found himself politically ostracized. Robertson also believed he was the senior local politician when another long-serving Labour councillor, Robert Middleton, was elected convener of Grampian Regional Council in 1990. For Middleton, who had spent years in political opposition, becoming convener was an opportunity to start achieving things. That led to friction with his Labour Group, but nothing like as much friction as there was between Middleton and Robertson over who should take the leading role in various local political activities. A little of that friction is often detectable between the lord provosts of the four cities and the convener of the regional tier. The antiquity of the Lord Provost title, plus the status of being the city's lord lieutenant, gives the post a public clout which the regional conveners lack and sometimes resent.

Though largely now a ceremonial figure, the lord provost cannot become detached completely from politics. In 1979, Lord Provost David Hodge of Glasgow brought massive disapproval on his head by meeting the South African ambassador. His successor, Michael Kelly, Lord Provost 1980–84, was a young councillor chosen to bring the job back within political direction. But Kelly unexpectedly fulfilled the ambassadorial job for the city of Glasgow in a dramatic way. It was his relationship with the public relations executive John Struthers that produced the 'Glasgow's Miles Better' campaign and the 'Mr Happy' logo. However, Kelly went out of politics and into public relations after his term of office. In 1988, and for the first time, two women became lord provosts—Susan Baird in Glasgow and Eleanor McLaughlin in Edinburgh—a development which many hoped would lead to more women becoming involved in the otherwise male-dominated world of local government.

The regional councils

The regions are the most powerful of the local authorities, none more powerful than Strathclyde Regional Council. Forty-five per cent of the Scottish population lives in its area. In 1991 it employed 85,000 people and had a budget of capital and current spending of just over £2 billion. In Strathclyde, the posts of chief executive and leader of the council are powerful enough, but there is little doubt that the ability and integrity of the occupants added immeasurably to the stature of the posts and the council.

From 1980 to 1992, the chief executive was Sir Robert Calderwood. He was born in Ayrshire but worked in local government in England, particularly Manchester where he was chief executive before moving north. As an official, Calderwood probably had as much influence in Scotland as a Scottish Office department head. In October 1991, it was reported in the *Herald* that some councillors were angry that Calderwood was going off on a month's tour of the Far East embracing two Council trade missions and a week's holiday, and thought a row might provide an opportunity to curb the chief executive's powers. But the report noted: 'However, it is understood the present Labour administration does not feel quite up to a confrontation with the formidable Sir Robert.'

The Council leaders have been equally formidable characters. Two Lanark-shire men have dominated the Council since the beginning: Dick Stewart, an ex-miner and leader 1974–86, and Charles Gray, an ex-railwayman and leader 1986–92. Gray met Stewart pre-reorganization when both were members in Lanarkshire County Council and whose murky reputation they cleaned up. To sit in Gray's office was to watch a powerful and decisive man at work. The phone rings, Gray listens, barks out a response, the phone is put down—a decision has been made. Gray's biggest political problem is his own party. In 1990, Labour won 90 out of 103 of the Strathclyde seats. However, Glasgow's left have been more interested in the District Council, leaving Gray to wrestle more with territorial divisions—Ayrshire and Lanarkshire suspicions of Glasgow, for example—than ideological conflict.

The size of Strathclyde Regional Council has been both a strength and a weakness. It is an organization large enough to achieve significant things but inherently inclined to be distant from its clientele. Strathclyde's outstanding achievement is its dealings with the EC. Much of that has been due to the way Calderwood has arranged his top management into a team of six assistant chief executives, and a depute chief executive. They have strategic responsibilities, such as coordinating technology changes across departments. One of his assistants, Dr Mike Greig, had a leading role in setting up links with the EC. The council was one of the first in Britain to establish its own office in Brussels. In the period 1975–86, it secured £157 million worth of grants and £154 million in loans from the European Investment Bank. But the crowning achievement came in 1988 with the securing of £378 million of EC funding for a £1 billion Integrated Development Operation, the largest of its type in the EC at that time. It involves spending on transport infrastructure, training, assistance for business start-ups and aid with technology investment for existing businesses. Other local authorities who have gone to Strathclyde to learn the secret of European success have found that the size of Strathclyde is a big factor.

The rationale for the regional councils was that of the economic planning region based on a city and its hinterland. The Scottish Office, which led the whole reorganization exercise, believed that such zoning would greatly enhance the work of the Scottish Economic Planning Department. But political considerations partly defeated this hope. The last Fife County Council convener and first Fife Regional Council convener, Sir George Sharp, successfully led a strong campaign to stop Fife being split between Tayside and Forth (now Lothian) regions.

Regions were required to work out economic plans, zoning land for various types of development, and in some areas this became the most visible part of regional activity. Grampian Regional Council inherited the North-East of Scotland Development Authority (NESDA) from the previous county councils, and kept the NESDA name, though it was in reality the council's economic development department, to which status it reverted in 1990. Tayside Regional Council gave its similar department a snappy name too:

Tayside Regional Industrial Office (TRIO). Otherwise, regional attempts to flex a little development muscle were patchy.

The district councils

The district councils' major job is housing. Indeed it is often said that they were only given that job at reorganization so they would have something to do. But the Conservative government was anxious to keep housing out of regional control, as Labour would tend to use rating income from the suburbs to subsidize council house rents. By allocating housing to districts, and by having quite small suburban satellite councils around Glasgow, the political problem was addressed. The importance of this decision was seen when reorganization was mooted in the late 1980s. A vigorous campaign was mounted by Conservative-controlled Eastwood, and Bearsden & Milngavie districts to stay out of Labour-controlled Glasgow.

Generally, apart from membership of the four big city councils with their large budgets, becoming a district councillor has not been an attractive proposition. It can involve long hours during the day, requiring time off work, and in the evening, eating into leisure time. The rewards are minimal financially. In 1990, the Scottish Office agreed a flat rate allowance system which gave, for example, the average Edinburgh district councillor £4 000 annually, and in East Lothian, £2 750 annually. By allocating responsibility payments to committee chairmen, payments increased to just under £8 000. Thus, many councils tend to be dominated by a mixture of the retired or unemployed, small businessmen or trade unionists, plus in rural areas, farmers and landowners. It has not made for dynamic district councils.

One interesting trend has been the growth in concern for the environment. District councils, who have statutory responsibility for environmental health, and rubbish collection, began to recognize that there was interesting work to be done here. Dundee District Council, largely through the energy of Council leader Mary Ward, and the cleansing manager Frank Mulgrew, established such a lead that in 1990 it was selected by the pressure group Friends of the Earth as 'Recycling City' in a scheme sponsored by British Telecom. The council enthusiastically organized the collection of glass, cans and paper, with the aim of recycling 25 per cent of domestic refuse by the year 2000. Many other projects were undertaken, ranging from trying to turn garden and kitchen refuse into compost, to inspecting all materials used by the council for their environmental friendliness. The Labour-controlled authority even helped neighbouring SNP-controlled Angus District Council with its glass collections.

Smaller councils have also tried various initiatives. Gordon District in 1989 was the first Scottish authority to publish a Green Charter, covering conservation, pollution control and recycling. For example, instead of just dumping old refrigerators, the council switched to using a private contractor who removed the ozone-damaging chlorofluorocarbon (CFC) gases. The fridges, 1500 of which were handled in the first year, were then sold as scrap. Hamilton District Council experimented with using a private contractor to sort rubbish being brought by people for disposal in skips into recyclable materials. Tweeddale District were first in Scotland to introduce bottle banks with separate containers for green, brown and plain glass.

Leisure and recreation became an area of some bold projects in the late 1980s. Some authorities, like Perth & Kinross and Motherwell invested quite heavily in water sports centres which attract people from up to 50 miles away. More ambitious yet was Monklands District Council's £16 million Time Capsule ice and water leisure centre, said to be the first of its kind outside the US when it opened in 1991.

The islands

Of all that came out of local government reorganization, the three islands authorities were long held to be the great success story. Their multipurpose structure, with social work alongside housing, was held to be a model for the future. But in 1991, disaster struck.

Orkney Island Council social workers, acting in the belief that children in a particular community had been sexually abused, removed the children to places of safety on the mainland. Not the least of the questions raised in the subsequent furore was whether the Council's social work department was capable of dealing with such serious matters. In the Western Isles, councillors woke up one morning to find that £23 million of the Council's money had vanished with the collapse of the Bank of Credit and Commerce International (BCCI), raising questions as to the ability of the finance department.

The reputation that the councils enjoyed prior to these dramatic events probably owed a lot to their handling of oil-related developments in the case of Shetland and Orkney, and to the creation of a cohesive local government structure in the case of the Western Isles.

In Shetland, Ian Clark, county clerk of Zetland County Council, which merged with Lerwick Town Council to become Shetland Islands Council with Clark as chief executive, decided that an Act of Parliament was needed if Shetland was to have the powers to cope with the Klondyke of oil. It was passed in 1974, enabling the council to purchase compulsorily the Sullom Voe oil terminal site. The income from rates on the terminal and other oil-related developments has been vast, enabling new schools and community halls to be built throughout the islands. More spectacular was a Disturbance Agreement, effectively royalties on oil landings which were paid into a charitable trust, and which the Shetland journalist Jonathan Wills has estimated can now be sustained at £100 million indefinitely. It funds island sport, arts and, Wills has written, a miniature welfare state of first-class support for pensioners and the disabled, including a £200 Christmas bonus. In 1976 Mr Clark left the council to work for the British North Sea Oil Company.

186

In 1974, the Western Isles Council and also the Western Isles Health Board were established, ending local government rule from Dingwall (Ross and Cromarty County Council) of Lewis, and from Inverness (Inverness-shire County Council) of Harris, the Uists, Benbecula and Barra. In 1987 Roger Haworth, then the Council's Director of Planning and Development wrote: 'For the first time, people felt a direct involvement in the government of their area; island problems and potential were seen and acted upon from an islands point of view. The council was a totally new authority with many new members and for the most part, new staff. This provided an opportunity for a new and fresh approach to local government and I think it would be fair to say that the last 12 years have been exciting, imaginative and innovative in this field in the Western Isles.' For example community schools have been built in Barra and Benbecula, reducing the need for children to travel to Stornoway (pre-1974 to the mainland) for secondary education, an incalculable social benefit.

In their glory days, the islands councils produced some remarkable political figures. Donald Stewart, Western Isles MP 1970–87 was a former provost of Stornoway. Sandy Matheson, the Western Isles convener 1982–90, was a politician to be reckoned with, as was Edwin Eunson, convener of the Orkney Islands Council 1978–90. Alexander I Tulloch, known simply by his initials 'A I', convener of Shetland Islands Council 1974–86 was perhaps the most notable of them all. In his book *A Place in the Sun, Shetland and Oil*, Jonathan Wills records a Scottish Office source as saying: 'Mr Tulloch is the only council leader I know who flies in a chartered aircraft to London, drives in state to Dover House, and grants an audience to the Secretary of State for Scotland.'

The Northern Islands have also spawned their own political movements: the Orkney Movement and the Shetland Movement. Their origins go back to the 1970s as irritation in the islands built up over a number of matters over which the Government was regarded as being insensitive: disputes over Council finance, ferry services, fishing rights, and others. The movements produced a manifesto demanding more local control of island affairs. In 1986, candidates from the Shetland Movement, the stronger of the two movements, gained four Council seats. In 1987, an extremely able member, John Goodlad, secretary of the Shetland Fishermen's Association, stood as a joint candidate in Orkney and Shetland at the general election, but caused scarcely a ripple, coming third.

The housing legacy

The desperate legacy of the vast, anonymous, and decaying council house schemes on the edges of Scotland's cities and towns has long been recognized as the most pressing problem which local authorities have to deal with. In 1914 there was no public housing; 90 per cent of homes were privately rented. By 1981, 55 per cent of houses were publicly owned, only 10 per cent rented and 35 per cent were privately owned. In 1990, there were 2.1 million houses in Scotland, with about 920 000 owned by local authorities. Something like 81 000 were estimated to be 'below tolerable standards', 145 000 were affected by dampness, and another 132 000 were affected by condensation. Add in unemployment, which can run at levels of 50 per cent and more in some schemes, and you have a picture of misery. The problems occur throughout Scotland, but on a frightening scale in Glasgow, where the District Council is Britain's biggest landlord with 170 000 houses.

People's lives on these estates have been graphically described by David Donnison, former chairman of the Supplementary Benefits Commission, and the author of respected work on poverty and housing. In *A Radical Agenda*, he related how some people were living on a Glasgow housing estate, although it could be any estate in Scotland. One was Gordon MacDonald, who had given up working down south as he was neither making money nor keeping his marriage together: 'His children have only once, during the last 12 months, been out of the housing estate where they live—to see their granny, seriously ill in hospital. They can walk safely only in restricted parts of their neighbourhood, because gangs of youngsters attack them if they stray on to their territory. Their chances of getting a decent job when they leave school are bleak. There's one health centre on the estate, open for a few hours a day, but no other doctors or nurses for miles.' Another was a widower, Pat McCarthy: 'When someone stole the boiler from the flat overhead, water poured through his ceilings for weeks before the council turned it off. Most of his possessions had to be thrown out, mouldering to bits. When I saw him, the new boiler overhead had been stolen once more. For two weeks he had been living under dripping ceilings; his bed in one dry corner, his television set in another, and one light still working. His doctor, a home help, and a health visitor had all written notes to the Housing Department about his plight. But nothing had been done. Eventually his neighbours marched in a body to the Housing Office and got some action.'

Strathclyde Regional Council had pressing social problems to deal with but was in danger of becoming remote and bureaucratic. This was recognized from the start by two influential councillors. One was the Reverend Geoff Shaw, a former member of Glasgow Corporation who ran a community ministry in the Gorbals, and became the region's first convener. He died in 1978, greatly lamented. The other was Ron Young, who had been social work chairman in Greenock before reorganization. With Greenock's director of social work, he had worked on policies targeted at poor areas and which involved the community. The director joined Strathclyde and Ron Young became secretary of the regional Labour Group. As a result of their influence, Strathclyde quickly produced a policy in which 45 areas within the region, 24 in Glasgow, were designated as Areas of Priority Treatment (APTs). The Council positively discriminated in its budgets in favour of these areas and they were put at the top of the list of applications for money from the government's urban aid programme. Seven areas, three in Glasgow, were in 1978 defined as special initiative areas, where both Regional and District Councils cooperated. Special area teams of officials under area coordinators were given the job of devising projects to secure urban aid funds and to boost community networks.

The special initiative projects were wound up in 1981. That same year, the six divisions of Strathclyde—areas with a degree of devolved management and decision-making covering Glasgow, Ayrshire, Argyll and Dumbarton, Lanarkshire, and Renfrewshire—formed divisional deprivation groups, to which three years later were added community development committees of all the councils in each division. Glasgow district in 1980 devised systems of area management to try and improve the sensitivity of their housing service, with matching consultative committees of all district and regional councillors and the local MP.

But tinkering with administrative structures was never going to solve the problem. In 1986 Glasgow District Council set up a Committee of Inquiry chaired by Professor Sir Robert Grieve, which reported that diversification of tenure, transfer of 25 per cent (more in the peripheral estates) of the district's housing stock to other owners within 10 years, was needed to reduce the Council's grip of the rented housing market in the city. At the same time, the Conservative Secretary of State Malcolm Rifkind reached much the same conclusion. The policy vehicle he came up with was Scottish Homes, which under its able chairman Sir James Mellon, had the specific objective of encouraging new forms of tenure and reducing councils' housing empires.

Both Scottish Homes and the idea that there might be better landlords than the district councils have met with a lot of resistance amongst more traditional Labour councillors. But attitudes have changed, and at the start of the 1990s, groups of new or refurbished houses are beginning to brighten up Scotland's urban landscape and the lives of people living there. Blocks of five-storey flats are being reduced to three floors and given pitched roofs to replace the leaking flat ones. Some tower blocks have been demolished, others have been refurbished and some have been let to students. New forms of ownership are springing up; by 1989, 2 700 houses in Glasgow were co-operatively owned. New types of management were being tried out. In Glasgow by 1989, there were 21 tenant management co-operatives covering 5 893 houses and a further 24 groups covering another 6 000 houses were considering making the move. Area management combined with housing redevelopment gained momentum in Glasgow. Comprehensive Area Renewal Strategies involving agencies like Scottish Homes, employed a variety of types of ownership and management and environmental improvement, using the work to train local people in a variety of skills.

Central government also pitched in, announcing in 1988 that the Scottish Office was going to lead four major initiatives. The four areas chosen were Castlemilk in Glasgow, with a population of 23 000 and unemployment at 30 per cent; Ferguslie Park, Paisley with 5 500 people and 30 per cent unemployment; Wester Hailes, Edinburgh, with 12 000 people and 22 per cent unemployment; and Whitfield, Dundee, which had 6 000 people and 25 per cent unemployment. Their problems were to be tackled with a multi-agency approach involving district and regional councils, the Scottish Enterprise (then Scottish Development Agency) local companies, Scottish Homes, the Department of Employment, local community organizations and other local companies.

The choice of Wester Hailes in Edinburgh caused some comment as it was not the worst area of poverty in the city, but was in the Edinburgh Pentlands constituency of the then Scottish Secretary Malcolm Rifkind. However it was said to have the most highly developed community network of any of the likely areas in Edinburgh. Two years on there were some visible changes in Wester Hailes. The council had refurbished some tower blocks, and demolished others to make way for low-rise, low-density housing. However, according to officials involved, there had been only marginal progress in the key to the success of the project, increasing the incomes and hence the purchasing power of the residents, 80 per cent of whom lived in a household whose income was less than £10 000 a year. It will be a long time before Wester Hailes becomes a town within a city, like Leith, but there are grounds for hope.

As a city, Edinburgh is one of the wonders of Europe, counted by some to be amongst the most architecturally splendid in the world, but also regularly cited as a place whose inhabitants enjoy a 'quality of life' as enviable as any in Britain. In character, however, and in the way it is run, it has been accused at various times of complacency, of lacking the energy and self-confidence that is such a marked aspect of its great rival in the west. And while at its heart lies a superb city vista, around its periphery there are some of the most run-down housing estates in Europe.

The capital

As the capital of Scotland, Edinburgh is the centre for a whole range of administrative functions. It is a political centre, where the Scottish Office is based; a religious centre; where the General Assembly of the Church of Scotland meets; a centre for the law, where the appeal courts of the land are sited; a financial centre, where the banks and the life assurance companies have their headquarters; and an administrative centre for a whole variety of public organizations. But it is not primarily, and certainly has never seen itself as, a great manufacturing city. As a result it lacks the central drive and cohesion that indigenous business activity can give a city. The bankers and the financiers, whose success depends on private discretion rather than public prominence, and most of whose business is outwith Scotland, let alone Edinburgh, are no substitute for the local manufacturers with their roots in the city who give Glasgow so much of its drive. Since Edinburgh has never in the past had to fight for business to come to the city, nor had to contend with the appalling problems of industrial decline that Glasgow has had to face, it has perhaps lacked a basic motivating force.

Until recently, Edinburgh suffered from another flaw. In the late 1980s there was a running battle between the public and the private sector, with the Labour-led district and regional councils seen as hostile to business and driven by left-wing ideology rather than any desire to help build the city's economy—again in marked contrast to Glasgow with its tradition of cooperation between the two sides. Latterly this mutual suspicion has largely evaporated, thanks to a series of council and business-led initiatives. But there is still a marked impression that 'getting things done' in Edinburgh is uphill work—the saga of its unbuilt opera house, the endlessly postponed appearance of its conference centre and the lack of a long-term traffic plan being called in evidence.

For those with Glaswegian experience, like Michael Kelly, former Lord Provost of Glasgow who coined the 'miles better' slogan and achieved so much for his city, trying to do the same for Edinburgh was a chastening experience. He has argued that there are so many educated and articulate groups in the city, conservation bodies like the Cockburn Association or the Old Town Trust, dedicated to the special interests of their own particular sector, that it takes time and immense effort to get planning on a large scale through. 'Glasgow doesn't have this sophistication or pretension,' he says. 'It just batters through with the decision.'

David Murray, the property millionaire, and one of the key figures in the future development of Edinburgh, says there is a reluctance by people in Edinburgh to get involved: 'There are too many people in life standing on the touchline giving advice and not getting involved in the game—too many voyeurs.'

Others, like Eric Milligan, convener of Lothian Regional Council, claim there is a gulf between the city's working class and its middle class, stemming from the famous private schools of Edinburgh. 'Edinburgh is socially divided,' he says, 'but people also accept it. There's no one fighting in the streets against it. People seem almost to be comfortable with it, it's so deep-rooted, so much part of the city.'

Given all of this, it is remarkable how Edinburgh has, nevertheless, thrived. Without any of the self-adulation of Glasgow, it has quietly expanded; its own industrial centres on the outskirts of the city, aided by one or two major businesses, like Ferranti, the defence contractors, have grown steadily; its city centre, cleaned of centuries of grime, and floodlit at night, looks better than it has ever done; the Old Town, now refurbished and transformed, has become one of Europe's major tourist attractions; Leith, though it is no longer sustained by thriving docks, has taken on a new life as a place of waterside restaurants and up-market accomodation. Leith seems likely also to be the site of the relocated Scottish Office.

In recent years there has been strong evidence of determined efforts to galvanize the city into change. A new spirit of cooperation between the public and the private sector has emerged, with the establishment of bodies such as Edinburgh Marketing and Edinburgh Vision to promote the image of the city. Lothian and Edinburgh Enterprise, the local enterprise company, chaired by Sir Charles Fraser and led by Dr Des Bonnar, has begun to drive forward a number of initiatives, with the emphasis on raising the city's profile and enhancing its appeal to inward investors. The continued success of the Edinburgh International Festival, together with other similar events such as the Science Festival, has been accompanied by growing sponsorhip of the arts from local businesses. The greatest success story of this new era has been the joint backing of the refurbished Empire Theatre, a £15 million project to give Edinburgh the opera house it has so long lacked, an enterprise enthusiastically backed by the Scottish Office, the District Council and the private sector.

Much of the argument about Edinburgh's future revolves around its property and how it is used. David Murray believes the conservationists will have to concede some of their principles if the office space so essential to Edinburgh's expansion is to be generated. George Kerevan and Donald Anderson, who at the start of the 1990s chaired the main economic committees on the district and regional councils, argue that Edinburgh needs to be seen in regional terms, with towns like Livingston in West Lothian providing the manufacturing base that the city itself lacks. Increasingly, they believe, central Edinburgh could revert to being largely residential, thus reversing the trend in larger cities whose centres are relatively empty in the evening. Financial services are still seen as a growth industry, possibly overtaking manufacturing in Lothian in 1992. Services will increasingly supply employment. It is interesting to note that in 1990, services provided 74 per cent of Lothian's employment, manufacturing 17 per cent, other sectors 9 per cent; by 2005 the percentages are expected to be 78, 13, and 9 respectively, which echo the projected pattern in London and are very different from those in 'provincial' cities like Glasgow and Birmingham.

As in Glasgow, however, the future of Edinburgh will be decided by the energies and commitment of a relatively small group of people, and they in turn view certain developments as pivotal to the city's future. Angus Grossart, merchant banker, pins much on the major conference centre due to open in 1995, but also believes that the Waverley Valley area, at present a huddle of railway sheds in the city's centre, must be redesigned if Edinburgh is to be counted a truly European city. Tom Farmer, ebullient boss of Kwik-Fit, has brought his entrepreneurial flair to developing some of Edinburgh's desperate and down-at-heel housing estates. James Miller, who heads one of the UK's most successful construction firms, is heavily committed to the arts and charities. And on the public side, though she stood down in 1992, the Lord Provost, Eleanor McLaughlin, was probably more instrumental than anyone else on the district council in breaking down the old barriers between business and the council. Alick Rankin, through his chairmanship of the brewers Scottish and Newcastle, a major employer in Scotland, is committed to a vast tourist development in Holyrood Park known as the Younger Universe, which will also refurbish the whole of the Old Town area at the bottom end of the Royal Mile.

Edinburgh, therefore, despite its critics, is thriving. It awaits essential developments such as a traffic plan and a truly international airport if it is to establish itself as a major European city, but its many advantages heavily outweigh its drawbacks. There is, of course, one change that most people agree would give it an enormous boost, and that is the establishment of a Scottish parliament. The building is there to house it—the Royal High School, which stands empty and expectant at the foot of the Calton Hill. But that is for tomorrow.

Trends in local government

Ever since the first elections to the new local authorities were held in 1974, there has been a trend of creeping politicization, and growing Labour Party control. In 1974, of the regional councils, the Conservatives controlled 2, Labour 4, and the Independents 3. Of the district councils, Labour controlled 17, the Conservatives 5, the SNP 1, and the rest had either no overall control or were Independent. By 1990, Labour controlled 5 regions, had a joint administration with the Liberal Democrats in another, and a minority administration in another, while the Conservatives controlled none and the Independents 2. Among the district councils, Labour controlled 26, the Conservatives 3, the Liberal Democrats 2, the SNP 1, and the remainder had no overall control or were run by Independents.

The decline of the Conservatives and the rise of Labour has been dramatic. In 1974, the Conservatives had 315 district and regional councillors and Labour had 600. By 1990, the Conservatives were down to 215 councillors, but Labour was up to 797, nearly half of the 1 682 councillors in Scotland. Though Labour swung left in the mid-1980s, it avoided the extremes. In 1984, it shocked the Tories by winning Edinburgh District Council. A hard left-winger, Alex Wood, became leader. He was bent on using the Council as a battering ram against the Government rather than just to win concessions. The Labour Group turned on him, and the softer left Mark Lazarowicz took his place.

The dominance of Labour, and the lack of real influence in local government among the other parties, has meant that few other people of influence or stature have emerged other than from Labour ranks. It used not to be the case. Malcolm Rifkind, Conservative Secretary of State for Scotland 1986–90 and Lord James Douglas-Hamilton, a Scottish Office junior minister from 1987, both cut their political teeth on Edinburgh Corporation. Rifkind was encouraged to go into politics by a council colleague, Brian Meek, who was leader of the Conservatives on Lothian Regional Council 1974–90 and council convener leading a minority Conservative administration 1982–86. Among the Labour MPs who had to give up council seats and posts on being elected in 1987, and who gained front-bench responsibilities in that parliament were Alistair Darling (Edinburgh Central), Nigel Griffiths (Edinburgh South), Tony Worthington (Clydebank and Milngavie) and Henry McLeish (Central Fife).

Again Labour's dominance can mean that changes within council groups have a greater effect on the politics of the council than elections. Such a case occurred in 1986, when an old-school left winger, Pat Lally, successfully challenged classics teacher Jean McFadden for the leadership of Glasgow District Council which she had held since 1977. Lally, who had been the city treasurer (finance convener) promised back-benchers they would have more say, but turned out to be an autocrat. His most infamous decision was in 1991 to take down a set of murals which had been gifted to the Glasgow Royal Concert Hall by Strathclyde Regional Council, basically, it appeared, because he did not like the paintings.

Another trend, mainly among Labour councillors, has been towards the full-time councillor, surviving on his allowance and perhaps some part-time work. These Labour councillors tend to be sharp, bright people, near the centre of the party, often with eyes on a parliamentary seat. Their determination means that they can achieve a good deal against difficult odds. A good example was the Labour group of 18 councillors elected on the 46-seat Tayside Regional Council in 1990. They formed a minority administration, led initially by Chris Ward, husband of Mary Ward, the Dundee district leader, and then by a printer, Bill Derby who became a full-time councillor. Among the councillors were Mervyn Rolfe, education convener and who became parliamentary candidate in Perth and Kinross, George Hood, economics development convener, and Raymond Mennie, the roads and transport convener. They formed the nucleus of a cohesive group and despite their minority position achieved policy advances, including the expansion of pre-school and adult education.

The newer breed of councillor also met a newer and younger breed of chief official, no longer the archetypal lawyer who has steadily worked his way though the council's legal department. In 1990, two councils, Nairn and Stirling districts, appointed chief executives aged 36. Geoff Bonner went to Stirling via Luton, the Midlands, and Highland Regional Council where he had been praised for the policy he devised for the development of Gaelic. He was appointed mainly because of his enthusiasm for decentralization and customer-orientated services. Although Stirling District Council were constantly berated by the Stirling Conservative MP Michael Forsyth for their left-wing eccentricities, there is little doubt that electoral competition for the Council has stimulated original thinking amongst the Labour councillors, who retained control in 1988 only by the cut of the cards. Bonner helped Stirling into a position to claim in 1991 to be the first authority in Scotland to draw up customer contracts specifying how and when rubbish would be uplifted and how to claim if it was not removed.

This kind of thinking arose partly because some councillors were genuinely committed to improving services, but also because of compulsory competitive tendering, introduced by the Conservative Government in 1980 and 1988. The Acts specified that building and street cleaning, rubbish collection, catering, ground maintenance, and vehicle maintenance, should all be put out to tender rather than undertaken by the councils' own staff. Many council functions had suddenly to be viewed as businesses, run to a high standard of service but on profitable lines. A furore was caused in local government circles, as trade unions predicted cowboy operators would pay poverty wages to win contracts. But out of the first wave of 44 contracts to be awarded, 41 were won by the councils' own workforces, often and perhaps significantly, renamed Direct Service Organization instead of Direct Labour Organization.

Compulsory competitive tendering also spotlighted the role of councillors as setters of policy rather than administrators. The remarkable thing about the 1974 reorganization was just how little was reorganized internally. Despite the bold talk of new corporate approaches as envisaged by the 1973 Paterson report, many new councils, staffed by officials from the old councils and controlled by members from the old councils, simply carried on in the old ways. Rigid departmental structures headed by departmental barons survived, as did the councillor who wanted to see everything the officials did listed on paper. Because the new councils were that much bigger, there had to be more committees, with more subcommittees and more minutes.

That is now changing as exemplified by Central Regional Council after 1990. A new wave of Labour councillors took charge after the 1990 elections, under the leadership of Corrie McChord, a 43-year-old who resigned his job as a local government training officer in order to become a full time councillor. Shortly thereafter, they had the chance to appoint a new chief executive, and they chose Douglas Sinclair aged 44, who had managed to help Ross and Cromarty District Council earn a national reputation in 1989 as the first Scottish council to come forward with an Environment Charter. The Council was reformed in a big way. The size and number of committees was slashed. Councillors spent half the time they used to do at meetings. Member and officer groups have been set up to discuss how corporate objectives, such as better communications within the Council and to the public, might be achieved. Under the previous regime, McChord, though a committee chairman, had never been in the chief executive's office. The policy and resources committee was divided into two, as the Council's work was being dictated by resources rather than being tailored to the policy objectives. A new committee, called Policy, Quality, and Performance Review, was created, the title describing exactly the role that the councillors believe they should fulfil, leaving administration to the administrators.

The other major trend in local government has been the concept of partnership; that no one organization is likely to be able to achieve successful resolution of a problem on its own, so a multi-agency response is better. A good example is that of the Grampian Initiative, formed by the 1986–90 Liberal Democrat and SNP administration of Grampian Regional Council. This brought together all five district councils in the region, colleges and university, and many local firms in the new and traditional industries in the region. Under the slogan 'Grampian's Going Places', the Initiative set up 'task forces' in food, sub-sea technology, tourism, and research, education, and training. The food task force, for example, under the chairmanship of Barrie Evans of Buchan Meat, has helped the international and local promotion of local produce and the further development of that produce through high technology units established on food parks at Forres and Inverurie. The tourism task force was chaired by Gordon Henry of the North-East of Scotland Tourist Authority, itself a partnership of local councils. Initially at least, the Initiative has had a big impact, and on a budget which in 1989/90 was just under £400 000.

The local authorities and central government

COSLA

The principal organ through which the 65 local authorities deal with central government is COSLA, the Convention of Scottish Local Authorities. Appropriately, its offices are at the opposite end of Edinburgh city centre from the Scottish Office, a few steps away from Haymarket railway station. It was set up at the same time as local government reorganization, a single representative body replacing the four associations which represented the outgoing 430 local authorities. Early expectations were that this single body would prove a force to be reckoned with, but these hopes were not to be realized until well into the 1980s. COSLA was initially dogged by great rows, more between rural and urban authorities over whether rural interests were being overshadowed by the power of the urban authorities, than along political lines, though the strength of the Labour Party machine was a factor. The disputes were so bad that in 1980, COSLA told the Stoddart Committee inquiring into the two-tier structure that it was impossible 'to submit a single Memorandum of Evidence which would be of any value to your committee and would at the same time be acceptable to a reasonably substantial percentage of the Convention's membership'.

The rows were eventually resolved by amending the structures until all concerned believed there was a rough balance, and also by the weight of Government legislation in the 1980s which pushed most authorities together into a common cause. COSLA was also helped by increasing both the quality and quantity of staff. In 1980 it had 17 staff but in 1990 it had 50 working to a tight budget of £1.8 million and headed by a secretary general, Roy MacIver, a former chief executive of the Western Isles. Key officials were also Bruce Black, the senior depute secretary, a personnel depute secretary Iain Roberts, and a finance depute secretary, Albert Tait, all of whom commanded respect for their knowledge of local government matters. A network of 150 advisers drawn from all councils also improved COSLA's professionalism.

On the elected member side, there are three leading posts, all elected by the 54-member COSLA executive committee for two-year terms. The president normally becomes the leading spokesman for the COSLA view of local government issues. In 1990, Jean McFadden, treasurer of Glasgow, succeeded

Eric Milligan of Lothian as president. Usually the senior vice-president rises up to the presidency, and Charles Gray, senior vice-president 1990–92, became president in 1992. There is also a junior vice-president, a post created to give rural authorities a voice in the hierarchy. For 1990–92 that was Duncan McPherson, the convener of Highland Regional Council. The presence of tough local politicians such as these in the top COSLA posts means that the organization's voice is a strong respected voice.

COSLA is not a statutory body, though the Scottish Secretary is obliged by statute to meet COSLA four times a year to discuss local authority finance. Its main job is to present views and opinions to the Scottish Office on government proposals, normally done by seeking opinions from all local authorities and then producing a collated opinion at a committee meeting. Since 1988, the latest internal constitutional settlement, there have been five 28-member committees of regional and island councils alone to consider regional matters: education, protective services (fire and police), roads and transport, social work, water and sewerage. The districts also have four 41-member committees to deal with arts and recreation, environmental services, housing, and miscellaneous matters. There are three 44-member joint committees covering economic affairs, personnel matters and planning, plus several other committees dealing with, for example, finance and rural affairs.

COSLA also acts as an employers' organization, handling pay negotiations with trade unions. As local authorities are big public sector employers, a dispute is a serious matter and can pitch the councillor chairing the joint negotiating committee into that national spotlight, as was the case with Strathclyde regional councillor and COSLA education committee convener Malcolm Green during the 1985 teachers' dispute. They also act as an information exchange between local authorities, and to bring together councillors from different parts of the country, particularly within political groups.

Strathclyde's huge size means that it inevitably has a big role in COSLA. Indeed COSLA without Strathclyde would be a ridiculous affair. But COSLA is so structured that Strathclyde does not have the share of committee places that it would be entitled to on a strict pro-rata basis, and this applies to the other big councils as well. Strathclyde has been careful not to abuse its position, aware that any division in local authority ranks reduces the effectiveness of an argument, and COSLA officials work hard at making sure the rural or independent council voice is heard. Labour's growing power in the 1980s led to the Scottish Office ministers complaining it was a wholly-owned Labour subsidiary. But what seemed like anti-local government legislation, particularly the financial squeeze of the early 1980s, meant that COSLA became cohesive across party lines, a cohesion which the poll tax further cemented.

COSLA is now at the cross-roads of the traffic between central and local government, and attempts to direct it as much as possible. Such has been the confrontation between central and local government in the last decade, that COSLA has only been really successful in altering Government proposals at the margins, or over politically non-controversial questions. Though it shaved some rough edges off the poll tax, the main body of the legislation went through unaffected.

The poll tax

The other links which are important are those between the Scottish Office and councils themselves, particularly at official level. Sometimes officials will attempt to sort out minor problems between themselves, although the politicians on either side get upset if they think the political process is being by-passed. The importance of relationships between central and local government at official and political levels, is illustrated graphically by the entirely different course of events in two dramas a decade apart. Both involve the same plot—a Conservative Secretary of State ordering a Labour-controlled Lothian Regional Council to cut its spending—but featured different actors in the title roles.

In the early 1980s, the Conservative Government introduced strict monetary control policies and curbs on public spending, particularly local authority spending which was felt to be a runaway gravy train. In 1981, 59 of the 65 Scottish local authorities had produced budgets which were above the guideline figures set by the Scottish Office. The Scottish Secretary George Younger and his local government minister Malcolm Rifkind were determined to squeeze council spending. Rifkind, as the Edinburgh Pentlands MP, faced many complaints from his constituents about rapidly rising rates bills. Thus it was no surprise when Lothian, which had planned spending 25 per cent above guidelines, was ordered in June 1981 by Younger to cut £53 million from its £319 million revenue programme.

Lothian's response was to dig in and fight back. Officials produced a document roundly condemning the government as knowing nothing about local government and threatening the jobs of 15 000 of the 35 000 employees. The ruling Labour Group's complexion had changed in the 1978 elections with an influx of young radical councillors. The result was a no-surrender policy, even when Rifkind announced in August, effectively, that cuts of £30 million would do. Exasperated ministers implemented the order, cutting the rate support grant at a weekly rate which would have fulfilled the £47 million cut by the end of the financial year. The move broke the nerve and the unity of the Labour Group. In late September, the Council implemented the full £30 million cuts package. The postscript to the affair was that in the 1982 elections, Labour lost control of Lothian to a minority Conservative administration with Rifkind's close friend Brian Meek becoming the council convener.

In May 1991, the Council found itself in the same position. The Scottish Secretary, now Ian Lang, decided Lothian's spending proposals were excessive, and ordered cuts so that poll-tax bills could be reduced by £50. Lothian officials estimated it meant slashing £25 million off the budget. The Labour administration was, however, of a different hue from that of 10 years previously.

The practical centre-left politician Eric Milligan, first elected in 1978, had become the regional convener a year earlier. The appointment so disgusted the remaining left-wingers on the Council they sat on their hands as the rest of the Council applauded Milligan. Keith Geddes, a housing rights worker who had become a full-time councillor in 1986, had been elected the Labour Group leader, while David Begg, an economics lecturer at Napier Polytechnic, was the finance convener. All three were in their thirties when elected to their posts in 1990.

The new administration rapidly proved that they would make the system work. David Begg in particular developed a reputation as a zealous collector of the poll tax in complete contrast to the previous 1986–90 Labour administration under John Mulvey. That administration dragged its feet over collection, frustrating officials who could see where the shortfall was leading and who had bitter memories of the 1981 confrontation with the Government. Under Mulvey's leadership, a dozen Labour councillors declared themselves to be poll-tax non-payers. But Begg cracked down hard on non-payment, even announcing that the allowances of the two remaining non-paying councillors were going to be arrested.

After Lang's request for cuts there followed a brief rhetorical war as fierce as any past exchange of words between the regional administration and the Scottish Office. But this time the officials did not join in. Lothian officials led by chief executive Graham Bowie, and Scottish Office officials under the guidance of Scottish Office Environment Department secretary Gavin McCrone met quietly, each knowing what the politicians would settle for, and each having a high respect for each other. After just four weeks, a compromise was agreed on: an £18.5 million package of spending cuts and a £37 poll-tax reduction. Considerable bitterness was caused amongst the Labour councillors, as the cuts cost them their much prized free bus travel for pensioners' policy. But the process was infinitely less painful than the 1981 15-week battle, and unlikely to cost the Labour councillors their credibility as their predecessors lost theirs.

The future of local government

Overall during the 1980s, local government faced a major setback mainly because of something that was imposed on them—the poll tax. The more the government attempted to cure the anomalies that kept cropping up, the more complex and hence unworkable the tax. The bigger councils dealing with areas where the the population was much less settled than in rural areas, and with residents who became increasingly determined to evade payment, were swamped in an administrative nightmare. Caught in a trap of unpopularity from above and below, the councils were abused by ministers for their low poll-tax collection rates, while voters abused the councils for trying to collect the poll tax from them. In April 1992, COSLA said that £118 million was unpaid from 1989–90, £203 million was unpaid from 1990–1, and that by

February of the third year of the poll tax, some £312 million of payments due had not been paid.

The poll tax was a disaster for local government, and had a lot to do with the call in the late 1980s for the regions to be abolished, and for single-tier local government to be instituted. In 1992, with the council tax projected to bring in only 14 per cent of local authorities revenues, it is unrealistic to expect central government not to want a big say in how that money is spent. If the council tax also proves unworkable, then it may well be that the system of local taxation will be broken beyond repair and local government will become entirely the creature of central government.

All this took place just as regions and districts had begun to work together better than ever before, begun to be responsive to the demands of the community, begun to cooperate with other sectors of society notably business, begun to accept a role as enabler rather than provider, and had begun to utilize new practices that promised to make for more dynamic, innovative local government. At the start of the 1990s, it seemed likely that this background, plus the institutional weight of opinion among Scottish Office civil servants and local authorities would make it very difficult to move to a single tier of local government.

What local government does do, more effectively than is perhaps realized, is provide a political counterweight to the Scottish Office, both to ministers and the civil service, a counterweight which would be broken under reorganization into smaller authorities. A Scottish parliament would of course bring the Scottish Office civil service under political control, but then, would there be a need to have a political counterweight to a Scottish parliament?

Scotland's Regional and District Councils

Council	Population 1990	Budget 1991–2 (£ million)	No of councillors
Borders Region	103 500	86.7	23
Districts:			
Berwickshire	19 070	1.6	11
Ettrick and Lauderdale	34 270	3.1	16
Roxburgh	34 990	3.4	16
Tweeddale	15 170	1.4	10
Central Region	272 100	213.2	35
Districts:			
Clackmannan	47 470	7.5	12
Falkirk	143 270	13.6	36
Stirling	81 360	12.3	20
Dumfries and Galloway Region	148 400	123.1	35
Districts:			
Annandale and Eskdale	36 580	3.9	16
Nithsdale	57 820	5.6	28
Stewartry	23 520	2.4	12
Wigtown	30 480	3.2	14
Fife Region	345 900	287.6	46
Districts:			
Dunfermline	129 910	16.5	34
Kirkcaldy	147 070	17.9	40
North-east Fife	68 920	8.2	18
Grampian Region	506 100	369.7	57
Districts:			
City of Aberdeen	211 080	30.7	52
Banff and Buchan	85 020	8.5	18
Gordon	74 600	8.7	16
Kincardine and Deeside	50 920	4.3	12
Moray	84 480	8.8	18
Highland Region	204 300	195.8	48
Districts:			
Badenoch and Strathspey	11 190	1.1	11
Caithness	26 790	2.4	16
Inverness	63 090	5.4	28
Lochaber	19 030	2.2	15
Nairn	10 420	1.1	10
Ross and Cromarty	48 910	5.5	22
Skye and Lochalsh	11 820	1.3	10
Sutherland	13 050	1.6	13

Scotland's Regional and District Councils

Council	Population 1990	Budget 1991–2 (£ million)	No of councillors
Lothian Region	749 600	600.1	49
Districts:			
City of Edinburgh	434 520	67.2	62
East Lothian	85 480	10.8	17
Midlothian	81 310	9.9	15
West Lothian	148 290	15.6	24
Strathclyde Region	2 306 000	1 874.5	103
Districts:			
Argyll and Bute	66 150	10.1	26
Bearsden and Milngavie	40 900	4.8	10
City of Glasgow	689 210	132.6	66
Clydebank	46 920	7.1	12
Clydesdale	58 560	8.5	16
Cumbernauld and Kilsyth	63 100	7.2	12
Cumnock and Doon Valley	43 030	5.5	10
Cunninghame	137 530	17.6	30
Dumbarton	79 750	10.7	16
East Kilbride	83 060	11.1	16
Eastwood	61 010	5.9	12
Hamilton	106 560	12.9	20
Inverclyde	93 470	11.4	20
Kilmarnock and Loudon	81 110	9.7	18
Kyle and Carrick	113 730	15.4	25
Monklands	104 460	14.3	21
Motherwell	146 760	17.0	30
Renfrew	201 030	29.7	45
Strathkelvin	89 660	11.8	15
Tayside Region	394 000	318.9	46
Districts:			
Angus	95 370	10.5	21
City of Dundee	172 860	24.7	44
Perth and Kinross	125 770	14.6	29
Orkney Islands	19 570	21.2	24
Shetland Islands	22 270	37.4	22
Western Isles	30 660	43.2	30

Sources: Chartered Institute of Public Finance and Accountancy, *Rating Review Estimates of Income and Expenditure 1991–2*, Summary Volume, Edinburgh, June 1991; Scottish Office, *Factsheet 28 Local Government in Scotland*, Edinburgh, 1991

Regional and District Election Results Summary Since 1974

Total numbers of Seats won, and Percentage Share of the Vote received, by each
political party across Scotland

Year	Labour No of seats % of votes	Conservative No of seats % of votes	Lib/Dems No of seats % of votes	Scot Nat No of seats % of votes	Indeps No of seats % of votes	Others No of seats % of votes
Regions						
1974	172	112	11	18	114	5
	38.5	28.6	5.1	12.6	12.4	2.9
1978	176	136	6	18	89	6
	39.6	30.3	2.3	20.9	4.9	1.9
1982	186	119	25	23	87	0
	37.6	25.1	18.3	13.4	5.1	0.6
1986	223	65	40	36	79	2
	43.9	16.9	15.1	18.2	4.8	1.1
1990	233	52	40	42	73	5
	42.7	19.6	8.7	21.8	4.5	3.0
Districts						
1974	428	241	17	62	345	17
	38.4	26.8	5.0	12.4	14.1	2.4
1977	299	277	31	170	318	22
	31.6	27.2	4.0	24.2	9.8	3.3
1980	494	229	40	54	289	18
	45.4	24.1	6.2	15.5	6.7	2.2
1984	545	189	78	59	267	11
	45.7	21.4	12.8	11.7	6.8	1.6
1988	554	163	85	110	227	16
	42.6	19.5	8.8	21.3	6.1	2.0
1992	468	204	97	150	225	14
	34.1	23.2	9.5	24.3	7.1	1.5

Notes: Liberal Democrat column includes all elections fought by the Liberal Party (1974–80), by the Liberal
Party and the Social Democrat Party whether separately or jointly (1982–90) and by the Scottish Liberal
Democrats (from 1992)

Sources: Bochel, John and Denver, David, *Scottish District/Regional Elections*, various volumes from
1974, Election Studies, University of Dundee, Dundee

10

The Glasgow Factor

Alf Young

Where should Glasgow be placed in the modern anatomy of Scotland?
Now that Scotland's largest city has been propelled on to the European
cultural scene—albeit with a 1991 hangover whose symptoms included gallery
closures and some unseemly wrangling in those national, but Glasgow-based,
institutions, the Royal Scottish Orchestra and Scottish Opera—should we place
it close to the national sense organs? Caledonia's eyes and ears perhaps? Or
Scotland's centre of artistic taste?

Ask the music-hall version of the typical Glaswegian male, the pinched wee
hard man in the bunnet, nursing his whisky and chaser in a well-scrubbed city
boozer, and he will unerringly go for the heart. 'Nae place on earth like it, son,'
he'll tell you, with the kind of irrepressible enthusiasm which seems impervious
to almost any privation. 'God's own city.' His modern comedy apotheosis, Rab
C Nesbitt, hasn't changed that fundamental refrain. Most Glaswegians have long
been convinced, not least by Mr Happy, that Glasgow is miles better: the city
that makes Scotland, as a whole, tick.

Some of them, particularly the many thousands without jobs, might also
wish that Glasgow still provided Scotland's industrial muscle, that the countless
Glaswegian hands which once made everything from railway engines to
chemicals, from ships to carpets, were still so productively employed. There
continues to be plenty of loose talk of Glasgow as a great centre of commerce.
But the facts of Scottish economic life in the 1990s suggest an altogether more
downbeat conclusion.

We might, given Glasgow's apparent obsession with football, look to Scotland's feet in our anatomical search. These feet might detain us a little
longer—'He's a left-fitter, by the way!'—when we recall the city's deep-rooted
reputation for sectarianism, on and off the football pitch. Or, given the genuine
poverty and ill-health still to be found in some Glasgow housing schemes,
notably those on the urban periphery, we might dwell on this crusted national
artery, that stomach bloated with a steady diet of fried carbohydrates, the ugly
red scar over there on that wasting limb.

What about the brain? Does Glasgow have any claim to control a slice of

Caledonia's grey matter? Certainly, the city's—and Scotland's—commitment to university education stretches back more than 500 years. But Glasgow is singularly under-represented in many of those broadly cerebral aspects of life north of the border—national government, civil law, church administration, finance—which are often taken as the primary dimensions of the Scottish identity.

Before we embark on this effort to chart Glasgow's place and functions within the anatomy of Scotland, I should, perhaps, lay out my own credentials for attempting such a sensitive task. I am not a Glaswegian by birth. My late father was. He grew up in Partick, but moved with his family down the Clyde to Greenock, where he met my mother. She had come, in her teens, like many before her, from Ireland. I grew up on the Lower Clyde, amidst shipyard craftsmen, and first knew Glasgow as the big exciting city to be visited on special treats, at the end of a long steam train journey. Living there came later, when I went up to Glasgow University in 1963. Apart from two short spells, teaching physics in Paisley and working for *The Scotsman* in Edinburgh—no more than five years in all—I have worked in Glasgow ever since. First in education, then politics, now in journalism. Although I lived in the city as an undergraduate in the 1960s and again from the mid-1970s to the mid-1980s, I am now a commuter, having slipped across that regional boundary under the Campsies, where Central Region encroaches on Strathclyde's west of Scotland dominance.

Glasgow since 1800

The first striking thing about Glasgow is its sheer size. As late as the early 1960s, its population was still in excess of one million, fully one-fifth of the entire population of Scotland. In its hinterland, within a modest radius, are many other substantial centres, towns like Paisley, Motherwell, Greenock, Kilmarnock, Airdrie, Clydebank, Hamilton and Dumbarton. Thus, simple numerical superiority gives Glasgow, and the west, a place in Scotland's anatomy.

That concentration of humanity was not accidental. It happened when Glasgow was industrialized in the 19th century. The city was dominated first by textiles with more than 12 000 handloom weavers by 1819, then, increasingly, by the burgeoning shipyards and heavy engineering shops, to the point where, by the end of the century, three-quarters of the male workforce was either skilled or semi-skilled. Immigrants were drawn, in their thousands, from elsewhere in Scotland and from Ireland. Glasgow was a magnet. Work, plentiful work was its attraction. Such spiralling population growth brought with it intense community pressures: dense overcrowding in inadequate housing, social distress as the utilities struggled to cope; slums, disease, crime. But Victorian Glasgow took that as a challenge. Michael Lynch writes: 'Glasgow was both the most advanced municipality in Britain and an imperial city. The Glasgow civic state—in which the Corporation ran everything from trams to telephones—was the 19th-century new town, in which notions of space and order, vital to the middle-class view of the world, were given physical form. Municipalisation was the Victorian version of Improvement—a new philosophy of patriotism, no longer North British but at once both civic and imperial.

'The city was the new reality, to which other, more ephemeral loyalties, both new and old, might stick. For the evangelists it was gospel city: the motto, Let Glasgow Flourish by the preaching of the Word, was the product of its mid-century zeal. For late Victorian civic reformers, it was the ideal city of the social gospel, a vast working model of Christian enterprise. Civic culture was confident and cosmopolitan—Glasgow was already in the 1880s being likened to a Scottish Chicago.'

Not all historians are agreed that Glasgow's apolitical public ownership of an ever-widening range of municipal services in the latter half of the 19th century—a phenomenon which drew admiring attention from across the Atlantic—had much real impact on the mass of working-class Glaswegians. 'The age of great industrial triumphs,' writes T C Smout, 'was an age of appalling social deprivation, not, certainly without amelioration, but with no solution for its terrible problems. I am astounded by the tolerance, in a country boasting of its high moral standards and basking in the spiritual leadership of a Thomas Chalmers, of unspeakable urban squalor, compounded of drink abuse, bad housing, low wages, long hours and sham education. I find it unexpected that there should be only such limited improvements in social welfare as late as 1918. What was the point of all those triumphs of the great Victorian age of industry if so many people were so unspeakably oppressed by its operations?'

There is a strong contemporary echo of these doubts in the way groups like Workers City and present-day observers of Glasgow, like the sociologist Sean Damer, regard events such as the year as Cultural Capital of Europe as an image-building pastiche of the real Glasgow. According to Damer 'Glasgow's problem is that it is a workers' city whose rulers resolutely pretend that it is something else'. Few of Glasgow's Victorian, under-educated working class had the time or energy to use the new parks and libraries, museums and art galleries. Workers City claims that 1990 left real Glaswegians in the housing schemes untouched. I am not so sure. What Scots in the rest of Scotland sometimes see as Glasgow's excessive conceit of itself—a 'here's tae us, wha's like us' defence mechanism which springs into blustering action at the slightest provocation—has deep roots. It is anchored, in nostalgic but powerful pride and respect for Glasgow's past achievements.

The shipyard workers didn't own the ships they built. Indeed, as launch day approached, depending on the state of the order book, more and more were given their cards and sent packing. Yet the community pride invested in each boat as she hit the water was tangible. Like the ships, the Garden Festival, the 1990 accolade, and, deep in the collective folk memory, the civic improvement programmes initiated by Glasgow's Victorian city fathers all buttress Glaswegian self-esteem. And Victorian self-help did bring fresh water to the city from Loch Katrine as early as 1859. Infant mortality dropped by a quarter between 1870 and 1908. Victorian Glasgow thought itself miles better too. But miles better than what?

No city judges itself in isolation. Glasgow has a convenient foil, less than 50 miles to the east, in Scotland's capital, Edinburgh. The rivalry which locks Scotland's two major urban centres in a never-ending sparring match is impenetrable to outsiders. But, as part of the bedrock of local humour, it seems to fulfil some deep psychological need in both places. Some comparative analysis of how these two great Scottish cities have developed and their present roles within the Caledonian body politic is essential.

While Victorian Glasgow was fashioning itself into an industrial and commercial powerhouse and using its new-found wealth to finance the civic state, 19th-century Edinburgh was the home of older money, much of it founded on the legal and landed establishments. But it remained, as it had done since 1707, a capital city without any of the meaningful trappings of government. There was no Secretary for Scotland until 1885. The new Scottish Office was in Whitehall, not Calton Hill. It was not until the 1930s that a fully devolved Scottish administration moved north. Edinburgh had itself flourished, but earlier, in the intellectual ferment of the late 18th century. The building of the New Town was a Georgian, not a Victorian achievement. For Edinburgh, the 19th century brought the shock waves of the Disruption of the Church of Scotland. From the 1850s through to World War I, Glasgow was in the ascendancy, with Edinburgh, always a much more socially stratified city, succumbing to a fractured complacency from which it has not yet completely emerged.

World War I was a watershed in Glasgow's fortunes. The prosperity enjoyed in the years leading up to the outbreak of hostilities, when the Clyde was one of the world's major shipbuilding rivers, could not be recaptured when the conflict ceased. The decades since the 1920s have been years of inexorable industrial and commercial decline. There were remissions, for example when Britain rearmed in the late 1930s and again, in the period of reconstruction once Hitler had been defeated. However, the underlying trend has been a persistent downward drift.

The Victorian civic state, intensely proud of its record of self-improvement, gave way to a much more politically divided city, desperately trying to manage the human consequences of decline: slum housing, mounting unemployment, poverty, the gangs. Glasgow developed the reputation as a dreich, mean and violent city, which stuck to it into the 1980s. Edwin Muir's *Scottish Journey* was published in 1935. In it he wrote: 'Since I began to write this book everybody whom I have asked for information about Glasgow has at once got on to the subject of the slums and enjoyed himself for an hour or two, without my being able to convince him that that was not what I really wanted. I have been told of slum courts so narrow that the refuse flung into them mounted and mounted in the course of years until it blocked all the house windows up to the second-top storey; and I have been given an idea of the stench rising from this rotting, half liquid mass which I shall not reproduce here. I have been told of blocked stair-head lavatories with the filth from them running down the stairs; of huge midnight migrations of rats from one block to another; and of bugs crawling down the windows of tram cars.

'The slums,' Muir continued, 'not only penetrate the lives of all classes in Glasgow, affecting their ideas and their most personal emotions, perhaps going with them into their bedrooms, but also send out a dirty wash into the neatest and remotest suburbs and even the surrounding countryside, so that it is possible for one to feel that the whole soil for miles around is polluted.'

Two years before Muir wrote that, Labour had gained political control of Glasgow, for the first time, from the Progressives. Labour ran Glasgow solidly for 15 years from the early 1950s until the SNP, capitalizing on its Hamilton by-election victory in 1967, made inroads at local elections too. Labour's answer to the slums was to sweep them away and rehouse their inhabitants in the emergent new towns, in overspill housing schemes in surrounding, smaller towns, and in the sprawling new estates created on the city's periphery. In a city with one of the lowest car ownership rates in the country, Labour councillors drove a motorway through Glasgow's heart.

Glasgow councils could build new homes for the city's people, in Drumchapel, in Easterhouse, and Castlemilk. But local government could not provide these new communities with enough productive work. In solving one set of problems, politicians and planners, however well-meaning, were creating a new generation of social ills, every bit as acute, in what the comedian Billy Connolly memorably dubbed 'yon deserts wi' windaes'.

They still argue today about who—John Struthers, the advertising man; Michael Kelly, the Lord Provost; Harry Diamond, the city's blunt-talking PR supremo—actually invented Glasgow's new image, back in 1984. What is not in doubt is the transformation in other people's perceptions of Glasgow, wrought by a combination of Mr Happy, the Miles Better slogan, and a series of exclamation mark events, notably the openings of the Burrell Gallery, the Scottish Exhibition Centre and the Concert Hall; the 1988 Garden Festival; the launching of the annual Mayfest; and the 1990 accolade of European City of Culture. After more than six decades of being very definitely out, Glasgow was in again.

The transformation was, in part, cosmetic, although it would be wrong to dismiss the present-day economic significance of the arts and tourism. But, as Stuart Gulliver, chief executive of the new Glasgow Development Agency points out, all this image work has only moved Glasgow out of the fourth division of European cities into the third. When his own agency was arguing (unsuccessfully) for British Rail to locate its new Scottish Eurofreight terminal in the city, part of its pitch was that Glasgow's unemployment problems are substantially worse than those of successful rival Lanarkshire, even following the closure of the Ravenscraig steelworks.

Glasgow has yet to find a new economic role for itself to replace the manufacturing dynamo which began to seize up as long ago as the 1920s. Promotional brochures emerging from the City Chambers still talk, in typically gallus if overblown style, of the city as the commercial and investment capital of Scotland. The hype, given the scale of Glasgow's problems, is surely forgivable since to achieve any new economic upswing requires self-esteem. That first stage of the recovery process has begun. The restoration of Glasgow's self-respect since 1984 has been achieved, in part, because the recent cultural renaissance, with all its associated PR froth, has tapped a deep tribal memory of the Glasgow of a hundred years before.

Business and employment today

Plant a city of Glasgow's size (albeit one where the population has shrunk from the million plus recorded in 1961 to less than 700 000 today) at the centre of a region containing half the entire Scottish population and you cannot fail to achieve some economic momentum. Glasgow is still a major retail centre in UK terms, a role enhanced by the lower average property costs and the higher net disposable incomes of those living in the city and its densely populated hinterland. The centre is still a hub of commerce, well served by banks, life offices, accountants, lawyers, surveyors, stockbrokers and the other professionals who make up the financial services sector. But, despite their numbers and a lively market in office building and refurbishment, Glasgow's claim to be, still, the epicentre of Scottish business life is increasingly difficult to sustain. Scotland's Top 200 companies are listed annually by *Scottish Business Insider*. In the 1992 rankings, 12 of the Top 20 companies were based in Edinburgh, 6 in Glasgow. If we consider only genuinely independent companies within the Top 50, Edinburgh can boast the two major Scottish banks; five life offices including the daddy of them all, Standard Life; our biggest industrial company Scottish & Newcastle; and a clutch of other leaders in various sectors: John Menzies, Dawson International, Christian Salvesen and Kwik-Fit Holdings. Edinburgh is also home (but not for much longer) to the newly privatized Scottish Hydro-Electric.

Glasgow, in comparison, has only two life offices: Scottish Amicable (shared with Stirling) and Scottish Mutual (since sold to Abbey National). It is home to Scottish Power and, again within the Top 50, to a clutch of nine other independent groups: Hewden Stuart, Weir, Lilley, Stakis, Highland Distilleries, James Finlay, Shanks & McEwan, Grampian Holdings, and Scottish Television. In recent years, four of these nine—Weir, Lilley, Stakis and James Finlay—have been subject to divestment programmes, reconstructions or full-blown rescues. In 1992 only Weir, the Cathcart-based engineering group, is again firing profitably on all cylinders. So, the listed company base in Glasgow looks too fragile to sustain the notion of ongoing commercial superiority.

Edinburgh is home, too, to some of Scotland's largest privately owned

companies, like the Miller construction and mining group, the Morrison Construction Group, and Murray International Holdings, owners of, among other
things, Glasgow Rangers Football Club. Glasgow's biggest private companies,
William Grant & Sons and Robertson & Baxter, are both whisky distillers, and
significant businesses. But, with honourable exceptions, the Glasgow economy
is not producing enough new indigenous fast-growth companies to replace
those being lost through hostile takeover or willing sale. Low rates of new
company formation are a Scotland-wide problem, but Glasgow seems to have
a particularly bad dose of it.

The Thatcher Governments of the 1980s had an industrial strategy to attract
inward investment from the USA and, latterly, Japan, to replace the capacity
and jobs lost in the declining traditional industries at home. Scotland was a
major recipient of such mobile investment capital, but the plants and the
jobs went, disproportionately, to the five New Towns and to other greenfield
locations. Glasgow—although it made some modest gains from civil service
dispersal and from back office functions, in the financial services sector and
elsewhere, moving out of the overpriced south-east—watched almost all the
new manufacturing investment pass it by.

The result has been endemic high levels of unemployment within the city.
By October 1991, Glasgow had the worst unemployment rate (15.0 per cent)
anywhere in Strathclyde Region. By comparison, the Motherwell rate, despite
the impact of steel closures, was more than three points lower at 11.4 per
cent. Glasgow's male unemployment rate, at 20.8 per cent, was easily the
highest in the region, and more than double the 9.9 per cent recorded in East
Kilbride New Town. Within the city boundaries, male unemployment rates in
some areas were sky-high. In September 1991, the city centre recorded the
highest rate (38.2 per cent), almost matched by Bridgeton/Dalmarnock (36.6
per cent), and closely followed by Easterhouse/Garthamlock (30.6 per cent)
and Ruchazie/Queenslie (29.6 per cent). That same month 12 other Glasgow
districts had male unemployment rates above 20 per cent; a level unrecorded
anywhere else in Strathclyde.

There is other evidence of Glasgow's comparative economic decline in recent
years. According to the Government's own figures, Strathclyde's per capita
GDP (as a percentage of Scottish GDP) fell from 96.6 per cent in 1977 to 94.3
per cent 10 years later. By 1989, manufacturing's share of total employment in
Strathclyde had fallen to 21.8 per cent, lower than Borders, Fife, Central and,
even, Dumfries and Galloway. Other than employment and unemployment
there is a singular dearth of official economic data on the performance of the
Glasgow economy. One is forced to use Strathclyde as an inadequate proxy.
But Mackay Consultants do produce estimates of economic output (GDP) by
district. Their latest estimates are for 1990. Glasgow emerges, unsurprisingly
given its still-dominant size, with the largest aggregate GDP, £4 681 million,
followed by Edinburgh (£3 827 million) and Aberdeen (£2 319 million). When
the figures are restated on a per capita basis, a very different picture emerges.

Aberdeen tops the table, with a GDP of £10 984 per person. Edinburgh is ninth, at £8 808. Glasgow comes in forty-sixth of the 56 authorities listed, at just £6 796.

The scale of Glasgow's unemployment problem may be overstated. Much of the white collar and professional middle class which works within the city has long since moved house to surrounding district council areas, where, unemployment rates are well below the Scottish average: to Bearsden and Milngavie (male rate in October 1991 5.1 per cent), Eastwood (5.3 per cent) and Strathkelvin (8.5 per cent). If this Greater Glasgow area is considered as a single labour market, the overall picture might not seem so bad. But such statistical aggregation would not obscure the fact that, in some parts of the city, between three and four men in every 10 are still officially unemployed, at a time when Scottish unemployment rates have, in general, tended to converge towards and, in the early months of 1992, fall below the UK norm.

Further reorganization of local government is back on the political agenda, barely 16 years after the two-tier system of district and regional councils was ushered in, in 1974. The Tories want change to break the stranglehold Labour now exercises over most councils. The other parties, including Labour, concede that their constitutional aspirations could not readily co-exist with so many levels of local government. So, whatever happens, a new council shake-up is under way.

For some leading Labour politicians in Glasgow District, including the former majority Labour Group leader, Councillor Pat Lally, a restoration of single-tier local government cannot come quickly enough. The city council has co-existed peacefully for the most part with Strathclyde Region. After all, Strathclyde, with its own headquarters in Glasgow, is a major source of employment and of non-domestic rate income. The public stushies, when they do erupt, tend to focus on issues of Clochemerle significance, like the infamous Concert Hall murals row: Strathclyde commissioned them, Councillor Lally didn't like them and said so. Amid threats of litigation and a fierce row about artistic censorship, the offending paintings came down.

Privately, the men and women in the City Chambers have never taken kindly to becoming a subordinate authority to Glasgow's regional big brother. They see their chance to recreate a 1990s version of the Victorian civic state. But some of them want to go further. In 1975, they managed to absorb Rutherglen. This time they have their eyes on the prosperous suburban districts, Eastwood, Bearsden and Milngavie and Strathkelvin, where so many of the Glaswegian middle and professional classes now live. That expansionism will, doubtless, be strenuously resisted. But Glasgow District is not alone in arguing that it needs access to that wider constituency. When plans were being laid to replace the Scottish Development Agency (SDA) and the Scottish functions of the Training Agency with a new integrated body, Scottish Enterprise, most of whose delivery would be subcontracted to a network of private sector-led local enterprise companies (LECs), the new Glasgow LEC, now known as the Glasgow Development

Agency, argued strongly with the Scottish Office that it should be allowed to expand its geographic area to include areas like Bearsden and Eastwood. Only then, it argued, would it have comprehensive responsibility for the training needs of the Glasgow labour market. The Glasgow Development Agency's pleas were rejected. They would have set a dangerous political precedent in areas the Tories either held or have hopes of winning back. The logic won't go away.

Regeneration projects

Refurbishing Glasgow's image in the 1980s as a major cultural centre and vibrant modern city was a natural follow-on from earlier attempts to regenerate parts of the local economy started in the 1970s. The biggest of these was GEAR, the collaborative, multi-agency Glasgow Eastern Area Renewal Project. Large tracts of the city's east end, acknowledged as one of the most run-down areas anywhere in western Europe, were subjected to a redevelopment programme which ran from 1976 to the spring of 1987. Some £300 million of public investment was committed, generating further private sector investment of some £200 million. Some of that private money came as industrial investment, for GEAR stretched as far as the site of the old Clyde Iron Works, known today as Cambuslang Investment Park. But as much was invested by private housebuilders, bringing owner-occupation to an area which had been, almost monolithically, housing for rent.

GEAR was coordinated by the SDA, founded in 1975 and itself head-quartered in Glasgow. The SDA alone spent some £70 million on GEAR over the project's 10 year life. Much of that money went on land acquisition, new factory building and environmental improvements. While few dispute that the physical fabric of the area was much improved by such sustained investment, controversy continues to rumble around just how much impact it all had on the local economy.

There were notable achievements. The Templeton carpet factory is now a bustling business centre, home to a myriad of small companies. The derelict site of the old Beardmore works at Parkhead Forge has been turned into a regional shopping centre. However most of the new jobs are inevitably in service industries, 'the worst paid, least unionised, most seasonal jobs, with the longest hours and the poorest conditions', according to Sean Damer. He cites academic studies showing that only 14 long-term unemployed east-enders emerged from GEAR as small entrepreneurs. And their efforts generated just 16 additional jobs.

Male unemployment in areas like Dennistoun/Carntyne, Parkhead/Shettleston, and Bridgeton/Dalmarnock remains stubbornly high at 21.8 per cent, 24.5 per cent and 36.6 per cent respectively (October 1991). Even officialdom acknowledges the limitations of its achievements. The 1987 SDA annual report conceded 'Unemployment in the area remains unacceptably high and the east end continues to battle against the economic tide.' In *New Life for*

Urban Scotland, published in 1988, even the Scottish Office admitted 'some difficulties, particularly the economic problems faced by residents, are very hard to solve'.

The response has been to launch sons and daughters of GEAR. The SDA launched area projects in Clydebank and Leith, Motherwell, Dundee, Coatbridge and Inverclyde. *New Life for Urban Scotland* ushered in major new initiatives in four peripheral housing schemes, including Castlemilk in Glasgow. Now Glasgow Development Agency, the local successor to the SDA has launched an £80 million regeneration project in the Crown Street area of Gorbals, on the cleared site of the notorious Hutchesontown E housing scheme. Lifting the image of an area by attacking the problems of its physical infrastructure remains a more readily achievable option for development agencies than creating new work for idle hands.

By the mid-1980s, as GEAR was winding down and the Miles Better image was being flagged up, a new SDA-inspired body arrived on the scene. Glasgow Action described itself, with typical Glaswegian understatement, as 'arguably the single most important initiative in the city's history'. With a board dominated by the most distinguished local business figures, chaired by Sir Norman, now Lord Macfarlane of Bearsden, Glasgow Action's main focus was the city centre. Its aim. 'To make the city more attractive to work in, to live in and to play in; to recreate Glasgow's entrepreneurial spirit; to communicate the new reality of Glasgow to its citizens and to the world.'

The creation of Glasgow Action flowed from a recommendation in a report commissioned by the SDA from international management consultants McKinsey. McKinsey's initial analysis of Glasgow's economic potential was bluntly realistic: 'Glasgow faces a possible spiral of decline,' it warned. 'The combined effects of dramatic structural decline in manufacturing and failure to share in the growth of service industries pose a severe threat. High unemployment and declining wealth creation are the immediate, debilitating effects.' But the ambitions set for Glasgow Action by the McKinsey team look, with hindsight, somewhat grandiose. It was to play its part in improving Glasgow's image, by improving the city centre. Building up the local tourist industry was also on its shopping list. Its blueprint was an ambitious, conceptual environmental plan for the city centre, drawn up by the distinguished urban design consultant Gordon Cullen. On top of that hefty agenda, Glasgow Action was to spearhead the drive to attract corporate headquarters to the city, help develop a local software industry, and encourage more local service industries to export their wares.

At the start Glasgow Action talked of generating between £200 million and £300 million of new expenditure over 10 years, most of it from the private sector. To underline that it was not seeking to stand on any local political toes, it invited leading councillors from both Glasgow District and Strathclyde Region to join its board. It sought active collaboration with the councils and other public agencies. But its own secretariat, though energetic, was extremely small. It had little money of its own with which to prime the pumps. Its contribution was primarily evangelical, indeed it even described itself as 'guardian of the vision'.

The new initiative's timing was good. In its five years existence, it straddled the late 1980s property boom and benefited from pressures in an overheated south-east to export office functions to lower cost areas in the north, Wales and Scotland. Glasgow's prime office district was ripe for redevelopment. In the early 1980s, new office completions had averaged some 15 000 sq m a year. From 1986 to 1989, that annual average leapt to around 64 000 sq m. Parts of the city centre seemed permanently cloaked in scaffolding.

Glasgow's reputation as a major UK retail centre was reinforced by significant new developments like the St Enoch Centre, the upmarket Princes Square and the Italian Centre on Ingram Street. The latter was just one example of a sustained programme to bring new life back to the old merchant city district. Redundant warehouses were turned into designer flats. Classy wine bars, restaurants, delicatessens, barbers, and dry-cleaners opened their doors to cater for this demanding breed of inner-city dweller. As well as the furious pace of new building and redevelopment, there was a sustained, subsidized programme to clean up the best of Glasgow's remaining Victorian sandstone facades. Emerging from decades of grime, the soft pink and buff tones gave the city centre an appealing new grandeur. Eyes drifted upwards again. Today's Glaswegians were brought closer to the monumental achievements of their Victorian forebears.

Creating new, high-tech office space was one thing. Finding the tenants to fill it was another. There was a great deal of trading up by existing Glasgow businesses. Everyone, from lawyers and accountants to insurance companies, was swapping the old green lino and standard-issue phones for computer-friendly environments with real art on the walls. There were incomers, too. In its final report, Glasgow Action claimed to have helped secure nearly 20 location decisions, representing more than 7 000 new jobs for Glasgow. One project, a Ministry of Defence dispersal, involving 1 400 jobs, had been decided before Glasgow Action came into being, and a second, the 1 800 jobs involved in the 1991 census processing project, had a very finite lifetime of two years. Many of the other relocations were back office processing functions and Glasgow Action was only too aware that these could perpetuate the city's reputation as a limb of the branch economy. Over the five years, no major corporate headquarter decided to relocate to the banks of the Clyde.

The initiative's efforts to encourage Glasgow's indigenous service industries to become more expansionist and export-minded enjoyed less dramatic success. The real breakthrough—and Glasgow Action was only a minor player in some of the key events which made it happen—was the rediscovery of Glasgow by short-stay visitors: tourists, conference-goers and culture vultures. Some 700 000 people visited Glasgow in 1982, spending an estimated £68 million. By 1988, the year of the Garden Festival, visitor numbers had risen above 2 million, and their spending is thought to have nearly trebled, to £190 million. Two years later, the year as Cultural Capital of Europe, brought more than 3 million visitors to Glasgow, part of the total audience of 9 million which participated in the 12-month Culturefest.

The end of Glasgow's year in the cultural throne coincided with the onset of recession in the UK. For the arts, 1991 was a sobering return to earth. The pioneering Third Eye Centre closed its doors. Both Scottish Opera and the Royal Scottish Orchestra were riven by mounting deficits and plummeting staff morale. Lewis's, the flagship store in the St Enoch Centre development, and a Glasgow institution, followed nearby Goldbergs into receivership. One of the biggest of the new office developments, Tay House, lay empty as the overhang of unlet new space depressed the market. Elsewhere paper plans, like those to redevelop the old Sheriff Court building and create a major new complex on a cleared site next to the City Chambers, stayed on the drawing board.

This painful, enforced pause is not unique to Glasgow. But it has come at a critical time. As the McKinsey study team observed after reviewing Glasgow Action's efforts, the turnaround in Glasgow's fortunes in the 1980s was just stage one of a long haul. If recession were to kill the momentum, however temporarily, the fragility of the achievements this far could be cruelly exposed.

Red Clydeside?

The McKinsey team saw Glasgow Action as a way of bringing private sector business people to the fore in Glasgow's regeneration effort. A high-calibre private sector board would encourage more business leaders to come forward and act as project champions. And, although the rest of the logic remained unstated, the emergence of private sector champions would reassure the rest of the world that Glasgow, in the 1980s, was more than a misplaced workers' soviet. If that was the way their minds were working, their innocence was understandable. Hadn't the Red Flag flown in George Square in 1919? Wasn't Glasgow then in a pre-revolutionary ferment, home to the Red Clydesiders? Hadn't Lenin appointed John Maclean as the first Soviet consul in Scotland? And hadn't that socialist tradition survived virtually intact? After Roy Jenkins's SDP by-election victory in Hillhead in March 1982, in House of Commons terms, Glasgow became a Tory-free zone. Labour enjoyed majorities of crushing magnitude in both Glasgow District and Strathclyde Region. The city remained Tory-free even after the 1992 general election.

And yet, the evidence was part illusion. If the McKinsey team had probed deeper they would have discovered that public/private, left/right collaboration was alive and well in Glasgow politics and community affairs, just as it had been at the height of the Victorian civic improvement drive and during the Red Clydeside era, when one of its leaders, David Kirkwood, revelled in the close working relationship he formed with the industrialist Sir William Beardmore.

Glasgow red in tooth and claw has always been something of a political

215

myth. Historians have long recognized that the George Square riot of 1919 was not planned, but the crowd's instinctive reaction to an indiscriminate police baton charge. Far from being the prelude to a planned general strike, the craft aristocrats of the Clyde Workers' Committee had been far too conservative to heed Maclean's appeals, from 1915 on, for a political strike as a way of ending the war. Six of the 10 Glasgow Labour MPs elected in 1922 were schoolmasters—inheritors not of a Leninist revolutionary tradition, but of the kind of municipal good works pioneered in Glasgow by their Liberal forebears. Some of them, like Kirkwood, were captivated by Westminster. He ended up Baron Bearsden, a title recently revived by the enobled Glasgow businessman Norman Macfarlane.

There is an instructive symmetry in that. Generations of Labour councillors in Glasgow's City Chambers have eschewed ideology for political pragmatism. At times, that pragmatism has tipped over into corruption, as with the allocation of some of the choicest new housing in the inter-war years, and some headline-grabbing trials in the 1970s. But, in the main, honest Labour politicians have been ready to work with anyone who would join them in advancing Glasgow's cause. From opposite sides of George Square, the Labour leadership in the District Council and the Conservative leadership of the Chamber of Commerce have long since sunk their political differences to collaborate on everything from trade missions to securing the funding for the new Royal Concert Hall. The Labour leadership in Strathclyde Region was quick to exploit the funding opportunities from Brussels, long before its party nationally had managed to swallow its distaste for everything the EC stood for.

The Glasgow business community is peculiarly receptive to this kind of municipal collectivism. The tradition stretches back a very long way. But there must be more to its resilience than simply its antiquity. I have worked closely with the business communities in both Glasgow and Edinburgh. They seem to me to be quite different from one another. Edinburgh's, where the financial sector predominates, has clearly-understood social pecking orders. There are also close-knit and readily traceable networks, the chosen sitting on each other's boards, and not always on speaking terms with members of rival networks. I see stratification, an overdose of genteel pretension—that laboured New Town drawing-room office style now, thankfully, coming to an end in some cases as the Charlotte Square exodus gathers pace—and too much time spent jockeying for social as much as business position. By comparison, Glasgow's business style is more demotic, its business community much more closely-knit. The Trades House, with its incorporations of Hammermen, Cordiners, Barbers and other antique skills, is one rather ritualistic hub. Although its main purpose today is charitable work, its trade structure provides yet another link with Glasgow's proud industrial past. There is more self-made money around. I am anxious not to perpetuate unsubstantiated stereotypes. But Glasgow is clearly a much less socially stratified city than Edinburgh. This is reflected in the Glasgow business community's readiness to work hand-in-hand with politicians whose allegiances they, in many cases, do not share. This may be due to the much smaller role played by private education in the west; in Edinburgh, independent schools, including boarding schools, take a very sizeable proportion of the secondary school cohort, in Glasgow the numbers are much smaller. Glasgow's independent schools are primarily day schools, and their pupils grow up within the wider west of Scotland community. All this adds to the cohesion Glasgow can summon up when attempting to change its image or alter its economic destiny.

There may be another important factor at work. As Scotland's capital, Edinburgh is home to most of the apparatus of government power north of the border, the Scottish Office. Glasgow does house one part of the Industry Department for Scotland, the bit which dispenses what's left of government support for industry and offers help to exporters. It's there, presumably, because that's where most of Scottish industry is supposed to be. But what is not there is more significant. Government administrative power is concentrated in Edinburgh. All the main political parties, except Labour, have their headquarters there, too. Edinburgh is home to the Scottish legal establishment and hosts the General Assembly of the Church of Scotland. If there is ever to be home rule, Edinburgh will dispense that, too. In all these critical areas of Scottish life, Glasgow, despite its guid conceit of itself, is the outsider, sitting on the margin of where the real power lies. Glaswegians look east the way the Milanese look south to Rome: with the unwilling supplicant's lack of respect and a firm determination to sink local differences, band together, and make the best of it.

In the dark decades of decline, when the unacquainted got their images of Glasgow from the pages of *No Mean City*, the place was indeed an outsider, a pariah even, beyond the pale of civilized society. Hype or not, Glasgow has clawed its way back far enough in the urban listings to be considered, in some quarters, a role model for the post-industrial metropolis. I've never been quite sure what that means, because I've never been convinced that man or woman can live by services alone. Glasgow seems to have solved its image problem. But it has a long way to go before it achieves economic momentum and work for all its people.

11

The Highlands

Torcuil Crichton

The Highlands—that vast region of rugged open landscape in the north—form an essential ingredient of our image of Scotland and have always exerted a powerful influence on the Scots imagination. Most people who count themselves Scottish, even if they have never travelled north of the Caledonian Canal, have a fixed impression of the Highlands, whether as one of the last great wilderness areas of Europe, a place of dramatic hills and shimmering islands; or as a romantic symbol of the past: last refuge of the clans, a rebellious outpost, victim of brutal repression.

The Highlands have had a political influence on the rest of Scotland, and indeed on London, far out of proportion to the size of their population, during most of their remembered history. From the 14th century when the Lords of the Isles ruled half Scotland, virtually a state within a state, and treated directly with the English kings; to the Clearances of the 19th century, when lurid stories of crofters burnt out of their cottages sowed seeds of a guilt complex which exists to the present day, the Highlands have been a source of irritation and frustration for central governments down the ages. But they have also been the focus for enormous efforts by governments and their agencies to inject new life into a rural economy which has been in a state of decline for as long as anyone can remember.

From Gladstone's Crofters Act of 1886 to the establishment of the Highlands and Islands Development Board (HIDB) in 1965, there have been efforts to reverse the decline in the Highland economy. Many have foundered on the rocks of climate, distance, or just Highland independence, not least the spectacular efforts of Lord Leverhulme who in the early part of this century, used his enormous wealth to establish a modern fish-processing industry first in Lewis, then in Harris, and turn the crofts over to producing milk and dairy products. He ran foul of local crofters, and when the price of fish dropped, his efforts came to naught.

More modern industries have also met with mixed fortunes, from aluminium smelting in the east to paper mills in the west, while the future of the nuclear industry, which revolutionized the economy of Caithness thanks to the advanced reactor at Dounreay, remains uncertain. More recently, however, the oil industry has had enormous benefits, particularly for Shetland and to a lesser extent Orkney in the north, while Easter Ross has also benefited from the boom. The rapid spread of fish-farming has been a modern phenomenon, and the biggest growth industry of them all, tourism, has meant that, during the summer at least, parts of the Highlands sometimes seem more like Blackpool on a bank holiday afternoon than the barren north.

Today, no geographical region of Britain has more agencies to administer it and to speak on its behalf than the Highlands. But whether there is any real political or economic power left in the area itself is open to question. The most basic resources, the land and the sea, remain firmly outwith the control of the people who live there, with fiscal and economic power exerted from further south.

Highlands and Islands Enterprise

In the past three decades no agency has been more easily identifiable with the area than the HIDB, the government-funded development agency which passed into history in 1991, some 25 years after being brought into being by a Labour Government. No aspect of life in the Highlands, with the possible exception of religious affairs, has been unaffected by the work of the Board. Nevertheless when it departed from the scene, the Fraser of Allander Institute noted that over the years of its existence, the economic well-being of the area had barely changed. It was hardly a ringing commendation of the agency which had for so long struggled with the problem of modernizing a scattered rural economy. Indeed such a judgement would be unfair for it would be hard to imagine many of the positive aspects of Highland economic life without the massive contribution the Board has made to them. For better or for worse the HIDB has created a place for itself at the very centre of the modern Highlands.

The Board has been replaced by a brand new institution, Highlands and Islands Enterprise (HIE), which took over the HIDB's commitment to the development and furtherance of the Highland economy, with additional responsibilities for training. HIE is a separate entity from its southern cousin, Scottish Enterprise, and perhaps brings an ideological as well as a practical approach to the problems of economic development facing the Highlands.

The old Board, of course, had to go. The concept of interventionism, anathema to a Thatcher Government, was carved deep into the ugly concrete walls of its headquarters on the banks of the River Ness. Ironically it survived Margaret Thatcher's spell as Prime Minister by five months, being replaced by HIE in April 1991. One of the factors which ensured that the agency continued in any shape or form was its chairman's ability to couch its grant-assisting ethos in the language of market enterprise in the last few years of its life. Sir Robert Cowan, who came from Hong Kong to chair the HIDB in the mid-1980s, also survived the upheaval and continued as chairman of the replacement agency. Unlike the previous Highland board, which was often portrayed as a top-heavy, bureaucratic civil service, the new agency was to be led by the business community in the Highlands through a cluster of satellite companies funded to deliver development and training services at a local level.

At the beginning fears were raised that the business community, barely surviving in a gloomy economic climate, would have little time or enthusiasm for the new set-up, but through a process of backdoor recruitment the members were found just in time for 10 Local Enterprise Companies (LECs) to be formed. It is within the new LEC structure that an increasing amount of the economic and developmental power in the Highlands should lie, according to the man who controls the new agency.

'The greatest distinction between the new organization and the HIDB is the dispersal of power of locally based bodies, and the drive to get decision-making to a local level,' says the chief executive of HIE, Iain Robertson. A son of the manse with a Highland background, Robertson cites this devolution of decision-making as one of the main reasons for leaving his post as a corporate lawyer with BP in the USA to take up the challenge of heading up the new agency. 'I see my job as passing more and more power out to the local enterprise companies, . leaving a central core here in Inverness to work on economic strategy and development.'

That upbeat analysis of the new structure has to be measured against the modest start-up budget which meant many of his training ambitions had to be left on ice. Some sceptics felt that the business community would use the LEC structure, which by necessity draws its members from the already established businesses in an area, to stifle new development and competition rather than foster it. But Robertson, administering a £70 million plus budget feels sure that, with the first year safely out of the way the LEC system will develop well: 'They are no different from regional or district councils in the area which tend to be dominated by businessmen . . . I think we're getting it right.'

In its first year HIE has produced major strategy documents on training, tourism, the environment, industry, social development and Gaelic, mapping out the developmental needs and broad developmental plans for each area. Out of this process some new thinking has emerged, but the exercise has also exposed the fact that policy-making in the Highlands remains heavily influenced by central government. For instance, a central commitment by the HIE is to a high-quality environment. But this is vulnerable to central government interference. It was under direct pressure from the Scottish Office that HIE dropped its objection to the expansion of nuclear reprocessing at the United Kingdom Atomic Energy Authority's Dounreay plant while drawing up its environment strategy. The HIE board, all government appointees, was poised publicly to oppose any expansion of the Dounreay work, the major source of employment in Caithness and a key element of the national atomic energy strategy. But between the HIE's draft statement and final approval, the Scottish Office, after representations from senior Dounreay officials, stepped in to protect their interests. As a result the final document addressed the issue in such vague terms as to disguise the HIE board's original position without offending members opposed to reprocessing. The fudge was, it is understood, much against the better judgement of Robertson, their chief executive, although he now defends the official board line convincingly.

A similar situation has developed with the contentious Skye bridge issue, where the Government supports a fixed link to the island on condition that the bridge is provided by a private company charging tolls equivalent to existing ferry fares in order to recoup the construction costs. Critics argue that the economic benefit of a high-toll bridge will be minimal and might even discourage tourists. Individual members of the HIE board publicly state their opposition to the scheme, but the whole board has adopted no position, except to welcome the project as an improvement to the transport infrastructure of the area.

The chief executive of HIE, who keeps a tight reign on the organization by grafting a go-getting US business attitude to the existing structure, is insistent that the new organization will stay politically neutral. 'We are an instrument of government,' says Robertson. 'We are not set up to advocate causes, we are here to maximize the benefit of government policy for the Highlands and Islands . . . my job, first and foremost, is creating jobs for the area—2 500 every year.'

Jobs, of course, do not just depend on the HIE. The newly privatized Scottish Hydro Electric Company, whose chief executive, Roger Young, is about to move its headquarters from Edinburgh to Perth, employs a total of more than 3 500 workers, many of them deployed in the Highland area. In its previous guise as the North of Scotland Hydro Electric Board this company probably did more to shape the Highlands both physically, in the form of vast dams and manmade lochs, and in terms of investment than any other single organization. There are entrepreneurs like the redoubtable Pat Grant whose Caithness-based company Norfrost now manufactures some 250 000 freezers annually, exporting them worldwide and employs 400 workers. And there are the more traditional industries such as whisky. Invergordon Distillery, which recently staged a management buyout, has become one of the components in a highly successful manufacturing zone in the Cromarty Firth area.

Local government and interest groups

Politically, the Highlands are a virtually Tory-free zone. There are no Conservative MPs, indeed precious few Conservative councillors. Their replacements at Westminster are mostly Liberal Democrats, drawing on the long-standing Liberal tradition of the area, and they are noted for a caretaker approach rather than the radicalism which is their heritage. You will look hard to find a common political agenda for the Highlands among the five Highland Liberal Democrat members. Even in the Western Isles, recaptured by Labour from the SNP in 1987, Calum Macdonald MP can be relied on to take a moderate approach to national and local issues. Political advancement in the Highlands, MPs of all shades have learned, comes through consensus and the steady build-up of the personality vote.

Despite the dominance of the Liberal Democrats at a UK parliamentary level, the Highlands and Islands electorate has consistently supported the SNP's Winnie Ewing in Euro-elections. Ewing, a star in the SNP firmament since winning the Hamilton by-election in 1967, has been the Highlands' first and only MEP since 1979, increasing her majority at successive elections. At the last count, in 1989, she had the support of nearly half the voters in the vast constituency. The SNP's early antipathy towards the EC may have helped her initially in the fishing communities of the north and west, but her own stature as a national and Euro-politician has undoubtedly strengthened her position. Ewing, the 'Madame Ecosse' of the European parliament, has become an institution. Her high profile as Highland, even Scottish, ambassador to Strasbourg, has arguably brought direct financial benefit to the area in the form of EC structural and grants support over the years, but more than that she has come to symbolize the growing relationship between the Highlands and Islands and the EC. Over the years, the Highlands, which are regarded as being economically disadvantaged by the EC, have attracted a fair amount of aid from Brussels. Although in recent years the region has slipped out of priority-help categories, Europe is still seen as an important source of funding for all major infrastructural and social developments in the area.

At local government level most councillors value their independence from party labels, preferring to build electoral support on personal reputations. On the Highland Regional Council—which has 52 members representing a scattered population of 0.75 million people—there is a small Labour grouping of 10 councillors with a none-too-strict party line.

The monolithic Highland Region looks set to survive the proposed reorganization of local government in Scotland as a single unit, overcoming criticisms that it is unwieldy and unresponsive to public opinion with arguments that it provides a democratic forum and a unified voice for the whole area and is best suited to coordinate public policy in the north. But the future structure of single-tier island authorities, once heralded as an example of how good local government should be practised, is currently open to question. The assumption that small, local councils are good councils has been blown apart by debacles which left two authorities picking up the pieces of their shattered reputations. In Orkney, Lord Clyde's long-running inquiry into allegations of ritual child abuse have exposed the Council's social work department to criticism. In the same year the Western Isles Council crashed more spectacularly when its borrowed funds were lost in the collapse of the Bank of Credit and Commerce International (BCCI) on 5 July 1991 leaving the islanders facing an uncertain economic future. In both cases it was claimed that the small councils had neither the expertise or experience necessary, at official or political level, to avoid or deal with the crisis which faced them. Among the lessons already learned from the

Western Isles' BCCI disaster, although not yet applied, has been that without political leadership from elected members, Council officials, to a large extent, dictate Council policy. With regard to the Council's investment policy, in BCCI or any other institution, officials were left to do as they saw fit because, as they later claimed, councillors simply were not interested.

The relative poverty of the Western Isles Council could not be contrasted more sharply than against the third and most affluent of the island authorities, in the Shetland Islands. Oil-rich, by a raft of measures which channel oil revenues from the Sullom Voe terminal into various development funds, Shetlanders enjoy a standard of local authority service second to none in the UK. The compensations of living on the same latitude as Helsinki include direct benefits for pensioners, suberb localized leisure and recreation facilities and a first-class roads system. The one worry is that Shetland is also on the same latitude as Prince William Sound where the *Exxon Valdez* oil spill wreaked havoc on the Alaskan environment. Sullom Voe's safety proceedures are a quantum leap ahead of those in place in Alaska at the time of the Exxon Valdez disaster but the risk of environment ruin accompanies every oil tanker that sails from the port.

Almost half the councillors on Comhairle nan Eilean, the Western Isles Council, are usually elected unopposed and on a strictly non-party basis. The only manifesto often placed before the electorate is a promise to improve amenities and roads in the locality. After four years in elected office, a member's record can usually only be judged against the number of street lights in his or her constituency. Typically, they are retired professionals or self-employed businessmen and women with time to spare. With few exceptions district and island councillors are drawn from the native population of the Highlands. Very few of the new Highland population—the 'white settlers' who have moved from the south of Scotland or England—have made an impact on local government or politics although in some areas these new rural dwellers (a kinder sociological description) make up more than half the population and have considerable economic power in the housing and employment market. Aware of the resentment their presence can generate, most incomers tread carefully around the established institutions.

They remain, however, a sizeable and not entirely unrepresented group, often finding expression on parent/teacher organizations, action groups or community councils. Of the plethora of interest groups, such as the community co-op movements, which have sprung up in the Highlands none has proved more effective or more professional, or genuinely representative of its members, than the Scottish Crofters Union. With over 4 000 members it has more subscribers than the National Union of Mineworkers in Scotland. Despite having a structure based on a trade union's branch, the organization is essentially a pressure group.

Since its establishment in 1985, with the academic and journalist Jim Hunter as its director, the Crofters Union has scored several successes in obtaining improved benefits and recognition for the crofting community. Having realized that European and UK government policy are both turning away from systems of agricultural support, the Crofters Union has been quick to present its case on environmental and economic grounds, portraying crofting as a viable means of maintaining a rural population while conserving the landscape and the habitat of wildlife. The Union is now involved in joint projects with conservation organizations which, although feared and even loathed in the Highlands for many years because of their tendency to interfere, are now increasingly viewed as allies.

Land ownership

The Crofting Acts which followed a long period of land agitation in the Highlands a century ago delivered security of tenure for the crofting community and greatly reduced the power of crofting landlords. Despite that, the land ownership issue is still regarded as central to unlocking the development potential of the Highlands. The most persistent campaigner against the traditional system of land ownership in the Highlands, is Brian Wilson, Labour MP for Cunninghame North. Now a front bench MP, Wilson was drawn to the Labour Party by the land issue, and it remains central to his thinking. 'I have no doubt that landowners remain the most powerful body of people within the Highlands and Islands,' says Wilson. 'They certainly exercise more power over public policy than any other elected or appointed body within the area by the fact that by-and-large nothing can happen without them agreeing it should.' His diagnosis, although general, is simple: 'You must have access to land in order to plan strategically for the development of rural communities. Where land ownership is identified as an inhibiting factor, the power must exist to sweep it aside.' Wilson's arguments are well-rehearsed in his regular column in the radical *West Highland Free Press*, based in Skye, which he helped found in 1972. The newspaper has influenced the thinking of a generation of young Highlanders in the West by rearticulating the radical tradition of the area.

Vast areas of the Highlands—the empty hills, glens and islands—are indeed owned by a relatively small number of landowners, but not all of them conform to Wilson's stereotype. There are those, like Viscount Thurso in Caithness or John Grant of Rothiemurchus, who live permanently on their estates, regard themselves as part of the community, and are committed to maintaining local employment. Even the absentee landlords, like the Duke of Westminster or the Vestey family, are major employers in the Highlands, responsible for a significant part of its economy. The owners of various Hebridean islands, who are often absentees, are perhaps a less reliable quantity, but those who do live on their islands, like the redoubtable John Lorne Campbell of Canna, often bring a fierce dedication to their community.

Most traditional landowners would see the future of the land as bound up with sporting rights, sheep and forestry, which sit in uneasy alliance with the greater access demanded by the modern industry of tourism, and would argue that Brian Wilson's approach would do little for the local employment they bring to tenant farmers, forestry workers, gamekeepers and ghillies. Patrick Gordon-Duff-Pennington, a shareholder in a 15 000 hectare Highland estate and former convener of the Scottish Landowners Federation, holds that landlords can, by example, show how the land can be managed for the benefit of all. 'Landowners are no better or worse than other people, but because of the position they are in, they have to make the best of what they've got for the people that live in their area,' he says. 'Of course there are bad examples of estate management, but equally many landlords are genuinely helpful and motivate development in their area. It is very easy for politicians to say that the whole thing should be turned over to public ownership, but I don't believe that would solve any problems. There would be insufficient investment in the land, and local people living and working on the land would take unkindly to being told what to do by remote bureaucrats or armies of do-gooders with environmental degrees.'

Control of the resources of the sea as much as the land is largely beyond the reach of those who live in the Highlands. Fishermen have seen local stock depleted by the incursion of the east coast and European fishing fleets which they have been powerless to stop. The 'klondikers', crews who bring factory ships from eastern Europe into Scottish waters, have been huge purchasers of local fish, but with the collapse of the former USSR and the decline in herring and mackerel stock, the end of the klondike era may have come. The west coast fishing organizations have little political or economic muscle, but like the crofters they are beginning to realize that by pushing their arguments for local control and conservation policies with the backing of the formal conservation lobby they have more chance of success.

The most modern of Highland industries, fish-farming, is controlled by the Crown Estate Commission, whose chairman is the Earl of Mansfield. As traditional owners of Britain's foreshore, the Commission leases plots of seabed to fish-farmers to whom they charge rental. Even the giants of the fish-farming industry, very much now the domain of multinational companies like Unilever or Booker, have to pay a tax per kilo of salmon produced on the sea sites belonging to the Crown, an income worth more than £3 million a year. There has been much controversy over the way in which the Commission is able to allocate sites without seeking planning consent. Lord Mansfield argues, however, that the industry could never have developed so rapidly and successfully without the Commission's ability to cut through bureaucratic delays. More recently, the Commission has been reinvesting funds in research and has attempted to broaden its consultative process.

The Church

Another body which still exercises control—though of a somewhat different nature—in the Highlands, is the Church. There are still large areas, particularly in the west, where it is the dominating force within the social system. That can have a political and commercial effect when, for instance, sabbatarianism, an issue which can still pack Highland village halls, opposes Sunday street sweeping and prevents ferries sailing. But the Church in the Highlands—even the dominant Presbyterian denominations, the Church of Scotland and the Free Church of Scotland—is an empire in decline. The Reverend Murdo Alex MacLeod, minister to the largest congregation in Scotland at the Free Church in Stornoway, acknowledges the extent of the decline, even though with an average 1 in 10 attending church, his predicament would be looked on nationally with envy. 'Church attendance in this island alone is now less than 50 per cent of the population,' says MacLeod. 'Attendance in the town itself has been maintained but that is at the expense of declining attendance in the rural areas. There isn't the same sense of need for the gospel in the communities as there used to be.' MacLeod denies that the native Highland population is turning away from the Church, but the community has been diluted. 'A sizeable percentage of the population now comes from other cultures. I have nothing against that but they conspicuously don't associate with the church. There is a challenge for us in that.'

Religion however still has some power. One of the Free Church's most notable victories of recent times was to stop the Caledonian MacBrayne's proposed Sunday ferry service to Harris. Cal Mac's state-subsidized ferry service is the lifeline of the west coast island communities. Without it, living on the islands would be nigh on impossible. Attempts at privatizing the service, during the Thatcher administration, had to be abandoned in the face of strong community opposition and sheer unpracticality, but the ferry company had to develop a new commercial ethos which led it to propose a Sunday ferry service much against the wishes of the communities it served. However, the success of the anti-Sunday sailing campaign was, in reality, a partial victory because the ferry company went ahead with Sunday sailings to North Uist.

The 'Gaelic Mafia'

As old influences wane so new structures emerge to fill the vacumn. In recent times a new type of political operator has been identified in the Highlands, an élite of 'agenda setters', as they have become known, who mainly through the success of their own initiatives have been elevated to influential positions in Highland society. They are the people who draw up the development plans, are consulted by the consultants, make the strategies, and are appointed to the institutions which affect life in the area. Not the least of these is the so-called 'Gaelic Mafia' which has emerged on the tide of revivalism and growing self-confidence in the indigenous language and culture of the Highlands. With the appointment of John Angus MacKay to the board of HIE, and then his success in becoming the director of the Gaelic Television Committee—the quango which will determine what television viewers throughout Scotland will see on the Gaelic television service from 1993 onwards—the ring of influence of the new élite would appear to be complete. In less than 10 years MacKay, from Arnol in Lewis, has gone the full circle from being an employee of the HIDB to sitting at the boardroom table on an equal basis with his former employers. In 1984 he was the successful applicant for the post of director of the newly established Gaelic language promotion agency, Comunn Na Gaidhlig (CNAG), set up in a determined effort to improve the fortunes of the language. Funded by various public and voluntary agencies, including local authorities and central government, it had the onerous task of attempting to reverse what appeared to be a terminal decline in Gaelic language and culture. 'CNAG was put together so that it could work equally well with the voluntary and professional sector. We were responsible and responsive to both,' says MacKay. 'I could have a valuable and worthwhile exchange of views with parents in the morning, and walk out of that situation into a meeting with civil servants in which we were equally well regarded and relevant.'

At the other end of the educational scale, in further education, MacKay helped develop Sabhal Mor Ostaig, the Gaelic business college in Skye, which was set up as a linguistic and cultural centre by Sir Iain Noble in the 1970s. Noble, an Edinburgh merchant banker with a strong enthusiasm for Gaelic, learned the language and speaks it fluently. He bought up land in South Skye and set about encouraging cultural and business initiatives, offering courses ranging from business studies through to television production, all through the medium of Gaelic. Sabhal Mor—literally big stable, the beautifully converted but cramped base in Sleat—is now emerging as a new force in the Gaidhealtachd. Under the guidance of Norman Gillies the college is becoming increasingly involved in economic development and training through the local enterprise network and the emerging Gaelic television industry. It has also found a role as an enabler, bringing together delegates from diverse parts of the Scottish community for major conferences on the environment, language and the arts in the Highlands. For CNAG, the development of cultural, economic and educational confidence is inextricably linked. On the economic front the organization was quick to grasp the opportunity afforded by the shake-up of the HIDB in 1991. MacKay became a founder member of the Western Isles Local Enterprise Company (LEC), one of the 10 self-appointed area companies established to deliver the training and development services of HIE at a local level. Latterly MacKay has given up membership of the LEC for a far more influential position as the only Gaelic-speaking member of the HIE board. As director of CNAG he had argued that it was vital that the new board had a Gaelic voice and, to his own surprise, he says, he ended up being it.

The most startling success of CNAG has been in persuading the Government to set up a Gaelic Television Fund to provide an extra 250 hours of year of Gaelic programmes. MacKay masterminded the campaign—a set piece of political lobbying over many months—and impressed the economic and cultural case on the Scottish Office, and in turn the Home Office officials, in order to hitch a Gaelic commitment on the back of the 1991 Broadcasting Act. MacKay's reward was to be the successful applicant for the post of director of the Gaelic Broadcasting Committee which will determine the programme menu for the extra hours of Gaelic television lined up for Scottish screens. In the arts the influence of the same professional approach adopted by MacKay has been profound.

Gaelic arts have flourished in recent years. The music of Runrig, Scotland's most successful rock band, is firmly rooted in the Gaelic tradition. Runrig, who were formed on Skye in the early 1970s, have done more to broaden the appeal of Gaelic culture than any other single factor. The language now enjoys a higher profile nationally, more funding and a definite renewal of confidence. Most of the effort in this direction has been channelled through the National Gaelic Arts Project, a development agency funded by a number of public bodies led by the Scottish Arts Council and CNAG. The embodiment of the Arts Project, set up in 1987, is Glasgow Gael Malcolm MacLean who lived and worked in Lewis as an itinerant art teacher before becoming the first Gaelic arts administrator. MacLean has worked tirelessly and not without some success to set up a framework for the development of the Gaelic arts.

At this point, a close but informed circle of influence in Gaelic affairs becomes evident. The report which led to the creation of the Arts Project was written by Finlay MacLeod, another Lewisman, and a founding board member of Acair, the successful Gaelic language publishing house. Acair is managed by Agnes Rennie, a recent appointee to the Gaelic Television Committee who is married to one of the most active promoters of community politics in the Highlands, Frank Rennie. A former employee of the Nature Conservancy Council, his freelance work in the field of social development has involved him in Gaelic arts, the LEC structure and the community co-op movement in the Highlands. Rennie was the first president of the Scottish Crofters Union and he remains on the Union council, its policy-making body. One of his major tasks after leaving the Nature Conservancy Council was to produce the business plan for the Western Isles LEC founded by, among others, John Angus MacKay. Thus the chain of influence comes full circle, for Frank Rennie is a keen supporter of the crofting trust principle espoused by Jim Hunter, architect of the Scottish Crofters Union. Hunter himself has now left the Crofters Union to become the driving force behind the Skye and Lochalsh LEC, and since then has been appointed to the board of HIE. He is also a member of Scottish Natural Heritage North West Regional board, along with Finlay MacLeod. And if this suggest that the same names increasingly crop up in Highland and Gaelic affairs, then that is simply a reflection of the reality of life. Whatever the methods, the results are plain for all to see. The lead agencies involved in economic development, language promotion, culture and the arts, publishing, television, crofting and the environment in the Highlands and Islands show a remarkable degree of cross-over in their membership. MacKay does not see his involvement in any of the multifarious organizations to which he belongs as anything else but an extension of his development work. 'Sure, I suppose people can see me in a number of positions in the Highlands and suspect that there is some kind of power base being built,' he says. 'I don't see it myself. I have always been committed to development in the Highlands and I get involved in these organizations because I see them as important levers. It is not automatic that when I speak people turn their heads to listen.'

Jim Hunter, now adjusting carefully to the role of policy-maker instead of adviser and commentator on Highland life, feels that the evidence of a new élite has encouraging signs as well. 'The phenomenon does exist to a limited extent, although it is not a new one, it has historical parallels. For example, when owner occupancy was pushed through in crofting by a small group of activists there was little the rank and file could do to change it. As we saw with the crofting trusts that simply can't be done. We have an active and articulate organization at grassroots and a group of people in their thirties and forties committed to working and improving the area. At one time there were very few people of intellectual ability in the Highlands, anyone with any academic ability left. That has now changed. Now we have a group of people who are living in the area and interested in getting things done. That is the change, and one for the better I think.'

12

The Economy

Keith Aitken

Part 1 Introduction

Preamble: Saturday, 14 July 1990

The last rays of the sun are fading and all round the grassy arena of Fallin Field
the fairground amusements, the stalls, the burger stands have fallen quiet. The
stage, borrowed for the occasion from Frank Sinatra, stands starkly lit against
the brooding backdrop of Stirling Castle. The mood among the loose-packed
crowd is mellow and expectant. Some of the smaller children have been driven
home to bed, others sleep on their parents' coats or dance happily amid the
debris of plastic beer glasses. The last hour has brought reinforcements, as the
young flock for the music of Runrig, Dick Gaughan and Hue and Cry.

At last the stage lights dim and a spotlight picks out the arrival onstage of a
group of middle-aged men and women, casually but conservatively attired. They
are introduced, to friendly applause, by a portly, florid man with thinning black
hair. Last to appear is a wiry, 52-year-old Welshman. Clive Lewis, divisional
organizer of the Iron and Steel Trades Confederation and this year's President
of the Scottish Trades Union Congress, has exchanged his chainstore jerkin
backstage for his son Steve's black leather motorcycle jacket, which he feels to
be more appropriate to the occasion. The cheer hits him like a wave and, on a
sudden impulse, he grabs the microphone. 'Ra-vens-craig! Ra-vens-craig!' The
crowd takes up the chant with a roar the bands might envy. A rock festival is
shouting itself hoarse for a steelworks.

The event is the STUC's 'Day for Scotland' and only in Scotland could such a
thing have happened in this, the 11th and final year of Margaret Thatcher's
rule. Only in Scotland would 30 000 people of all classes, creeds and ages mass
at the invitation of organized labour to celebrate their nation's hopes for itself.
Only in Scotland would they turn instinctively to a threatened industry as the
defiant symbol of those hopes.

Any examination of what is distinctive about Scotland at this uncertain time in its history comes swiftly to confront the continuing preoccupation of Scots with industrial matters. Part of the legacy of the 1980s in Britain was to depoliticize industry: to sap the confrontational potential of the trade unions, foreclose political intervention, and leave destiny to take its chances in the marketplace. Closures are elsewhere regretted as sad but inevitable, like the last of the steam trains. But in Scotland, industrial decline remains a powerful motif of plays and songs and poems, a talisman of national grievance. Among those to realize this has been the SNP, which has increasingly drawn on industrial resentments, once the prerogative of the labour movement, to promote the case for independence. What industry has become is the totem of the Scottish consensus, and totems romanticize reality. After all, Scottish popular culture has never been best known for its faithful portrayal of inconvenient truth. The industrial campaigns of the past decade have, it might be argued, been founded on a theme-park caricature of a past that never was, where fine-limbed Scots beat great machines from raw metal and spent their evenings at the Workers Educational Association; an urban kailyard of honest toil and good neighbourliness, sheltering from a privileged enemy who is never properly defined but who takes his orders and his danegeld from somewhere beyond the Cheviots. It has lately been the signal misfortune of the Scottish Conservatives to find themselves on the wrong side of all this heady treachery.

Caricatures distort. More Scots now work in fish-farming than in coalmining. As many work in forestry as in shipbuilding. Salmon-dumping by the Norwegians has lately threatened the fish-farms; in Scotland, due concern has been expressed, but no one is marching or rallying. At the height of the Ravenscraig campaign, Ian Lang, then Scottish Industry Minister, took to pointing out that there were 30 bigger-employing industries than steel in Scotland. He was right, but it was the wrong thing to say.

In attempting to assign Scotland's industrial and commercial communities their proper place in the power structures of the land, this chapter concentrates on two broad objectives: first, to straighten out the caricatures and arrive at a more accurate picture—sectioned, to show its workings—of the Scottish economy; and secondly, to attempt to reconcile Scotland's feisty insistence on still caring deeply about its industry with the profound changes which the profile of the Scottish economy has undergone. Except where stated, the statistics quoted come from official sources and publications, but the interpretation placed on them does not.

Origins

Scotland's sense of itself as an industrial nation draws from a fairly recent past. The Newbattle Charter may show that the Cistercian and Augustinian monks of Fife and the Lothians were mining coal as early as 1218 and using it as fuel to pan salt, but it was mining of a form closer to agriculture than industry.

231

Even by the 1550s, the national coal output was only around 40 000 tonnes a year: the Longannet pit today produces as much in a week. It was another 150 years before mechanical pumps were used to free the workings of water and 50 more before mining began the transition from landowners' sideline to industrial catalyst.

Coal is inseparable from Scotland's industrial history. For nearly 200 years, Scotland's miners and their families were retained as serfs, breaking free from their chains only in the last year of the 18th century. Coal became the fabric of the Industrial Revolution, the herald of its onset and its decline. There is still symbolism enough in mining to bring the crowds out to cheer when Scotland's depleted mining union—reduced to one working pit and a couple of thousand members—marches to the Queen's Park in June for its annual gala. There are other miners' galas, many better attended; but there is none which bears the same weight of national self-recognition. For one thing, none of the others takes a short cut through a Royal Palace.

Some industries pre-dated the industrial development of the coalfields. It was New World trade, in tobacco, linen, paper, (latterly) cotton, and the 'inkle' binding which Americans dimly remember as 'Scotch' tape, that turned Glasgow in the course of the 18th century from a rustic community of 13 000 to a 70 000-strong industrial port. But it was heavy industry, founded (sometimes literally) on coal, which in the century that followed built Lanarkshire's population to the size Scotland's had been then, and took Glasgow's to 0.75 million.

Industrialization came neither smoothly nor suddenly. Though the steam condenser was invented by a Scot, James Watt, it was received cautiously in his native land, where the abundance of running water deterred the mills from converting. By the beginning of the 19th century, however, it was powering a spreading range of industries. Iron smelting was an early strength, fortified by the discovery of ironstone—iron-bearing coal—in Lanarkshire and by James Neilson's invention of the hot blast furnace. Shipbuilding, previously a small-scale trade, gained industrial impetus from the development of the steamship—mainly by Scots like William Symington, Patrick Miller, James Taylor and Henry Bell—and later from the advent of the metal hull. This growth, in turn, spawned marine engineering innovations like James Howden's Scotch boiler. On these great foundation stones, industrial Scotland was built. New industries sprang up, like shale oil mining, rubber and chemicals; older ones, like wool and cotton, drew fresh momentum from mechanization, industrial organization and the innovative current of the age.

The social implications were profound. Innovation and coal were not the sole reasons for the transformation. The availability of cheap labour was an asset which industrial capital was keen to preserve from depreciation. It was the age of the urban peasantry: tens of thousands flocked to west-central Scotland from the Highlands and from Ireland. A grim existence awaited them. Cramped, insanitary and hurriedly erected housing; a working day of 14 hours (longer after the advent of gas lighting) for men, women and children alike; dirty and dangerous working conditions, subsistence pay, and inadequate diet: in all these lay the paradox, intuitively familiar to the modern Scot, of a nation's wealth being built on the poverty of its people. Diseases—smallpox, cholera, rickets, tuberculosis—shrivelled the physical stature of the Scots-Irish people, and killed them in numbers which only continuing waves of immigration could keep economically viable. Average life-expectancy in Glasgow in the late 19th century was 30; 16 years below the national figure. As late as the eve of the World War I, nearly two-thirds of the city's population lived in homes with two or fewer rooms; and nearly 15 per cent of children died before the age of one.

From this emerged a bree whose flavour pervades the modern Scottish character and caricature. The music hall Scot—small, mean, cunning, pugnacious and drink-obsessed—may dress like a Balmoral ghillie, but his traits are urban. An 1841 census estimated that Scots were drinking nearly six times as much spirits as the English. In the teeming slums, it induced violence and petty crime, unconstrained by the dire penalties of the law. The influx of Irish migrants, ready to accept lower wages than their native counterparts, added the seasoning of religious rivalry. Voices grew loud and harsh to penetrate eardrums deadened by factory noise. The old feudal simplicities gave way to a complex industrial class structure, still discernible in Scotland's social geography. Mechanization subdivided skills, and managers introduced intricate demarcations to keep their best workers. The unskilled, semi-skilled, artisans, engineers, clerks, foremen were subtly differentiated by dress, habits, and housing. A pervasive work ethic, sponsored by a stern Kirk which also dispensed such poor relief as existed, swiftly ranked these distinctions on a moral scale running from disreputable to respectable. Social mobility was minimal, particularly while children from the lower orders were worked rather than educated. The 'lad o' pairts', bettering himself through the universal opportunity of a fine education, has had a stronger grip on Scotland's mythology than ever he had on its history, at least so far as the urban proletariat was concerned. By the mid-19th century, 1 in 205 Scots reached secondary school. It compared well with England's 1 in 1 300, but it was scarcely universal opportunity.

There was reform, often stemming from the consciences of enlightened paternalists, but it was slow and erratic. The New Lanark of David Dale and his son-in-law, Robert Owen, is the best known example, even if its radical notions of friendly societies, sanitation, education and restrictions on child labour are better recognized by today's labour movement than they were by the millworkers of the time, who regarded them as an assault on family earning potential. Other reformers, Scots whose influence spread wider, included Thomas Chalmers and William Quarrier. There was also sporadic legislative reform, notably the 1819 Factory Act, an early restraint on child exploitation, and its successors; various Improvements Acts, aimed at reducing the menace to health posed by slum housing; measures like the 1842 Mines Act, which restricted the employment of women and children; and, most importantly, the 1872 Education Act, which made school attendance compulsory to the age of 13, though with numerous loopholes.

In the early years, social change grew more from enlightenment than pressure. The venerable Scottish tradition of the mob took a long time to sound an echo in working-class solidarity, which remained deeply fissured by craft jealousies, class and the power of the employer. The handloom weavers, though celebrated in folklore, were essentially luddite. Political movements like the Scottish Friends of the People or the Chartists rarely reached further down the social scale than the artisans, though they did implant ideas which would ultimately find expression in the co-operatives and the trade unions. With the collapse of the Chartists, radicalism in Scotland was left largely a rural phenomenon, which did not gain the urban stimulus of socialism until the 1880s; a stimulus which, despite its debt to Scots like Keir Hardie, came to Scotland relatively late.

The rural heritage was evident in the structure of Scottish capital through the Victorian age and beyond. The company, like the farm, was a family concern to be passed on to succeeding generations. Those which grew did so largely from self-generated success, rather than from credit or amalgamation. Only in the 1880s did the system begin to rationalize, and even then the engine of change was the defence of markets rather than strategic expansion. It was the time of the great industrial and financial dynasties: the Tennants, the Finlays, the Stephens, the Colvilles, the Murrays, the Lithgows, the Wemysses and the rest. Today, when ownership often lies vested in distant, faceless institutions, this era can assume a golden glow, but there are good reasons for seeing in it the origins of a deadly inertia. The dynasties grew closer to each other, bound by ties of marriage or by interlocking directorships; sometimes, as a means of regulating markets or of raising 'joint stock' capital, businesses merged beneath the umbrella of holding companies. But scant industrial restructuring occurred and little attempt to enhance efficiency or streamline production. By contrast, in the rising industrial economies of the USA and continental Europe, the banks were actively promoting amalgamations as a means of creating rationalized, corporate structures. From these would ultimately flow systems of mass production and trans-national marketing that would leave Scotland's muscular craftsmanship mired in the past.

Hindsight discerns in the decades before 1914 the seeds of the long decline that was to follow. At the time, they were deeply buried. Trade was booming, powered by the shipbuilding might of the Clyde, and extending the market for Scots goods to every corner of the world. Abundant raw materials like coal and iron ore seemed unassailable. By the eve of war, Scotland was outputting more than 42 million tonnes of coal a year and close to 1.5 million tonnes of pig iron. Scottish engineering remained world-class. There was little incentive to diversify from heavy industry, and little apparent cause to worry as the growth of the holding companies drew corporate ownership from Scotland; after all, partnership with English firms, even junior partnership, brought fuller access to the opportunities of empire. There were exceptions—J & P

Coats, under the management of a Prussian, Otto Philippi, systematically swallowed smaller rivals to become one of the first true multinationals—but they were rare. Booming demand encouraged neglect of design and discouraged investment in new technologies. The Clyde built 40 per cent of the British warships commissioned from private yards in the half-century to 1939 but only Yarrow's—significantly, the only one now surviving—made a consistent success of design.

The coming of war hastened the inevitable reckoning. Exports were severely disrupted, both by the naval threat and by the diversion of heavy industry to the war effort. Though some industries enjoyed a brief post-war boom, many overseas markets had been lost forever. Confiscated German shipping was sold at bargain prices, to the lasting injury of the Clyde yards. Across Scotland's mainstay industries capacity, swollen by the demands of war, massively exceeded demand. Prohibition in the US savaged whisky exports. New products and methods had grown up and the war had helped centralize the lighter industries closer to London.

Though the depression of the 1930s took a terrible social toll on Scotland—in 1933, male unemployment touched 35 per cent—the chronic nature of the decline among core industries remained to some degree masked. Everywhere, after all, was in recession, and there were some encouraging structural changes. Holding companies began to rationalize, a few rising to command their sectors. Acquisitions grew, as the banks took on an increasing industrial role. This coincided with a general upsurge in the financial sector, notably in investment trusts. These sometimes invested in industrial concerns, but more often sought higher returns from government or foreign stock, having been started, in the 1870s, to divert manufacturing profits into more lucrative deployment than industry. A cross-fertilization began, and continues, between the boards of manufacturing firms and financial institutions. The institutions, while willing to invest in industry, had little interest in running it. Manufacturing remained largely under family control, if no longer outright ownership. There were instances of managers reaching boards, but usually through dynastic sponsorship or because the controlling family lacked a mature heir. The acquisitions and mergers process also set in train another trend that was to show great staying power; the seepage of headquarters and therefore of strategic control to London. The two economies were drawing closer than at any time since the Union of 1707. Increasingly, Scots firms might buy basic supplies from England, process them, and send products back south for assembly or finishing. They were also learning to shop around for capital, often looking to London.

With the end of World War II, the outline of today's Scottish economic profile becomes increasingly recognizable. Groups like the Scottish Development Council had long worried about the rigid reliance of the Scottish economy on declining staples, and had tried to graft on newer and lighter industries. But the decay in the manufacturing base was becoming clear. Output in industries like coal, shipbuilding and heavy engineering was falling, taking productivity with it. Scottish coal output halved between the eve of World War I and the end of World War II. By 1948, Scotland was contributing just 8.9 per cent of the national income against the 9.8 per cent it had provided in 1924, and by 1960 it was down to 8.7 per cent. For a while, employment levels held up against the odds: peaking in engineering and shipbuilding in the mid-1950s, and in mining (where a massive reconstruction programme was mounted) in 1958. But when the crash came it was brutal. Shipbuilding, with the localized sourcing which still supported around 15 per cent of Scottish manufacturing into the 1960s, painfully subsided. Between 1962 and 1977, Glasgow alone lost more than 85 000 jobs, nearly 40 000 of them in metals, shipbuilding and engineering. The 187 Scots pits working at the end of the war dwindled, by the late 1970s, to 18. Textiles employed 125 800 in 1966 and 88 200 in 1978 (the figure is now below 50 000).

Against this background, other profound changes were taking place. Nationalization, much debated in the pre-war years, became a central drive of the Attlee Government: the coal mines, the railways, the electricity industry, the gas boards, the airways, and steel (later successively denationalized, renationalized, and privatized!) were all brought into public ownership. To the coal industry, it brought the faith that 'a painful record of exploitation, poverty and beggary' was coming to a a close. It brought the 1950 *Plan for Coal* and 1955 *Scotland's Coal Plan*, which set forth an ambitious investment programme to return Scottish production to the pre-war level of 30 million tonnes. The programme was a noble failure. Of 15 new sinkings, six were moderately successful, two less so, one abandoned and six travesties. The Rothes, sunk at huge cost and intended to last a century, closed after five years. The bigger problem with nationalization was the effect it had on Scottish coalfield economics. Scotland, with the biggest investment programme, shouldered the biggest burden of expectation. Pre-war, the coalfield had achieved appreciably better productivity and costs (though poorer pay and conditions) than those elsewhere in the UK. It had its own local markets which it knew how to address. But as it struggled to square the circle of a doomed reconstruction programme, a reputation grew for hurling money down mine-shafts at hard-won, low calorie, high-cost coal. From the 1980s, as the industry faced the pains of rapid market loss and retrenchment, the Scottish pits slid inexorably to the bottom of a centrally drafted agenda. In 1992, only Longannet remains in operation.

Industrial structures which had made sense in Scotland—steel for example—made none once dashed on a wider canvas. Nationalization may have given some industries the strategies they needed but its enduring impact on Scotland was to externalize and depersonalize ownership, control and capital. The industrial dynasties were meanwhile discovering that money could work harder put elsewhere than in their family firms. Those that did not sell out to the state, took to selling blocks of shares to the financial institutions, particularly insurance companies and pension funds, and investing the proceeds in high-yield portfolios that had nothing to do with Scottish manufacturing.

In some cases, the families, now often minority shareholders, were allowed to retain control of the companies that bore their name; in others they simply took the money and their grateful leave. A further post-war trend to diminish Scottish ownership was overseas inward investment. Inward investment has taken Scottish manufacturing into new markets which it could not otherwise have addressed. Yet it has also created an economy which lies at the mercy of distant strategic decision-making.

Both foreign and domestic capital was marshalled into Scotland by proactive regional policy. This is now fashionably derided as the product of fumble-fisted planning policies which could not distinguish between cause and effect, perceiving the problems of disadvantaged areas in no more penetrating terms than as an excess of labour supply which could be rectified by fabricating demand. Nevertheless, it is hard to see that the orthodoxy which has followed—that the market, left to its own devices, will ultimately create equilibrium between congested and deprived regions—has achieved more: nor that the raising of interest rates throughout Britain to cool economic overheating in southern England is a measurably more sophisticated instrument of intervention.

The early 1960s brought a marked shift in regional policy, occasioned by two seminal documents: Sir John Toothill's report for the Scottish Council Development and Industry (SCDI): and the Government's white paper on revitalizing central Scotland. These preserved the central objective of increasing employment, and so of reducing emigration, but saw the means increasingly in terms of promoting the environment for sustainable growth in new industries like electronics, rather than providing relief for unemployment blackspots.

Cross-party consensus on this persisted into the 1970s. It was a Conservative government which brought a strip mill to Ravenscraig, the British Motor Corporation to Bathgate, the Rootes Group to Linwood, and Wiggins Teape to Corpach; and which mustered £47 million to save Upper Clyde Shipbuilders. But the consensus shattered with the general election of 1979. Recession swept across Scotland, chilled by the upward pressure of oil production on the value of the pound and by the disengagement of a government determined to deny shelter to those unable to weather the storm. Between 1979 and 1981, Scottish manufacturing lost 11 per cent of its output and 20 per cent of its jobs. One by one, the post-war towers of hope tumbled; Linwood, Bathgate, Corpach. The aluminium-smelter at Invergordon, centrepiece of the Highlands and Islands Development Board's dream of an industrial crucible in the Highlands, followed. So did more ancient obelisks. Scotland's oldest company, the Carron iron works at Falkirk, called in the receiver. The decade-long demise of the Scottish steel industry began. The Singer sewing machine factory at Clydebank, which had once employed 23 000, closed.

It is customary now to argue that this surgery was inevitable and that the medicine would have been less bitter had it been administered in earlier and more gradual doses. There were also developments elsewhere to sweeten the pill. Off Scotland's shores, production of oil and gas was swelling rapidly, fuelling financial services employment in Edinburgh and Glasgow, and turning Aberdeen into an unlikely boom town. In bright, modern factories, a state-of-the-art electronics industry was developing, just as Toothill had said it should all those years before, powered by an apparently insatiable demand for computers small and cheap enough to sit in every office, school and home.

These were the new strategic industries. Yet strategic importance had been given little thought in recession. Endurance was the sole criterion for survival. In March 1981 directors of the Weir Group spent a day in the company's Cathcart boardroom debating whether to declare the firm bankrupt. Eventually they decided to make one last bid for survival. The Scottish Development Agency (SDA) put together an emergency rescue package involving no fewer than 12 banks. Sir Francis (now Lord) Tombs was called in as company doctor to oversee a massive restructuring. A quiet-spoken career engineer at the firm, Ron Garrick, was appointed chief executive. Against the odds, and unlike so many contemporaries, Weir survived. Ten years later, it is the jewel of Scottish engineering, exporting equipment and buying companies across the globe, and recording profits approaching £30 million on turnover in excess of £300 million. A 'sunset industry' has produced one of Scotland's brightest economic lights of the 1990s.

Strengths and weaknesses

The Scottish economy of the 1990s bears little resemblance to that of the 1970s and before. The old mainstays, the shipyards, pits and steelworks, have shrivelled, though they continue to engage the attention of the commentators and the affections of the people. The car industry, implanted with such determination in the post-war years, has been uprooted, never a hardy shrub. Scotland now has a lower proportion of its people engaged in manufacturing than the UK average. Manufacturing employed 800 000 Scots in the early 1960s: and around half that number in the early 1990s. Even adding in sectors like construction, water supply and energy fails to bring the proportion of the workforce engaged in production up to one-third. In 1989, the service sector provided 64 per cent of GDP output and 68 per cent of employment; manufacturing contributed 22 per cent and 20.5 per cent respectively.

It is wrong to see this as a simple picture of decline. There have been areas of significant growth, and not merely in services. Over the 1980s, the computers sector chalked up a remarkable average annual growth rate of more than 30 per cent. One third of the personal computers sold in the EC were made in Scotland. Whisky continues to be a fine export performer, establishing its chic in new markets, like the fringes of the EC. The quality end of the clothing market, too, has carved deep niches in many overseas markets. Scotland, long resigned to a reputation for dowdiness, has surprised itself with a growing recognition for fashion prowess.

But these manufacturing growth areas have not significantly generated employment: electronics achieved a net gain of just 4 000 jobs across the 1980s. Service sector employment has risen by more than 310 000 since the mid-1960s (though that figure includes part-timers), and from under 50 to nearly 70 per cent of the workforce. Virtually all parts of the sector have grown in output and employment terms. The financial services sector, buoyed on the flow of oil and gas, has been increasing employment at an annual rate of 3.25 per cent up to the late 1970s, and at around 4 per cent since. The total now stands at close to 187 000, well over twice the level of the mid-1960s. The past quarter-century has also brought significant employment growth in tourism and leisure-related services, health care, telecommunications and distribution.

Does this shift from manufacturing to services matter? There was a vogue in the mid-1980s for arguing that it did not; that it was perfectly possible to build a diverse and robust economy on the provision of quality services. That argument has subsided of late, helped on its way by a record trade deficit and by the recessionary effects of the high interest rates introduced to suppress imports of foreign consumer manufactures. A deeper understanding now exists of the extent to which manufacturing underpins services. This is persuasively explained by the Scottish Enterprise strategy paper. It calculates that services constitute roughly two-thirds of both jobs and output, and productive industry one-third. But a different picture emerges from an analysis of demand, that is, final sales. There, goods rather than services predominate, constituting 55 per cent of home sales (rising above 60 per cent if, perhaps tenuously, housing rent is added to the production side of the equation) and fully 75 per cent of exports. The paper forgivably presents this in simplified terms. Services, it says, are two-thirds of the jobs but only one-third of home sales and one-quarter of export sales. That does not mean production employees work harder; merely that services like marketing or consultancy are an intermediate input to, and therefore dependent on, the productive process. Scottish Enterprise reckons this to apply to around half of all service jobs. It wants to build an economy which can produce, sell and export quality manufactured products that embody high added value—part of it provided by service sector industries.

How well-equipped is the modern Scottish economy to attack such an ambitious goal? The answer is far from simple. Scotland's economy is closely integrated with that of the UK. On many indicators it registers a distinctive performance only at the margins, though with a consistency remarkable for such a small and volatile economy. Nevertheless, it does have a number of clear structural idiosyncrasies.

Some of these count as strengths. Scotland still exports a higher proportion of its manufacturing output than does the UK, though the differential is erratic and appears to be narrowing. In 1990–1, according to SCDI estimates, Scottish manufactured exports totalled £8.6 billion and sustained 93 215 jobs. Some 70 per cent of sales were to Western Europe, reflecting a successful transition from older mainstays, like the Commonwealth and the US. Germany and France are now more important markets than the US. Export orientation should prove an appreciating asset with fulfilment of a European single market, the opening up of economies east of the Elbe and the currency stability brought by membership of the EC Exchange Rate Mechanism. A further strength lies in the orientation of Scottish manufacturing towards the more gentle demand curves of capital investment. Around 27 per cent of Scottish industrial output is in the capital goods sector, compared with a UK figure of 19 per cent. Moreover, Scottish manufacturing consistently outpaces the UK in terms of productivity; currently about 3 per cent ahead overall, and in front in seven of the 11 standard sectoral categories.

But these strengths need to be weighed against some significant structural weaknesses. Exports are greatly dominated by just two products, electronics (mainly computers) and whisky, which together account for two-thirds of the total. Shorn of these, Scottish manufacturing is significantly *less* export-orientated than the UK. Overall, Scottish share of UK exports has fallen in recent years, settling at around 9.5 per cent. It is a narrow base for the weight of hope piled upon it, and one which remains at the edge of an increasingly homogeneous market. Peripherality is a problem which bears ever more heavily on the minds of Scottish industry; so much so that the Confederation of British Industry (Scotland) has set aside its customary anxiety about public spending to demand that the Scottish Office come up with an extra £1.5 billion over the next decade to upgrade Scotland's transport infrastructure. The CBI is particularly exercised about roads—Scotland's splendid internal motorway system that connects so poorly with the main routes south—but others are just as worried about the coastal rail routes. Moreover, the perennial congestion in and around London takes its toll on Scottish goods reaching export markets. The biggest traffic jam in Scotland, one business leader told me, is the M25 motorway orbiting London. Scottish exports too often seek to compete on grounds of price rather than quality or innovation, leaving them vulnerable to attack from emergent low-wage economies and heavily reliant on solving transportation problems. Scotland's share of world trade, computers notwithstanding, is less than half of what it was in the immediate post-war years; and has failed to grow in line with rising international demand.

Productivity, too, lags behind principal international competitors. Investment levels in British industry remain below those of other industrial economies, reflecting the City's consistent preference for speculation over investment. Value added tax per person, according to the CBI, was little more than half the West German figure in 1980, and is still only 71 per cent, despite transformed working practices. The hardest workers in the world can only do so much with out-dated equipment. Nor is the capital goods orientation always the advantage it might seem. Capital goods are one step removed from the switchback of consumer demand, but only one. Many of Scotland's capital goods manufacturers rely heavily on consumer producers for their staple custom. Capital investment is not always the first indicator to dive come a recession, but it is usually one of the last to resurface.

Where there is high investment and high productivity, for example in electronics, the consequent prosperity can yield little pay-off in employment terms. Domination by remote branch plants, some doing little more sophisticated than sticking widgets together, greatly restricts the business generated for financial services. More than half Scottish industry is owned from outwith Scotland and more than a fifth from outwith the UK. The headquarters haemorrhage is one respect in which the destiny of the Scottish economy lies to an uncomfortable degree outwith Scotland's control.

Another is policy-making. Scottish economic policy is determined centrally in a unitary British state. This might seem apt enough given the integration between the Scottish and UK economies, yet its efficacy is questionable, appearing the more so with the recession of the early 1990s. Ministers argued, justly, that Scotland's path in the recession was shorter and shallower than the UK's in general, and southern England's in particular. But a longer perspective suggests a similarly flat curve to the upward slopes of the cycle. What becomes clear is that the Scottish economy responds equally sluggishly to every sort of policy stimulus, be it positive or negative, inflationary or deflationary: the et cetera of Treasury strategy.

Compare the following graphs, which aggregate Employment Department data into broad regional groupings. Figure 1 shows the paths followed by regional unemployment levels over the initial phases of the 1990s recession. Taking January 1989 as the starting point, we see that unemployment did indeed rise earlier and faster in the south of England than in the rest of the country, and that Scotland did make a later and lesser sojourn into the badlands. But then look at Figure 2 which charts unemployment across the full economic cycle, taking 1979 as its outset. What it shows is that unemployment in Scotland rose least markedly of all the groupings during the early 1980s recession, recovered least well during the growth phase, and then worsened least severely as the cycle moved back into recession. This, of course, is a measure of *relative* movement. Figure 3, which compares unemployment *rates*, shows Scottish unemployment to have been more inert than in any other part of the UK, and perhaps more endemic. What is also striking is the unchanging ranking of the regional agglomerates. Whatever the cyclical phase, the further a region is from the south-eastern centre of policy-making power, the less effect economic change has on its unemployment levels.

True, unemployment is a lethargic indicator. But other more volatile measures—average earnings, employment share, output, disposable income, self-employment—all show a relative decline for Scotland in comparison with the UK across the economic cycle of the 1980s. The inference is that, Scotland is doing better than it did, but worse than its neighbours; and that this divergence seems likely to continue.

Figure 1: Regional unemployment levels, 1989–91

Figure 1: Regional unemployment levels, 1989–91

Legend:
- South of England
- North of England
- Whole of UK
- Scotland
- Midlands & Wales

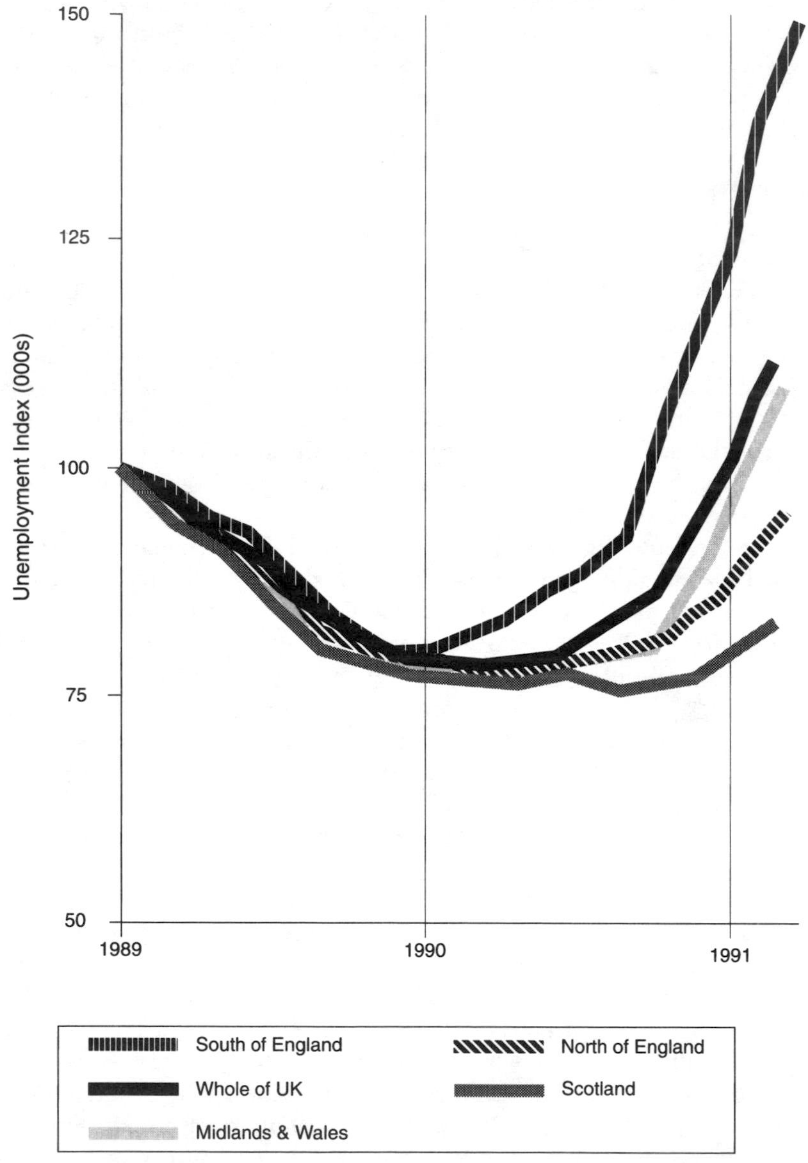

Figure 2: Regional unemployment levels, 1979–90

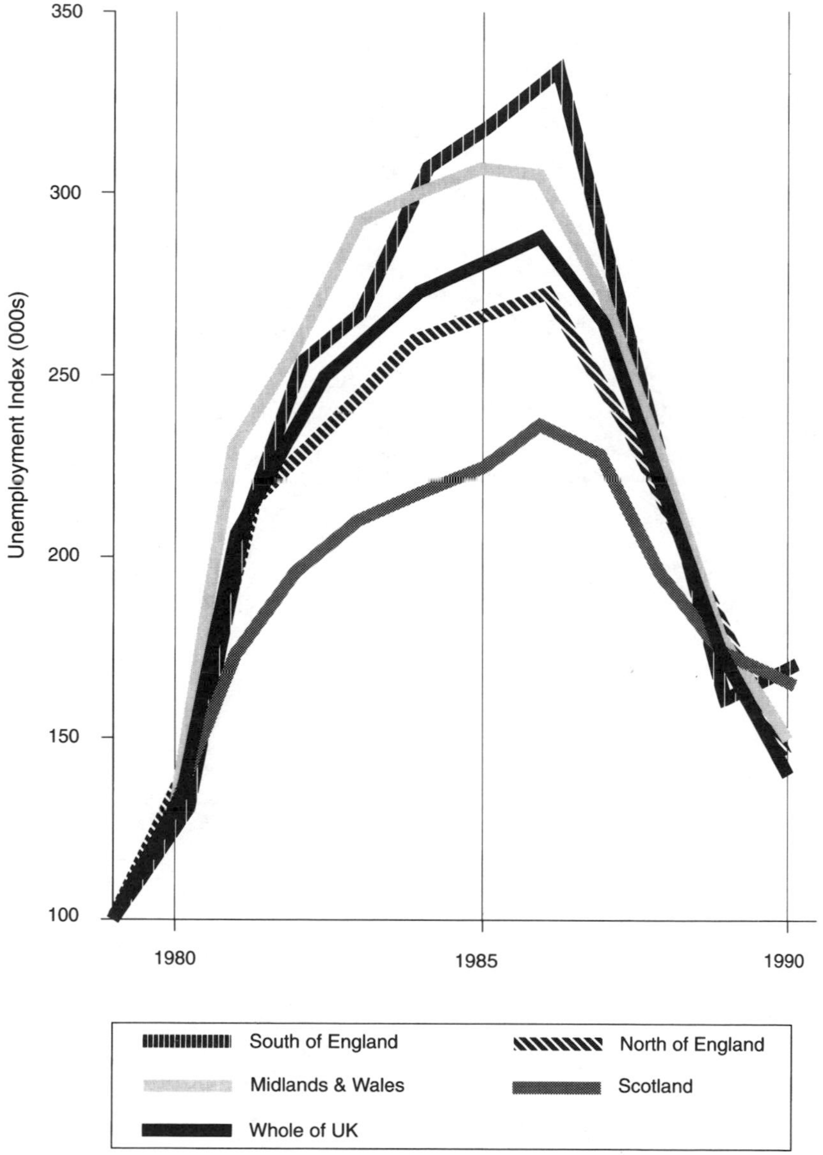
350
300
250
200
150
100
Unemployment Index (000s)
1980
1985
1990
South of England
North of England
Midlands & Wales
Scotland
Whole of UK

Figure 3: Regional unemployment rates, 1979–90

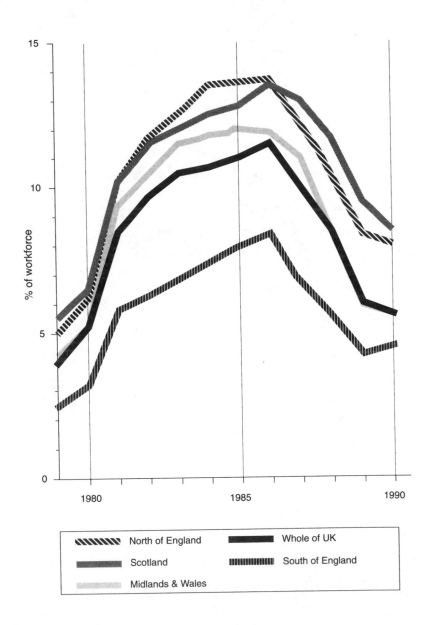

There is one last specific, but considerable, weakness to note in the Scottish economy; its high dependency on defence spending. In the cold war frosts, defence budgets were among the least vulnerable sources of demand. But that has changed abruptly with the collapse of the old Communist regimes. The Ministry of Defence's 1991 *Options for Change* review has made it plain that no area of defence expenditure, except for the Trident programme, is sacrosanct. Over the past two years, Scotland has lost defence-related jobs at GEC Ferranti (where damage was heightened by Ferranti's ill-conceived US adventure), GEC Yarrow, GEC Marconi, Yard, Rosyth, Barr & Stroud, Rolls-Royce, the Holy Loch and many more. The Scottish socio-economic structure is particularly exposed to this process. Scotland has a relatively high share of direct MoD spending—in 1988, 8.5 per cent of direct employment, 7.5 per cent of procurement budgets and 9.5 per cent of defence contractor employment. The defence unions estimate that around 1.5 million UK jobs are sustained directly or indirectly by defence expenditure, of which Scotland's share is 8–10 per cent; perhaps 150 000 jobs. But they are jobs of exceptional social and strategic significance. For one thing, many are in remote communities, where the impact of their loss strikes every sort of business from caterers to jobbing builders. For another, a great preponderance of research and development in Scotland's high-tech industries is dependent on the business of war, as is a high proportion of output. Scots may have become accustomed to seeing their electronics sector as a sleek producer of desktop technology, but around a third of its turnover is financed out of defence budgets.

The pages that follow consider how these currents play on five selected sectors. Electronics is chosen as an area of manufacturing generally supposed to be in the ascendancy, shipbuilding as one held to be in chronic decline; tourism is there to represent a celebrated service industry; whisky as a distinguished niche export. As to the oil and gas sector, it is arguably the most dramatic thing to happen to the economy of (or, at least, in) Scotland over the past three decades.

Electronics

Silicon Glen, as the electronics industry in Scotland is popularly and inaccurately known, pre-dates its recent hyperbole. Its foundations were laid with the first big wave of inward investment in the 1940s and 1950s, which brought settlers like Ferranti, IBM, Honeywell and NCR. The hype is of more recent vintage, dating from the late 1970s when the industry underwent rapid growth thanks to a renewed surge of investment allied to the personal computer revolution. The Glen, incidentally, does not accord with any topographical feature, unless the Highland Boundary Fault is taken to be the northern escarpment of a single valley. Electronics plants are spread across central Scotland from Tayside to Ayrshire, with the main concentration in the five New Towns, but there is also a sprinkling of operations elsewhere.

Is it reasonable to talk of hype? By some measures electronics, particularly computers, are of great importance to the Scottish economy, and have gained distinction as other industries contracted. Electronics alone accounts for such growth—not quite 20 per cent—which Scottish manufacturing managed to achieve across the 1980s. Output growth in electronics averaged 14 per cent a year over the decade, with computers averaging a lustrous 30.1 per cent. It has also been a potent source of investment, ploughing in more than £200 million in 1988. Above all, it has become Scotland's biggest exporter. In 1990, according to the SCDI, computers accounted for 33 per cent of Scottish manufactured exports, and electronics in general for 42 per cent. Computers achieved overseas sales of £2.8 billion, over 90 per cent of them in Europe.

These are considerable achievements, yet they could not be said conspicuously to have galvanized the Scottish economy. Electronics could never have replaced the other industries allowed to wither in the 1980s. For one thing, it is a high-performing generator of wealth, but a low-performing job creator. Output grew 10 times as fast as employment in the 1980s. At the time when output first began to soar in the early years of the decade (while the rest of the manufacturing base was crumbling in recession) electronics was actually *shedding* jobs. Across the 1980s, electronics employment rose by fewer than 5 000 while manufacturing as a whole lost more than 200 000 jobs, The 47 000 Scots working in electronics are a smaller workforce even than in mechanical engineering, and less than a quarter the number employed in retail distribution. Broadening the focus to the standard industrial classification of electrical and instrument engineering shows employment to have fallen from 62 900 in 1966 and 70 000 in 1978 to 59 900 in 1990.

In the early 1980s, there was much eager talk of the industry achieving *critical mass*. This meant that inward investment would reach a volume and animation whereby it started spontaneously to give off entrepreneurial energy and so generate indigenous growth. It simply never came about. The proportion of the industry owned within the UK is smaller now than a decade ago: 48.9 per cent of electronics employment in 1989, against 54.3 per cent in 1979. More than two-fifths of jobs are in US-owned plants. The number in Scottish-owned firms is unrecorded, but certainly small; in 1985, Andrew Hargrave put it at 10–15 per cent and it has probably since shrunk.

There have been some successful Scottish start-ups in the industry—Prestwick Circuits, Linn Products—but the failures have been at least as signal: Rodime, Domain, ESI, Hinari. It is perhaps a measure of Scotland's faith in her own competitive capabilities that the last of these, a valiant but over-impetuous assault on the consumer electronics market, was deliberately named by its Glasgow-based founders to sound as if it was Japanese. Where Scotland has succeeded in nurturing indigenous start-ups, they have generally been on the innovative fringes of the industry. Software, despite sustained cultivation from the SDA and others is an area of obvious potential which has not flowered commercially. Scotland produces many software talents, and numerous seedling companies, but few spread their roots.

A number of explanations are advanced for this entrepreneurial inertia. Dr David Simpson, who set up one of Scotland's first semi-conductor plants for Howard Hughes at Glenrothes in 1960 and was later involved in bringing Hewlett Packard to South Queensferry, identifies three key differences between Scotland's electronics industry and that of the US, where he spent much of his career. These are: the lack of an adventurous and well-infrastructured local market; the lack of sufficient fiscal incentives for entrepreneurship; and the lack of knowledgeable, audacious or resilient sources of venture capital. He writes: 'In Scotland I have seen examples of companies taking millions of pounds of the investors' money, failing to meet their projections and ending up in receivership—despite the fact that they have world-class products and good market acceptance. Instead of moving in with help at the crucial time, the investors took cold feet and ran for cover.' No doubt there is much wisdom in that, and particularly its comment on a timid and short-breathed financial sector. There are investment houses which have put money into electronics start-ups—3i (Investors in Industry), Murray Johnstone, Ivory and Syme—but they are relatively few and the scale of the stake usually small. Yet, there is also surely a much more fundamental factor at play: namely, that the structure of the electronics industry in Scotland actively militates against the indigenous start-up.

Silicon Glen is dominated by the US presence, the product of decades of focused inward investment effort. Scotland has 1 in 7 of the US manufacturing jobs in the UK; more than 180 plants, of which a third are in electronics. As James McCalman of Glasgow Business School has written, 'What we have is largely what we consciously set out to develop: an American-derived industry comprising production-oriented subsidiary operations.'

Yet, theoretically, there was valid reason in the early days to anticipate critical mass. That, after all, had been the experience in the USA, where the big successes of California's Silicon Valley and its East Coast equivalent around Boston—companies like Data General, Wang, Apollo—were spin-offs from older-established companies, created by young specialists with the will and opportunity to capitalize on innovations. Moreover, since original equipment manufacturers (OEMs) generally make few of their own components there seemed ample opportunity to generate local supplier networks. In the event, neither process has achieved any real momentum in Scotland. There are remarkably few successful Scottish suppliers. Recent estimates suggest that no more than 15 per cent of the input to the Scottish electronics industry is Scottish, and that includes utilities like electricity supply. Nor has the quality reputation of Scottish component makers been unsullied, though it has improved, and their product range is restricted. A recent corporate reshuffle within IBM has given its Spango Valley plant at Greenock greatly enhanced purchasing authority, and the plant has long sought to buy Scottish whenever it can. But its managers can find relatively few suitable indigenous suppliers with whom to spend a £1.1 billion purchasing budget. Even the gradual adoption of just-in-time (JIT) manufacturing, which US firms have been slow to implement but which gives advantage to local suppliers, does not necessarily help. Motorola has established its personal telephones plant at Easter Inch in West Lothian, hopes to persuade its normal global suppliers to set up operations in Scotland rather than to build new relationships with indigenous firms.

More important than purchasing policy is the profile of US-owned plants. McCalman points out that most US electronics manufacturing adheres to the Fordist assembly line structure, in which assembly operations are separated from the higher corporate functions like research and development (R&D), marketing, and strategic policy-making. Typically, it divides skills into rigid specializations. US plants in Scotland are often characterized as low-skill operations; but while this is true in sectors like semi-conductors, the more common feature is *narrow* skills. The effect is to limit the potential for spin-off ventures. As Dr Jim Love of the Fraser of Allander Institute put it, 'We still make an awful lot of boxes.'

Most Scottish subsidiaries of US electronics firms lack the higher corporate functions, and particularly R&D. There is some dispute about this: an SDA survey in October 1990 found that 55 per cent of US manufacturing plant managers in Scotland (not just in electronics) claimed to have in-house R&D, and 65 per cent sales or marketing responsibilities. Much of this activity however, may simply be addressing standard products to local markets. Original product development in the electronics field does not appear common. The autonomy enjoyed by NCR's managers in Dundee, who develop their own products and control the marketing of them in more than 70 countries, is unusual if not unique. Few if any of the US electronics firms in Scotland have provided the sort of nursery for tradeable talent which Ferranti has been over the years, nor the opportunities for technology transfer which that offers. Moreover, many US firms operate systems of positive incentive to keep their executives from leaving the parent company. Some offer share packages or profit-share schemes; others deliberately move executives around their global operations, from post to post and plant to plant. Walk into any Digital operation in the world and you will hear Scottish accents. That affords Scots who become involved in electronics exciting and satisfying career prospects. It does not encourage them to venture forth on their own.

By the same token, the remote nature of foreign-owned plants limits their capacity to generate business, and therefore jobs, in local services, particularly the financial sector. The full range of business services—banking, consultancy, financing, accounting, legal services—are employed by headquarters, not branch manufacturing plants. These services, whose vigour is central to indigenous company foundation, gain remarkably little sustenance from Scotland's electronics sector.

McCalman's analysis sounds one note of qualified hope. The past decade has seen a steady seepage of the world market share in electronics from the US to Japan. At the same time, the long concentration of Locate in Scotland (LiS) on the US target has paid diminishing inward investment returns. This has been part-balanced by a slow-growing success in the Far East, principally Japan. McCalman argues that the Japanese model of electronics development holds better promise for stimulating indigenous growth, thanks to its devolved workforce patterns of flexibly skilled teams, its close relationships between producers and suppliers, its readiness to nurture spin-offs within the corporate family and its integration of innovation with production. Japanese manufacturers do seem to interact more readily than US companies with local business infrastuctures. But it seems possible that Scotland is coming to this too little and too late. The onset of the single European market has been a stimulus to Japanese companies to build European bases, but most of the big players are already established. Moreover, Japanese firms generate their own critical mass; they like to locate near each other, and preferably with easy access to the best available transport links. In Britain, the main focus for Japanese electronics investment has been the M4 corridor between London and south Wales, rather than Scotland with its indifferent transport connections. The UK already has an exceptional share of Japanese investment to Europe, and may now have to reckon with Japan's native chariness about putting too many of its eggs in a single basket: also with the implication for investment of a depressed Japanese stock market.

The early 1990s are proving transitional for the electronics industry. The personal computers bubble has burst, and the falling demand of recent years both preceded the recession in the UK and the USA and extended to markets little affected by it. It is a time of cusp between technologies, with no certainty where demand may move. This has engendered a gradual acknowledgement by the Scottish development community that the days of attracting the big electronics manufacturers are largely over, and a consequent refocusing on more specialized targets like communications equipment, peripherals and automotive components. 'We have to cherry-pick,' the LiS director, Robert Crawford, told me. 'We have to niche-market. We have to get out of the markets where the competition is strongest.' This approach may continue to yield projects, but they are likely to be of greater strategic than employment significance.

Scottish Enterprise's 1991 strategy paper implied a shift of effort away from inward investment attraction towards stimulating indigenous development. Its central thrust was towards enhancing the competitiveness, growth and start-up rate of domestic companies, rather than soliciting investment overseas. How much impact that can now make on the sort of structure which electronics has developed in Scotland is hard to judge. Markets and the preferred means of addressing them can change rapidly. The trick for Scottish Enterprise is to spot the coming growth sectors, like opto-electronics, and try to nurture the indigenous expertise to exploit them. Some of the developments coming out of Scottish research in recent years show promise. Yet how soon, or whether, they evolve into high-volume business is anyone's guess. For the time being, the electronics sector represents a lush oasis of success within Scottish manufacturing; but one whose irrigative effect on the surrounding economy remains disappointing.

Oil and gas

As a political slogan, 'It's Scotland's Oil', the Nationalist battle-cry of the 1970s, spoke with greater resonance than meaning. In the legal, constitutional or fiscal senses, it was not Scotland's oil. The revenues, totalling some £80 billion since the first oil came ashore in 1975, have been paid into the British, not a Scottish, Exchequer, and used to Scotland's benefit only in accordance with the normal dispensations of public expenditure policy. Their principal use has been to underwrite the economic reconstruction of the UK which the Thatcher Government, whose election in 1979 coincided with the first great surge of North Sea production (up from 1.6 million tonnes in 1975 to 80 million), felt to be opportune and necessary. The common allegation that the dividend of North Sea oil has been squandered on maintaining record levels of unemployment is merely to lend subjective innuendo to objective fact. The industrial shake-out of the early 1980s, of which unemployment above 3 million was the consequence, was indeed financed with the considerable help of the oil revenues. It can also be argued, cogently, that the oil worsened the shake-out, since it pushed the value of sterling relentlessly upwards at a time of spiralling wage inflation, making it all the harder for British manufacturers to compete in overseas markets. Britain has been a net exporter of oil since 1980 and in 1985, when production peaked at over 122 million tonnes before the price slump of the following year, North Sea oil recorded a balance of payments surplus of £8 billion. Britain is now the fifth-biggest oil producer in the world, and the biggest natural gas extractor in Europe. In macro-economic terms, then, it has been unmistakeably Britain's oil.

But its impact on the Scottish economy has been, and remains, profound. Scotland may not have had the revenues but it has enjoyed substantial gain, including employment. In mid-1990, according to an SDA/Training Agency/Scottish Office survey, one in 20 Scottish jobs was directly related to the oil industry; 64 100 were in wholly oil-related employment, and a further 32 900 were indirectly sustained by the offshore industries. Many, admittedly, are migrant workers, who commute on and off installations from all over Britain, making scant donation to the Scottish economy as they pass through. Nevertheless, the offshore sector was an important place of refuge for men from occupations like shipbuilding, fishing and the merchant marine as these industries contracted during the 1970s and 1980s. It has also benefited a number of other sectors. The development of petro-chemical complexes like Mossmorran in Fife have helped give Scotland a 17 per cent share of the UK chemicals industry, which in turn has 16 per cent of European production. Scotland's engineering tradition, which had been running out of applications, gained a new lease of life, with firms like Weir, Yard and Babcock developing technologies for winning oil from inhospitable and previously marginal reserves which have found worldwide markets. Moreover, the discovery of oil provided a powerful stimulus for the rapid 1980s growth of the financial services sector.

Not all the effects have been beneficial. Oil and gas are cyclical industries, but they cycle at a different pace from the economy in general. Concentration of oil-related activities renders Scotland particularly prone to boom-and-bust volatility. This has been evident in construction yards like those at Nigg, Arnish, Ardersier and Methil, which have lurched between clamour and closure for much of the past 15 years. The 1986 slump in oil prices cost 20 000 jobs in Scotland, registering a severe impact across the breadth of the Scottish economy, at a time when UK recovery was accelerating out of recession, with the consequence that Scotland did not share in the economic boom of 1987–90 until a very late stage. Indeed, Scottish production output did not catch up with UK growth rates until the winter of 1989–90. On the other hand, a North Sea mini-boom, boldly predicated on a price for crude of around $20 a barrel, helped cushion the Scottish economy, particularly employment levels, from the early ravages of the 1990s' recession. A Labour Party study showed that in the year to July 1991, while UK unemployment rose steadily, unemployment in the oil-dominated Gordon constituency in Aberdeenshire actually fell by more than 43 per cent. In 1989, exploration and development hit its second-highest level on record, with 125 licence applications being lodged, 105 licenses being granted and 328 wells coming on stream.

Yet the memory of 1986 stands as a reminder of how abruptly such vigour can subside. Houses in Aberdeen which were unaffordable in 1985 were unsaleable by 1987. Ian Wood, chairman of the UK's biggest energy services company and now also of Grampian Enterprise, sees a further hazard: 'If you look back at the past 20 years, there is a significant erosion in the breadth of economic activity in Grampian. It is a massive vulnerability that exists.'

Nor has the offshore industry always benefited its neighbour sectors in Scotland. The discovery of cheap 'sour' gas in the Miller field has borne directly on the rapid decline of the Scottish coalfield, since it has been bought up in large quantities for use at Peterhead power station in place of coal, and may cost Scottish opencast coal business in Northern Ireland. It will also provide cheap power for industrial users on Teesside; among them British Steel, which intends to transfer its Lanarkshire platemaking operations there.

The development of the industry since exploration began in the UK sector in 1964 has had sociological as well as economic significance. Small, remote communities have suddenly found themselves courted by some of the world's biggest conglomerates, a circumstance memorably satirized in the movie *Local Hero*. Experiences have varied widely. Orkney and Shetland have coolly banked a handsome income from the terminals at Flotta and Sullom Voe, the latter

Europe's largest. By contrast, Ross and Cromarty, like Dundee or Fife, rode the bumpier path of unstable construction demand. Early disquiet about the possible environmental consequences of North Sea development has been for the most part soothed, and the bigger concerns have focused on the petro-chemicals end of the industry. A higher price has been the continuing toll of lost lives in the North Sea. A nation used to the fatality rates of mining, civil engineering or fishing was nonetheless stunned by the explosion on the Piper Alpha platform, 110 miles north-east of Aberdeen, which claimed 167 lives on the night of 6 July 1988.

One consequence has been an upsurge in industrial action offshore, as union activists agitate for the recognition which they believe to be essential to decent safety provision. Both unions and employers are fragmented. No more than a quarter of those who work in the industry are directly employed by the oil companies. Most work for a variety of contractors and service companies, often on a self-employed or short-term contract basis. The eight main unions have a long-standing umbrella body, the inter-union offshore oil committee, set up in 1974 and chaired by Tom Maclean of the Amalgamated Engineering Union. But it is a creature of shifting alliances and rivalries, and the main impetus for direct action since Piper Alpha has come from an unofficial cross-union grouping, the Offshore Industry Liaison Committee, chaired by the forceful Ronnie McDonald, which has now claimed the status of a fully fledged industrial union. On the employers' side, the most powerful body is the UK Operators Association, representing 36 operating companies. It wields considerable influence over the Offshore Contractors Council, representing some 200 companies in the construction, electrical and service sectors, and over other trade groups. In 1991, a single 'hook-up' agreement was reached covering onshore and pre-production work, but despite several years of unofficial stoppages—resulting in 729 dismissals and widespread blacklisting—recognition for production workers remains elusive.

The investment stakes offshore are gigantic, and Scotland's input to development has been variable. In the early days, British companies in general, and Scottish companies in particular, were slow to exploit the opportunities for supply and servicing which the industry presented. It took positive governmental intervention, mainly through the Offshore Supplies Office in Aberdeen, to bring the British contribution up to two-thirds by the late 1970s, and it is now above 80 per cent. Some Scottish companies, like Ian Wood's Aberdeen-based Wood Group, have prospered, but according to Wood, the UK is still doing very poorly in the world market: 'The North Sea supply industry has largely been developed by branch offices of overseas companies. It has not yet graduated to become a worldwide servicing centre.'

Development in the early days was largely financed by foreign capital, though by the late 1970s all three Scottish clearing banks had established oil divisions and around 10 per cent of their advances were related to offshore development. The merchant bank Noble Grossart and stockbrokers Wood MacKenzie were swiftly into the field, as were finance houses like Ivory & Syme, with the establishment of picturesquely named offshoots like Pict Petroleum and Caber Oil to invest in exploration. This may have had a marginal impact on the momentum of North Sea development, but its effect on the restructuring and growth of the Scottish financial sector was considerable. Yet few of the levers of real power in the industry are in identifiably Scottish hands. Licensing policy, the means by which the Government controls the pace of development, rests with the Department of Trade and Industry, not the Scottish Office. The operator of a big field is often senior partner in a consortium which, in the case of a field like Forties, can run to more than 20 member companies, many based overseas. Some of these companies have substantial onshore presences in Scotland, though strategic decision-making is rarely much devolved.

A significant development came with the takeover of Britoil by BP in 1988. Britoil had begun life in 1976 as the British National Oil Corporation, a public body established to bring the state some direct share in North Sea profits and to monitor the behaviour of the operators. It was privatized from 1982. Though Britoil was a creation of Westminster, its 1 600 onshore staff worked in Aberdeen and Glasgow, and it could be reasonably regarded as a Scottish-headquartered company: indeed, it headed *Scottish Business Insider*'s top 10 Scottish firms for 1985. Its interests were almost all in the North Sea. BP, by contrast, is global in its operations, and headquartered in southern England. Since the Government maintained a 'golden share' in Britoil, it was able to insist on the maintenance of job levels in Scotland and of Britoil's managerial structures. Britoil duly became integrated within BP's Exploration North-West Europe division, headquartered in Glasgow. BP transferred some 470 professional posts to Glasgow and recruited around 150 support staff. By August 1989, total staffing was 27 per cent up on the pre-takeover components. But the following month, BP announced 1 700 redundancies, 970 in Scotland. That left numbers in Scotland still up on the pre-merger position, but BP's adherence to its commitments open to doubt. For one thing, BP had already been planning North Sea expansion prior to the merger, and for another prospects in the sector had improved. In other words, both companies would have been likely to grow regardless of the merger. Moreover, the redundancies corresponded with a major restructuring in which the Glasgow executives appear to have had little say. Behind it lay a BP global strategy of offloading older or declining fields and refocussing resources elsewhere. It has disposed of some North Sea assets, including some inherited from Britoil. The takeover thus arguably affected job numbers in Scotland, and deprived a substantial tranche of North Sea assets and employment of a specifically Scottish perspective. In June 1992, BP announced that it was moving the office to Perth, with the loss of 350 jobs.

What was noticeable about this saga was how little public fuss it created. True, the issues were complex and the outcome ambiguous. Perhaps few Scots thought of Britoil as an essentially Scottish company or of BP as an alien one;

after all, in earlier times. BP had absorbed the remnants of Scotland's shale oil industry. But perhaps the bigger reason is that the North Sea industries have been seen as being done in and to, but not really *by*, Scotland; a passing phenomenon from which benefits are to be extracted but which is somehow incidental to the indigenous industrial machine. We have grown accustomed to gloomy predictions of when the reserves will run out; in fact, new finds and better technology have prolongued the industry's life expectancy. Barring global market upheavals, production is now expected to continue well into the next century. The degree to which it really was Scotland's oil may never have been great, and may even have diminished over the past couple of decades; but it is, and remains, an important and unpredictable factor in determining the performance of Scotland's economy.

Tourism

A splendidly pointless argument is sometimes to be heard about whether tourism or financial services constitute Scotland's biggest-employing service sector. The Scottish Tourist Board (STB), betraying little doubt on the matter, describes tourism as 'the country's biggest industry', calculating direct employment at 180 000, or 8 per cent of all Scottish jobs. The financial services sector, however, claims a payroll of nearly 187 000. Both figures are open to dispute. Tourism includes some 25 000 in self-employment, together with a large proportion of seasonal and part-time jobs. The financial services total also includes a lot of part-timers, together with such loosely relevant trades as law and public relations. Both figures fall below the 193 000 in retail distribution, though tourism and possibly financial services too might claim some of these for their own.

None of this, of course, matters in the slightest. What is pertinent is that tourism is a major and growing part of the Scottish economy. The STB put its value in 1990 at £1.8 billion, equivalent to 5 per cent of Scottish GDP; a full percentage point ahead of electronics, and two points ahead of the drinks sector (though well behind financial services, which claims 15 per cent). It is worth £350 a year per resident in Scotland, compared with a UK figure of £300, and gives Scotland an estimated tourism balance of payments surplus of £125 million, against a UK deficit of £2.4 billion.

This prosperity rises above a heap of paradoxes, not the least of which is an abiding native suspicion of the whole business. It is not hard to detect the view that making beds for visitors is not a real job, a *man's* job. 'We must rid ourselves,' warned the STB chairman, Ian Grant, in a recent speech to the CBI Scottish Council, 'of the notion that unless you are hewing coal, building ships or pressing steel you are not engaged in gainful employment.' It is possible that the Scots' ambiguous national status encourages them to resent the varnishing of their heritage for purposes of commerce. That is not to belittle Scotland's famous hospitality, which at its best can be superlative. But there has been a lingering belief in the sufficiency of genial amateurism, a faith in the peerlessness of Scotland's natural and human assets, which has obliged the STB to battle long and hard to instil the professionalism appropriate to a competitive tourism market. To be fair, the argument does not run all the one way. Pay, conditions and training levels in the industry—not least in some of its grandest hotels—can be lamentable. Some developments, like the Aviemore Centre, have arguably been ill-conceived, alien and tacky. The eternal conflict between developers and environmentalists is at its most intense when plans are afoot to adapt untamed Scotland to the demands of the 'leisure industry'. The protracted struggle over ski developments like Lurcher's Gully in the Cairngorms is a case in point. There is also, though it is mercifully less evident than of old, a kitsch tartanry about some of the promotion. The recent trend up-market from 'souvenirs' to 'crafts', is only half an answer. We may no longer import so many tartan ashtrays from Bulgaria with 'Frae Bonnie Scotland' scratched on the bottom, but traditional lasagne sets croft-crafted by a retired tax inspector from Guildford are not necessarily much of an improvement. Every tourist country does it and of course to present is inevitably to falsify. Nevertheless, the tourist vision of Scotland is not always one Scots would cherish.

The market also has its paradoxes. At time of recession, Scotland benefits from British visitors who cannot afford to go overseas. But the British, Scots included, are rather fickle patrons. To the STB's chagrin, many Scots still think of their country as the place to holiday when they cannot raise an air fare to the sunshine. In 1990, according to the STB, the volume of overseas visitors grew for the seventh successive year (1.5 million, staying 14.1 million bednights, pumped £405 million into the economy), while the numbers from elsewhere in the UK reached 7.7 million trips, yielding 37.4 million bednights and £1.04 billion. Of the overseas visitors, 48 per cent came from western Europe, 32 per cent from North America and 20 per cent from the rest of the world, notably Japan. But 60 per cent of tourism expenditure *by Scots* went overseas. The STB responded with a 'Holiday at Home' promotion, coupled with an audacious advertising campaign in London which suggested, to the great ire of the London Tourist Board, that there was nothing like spending time in London to heighten the appeal of Scotland. Still more fickle is the Scottish climate. No amount of expenditure on ski facilities can overcome the deterrent effect of successive winters without snow. And when it rains, as has been known, in Achiltibuie in August, or when the infamous midges swarm, visitors can hardly take to the casinos. On the other hand, the Highlands at their best are simply unbeatable; that is a gamble which visitors must be ready to take, and one which can only be partly offset by the development of designated visitor attractions.

How do you enhance the unspoiled without spoiling it? This is a question which, not surprisingly, the tourism authorities tend to shrug off. Tom Band, the STB chief executive, recently observed testily: 'As far as tourist pressure in Scotland is concerned, there is pressure in Edinburgh Old Town for three weeks in August. Other than that, we can't honestly say there is an overabundance of tourists anywhere.' Others, queuing to park in Pitlochry, or crammed into a Scotrail Sprinter en route to Fort William, or confined behind a procession of caravans on a single-track road in West Sutherland might disagree, but 'overabundance' is not an objective measure. Compared to the Place du Tertre in high season, or Disneyworld, or the Ponte di Rialto, or the departures lounge at Athens Airport, Scotland is indeed an oasis of quiet. The STB, to its credit, recognizes that relative tranquillity as an asset worthy of due respect.

The industry is greatly diverse, which is mostly a strength but occasionally a weakness. Accommodation ranges from Gleneagles to Mrs McGinty's back room in Ballachulish. Visitors come to climb in Glen Affric, fish the Tay, caravan in Assynt, ski at Glenshee, water-ski on Loch Earn, bird-watch at Boat of Garten, excavate in Orkney, monster hunt at Loch Ness, festival in Edinburgh. That broadens the market, but makes standards harder to maintain. The STB has run a grading scheme for accommodation since the mid-1980s and supports the parallel Taste of Scotland scheme for catering. The accommodation programme now embraces some 4 000 members—60 per cent of hotels and guest houses, 48 per cent of self-catering and bed-and-breakfast premises.

Almost as diverse as the industry is the apparatus to promote it. The Scottish Office has established the Scottish Tourism Co-ordinating Group, chaired by the Scottish Tourism Minister, and charged, as its title implies, with co-ordinating the efforts of the various bodies in the field. This was, oddly, just the remit given to the STB when it was established in its present statutory form by the 1969 Development of Tourism Act. Tourism promotion is not new. More than 60 years ago, there was a body called the Come to Scotland Association. It did not receive public funding until it became the Scottish Tourist Development Association, in which guise it received from the Treasury, in 1939, the magnificent sum of £250. In 1945, under pressure from the Scottish Secretary, Tom Johnston, it became the Scottish Tourist Board; autonomous from London, but still resolutely amateur in character.

In fact, even the 1969 Act left this autonomy in doubt. Prime responsibility for overseas promotion lay with the British Tourist Authority (BTA), not the 'regional' tourist boards. Helpfully, this distinction is increasingly honoured in the breach, defusing the anomaly of, say, a regional council or the Highlands and Islands Development Board (HIDB) being entitled to undertake tourist promotion overseas while the STB was not. Now, the STB mounts overseas missions and promotions, including running a valuable agents' network of more than 800 SCOTS (Specialist Counsellors On Travel To Scotland) in the US, though still technically in consultation with the BTA. It is clearly the lead Scottish body, but it is not the only one. Beneath the modish talk of partnership there remains considerable fragmentation. In particular, the tourism remit of the HIDB, now Highlands and Islands Enterprise (HIE), has been a source of friction, much of it, a former HIDB official told me, dating back to the STB's voluntary days. Tourism constitutes 20 per cent of the highland economy, calculated by HIE at 20 000 full-time equivalent jobs, and generating £500 million a year.

The STB is headed by a chairman, Ian Grant; a chief executive, Tom Band; a six-strong board, appointed by the Scottish Secretary; and a team of five senior executives. Based in western Edinburgh, it received just under three-quarters of its funding—some £12 million in 1990—from Scottish Office grant-in-aid. The remainder comes from commercial activities; between 1986–7 and 1990–1, the Board's income from the Government rose by 38.7 per cent, while its overall income rose by 43 per cent. Its spending, over the same period, rose by 41.6 per cent, and in 1990–1 total outgoings of £15 639 000 exceeded its income by £64 000.

Around half this expenditure goes on investment and promotion. Like all public agencies these days, the STB is required to have regard to *leverage*—the proportion of private sector investment it can attract for every £1 of its own money—and in 1990 it managed a ratio of nearly 4:1. In all, the board's £3.8 million helped pump-prime investments worth an eventual £18 million. Its promotional activities achieved a less impressive leverage rate, attracting £2.7 million from the trade for a £3.5 million STB budget. It also undertakes extensive research into the industry's performance (though surveying of overseas visitors remains a BTA responsibility), and has put increasing amounts of money and effort into training, in partnership with other bodies. It subsidizes, to the tune of £1.1 million in 1990–1, a network of 32 Area Tourist Boards (ATBs), which are also supported financially by more than 14 000 trade members, the local authorities, the enterprise networks and other commercial income. These, in turn, administer 170 tourist information centres which, in 1990–1, handled 6.7 million inquiries and made 327 900 accommodation bookings. The ATBs have their own liaison mechanism, the Scottish Confederation of Tourism, which holds bi-annual meetings and acts as an industry-wide lobby. Liaison groups are not scarce in the Scottish tourist industry. Perhaps the Scottish Tourism Co-ordinating Group is best regarded as the forum through which the liaison groups liaise.

All this fragmentation has its positive side. It reflects a perception by the trade itself of the need to market diverse wares, to behave like an industry instead of a rummage sale, while competitiveness helps preserve Scotland's infinite variety against the blandness of grand marketing strategies, and perhaps prevent the transformation of a nation into a theme park.

Drinks

Food, drink and tobacco, customarily lumped together in official statistics, is now the biggest-employing sector in Scottish manufacturing, registering a combined total of some 70 000 employees. We can discount tobacco from the equation; the closure in 1991 of Imperial Tobacco's Glasgow plant marked the final demise of one of the colonial industries on which the city was founded.

The food sector is diverse, ranging from family fish-smokers to big, sometimes little-known, combines like Wittington Investments (who own City Bakeries), United Biscuits and Rank Hovis McDougal. Recent years have concentrated the industry increasingly in big, often non-Scottish, corporate hands. Many of Scotland's best-known independent manufacturers—like Lees the macaroon maker, which famously sold its snowballs to the Eskimos—have gone, though others like Tunnock's, of caramel wafer celebrity, and Baxter's, the exporter of high quality convenience food which has now resisted more than 100 takeover bids, remain as family concerns.

The drinks sector is of greater macro-economic consequence. Brewing, dominated by two large manufacturers—Scottish & Newcastle, and Tennant Caledonian (owned by Bass Charrington)—is probably the bigger employer, but its main market is domestic. Distilling, employing 13 000, is Scotland's biggest volume exporter, and in the UK top five. It is also the product for which Scotland is best known in the 190 countries across the globe where it is sold. In 1990, export sales approached £1.6 billion. But according to the Scotch Whisky Association, the industry's influential trade body, that growth masked a sharp decline in the *volume* of sales: down 12 per cent in the year to June 1991. The decline would have been greater had it not been for a 15 per cent rise in sales to the EC, where trade in the Mediterranean countries has rapidly grown as the US market, traditionally a mainstay, has faltered.

The spirits industry is much at the mercy of policy. A protracted battle won deferment to 1999 of EC plans to abolish duty-free sales, but a more serious danger is posed by proposed reforms in excise duties which would sharply reduce minimum rates on wine and beer at the expense of a much higher rate for spirits. The price of a bottle of whisky in the Mediterranean countries would rise by up to £2.50, according to the Scotch Whisky Association. The Association is not prone to understate its problems, which makes it a better lobby than barometer; nevertheless, Scotland's most prestigious export faces a less than assured outlook.

The 1980s was a period of traumatic restructuring in the whisky industry, much of it long overdue. Many distilleries closed, sometimes with a severe impact on small communities. The result has been a more rationally structured industry, but one where ownership lies in relatively few, sometimes remote, hands; and where uncertainty is the only constant. For example, Whyte & Mackay, which lost a 12-week £350 million battle to take over Invergordon Distillers in 1991, has itself changed hands with bewildering frequency: independent in the 1970s, then passing to SUITs (Scottish and Universal Investment Trust), Lonrho, Brent Walker and ultimately (via an unsuccessful management buy-out bid) to American Brands, owners of the tobacco giant, Gallaher. Fewer than a fifth of distilleries are now owned by private companies.

Both brewing and distilling have generated a succession of takeover battles over the past decade. Scottish & Newcastle saw off a hostile bid from the Australian lager-maker, Elders IXL, after a vigorous resistance campaign, led by its chief executive Alick Rankin which ultimately persuaded ministers to refer the bid to the Monopolies and Mergers Commission (MMC). That response may have been in part prompted by aching memories of the earlier debacle over Guinness's 1986 acquisition of the Distillers Company, now trading as United Distillers. Guinness's tactics in that affair, which culminated in gaol sentences for some of those responsible, provided the major British financial scandal in a decade rarely short of them. More bitterly resented in Scotland was Guinness's broken promise to relocate its corporate headquarters to Edinburgh. The episode stands as a monument to City rapacity at its worst, though not one that has brought conspicuous reform. The Eleventh Commandment, Thou Shall Not be Found Out, appears to have been fortified rather more than the other ten. The compensation of a Scottish cadre of directors on the Guinness board did not much sweeten the realization that even the most Scottish of Scottish industries was prey to the anarchies of a distant jungle. Nor had Scottish financial institutions proved notably loyal. This last observation had already arisen with the Elders incursion, and was to surface again in Whyte & Mackay's bid for Invergordon, after which Invergordon's chief executive, Dr Chris Greig, remarked with commendable restraint: 'It was perhaps a little disappointing that the Scottish institutions figured more prominently in the selling out.'

The industry's restructuring, though painful, has, however, left it on a firmer footing. Guinness may command more than a quarter of home spirit sales and over a third of the export market, but its revitalization of the docile Distillers, and of Bells which it had acquired a year earlier, created a beneficial ripple effect throughout the industry. Even its rivals are ready to acknowledge this. Michael Lunn, the Whyte & Mackay chairman, said in a speech to the Institute of Directors in 1990: 'It would have taken perhaps five or 10 years longer to achieve as much by natural evolution and, though I did not like the policies, that time will be looked back on as a period of immense value to the industry.'

An increasingly multinational ownership has also brought new marketing strategies. The rugged machismo of old has given way to slicker, shrewder targeting, aimed at neglected but lucrative consumers such as women drinkers and the upwardly-mobile young. The most rapid growth has been in sales of single malt and de luxe blended whiskies. Familiarity with a world stage has broadened vision. Seagram may be associated in Scottish minds with the colourful chairman of its Scottish subsidiary and of Ayr racecourse, Major Ivan Straker. But the export success of brands like Glenlivet and Chivas Regal owes much to the way its Montreal-based owners apply the same marketing drive to Scotch as to products like Martell cognac. The lessons taught by the multinationals have been learned by the remaining indigenous producers.

Just as well, perhaps. Though the value of whisky sales continues to climb into the 1990s, the volume is falling steadily: a trend that cannot be indefinitely sustainable. Some analysts put over-capacity in whisky production as high as 10 per cent. In both home and export markets, tough times may lie ahead. In the last decade, the industry has been through trial by fire, but it has emerged better equipped to confront the challenges of the future.

Shipbuilding

Among the many unattractive contributions of the 1980s to the economic lexicon was the concept of the 'sunset' industry. This crass usage was probably applied more frequently to the Scottish shipbuilding industry than to any other. Anyone who has been privileged to see the computer design facilities at Govan or Yarrow knows them for sunrise technologies a world away from primitive metal-bashing. Still, the decline of the shipbuilding tradition, particularly on the Clyde, has been a central fact of Scottish economic change, and a grievous loss to the culture of the west of Scotland.

The fragments that remain, though well-equipped and highly efficient, are mostly owned from outwith Scotland and are still uncertain in their outlook. On the Clyde, just two big yards survive, one (Kvaerner Govan) a merchant yard and the other (GEC Yarrow) building warships. There is a naval dockyard at Rosyth, now under the privatized management of Babcock Thorn and, despite brave attempts to diversify into fields like refurbishing tube trains, heavily dependent on declining naval budgets. It shed 1 000 jobs in 1991. There is also a scattering of marine engineers—such as Brown Brothers of Edinburgh, owned by Vickers—and high-tech consultants, like Yard of Glasgow, once part of Yarrow and now run as a joint venture by British Aerospace and Sema-Metra of France. Govan was sold by British Shipbuilders to Kvaerner Industrier of Oslo in 1988 for the knock-down price of £6 million. The sale was greeted with suspicion in Scotland, and not just because of the price. Kvaerner, a polymath with international interests in ship-owning, oil and gas, and engineering, had just closed Norwegian yards at Frederikstad and Moss because they could not be competitive without access to EC subsidies. But, even subsidized, EC yards were finding it hard to compete with cheap-labour economies like Korea and the subsidies were in any case being gradually withdrawn. The recent traumatic closure of the successful Caterpillar plant at Uddingston by its troubled US parent had left many Scots sceptical about the benevolence and loyalty of foreign owners.

On the other hand, the probable alternative to sale was closure; indeed, Eric Mackie, the Govan managing director, had been sent there in 1979 with a mission to close the yard and, though he had staved that off by agreeing radical productivity reforms with union leaders like the incorrigible Sammy Gilmore, and by tendering—in Gilmore's phrase—for everything except the *African Queen*, the axe remained poised. Kvaerner was looking for somewhere to build highly specialized liquid petroleum gas carriers and was initially interested in an English yard, now closed. It was pointed at Govan by the then assistant director of the CBI and a former Govan director, Keith MacDowall (husband of the print union leader, Brenda Dean), who happened to know one of the senior executives. There have also been suggestions that it was guided there by incentives from a Government keen to recoup some of its dismal standing in Scotland. Though the takeover would mean several hundred job losses, the Norwegians came armed with substantial investment plans, a clutch of ready orders and a promise to leave local management in charge and intact. For a Government determined to get British Shipbuilders off its books one way or another, the offer was irresistible and the price inconsequential. The cost of the sale to the public purse has been estimated at £50 million.

Despite early scepticism in Scotland, Kvaerner has delivered most of what it promised. One expected package of orders, from a Kvaerner-led shipping consortium, failed to materialize, but the yard has been kept busy. Though Mackie was in due course succeeded by a Norwegian, Steinar Draegebo, the bulk of the management team remained and, more importantly, retained reasonable autonomy. Above all, an ambitious £26 million investment programme, including a magnificent modular construction hall, was implemented. Though the yard has yet to venture far beyond its gas-carrier specialism, the doubts about Kvaerner's commitment have been for the most part subdued, and a £200 million tranche of orders in late 1991, the biggest ever for a British merchant yard, has secured its future at least to mid-decade.

For many years, as world shipping demand slumped and the low-cost Far East yards cleaned up the available scraps, the future for British merchant shipbuilding grew rapidly bleaker and only the warship yards, cushioned by 'cost-plus' defence procurement contracts, looked at all secure. The past couple of years, however, have reversed that position. Govan may have lurched from order to order, but its specialization is a useful niche in a slowly reviving world market. By contrast, Yarrow, long kept busy by the Government's commitment to a 50-strong surface fleet, has faced rather greater uncertainties.

Yarrow, originally Alfred Yarrow & Co, is one of Scotland's most enduring inward investments, having transferred its business to Scotstoun from Poplar as long ago as 1907. Its mainstay in recent years has been the Type-23 frigate, which it designed. It built six of the first seven commissioned. But in December 1989, it was outbid by Swan Hunter on the Tyne for a long-awaited batch of three, worth more than £300 million, on which it had been depending. The unexpected loss gave rise to speculation that the Swan bid, which kept that yard from closure, had been shorn of such fripperies as a profit margin; or that the Ministry of Defence, facing intensely competitive lobbying, had decided late in the day that it needed to retain a choice of suppliers. Chastened, Yarrow cut its workforce to below 3 000, pursued stop-gaps like Malaysian corvettes and meticulously planned its bid for the next frigate round, which it won by a reportedly handsome margin in January 1992.

It is, by common accord, just about as proficient and competitive a warship yard as any in the world. But the peace dividend has put a drag anchor on naval ordering, stalling timetables and subjecting procurement plans to perpetual review. Competitiveness is of little help if demand evaporates, and if Yarrow went, a question mark would then arise over the future of Govan, which would have to absorb more of the cost of dredging the river. The yards have survived against the odds into the new dawn of high technology and sleek competitiveness; but sunset may yet return.

Part 2   Owners and Entrepreneurs

Owners

A company is a system of authority, not of democracy; at least not usually in this country. In countries like Italy, where a third of companies are some form of co-operatives, democracy has rather a better industrial than political track record. In Britain, the reverse is true. Most companies operate on a pyramidal structure, with power focused at the apex: the chairman and board, acting in the name of the owners.

Within the pyramid, there can be devolution. Scotland's best-performing engineering company, the Weir Group, grants its 20-odd subsidiaries considerable operational and strategic autonomy, provided that their detailed and daily financial returns to the central managerial core continue to meet prescribed targets. Kvaerner Industrier, owner of the Govan shipyard, consists of just a tiny handful of executives in Oslo, keeping watch over the performance of a clutch of distant companies. Japanese manufacturing, with its shopfloor work teams intently discussing how to solve production problems, is arguably still more devolved, though ruled by rigid centrally determined quotas. These variations can make a difference to the performance of a company or its congeniality as an employer. But they rarely impinge on matters of strategy: the move to a new market, or new product; the decision to acquire, or expand, or to close. These are the higher corporate functions and they belong in the higher corporate reaches—the boardroom and the headquarters.

Scotland in the 1990s is conspicuously, many believe alarmingly, short of headquarters. Accurate figures are hard to come by. Those generated by government sometimes distinguish between UK and overseas ownership, but not between Scottish ownership and the rest. However, there are sufficient unofficial sources available to paint a representative, if not a comprehensive, picture. Consider this calculation by the management consultants, PE Inbucon. In two years alone, 1985 and 1986, external takeovers reduced the amount of capital controlled by Scottish-registered commercial and industrial companies by more than half: from £4 672 billion to £2 278 billion. Those snapped up, moreover, were unsurprisingly the better-achieving firms; they represented 37 per cent of turnover, but 49 per cent of profit income. Now, these were two exceptional years, which saw such massive acquisitions as Arthur Bell, House of Fraser, Coats Paton and Distillers. But if the scale of the outflow was exceptional, the pattern was not. Firms like Teachers, Barr & Stroud or SUITs passed out of Scottish ownership in the 1970s, not the 1980s. Indeed, at UK level, the numerical takeover rate during the years of the Heath Government rivalled that of the predatory 1980s, though the value of the firms involved was smaller. Between 1965 and 1980, an average of 2 000 Scots jobs a year passed outwith Scottish control; that 1985–86 spree took out 50 000.

Ownership of Scottish industry has been flowing out of Scotland throughout the post-war period. In 1950, just 4.3 per cent of Scottish manufacturing employment was with overseas (ie non-British) companies. By 1989, the proportion was more than five times as great. It is a share which has continued to grow steadily regardless of wider economic trends, like the decline in manufacturing's overall share of employment or of GDP. Between 1970 and 1989, the *numbers* employed with overseas firms fell from 112 900 to 78 100 but the *share* of manufacturing employment represented by the foreign firms rose from 16.6 to 22.2 per cent. According to one assessment, only five of the top 50 manufacturing companies active in Scotland are headquartered here. No more than 90 Scottish companies, even on a cosmopolitan definition of Scottish, have stock exchange listings. Over the past decade, new listings by Scottish companies averaged fewer than three a year, while takeovers from outwith Scotland ran at around two a week.

Does it matter? A case can be made that it does not. Markets are increasingly international; perhaps it is inevitable for the structure of capital increasingly to mirror the structure of trade. Public companies, wherever their headquarters, are owned by institutions, to whom the national interest is a quaintness that has nothing to do with fiduciary obligation. Takeover can sometimes save an ailing company from decline or oblivion; it can take it into markets which it could not approach on its own, and takeover, or the threat of it, can act as a spur to management to improve efficiency and competitiveness. Besides, the traffic has not all been one way; Weir has been an energetic acquirer, in Europe, Australia and in the US. Grampian Holdings, Bill Hughes's Glasgow polymath, has also successfully bought overseas, including in allegedly impregnable France; Howden purchased Wirth in Germany. Foreign ownership is not just the product of takeovers; it is also the result of inward investment, calculated to have brought Scotland 50 000 jobs in the decade to 1991. Overseas ownership need not mean instability: according to the Scottish Office's regional data system, employment in foreign-owned manufacturing plants in Scotland dropped by less than 28 per cent in the decade to 1989, whereas the fall in the UK-owned plants was nearly 40 per cent.

But this is a pretty threadbare case. These last figures can equally support the view that predators have picked the plums and left the crab apples alone, as suggested by the Inbucon study. As to Scottish firms taking over external rivals, the numbers are small compared with the reverse flow, as is the size of the transactions. Relatively few Scottish firms seem to be able or willing to shop abroad; Richardson and Turok identified 178 takeovers outwith Scotland by Scottish firms between 1982 and 1989, but found that three-quarters of them were undertaken by just 27 Scots companies, and 55 per cent by just 16 firms. For most Scottish, indeed British, companies the effort of navigating a path through the obstacles, overt or hidden, erected by other countries against predators is regarded as more trouble than it is worth. By contrast, Britain's securities market is probably the most open in the world, making it the favourite target for non-EC companies seeking bases in an integrated European market. Some cultures, like the Japanese, have preferred to register their presence through greenfield inward investments, but others have found buying more convenient than building.

It is the effect of ownership seepage on the dynamics of Scottish industry that is most unsettling. True, takeover can open new markets for a company, but it can also close them off. In 1982, a South African-originating multinational, Charter Consolidated, took over Anderson Strathclyde, now the Anderson Group, a world-renowned manufacturer of mining equipment, based in Motherwell (also, at that time, Glasgow, East Kilbride and Glenrothes). The takeover came as both global and domestic markets for heavy colliery kit were shrinking. Anderson had already shown some talent for diversification, and might have been expected to show more. But takeover had turned it into the mining equipment division of a diverse multinational, even if, as its chief executive, Alasdair MacLauchlan, told me, it also brought stability. As Anderson's core business withered, it had no choice other than to shed capacity and jobs.

In the case of the pure branch plant, the effects can be still more extreme. Caterpillar in Uddingston, Wang in Stirling and Unisys in Livingston are among examples of efficient and successful Scottish plants closed because their multinational parent found its global business in trouble. The closure that claimed 1 200 jobs at Caterpillar in 1987 had nothing to do with the Uddingston plant—which less than four months earlier had been promised a £62.5 million investment programme entitled, with tart irony, 'Plant with a Future'—and everything to do with international factors such as the steady erosion of Caterpillar's market share by Japanese producers like Komatsu, and a devalued US dollar which made European plants more advantageous to close than US ones. Besides, when you prune a tree, you lop the branches not the trunk.

Trees feed through their roots, and branches are a long way removed from these. This is particularly true of US manufacturers, the dominant foreign owners in Scotland, who classically centralize not just managerial control but also the more cerebral functions like design, or research and development. The consequences of this have already been discussed in relation to the electronics industry. They include: reduced opportunity for innovation and product-based spin-offs; reduced contact with local financial services; a discouragement of entrepreneurial endeavour; emigration of technical or managerial talent; inflexibility towards local markets; little commitment to local communities; and a lack of technology transfer to indigenous industry. The price Scotland has paid for welcome inward investment has been to see strategic control of the economy slip further from Scottish hands.

For a time in the latter part of the 1980s, it looked as if the seepage might be stemmed. Takeover activity in Scotland had diminished from its mid-decade peak, possibly because many of the best prizes had already gone. Hope for a while focused on two related trends of the period, the 'unbundling' of unwieldy corporate agglomerates (selling off diverse activities to concentrate on core activities), and the management buy-out (MBO) or buy-in (MBI). MBOs were particularly in vogue during the 1980s, even in Scotland where the venture capital community is small and notoriously cautious. MBOs like Caithness Glass or MBIs like the whisky blenders, Burn Stewart, sometimes lent fresh momentum to sluggish businesses. Despite some spectacular failures, their success rate raised the hope that bits of some of the big companies which had been snapped up could return to local control.

They became, too, an answer for the Government to the criticism that privatization too often turned public monopolies into private ones. So, for example, the legislation enabling the break-up and sale of the Scottish Bus Group included a modest measure of positive discrimination in favour of management or management/employee buy-outs. But the problem with MBOs was leverage; they were often financed by huge borrowings. High interest rates severly penalized that, and it is too early yet to say whether the MBO trend will resume as interest rates subside. Moreover, while MBOs have in some cases restored vigour and local control to existing businesses, they may have done so at the expense of start-ups, which present a more daunting risk to venture capital houses. Besides, there are swathes of the economy where MBOs are simply not an option, precisely because of the branch plant proliferation. They have been a comparative rarity in electronics: at the fringes of the sector, there have been some—like the secession of Pentland Systems from the Livingston-based US component maker, Burr Brown—but the bulk of the industry is dominated by plants which quite simply lack the structures to become or to spawn self-standing businesses.

The takeover vogue of the 1980s raised issues that extended well beyond the Scottish economy. Britain's lacklustre industrial investment record can in part be attributed to the need to maximize returns to shareholders or face being boarded with cutlasses. While there was money to be had for the asking, acquisition could always offer faster expansion opportunities than organic growth: why toil to build a successful brand when you could buy one ready-made? But in a small economy like Scotland's, ownership seepage has particularly destabilizing consequences. Regional economic or employment impact remains a valid ground for referring a bid to the Monopolies and Mergers Commission, but ministers have generally regarded competition as the sole justification for referral.

Perhaps there is some irony in the fact that Margaret Thatcher's Government, while steadfast in defence of political sovereignty, appeared so tolerant of the loss of economic sovereignty. In Scotland, the linkage between the two has been more consistently understood. The Scottish Constitutional Convention attached high priority to giving a Scottish parliament powers to stem the loss of ownership, including control over mergers policy and a right to bring companies into public ownership. The Standing Commission on the Scottish Economy came up with the idea, never convincingly fleshed out, of a 'white knight agency' to protect Scots firms against hostile takeover. Such notions may or may not be practical in a free market, but they reflect the high place which the issue of who owns Scotland's economy has come to command on the Scottish political agenda. The 'dependency culture' which most concerns Scots is their economy's reliance on the whims of distant decision-making.

Entrepreneurs

'But the Scots *invented* Thatcherism,' Margaret Thatcher was prone to say in moments of mystification at the resistance which she and her policies met from ungrateful Caledonia. It was a remark intended as a compliment, a tribute to what she perceived as the Scottish virtues of thrift, financial acumen, and the pursuit of grace through individual toil: also to the 18th- and 19th-century Scottish school of economic philosophy—Hume, Stuart, Rae, above all Adam Smith—which so influenced 20th-century monetarist writers like Friedrich von Hayek or Milton Friedman, who provided much of Thatcherism's intellectual foundation.

It was not just the Scots' dogged preference for collective remedies to their problems that jarred. Right-wing commentators, both within and beyond Scotland, asserted that the vocation of entrepreneurship, the dynamic acquisitiveness fashionably (and imprecisely) celebrated as enterprise, had fallen into neglect north of the Tweed. As Margaret Thatcher was crediting Scots with inventing Thatcherism, her Chancellor, Nigel Lawson, was rebuking their failure to measure up to it. Speaking in Glasgow in November 1987, he belaboured Scotland's 'hostile attitude to wealth creation and to the enterprise culture on which economic success in a free society depends'. We began to hear of Scotland's 'dependency culture', a slander culminating in a famously intemperate leader in the London *Evening Standard*, alerting the M25 precinct to the nation of 'subsidy junkies' 400 miles to the north.

The allegation about subsidy addiction is a canard; taking public spending in the round—public procurement patterns in particular—southern England's palm is rather more generously hanselled. Yet the suspicion that entrepreneurship is a sickly plant in late 20th-century Scotland is not so easily dismissed. It is as foolish to ignore the entrepreneurial achievements of Tom Farmer in automobile services, David Murray in steel stockholding, the Baxter family in food processing, Anne Gloag in coach transport, or Bill Miller in electronics, as to pretend that they are somehow typical of a vibrant entrepreneurial class. This is a matter with which Scottish debate often seems uncomfortable. A leaked SDA study in February 1990 on the question earned the Agency, then painfully transmuting into Scottish Enterprise, a blistering reproach from the Scottish

Enterprise patent-holder, Bill Hughes. The preference is for accentuating the positive. A Scottish Office report in May 1991, *Small Firms in Scotland*, proclaimed a 'massive' net increase of nearly 20 000 new businesses established in Scotland during the preceeding decade, with company registrations rising from 3 270 in 1980 to 6 794 in 1989, and an increase of nearly 100 000 in self-employment. In fact, that picture distorts in deeper focus. Business start-ups and self-employment have indeed grown in absolute terms, but the Scottish proportion of UK activity in these fields has consistently declined. Scotland's share of UK self-employment fell from 8.4 per cent in 1979 to 6.8 per cent in 1987.

For its final report in November 1989, the Standing Commission on the Scottish Economy asked Strathclyde University's Fraser of Allander Institute (FAI) to test the mettle of Scottish entrepreneurship. The exercise was instructive. First, the FAI looked at the raw measure of VAT registrations per thousand of working population in the period 1980–6 and came up with a figure of 35.11; not much more than half the rate in southern England, well behind both Wales (49.35) and Northern Ireland (40.48) and a dismal tenth out of the 11 UK regions and nations. But, converting that to a *net* figure, Scotland rises to eighth place, suggesting a relatively high survival rate for new Scottish ventures. If the survey period is condensed to 1984–6, Scotland rises to fifth place in the net registrations table, adding to the weight of evidence that Scottish recovery from the recession of the early 1980s was painfully slow.

Yet, the indifferent showing in these UK league tables came in a period when regional policy was more active than is now the case, when the SDA and HIDB were at their most vigorous and before falling oil prices had sapped the pace of Scottish recovery. Is this a symptom of subsidy addiction? The FAI drew up a list of factors which it supposed might influence capacity to generate new ventures, and measured Scotland's score against other parts of the UK. The choice of indicators might be questioned, but three inherent characteristics did appear to be significant weaknesses: a low level of personal wealth, as measured by characteristics like home ownership and average incomes; a social structure in which education, managerial and professional skills were poorly represented; and an industrial plant structure which militated against Scots gaining ready experience of small firms. The implication was that Scotland lacked entrepreneurial *opportunity* rather than will.

There is room here for an argument about cause and effect. Anyone who deals regularly with industries furth of Scotland finds a ready abundance of successful Scots in senior executive positions. Is Scotland's business culture infertile because the gifted depart, or do they depart because they find so few opportunities at home? The answer to that lies deeply buried, but the implications weigh against the proposition that lack of business flair is some sort of ethnic trait. The low level of indigenous development stimulated by inward investment to Silicon Glen, the failure of the much-heralded 'critical mass' to go critical, has already been noted. Yet many Scots have achieved success at the leading edge of the US electronics industry; Crawford Beveridge, the Scottish Enterprise chief executive, is one, Don Burns of Motorola another, Dr David Simpson, one of the true begetters of Silicon Glen, a third. Each has subsequently, in his own fashion, shown faith in the potential for business growth in Scotland; yet each found emigration the path to opportunity. The ambitious Scot all too often finds that promotion leads him away from the constraints of Scottish manufacturing.

This brings us to familiar territory; Scotland's 'branch office' economy. Plants which are remote lack opportunities for the able or ambitious. The higher career options lie with the higher corporate functions and these have steadily drained from Scotland. This shortfall is not confined to the private sector. With the exception of the Scottish Office, promotion for Scottish civil servants beyond the lower-to-middle grades usually means London, an impasse which successive drives to 'disperse' posts from London have largely failed to redress.

Development agencies, like the one which Beveridge now commands, have to act where markets fail, which requires understanding of the reasons for failure. SDA research suggests that Scottish start-ups tend to grow at much the same rate as those in other parts of the UK for their first six or seven years, and then to stagnate; with the consequence that their potential as generators of employment is stunted. The February 1990 paper estimated that 1.6 per cent of the Scottish workforce—some 40 000 people—were employed in independent companies set up in the period 1980–2. This compared with 4 per cent in south-east England. In both cases, the bulk of the jobs were located in a small elite of 'high-flier' companies; but a greater proportion of the English start-ups became high fliers, and they flew higher, particularly in the service sector. The report summarized thus: 'The more dynamic regional economies have high birth rates generating competition within the region, higher death rates but with overall higher growth. There is little evidence of this type of internal competitive flux within the Scottish economy.'

The explanation for this is neither simple nor certain. The FAI analysis may carry some implications for demand levels, but it cannot fully explain the sluggish performance of new Scottish firms; particularly since *disposable* income in Scotland is relatively high, the more so since the southern property boom. Scotland has an elaborate network of development agencies and a celebrated financial services sector. It has educational institutions with established reputations in high-tech fields like micro-electronics and biotechnology; yet high-tech employment fell during the 1980s.

Much discussion focuses on the availability of both venture and growth capital to young Scottish companies. Only 1 per cent of the money invested by venture capital firms in the UK is seeded in Scotland. Even a house like 3i, with high-profile operations in Edinburgh, Glasgow and Aberdeen and a commendable specialism in start-ups, invested less than £30 million in Scotland in 1990–1. Reid and Jacobsen propose a number of features common to small entrepreneurial Scottish firms: a reliance on banks for advice and external finance, often secured by personal guarantee; a reluctance to risk high gearing, even for relatively short periods; poor market research and lack of personal finance as the usual reasons for failure to gain financial backing; a reliance on debt capital, rather than equity, to fund expansion; and a tendency to cash-flow problems, due mainly to bad debtors and insufficient overdraft facilities. The same authors also identify several market restraints on small business growth, notably a tendency, through poor resourcing and inexperience, to be better at creating than defending market niches; and a proneness to settle for a comfortable if modest subsistence on contracts too small to be worth the while of the bigger players, who would in any event react fiercely if challenged on their high-volume business. Several commentators have diagnosed a general susceptibility to undermanaging, particularly in fields like marketing.

To this has to be added a perhaps more culpable characteristic of Scottish entrepreneurial activity: its lack of staying power. Recent years have seen many start-ups which, having achieved success, were sold out by their founders to the highest bidder, who rarely hailed from Scotland. Examples include Apollo Blinds (English purchaser), Thor Ceramics (German), Bauteil Engineering (English), Office Workstations (Japanese), and PR Consultants (English). These 'earn-outs' are perhaps too readily characterized as taking the money and running. In some cases, the founders have stayed on under the new owners to continue to develop the businesses. The options for the fast-growing start-up doubtless seem clearer in retrospect than they do at the time. Certainly, achieving a market listing is no longer the entrée to the super-league that once it seemed. For those few Scots firms which have tried it in recent years, the experience has often been harrowing: the Fife children's wear manufacturer, Babygro, was sold to an English firm in 1988 at little more than a quarter of the value placed on it when it was first floated a year earlier. Exposure to the rapacious attentions of the City, or continuing with the limited resources of the private firm is not an attractive choice, and many entrepreneurs have instead opted for the consolation of a cash-filled nest-egg.

It is easier to document these weaknesses than to explain why they should prevail particularly in Scotland. It is not sufficient merely to blame the stuffiness of the Scottish financial sector, though many finance houses do have a cultured disdain for start-ups, and little enthusiasm for refinancing. From the peculiar vantage point of recession, this is not entirely deplorable. Scottish institutions were cannier than their southern counterparts during the 1980s boom years, and so avoided the retribution of high interest rates on the over-extended and over-leveraged. But bank overdrafts are a stodgy growth stimulant (at least in this country; the German banks' patient relationships with businesses of all sizes provide valuably long-sighted investment). Scots firms seem doggedly thirled to their banks. They have little choice. The expansion of Scotland's financial community in recent years has done little to extend the availability of venture or development capital, particularly to the smaller player; and even the few houses that are in the field have been drawn to the safer bet of the buy-out market.

Yet the financial community denies the charge that it is reluctant to back start-ups. 'There is no difficulty getting money for a well worked-out business plan,' one senior figure told me. 'What Scotland is short of is business plans. In California, start-up finance means $60 million. No one wants to give Willie in Pilton a new ladder.' His suspicions had to do with the quality of life available in Scotland to those with secure employment, and with the inheritance from the protestant work ethic of a fear of failure: 'Wealth is that part of your income that you don't spend. Wealth is not going out on your bicycle, like that idiot politician said, and starting your own electronics business in Glenrothes.'

The SDA battled wilfully, if never decisively, against this tendency to entrepreneurial atrophy, through its remit to provide or path-find venture capital at higher risk levels than the private sector would entertain. But this facility was progressively weakened as governmental pressure required the agency to maximize returns on its investments and jack up its leverage ratios. The result was to lower the level of risk acceptable even to the SDA. It focused increasingly on a small group of potential growth sectors—electronics, biotechnology, advanced engineering—and on helping academics market their innovations. In one experiment, it set up a bespoke electronics company, Domain Power, to fill an identified market niche, though the venture was but a partial success. Domain floundered amid under-financing and management problems, and was sold at a loss to a US (and, subsequently, a Japanese) manufacturer.

The Agency often backed winners who would have found support otherwise hard to come by, but the overall impact on Scotland's entrepreneurial performance remained at the margins. Its direct investment function was subject to growing constraint, culminating in the enforced sale of most of its property and investment portfolios. Its efforts were increasingly directed towards the inward investment target, which made for better press conferences; though returns in that field are fast diminishing. This rundown, coinciding with the transition to Scottish Enterprise and its more micro focus, may bring more effective efforts to nurture indigenous growth. On the other hand, the pressure to get out of investments at the earliest possible date seems destined to remain, with the consequence, predicted by one former SDA director, of 'Scottish Enterprise being at most a minor player in the development and venture capital scene in Scotland'. That leaves open the question of who will be a major player. Recent years have seen a number of venture capital clubs, like Strathclyde Innovation, set up to back promising novices. The Prince of Wales has set up the Prince's Scottish Youth Business Trust, which aims to launch 600 small businesses a year from 1991–92. Worthy initiatives, but they are unlikely to make more than a modest impact.

What of the managerial inadequacies identified by Reid and Jacobsen? Here, considerable effort has been directed to making better advice and expertise available to fledgling businesses; also to trying to overcome the perennial problem, by no means unique to Scotland, that the individual with the brilliant idea is often ill-equipped by talent or temperament to exploit its commercial potential. The SDA and HIDB and their successor networks have run a wide range of programmes to help companies access or pool technical, financial or business development expertise. Finance is available to assist firms to devise marketing or product development strategies, to penetrate export markets, to exploit new technology and to improve business skills and practices. The Department of Trade and Industry runs a range of schemes on the Enterprise Initiative theme, particularly for small firms. Mostly administered by or for the Scottish Office, these include the Consultancy Initiative, Better Business Scheme, Business Expansion Scheme, Loan Guarantee Scheme, Enterprise Allowance Scheme, and others. They provide assistance for firms seeking help with quality, design, marketing and new technology. Take-up has sometimes been disappointing, possibly because of entry criteria which debar those small operations—70 per cent of Scottish manufacturing—which are subsidiaries of larger companies. A more favourable, if patchy, response has been achieved by the network of more than 40 enterprise trusts. Funded through ScotBiC (Scottish Business in the Community) by the private sector, Scottish Enterprise/HIE, the local authorities, the Government and the European Commission, these aim to provide entrepreneurs with access to information, advice and finance. They are in some respects a forerunner of the local enterprise companies (LECs) set up under the Scottish Enterprise/HIE reforms, and now often work closely with their parent LECs. Despite small core budgets, their motif of 'business talking to business' has proved popular with the smaller small businesses, up to 20 000 of which a year make use of their services. In addition, the regional authorities maintain economic development departments and a range of specialist sectoral services are offered through bodies like the STB, Scottish Engineering, industrial training boards and local business collectives.

There is plenty of advice available: Labour's Gordon Brown made the count, at November 1990, 34 urban assistance schemes and 45 small business programmes operated by at least five Government departments. Surveys show that small businesses have in general a fair idea of the sort of assistance available and of where to look for it. It is possible that the relatively low failure rate of Scottish small businesses owes something to these sorts of schemes. Yet it is harder to say how much they can do to make small firms grow into big ones. There, more than advice is needed. Scotland may or may not be a congenitally entrepreneurial nation, but it seems to lack an entrepreneurial economy.

Part 3   Managers and Workers

Management

The Scottish polity is like a flask. All sorts of elements get tossed together above the intense flame of a small country with a vigorous media and a gift for introspection. Nothing, meaning no one, need be left out. Occasionally, against the odds, the formula yields a coherent compound of consensus. At other times, the compound fails to absorb every element, leaving some to flare off into the atmosphere. When Jim Sillars sensationally won the Govan by-election for the SNP on 10 November 1988, the heat was turned high, causing the contents of the flask to sizzle and spit. The mixture briefly broke down into its constituent parts, though before long much of the previous compound had reassembled under the guise of the Scottish Constitutional Convention, the anti-poll tax campaign, and the Standing Committee for the Defence of the Scottish Steel Industry. *The Scotsman*, like other newspapers, entered gleefully into the spirit of the moment, publishing a series of articles called the 'Govan Debate'. For one of these I went off to interview industrial figures about the constitutional questions which Govan had revitalized. It was a salutary reminder of how small the flask is, and how generic the substances within it. On successive days, Campbell Christie, general secretary of the STUC, and John Davidson, the late director of CBI Scotland, sat at the same table in the same Glasgow restaurant (their offices are only a few hundred yards apart) and expressed views more striking in similarity than divergence. But Davidson offered one thought that was truly unexpected: while most industrialists were indifferent to constitutional reform and hostile to the idea of a devolved legislature with revenue-raising authority, they might warm to Sillars's vision of independence within Europe if Margaret Thatcher made many more speeches like her Bruges tour de force.

These comments caused something of a stir. For one thing, they contradicted an unscheduled speech by his chairman, Bill Hughes. But there was greater surprise that the CBI should have so broken cover. The late Sir Alex Fletcher, a former Tory Scottish Industry Minister, once remarked in frustration that any stranger arriving in Scotland would come swiftly to the conclusion that the STUC was Scotland's spokesman. It was intended to ginger business into taking a fuller part in the debates that engage Scotland. That is the point about the Scottish debate: no one is excluded who does not want to be. The managerial lobbies seem sometimes to want to be. For their presumed allies in the Conservative Party, this reticence is a source of perpetual distress.

Public diffidence is often supposed to mask private influence. But while business leaders have gained power in the past decade, business lobbies have not. In Scotland, as elsewhere, boards of public bodies have acquired numerous business executives, to the extent that demand outstrips supply and the same faces pop up in all sorts of corners. Scotland never seems a smaller place than when you compare board lists. Time has not hung heavy, for example, on Sir David Nickson. As well as successive day jobs at the head of William Collins, Pan Books, Scottish & Newcastle Breweries and the Clydesdale Bank, together with directorships of Scottish United Investors, Edinburgh Investment Trust, General Accident, Radio Clyde and Hambros, he has found time to govern us from a variety of platforms: the Scottish Industrial Development Advisory Board, Scottish Economic Council, National Economic Development Council; Design Council, Countryside Commission, Top Salaries Review Body, Atlantic

Salmon Trust, Association of Scottish District Salmon Fishery Boards and, of course, as last chairman of the SDA and first chairman of Scottish Enterprise. During this period, he has also chaired the CBI, both in Scotland and at UK level. Yet, it is as an individual that his influence has been strongest.

It is possible to see such people, still mostly men, as fulfilling some of the characteristics of a new Establishment. The 1980s have been the decade of the businessman, a small and fairly close-knit group whose members have been propelled into supervisory positions in many Scottish institutions by the patronage of a governing party increasingly short of elected sympathizers. It is a phenomenon subtly different from the list of 'great and good' from which successive governments have appointed those who sit on quangos. The commercial analogy at the heart of the Thatcher Government's view of public bodies created boards where none had previously existed (or reshaped those which had) and staffed them with appointed businessmen, presumed to be rich in entrepreneurial or managerial expertise. Nickson's spread of interests is not exceptional; businessmen have been moved into oversight of institutions across the spread of Scottish public life: education, arts, health, heritage, conservation, economic development, broadcasting. Many sincerely regard their role as service to the community, while remaining aware of the element of political convenience involved.

The problem, though, is that in contemporary Scotland influence on government is not enough. St Andrews House may still represent the inner circle of executive power. But the consensus formed against it over recent years is not just a vehicle for left-wing or nationalistic protest; it also engages areas of significant power—the local authorities, for example—with which business has to interface. It raises and ventilates issues in which the views of business are, or ought to be, of some relevance. The absence of a strong, consistent business voice in the wider Scottish debate is an imbalance which is satisfactory to no one. Both Malcolm Rifkind and Ian Lang, as Scottish Secretaries, have openly appealed to the business community to involve itself in constitutional debate, in which Rifkind called it the 'glaring omission'.

That may presume a coherence of view which business groups infrequently achieve. Their contribution to the revived home rule debate of the 1990s, for example, was belated, flustered and unharmonious. The presumed vehemence of business opposition to constitutional reform is in any event over-stated. While soundings by groups like CBI Scotland, Scottish Financial Enterprise and the Scottish Chambers of Commerce certainly show little enthusiasm for change, the low return rate does not imply that the depth of apprehension proclaimed by a handful of financial institutions in suggesting prior to the 1992 election that they might withdraw from a self-governing Scotland is widely shared. The Federation of Self-Employed participated in the Scottish Constitutional Convention, while a group of smaller—and indigenously Scottish—firms formed the 'Business Says Yes' lobby in early 1992. It is an ill-kept secret that the hierarchy of the banks contains a sizeable nest of nationalists; it is, after all, only a few years since the

Royal Bank employed a bright young oil economist called Alex Salmond, now leader of the SNP. Perhaps that should not be a cause for surprise. Other nations do not assume a flawless adherence by their industrialists to any one political party. Perhaps we in Britain only ascribe them such lumpen tendencies because we hear so little of them speaking for themselves.

CBI Scotland

The most active and best known of the employers' lobbies in Scotland is CBI Scotland, sometimes seen as nature's counterpart to the plaintive exuberance of the STUC, though the comparison is seldom fulfilled. Its 50-strong council, which meets quarterly, includes many of Scotland's biggest employers, and is a notable forum for the Scottish heads of UK and multinational companies, both public and private sector; much as the STUC general council consists largely of Scottish officers from UK unions. Though the main focus of the CBI's membership is manufacturing, its council also includes representatives from other sectors, such as the director of ScotRail, the chairman of the Scottish Tourist Board, heads of the privatized utilities and the president of the National Farmers' Union of Scotland. It publishes a regular industrial trends survey among member companies which is, along with the Scottish Chambers survey, one of the principal instruments for taking the temperature of the Scottish economy, and it maintains a sizeable industrial archive.

Not uncommonly among business collectives, CBI Scotland's procedures are an odd mix of election and appointment. Its principal lay officer is the chairman, who serves a two-year term. The job is somewhat ill-defined, or rather is defined by the personality and drive of the incumbent. One of the more flamboyant of recent times was the ubiquitous Bill Hughes, chairman of Grampian Holdings, who used the post to establish himself as a force on the Scottish right (he became deputy chairman of the Scottish Tories). A steady procession of eminent Scottish figures, and numerous journalists, were lunched at Grampian's riverside headquarters and, in due course, it was Hughes who introduced to the nation the grand design for Scottish Enterprise, somewhat to the distress of those CBI figures who found themselves abruptly identified with an initiative they had not had the opportunity to discuss. Hughes's successor, Alistair Mair of Caithness Glass, was more shy and reserved, handicapped by the death of the CBI's erudite Scottish director, John Davidson. Mair's successor, Alasdair MacCallum of Don & Low, is more outgoing, with a refreshing frankness.

Despite his importance to the organization's profile, the chairman is not directly elected. Every other year, the sitting chairman, vice-chairman and director meet to nominate a council member to serve first as vice-chairman, then succeed to the chairmanship. The outcome is then presented to the council for approval. Council members are elected to serve a three-year term, and are restricted to two consecutive terms. The lack of a directly elected figurehead does not greatly hamper the CBI's capacity to argue its corner in Scottish debate. But two other constraints do. The first is a quaint self-denying ordinance which prohibits comment or intervention in any matter relating to the affairs of a member company; the second is the lack of autonomy enjoyed by the Scottish Council within the CBI. Both have the effect of stifling the CBI voice in Scottish industrial causes célèbres. When, in 1990, Mair turned up at a meeting of the broad-based campaign to save the Scottish steel industry, it earned him a rebuke at the next council meeting from the manager of Ravenscraig for interfering in British Steel's affairs; irrespective of the impact of steel closures on the wider Scottish economy. Similarly, the brink-wrestling of 1988–90 between the South of Scotland Electricity Board and British Coal over supply prices stirred comment from almost every lobby except the CBI: the Scottish heads of both bodies sat on the council and, though the issue bore directly on the interests of many member companies and was discussed on the council, no public comment was made. CBI staffers betray occasional exasperation at being expected to follow debates from which they are debarred.

The second restraint is the more telling. Occasionally, a proposal arises to turn CBI(S) into SCBI or even CSI, but it never gets far. Nor is there any obvious channel through which to pursue it. CBI Scotland has no policy-making conference and, indeed, no systematic policy of its own. Its status is as one of 13 regional councils. All staff appointments are made by the CBI's headquarters at Centrepoint in London and the Scottish director, David MacLehose, is directly accountable to the CBI's Director of Regions and Smaller Firms, a post long-held (until her retirement in 1992) by the formidable Sonia Elkin.

Centrepoint's hand weighs heavy on the Scottish 'region'; the more so since the loss of Davidson, whose intellectual stature afforded him a certain licence in adapting CBI policy to the Scottish milieu. CBI Scotland is supposed to operate within the context of the policies decided at the CBI annual conference. In practice, this leaves a measure of flexibility on purely Scottish matters, though it is not unlimited; MacCallum, at his first press conference as vice-chairman, was memorably corrected by Elkin midway through a hearty endorsement of regional aid. Regional aid is not CBI policy. London also keeps a tight budgetary grip. Member companies pay subscriptions—calculated on a complex formula—to Centrepoint, which makes the disbursements and employs the 250-plus central and regional staff. Staffing at Beresford House in Glasgow's west end now comprises the director, four assistant directors (one of whom comes on secondment from the private sector, usually from a bank; and another of whom acts as press officer), an administrative officer, a clerical assistant and two secretaries. There are around 1 200 member companies in Scotland, a figure which has fallen thanks to mergers and to company headquarters moving south. One of Davidson's many innovations was the annual CBI Scotland dinner in September, which attracts around 600 industrialists and politicians and can credibly claim to be Scotland's premier business gathering of the year.

CBI Scotland's voice in Scottish public debate is intelligent, yet muffled. This is not just a matter of its constitutional dilution. It also has to do with the innate conservatism—in an apolitical sense—of its members. Businessmen, unlike trade unionists, do not seek or achieve eminence through a sense of ideological mission. They are often the Scottish agents of companies based furth of Scotland or even of Europe. Of course, most members of the STUC general council are in a broadly similar position. Yet, throughout the employers' lobbies there is a diffidence which contrasts dimly with the dialectical sparkle of the STUC. Rather often, their preferred course amounts to better the devil they know. A membership survey in April 1991 found more than half vaguely dissatisfied with the way in which Scotland is governed, but 80 per cent opposed to a Scottish parliament (rising to 90 per cent were the parliament to have revenue-raising powers). Attempts by MacCallum in 1992 to edge the CBI towards a more positive stance on Home Rule were reined in sharply by a deputation of grandees from the council.

Occasionally, these constraints encourage guile of a form made possible by the tight-knit nature of the Scottish industrial community. It has been known for discreet contact to take place with, say, the SCDI—even, on occasion, the STUC—thus providing an outlet for ideas which CBI Scotland would be uncomfortable promoting on its own. After all, over the past decade particularly, the shared belief of CBI Scotland and the STUC in the importance of a strong manufacturing base has found ample common ground against what both perceived to be governmental indifference.

The Thatcher era shut corporate lobbies like the CBI out of the decision-making process almost as thoroughly as it excluded the TUC, paying less heed to their views than to those of favoured individual businessmen. A recent radio interview found MacLehose admitting some attraction to Labour's proposal for a National Economic Assessment, which would have restored the CBI and the unions to tripartite discussion of economic strategy with Government. There is a further paradox here: a Scottish parliament, with the sort of muscular economic remit envisaged by the Scottish Constitutional Convention, would wish to consult the industrial community extensively on economic matters. Yet CBI Scotland remains suspicious of devolution. It would in any event need to change its own constitutional status to play the part credibly.

As it happens, change may well be in prospect, though Scottish constitutional aspirations are not the reason. In Scotland, as in the UK as a whole, the business lobby does not speak with anything approaching a single voice. It is not a simple left-right axis, though it seems often the case that the National Federation of the Self-Employed fires to the left of the chambers of commerce, which fire to the left of the CBI, which fires to the left of the Institute of Directors (IoD). More usually, the inconsistency reflects different sectoral interests. For example, the IoD, whose 1 650-strong Scottish membership includes financiers and retailers, shares neither the CBI's preoccupation with reviving manufacturing nor its abhorrence of the investment practices of the City. They coexist perfectly civilly, but in different spheres.

The fall of Margaret Thatcher—with her well-developed distaste for collective lobbies of whatever provenance—may have provided one stimulus for change, and the return of recession a second. Management lobbies are instinctively more muted under a Conservative Government: Terence Beckett, the then CBI director general, may have threatened Thatcher with a 'bare-knuckled fight' over interest rates in 1980, but bodies like the CBI feel reluctant about scrapping publicly with their Tory allies even when, as with the decimation of manufacturing in the early 1980s, they are profoundly unhappy. Nevertheless it is possible that they see in John Major's Downing Street and Michael Heseltine's Department of Trade and Industry, the potential for a bolder dialogue than in the recent past. Whatever the reason, things seem to be moving.

Little of the impetus is identifiably Scottish, though the implications may strike deeper in Scotland than elsewhere. The Scottish Engineering Employers' Association, for example, relaunched itself in April 1991 under the banner of Scottish Engineering, with a beefed-up executive team, a broader range of membership services and the objective of becoming a stronger proactive ginger group on behalf of the industry. Its chairman, John Ferrie of Rolls-Royce, said at its launch: 'We have no intention of going to St Andrew's House for afternoon tea and sympathy.'

The Scottish chambers of commerce

Something of the same sort is also happening in the chambers of commerce. In Britain, the chambers have never been the semi-statutory force that they are in many European countries. In Germany and France, for example, they have formal status under public law and a range of quasi-statutory functions, notably prime responsibility for training and vocational education. In both countries, membership is compulsory for all sizes of commercial companies. The German chambers devote around a third of their budget to vocational training, while in France every member company has to contribute 1 per cent of its payroll to education through the chambers. The German chambers are also licensing authorities; they regulate trading hours; they run the stock exchanges; they settle disputes over advertising or trademarks. The Italian, Dutch and Greek chambers are responsible for company registration. The French chambers are tourist-promotion authorities; they share in the funding and management of science parks, industrial estates, ports and airports, motorway services, and housing provision. In many European countries, the chambers have a prominent role in commercial courts and in local government. Only a faint shadow of that prestige applies in Scotland, where membership is voluntary. Most chambers have full-time staff who endeavour to provide business services and lobbying, but their effectiveness varies widely. They have increasingly sought a more focused voice through the Association of Scottish Chambers of Commerce. In the past, acting individually, the chambers' public lobbying has prevailed mainly at local level, though that can occasionally carry through into national issues; an example being the role played in the campaign to remove Prestwick

Airport's transatlantic monopoly by the Glasgow chamber. Glasgow, formed in 1783, lays claim to being Britain's oldest chamber and its chief executive, Ewen Marwick, is probably the best-known figure in the Scottish chambers.

Proposals are afoot to restructure the Scottish chambers, which have 8 000 member companies, into about five major chambers of around 1 000 members each in the main Scottish cities. Smaller chambers would link in to these, pooling resources to access better information and support services. The Scottish Chambers director, Andrew Moore, has hinted that they could take over some of the business services currently provided by local enterprise companies. An alternative view is that the LECs have taken on many of the attributes of the continental chambers, and are a truer analogue for what happens elsewhere in Europe. In any case, the origins of the reform proposals are not Scottish: they derive from a report commissioned by the British Chambers from Professor Bob Bennett of the London School of Economics.

John Banham, the CBI director general, has floated a plan for a single umbrella organisation, the National Manufacturing Roundtable, to represent the interests of manufacturing. Made up of around 100 top companies and trade associations, it would have a permanent staff and a director who, in due course, would take over Banham's own role. Banham has been pursuing these ideas for some time in a round of discussions with the Engineering Employers Federation, the British Chambers and others; seeking consensus for a realignment to give employers a more focused view. Some see the biggest companies being organized through the CBI, or a successor like the Roundtable, while a federation of chambers with enhanced powers would represent smaller firms, possibly taking over from the present structure of CBI regional councils. That would certainly change the topography of economic debate in Scotland. Whether replacing one London-determined structure with another would make the business voice any more influential is less certain.

The unions

The image of trade unions, in the last decades of the century, is rather like a split-screen movie. There is the shot in the heritage museum: the bands, the banners, the sepia infamies of Tolpuddle and Taff Vale. Concurrently, there is a monochrome close-up of unglamorous, workaday structures still available to more than 8 million of us if we have a problem about overtime rates or holiday entitlement. More recent years have interposed a third scene: smudgy newsreel footage in which the anoraked dragons of a dimly remembered recent past bellow angrily from behind their picket-line braziers; dragons now slain in the interests of efficiency, but whose burial grounds still need to be exorcised for fear of resurrection.

Scots are not immune from this disjointed perception. Most are aware of the part mighty industries played in shaping the nation's character and of the collective traditions that were their proud corollary. Yet, much of what remains seems the relic of a bygone age, like the miners' welfares in Ayrshire and Lanarkshire and Fife which still prosper long after the pits have gone. The Scotland of the business pages and the New Town advertisements is a very different place. In the big growth sectors of the past 10–15 years, like electronics and financial services, union organization is either sanitized or non-existent. The Thatcher labour legislation applies as much in Scotland as anywhere, the destruction of the unions' traditional breeding grounds in heavy industry all the more so. Union membership in Scotland stood, in 1991, at 829 763: just 38 per cent of the workforce.

And yet, over the past decade, as the UK has voted one way and Scotland increasingly another, it has been to organized labour that Scots have intuitively looked to give voice to their collective frustrations. Whether or not trade unions remain, as the STUC general secretary, Campbell Christie, has claimed, engrained in Scotland's political culture, there are few corners of the Scottish agenda where their voice goes unheard. To understand the role of Scottish trade unionism, and particularly of the STUC, is to understand much of what is distinctive about the Scotland of the 1990s.

The Scottish TUC

The focus for trade unionism in Wales is called the Wales TUC. The focus for trade unionism in Scotland is called the Scottish TUC. In that distinction between a noun and an adjective lies a world of difference. Unlike its Welsh counterpart, the STUC is not a regional council of the TUC: not the TUC-in-Scotland, but the *Scottish* TUC. Since its founding congress at the Berkeley Hall in Glasgow in March 1897, the STUC has been independent of its elder cousin in Bloomsbury; constitutionally, politically, temperamentally. Over the past quarter-century, its industrial importance as the high command of union organization in Scotland has steadily diminished; yet its eminence as a vehicle for national grievance, as interim convener of the provisional assembly-in-waiting, has grown. It is much bigger than the sum of its parts, more Scottish than TUC, and bears a status in contemporary Scotland that consistently rises above the faded prestige of trade unionism.

Part of the STUC's resilience comes from its habit of leading from the back. That is not to suggest that it is timid in giving a policy lead—quite the reverse—but rather that it has been careful to keep pace with the mood of the rank-and-file and adept at identifying that mood. It is very often the lot of the trade union official to moderate shopfloor instincts and dilute expectations. The STUC, possibly reflecting its lack of real industrial power, takes these aspirations and tries to mould them into coherent policy. This has sometimes attracted the sneer from UK union leaders that the STUC is just a glorified trades council which lacks the discipline of responsibility.

The STUC arose from a schism within the union movement in 1894–97, the immediate cause of which was the TUC's decision to exclude trades councils from affiliation. This apparently arcane issue was cypher for a whole nest of political and strategic disagreements, and reflected quite significant structural differences between the movements in Scotland and England even then. Trades councils in Scotland have declined through a chequered history to a position now of limited influence; yet many of the arguments of the time remain current. Much of the STUC's distinctive approach is rooted in its origins, and habitually justified by reference to them. It retains a reputation, generally merited, for being both more left-wing and more radical than the carthorse of Bloomsbury's Great Russell Street (one modern example was its pace-setting mobilization of union opposition to Barbara Castle's *In Place of Strife* industrial relations reforms). But the more important distinction was summed up in the rubric offered for the new organization by its first president, Duncan McPherson of the tinplate workers, at the Berkeley Hall: 'There are many questions which affect Scotland particularly to which our English fellow trade unionists cannot be expected to devote the necessary amount of time and attention they deserve.'

The STUC is now mainly composed of unions based south of the border, yet it has continued to place Scottish issues above all others. For example, the post-war nationalization programme, an unblemished good as far as the TUC was concerned, was regarded by the STUC as at best a mixed blessing, which it realized would centralize industrial decision-making away from, and to the detriment of, Scotland. That same Scottish-centredness has also sometimes soured relations with Labour's Scottish high command. Prolonged electoral dominance has left Labour in many respects the political establishment in Scotland, a position made all the more uncomfortable when it is in opposition at Westminster and accordingly less able to deliver what the STUC and other Scottish lobbies expect of it. As a UK-based party, it is also exposed to the charge, most raucously from the SNP, of being reluctant wholeheartedly to back Scotland against other parts of Britain in the competition for economic benefits. The STUC, by contrast, suffers no such inhibitions; a viewpoint which has led some English union leaders to dismiss it as a nationalist front. The nationalists, in turn, tend to see it as a Labour Party front, a view greeted with grim derision at Keir Hardie House.

That might imply a reputation as a political jack o'lantern, but it is the key to the STUC's survival in the face of all those forces which ought to have marginalized it in recent years. There is a distinction between opportunism and pragmatism, and the STUC has thrown up successive leaders shrewd enough to know where it lies. Through much of Scottish politics runs an instinctive synthesis of nationalism and collectivism, of which no one party has the monopoly. The STUC's achievement, sustained by finesse, has been to approach issues on a loose enough basis to find and consolidate this consensus. The result has been broad-based, often dynamic campaigns on issues like steel, coal, health and the poll tax. These have typically brought together politicians, trade unionists, performers, churches, youth groups, local authorities—aggrieved Caledonia, addressing an uncomprehending London.

Quite how this role has developed is open to debate. Doug Harrison, who recently left the STUC after 14 years as assistant secretary, sets its origins with George Middleton, who was general secretary from 1949 to 1963. That period, particularly the latter part of it, was in retrospect something of a golden age. With Scotland's traditional industries locked into their long decline, a fiercely proactive regional policy sought to revitalize them and to diversify into other sectors. The STUC gradually became a lead voice in the clamour for economic aid—Middleton proudly boasted to the 1961 congress that the STUC had issued more statements about the Scottish economy than any other organization—and, under campaign themes like 'Jobs for Scotland' and 'Quest for Jobs,' led broadly recruited economic raiding parties to Whitehall, sometimes returning with spoils.

If Middleton did lay the foundations, each of his successors added something to the strategy and reshaped it to changing circumstances. James Jack (1964–75) had, as Middleton's deputy, provided the often meticulous research that strongly underpinned the campaigns. That mission to expose and explain helped adapt strategy to the advent of a Labour Government, and to forge many of the links with outside bodies that continue to serve the STUC well. During the 1971 Upper Clyde Shipbuilding campaign it took the form of a committee of inquiry, calling evidence on the yard's plight, while later there were two broad-based 'Scottish Assemblies' convened by the STUC to debate Scotland's future. In this latter initiative lay the seeds of two of the most prestigious coalitions of the 1980s; the Standing Commission on the Scottish Economy and the Scottish Constitutional Convention.

Jack's successor was, in his different way, just as influential. Jimmy Milne, who had long represented Aberdeen trades council on the general council, was general secretary from 1976 to his death in 1986; a period when, all logic suggested, the STUC's star should have dimmed. Milne's achievement was to ensure it did not. He was primarily a political animal, one of a handful of forceful left-wingers who had challenged the right's post-war domination of the general council (Alex Kitson from the Scottish Horse and Motormen and Abe Moffat from the miners were others). But he had also, as the first trades council delegate to chair the general council in 26 years, been a key mover at Middleton's elbow in the push for regional policy gains. George Bolton of the Scottish miners is among those who see as much of Milne as of Middleton in the tactics of that period, and credit Milne more than anyone with the strategy of the consensus campaign. It certainly has deep roots in the Scottish Communist tradition of which Milne was a stalwart.

Despite his background, Milne's leadership also brought warmer relations with the Labour Party in Scotland, though they have periodically chilled again since then. Labour leaders, uncharmed by Christie's occasional tendency to think with his mouth, grumble that the STUC leadership lacks the salutary discipline of accountability to the electorate: STUC leaders fret that Keir Hardie House is prey to the Walworth Road prejudice, which they regard as irrelevant in Scotland, that consorting with union leaders is bad for your image. Certainly, the STUC can sometimes force the pace on delicate policy questions. This is not a new phenomenon: Mick McGahey won congress over to home rule in 1967, seven years before Labour fully bought the package. More recently, it was the STUC which honed the policy edge on issues like electoral reform, the poll tax and economic powers for a Scottish parliament. The suspicion sometimes forms that this is a useful facility for Labour's Scottish command, enabling them to slipstream as Christie gallops recklessly across dangerous ground. But the evidence is persuasive that Labour is more often discomfited than convenienced, and perhaps a touch resentful at the glamour of STUC populism.

Milne's legacy to Christie was an STUC which, at the mid-point of Thatcherism, was in remarkably good shape. Christie, the son of a Carsluith quarryman, had risen through the ranks of the civil service unions during the 1960s in London, where as part of the 'Sauchiehall Street Mafia', he had helped transform the Society of Civil and Public Servants from a small and docile staff association into a large and disciplined broad-left union. In the process, he had become the left's tactician in the TUC and widely seen as its prodigy of that generation. His departure to the celtic backwater of the STUC met with dismay. But Christie has always set a Scottish parliament at the heart of the STUC's aspirations, and saw a chance to help bring it about. Scottish public life is a small stage and he has the personal and campaigning qualities to loom large upon it. The years of Tory rule have edged the STUC from many forums: its nominees on Scotland's 15 health boards, to take just one example, have been steadily reduced in number from 36 in 1979 to none in 1991. But Christie retains a beefy portfolio of involvements, and a high profile in all of them: European social fund, Scottish Economic Council, National Economic Development Office, SCDI, ScotBic, Scottish Constitutional Convention, Glasgow City Aid, Glasgow Development Agency and more. Identification of the STUC with the personality of its general secretary creates occasional tensions in the hierarchy, but fewer than might be expected. The general council has its factions—the patrol of 'young turks' like Jim Martin of the EIS and Pat Kelly of the civil servants is perhaps the most engaging—but there is no regular cabal. Christie came closest to trouble in 1990, when he accepted a seat on the board of Guinness. He was challenged less on policy grounds than for his failure (on, he says, Guinness's insistence) to consult sufficiently among colleagues before taking the post. In forcing him to relinquish the appointment, the general council was gently reminding him that the general secretary is a functionary of congress and not the other way around.

But dynamism levies the price of licence. The union movement is a ragged battalion, redeemed in Scotland by the freewheeling flair of the STUC. The secretariat at Middleton House is small and committed: besides Christie and his deputy, Bill Spiers, the executive officers number just five. Travelling that light requires improvisation within the broad policy outlines set by the annual congress, the general council (which meets eight times a year) and the various general council and ad hoc committees. The workload is formidable. Jimmy Jack's bequest of careful research remains a guiding light. STUC publications are often very good indeed; the 1987 *Scotland—A Land Fit for People* was a solidly assembled, attractively written commentary on the Scottish economy which may have been the inspiration for the following year's Scottish Office publication *Scotland—An Economic Profile*.

Christie's STUC is essentially a protest vehicle, a tribune for dissent. But how secure is that role? Margaret Thatcher's departure may not have obviated Scottish grievance, but it did remove a terribly handy demon. Politics then seemed a stark affair, painted in primary colours. John Major simply does not provoke the same delicious rage. Where would the coalition strategy go if Labour ever returned to office? It is not hard to picture Christie arguing the toss with Mr Secretary Dewar, but it would be a different type of dialogue, demanding a less fortissimo soundtrack. Some coalition partners, like the local authorities, could be expected to make their excuses and leave. What, too, if a parliament of sorts made its appearance in Edinburgh? Even if it lacked the ambitious remit proposed by the Scottish Constitutional Convention, it would surely diminish the need for the sort of three-ringed circus the STUC has regularly staged to catch Westminster's attention.

There is, too, something in the SNP charge that the issue coalitions, while emotionally fulfilling, have actually achieved little. The coalition campaigns, though often magnificent, did not save Gartcosh and have not saved Ravenscraig. This last, perhaps, will come to be seen as a turning point for this brand of populist pressure politics. Ravenscraig, after all, had long been hoist as the idol of Scottish industrial virility. True, the campaign was not solely an STUC production; and true, it was actively, if unconstructively, scorned by the nationalists. But at the end of the day, it achieved little more than its own unravelling. The wanton smashing of the virility symbol left the impression of something very like impotence.

The day-glo politicking which the STUC has done so well in recent years has masked a lack of real *industrial* muscle. Christie, indeed, has admitted that he feels uncomfortable with the idea of union power, and more comfortable with argument and persuasion. That is honestly meant, but rather a Hobson's choice. The days of indigenous Scottish unions have long gone: only five out of 52 STUC-affiliated unions are Scottish-based, and only the Educational Institute of Scotland is of any size. They hold just two out of 34 general council seats, three if you count the trades council delegate. While the degree of autonomy accorded the senior Scottish official in UK unions varies considerably, many wield only limited delegated authority, rather like the managers of the branch plants in which many of their members work. Unions have repeatedly chosen TUC rather than STUC procedures to resolve inter-union disputes even where they relate solely to Scotland: for example, in the cases of Ford at Dundee or Caledonian Paper at Irvine. The STUC has tried to negotiate an automatic right of referral from the TUC in such cases, and has been told, politely but unamendably, to get lost.

An altogether more serious failure has been the inability to win union recognition from the inward investors who have provided the bulk of new manufacturing capacity. Silicon Glen is virtually a union-free zone. This is particularly infuriating to STUC leaders because the Wales TUC has scored highly among overseas investors and, jealous of the STUC's independence, rarely neglects to remind Christie and his colleagues of the fact. In some measure, this reflects differences in the respective inward investment patterns. Scotland's mainstay has been the US electronics sector where, particularly since the 1960s, non-unionism has been the norm, variable only where host governments insist. The Welsh, by contrast, have hunted most successfully in Japan, and Japanese companies are not dogmatically anti-union, though they generally cede recognition only on their own terms. But the Wales TUC also has a standing agreement with the Welsh Development Agency whereby it is afforded an early introduction to potential inward investors and takes part in developing the bid package. The STUC, by contrast, learns of inward investments when they are announced at press conferences, and has long suspected that Locate in Scotland actively promotes as an incentive to inward investors the impunity which which non-unionism can be maintained in Scotland. LiS denies this, but admits that it tells firms who ask that they need not recognize unions if they do not want to do so. It is also clear that Ford's abandonment in 1988 of its planned components plant in Dundee casts a long shadow over the LiS psyche. That affair was not strictly about recognition. All the same, the abiding memory is of unseemly inter-union acrimony and it has left LiS determined to have as little to do with unions as possible. The STUC, which believed it could have resolved the dispute where the TUC failed, may see that view as unjust, but can do little about it.

This is a major weakness for the STUC. As traditional manufacturing has declined, its affiliates have done moderately well in recruiting more white-collar members. But their influence remains scant in most of the Scottish economy's principal growth sectors. Aside from the earlier incomers, like Ferranti, electronics is largely non-union. A series of bitter disputes on North Sea installations, led by the Offshore Industry Liaison Committee, has made only limited impact on the resolute hostility of offshore operators and contractors to union recognition. In the service sector, now 70 per cent of Scottish employment, much of the jobs growth is part-time or casual and therefore resistant to union organization.

Shop stewards

In industrial disputes the STUC's role is supportive rather than executive. It raises funds and popular consciousness, it lobbies and declaims. Rarely does it direct strategy or intervene to broker a settlement, and it would be unthinkable to do so without the consent and invitation of the shop stewards. Sometimes, particularly when the opponent is the Government, the STUC's muster of a bugle-blowing militia can be important. The noise raised over Ravenscraig twice in the 1980s persuaded ministers to retrieve the plant from the dead cart. But that is part and parcel of the STUC's political, rather than industrial, clout; contingent as much on the weight the Scottish Secretary of the day wields in Cabinet as on the STUC's own influence.

The Thatcher industrial legislation severely curtails the ability of trade unions to mount action in support of colleagues' disputes. But the STUC must also bow before the Scottish tradition of a strong shop stewards' movement. It is for the workforce, through its stewards, to embark upon and conduct industrial action; it is for full-time union officers and the STUC to provide the help required. This is an etiquette prone to generate tensions, particularly when job losses are the issue. If the workforce resists, it often expects more support than is forthcoming; if it does not, its readiness to 'sell the jobs' can frustrate union officials.

Relations are better outwith battlefield conditions, but the tensions remain and the proprieties are observed. They rest on a long history. Particularly in the engineering industries, which remain the heart of the shop stewards' movement, the tradition of workshop autonomy stretches back to the earliest days of the movement and, especially in Scotland, to the opposition to union centralization. The 'Red Clydeside' legend sprang from shop stewards', rather than trade union, militancy. A landmark dispute took place in 1915, when the refusal of the engineering union to support a pay strike prompted stewards to form the Clyde Labour Withholding Committee (CLWC), which succeeded in pulling out 10 000 workers at 26 plants. The CLWC evolved into the Clyde Workers Committee (CWC), the radical demands of which, particularly in munitions factories, struck fear into the wartime Government, provoking arrests and deportations. These fears, intensified by the Russian Revolution, remained after the armistice, culminating in the infamous use of troops in Glasgow's George Square to dispel a rally called in support of a CWC general strike over working hours. Mass unemployment in the 1930s sapped union strength, but World War II brought an influx of new workers, particularly to the engineering plants. The shop stewards' movement regrouped around the Engineering and Allied Trades Shop Stewards National Council, a forebear of the present-day Confederation of Shipbuilding and Engineering Unions (generally known as the Confed). Local activism was also to bring unofficial pit strikes against closures and, perhaps most importantly, a series of strikes in the Clyde engineering plants over the right to organize apprentices. These drew young, often Communist, talent into the movement and, indeed, threw up several of those who would later stage the successful work-in in defence of the Upper Clyde Shipbuilders' shipyards.

The Confed, which is headed by a Scot, Alec Ferry, has an annual policy-making conference but its main importance is as a network rather than a lobby. Ironically enough, its greatest success of recent years has removed one of its prime functions. Its unexpectedly triumphant campaign in the late 1980s to shorten the standard 39-hour working week has, while falling short of the ultimate target of 35 hours, succeeded in establishing 37 or 37.5 hours as the industry norm. But the victory also saw the Confed's managerial equivalent, the Engineering Employers' Federation, call a halt to national bargaining on minimum pay and conditions.

Trades councils

Trades councils represent another stratum of union activity in Scotland, but one buried rather deeper than the shop stewards' movement. They remain a living reminder to the STUC of the obligations of its heritage, but their modern function is less clear and their strength uneven. Some, like Aberdeen, are well entwined in the fabric of their local communities, most much less so. A few have been targets for far-Left infiltration. In all, 48 remain affiliated to the STUC. In an interview in 1987, Mick McGahey commented: 'I am always pleased to boast about the difference between the TUC and the STUC, because the rank-and-file participate at the Scottish TUC. When we go to the TUC it is the "heid yins" who do all the talking, but in the STUC there is rank-and-file participation because of our trades council involvement.' Certainly, the trades councils remain closely enmeshed in the STUC, proof of its success in holding together the strands of the movement in Scotland. Yet, beneath the historical symbolism, their real influence on policy is slight. They press constantly, and so far unsuccessfully, for stronger representation in the STUC, citing their often considerable role in mobilizing financial and organizational support in major disputes. In the post-war years, when the general council was firmly in the hands of the right, the trades councils were the conduit through which the left, principally the Communist Party, could inject its thinking onto the STUC, and wider Scottish, agenda. But the shift to a more left-wing general council has eroded that role, and the young activists who once cut their teeth in trades council debates are now better valued, and cultivated, by their unions. About some, though not all, trades councils there is an air of ageing, even of decay.

Only a history of resilience cautions against the conclusion that the 1990s bode ill for the trade union movement in Scotland. By all logic, nemesis, or at least steep decline, should have visited the STUC and its satellites in the 1980s. Talented leadership, political élan and a heightened sense of its own place in Scottish culture prevented that happening, and may do so again. Scots seem content that their society should have room for a powerful voice to speak on the workers' behalf, and may not trust to a repackaged Labour Party, in or out of office, to articulate that voice alone. The STUC's strength lies in its retention of a popular identity delineated by populist politics. But the 1990s, while more tolerant than the preceding decade, are unlikely to bring a structure of employment any more accessible to union organization. The division of the workforce into full-time skilled core and part-time, casual or subcontracted periphery, seems destined to continue, and the task of recruiting in either group to grow harder. For the STUC, the challenge of remaining relevant will be at least as daunting as in the 1980s, and it will have to go about it a different way.

Part 4   The Financial Sector

Charlotte Square

Charlotte Square is rather more a brandname than a place. The graceful Georgian square at the west end of George Street in Edinburgh's New Town houses all manner of establishments. There are the official residences of the Scottish Secretary, and of the Moderator of the General Assembly of the Church of Scotland. There is an hotel, a solicitors' office, an annex of Register House. None of that is what is usually meant by Charlotte Square, which either as a noun or an adjective, denotes the Scottish financial community in precisely the light which that community most relishes: elegant, unflustered, understated, reaching prudent decisions in old drawing rooms beneath crystal chandeliers.

A fair cross-section of the community does indeed shoulder the burden of Charlotte Square leases: fund managers like Ivory & Syme and Martin Currie; insurance companies like Colonial Mutual and Legal & General; investment houses like 3i and Northern Venture; Adam & Co, the upper-crust bank. Yet much of the Scottish—even the Edinburgh—financial community is elsewhere. The clearing banks always stood their headquarters apart. The stockbrokers are thicker on the ground in Glasgow than Edinburgh. Some Edinburgh institutions—like Martin Currie, or the accountants Peat, Marwick McLintock—are abandoning the Square for Saltire Court, the fresh-built financial centre erected in one of Edinburgh's notorious holes-in-the-ground at Castle Terrace. Others have long roosted outwith the magic quadrate: Noble Grossart, the merchant bank; many of the biggest fund managers (Edinburgh Fund Managers, Dunedin, Scottish Investment Trust); brokers like Wood Mackenzie or Torrie & Co. Yet, all these carry the Charlotte Square kitemark.

On 14 January 1991, Ian Lang, the Scottish Secretary, made a little-reported speech to the biennial dinner of the Institute of Bankers in Scotland. It repays closer study. The tone was one of careful praise for a sector which had achieved substantial growth in the preceding decade; the sub-text was of eloquent frustration that this growth had not brought greater regenerative benefit to the Scottish economy. Lang began by describing the financial institutions as 'one of the major bulwarks of Scotland's economy through the years', with a vital contribution to make to Scottish life. They were, he told them, already contributing a good deal: creating employment, demonstrating 'social responsibility' through sponsorship, underwriting the Government's loan guarantee scheme, supporting enterprise trusts and the like. 'I would like however to suggest some ways in which the financial sector's contribution could be more effective still. I do so, of course, in the knowledge of the duty owed by financial institutions to their investors and shareholders. But I believe that, within that responsibility, there is scope for effort and involvement which would not only benefit the wider community, but enhance the status of the sector itself.'

Two phrases merit expansion. The duty owed is what is called fiduciary duty, the trust placed upon those who manage the assets of others to seek maximum return on investment. It is the justification pleaded by the financial institutions in their own defence when they are accused of acting more in the interests of mammon than of Scotland. The second is Lang's reference to enhancing the status of the sector itself. What he was addressing, and therefore acknowledging, was a popular perception that the advancement of the Scottish financial community had brought no great obvious benefit to the common weal; that the presence here of what claims to be Europe's second financial centre has done little to stop much of the Scottish economy subsiding into the swamplands; that Scotland's investment-starved industries have floundered while Charlotte Square has blithely sent capital overseas in search of a faster fix. Lang was not, of course, buying these prejudices in their totality. But he was warning the institutions that they had an image problem that reflected unkindly on a Government which had provided a policy framework for their prosperity. It was, at root, an appeal: 'Come on, guys; we've done our bit for you. Now, give us a break, huh?'

It came at a time when yet another Scottish industry, steelmaking, was being closed down for no better reason than the strategic convenience of a distant owner. Europe's Second Financial Centre had taken a look but shown no great interest in taking the industry over, whatever its potential viability. Not long before, Scotland's biggest brewer had faced a hostile bid from Australia in which several venerable Scottish institutions had lined up with the predator. Before that, too, several had signed up with the subsequently disgraced Ernest Saunders of Guinness against Distillers. Recession was once more looming, raising the prospect of fine Scottish firms sinking for lack of capital. What was it that Scotland got from all this wealth being created in its midst?

It is a question rather resented in the Square. One pillar of the place declared testily: 'It is an idiotic question—they [the institutions] are not structured or formed to invest in Scotland. That's not what their articles of association say.' Francis Bacon had put it more pithily: 'Money is like muck, not much good except it be spread.' Lang was not asking them to buy Ravenscraig. But he was telling them that they were not doing enough for the community they inhabited. Specifically, they could be doing more to help the Government's initiatives in peripheral council estates, by becoming more involved in the business support groups set up in these urban deserts: 'I believe that many residents in these estates could benefit greatly from professional advice on money matters,' he said, conjuring up a vision of *le tout* Charlotte Square descending on Drumchapel in a fleet of Porsches and urging the locals to get out of bonds and into equity. He also suggested that the fund management sector might care to cast its eye over the industrial property market, which the SDA was being required by the Government to vacate; and that the banks and others should be more ready to plough more money into business start-ups and expansions through the enterprise networks.

They had, by their lights, done their bit, of course. Some of them had done a great deal. Like all élites, particularly those which are the product of expensive education, the financial community is prone to peer group jargon, of which a favourite is to describe its more energetic denizens as 'movers and shakers'. This concept has attracted ministers, who have eagerly co-opted them to move and shake organs of public policy. Take Sir Charles Fraser, the Charlotte Square lawyer. It might reasonably be thought that a man with 41 past and present directorships on his CV had enough to keep him occupied. But Sir Charles, a man of considerable charm and unrivalled contacts, has found time to move and shake in the public sphere as well. He chairs the Lothian local enterprise company, Lothian and Edinburgh Enterprise Ltd, and sits as a director or trustee on the Scottish Civic Trust, the Edinburgh Old Town Trust, the National Trust for Scotland, the court of Heriot–Watt University, the University of Edinburgh Foundation Fund, ScotBIC, and the council of the Law Society of Scotland (he is also, for good measure, a member of the Hon Company of Edinburgh Golfers, ex-governor of Fettes College, Assistant Purse Bearer to the Queen and a self-confessed bagpiper). By all accounts, he is wholly generous in the time he gives to the unlucrative business of public administration. Des Bonnar, chief executive of LEEL, told me he had always found Sir Charles accessible and ready to get involved, while Sir Charles himself spoke to me of his LEC work with unmistakeable enthusiasm: 'It is exciting that LEEL is working so well with the region and the districts and with local business people. LEEL is a marvellous opportunity for all these different organizations to collaborate—we are a great focus for collaboration.'

There are others, too, who do their bit (though some who do not; manufacturers outnumber financiers on the LEC boards by nearly 7 to 1). But it was not principally their time Lang was seeking. It was their money, or rather the money they move about on behalf of their clients. In the second half of the 1980s, the total value of funds under management in Scotland doubled to £140 billion; around 12 times the annual budget of Lang's own department. Yet, as we have already seen, precious little of that is available to start, expand or save Scottish companies even in the most vibrant sectors.

The familiar response is fiduciary duty. It was put with characteristic frankness by Professor Jack Shaw, then executive director of Scottish Financial Enterprise, in November 1989 at the third and final economic summit called by the Standing Commission on the Scottish Economy: 'It is inappropriate to expect Scottish fund managers to invest in Scottish enterprises if better profitable investment opportunities exist elsewhere which will give funds of international origin a better return with greater security. The challenge for Scottish business—including financial businesses—is to justify, on the basis of international competition, their attractiveness for the investment of capital resources generated in all parts of the world.' Perhaps so, but the challenge has to overcome not just objectivity but long preconception. Prudence is rarely an absolute. The large-scale export of capital has, since the early years of the century, been a notable British pastime, undiminished by the loss of empire. Scottish capital, though always keen to distinguish its practices from those of the south, has played a full part in that. The practice of investing overseas, particularly in North America, dates back to the earliest days of the investment trust movement, which generally has at least a third of its holdings in non-British equity. The Scotland of the industrial revolution, as one senior financial figure put it, 'had more money swishing about in it than its economy required. There wasn't a need for that capital in Scotland, there was more than the community needed. The community in America was capital-short, but income-long. The opportunities existed.' The banks have concerned themselves rather more with the Scottish scene, but have an engrained wariness of long-term lending, and a continuing orientation to the retail, personal side of the business.

A recent newspaper survey of the Scottish financial sector's involvement in electronics investment highlighted this disconnection. Sixteen appropriate institutions were asked whether they had put money into Scottish electronics over the previous two years. Nine had either made no investments in the sector or (in one case) declined to comment. Of the seven which had, five reported a single investment. In almost all cases, the investment was either development capital or backing for a buy-out. As far as start-ups were concerned, the score was negligible. Even the SDA had only seeded £1 million in electronics start-ups, against £2.75 million in established companies.

It has been a recurrent theme of this analysis that economic success in Scotland, though less exceptional than the broad indicators might suggest, seems to take place in peculiar isolation; that the economic structure lacks the conductive materials to spread the benefits of prosperity. As with electronics or the offshore industries, so too with the financial sector; which should, perhaps, itself be an instrument of conduction. The economic audit conducted by LEEL in the preparation of its business plan brought this into sharp focus. Using the annual turnover league table compiled by *Scottish Business Insider*, it found that 14 of Scotland's top 25 companies are headquartered in Edinburgh. Eight of these (11 of the 25) are financial institutions. Yet Lothian's company formation rate ranks sixty-first out of 64 UK regions.

Employment in financial services in Scotland increased by around 50 per cent over the 1980s, with growth fastest in the portmanteau category of 'business services', which includes accountants, lawyers, consultants, estate agents, computer bureaux and advertising agencies. This category accounts for just over half of financial sector employment, with the remainder divided between banking and finance (just under a quarter) and insurance, real estate and leasing services (just over a quarter). Overall, the sector now accounts for nearly 15 per cent of GDP. But the growth needs context. According to a study by the Cambridge economist Iain Begg for the Scottish Foundation for Economic Research, Scotland actually lost ground among the UK nations and regions during the 1980s in terms of financial sector employment.

There is also an element of squinting out of a half-closed eye in this claim to be Europe's second financial centre. First, you have to confine your comparison to the value of equities under management. Then you have to confine your definition of Europe to the EC, thus excluding Geneva and Zurich. Then, you have to argue that Edinburgh and Glasgow are essentially a single centre, and deny the same tolerance to Dusseldorf and Frankfurt. Having done all that, Scotland squeezes ahead of Paris and into second place behind London.

Growth patterns, and the factors behind them, have been neither simple nor even. The Scottish financial sector, particularly the banks, benefited from an initial surge of growth (and attendant restructuring) before the 1980s, thanks to North Sea oil. Young Scottish financial talent, previously drawn to London, began to see its career prospects closer to home. Therefore, we should be careful about drawing stark conclusions from comparisons of relative transformation during the 1980s; the SDA calculated employment growth in the 15 years from 1973 at more than 70 per cent. All the same, the rapid change in the UK financial infrastructure over the past decade has not left Scotland unaffected. Deregulation has increased competition and demand. The differences between the activities of, say, banks and building societies have diminished markedly. Technological change has had a mixed effect on employment; reducing numbers of tellers and clerks and accelerating the trend towards part-time employment; yet at the same time generating employment growth in fields like credit processing.

It was in Edinburgh, in February 1984, that the Governor of the Bank of England first sketched the outline of the opening up in financial markets that was to reach its climax with the 1986 'Big Bang' reforms, the Financial Services Act. Big Bang was viewed with some suspicion by the Scottish institutions, whose main preoccupation was to protect their specialized niches from the predators whom they expected to come hunting. Charlotte Square legend, gilded by retrospection, has it that the Scottish institutions quietly grasped the opportunities implicit in a less fragmented sector, while forswearing the excesses that possessed the City; with the result that when the following year brought the stock market crash and a series of lurid City scandals, Scotland's reputation for probity paid dividends. Certainly, the funds poured in: not just from London, but from elsewhere in the world, too. 'We have a lower greed threshold . . . less yuppiedom,' Shaw explained to a strolling *Guardian* reporter with evident satisfaction. Scotland's financial sector was 'the fellow sitting quietly in the corner' while the hucksters screamed, and his patience had brought 'a constant procession of people' north in search of old-fashioned coolness and honesty. 'Black Monday cheered up the Tartan City no end,' the *Guardian* concluded. 'In Scotland, the crash of '87 left few discernible scorch marks on portfolios, in marked contrast to the London City.'

Well, maybe. The downside of caution is inertia. What is certain is that the post-Big Bang contrast between the placid dignity of Charlotte Square and the tantrums of the City worked to the former's favour; also that the Scottish houses were altogether more circumspect in the silly money days of 1986–87. But how much of this was wisdom, how much irresolution, and how much a consequence of the concurrent downturn in the oil industry, to which some Scottish institutions were heavily committed? What we do know is that a wide-ranging study of the Scottish institutions during this period conducted by Strathclyde Business School found complacency, reluctance to consider coherent development strategies and insufficient awareness of the need for marketing. It concluded that players in the industry lacked the linkages with each other that a properly integrated financial sector demanded, possibly because so much was UK or internationally oriented. It also took a stage further the familiar charge of reluctance to back start-ups in Scottish industry, by remarking the sector *itself* had a conspicuously low rate of new firm foundation, given its output growth.

It is a matter of judgement whether the Scottish financial sector would do well to trade some of its reliability for a greater propensity to risk. On the credit side, its reputation for integrity, for rigorous analysis, and for disregarding City investment fads, is certainly bankable, particularly with US companies looking to Europe for finance. The recession of the early 1990s once again demonstrated the relative resilience of Scottish investments: the value of funds managed by the independent fund managers fell by 7.8 per cent over the first 12 months, compared with an 11.4 per cent decline in the FT All Share Index; equally, turnover among the Scottish life assurance offices was up 10 per cent, against a UK average of just 7 per cent. Yet, when activity levels are high elsewhere, that same steadiness can look like under-performance, alerting potential predators. There has been something of a trend in recent years for investment trusts to be swallowed up by larger external institutions, while one of the stalwarts of the life assurance sector, Scottish Mutual, has lately been absorbed by the Abbey National. Scotland has been accused of failing to spot and exploit the rapid growth of the unit trust business. Charlotte Square elders tend to plead guilty to over-caution, though only as a long-discharged offence. 'There was a slight stodginess in the 50s and 60s,' one confessed to me amiably. 'Now there is a much more aggressive young man in charge of the houses, and they do well.'

The sector has some significant structural gaps. Growth, depending on definition, may have been impressive in recent years, but some limbs remain stunted. Building societies, for example, have been historically slow to develop in Scotland, and although the number of branches has risen sharply to more than 470 by the end of 1989, only three societies are headquartered in Scotland and only one, the Dunfermline, is even on the fringes of the major league. Merchant banking, despite the high hopes of the 1960s, has never really broken free of narrow niches to compete with the London houses. Aside from General Accident, standing in splendid (if troubled) isolation at Perth, insurance representation is confined to life offices.

That does not make the sector necessarily weak, merely specialized. Yet the global trend over the past decade has been away from specialization and towards diversity. That may well accelerate with the coming of the single market, which threatens to intensify the concentration of financial activity in the London–Paris–Frankfurt triangle. It is not just in Scotland that this development arouses concern. The EC Commission has encouraged the formation of associations of firms in fields like venture capital and securities trading, to enhance the connections between regional centres like Munich, Lyons or Barcelona, and the central hub. Scottish Financial Enterprise, formed in July 1986, has built alliances with various European regions, as well as endeavouring to persuade institutions to develop at least as much understanding of Europe—east and west—as they have long had of North America. It has pitched, as have others, for a central EC financial agency to be located in Scotland. But the path has not been easy. James Provan, a former Tory MEP turned Euro-consultant, was appointed to succeed Shaw in 1990 with the specific objective of gingering the Scottish financial community to address the challenges of 1992. But he found a resistance to collective initiatives or promotions and, worse, 'parochialism and even anti-Europeanism' among some firms. He quit after just 18 months in the job.

SFE's first and greatest challenge as an umbrella organization was to persuade the financial sector to think collectively. Some big institutions continue to stand aloof, preferring to make their own way without breaking bread with rivals. In some measure SFE has succeeded in this primary aim, but it has done less well in turning that into the projection of Scottish finance as a coherent entity beyond Scotland. Overseas, even in London, the image is indistinct, defined more by the reputations of individual institutions than awareness of the sector as an integrated whole. SFE has been accused of placing too much importance on specialisms, of neglecting the bigger game. Perhaps that wider perspective will gain from the appointment as Provan's successor of James Scott, a long-time career civil servant and, latterly, caretaker chief executive of the SDA.

The Scottish financial sector is an odd mix of recent growth and long history. Neal Ascherson has pointed out that the post-oil revival of Edinburgh finance has restored the employment patterns of the 16th century; the profile of a court city, albeit one without a court. Edinburgh now has three-quarters of its workforce in services and less than a sixth in manufacturing, the same proportions as London, and quite different from those of cities like Birmingham,

Manchester or Glasgow. Its financial sector has become part of its claim to be a capital city.

The bankers

In employment terms, two sectors dominate Scottish finance; banking and insurance. In 1989, banking employed just under 42 000 people and insurance just over 22 000. There are three Scottish clearing banks, the Royal Bank of Scotland (RBS), the Bank of Scotland and the Clydesdale Bank; the first two are headquartered in templar splendour in Edinburgh, the third in less assuming, though still handsome, premises in Glasgow. Scots were the originators, and most loyal adherents, of the trustee savings bank movement, though the 1986 flotation of the TSB to create a unified, and troubled, new force in British banking has removed much of what remained Scottish about it, along with its trustee status. Scotland is also the headquarters of the National Savings Bank, which moved to Glasgow in 1966, and has a small merchant banking presence.

Most Scots bank with one of the three clearers; the English 'High Street' banks have made scant impression on Scottish high streets, except through periodic holdings in Scottish banks. For the first half of the century, there were eight Scottish 'joint stock' banks, but a series of mergers and amalgamations between 1950 and 1969 produced the present three-bank configuration known, from 1971, as clearing banks. Their traditions differed in a number of respects from those of their English counterparts, though the distinctions count for less as time passes. Their central funds came largely from deposits, rather than investment or interest on advances, which ran at lower levels than in England; they had a much lower level of non-interest bearing accounts, with most Scots until quite recent times preferring the bank book to the chequebook; they were congenitally wary of long-term lending, except in agriculture, and though they were involved in industrial development, particularly in the 19th century, it was generally through short-term, self-liquidating loan forms. Increasingly, their role in lending to manufacturing has diminished, due in part to the externalization of industrial ownership.

If the configuration has been stable for more than 20 years, the banks' fortunes have not. For decades, they had enjoyed a cooperative, at times soporific, relationship, quietly agreeing common interest rates and charge levels between them. But a combination of legislative reform and economic upheaval in the 1970s changed all that. Soaring interest rates in the capital markets saw private companies turn increasingly to banks for funds. The Scottish banks became involved for the first time in heavyweight international syndicates to finance oil development. Though personal retail business remained their most important activity, the three clearing banks entered the 1980s more diverse and supple than they had been a decade earlier.

The banks are the financial institutions with which the public has the closest contact and the greatest understanding, and their fortunes arouse stronger interest than those of the shadowy institutions behind the Georgian doors of Edinburgh's New Town. Each retains a distinctive public image, and considerable customer loyalty. The 1981 battle for control of the RBS between Standard Chartered and the Hong Kong and Shanghai Bank (alias The Honkers and Shankers) stirred deep public passions, while flotation of the TSB in 1986 was opposed by a militia of Scots deposit holders. The Scots seem to see their banks, despite many reasons for not doing so, as expressions of national character.

The Royal Bank of Scotland

The biggest, and second oldest, of the clearing banks is the RBS, incorporated in 1727. It commands 6 per cent of the UK market, and can justly claim since it merged in 1985 with its long-time English partner, Williams & Glyns, to be the most 'national' of all banks, having branches from Shetland to Truro. Despite an increasingly unsentimental business strategy, it retains some endearing eccentricities; it is the only bank still printing £1 notes, the only one with a Ladies Branch (at the west end of Princes Street in Edinburgh), and was the first to offer currency exchange by cash dispenser. Its business initiatives of the past decade have been equally dashing, ranging from the successful to the hapless. Of the three, it has ridden the bumpiest road, and is now paying the price with a £25 million restructuring exercise expected to cost 3 500 of its 20 000 jobs. Like all banks, it was hit hard by the recession of the early 1990s, which dried up demand for advances and greatly increased the burden of bad debt. In 1990, profits fell 28 per cent to £241.4 million, and the first half of 1991 saw them drop a further £101 million on the equivalent period of the previous year.

What became known as the 'Battle Royal' in 1981 was not the first tussle for the soul of this peculiar institution. It had already seen off a challenge from Lloyds (owner of an RBS ancestor, the National Bank of Scotland), which had maintained a 16 per cent share. It was partly fear of predators that persuaded the then RBS chairman, Sir Michael Herries, to arrange a marriage with Standard Chartered, a London-based bank with South African connections. This, in turn, brought the Honkers and Shankers a-courting. Like a foretaste of the Westland affair, this relatively arcane issue divided not only public opinion but also Whitehall, with the Foreign Office, then facing delicate negotiations with China over the future of Hong Kong, throwing in its lot behind the Honkers. The whole affair was eventually tossed to the MMC which seized, unusually, on Scottish angst over the branch office syndrome to rule out both mergers. Retrospect suggests that this solution was best for the Royal, though it has not always been a clear judgement. The 1985 integration with Williams & Glyns, motivated in part by an overestimation of the unifying powers of computer technology, forced together two quite different cultures and structures, with disruptive results. At the time, the chief executive, Charles Winter, laid out a 10-year plan to close 80 of the 550 Scottish outlets and add 80 to the 314 in England and Wales. Six years later, the score was that Scotland had lost 117 branches and England and Wales gained 32.

The Royal has been diversifying, not always successfully. On the credit side of the balance, in 1988 it formed a partial merger—essentially, a share-swop—with the prosperous Banco Santander of Spain, which brought it outlets in Germany, Belgium and Portugal as well as Spain, and which operates via a sophisticated electronic money transmission system. The alliance has also helped protect the RBS against hostile takeover, since Santander cannot sell its 9.9 per cent holding in the Royal without the Royal's approval. In the same year, it became the first Scottish bank to make a major overseas acquisition, when it bought Citizens Financial of Rhode Island. Other diversifications included Charterhouse, its merchant banking and stockbroking subsidiary (which it is now offering for sale); two insurance subsidiaries, Direct Line and Royal Scottish, the latter a joint venture with Scottish Equitable; a trade finance service to European importers and exporters; and an investment management arm, Capital House, which had £113 million under management in 1990.

But the debit side has also been considerable. There was an ill-starred sojourn into travel agency, described privately by one executive as 'insane'. There was an abortive £88 million bid to buy a second US base, the Bank Worcester of Massachusetts, at a time when the RBS was closing down other US outlets acquired in furtherance of its oil interests in the 1970s. There has been heavy exposure in some of the decade's least enduring buy-outs, notably Lowndes Queensway and British & Commonwealth. Perhaps worst of all was the 'Spanish Gold' adventure in 1990, when the RBS and Santander went into partnership with Gibraltar-based Alomar to set up a mortgage service. Within a year, contracts had been terminated in expensive disarray.

With the restructuring comes an altogether more streamlined and, as it were, younger RBS. Herries's successor is indeed George (now Lord) Younger, the former Scottish and Defence Secretary, whom Herries first approached about the job in 1983 (despite Younger's role in blocking the Standard Chartered merger) and who became group chairman in 1991. In charge of the restructuring is Dr George Matthewson, who joined the bank in 1987 after a much-admired stint as SDA chief executive, and succeeded Winter in 1992. Both are representative of major changes taking place. There has been a rigorous clear-out of middle-management, a flattening of the Royal's baroque divisional structure, and the ascendancy of a carnivorous executive class, many just in their forties. Further restructuring seems certain.

The Bank of Scotland

Older than the Royal by 32 years, and possessed of a rather more conservative reputation, the Bank of Scotland has also been through unsettled times. In 1990–91, the Bank, which has a £23.9 billion asset base and 4 per cent share of the UK market, suffered its worst upset in 17 years when pre-tax earnings fell by 30 per cent to £134.1 million. It responded with a £194 million rights issue, and at the same time bought out the remaining 25 per cent of Bank of Wales, which it now owns outright. Though less ruthless than the RBS in closing branches, it shed 300 staff in the year to 1991, and now has one of the best cost–income ratios in the business. Its 1991–2 results showed some improvement, though bad debt remained a problem.

Despite its reputation for caution, the Bank has done its bit for innovation. It was one of the first explorers from the banking world into the mortgage business, and now has a £3.7 billion mortgage book. It has experimented extensively with new technology, developing the successful ARTIS electronic share dealing system and an electronic payments system for international traders, EDIPAY, which it claims to be the first in Europe. It has also formed an ambitious joint venture with a German partner, the Quelle Bank, with whom it shares its impressive new credit-card processing operation at Pitreavie in Fife, and which offers the prospect of possible expansion in eastern Europe. It also reportedly nurtures ambitions to expand in England.

In June 1991 it signalled a further departure when, after 296 years, it combined the posts of governor and chief executive, in the relatively youthful person of 53-year-old Bruce Patullo. Patullo, a product of Edinburgh Academy, Rugby and Oxford, started with the Bank as a graduate trainee and served a long stretch as chief executive to the splendidly named Sir Thomas Risk. His accession may presage a more adventurous path ahead for the Bank, a prediction fortified by the appointment of the energetic former Scottish Financial Enterprise director, Professor Jack Shaw, as deputy governor.

Unlike its bigger cousin the RBS, the Bank of Scotland has benefited from a stability of ownership since Barclay's (which, like the RBS with Lloyds, it had inherited through the merger process) sold out its 33 per cent stake to Standard Life in 1985 for £155 million. It too has constructed an elaborate structure of subsidiaries besides its presence in Wales. With a characteristic eye to history, it preserved the venerable name of the British Linen Bank in 1973 as a merchant banking subsidiary, though with inconsistent results. It has a consumer finance subsidiary, NWS, which is doing well and a factoring arm, Kellock, which has been doing badly. It also has a 50 per cent share in Dunedin Fund Managers and, more colourfully, a 30 per cent share in a recently established Greek bank, Dorian. Like the RBS, it too fell victim to the 1980s buy-out craze—MFI was one of its less prudent exposures—and more recently lost up to £14 million in loans to English property companies, later contaminated by scandal.

The Clydesdale Bank

If the Bank has benefited from stable ownership, the smallest of the Scottish clearers, the Clydesdale, has benefited from breaking loose from stable ownership. The product of a 1950 merger between two wholly-owned subsidiaries of the Midland Bank, the Clydesdale suffered for years from chronic under-investment and under-ambition beneath the dead hand of the Midland. In 1987, the Midland sold it to the National Australia Bank (NAB) for £360 million and it began to awake from a decades-long torpor. In the next three years, profits trebled. Though it is far smaller than its two rivals—with a third the staff of the Royal, and a quarter the asset base of the Bank—it has so far ridden out the recession better than either, recording a 20 per cent rise in profits to a record £70.2 million in 1990. It has lately followed its rivals in announcing staffing cutbacks, though on a more modest scale: it has a poorer costs–income ratio than they, but a better profitability relative to assets. More radical surgery looks unlikely, however. The NAB has troubles, but they are mostly in Australia and the US, and its British operations provided 35 per cent of group profits in 1990.

The Clydesdale has the narrowest spread of business interests of all the Scottish banks, largely a legacy of the Midland years. But it had also hoped for better things from the Australians. The purchase certainly roused its competitive spirit, but its hopes of becoming NAB's UK flagship and of expanding south of the border evaporated in 1990 when NAB bought the Yorkshire Bank. The Australians, one senior executive told me, are supportive of Clydesdale investment and do not interfere in decision-making, but they are only really interested in it as a retail bank. It has a small, though useful, sideline in insurance broking and asset finance (through Clyde General Finance) and a modest but busy corporate division; it has a long-standing reputation, particularly in north-east Scotland, as a farmers' bank; it occasionally hints that it may buy a UK insurance company, or that the Australians may buy a building society; but its central strategy is to concentrate on improving its core retail business.

For all its success, the Clydesdale, too, is undergoing change at the top. The engaging Sir Eric Yarrow retired as chairman at the end of 1991, to be replaced by the Scottish Enterprise chairman, Sir David Nickson. Nickson's appointment caused some surprise; in 1988, as chairman of Scottish & Newcastle, he resigned from the board of the Clydesdale in protest at the Bank's support for the bid by Elders IXL (a valued NAB client in Australia) for Scottish & Newcastle. He returned a year later, though his pitch had been presumed queered. Perhaps more upsetting was the unexpected decision by Richard Cole-Hamilton, a driving force behind the transformed performance of recent years, to retire early after 10 years as chief executive. There is little doubt, and fears in some quarters, that these ructions afford the Australians an opportunity to stamp their identity more firmly on the Clydesdale. But it is hard to see why they should. The Clydesdale does less than the other Scottish banks but it does it rather well.

The TSB

A less uplifting recent history attends the TSB. It has been shedding staff, streamlining its operations, and looking about it with some apprehension for predators as the Government's 'golden share' expires. It should have done so well. The flotation turned a loose federation of savings banks with loyal customer bases into a national organization, and provided a bounty of £1.5 billion to be ploughed back into the business. It became, at a stroke, Britain's sixth biggest bank. It acquired, in 1989, the respected former Stock Exchange chairman, Sir Nicholas Goodison, at its head. But destiny seems undecided about 'the bank that likes to say yes'.

Its tribulations are being watched with particular sourness from Scotland. It is a Scot, the Reverend Henry Duncan of Dumfries, whom history credits with founding the savings bank movement in 1810, with its ethos of recycling profits among savers. The 1986 flotation was bitterly opposed, both because of the undermining of that ethos and because of fears that Scottish distinctiveness would suffer. Partly to assuage this opposition, undertakings were given that net employment levels in Scotland would be maintained and that TSB Bank Scotland, as the new edifice was cumbersomely styled, would remain a separately managed Scottish bank. Neither assurance has proved watertight. Cancellation, in 1991, of plans to transfer 300 staff from TSB's beleaguered mortgage wing, Mortgage Express, to Scotland cast doubts on assurances of incoming jobs to replace the hundreds shed in Scotland. A restructuring extended the territory of its admired chief executive in Scotland, Charles Love, into England and left the Scottish banking operation responsible to a divisional board with no non-executive members. Scotland remains the jewel in TSB's tarnished crown, with profits rising 32 per cent in 1990 to £61 million, a successful mortgage business and ownership of Scotland's biggest estate agency, Slater Hogg & Howison. But elsewhere, recession is taking a heavy toll: particularly for Hill Samuel the merchant bank purchased by TSB in 1987.

How will the Scottish clearers fare in the ructions promised by the single European market? They have shown themselves alive to its implications both by restructuring and by forming continental alliances. Yet they may need a more ambitious scale of partnership to compete in, and avoid emasculation by, the big-table market that lies ahead. As one of Charlotte Square's more acute observers put it, 'In a world of supermarkets and boutiques, they are neither.'

Merchant banking

Scottish merchant banking, meanwhile, remains popularly synonymous with the name of Angus Grossart, much as it was 20 years ago. Merchant banks developed late in Scotland and on a relatively small scale. In the 1960s, the clearing banks established subsidiaries in the secondary or wholesale banking field, which were able to become fully-fledged merchant operations after legislation in 1971. The period saw other start-ups: James Finlay, one of the great survivors of Glasgow's colonial trade; McNeill Pearson and, in 1969, Noble Grossart. Several of the big London names, like Morgan Grenfell and Hill Samuel, established Scottish branches. Much the same was happening elsewhere in the 'provinces', partly because of growing demand from local authorities for long-term borrowing, though Scotland offered the added promise of a robust financial infrastructure and of developments in the North Sea. Yet, while many of these banks remain and some have prospered, the anticipated growth has not taken place. As the Scottish Office observed in 1991: 'Existing merchant banks tend to operate in niche markets exploiting local knowledge, but have not competed successfully for "big business", where competition is intense.'

Grossart, an advocate by training, remains the star of the sector; a tireless mover and shaker, with involvements across the financial industries and a personal fortune, according to one recent estimate, of between £8 and £16 million. He founded the company in 1969 with Sir Iain Noble (nephew of Michael, the former Tory Scottish Secretary), who later withdrew. The venture was backed by Sir Hugh Fraser's SUITs group, four investment trusts and the engineering-to-retail group, Stenhouse Holdings. Its rapid growth came in the 1970s, largely on the back of oil. Noble Grossart was not the only merchant bank to become involved, but it was probably the most successful, managing investment ventures like Pict Petroleum, Caber Oil and North Sea Assets. At the same time, it was building a reputation for sound matchmaking advice, notably with the Kuwait Investment Office's £100 million takeover of St Martin's Property.

The 1980s found Grossart increasingly moving on a wider stage. He backed Eddie Shah's newspaper revolution, raised finance for David Puttnam's movies, and was heavily involved in two of the decade's biggest Scottish takeover battles, Coats Paton and Distillers. He has also been an adviser for flotations like TSB and Scottish Power. At the same time, Grossart built up his company's investment wing, buying out the other shareholders in 1988. Its strength lies in sizeable stakes in many of Scotland's leading unlisted companies, and the total worth of the portfolio is estimated at up to £50 million.

Nonetheless, Noble Grossart retains the structure of a small, private concern. 'Angus has done a good job, but he has kept himself small,' one long-time friend of his told me. 'Angus in my book is a one-off.' Certainly, Grossart is distinctive in the ease with which he moves on the international stage. But he is also a presence in many corners of the Scottish economy. Adding the investment portfolio to the advice client list, the range of Noble Grossart involvements includes retail banking, fund management, insurance, health care, metals, plant hire, television, offshore development, textiles, confectionery, advertising, art, hotels, coach travel, brewing and distilling, sports clubs, food manufacturing, electronics, haulage, electricity and retailing. Merchant banking may have failed to take off as an indigenous Scottish growth sector: but it has produced probably Scotland's single most influential financial figure.

The insurers

Scotland's strength in the insurance field is at once substantial and lopsided. Insurance has many strands but, broadly, the business divides into two main segments: life assurance; and composite or general insurance. Scotland is skewed heavily to the life sector: its nine offices (six based in Edinburgh, three in Glasgow) together command between a sixth and a fifth of the UK life business. Despite the Caledonian motif which persists in many of their names—Scottish Widows, Scottish Mutual, Scottish Amicable—far the greater part of their business takes place outwith Scotland. As one senior financial figure put it to me, 'They happen to be in Scotland and to be managed by Scots.' Equally, most Scottish insurance business is placed with non-Scottish companies, some of which are products of mergers involving former Scots firms, and many of which retain substantial representation in Scotland. But life assurance is not quite the whole picture: Scotland has only one big general insurer, General Accident of Perth. But it is the biggest insurance company in Scotland, with some 15 000 employees, and is a significant player on the British stage.

Standard Life

Far the most important of the life offices is Standard Life, Europe's biggest mutual life assurance company. It has 5 500 employees, of whom more than 3 000 are in Edinburgh, where both Standard and its nearest local rival, Scottish Widows, have erected splendid head office buildings in recent years. Employment and fine buildings are perhaps the most conspicuous public manifestations of the life offices. No doubt reassuringly for policy- and pension-holders, they emit an air of urbane continuity. Dullness would be another word. They also have their clubbish side. 'I always think of them as being like the Brigade of Guards,' said one financier. 'They recruit similar types, you are there for life, you become embedded in the company culture. They are strong on team spiritedness, on esprit de corps.'

Standard Life has been called the 'sleeping giant' of Scottish business, but the giant aspect of that is at least as valid as the slumber. It is a formidable concentration of capital. In 1990, despite an 8 per cent fall in UK new business, Standard Life raked in premiums worth £1.72 billion. It had £20 billion of funds under management, a portfolio which represents fully 2 per cent of the UK stock market. Among its holdings are a one-third share of the Bank of Scotland, acquired from Barclays in 1985. But, inevitably, the bulk of its equities are in non-Scottish firms, and transacted through London rather than Edinburgh or Glasgow.

Nor does Standard Life's management, headed by managing director Scott Bell, entirely merit the 'sleeping' side of the nickname. The past decade has brought significant change in the life market, notably a marked shift away from endowment mortgages—long a Standard Life specialism—and a rapid growth in personal and profit-linked pension schemes. The consequence has been to forge new or stronger links between the life offices and other financial institutions, for example taking the insurance companies increasingly into the unit trust business, an area in which Scotland is indifferently represented. The 1986 Financial Services Act required all investment advisers to register as either tied or independent agents, further encouraging institutional linkages. Standard Life was the first life office to sign a big building society—the Halifax—as its agent, giving rise to later joint ventures, and, in 1989, also recruited the Bank of Scotland as an agent, recommending only Standard Life products to customers.

General Accident

The other giant of the Scottish insurance scene, General Accident (GA), has been neither sleeping nor particularly sitting comfortably. General insurance is, by its nature, a less stable business than the life sector: escalating crime rates and the imponderability of natural or manmade disasters see to that. Companies accordingly rely for their profits not on their insurance underwriting, but on their investments; few more so than GA, which has made consistent losses on its underwriting activities, totalling £1.8 billion in the decade to 1990. One analyst was quoted describing GA as 'an investment trust with an expensive hobby.' These investments grossed GA £2.9 billion over that same period, more than offsetting the underwriting costs. But in 1990, global stock markets dipped, leaving GA's investment income £121 million short of its £461.7 million insurance losses.

GA has sought, in response, to diversify but its ventures have not gone entirely well. It bought a New Zealand bank and a chain of 450 estate agents, intended as a means of drumming up business for its York-based life division. Between them, the two diversifications lost £120 million in three years. Rather more successfully, the chief executive, Nelson Robertson, is reducing costs and has already made inroads, though further rationalization of GA's elaborate structure seems inevitable.

It comes at a time of ever tougher competition in general insurance, both in the UK and overseas (GA has substantial interests in North America), which is pushing down premium charges and making traditional broker-based sales seem increasingly unviable. Equally, the life offices are uneasy about the implications of the single European market. Life policies are cheaper in the UK than in continental Europe, yet rumours of EC predators persist. It seems possible that Scotland's insurance firms may be facing a more turbulent few years than they have known in recent memory.

The building societies

There is a tendency in Scotland to think of building societies as something of an alien concept. It is not strictly so; at the turn of the century, there were 140 native Scottish societies, though only 14 of them survived to the end of the

1970s, and by the end of 1989 the Building Society Association affiliated just three Scottish members. But the indigenous Scottish sector was always small in scale. Scots, though diligent enough savers, historically tended to vest their faith and the fruits of their thrift in banks, particularly trustee savings banks, and in Post Office savings. A much lower level of home ownership than in the rest of the UK—until the Thatcher Government's council house sales programme, only a third of Scots were owner-occupiers—restricted demand for mortgages.

Owner-occupation is now over the 50 per cent mark, and recent generations of Scots have come to regard building societies as part of the fabric of life. Over the last quarter-century the building society presence has rapidly grown, boosted by rising home ownership levels and by the introduction of Save As You Earn in the early 1960s. Between 1965 and 1980, the number of branches in Scotland quadrupled, and in 1989 it stood at more than 470. At the same time, the demarcations between building societies and other institutions have been eroded. Banks have moved increasingly into the mortgage business, building societies have begun to offer current accounts and cash dispensers. Both also act as conduits through which their customers can access intricate networks of alliances with insurance companies and stockbrokers.

What has not greatly changed is the small Scottish indigenous share of the market. Far the biggest Scottish society, with assets totalling £607 million in mid-1991, is the Dunfermline, headed as chief executive by a solicitor, David Smith. Yet the Dunfermline scarcely registers in the UK major league. It has around 40 branches throughout Scotland and a reputation for being well-run. It took the Dunfermline from 1869 to 1981 to lift its asset base to £100 million: and only until 1990 to increase this to £500 million. In 1990, despite a sluggish housing market, it increased profits for the second successive year by 40 per cent, to £9.3 million, helped by a marketing campaign emphasizing its Scottishness, which seems to have been a hit both with new borrowers, such as council house purchasers, and new savers, attracted by schemes like TESSA (tax-exempt special savings accounts). Smith has, however, resisted the vogue for offering current accounts in competition with the banks, arguing that he does not need the overheads involved in establishing cheque-clearing facilities. It does not seem to have done much harm.

The brokers

As recently as the early post-war years, Scotland had five stock exchange floors. First to go was Greenock, followed by Aberdeen (closed 1963), Dundee and Edinburgh (both 1971). Like other 'provincial' exchanges, they had handled a diminishing volume of business as private investors became an increasingly marginal corner in a market dominated by big London-orientated institutions. In the wake of the Aberdeen closure, they federated into the Scottish Stock Exchange, but both business and the numbers of brokers engaged in it continued to decline. In 1973, Scotland's last exchange, Glasgow, joined the five other provincial exchanges which had survived in a single unified structure run from London. Though the building in Nelson Mandela Place is still generally referred to as the Glasgow Stock Exchange, its proper title these days is the Scottish Region of the London Stock Exchange.

Technology, starting with the telephone, had steadily decreased the importance of local exchanges. It meant that, in theory at least, any stock could be traded anywhere, though a tendency remained for smaller local stocks to be listed and traded locally. The 1973 reform changed that, by instituting a central list. Meanwhile, the market in unlisted stock had diminished. It seemed to add up to an inevitable decay of the smaller exchanges. But in the event, the past decade has seen a significant revival in stockbroking activity in Scotland, particularly Glasgow, and in the other provincial exchanges. On-screen dealing systems have meant that business can be done as readily from Lerwick as from London. Moreover, business has increasingly divided between big institutional dealers and the smaller, client-based transactions. The big London houses, facing escalating overheads and therefore requiring to charge ever larger fees, have found the private client sector decreasingly worth the trouble. Centres like Edinburgh and Glasgow had a long expertise in this sector. Therefore, the past decade has seen UK broking houses establishing a steadily growing presence in Scotland, mostly by acquisition, though also by moving some 'back office' functions north.

A senior manager in one Glasgow house told me that he reckoned Glasgow to handle on an average day around 8 per cent of all stock market transactions in Britain, with his own operation perhaps accounting for about 2 per cent of trades. The proportion in value terms would be much smaller; there is little institutional business done in Scotland, and big Scottish institutions, like insurance companies, mostly deal through London. Nevertheless, the Glasgow Stock Exchange now reckons close to 50 per cent of retail—non-institutional—transactions to be traded in Scotland.

Just how *Scottish* a business it is lies more open to question. Few of the main players in Glasgow or Edinburgh could be said to be entirely Scottish. Equally, only one Scottish firm—Wood Mackenzie of Edinburgh—has really made the UK major league in recent times, with a business built on its oil and gas analysis in the 1970s, and it is now part of National Westminster, though retaining a substantial presence in Scotland. Among the other important players are Barclays, which channels much of the private client stockbroking business it generates throughout the UK through its Glasgow stockbroking operation; Parsons Penney also in Glasgow, which is part of a nationwide network, Allied Provincial Securities; and Bell Lawrie White, based in Edinburgh but owned by TSB. There are a few purely Scottish houses remaining: Speirs & Jeffrey in Glasgow, Torrie & Co in Edinburgh, for example. There are also two Glasgow 'market-makers', Aitken Campbell and F A Maclean. Market-makers are the descendants of what were previously called jobbers; in essence, the wholesalers of the equities business. Unlike the brokers, they make their living not from commission but 'on the turn': by selling the shares on at a higher price than that at which they bought them. Both these firms operate from the stock exchange floor, though more for traditional than practical reasons. 'The presence of a floor now is fairly irrelevant,' said one Glasgow stockbroking source nostalgically. 'The old days of the floor meaning anything have gone.'

The fund managers

If there is a glamour stock in the Scottish financial community it is probably the fund managers. The function they perform is neither more conspicuously useful nor demanding than those of the bankers or the brokers, but the search for a quintessential Charlotte Square institution would almost certainly fetch up with a fund management house.

One reason is that it is an area of celebrated Scottish strength. Scotland's forte is the investment trust, a concept reputedly invented, and certainly pioneered, in Dundee and Edinburgh from the 1870s as a way to capitalize on the surplus profits from industries like jute. Unlike other Scottish innovations of that age, it has remained a strength. Around 35 per cent of the resources vested in investment trusts in the UK are managed from Scotland. It is a trade at which Scottish houses also prosper abroad. Several of the big houses are active in North America or around the Pacific rim.

Investment trusts have, for much of the past 20 years, enjoyed rather less vogue than unit trusts. A distinction between the two concepts, neither of which is a trust in the commonly understood sense, is complicated by the variety of specialisms which both forms can take. They might be designed to track a particular market, or might concentrate on a specific type of stock: the old-established Edinburgh house, Baillie Gifford, for example offers an investment trust specializing in smaller overseas companies, or a unit trust focused on energy stocks. Broadly, investment trusts are companies (or subsidiaries) whose assets are funds, mostly held in the form of equity in other companies. These holdings are traded to the benefit of shareholders in the trust, whose numbers are limited—a closed-end fund, in the jargon—and shares in the trust itself are also traded. The unit trust, aimed more at the small investor, is open-ended, with the number of units issued to customers being governed by demand and the price moving fluidly with the values of the investments the trust makes.

Scotland manages only a tiny proportion of the funds vested in unit trusts. Those who believe Charlotte Square to be a touch stolid in outlook point to the reluctance of Scottish institutions to venture an earlier or greater involvement in unit trusts as their popularity grew in the 1970s and early 1980s. One grandee of the financial community, not a fund manager, told me: 'The investment trusts have done well, but they are closed-end. In the modern world, investment packages are sold, not bought. You don't sell investment trusts, you buy them. Marketing and selling has not been Scotland's skill—we are a product-orientated society.' The balance has been redressed somewhat in more recent years: 10 of the 24 fund management houses listed in the current *Scottish Financial Yearbook* offer a unit trust option. But few can boast long experience in the field.

One which can is Edinburgh Fund Managers (EFM), in recent years the most profitable of the Scottish houses, with a pre-tax profit in 1990–91 of £4.2 million and around £2 billion of funds under management. EFM, chaired until 1991 by the ubiquitous Angus Grossart (and since by Colin Ross), first tested the waters of unit trusts as far back as 1972. It has retained its faith in them and in 1991 acquired four more, bringing its total to 14, with a total subscription of some 23 000 unit-holders.

In recent years, the pendulum of investment vogue has begun to swing back towards investment trusts, thanks to the development (often in Scotland) of innovative savings schemes making them more accessible for small investors, to changes in the regulatory and fiscal regime, to the ravages of the 1987 stock market crash on unit trusts, and to their generally lower management charges. But they are not a particularly stable business. When world markets dip so too do the profits of the fund managers, though Scottish houses have an enviable reputation for minimizing the damage to both their clients' money and their own income. That reputation traded at a premium after the 1987 crash. But it also brought predators into the Charlotte Square clearing. EFM, which had built up a particular reputation in the Far East markets, lost three investment trusts in the space of a year. There was a period in the early 1980s when the rapid expansion of the investment business, particularly of pension fund management and unit trusts, meant the Edinburgh houses could achieve solid growth without worrying about increasing market share. But the cycle has moved on, and competition has intensified. It has been a time of some turbulence; nowhere more so than at No. 1 Charlotte Square, home of Ivory & Syme.

Ivory & Syme would lead nominations for the institution which most typifies *le vrai* Charlotte Square. Its glory days were in the 1970s, when it set the pace (along with Grossart, and the team at Wood Mackenzie) for the Scottish financial community's rewarding involvement in North Sea development. That adventure, powered by investment funds, brought the firm an international reputation. Yet, perversely enough, it also paved the way to a decidedly uneven 1980s, and Ivory & Syme found itself over-exposed on oil investments when the price of crude collapsed. These troubles cost the firm its top slot among Scottish fund managers, in business if not in prestige terms. No longer the undisputed champion of the investment trust business, it remains nonetheless a champion. It resisted the temptation to follow its competitors into the unit trust sector and has increasingly concentrated on a stable of nine investment trusts, some of which have been among the best-performing in the country. It also has a development capital wing, a pensions operation and a management services division which tends its operational departments.

The phrase 'formerly of Ivory & Syme' appears on many Charlotte Square

CVs. Rather like Ferranti in the electronics field, the company has acted over the years as nursery for an impressive succession of youthful talents, many of whom have since ventured forth on their own. Among the better-known graduates is Peter de Vink of Edinburgh Financial and General Holdings, one of the Square's more flamboyant figures and its arguably foremost deal-monger. This incubator role, unusual in the sector, evolved under the chairmanship of Jimmy Gammell between 1975 and 1985, who regarded the periodic departure of his young dynamos as a fair price for the energy they generated. As Ivory & Syme's soil began to tire in the mid-1980s, the departures became less controlled; culminating, in 1990, in the en bloc defection of the core management team installed by Gammell's successor, Alex Hammond-Chambers, to restructure the firm's business. The managing director, David Ross, and five key directors departed and Hammond-Chambers himself relinquished his executive duties.

In a financial village where everyone knows everyone else, this was a drama of scarcely containable proportions. It is a community which readily believes its own reputation for imperturbable serenity, though the executive turnover is actually rather greater than sometimes imagined. Salaries are commonly tied to company performance, and when times are bad, or when expansions squeeze profits, it is unsurprising that acquisitive minds turn to independent ventures. Several of the bigger houses went public during the 1980s, netting windfalls for the directors of the time which later recruits have not shared.

Recession notwithstanding, Ivory & Syme is back on a fairly even keel. Profits in 1990–1 rose 13.7 per cent to £2.9 million. A new management team, headed by David Newbigging and Allan Munro, has concentrated on improving performance rather than essaying new ventures, and on cost-cutting. At the same time, the company has acquired a London-based management operation, Argosy Asset Management, through a joint purchase with the north-eastern house, Aberdeen Fund Managers. That deal has added some £500 million to the funds under management by Ivory & Syme, bringing the total to over £3 billion.

The fund managers represent a sphere of acknowledged Scottish expertise whose reputation works, to some extent, to the benefit of the wider Scottish financial community. The respect they command has helped Scotland maintain an edge over up-and-coming financial centres like Dublin, and played a part in making it an alternative to London for the back office jobs of UK institutions, though so far on a fairly unspectacular scale. But the fund managers are not in themselves big employers: a ratio of £20–25 million of funds under management per employee is not exceptional. Nor do they seed much of the capital they handle in Scottish soil. The investment trust movement was, from its earliest days, a vehicle for sending capital overseas (the oldest of them all, the Dunedin Income Growth trust, was until 1990 know by its old name of First Scottish American) and, though recent years have seen something of a retrenchment to British stock, there is little sign that the proportion of funds invested in Scottish firms has significantly grown. Some houses run investment trusts which specialize in smaller companies and a few, like Murray Johnstone and Ivory & Syme, have modest venture capital wings. In general, though, it is hard to see that Scottish industry draws much investment benefit from having an international centre of investment excellence on its doorstep.

Part 5   Mediators and Monitors

It is possible that the preceding pages have given an impression of the Scottish economy as a somewhat sickly patient, with strong limbs but a weak heart. If so, it is a patient which is kept under intensive observation, its symptoms rigorously analysed by a widening circle of diagnosticians in the business schools, the political world, the consultancies and the media. It may lack the vigour of more robust economies, but it certainly does not want for attention.

There is a steady flow of academic analysis. The best-known source is Strathclyde University's Fraser of Allander Institute (FAI), which maintains an increasingly refined medium-term Scottish economic model and has recently developed a short-term version. It houses a team of prolific commentators including its director, Brian Ashcroft, its chief modeller, Jim Stevens, and Jim Love, until recently the editor of its quarterly *Economic Commentary*. The *Commentary* is a consistently authoritative chronicle of the Scottish economic scene. The FAI also contributes to debate through its stewardship of the Scottish Chambers' Business Survey, the most comprehensive sounding taken among Scottish businesses. But there are numerous other commentators, in the business schools and higher education colleges. Many of the banks, finance houses and consultancies issue regular publications: the *Royal Bank of Scotland Review* is perhaps the best known. Among the consultancies, the Strathclyde Institute, set up as a joint public/private sector venture to promote computer-integrated manufacturing, is an enthusiastic pundit. Its chief executive, David Pearson, is coming to rival the SCDI's Hamish Morrison as a ubiquitous source of Scottish economic comment. Add to that the various economic think-tanks spawned in recent years, not all of which involve Sir Kenneth Alexander, and it is tempting to conclude that analysis of the Scottish economy operates in inverse proportion to achievement.

This analysis is gratefully gathered up by the Scottish media, which adds its own conjectures. All the main Scottish newspapers maintain stables of business and industrial correspondents, as do the indigenous radio and television stations. There are several specialist publications, of which the best known is *Scottish Business Insider*, and a number of trade union journals, notably the quarterly *Scottish Trade Union Review*, produced by Glasgow Polytechnic's Trade Union Research Unit, in conjunction with the STUC. This stream of economic reporting, analysis and invective injects into the bloodstream of Scottish political debate, often producing lively reaction. The business surveys and the more widely reported publications generally stimulate responses from the main political parties, often headed by the Scottish Industry Minister. It is the debate which might otherwise take place in a Scottish parliament, and is unconstrained by the lack of such a forum.

Yet the Scottish economy is not just encircled by commentators. Despite the resolute march towards deregulation, it is also surrounded by a diverse and remarkably intricate institutional framework. This comprises government (both national and local), its agencies, and a rich blend of others: relics, retreads, regulators and rhetoricians. Some have a specific purpose and function, like the regulatory body for the privatized Scottish electricity industry, the Offshore Supplies Office, or the sectoral consumer councils. Others have more wide-ranging remits and it is on these that the following section focuses. Some have and exhibit real power; some have little, but pretend to more; some have an abundance, and keep it carefully out of sight. Many have members in common—after all, this is a small country. Beyond that, their only common feature is a certain disjuncture between mission and deliverance.

The Scottish Office Industry Department

In 1990, the Scottish Office spent more than £100 000 on a revamp of what is modishly called its corporate identity. Among the cultural enrichments ensuing was a new letterhead, on which the official crest gained an oval border and a rather fetching blue tone. A further innovation was to give the various departments more cumbersome names than they had previously borne. Each had to include the words 'The Scottish Office'. This was conceivably prompted by evidence that these words provoke blank stares from large sections of the populace, rather than the deference proper before such majesty. In any event, the Industry Department for Scotland, familiar to all acquainted with it as the IDS, became the Scottish Office Industry Department (SOID).

It was not the first change of name, and seems unlikely to be the last. The Department's modern form dates only from 1974, when the incoming Labour Government decided that the Scottish Economic Planning Department (which became the IDS in 1983) should take over the Scottish Industrial Development Office in Glasgow (part of the Department of Trade and Industry, though liaising closely with the Scottish Office) and hence the administration of regional aid in Scotland. The authority of the Scottish Office over industrial policy in Scotland has been uncertain since the office of Secretary of State was established in 1926 and, while some have seen the establishment of the SDA in 1975 as finally validating the Scottish Office's credentials as an industrial ministry, many ambiguities, overlaps and anomalies remain. For example, the Scottish Secretary has the power to refer takeovers involving Scots companies to the MMC, but by custom and practice only the Trade and Industry Secretary does so.

In any event, having established what the department should now properly be called, the more pressing question arises of what it is supposed to be *for*. It does not come particularly cheaply: in the Government's 1991–2 spending plans, the SOID accounted for 6.4 per cent of the Scottish Secretary's £11.052 billion budget: £706 million. This was more than double the previous year's £311 million allocation, thanks largely to the Scottish Enterprise reforms which transferred responsibility for volume training schemes from the Employment Department to the Scottish Office. It was, however, projected to fall back to £670 million by 1993–4, a figure not wildly adrift from the £658 million spent in 1986–7: before the transfer of training responsibilities, but also before the abolition of the biggest element in regional policy, Regional Development Grants (RDG). Departmental running costs, in 1990–1, were a not inconsiderable £6.7 million. The Department's expenditure, then, is a somewhat erratic figure; reflecting, in part, the impact of cyclical factors on variables like inward investment incentives, but also the changing policy framework within which the Department operates.

There was a time when the purpose of government industry departments was self-evident. They were there to supervise publicly owned industries and divert markets to social ends; for example by intervening to save deserving casualties, or by injecting money through devices like RDG to stimulate areas the markets' omniscience had disdained. That orthodoxy, like so many others, evaporated after 1979. Since then, government has rigorously deferred to the market, holding its deliverances to be embellishable at the margins, but fundamentally inviolable. It has dispensed with much of the public sector and expected what remains to behave commercially. It has phased out RDG in favour of discretionary Regional Selective Assistance (RSA), cutting the real value of regional aid in Scotland by more than half. And it has resolutely refused to intervene, except by self-conscious ministerial declamation, in commercial decisions, even where their social, and therefore political, implications were considerable.

The Department's remit, determined by the Secretary of State, is contained in charters of aims and objectives. Neither rubric is notably informative. The aims are generally of the 'make Scotland great again' type: maximizing value added tax, enhancing the role of private enterprise, encouraging investment and so on. The objectives, presented as a three-year programme, are more specific: to oversee the enterprise agencies; to privatize the non-nuclear electricity companies (completed in 1991) and monitor the nuclear rump; to begin the wind-up of the New Town corporations; to develop partnership programmes for problem housing estates; to help out areas with particular economic problems; to stimulate private sector provision of property and capital; to have a tourism policy; to ensure uptake of assistance programmes; to secure inward investment; to lighten regulatory burdens on business; to get the most possible out of the EC; and to encourage energy efficiency. Much of this is farmed out to SOID-sponsored bodies, like Scottish Enterprise, Locate in Scotland and the Scottish Tourist Board. In other respects—deregulation, or interface with Brussels—the Scottish Office is rarely the lead department, and has at best limited policy autonomy. If there is a sense of mission in all this it is hard to pinpoint.

The Economy

I once put this question of what purpose a Scottish Industry Minister serves in a Government unwilling to play gooseberry in affairs of the mart to the incumbent, Allan Stewart. Stewart, a thoughtful and engaging figure who has held the job twice, replied as follows: 'The purpose is twofold. First, to oversee the organisations which are in the field, notably Scottish Enterprise; and secondly, to consider and act on particular situations, such as Lanarkshire, which has been naturally and rightly a focus of activity. In addition, there are situations when the Scottish Office has to know what is happening and liaise with Whitehall—an example of that would be Rosyth.' That is a full and measured answer, worth decoding. True, Scottish Enterprise and its highland equivalent were, essentially, creations of the Scottish Office, with a little help from Bill Hughes of the CBI and rather more from Norman Fowler, the then Employment Secretary. True, too, their core strategies are approved by the SOID and constrained by the budgets it allocates. But the largest part of those budgets is committed to the deliverance of Government-prescribed training schemes, like Youth Training and Employment Training, to which the Scottish Office's policy input is slight. More importantly, the central logic of the reformed structure was to pass the focus of decision-making to boards dominated by responsible businessmen. Once the network is properly established, there seems little for ministers to do except to ask it periodically—and nicely   to undertake assignments of economic, social or electoral advantage; try to get as much as possible of its budget past the Treasury; and share the glory of its achievements and spend.

Rosyth, as is related elsewhere, was notable chiefly for a covert closure plan, leaked before the Ministry of Defence had got around to telling the Scottish Office about it—an inventive definition, perhaps, of Whitehall liaison. This brings us to Lanarkshire. Lanarkshire's economy has, over the past decade, absorbed body blows like Joe Bugner on a bad night. In 1983, the closure of Cardowan Colliery had obliterated a mining county's last pit (and a steelmaking county's last local source of coking coal). In 1986, closure of the Gartcosh cold-rolling mill left the biggest employer, the steel industry, 200 miles away from the finishing facility for its product. In 1987, the troubled US multinational, Caterpillar, closed its Uddingston tractor factory just 16 weeks after promising it a £62.5 million investment programme. Then, in 1990–2, a newly privatized British Steel, seized with the conceit of licensed near-monopoly, shook and toppled the remaining pillars of the Scottish steel industry. Gartcosh was already gone, taking with it much of Ravenscraig's added value. Next came the 'Craig's hot strip mill, and half its blast furnace capacity; the Clydesdale seamless tubes plant at Bellshill; the Dalzell plates mill at Motherwell was also earmarked for closure. Even before the final blow was administered to Ravenscraig in January 1992, the end for a proud industry was clearly in sight.

In fact, it had been in sight for a long number of years. Regional policy, coupled with jarring alternation between the public and private sectors, had left Britain's steelmaking capacity shared between a number of integrated sites, while its competitors, like Japan, were producing similar volumes from fewer, more modern, plants with consequent price advantages. In particular, the Macmillan Government's political decision to split new stripmaking investment between Ravenscraig and South Wales rankled with the steelmakers. Industry veterans—notably Sir Robert 'Black Bob' Scholey, who became chairman in 1986—rarely bothered to disguise the view that Ravenscraig's strip operations should never have been built in the first place. By the late 1970s, a clumsily nationalized British Steel Corporation was losing £30 a second. It became evident that when the inevitable rationalization arrived, as it did at the outset of the 1980s, Ravenscraig and the plants around it were in the bed nearest the ward door.

The trouble was that the Lanarkshire plants had assumed rather a keystone position in the Scottish economic base. True, they no longer had a car industry or much shipbuilding to supply, nor coking coal pits to sustain. But they remained the biggest electricity customer in Scotland, and provided half Scotland's rail freight traffic. Their imports of ore and coal through Hunterston generated a third of revenues that kept the Clyde dredged. Though much of their output was invoiced to London, their biggest customer was the North Sea oil and gas industry, with its construction yards like RGC at Methil, UIE at Clydebank, Highland Fabricators at Nigg and McDermotts at Ardersier; and its need for quality steel products like well-casings, made from Clydesdale tube. To contend, as British Steel (BS) often did in the 1980s, that the closure of the Linwood car plant in 1981 and of most of the Clyde shipyards, had robbed the mills of their local markets was disingenuous; besides no one argues that Scotland's whisky or electronics industries should be shut down because the bulk of their output is sold outwith Scotland.

From the early 1980s, Ravenscraig, which had once pioneered techniques like continuous casting (concast), was progressively starved of investment, in favour of the Teesside and South Wales plants. When demand was high, small doses of investment were injected to keep its decaying kit ticking over. But strategic investment was denied, with sometimes absurd consequences. For example, Ravenscraig had developed a trade as BS's specialist odd-jobs plant, producing high-specification steels in small batches for electrical or armaments users. Yet it remained the only one of the integrated plants to be refused automatic roll-changing equipment, a facility which greatly shortens down-time between batches and a paltry investment which BS had readily sanctioned at high-volume plants where the gauges could go unchanged for days and weeks on end. Similarly, Dalzell was denied the relatively inexpensive machinery to turn plate into welded pipe, with the result that the North Sea mini-boom of the late 1980s found the port of Leith submerged in German and Japanese pipe bound for new pipelines off Scotland's shores. Admittedly, that spectacle was less risible from the perspective of BS, which had by then bought up much of the UK steel stockholding business and was making good money from handling imports, though scarcely to the advantage of a record trade deficit.

Against this dispiriting strategy, the steelworkers mounted a resistance that was, in its patient way, remarkable. Believing BS determined to prove their plants uneconomic, they agreed sweeping productivity reforms and worked the crumbling kit for all they were worth. It was, in essentials, as much a work-in as the Upper Clyde Shipbuilders' battle 15 years earlier; less flamboyant, but every bit as impressive. BS sourly declined to publish performance results for individual plants, claiming commercial sensitivity. What we do know is that, when demand boomed in 1988–9, Ravenscraig was reliably reported to be producing at 2.33 man-hours per tonne, against an industry average of 4.7. Equivalent figures for the investment-rich but troubled Llanwern would have been instructive: even by 1990, when Ravenscraig was being turned on and off as demand fluctuated, it was consistently out-producing the larger Llanwern. In its last three years of full production, Ravenscraig was almost certainly profitable. Whether BS was, as it claimed, loading its lowest-cost plants or, as Ravenscraig's union convener, Tommy Brennan, suggested to me, loading those with the highest investment costs to recoup must remain questionable.

Throughout the 1980s, the steelworkers shrewdly built an unparalleled political coalition in Scotland. Under the leadership of the charismatic Brennan, they countered a secretive employer with leaked information and boisterous campaigning, including a 400-mile march to London when Gartcosh closed. They took care to exclude no party from their cause—this was pointedly not Scotland against Thatcherism—and prominent Tories like Michael Hirst were signed up. The legend grew that Ravenscraig was politically uncloseable.

The Scottish Office, initially at least, helped write the legend. Twice in the early 1980s, BS moved to close the 'Craig. But the corporation was still in public ownership and the political tide swept the decision to Cabinet, where George Younger, the Scottish Secretary, let it be known that he regarded the plant's survival as a resignation issue. A bemused Margaret Thatcher once asked a senior Scottish party official why Ravenscraig was so special compared with other factories which had closed. The answer came that while any other closure might cost a few thousand votes, Ravenscraig's could cost every seat in Scotland. But, each escape left other ministers less tolerant, yielded ever weaker guarantees and brought privatization closer. In November 1987, the best that Younger's successor, Malcolm Rifkind, could wring from Scholey was that steelmaking on the site was expected to survive to 1994, subject to market conditions. Rather incautiously, Rifkind described this waterlogged undertaking as 'superb news for Ravenscraig'.

When a now privatized BS launched its third and final assault on Ravenscraig in May 1990, the Scottish Office had lost the will, and much of the means, to fight. It had become, in what was to be a familiar phrase, a commercial matter for BS to determine. But Scottish ministers nevertheless faced a dilemma. Given the recent history of Younger's brinkmanship and the plant's residual public prestige, they could not simply do nothing. Equally, whatever they did was unlikely to succeed: as members of the Government which had designed BS plc, they were well aware of its impunity. They were accordingly left with no option more congenial than forlorn endeavour. On the stewards' prompting, they demanded of Scholey a detailed account of the commercial justification for closure and were, like the Commons Industry Committee, brusquely told it was none of their business. They fumed and fulminated, for want of any more constructive course. They ordered an ill-pleased SDA to commission a study into the plant's negligible prospects as an independent slab-maker. And so it went on. In January 1992, BS announced that Ravenscraig would close by the following September, and production finally ended in June.

It is tempting to see this episode as responsibility without power, an unwonted concept of executive government. The responsibility is freely acknowledged: Rifkind, in particular, used to excuse his occasional tentative ventures down the path of intervention by observing that he held overall responsibility for the welfare of the Scottish economy. At another level, there is the responsibility for picking up BS's detritus. It is the Scottish Office, through the Scottish Enterprise network and local authority budgets, which must find the means to reassemble Lanarkshire's shattered economy. BS has contributed modestly to this task, but has so far refused to meet the costs—estimated at over £200 million—of rehabilitating its abandoned sites.

What has been less consistent is the exercise of power in discharge of these economic responsibilities. When three years of acrimony over prices between the then South of Scotland Electricity Board (SSEB) and British Coal threatened to obliterate the last fragments of the Scottish deep-mining industry, Rifkind—after months of insisting that he could not intervene in a commercial dispute—finally played ACAS or, as he put it, banged heads together, to procure an outline settlement. It was, of course, a row between two corporations which were both then in public ownership, though only the SSEB fell within the Scottish Office's direct purview. Yet Stewart, in that same *Scotsman* interview insisted that even among private companies non-intervention did not equate with ministers doing nothing. 'To say that management must manage is not to say that there is some divine right of managements always to get things 100 per cent correct. It is perfectly proper to undertake a study, it is right and proper to emphasise our belief in a study if we believe in it. That is an improvement on the amount of information a company has. But, ultimately, you have to say it is a commercial decision for the company.'

Government by consultancy? Certainly, the SOID has the expertise. It collects and publishes a lot of data, and its economic and sectoral analysis (such as the index of production and construction output, the *Scottish Economic Bulletin* and two excellent editions of *Scotland—An Economic Profile*) is authoritative and often useful. Yet, the doctrine makes for uncomfortable politics. The shop stewards' case for developing Dalzell so impressed ministers that they asked the SOID to produce its own analysis of the plant's potential, unusually publishing the study amid some fanfare. Scholey simply shrugged it off at the ensuing BS AGM. There is a sense, in looking at the SOID, of a powerful engine left unconnected to Scotland's economic wheels.

It is significant that when the Scottish Constitutional Convention published its draft proposals for a Scottish parliament in the autumn of 1990, the one area where it felt the need to spell out powers in some detail was in relation to the economy. It saw purpose in adding a whole range of functions to those the SOID currently chooses to fulfil. Owing much to the influence of the STUC, these were unashamedly interventionist. They included strategic economic planning powers over key industries with more or less self-standing Scottish structures; a parallel co-ordinating role for the Scottish end of UK businesses; responsibility for inward investment; policy authority over training; a licence to initiate public ownership or control of industries; a duty to stimulate research and development; monopolies and mergers authority; exports promotion; representation in Brussels; and a duty to give Scots firms the opportunity of commercial advantage. It was an ambitious manifesto, but it also reflected the perception that deepening enthusiasm for a parliament in Edinburgh stemmed in no small measure from the belief that Scotland's idiosyncratic economy needed an understanding and powerful friend.

Meanwhile, the SOID publishes its statistics, hands out RSA to variable effect, administers or delegates programmes on behalf of the Department of Trade and Industry and fulfils what is, perhaps, its most conspicuous role: that of the wall against which Scotland's economic players, pundits and agitators wail for deliverance from woe. That function has its uses, but they are never so great as to dispel the thought of what might someday be achieved.

The enterprise networks

On 1 April 1991, two familiar giants of the Scottish economic scene passed into history. The Scottish Development Agency and its elder sibling, the Highlands and Islands Development Board (HIDB) became Scottish/Highlands and Islands Enterprise (S/HIE) each consisting of a core body and a network of local enterprise companies (LECs). Both agencies had inspired the (sometimes exasperated) affections of the people they existed to serve, and the respect, expressed in emulation, of their rivals beyond Scotland, though they had rarely been free of political suspicion and review. Accordingly, their demise was accomplished on a scaffold garlanded with laurels. The reforms, it was insisted, had the objective of fortifying a winning formula, of lending fresh impetus to a praiseworthy momentum of achievement. Whether this was widely believed, it could not dispel the impression that the two agencies had been fixed without ever being shown to be broken.

In essence, the reforms were simple. They merged the two agencies with the Scottish end of the Training Agency, the Employment Department subsidiary which ran volume training programmes like Youth Training (YT) and

Employment Training (ET); and, at the same time, introduced a devolved tier of LECs which, like the boards of the core bodies, would comprise at least two-thirds private-sector employers. Simple in outline, but an administrative nightmare, as Crawford Beveridge, the Scottish Enterprise chief executive, told me: 'This was a massive, massive organizational change. I have rarely been with companies that have gone through as much as we expected people to go through, because we took two companies and merged them and, at the same time, decentralized it all. Very few companies would ever do that.'

The HIDB was the elder of the two agencies and the more obviously demand-inspired. Its founding legislation was the first Bill in the first Queen's Speech of Harold Wilson's first Labour Government in 1964. Though it was initially opposed by the Tories, by the time the Board came into being on 1 November 1965, it had the benefit of a broad and largely enduring political support; a recognition that something had to be done to prevent the Highlands from dying. 'It was,' Wilson later wrote, 'one of our proudest achievements.' Distinctively among development agencies, the HIDB had a social as well as an economic remit. A central objective from the outset, reinforced by chairmen like Sir Robert Grieve and Sir Kenneth Alexander, was to stem the relentless outflow of population, a goal which required the enhancement not merely of opportunity but also of morale. Thus, besides initiatives to stimulate manufacturing, fisheries, agriculture, forestry and tourism, there was a role as a planning instrument, a provider of schools and community facilities, and an active element in cultural development, notably of the Gaelic language. Experience drew these two strands increasingly closer as the years passed. By 1991, the population of the HIDB's 3.5 million-hectare area—almost a sixth of Britain's land mass and nearly half of Scotland's—had stabilized at around 370 000, some 7 per cent of the Scottish total and back to the level of the inter-war years. The HIDB could not and did not claim sole credit for that, but few would deny it a significant effect.

The SDA, by contrast, was born of political compromise and destined to be forever compromised by politicians. Its creation in 1975 by the restored Wilson Government reflected a desire less to emulate the HIDB or Ireland's Industrial Development Authority (IDA), than to quell the rising tide of nationalism. The calculation in those origins left the right disinclined to give the SDA the benefit of the doubt, and neither its willing pragmatism nor its eventual success ever wholly insulated it from the charge of interventionism. The pliancy of its high command in Glasgow's Bothwell Street, ever sensitive to criticism and the prevailing political orthodoxy, could never quite erase it from the Tory agenda. Once the Conservatives regained power in 1979, the nobbling of the SDA was more a question of how than whether. Scottish Enterprise may prove a worthy, even superior, successor, but it was not invented out of admiration for the SDA.

The SDA had its failures, some of them culpable. But its successes,

316

and eventual popularity, came despite rather than because of the political environment in which it was obliged to operate. When I asked a senior IDA executive why his organization had achieved so much in moving Ireland from an agricultural to an increasingly industrial economy, his answer was political stability. Stability is not the first trait that comes to mind for Irish politics yet, as he pointed out, since Sean Lemass first addressed the industrial target in the 1950s, there had been consistent centre-right government and unwavering support for the IDA as part of an integrated economic armoury. Irish politics rarely involve the depth of turbulence which the froth generated might suggest, and can have a deceptive purposefulness. In Scotland, rather the reverse is true. Politicians of both parties smiled on the work of the SDA, and claimed credit for its achievements; yet it was saddled with the burden of having constantly to justify itself and to adapt to the nomadic whims of political masters. This it did with a will, striving to anticipate changes before it had to be asked to make them, and always insisting afterwards that it had good practical reasons for shifting direction. A little more spirit might have been seemly, but the end result was always likely to be the same. One newspaper suggested the apt epitaph, 'Here lies the body that tried too hard.'

The SDA was established with a then-impressive budget of £200 million and a remit which innovatively combined economic and environmental development. It absorbed three existing bodies: the Scottish Industrial Estates Corporation (which brought it a ready portfolio of 25 million sq m of factory space), the Small Industries Council for the Rural Areas of Scotland (a regional policy instrument for smaller towns) and a section of the Scottish Development Department responsible for derelict land clearance. In a phased transfer, it also took over the SCDI's lead role in inward investment. To these were added some newly prescribed functions: industrial investment, particularly through equity and longer-term risk capital; business advice and consultancy; and urban renewal. It was, from the outset, charged with securing the maximum private sector input to what it did and, at its best, achieved leverage ratios of up to 7:1. That level, however, was usually possible only in times of relative prosperity, when investment optimism was high. Scottish Enterprise inherits the paradox, common to many remedial agencies, that the need for their work is highest when the resources to underpin it are at their lowest.

From the outset the SDA's investment function, rarely much more than 10 per cent of expenditure, attracted the most controversy. Though the Agency could offer loans or guarantees, its earlier investments mostly took the form of equity. The idea of setting up its own companies to plug product gaps, latterly and unhappily attempted with Domain Power, was present from an early stage, as was the notion that the Agency should approach companies with suggested ventures and offer help in addressing them. This was a new departure in regional policy, which had previously responded to requests generated by industry itself, but more important was the implicit assumption, not always entirely evident, of coherent strategy. This taint of planning, coupled with some early investment failures, further unsettled the right.

Though the investment portfolio improved with maturity, these failures in turn did little to encourage the financial sector to hazard the venture capital game. Later, as the Agency's reputation grew (and particularly after investment decisions were transferred from the industry directorate to a specialist unit), private venture capital was more forthcoming, though often only when the SDA was ready to give a lead. The cultivation of a vibrant private venture capital sector in Scotland cannot be counted among the Agency's achievements, but provision would undoubtedly have been poorer without the SDA's pathfinding role.

The 1979 general election brought to the surface a debate within the Conservative Party between those who wanted the SDA scrapped and those who believed it should be retained but channelled to other ends. George Younger, Margaret Thatcher's first Scottish Secretary, found the Agency a useful arms-length tool for repairing some of the effects of untrammelled recession, and countering accusations of governmental indifference. He set in motion a twin-pronged strategy to realign the SDA along more commercial lines and to reflect more of its popularity on what was fast becoming an unpopular Government. In January 1980, the Agency was issued with fresh guidelines which reduced its employment-protection role and charged it to facilitate rather than provide investment; to be a catalyst for the forces of the market, rather than a defence against them. The following year, the inward investment function passed to a joint SDA-Scottish Office bureau, Locate in Scotland (LiS). This move, which coincided with a heightening public profile for inward investment, was something of a fiction, in that LiS usually traded overseas under the SDA brandname and was responsible in practice to the SDA (and now Scottish Enterprise) chief executive. Still, the idea was reinforced in 1988 by the creation of a LiS supervisory board, a committee which has rarely appeared vital, chaired by the Scottish Industry Minister. With the coming of Scottish Enterprise, LiS was finally obliged to fly its own colours in its encounters with foreign capital.

For the first half of the 1980s, these changes took some of the political heat off the SDA. Inward investment boomed, particularly in micro-electronics. LiS, though arguably over-reliant on the North American target, proved adept at persuading a new generation of US corporations to join the IBMs and Motorolas in Scotland, aided by an informal masonry of expatriates in the upper ranks of US business, among them Crawford Beveridge. Yet the unease remained in some quarters and, particularly from mid-decade, the Agency found itself under almost constant review.

It underwent a widely focused inquiry in 1980 by the Commons Scottish select committee, and then its investment activities (like those of the HIDB) were twice examined by the Commons public accounts committee, leading to a more rigorous investigation in 1985 by the National Audit Office. A further wide-ranging review, covering financial policy and management, was initiated by the Scottish Office in 1985. One consequence was to hasten the disposal, already begun, of the Agency's property portfolio. This culminated in 1990 with the sale of most of the portfolio; the initial remit of advance factory provision is now greatly diminished, raising disquiet over whether Scotland has sufficient ready accommodation to meet any revival in inward investment, since there is little sign of the private sector hastening into the breach. The SDA was also required to rid itself more systematically of its investment portfolio, turning the proceeds over not to its other activities but to the Treasury. Yet, in general, the 1985 review commended the manner in which the SDA had adapted to a changed political environment. Its report, the product of exhaustive examination, was published in 1987. A year later came the back-of-an-envelope design for Scottish Enterprise.

Other forces were in play at the time. In 1988, the SDA, under its own momentum, introduced a devolved structure of seven regional offices to enhance local delivery and relevance of its smaller projects (at any time, it had around 5 000 projects in progress). The resulting upsurge in demand threw the Agency's finances into atrophy, creating resented delays in funding projects. At the same time, the Agency fell foul of the National Audit Office over its stewardship of the Glasgow Garden Festival, the budget for which had doubled to £23 million, and which had involved a controversial property deal with Laing Homes. The flood of electronics investments was subsiding. Another NAO report found that around a third of the jobs proclaimed by LiS failed to materialize, a charge no less embarrassing for being equally applicable to other inward investment agencies. Changes in the structure of regional aid were shrinking the incentives on which both LiS and the SDA could call. Aid for development or intermediate areas had operated through two main instruments: regional development grants (RDG), which were automatic; and regional selective assistance (RSA), which was discretionary. In 1988, the Government, asserting a need for better targeting, began to phase out RDG. Ministers argued that automatic grants gave resources to developments which would have happened anyway, and had earlier tightened the criteria. RSA, on the other hand, required someone to pick winners. It was also, being discretionary, an often marginal consideration in location decisions by mobile investors. The net effect was to halve the provision of regional aid in Scotland. In 1986–7, £41 million of RSA and £166 million of RDG made a total of £207 million; in 1992–3, according to Scottish Office spending plans, the total will be just £100 million, falling to £90 million the following year as the last residual RDG payments drop out of the sum.

This was the scene in 1988 when, as legend has it, Bill Hughes, chairman of CBI Scotland, conceived the Scottish Enterprise design during a car journey. To stick momentarily with the folklore, he sold the plan to the Scottish Secretary, Malcolm Rifkind, and thence to Margaret Thatcher who duly endorsed it as 'a Scottish solution to Scottish needs' at that September's CBI Scotland dinner. Its effect on the SDA was like a grenade in a crowded shop; people dived for cover, and the more agile for the exits. Many of the Agency's finest executives departed. Once the charge had detonated, the survivors summoned courage in adversity, told each other it not been so bad, and did their best to live with their injuries. Nevertheless, for the last two years of the SDA's life, reconstruction did not leave much time for trade.

There is no doubt that the SDA was the prime target of the reform. Hughes rarely troubled to disguise his distaste for an agency of 'pen-pushers and academics'. Indeed, in the early days, he appeared uncertain as to whether the formula, which he rashly predicted could eradicate unemployment in a decade, should be applied to the HIDB. A subsequent leak of his submission to Thatcher showed that he had promoted his ideas privately in terms of enhancing flagging Tory fortunes in Scotland, involving the private sector more in development (particularly at the expense of the local authorities) and spreading the Thatcherite message. Hughes himself later defended this as merely the political sales pitch for a jobs-inspired proposal, which is plausible if not entirely conclusive. It neglects the awkward fact that the Agency had already implemented much of the central thrust of the change; it had realigned itself along more commercial lines, and had already devolved its own regional structure. The case for 'Scottish needs' is unconvincing.

Nor is the case for a 'Scottish solution' wholly persuasive. Doing something about the Training Agency was a Whitehall priority. The Agency was the mutant child of the old Manpower Services Commission (MSC). Ministers' patience with the MSC had snapped when it impeded the Job Training Scheme, precursor to the unloved Employment Training (ET). It became, first, the Training Commission, then the Training Agency, its tripartite structure abandoned. Ministers were also increasingly concerned at the cost of such schemes, and had been looking for some time at US experiments with farming out training to private sector-run authorities. Plans were already advanced to set up training and enterprise councils (TECs) in England and Wales by the time Hughes conceived of LECs for Scotland.

In Scotland, opposition to the reforms was curiously muted, and mostly confined to the packing of the boards with businessmen. There were two reasons for this unaccustomed diffidence. First, many saw merit in integrating training with economic development: indeed, the STUC had suggested much the same a year earlier. Second, the plan could be sold as an example of administrative devolution, since training responsibility was being passed from the Employment Department to the Scottish Office. Time has cast doubt on the authenticity of this devolution. The Employment Department retained the *policy* role on training, leaving neither the Scottish Office nor the LECs much scope for improvisation. A subsequent leaked letter from the Treasury Chief Secretary to the Employment Secretary made clear that the latter continued to negotiate the training budget for the whole of the UK, leaving the Scottish Secretary at best a secondary role in determining spending. The first year of Scottish Enterprise saw training budgets severely cut—ET spending was down by 40 per cent, though part of the reduction was later restored. Ministers had clearly hoped the reforms would persuade the private sector to dig into its own pockets for more of the training bill: the Scottish Enterprise White Paper spoke delphically of giving business 'a sense of ownership' over training provision. TEC and LEC directors were vocal in their displeasure at being made instruments of Government cutbacks.

LEC training directors are doing their best to encourage innovation at the fringes of provision, and to integrate training with economic development projects, but the twin constraints of budget stringencies and of the obligation to deliver Government guarantees on ET and YT leave scant scope. The irony was that the initial transition left some LECs hard-pressed to spend their development budgets; yet the rules, subsequently renegotiated, allowed little leeway to juggle funds between spending blocks. So far, neither the promised skills revolution nor the dispersal of training authority has conspicuously taken place.

Though the Training Agency brought more staff (and budget) to the merger than did the SDA, Scottish Enterprise in its early days is built largely in the SDA's image. Only one of its 13 LEC chief executives came from the Training Agency and the core structure, though subsequently streamlined, corresponds closely to that of the SDA. In part, this stems from the fact that the Training Agency, as the remote arm of a Whitehall department, had little managerial structure in Scotland. But it also reflects the preference of many Training Agency staff to remain in the civil service, believing, with some justice, that the alternative was to be tacked onto a structure largely designed by, and a culture inherited from, the SDA.

LECs have to secure the core's sanction for project expenditure above certain prescribed limits, which for development spending are a modest £250 000. That threshold gives them, according to Bothwell Street, discretion over about 80 per cent of projects but only 20 per cent of expenditure. Some LEC chairmen have protested to ministers, indeed to Downing Street, about this curb on their authority, and the pressure is likely to continue. Businessmen have reluctantly had to accept that they cannot deal with the Treasury's money as they do with their own companies' current accounts. The trade unionists and councillors who used to man quangos probably knew, whatever their other shortcomings, rather more about public accountability than those installed in their place.

The LEC boards were essentially self-appointed. Business leaders in each area were invited to form consortia to bid for three-year rolling contracts, in most cases without competition. All but one have local authority representation (the exception is Moray, Badenoch and Strathspey which, uniquely, is part of both Scottish Enterprise and HIE. 'How does that work?' I innocently asked one senior Scottish Enterprise executive. 'It doesn't,' he replied). Five have trade union representatives. The paucity of union presence has outraged the STUC, which has several times come close to formally withdrawing co-operation. In mid-1990, the consortia were given six-figure grants from the Scottish Office to commission business plans on the basis of which funds would be allocated them.

It was a rewarding time to be a business consultant. In Scottish Enterprise's case, only one LEC received the full first-year budget it sought. It was not for want of fine intentions. The core had been told by ministers to decentralize towards the target that, by year three, 80 per cent of spending was delivered through the LECs. In fact, year one saw the core hand the LECs 83 per cent of budget. 'I don't know that that was the healthiest thing we could have done,' admitted Beveridge later. Ministers too appeared taken aback, not for the first time, by Bothwell Street's habit of over-fulfilling its quota. Allan Stewart said he did not envisage any further radical change in the figures. Yet, the 1992 allocations saw a further small shift in the LECs favour.

Budgets are not the only expression of inter-institutional relationships, though they are often a faithful trace of power flows. The initial allocations to LECs were made before either network had evolved its core strategy or, indeed, completed its core staffing. This novel state of affairs left the convenient impression that the LECs were in the driving seat, but also suggested that the reforms had dissipated any coherent strategic thrust. The strategy papers that followed were well received by the LECs, though that assent requires the test of further budget rounds, in which allocations will be expected to accord with the core strategy. The dispersal of staff from the old agencies has also made for some spicy anomalies of rank, which typify the untried ground between the two tiers. Old SDA or HIDB hands who have gone off to run LECs can find themselves seeking spending approval from core managers who were previously several grades their junior. Equally, there are core executives now obliged to reason with LEC staff whom they used to command by memo. Between the professionals a protocol will evolve. Whether the same facility develops at board level is less clear. Ministers were justly gratified at the calibre of business leaders who came forward, but that in itself creates tensions: a successful entrepreneur does not take kindly to being told no by a distant official in Bothwell Street (or, worse, St Andrew's House). Nor does the evident enthusiasm of several LECs for freelance ventures overseas fit comfortably with the single-door approach of LiS. In theory, LiS was left untouched by the reforms. In practice, it will have to cope with the institutional tensions of Scottish Enterprise, and the implications for the strength of the Scottish Enterprise core, on which it relies for professional and operational resources.

The reforms promise subtle changes to the relationship between the development agencies and the Scottish Office. Bodies like S/HIE are products of a recurrent theme of the Thatcher Government: the blurring of distinctions between public and private sectors. Privatization, opting out, competitive tendering and agency status have all contributed to the ambiguity. So too the enterprise networks: funded in part from the public sector, in part from the private; agencies of public policy, got up to look like private companies and obeisant to market forces; supervised by businessmen appointed by ministers; constituted in a tangle of public legislation and commercial contracts. The mixed economy may be out of vogue, but hybrids like the enterprise companies are essentially the mixed economy in microcosm.

This is not just a matter of abstract theory. The old agencies, as wholly-owned subsidiaries, had a political usefulness to the Scottish Office which was incidental to their primary function: as a convenient depository for unwholesome issues. An example, from the dying days of the SDA, was steel. For ministers, under pressure to do something, the option of ordering the SDA to mount a study was a useful expedient, though one always more likely to produce scapegoats than solutions. The SDA was furious, but helpless. Now, seized with its status as a commercial look-alike, it would be better fortified to resist. Similar stirrings were audible within Scottish Enterprise when it was given the task of devising the Scotland Europa bureau in Brussels. Executives were in two minds about the concept; they believed it offered potential economic advantage, but were conscious that it was a commercial answer to what were, fundamentally, political demands. This time, they toed the line. But, as one of them remarked to me grimly, the day might soon come when ministers reached for the familiar lever and found it was no longer connected to anything.

The enterprise reforms will ultimately be judged by what they deliver. It was, perhaps, fortunate that the recessionary gale did not blow more fiercely in Scotland while the new vessels were still undergoing sea trials. All the same, major challenges lie ahead: defence dependency, European integration, an unsteady electronics market, declining inward investment potential. The new apparatus was conceived at a time of relative economic well-being, when employment, output and investment were growing. Its emphasis on stimulating local initiative and aligning skills provision to economic development can be seen as a response to the growth momentum of that time. Yet the networks must prove adaptable and applicable across the span of the economic cycle. If they can achieve that, they will establish themselves as worthy successors to the distinguished bodies they replaced.

The Scottish Council Development and Industry

The SCDI (it dropped the brackets around the D & I a few years ago in a hopeless attempt to make its title punchier) is the exception Isaac Newton missed. By all logic, it should have tumbled from the skies years ago. Its founding purposes, like the consensual milieu which it typified, have receded into the mists of time. Yet, what it now lacks in influence, it compensates for in ebullience. It exudes an air of impish common sense, and an endearing belief in its own licence to say what it likes on any subject it pleases. Whatever the debate, the SCDI tends to be found in its midst, saying interesting and provocative things. Like so many Scottish institutions, it seems bigger than the sum of its functional parts, an illusion sustained by its articulate officials.

It has a quite dazzling talent for improvisation. Nearly all the things it has existed to do during its 60-year history are now done by others, or no longer done at all. In part a creation of the Scottish Office, it worked in close partnership with it for two decades, often promoting ideas, like a Scottish Development Department, that were expedient but politically injudicious for ministers who had their UK colleagues to placate. That relationship began to break down with the arrival at St Andrew's House in 1964 of Willie Ross, who was suspicious of the Council's largely managerial membership and what he saw as its quasi-nationalist emphasis on Scottish interests. As its formal functions have diminished, it has settled to an existence as a stylishly independent voice, sometimes critical of Government policy yet clinging to a creed of trying to work with the prevailing political grain. It retains, as Kellas observed, the capacity as a lobby to invest issues with the aura of national struggle: unshakably pro-industry, but lacking partisan affiliation to any one faction. Yet even that role has been, to a degree, usurped by the STUC-led issue coalitions, and their more solemn offshoots in the Scottish Constitutional Convention and the Standing Commission on the Scottish Economy. Hamish Morrison, the SCDI's rubicund chief executive, is an eloquent presence at these gatherings, but one among many.

Like so many of the institutional foundations of contemporary Scotland, it was largely the creation of perhaps the greatest of all Scottish Secretaries, Tom Johnston, though one of its antecedents preceded his tenure. The Scottish Development Council was a group of industrialists formed in 1931 by the shipbuilder Sir James Lithgow, with the twin objectives of attracting new industries to Scotland and of countering the country's reputation for left-wing mischief. Its 1936 offshoot, the Scottish Economic Committee, was influential in promoting the business case for industrial diversification, better marketing, design and training in the new, lighter trades. It was also an early advocate of inward investment and, together with the Scottish Development Financial Trust (a venture capital body set up by the Earl of Elgin), was pioneer of the sort of territory later settled by the SDA. In evidence to the Barlow Commission in 1938, it urged the creation of a broad-based central planning authority for Scotland, reporting to the Scottish Secretary. This finally convinced Whitehall of the Council's unwholesome national leanings. But it also stands as a reminder that the Scottish consensus which has flowered in recent years has old and deep roots that spread wider than its visible foliage.

It was Johnston who moved this policy forward. In 1941, the year he took charge at St Andrew's House, he had set up the Council of State, composed of all his surviving predecessors, to identify and address the economic problems that would beset post-war Scotland. In his memoirs, he recalls the response of a bemused Churchill on being told of this extraordinary innovation: 'That seems a sort of national government of all parties idea, just like our Government here. All right, I'll look sympathetically upon anything about which Scotland is unanimous. And what next?'

What was next was to provide his baby-grand coalition with what he conceived as an industrial parliament. In 1942, he formed the Scottish

Industrial Council, later the Scottish Council on Industry, which drew its members and funds from the local authorities, Chambers of Commerce, STUC, Scottish Development Council and the banks. Johnston was unambiguous in regarding this apparatus as a means to draw decision-making north of the border and, despite Whitehall resentment, it achieved a quite remarkable series of far-reaching initiatives during those distracted wartime years. The North of Scotland Hydro Electric Board and the Scottish Tourist Board were the best known. Johnston would later chair both.

By 1945 Johnston and his coalition had brought 700 industrial developments to Scotland and wrung £12 million out of the Treasury for factories and plants. It was, as Pottinger observes, simply the most effective pressure group in Britain, and its merger in 1946 with the Scottish Development Council should have consolidated its power. But, by then, Johnston had left St Andrew's House to be followed in the post by a succession of weaker figures, and the wartime mood of inspired improvisation had given way to a dour austerity which encouraged Whitehall to reassert its authority. The Scottish Office would never again enjoy such self-assured autonomy; and the SCDI, while having decades of considerable achievement ahead of it, would never quite recapture the grandeur of these early years.

It remained, nevertheless, a doughty champion of Scottish development in the post-war years. It campaigned successfully for the establishment of industrial estates and, continuing the example of its development parent (updated by far-seeing analysts like Sir John Toothill and Sir Alec Cairncross), focused on newer industries which could be overlaid on Scotland's traditional industrial base. Its pursuit of inward investment helped attract some long-stay arrivals, particularly from the US but also from other parts of Britain: Ferranti (1943), NCR (1946), Honeywell (1948) and IBM (1951). These plants formed the contours of what, with rather greater fanfare, would be proclaimed as Silicon Glen a generation later. The council was at the same time showcasing Scotland in an ambitious exhibitions programme which led on from 1960, to the trade missions that were to become its mainstay. By the mid-1960s, the Scottish Office reckoned the SCDI to have brought 265 000 jobs to Scotland. In the process it had written a lasting rubric for development authorities in the UK and beyond. Ironically it was the establishment of just such an authority, the SDA in 1975, that left the SCDI conspicuously short of a raison d'être.

That is the SCDI's heritage, and it justifies pride. In a sixtieth anniversary celebration paper in May 1991, its chief economist, Craig Campbell, describes it as Scotland's economic watchdog. But these days it is a watchdog whose bark, lacking the menace of teeth, has lost much of its temerity. It continues to worry at trends which it sees as harmful to Scotland, such as loss of corporate control and short-termism, and tirelessly petitions select committees and the MMC. But its alarms are less regarded than of old, as are its often perceptive economic policy ideas, which can, despite its secular composition, be shrugged off as Scottish special pleading. And, to be fair, some of them (like the 1970s

Oceanspan/Eurospan concept of developing central Scotland into a prosperous manufacturing transit camp between North America and continental Europe) have verged upon the over ambitious.

Though the SCDI clings faithfully to the doctrine of working within the shifting parameters of political fashion, it has proved ill-suited to the dogmatic polarisation of the 1970s and 1980s. Loss of inward investment responsibility to the SDA marked the end of its role as a significant agent of government policy; and the onset of Thatcherism evicted it from the policy-making chamber with the rest of the tripartite furniture. Campbell says that, recognizing the disregard for its thinking, it has concentrated on *doing*. It now earns more from project contracts than from subscriptions. But, while activities like delivering the Enterprise and Education Initiative no doubt benefit the common weal, they also leave the impression of an organization looking for things to do. The dynamism of chief executives like Willie Robertson and Hamish Morrison never quite purges the taint of anachronism.

That taint permeates the SCDI's structure which, like its title, bears the elaborate stamp of the original patents. Including the chairman (Richard Cole-Hamilton), president, two deputy chairmen and 13 vice-presidents, its executive numbers more than 70. There are delegations representing corporate members, private members, the STUC, COSLA, the banks, the chambers of commerce and the Scottish Secretary: and nominees of timber growers, farmers, professions, heritage bodies, trade groups, development agencies, Churches, New Towns and more. It is *Who's Who in Scotland* made flesh, but a Council of Europe to Scottish Enterprise's Berlaymont. Recently, a more functional 18-strong board has been constituted.

Morrison, a volume manufacturer of quotes and sound-bites, enjoys particular licence as the Council's public voice. The senior staff number around a dozen, supplemented by secondees from industry and commerce. In addition to the elegant New Town headquarters in Edinburgh's Chester Street, the Council retains offices in Glasgow's west end (run by the general manager, Alan Wilson), Inverness and Aberdeen. It issues a number of regular publications, of which the most celebrated is its annual exports survey, the only systematic chronicle of Scotland's export trade. There is little doubt that the Council's trade missions, which average about one a month, have helped Scottish firms find niches in markets they would not otherwise have addressed. Towering over a tireless round of seminars and conferences is the annual International Forum, the brainchild in the late 1960s of Sir William McEwan Younger, which has gained prestige as markets internationalize.

If the SCDI was not doing the things in its busy diary, many would have to be done by someone else. In an unforgiving age, that is not quite a justification, still less a guarantee, for survival. John Major's accession has made consensual bodies less heretical, but not yet noticeably more influential. The return of a Labour government would certainly further warm the climate; but a Scottish parliament with wide-ranging economic powers would surely usurp much of the

Council's remaining purpose, leaving it little more than a top-heavy think-tank in a market already flooded with them.

The Council's last major executive function, trade promotion, had long been viewed with a predatory eye by Bothwell Street. There was obvious sense in reuniting the inward investment and trade promotion functions which the SCDI itself once combined, and there is also more to export promotion than trade missions.In October 1991, Ian Lang suddenly announced a new trade promotion body, Scottish Trade International, to pull together the advisory services, such as they are, of the Enterprise networks and the Scottish Office. It is to be overseen by Scottish Enterprise, informed by a twice-yearly Scottish Exports Forum, in which the SCDI will take part. Morrison's reaction was characteristic of SCDI restraint: the Council welcomed the more co-ordinated approach, and hoped there would be a place for experienced agents like itself. It was a brave face, but the new structure unmistakeably shifts the centre of gravity from Chester Street to Bothwell Street, potentially leaving the SCDI as merely a contracted provider of trade missions. The Scotland Europa office in Brussels, managed by Scottish Enterprise, is a shift in the same direction. The SCDI was among those (others included the STUC and COSLA) who criticized the arms-length posture of the venture, believing it should be a red-blooded, political champion, lobbying in the name of the Scottish consensus, rather than a consultancy for strolling traders; though the shrewd appointment of Grant Baird, independent-minded chief economist of the Royal Bank of Scotland, to head it has gone some way to pacify the dissenters.

Rationalization of the Scottish development community was arguably over-due. Scottish Enterprise is emerging the clear favourite of ministers, but the last thing it represents is the Scottish consensus. Instinct says the SCDI is more likely to emerge from the changes redundant than reborn. But the same instincts would have got it wrong in times past.

The Scottish Economic Council

The Scottish Economic Council appears more often in CVs than headlines. It is, like the SCDI, broad-based and composed of eminent industrialists, trade unionists and others. It is appointed and chaired by the Scottish Secretary. Yet its proceedings take place, for the most part, in douce obscurity. It is little troubled by the public gaze, and many Scots must have little idea it exists.

Does this mean it discreetly exercises great power over Scottish industrial policy? It does not. That is not to say that the Council is useless; in recent years, its reports on the European Single Market have been well-conceived and well-heeded. But it is essentially an anachronism, possibly the last surviving remnant of Harold Wilson's Department of Economic Affairs. That edifice, conceived as a foil to the Treasury and an instrument of economic planning, lasted just five years, from 1964 to 1969. One of its by-products was a nationwide network of broad-based regional planning councils. The Heath Government abolished them; all except for the Scottish one, which the Scottish Secretary, Gordon Campbell, chose to retain, though he excised the word 'planning' from its title. It survives as a sounding board for economic policy which the Scottish Secretary can heed or ignore as he pleases. It meets three times a year in the old Royal High School building, the Edinburgh doric temple which awaits a Scottish parliament, and reputedly generates lively debate. Its 29-strong membership is distinguished. The current line-up includes senior figures from companies like NCR, Scottish Equitable, BP, Weir, Hewden Stuart, Murray Johnstone, Christian Salvesen, the Wood Group, the Miller Group; there are three trade unionists, led by Campbell Christie; the chairmen of the enterprise networks, the Scottish Tourist Board, the SCDI, the Scottish legal aid board, the Rural Forum; there are academics, a pundit, a councillor. Members are appointed, as is the fashion, on personal rather than representative grounds, though the ratio of businessmen to trade unionists seems to change little. It is an impressive, and inexpensive reservoir of expertise: in 1988, it cost just £1 000 a year, which presumably covered mileage, stationery, coffee and biscuits. But it is not the only such resource, nor for Conservative ministers, the principal one. That position belongs to the Scottish Conservative Business Group, with which the Scottish Economic Council has some cross-fertilization (James Gulliver, Bill Hughes, Sir Matthew Goodwin, Peter Runciman), but which carries the additional influence of helping to sustain party coffers.

The Scottish Industrial Development Advisory Board

If few Scots know of the Scottish Economic Council, it seems likely that fewer still are aware of the Scottish Industrial Development Advisory Board (SIDAB). Like the Council, it is a remnant of a consensualist past; there are more of them around than the stridencies of the past decade have accustomed us to believe. But unlike the Council, it wields real power.

SIDAB's statutory purpose is to advise the Scottish Secretary on applications for Regional Selective Assistance (RSA), the main surviving regional aid incentive. Its effective function is to disburse RSA. Grants worth £176 million passed through its hands in 1990–1, aid calculated by the Scottish Office to have created or safeguarded nearly 22 500 jobs in projects worth more that £1.1 billion.

Like much of Scotland's institutional structure, SIDAB is descended from a similarly named body of rather different function. The Scottish Development Advisory Board was established by the Heath Government's 1972 Industry Act to provide a Scottish input to the disposal, by the DTI, of what was then called Selective Financial Assistance. It gained the 'industrial' in its title, and its statutory status, through the 1975 Scottish Development Agency Act. The Act denied the SDA control over selective assistance—unlike its Irish counterpart—but instead transferred responsibility from the DTI to the Scottish Office. SIDAB became the instrument of that responsibility, a role which has grown in importance with the phasing out of Regional Development Grants in favour of RSA.

The Board meets monthly at Alhambra House, the SOID building in Glasgow's Waterloo Street, just two minutes' walk from Scottish Enterprise and LiS. The proximity is appropriate, given RSA's importance to LiS in attracting inward investment. SIDAB is chaired by Duncan Macleod of the accountants Ernst Young, who succeeded Sir Robert Smith in December 1988. His appointment prompted a rare Scottish Office statement about SIDAB, listing its members, functions and activities. The 12 board members, appointed by the Scottish Secretary for renewable three-year terms, comprised eight from industry and commerce, two from the unions and two from the financial sector. In the previous five years, the statement said, nearly a thousand RSA offers had been made: £307 million of grants to projects worth more than £3.5 billion, creating or safeguarding 78 000 jobs.

SIDAB's discretion in approving these offers is considerable. RSA is subject to broad criteria: a project must be in a development or intermediate area, must strengthen the regional or national economy, must create or safeguard jobs, and is entitled to the minimum assistance needed to enable it to proceed. But the spending is not cash-limited. Indeed, the most common criticism of RSA is that it does not attract sufficient applications. SIDAB has virtual autonomy within these criteria. It is staffed by a dozen civil servants from Alhambra House, headed by an under-secretary, Hugh Morison, who assess and present applications for board consideration. The staff can themselves decide on applications below £100 000, and need merely report these approvals to the board. They also sign the cheques and monitor recipients' performance thereafter to ensure the criteria are met. RSA is often paid in tranches as projects develop over a period of years, and in 1990–1, around 500 projects were receiving funding.

All of this is done in the name of the Scottish Secretary, yet his direct involvement is minimal: 'Under present arrangements, he exercises his responsibility through his officials; it is exceptional for the circumstances of a particular case to be brought to his attention, and unknown for SIDAB's chairman to consult him about an individual project.' SIDAB is an oddity rarely mentioned in Scottish Office publications, unlike other advisory bodies, and yet what it does is much more than merely to advise. In essentials, it is an executive authority which sits at the heart of the Scottish development community, holds the public purse-strings of economic regeneration, but is subject to the loosest democratic or public accountability. And hardly anyone knows it is there.

The Scottish Business Group

The Scottish Business Group is a creature of politics, not administration. That needs to be stressed in considering the influence which it has sometimes appeared to exercise over ministers, and the linkages it enjoys with bodies of rather more public provenance.

It was set up by the Scottish Conservative Party in 1987 'to provide expert advice on business and economic matters as well as fundraising support for the Scottish Conservative Party.' In March 1989, a 13-strong Scottish Young Business Group was formed. Its chairman was the Charlotte Square financier Peter de Vink (who also sits on the senior group). He declared: 'We will have the opportunity, on a regular basis, to present our views on a wide range of issues to Government ministers and to senior officials of the Conservative Party . . . our views will not be confined to the problems or opportunities of the business community, but will take in current and potential social and economic issues of concern to everyone.'

A dual mandate, then: to advise and lobby on economic and wider matters; and to raise funds for the party. How effectively it does either is difficult to establish. It is not the sort of organization that has a press bench at its meetings. Notwithstanding its party fund-raising activities, it is more than an instrument of party policy. It has access to ministers, *as ministers*. The Scottish Secretary attends Scottish Business Group meetings, along with senior party officers; and de Vink's expectation of regular access by the youth business group to ministers presumably reflects his experiences on the full group. Place that alongside the group's role in canvassing the business contributions which make up the vast bulk of the funds the party raises annually in Scotland and you have channels that run deep.

Chaired by James Gulliver, the fallen hero of the Guinness debacle (subsequently also to fall, less heroically, at Lowndes Queensway), it includes Sir Hector (now Lord) Laing, a close confidant of Margaret Thatcher; Angus Grossart; Viscount Weir, paterfamilias of Scottish engineering; Bill Hughes and Alistair Mair, successive chairmen of CBI Scotland; Sir Ian MacGregor, the diminutive titan of the miners' strike; and Wallace Mercer, the unbashful property developer and chairman of Hearts football club: key figures from most of the power centres, institutional and informal, of the Scottish economy. Ministers would be hard-pressed to dismiss the advice of such an eminent, if partial, brains trust.

Its party fund-raising activities confer an additional edge; not just in advising ministers, but also within the Scottish Conservative Party. It was widely believed to have played an important part in the downfall of the evangelical Thatcherite, Michael Forsyth, from the Scottish Tory chairmanship. Relations between Forsyth and Malcolm Rifkind had, by August 1990, deteriorated to the point of open conflict between their respective supporters. Amid unaccustomed publicity, the Business Group held a crisis meeting, after which Gulliver emerged to tell reporters that group members had 'expressed their total support for both the Secretary of State [Rifkind] and the chairman of the party . . . they made certain suggestions which are being communicated to both and which will remain private'. Certain suggestions, from the people who fill the coffers, are not lightly disregarded. According to one inside figure, the flow of business contributions had already begun to dwindle as the ructions escalated. He told me: 'The message that came out of that meeting was, if there is one step more, we are pulling out.' This message, in essence 'Forsyth must go', was conveyed to the party hierarchy by emissaries chosen for their influence within the structures of the party. This particular source thinks that one at least of them reinforced the warning by adding 'and that goes for me, too'. Laing in particular, admired for his work in humanizing the image of business through ScotBIC and the Percent Club corporate charity scheme, was actively canvassing the views of the party's business support, and passing down to London the view that Forsyth had become a liability. Within a short time, and against Margaret Thatcher's personal instincts, Forsyth was out.

It is tempting to draw parallels between the inside influence which the Scottish Business Group commands and that which Tories habitually claim the unions would exercise over a Labour government: the charge that Labour will always be 'in the unions' pockets'. But there is nothing quite like the Group in the labour movement; certainly no such clout attends the liaison committees between party and TUC in either London or Scotland. The Scottish Business Group does not debate composite motions or wield block votes before the public gaze. But it does constitute a policy input at the highest level for the Tories' paymasters in the Scottish business community.

The New Town corporations

One Scot in 20 lives in one of the five Scottish New Towns; more than 0.25 million people. The oldest town, East Kilbride, was designated in 1947 and is now Scotland's eighth biggest burgh, with a population of 70 500. The others—Glenrothes (1948), Cumbernauld (1955), Livingston (1962) and Irvine (1966)—are also all substantial communities: only Glenrothes has fewer than 40 000 inhabitants. Their initial purpose was two-fold: to relieve overcrowding in the main conurbations, particularly Glasgow; and to attract industry and employment, through the provision of bespoke facilities and special incentives (Glenrothes was initially an exception; built to house miners transferring to the burgeoning Fife coalfield from Ayrshire and Lanarkshire, it fell into the same pattern as the others when the coalfield stopped burgeoning).

By the end of the 1970s, the first of these objectives had run its course. The towns' population had stabilized at around 250 000 and, in some cases, had begun to fall. There is nothing so unfashionable as the previous decade's high fashion, and people began to leave the bland, rented houses of the New Town estates for older properties in the cities, often commuting back to New Town jobs. But the second objective is more debatable. The rapid growth during the 1980s of the high-tech industries, particularly electronics, was at its strongest in the New Towns, drawn both by the presence of manufacturers from the early waves of inward investment, and by the activities of the New Town corporations, which had developed considerable expertise in stimulating, attracting and retaining technologically advanced industries. As we have already seen, rapid growth in sectors like electronics does not generate many jobs; nevertheless, while the population of the towns increased by less than 2 per cent between 1978 and 1989, employment within them grew by 19 per cent. In Livingston, latterly the outstanding high-tech magnet, the employment growth was a remarkable 114 per cent. LiS calculates that the New Towns landed 30 per cent of inward investment jobs during the 1980s, and that is probably an underestimate. Would Motorola, for example, have sited its personal telephones plant, promising 2 000–3 000 jobs, at poor, battered Bathgate without the thriving electronics infrastructure of nearby Livingston?

If there was wide consensus that the corporations had largely fulfilled their mission, there was less about what should replace them. The Government's answer, contained in the 1990 Enterprise and New Towns (Scotland) Act, brought these divisions into the open. It provided for the corporations to be phased out in successive three-year programmes (soon extended to four years) in order of designation; East Kilbride and Glenrothes would begin in 1991, Cumbernauld in 1993, Livingston in 1995 and Irvine in 1996. The most contentious aspect of this was the Government's initial reluctance to allow New Town tenants to transfer their tenancies to the district councils. But there is also concern about whether the considerable economic development momentum of the corporations can be maintained.

The equivalent process in England provides for the creation of a residuary body to take charge of all remaining commercial and industrial assets after the New Town corporations are wound up. But there is no such provision in the Scottish measures. Instead, the development teams are expected to become private development companies and contract with LECs to continue their work as before. There has been encouragement for the teams to privatize themselves, though little indication of how this might be achieved. The obstacles seem substantial. The corporations, acting with LiS, have skillfully tailored solutions to customer needs, drawing together rent concessions, temporary residential property and customized business premises, without the need to consider profit margins (though East Kilbride has been heard to boast that it is Britain's only self-financing public agency, thanks to its property sales). Legend has it that the Japanese firm OKI, while impressed by Cumbernauld's inward investment package, was finally won over by the concessionary corporate membership rate offered at Westerwood golf course! Whether the development teams, acting commercially and without recourse to the other elements of the corporations' remits, could rival that service is highly uncertain. On what terms, for example, would they be able to offer property, now being sold off, to investors? Would LiS and the LECs be ready or able to pay for a partnership they currently get free? Could the professional expertise in the teams be kept intact through the transition? The experience of the SDA, as it mutated into Scottish Enterprise, suggests not.

The New Town corporations have, for more than four decades, provided an engine for economic regeneration that has helped secure substantial mobile investment, modernize and diversify Scotland's economic base, and underpin export trade. But international competition for high-tech investment grows ever more demanding. If the Scottish New Towns can no longer offer competitive incentive packages, there are plenty of other locations that will.

This chapter has attempted to chart the progress of an economy in transition. If the point of departure has been more clearly described than the eventual destination—or even than the course set—it is perhaps because the rudder is in so many different hands. If there is a cause for concern when looking ahead, it lies less in the crumbling of the old strengths of Scottish industry than in the uncertain prospects of those that are to take their place.

What is not in doubt is that the Scots will continue to regard economic development as a key measure of the health of their nation.

13

Sport

Roddy Forsyth

King James II of Scotland banned golf in 1457 because it interfered with archery practice. Considering that he prohibited football when it was felt to be similarly hampering the nation's defence against England, it is an abiding irony that, five centuries later, sport can claim not only to have been the most popular manifestation of Scottishness within Scotland, but actually to have been its distinct assertion of nationality. Sport in Scotland also ventilates certain yearnings and frustrations which are accommodated by the country's political life. Perhaps football and rugby permits the expression of shifts of feeling within Scottish life before the same trends surface in the political arena.

Why should sport enjoy this undoubtedly singular status—and bear such a ludicrous weight of expectation—in Scotland? A succinct answer was offered by Dr Henry Drucker, formerly lecturer in politics at Edinburgh University, in 1985, when he wrote that football in Scottish life 'is much more than a sport. It's really the arena in which Scotland and Scots assert themselves and play a role in international affairs. There is no genuine focus for Scottish life, no arena for the Scottish identity to be seen. So football, which is the sport of many working class people, particularly in the west of Scotland, has come to play this role.

'After the Union of Parliaments in 1707, the Church, educational system and Scots law all helped to unite Scotland but the distinctiveness of these institutions has declined. If there was some kind of British league I think that would be a terrible moment for Scotland.'

Football, of course, has held a special appeal for most Scots for over a century and its attraction remains powerful today. It is Scotland's principal sport, if one takes into account the number of practising players along with its live audiences, followed on these counts by golf and rugby. The Scottish Sports Council report for 1991 listed 55 grant-aided governing bodies, from aeromodelling to wrestling.

Sport in Scotland does, however, have to contend with a number of inhibiting factors. Although Scotland does not usually endure the extremes of heat or cold of continental Europe, its climate is not conducive to prolonged outdoor exercise for much of the year. The number of all-weather surfaces has increased in recent years but as anyone who has played outdoor games or run their prescribed quota of laps can testify, when an Arctic wind propels icy raindrops with the force of a shotgun discharge, outdoor sport is purgatory rather than pleasure. The combination of a northerly latitude and maritime climate means that a large number of indoor facilities are required but the provision of these is still inadequate and not likely to meet the need for many years to come.

Perhaps for climatic reasons, too, northern European countries tend to have particular health problems, notably alcoholism and heart disease. In Scotland, especially in the west, consumption of alcohol, tobacco and fatty foods remains disturbingly high. In this context, the promotion of physical wellbeing through sport becomes a social necessity, but Scotland's approach to the development of its sporting talent remains generally haphazard. Moreover the population is compressed into the Central Belt with its many council housing schemes, and scattered sparsely across the rural Borders and the Highlands and Islands. The provision of good-quality sports facilities in such circumstances is a social need which is not adequately met.

The contribution of school sport has greatly diminished. Until the mid-1980s pupils played much of their sport in school time or under the supervision of teachers at weekends. When a bitter dispute about pay and conditions led to the teachers' strike in Scotland in the mid-1980s, the result was an erosion of extra-curricular activities which in some cases amounted to a collapse. The number of school football players, for example, dropped by 90 per cent as a result of the dispute and other team sports suffered similarly, although falling school rolls have also contributed to the declining totals of young participants. Since most people take up sport in their juvenile and teenage years, an invaluable natural resource is in serious danger of drying up. However, the principal governing bodies of Scottish sport have recognized the hazard and have to some degree turned a problem into an opportunity.

At the level of international competition small countries simply cannot be expected to dominate in several sports and Scotland is not an exception. Small countries may succeed by specialization: New Zealand, with a population of 3.5 million, offers a useful sporting comparison with Scotland. New Zealand enjoyed a fertile period in the 1980s when its cricket side was perhaps the best it has ever produced, with Sir Richard Hadlee acknowledged as the world's finest opening bowler, while its yachting fraternity was able to mount a credible challenge in the Americas Cup. But in rugby New Zealand has enjoyed a remarkable ascendancy, one reason being that the All Blacks are drawn from a pool of 250 000 players, with the consequent benefits of intense domestic competition and an undisguised financial input which has not yet been countenanced by the game's authorities in the northern hemisphere. Scotland, by way of contrast, is home to only 15 000 adult players and the main concentration of the game can be found in the moderately populated Borders. Nevertheless, in 1984 and 1990, Scotland won two Grand Slams, beating England, Ireland, Wales and

France in the Five Nations Championship, which meant that the Scots were recognized as the champions of the northern hemisphere. In the 1991 Rugby World Cup Scotland were bronze medallists, losing the playoff for third and fourth places to the All Blacks at Cardiff.

In the 1980s Scots were prominent in a number of sports. In athletics, for which the Scotsman Frank Dick is the British national coach, Allan Wells won the 1980 Olympic 100 metres gold medal and Tom McKean won gold over 800 metres in the Europa Cup (1989) and European Championships (1990). Yvonne Murray was the women's 3000 metre winner in the same European Championships and Liz McColgan became the women's world 10 000 metre champion in 1991, when she was also the fastest debutante in the New York marathon by a margin of over three minutes, the first woman home in a field of almost 26 000 runners. Jim Watt won the world lightweight boxing title in 1979 and defended it successfully for three years; in 1990 Donnie Hood became the WBC (World Boxing Council) International bantamweight champion and in 1992 Pat Clinton became the WBO world fly-weight champion. Sandy Lyle, although born in England, proclaimed himself a Scot by parentage and inclination, and Scotland was officially accorded the achievement when he won the Open championship in 1985 and the US Masters three years later. Robert Miller was the first—and in 1992, the only—British rider to win the King of the Mountains title in cycling's Tour de France (1984). Willie Carson has been British champion jockey five times, the European squash champion in 1991 was Mark Maclean, and Loretta Cusack held the women's world judo title between 1982 and 1984.

The list of winners also includes Richard Corsie, the world indoor bowls champion in 1989 and 1991 and Freuchie, which to general surprise north and south of the border took the English village cricket championship ahead of 11 000 other contenders. Whether snooker or darts are counted as sports is debatable—the Scottish Sports Council recognizes the former only—but each saw a Scot hailed as supreme exponent. Jocky Wilson was the world professional darts champion from 1982 to 1989 and in snooker Stephen Hendry set a remarkable sequence of records, becoming the youngest winner of a major title (Rothmans Grand Prix) in 1987, the first player to win four consecutive ranking tournament titles (1990) and first to win five ranking tournaments in a single season the following year. He also achieved the world record for consecutive tournament wins with 23 victories in 1990 and took the world title again in 1992.

Finally, in 1990 Scotland reached the finals of the football World Cup for the fifth time in a row, and qualified for the 1992 European championship finals for the first time, while at club level Aberdeen won the European Cup Winners Cup in 1983 and Dundee United reached the Uefa Cup final in 1987. In 1991 Scots featured remarkably, but not untypically, in English football where the championship was won by Arsenal, managed by George Graham from Bargeddie. Alex Ferguson became the first British manager to win the Cup

Winners Cup with two clubs when Manchester United emulated Aberdeen's earlier feat, and the biggest story in the English game was the resignation of Kenny Dalglish as manager of Liverpool, to be succeeded by his fellow countryman, Graeme Souness. Scotland also contributed the English player of the year, Gordon Strachan.

Taken together, these constitute a remarkable body of achievements, all the more notable because in several instances the successes were achieved against the odds or despite the indifference of the Scottish public. Few Scots have much idea of the obstacles which must be surmounted by their sportsmen and sportswomen. The complaint which was most commonly made by the sporting representatives I have consulted was that where Scotland succeeded, it usually did so in spite of itself.

Not everyone likes sport and it is often said that more people visit museums in Scotland annually than attend Scottish league matches. The two are hardly comparable, of course, since anyone who wants to contemplate Old Masters does not do so by standing for two hours in rain or sleet, having paid £6 or more for the privilege. Whatever sport adds to the spiritual, social or physical wellbeing of the citizens, it makes a surprisingly large contribution to the economy of Scotland, not to mention the British Treasury, and it generates both wealth and employment

The economics of Scottish sport

In 1984 the British Government was asked by the Council of Europe to pioneer the investigation of the impact of sport on the economies of Council members and a side effect of this request was the appearance of a number of studies of sport in the British economy, the first of which, covering the whole of the UK, appeared in 1986, with an updated version published in 1991. Because of differences between the Scottish economy and that of the rest of the UK, it is not possible to extrapolate with certainty the financial impact of sport in Scotland. To remedy this absence of accurate information, the Scottish Sports Council commissioned a research study, published in November 1991, titled *Sport and the Economy of Scotland* which provides some useful figures and estimates. The authors of the document assessed the importance of sport by measuring employment, expenditure and the amount of wealth created by sport for the community so that, for example, sport-related activity such as the processing of wood for hockey sticks or golf clubs was included in the survey, but separated from what was termed sport-core employment: the direct production and provision of sports goods or services, excluding retailing but including the teaching of sport.

On this basis sport-related activity accounted for no fewer than 57 350 jobs, compared with 105 900 in hotels and catering, and more than created by banking (43 100) or electronics (40 600). Of these, 28 000 jobs fell into the category of sport-core employment, but no estimate was attempted of sports-related expenditure on newspapers and it was not possible to calculate with accuracy how much newspapers themselves spent on sport coverage, because too many declined to respond on the grounds that the information was commercially sensitive. It was possible to make an educated guess at the kind of broadcast time devoted to sport and the figure ultimately produced suggested that the BBC, for example, spent around 11 per cent of the licence fee on sport. Sport-related expenditure of the average Scottish household was £591 per annum, making up a national total of £1100 million. When material inputs and services used in production and distribution of sport-related goods was calculated, the additional total was £1000 million, greater than that of the Scottish mechanical engineering industry and 70 per cent of the level in the electronics industry. Of the jobs directly supported by sport, it was found that career opportunities were wide ranging, with many unskilled and part-time jobs but also a managerial or professional staffing rate of 17 per cent.

Since sport generates substantial wealth it benefits central government accordingly. Tax and other revenues raised from Scottish sport were estimated at £560 million and central government spends £160 million on sport in Scotland. It should, in fairness, also be pointed out that local government is a major net spender on sport, disbursing £250 million while accruing the far smaller income of £70 million. Most Scots would be unsurprised at the scale of sport's contribution to the Scottish economy, but this is not the full story, because the survey excluded certain activities in order that comparisons might more easily be made with similar investigations conducted elsewhere. For example, racing and snooker were included, but greyhound racing and darts were not. Nor was hunting, which in Scotland means stalking rather than foxhunting. Stalking is both an ecological necessity, because of the overpopulation of deer in Scotland, and a contributor to the economy because it also generates revenues from tourist expenditure and the sale of venison and antlers. Gambling expenditure was also excluded. It was felt that sport provided an occasion or opportunity for gambling rather than being a cause for gambling. However, gambling, outside of casino betting, thrives at least in part because of a widespread interest in sport, so that although some gamblers would bet whether sport existed or not, others only place wagers because of their interest or knowledge of an individual sport, particularly racing or football.

Perhaps the most interesting implication of the economic impact of sport in Scotland—one which is true of the UK as a whole—is the fact that the governing bodies of Scottish sport have yet to realize the political clout they may be able to wield in their dealings with central government, especially since north of the border, sport has a political dimension which is not apparent in England. If the Conservative Government had declared in 1992 that it was about to spend £50 million equipping Scotland with a custom-built national football stadium seating 70 000 spectators, the number of votes it might have won from such a scheme would probably not have amounted to a tenth of the arena's capacity. But if it was felt widely that the Conservatives were willing to see Hampden abandoned in favour of Murrayfield because of the fact that Edinburgh returned Tory MPs and Glasgow did not, another profound grievance would be nurtured against the Party in Scotland. It was because of an awareness of such a potential for alienation that Michael Forsyth, in his capacity as Scottish Office Sports Minister, supported the idea of a national football stadium largely funded by central government finance. In fact, when government assistance for the refurbishment of Hampden Park was announced in February 1992, the allotted sum of £3.5 million—which had to be matched pound for pound by the Scottish Football Association—was widely criticized for being niggardly and hedged about with so many conditions that it seemed to have been designed to be turned down by the football authorities. It was also noted that the Secretary of State for Scotland, Ian Lang, was a former pupil of Rugby School who was known to favour the use of Murrayfield for rugby.

In addition, the case for a national lottery to provide funds for such areas as sport and the arts has now been accepted. Hitherto the UK and Albania have shared the distinction of being the only European countries not to operate such lotteries. The Republic of Ireland, with a population of 3.4 million, generates an annual lottery income of £55 million. However, one must also estimate the effect of a lottery on the football pools, which return £40 million a year to the game in Britain as well as £60 million to the Foundation for Sport and the Arts which disburses £40 million to other sports.

In order to keep pace with the provision of sports facilities in most of Europe, an additional £70 million will have to be spent in Scotland in the next decade. From whatever source it may be derived, this money should constitute a social priority. As the Health Education Board for Scotland has stated, Scottish children are less fit and active than their counterparts in Europe, and the gap is widening. Sport has such an evident contribution to make towards remedying this situation that a greater application of political muscle from the sporting sector in Scotland would benefit the country as a whole. It is for this reason that any additional awareness of sport's contribution to the Scottish economy should be applauded widely.

Golf

The visitor approaching St Andrews from the direction of Cupar comes upon a sporting vista when the road draws alongside the University playing fields. Beyond the trimly maintained rows of rugby, football and hockey pitches can be seen the rim of the sand dunes of St Andrews Bay, the location of the opening shots of the film *Chariots of Fire* which dramatized episodes from the life of Eric Liddell, the renowned Scottish athlete who won gold over 400 metres at the Paris Olympic Games in 1924. But if the visitor is a golfer then another aspect of the view catches the eye and heart: the sight of the grey sandstone clubhouse of the Royal and Ancient Golf Club of St Andrews at the head of the Old Course itself. This is the Mecca of the sport and if golfers, particularly those from abroad, approach it with a certain awe, the next most frequent reaction is usually surprise when they learn that the Old Course does not belong to the Royal and Ancient (R & A) at all. There are actually five courses on the St Andrews links, four of 18 holes and one 9-hole course for the use of beginners and children. What most astonishes non-Scottish golfers is that all are open to the public for no greater charge than the payment of a green fee. It is only since 1946 that St Andrews ratepayers were obliged to pay at all. Here, then, is a pleasing contrast: the headquarters of the ruling body of world golf (outside North America), and the most famous course in the world, open for all to play.

Since many foreign golfers, particularly from Japan and the US, find the sport to be both expensive and exclusive, they are astounded by the accessibility and cheapness of Scottish golf as exemplified by St Andrews. It is certainly true that Scottish golfers enjoy a provision of facilities which is not only the envy of outsiders but also of other sports within Scotland, but any analysis of Scottish golf must also take account of the fact that while demand is spread evenly throughout the country, facilities are not.

Golf was well established in Scotland in the 15th century and despite royal proscriptions on its practise it was taken up by a succession of monarchs such as James IV, Charles I and James VII. The first club to be formed was the Royal Burgess Golfing Society of Edinburgh in 1735, followed by the Honourable Company of Edinburgh Golfers in 1744. The Society of St Andrews Golfers came into being in 1754 but moved up a division in social standing when King William IV became the Society's patron in 1834, a favour which occasioned the change of name to the Royal and Ancient Golf Club of St Andrews.

The primary function of the R & A is a private golf club and its membership is fixed at 1 800 of whom 750 are foreigners, recruited from Australia to Zimbabwe. Most of the UK members are Scottish, many from the club's hinterland, Fife and Kinross; in 1991 they paid £183.75 plus VAT for the privilege. Members from the rest of Britain paid £130 and overseas golfers £105. There is a waiting list of 500, who must be patient for an average of 10 to 12 years until they can be proposed and seconded by two members. The Club employs a small staff at its headquarters, 22 purely on administrative work and a further 22 domestic employees.

The R & A's external activities are demanding. The first written rules of golf were established by the Gentleman Golfers at Leith in 1744 and their successors, the Honourable Company, inherited the status of custodians of the law. However, a degree of disarray in the Honourable Company coincided with the St Andrews club's receipt of royal patronage and the mantle passed to the R & A. By 1897 the growth of golf dictated a need for a governing authority and the R & A Rules of Golf Committee was formed to legislate for all countries outside the USA and Mexico, where the United States Golf Association is the ruling body. The Royal Canadian Golf Association legislates for Canada but is affiliated to the R & A. Every four years the R & A, which consults extensively with over 50 affiliated unions, meets with the United States Golf Association to review the rules of golf.

There is also the administration of the Open championship and the Amateur championship. For over half a century after the first Open in 1860 the conduct of the tournament was the responsibility of the host club but in 1919 it was decided that the R & A should govern both championships and the R & A Championship Committee was formed. The Committee now also administers the championships for Boys, Youths and Seniors. The running costs of the Open are now around the £3 million mark but the profit it makes subsidizes the other championships and gives grants to golf unions and grants and loans to clubs, the Golf Foundation for coaching and its schools' championships. In the five years to 1991 the R & A disbursed £7 million, principally in the UK but also as far away as New Zealand and in countries developing golf, such as Hungary, Czechoslovakia, Poland and Yugoslavia.

Michael Bonallack, the present secretary of the R & A, is a golfing thoroughbred who won the British Boys championship in 1952 at the age of 17. He took the English Amateur championship five times between 1962 and 1968 and was five times British Amateur champion between 1962 and 1970. He was selected for the British Walker Cup side continuously from 1957 to 1973 and was ever present in the World Team championship between 1962 and 1972. He became chairman of the Golf Foundation in 1977, president of the English Golf Union in 1982 and secretary of the R & A in 1983. Given his formidable pedigree and the enormous prestige of the R & A, it is reassuring to find that Bonallack still settles down to work each morning at a table in the secretary's room on the first floor of the Clubhouse, overlooking the 1st tee and the green of the 18th on the Old Course.

How many golfers have their passion ruled from this homely scene is not known. Bonallack's guess is 15 million, but the figure may be greater. The Open championship tends to generate more money for the local economy when it is staged at the Scottish venues—Muirfield, St Andrews, Troon and Turnberry—than it does in England. According to Bonallack, when the competition is held at St Andrews, which attracts the largest attendances, 'the benefit to north-east Fife is in the nature of £10 million, not to mention the free global publicity for the Scottish Tourist Board'.

As well as being the home of golf, Scotland must also cater for its golfers at home, and this is largely the realm of the Scottish Golf Union, based in Edinburgh. There are around 260 000 golfers in Scotland and they are well catered for by comparison with other countries. At the beginning of 1992, 454 courses served a population of 5.09 million, which meant a ratio of one course to 11 220 people, compared with one for each 42 000 in the Home Counties of England. There is plenty of scope for variation within the averages, however. A Scottish Sports Council survey of Scottish golf provision found that in the Highlands and Islands and in the Borders and Dumfries, less than half of the courses are 18-hole but the ratio is 9 000 people to each 18-hole course.

Most clubs have no waiting lists and green fees from visitors often account for more than half of a club's income. The picture in the Lowlands, is markedly different, with 77 per cent of courses being 18 hole, a ratio of one to 15 000 people, with club waiting lists common and club income derived predominantly from membership subscriptions. In the cities, the variations are even more pronounced. In Edinburgh there is one 18-hole course for each 17 100 of the population, in Aberdeen the ratio is 1:19 500, in Dundee, 1:34 000 and in Glasgow there is a sharp rise to 1:77 000. The Scottish Sports Council survey calculated that 15 per cent of the adult population had played golf in 1990, up from 12 per cent in 1973, and it appears that men outnumber women by 5 to 1 on the golf course. This situation can be expected to change over the next decade because, of the estimated 30 000 players on club waiting lists, 16 000 were men, 7 000 women and 7 000 juniors of both sexes. Although a high proportion of Scots play already, the international golf boom is likely to increase the numbers still further, with a consequent increase in the number of courses needed.

To satisfy current demand the equivalent of another 60 18-hole municipal courses, concentrated around the four main cities and their hinterlands, is required. In 1991 there were over 90 proposals for new courses but most of these were in rural areas, with Glasgow feebly represented, and a significant number also involved related housing, leisure or time-share facilities, reflecting the dominant trend in most other countries. In any case, a good many of these projects will not come to fruition because of lack of finance or refusal of planning permission. The construction of an average 18-hole course in Scotland requires between £500 000 and £750 000 for the purchase price of the land, and anything between £500 000 and £1.5 million for course construction, with the cost of clubhouse, car park, etc, to be added. This is why so many course proposals involve ancillary housing or leisure projects. However, although the number of such schemes will grow in the near future, Scotland will continue to sustain a gratifying number of municipal courses. These represent an investment by local government unmatched elsewhere. In Germany, for example, there is only one municipal course and golf in Europe would appear to the average Scottish golfer to be very much an élitist occupation. When the European Team championship was held in Madrid in 1990, no spectators were permitted on the course, a situation which would be inconceivable in the open tradition of Scottish golf.

While it is a myth that golf in Scotland is a classless occupation accessibility is a feature of Scottish golf, which can be said to be more the sport of the common person than it is elsewhere. Club members belong to 1.3 clubs on average, which means that three Scottish club members represent four club memberships. The typical turnover of a Scottish club ranges from around £100 000 to £250 000 per annum, with membership fees making up half the income and green fees, bar and other income accounting for a quarter each. Expenditure is evenly split between greenkeeping staff, course maintenance, clubhouse and administration.

The Scottish Professional Golfers' Association (SPGA) is a regional association of the Professional Golfers' Association, whose national headquarters is at The Belfry. The SPGA is run from Glenbervie Golf Club at Larbert and the secretary, appointed in January 1992, is Ian Bird (46), who was a housebuilder until his business fell victim to the recession. He oversees eight full-time employees and a variable part-time group which usually numbers six. The SPGA has a committee which runs its business in Scotland within the guidelines of the UK Association.

There are several classes of membership of the SPGA, the largest being class A with 184 members who are the nominated professionals on club courses inspected and approved by the Association. Class B, with 38 members, is for qualified assistants who have finished training and who are waiting for a professional vacancy. Class C accomodates 11 tour-card holders, class D is for workers on SPGA establishments who do not fall into the class A category (six in 1992), whilst class E includes 27 honorary life members. There are also 148 trainees waiting to take either class A or B membership.

The SPGA's income in 1991 consisted of a prize fund of £550 000 raised from sponsors, membership subscriptions of £16 500, competition entry fees of £84 000 and tournament levies of £33 000, a total of £683 500. The Association staged 80 pro-am tournaments in Scotland plus six major 72-hole events such as the Scottish Open and the Northern Open, and a programme of assistants' tournaments. With the expectations of the average Scottish club golfer rising markedly during the 1980s the SPGA has emphasized the need for thorough training of club professionals. In 1992 the training programme was reviewed to take account of the fact that even small golf clubs were making substantial demands on their professionals.

The golf clubs in Scotland are divided into 16 areas, and each club has a member on its county association. Each county is represented by a delegate to the Scottish Golf Union (SGU), whose secretary is 45-year-old Ian Hume, a former stock exchange dealer with the Edinburgh firm of Bell Lawrie McGregor who served for seven years on the SGU's championship committee on a voluntary basis before making golf administration his full-time occupation.

The SGU had an income in 1991 of £390 000, of which £328 000 came from club membership subscriptions, with £34 000 from sponsorship and the rest mainly accrued from interest on capital and grants from the R & A. The Union's principal expenditure—£153 000—went on administration, including the wages of its four employees, travelling expenses for members on the European golf committees, the Golf Foundation, and such like. International matches accounted for £84 000 and domestic championships for £34 000. Coaching at all levels cost £47 000, but this should be compared with the £90 000 spent in Sweden solely on the coaching of boys. Bob Torrance, the Scottish international coach, devotes 40 days a year to coaching his teams.

The SGU emphasizes its commitment to coaching, particularly at schools level, but an interesting development of its approach in recent years—one reflected in the growing professionalism to be found in golf-related occupations—is the training of greenkeepers. In future, we may expect to find that greenkeepers increasingly become course managers. Because many golf courses in Scotland have been established for some time, they tend to be shorter than the newer European courses; 6 400 yards compared to 7 000 yards. Nevertheless, of the 9.8 million rounds of golf completed in Scotland each year, 22 per cent are played by foreigners, a statistic which by itself is sufficient to establish golf as a productive national asset.

Rugby

Rugby in Scotland became a recognized sport on Monday, 3 March 1873, with the formation of the Scottish Football Union (SFU) at a meeting in Elmbank Street, Glasgow, 50 years after William Webb Ellis chose to run with the ball in his hands during a match at Rugby School, and in effect created the handling code of football. In 1815, during a game organized by Sir Walter Scott at Carterhaugh, one Walter Laidlaw picked up the ball and passed it to his team-mate, William Riddell. Riddell set off on a sprint and it is said he would have scored but for a spectator on a horse who ran him down. However, it was only in January 1871, with the formation of the Rugby Football Union (RFU) in London, that the handling code diverged permanently from the Association game, which was known initially in England and Scotland by the abbreviated name of soccer. The world's first rugby international was staged at Raeburn Place, Edinburgh, on Monday, 27 March 1871, and Scotland beat England by 1 goal and 1 try to 1 goal.

Apart from governing the game in Scotland, the most important function of the SFU was to hammer out the laws of rugby with the RFU. A significant example occurred when the English proposed that residence should be the qualification for selection for an international side, but the SFU insisted that parentage or birthplace should be the decisive element. This denied England the advantage of selecting Scots who had migrated south. Having established its authority both in Scotland and beyond, the SFU helped form the sport's International Board in 1886, and as a consequence Scotland maintains an independent voice on the game's legislating body to this day. In 1924, the Scottish Football Union changed its name to the Scottish Rugby Union, thus avoiding confusion with the Scottish Football Association, the ruling body of Scottish soccer. Nearly 40 years earlier the two codes had diverged rather more dramatically in practice when the Scottish Football Association recognized professionalism, a doctrine which was anathema to the rugby administrators.

Today 15 000 players come under the supervision of the SRU. There are 189 clubs which play rugby each Saturday and 80 on other weekdays and all are affiliated to the SRU either directly or through one of the five district unions. Full member clubs number 113 and each sends two delegates to SRU meetings, while the district unions (with a membership of 156 clubs in total) send five each. The SRU committee consists of 18 members, nine of whom are elected annually in the districts, while six are special representative members, elected every three years at the annual general meeting. The president and the two vice-presidents come up for election annually and are generally unopposed. In 1992 the president of the SRU was Gordon Masson, senior partner in the Aberdeen firm of Burnett & Reid, advocates, solicitors and estate agents. Born in 1933 Masson played scrum-half for Gordonians, but although he was never capped for Scotland he was good enough to be selected at district level for both North & Midlands. The SRU has 30 employees, six of whom are ground staff. The secretary since 1983 has been Bill Hogg, born in 1940. A chartered accountant by profession he refereed club rugby for many years and was the honorary treasurer of Watsonians before he became treasurer of the SRU in 1978, moving to his present position in 1983. There are six youth development officers whose direct responsibility is the nurturing of young talent.

Almost all of the annual income of the SRU is derived from the international matches played at Murrayfield which with gate money, broadcasting rights, sponsorship, ground advertising, programme sales and the dispensation of commercial hospitality bring in approximately £850 000 per match. Undoubtedly, SRU officials are sensitive to criticism that the commercial sector has prospered at the expense of the ordinary supporter when it comes to access, often much prized and highly valued, to Murrayfield games. The SRU accounts never reveal how much revenue comes from this area but according to the secretary and chief executive, Bill Hogg, 'It is a fact that only 1 000 tickets—from a total of 54 000—are allocated to commercial hospitality. The SRU is not run to make a profit but the easiest way to make extra money would be to raise the price of match tickets. That would be a non-starter because we distribute most of the tickets through the clubs and they would soon let us know what they thought of any proposal to make them more expensive. In any case, our main aim is to raise sufficient revenue to finance Scottish rugby and at the moment we bring in about £2.5 million per annum.'

In common with the English, Irish and Welsh unions—and unlike the four home football associations—the SRU owns its international home. However, while sports stadia represent an asset of uncertain value they are also a drain on resources and Murrayfield is not an exception. The stringent safety regulations which were drafted for sports venues in the aftermath of the Hillsborough Disaster in 1989 meant that Murrayfield, like most other stadia, had increasingly to use seating rather than terracings to accomodate its spectators. With patchwork alterations, such as that made to the South Terracing in 1986, consuming large sums of non-recoverable money, the SRU decided in the autumn of 1991 to lauch a debenture scheme whereby spectators could purchase the right to buy tickets for a seat for 50 years for as little as £1 200. It was hoped to raise a total of £37 million to construct a custom-built, all-seated and all-covered 65 000 capacity ground on the existing Murrayfield site. Within six weeks of the launch of the project, commitments totalling £22 million had been lodged. The success of the Scottish international team was instrumental in creating enthusiasm for such a scheme and it was the good fortune of the SRU that the debenture launch coincided with a Scotland side, arguably the best ever to emerge from north of the border, which reached the semi-finals of the 1991 Rugby World Cup. This event was the climax of a stirring decade for the game in Scotland. In 1984 under the stern guidance of Jim Telfer the Scots registered their first Grand Slam triumph since 1925 (and only their second ever), a feat which was repeated on an afternoon of highly charged emotion at Murrayfield when, on 17 March 1990, Scotland beat a greatly fancied England by 13–7. Such was the enthusiasm engendered by that victory and by the Scots' achievement in finishing fourth in the 1991 World Cup that there was little difficulty in finding willing spectators for the next half century. Whether the quality of the game in Scotland was likely to be maintained with such ease was the pressing question which faced the SRU.

The game in Scotland operates from a very limited base, the main platform being the Borders clubs. At school level there are 11 500 players, compared with 15 000 in the mid-1980s when, like all other team sports, rugby was seriously affected by the teachers' strike. The SRU's response was to encourage clubs to develop mini and midi rugby sections and financial assistance was made available. There has been notable success including in the Borders where every club is involved in mini/midi rugby, played on Sunday—two outstanding examples are Stirling County and Melrose. However, throwing money at youngsters is not a complete answer. Whereas the RFU in England estimated that the number of young players rose by 18 per cent after the 1991 World Cup, the SRU confessed to being handicapped by the lack of adults available to coach and supervise the equally large influx of youngsters. At the same time, the Scottish Sports Council, who appointed a rugby co-ordinator shortly afterwards, urged the need in Scotland for a system which would produce properly qualified coaches in the required numbers.

One invaluable piece of good fortune for the SRU has been the appointment of Ian McGeechan as national coach. Capped on 32 occasions for Scotland, 20 at centre and 12 at stand-off, he was captain of the international side nine times. Selected for the British Lions' tours of South Africa in 1974 and New Zealand in 1977, he played in four Tests in each series. McGeechan was assistant coach when Scotland took part in the 1987 World Cup in New Zealand and was promoted to coach in 1988–9, in time to supervise the historic Grand Slam season which culminated in the defeat of England at Murrayfield in 1990. His commitment to rugby caused him to be concerned about his ability to continue working as a schoolteacher in Leeds but the matter was happily resolved when Scottish Life in Leeds offered him a position as a marketing manager, making generous allowance for his sessions with the Scottish squad. Speaking at a sports conference in Glasgow in November 1991, McGeechan said, 'To utilize every good player in Scotland the system has to be right. We cannot afford to miss any potential. That is why we now have to link clubs and schools, develop under-18 and under-21 levels of rugby, bring the emerging players through into a developed squad, and play a development team plus an A team plus a national team, all of which will have to come under the control of one or two people. It needs a coaching structure. As yet there is not one in place nationally and it needs to use the obvious strength of national identity that we have in bringing together schools, clubs, local authorities, and the governing body in developing players and coaches together.'

The other obvious challenge which will face the SRU in the near future is the growth of professionalism in the world game. 'I speak to players all the time,' said Bill Hogg, the SRU Secretary, 'and they say again and again that they don't want to play for money.' However, players increasingly feel that they should benefit from the revenue raised by the tournament and from fringe activities, such as product endorsement, as permitted for the Australian and New Zealand players. Perhaps the most alarming possibility for Scottish rugby was talk of the formation of a professional union league in Britain, a move which would have a dire impact on the financially fragile Scottish domestic game. After almost 120 years of existence, the SRU has entered what seems likely to be the most crucial phase of its existence. The welfare of the game in Scotland is likely to depend, for many years to come, on the wisdom of the 1990s.

Football

The Scottish Football Association (SFA) was founded in 1873 as the ruling body of the game in Scotland and the Scottish League was formed in 1890 to cater specifically for the country's professional clubs. Although the world game is administered by Fifa, the laws of football are still regulated by the International Board, in which Scotland has a constitutionally guaranteed existence.

Football was so enthusiastically received in Scotland that by the turn of the century Glasgow boasted the three largest sports stadia in the world: Hampden, Ibrox and Celtic Park. All three are still in use but only Ibrox, the home of Rangers, has been transformed into a venue suitable for modern needs. Hampden Park, which belongs to Queen's Park and which is the home of the international team, requires modernization and was ruled unfit in 1991 to accommodate games designated as high-risk by Fifa. Likewise, Celtic Park, on a site of poor commercial value in the east end of the city, is in a serious state of dilapidation. This raises the question of whether Scotland requires three such large stadia devoted specifically to football, but so entrenched are the interests of the parties involved that it seems probable that some such arrangement will continue for the foreseeable future. The situation in other cities is similar. In Edinburgh, Hearts would like to move from Tynecastle, which is adjacent to Murrayfield but, unlike the rugby stadium, confined by warehouses, tenements and narrow streets. Hibernian, too, are looking at the possibilities of a move from Easter Road. Aberdeen are an exception, having decided in the mid-1970s, to halve Pittodrie's capacity and convert it into a fully seated and covered stadium.

The structure of Scottish professional football itself has been overhauled in recent years. The SFA has expanded its operations notably in the past decade or so and at its headquarters in Park Gardens in Glasgow there are now 40 employees, spread over 10 departments. There are 77 member clubs and six affiliated associations and the SFA Council, with 48 members, is the principal legislative arm of the SFA. In 1990 the income of the SFA was £7 848 248, of which £3 905 412 came from match receipts and £3 943 016 from broadcast rights and sponsorship deals. Staff costs of £1.1 million, variable refurbishment costs for Hampden Park, the organization of international matches at home and abroad—the Scottish squad is insured for £3 million on each foreign trip—and participation money for competing teams in the Scottish Cup and the Scottish Qualifying Cup account for the bulk of the expenditure. The SFA's main assets are its headquarter buildings, an investment portfolio and capital reserves of around £3 million. Ten years previously the SFA's turnover was £2 million.

The secretary of the SFA is Jim Farry, who joined the organization in 1972 when he was 18 years old. He was promoted to assistant secretary in 1978 and left in 1979 to become secretary of the Scottish League. After 10 years in the League headquarters in Glasgow's West Regent Street, he returned to Park Gardens as secretary elect in January 1990, succeeding Ernie Walker in May. His designation was subsequently changed to chief executive and he oversees a continuing policy of expansion at the SFA. 'By current standards the Scottish Football Association will be unrecognizable,' is his opinion of the likely situation in the year 2000. 'Every Scottish League club will have a community officer, every region will have a development officer and there will be a far greater extension of our Football Fun schemes for children. Youngsters will have much more access to properly trained coaches. We also intend to turn Hampden into an all-seated, all-covered ground with a capacity of 50 000. We estimate that this will cost £24 million with financial aid coming primarily from the Football Trust. We are considering a debenture scheme, but we must bear in mind that a high proportion of Scottish supporters already have a club season ticket and it may be corporate debentures that take us along part of this road.'

The Scottish League looks after the interests of Scotland's 38 league clubs from its base in the centre of Glasgow. The annual turnover of the League is around £2 million and it has begun to work with the SFA in securing commercial sponsorship, a move which may prefigure an increasing convergence of interests which many would say is overdue. On the playing side the League is divided into three divisions, the premier division having been expanded from 10 teams to 12 in season 1991–92. The first division also consists of 12 teams and the second division has 14. Power is divided accordingly, the premier clubs having four votes each while first division clubs get two each and a second division club has one. Economic power is much more concentrated. Rangers, Celtic, Hearts and Aberdeen are the Big Four of Scottish football. Even in this quartet there is a boundary line, with Rangers and Aberdeen relatively free of concern about their grounds, while Celtic and Hearts will require very large capital investment to keep pace. Dundee United, after 20 years of astute guidance by Jim McLean, are an example of good husbandry within modest means but most of the others survive on precarious margins.

Scotland's population is too small, by 2 or 3 million, for the premier division to strike the happy balance of having at least half a dozen genuine contenders for the championship. A division of 16 teams would reduce to two the frequency of league meetings between teams but it would also involve too many meaningless fixtures in the middle and lower layer, the curse of the old 18-team First Division. Ten teams with two relegated at the end of each season involves too great a failure rate, but 12 teams, as was demonstrated in 1991–2, means a congested fixture list and declining attendances. Fresh proposals from Aberdeen and Rangers at the beginning of 1992 offered the possibility of a league dividing into two at the midway point, with the bottom four clubs in the premier division playing in a new league competition along with the top four in the first division. This schedule, which theoretically offered four promotion places to the first division, also had the merit of reducing the fixture card to 36 games, with a midwinter break, only two midweek programmes and a guarantee to the national coach that he could assemble his home-based players for six days prior to any international match. It was an attractive idea which did not receive sufficient support.

In the 1980s Scottish football was drawing upon a limited resource in terms of spectators with total attendances for all competitions not exceeding 4.5 million in a season. Ironically, by attempting to supplement gate money from other sources, the game's authorities inadvertently reduced attendances. British Satellite Broadcasting struck a £12.25 million deal with the Scottish League and the SFA for live screening rights to matches, a contract which was inherited by the amalgamated company, BSkyB. The fees for clubs whose games were televized were handsome—at £60 000 a time few directors would quibble about admitting cameras to their ground—but the unexpected benefactors were pubs and clubs, which installed satellite dishes. A sizeable pub might attract an extra 200 customers on a big match night, for which the satellite company received only one subscription and the football clubs found that some supporters were losing the habit of attending games altogether. By March 1992 an unforeseen problem with satellite coverage arose. BSkyB signals are received in Ireland and the football authorities, both in the Republic and Ulster, began to veto almost every Scottish match scheduled for screening, on the grounds that attendances at their own fixtures would be reduced. The Football Association of Ireland, the ruling authority in the Republic, made it clear that they would withdraw objections if they were compensated. The sum involved was thought to be around £250 000. Since Irish crowds are low and few satellite dishes had been sold in Ireland in any case, the ploy was viewed by the broadcasting company and the SFA as virtual blackmail. BSkyB refused to lay out more cash on the grounds that it had already paid for games which were not being transmitted. The SFA refused to pay because they were making the games available and nothing was being screened. The effect was to force BSkyB to threaten to refuse to renew the contract in the summer of 1992. Meanwhile, the B&Q chain of DIY stores declined to renew its £2.25 million sponsorship of the Scottish League because of the recession.

This occurred at a time when the whole climate of Scottish football was changing radically. Business acumen, rarely an obvious asset in the directors' box, was becoming indispensable not only for clubs with genuine ambition but for those whose survival depended on maximizing slim resources. Into this category came Motherwell who in the mid-1980s were in debt to the tune of around £750 000. They were hauled back from the brink of insolvency by Tommy McLean, formerly a gifted winger with Kilmarnock, Rangers and Scotland and assistant manager of Rangers under John Greig. He was the youngest of three footballing brothers from the mining village of Ashgill in Lanarkshire, all of whom became managers. He achieved the feat of keeping Motherwell in the premier division while selling players shrewdly to reduce the overdraft, all the while nurturing promising youngsters on a slender budget: Tom Boyd, later sold to Chelsea for £850 000 was taken on by the club through the Government's Youth Training Scheme. The club acknowledged its debt to Tommy McLean by making him a director and Motherwell's progress continued when they won the Scottish Cup in 1991, beating Dundee United 4–3 in a thrilling final at Hampden Park.

Ironically, had United won the trophy it would have filled the obvious gap in the career of the middle McLean brother, Jim, who later the same year celebrated 20 years as manager at Tannadice, a tenure which made him the longest serving single club manager in Britain. United were not in danger of insolvency when he took over the team in 1971, but it was as a result of his extraordinary eye for juvenile talent and his equally remarkable ability as a coach that the club was able to sell several players at a premium while retaining sufficient home-grown talent to win the championship for the first time and the Scottish League Cup twice. United also reached the final of the Uefa Cup, losing to Gothenburg in 1987 and the semi-final of the European Cup in 1984, when they were defeated 3–2 on aggregate by AS Roma. On five occasions United reached the Scottish Cup final but the trophy remained elusive. Like his younger brother, Jim McLean moved into the boardroom to become first a director and then chairman and managing director of the club he had almost single handedly transformed.

In Edinburgh, Heart of Midlothian were revived during the 1980s after the club had been bought by an Edinburgh property developer, Wallace Mercer, whose style was mercurial but effective. In 1990 he attempted an abortive takeover of the other city club, Hibernian, and then turned his attention to plans to move Hearts to a custom-built, all-seated stadium on the outskirts of the capital.

Another Edinburgh businessman, David Murray, had a more dramatic impact on Scottish football. Murray, who had been obliged to leave Fettes College when his father could no longer afford the fees, began his entrepreneurial career by dealing in scrap metal, but he suffered a devastating setback when he crashed his car into a tree while driving home at speed after playing rugby, an accident in which he lost both legs. At this time, in 1976, he was 24 years old but he overcame his disability to supervise the phenomenal growth of his holding company, Murray International which by 1991 was an umbrella for 50 companies, paying Murray a salary of £116 000 and annual dividends of £1 702 000. He bought the controlling interest in Rangers in November 1988 and took an active part in supervising the building of a new tier of 7 500 seats at Ibrox, sold under a debenture scheme copied from US precedents.

In the summer of 1991 Rangers set a new Scottish transfer record for buying a player when the Soviet international, Alexei Mikhailichenko, arrived from Italy for £2.5 million and Trevor Steven set the record for a player sold from Scotland when he went to Marseilles in a deal worth £5 million. In all of these dealings Murray consolidated and expanded the trends which had begun with the arrival of Graeme Souness as Rangers manager in April 1986, a move which revolutionized both the club itself and the game north of the border, reversing the traditional flow of talent to England and sending players' salaries on to a dramatic upward spiral. In fact, Souness merely prepared the Scottish game for the conditions which would prevail in the 1990s. 'The mobility of players will accelerate,' says Jim Farry. 'There will be far fewer testimonials for long service—maybe none at all—and the concept of playing for the jersey, of devoting a career to one club and one locality, will fade. In all of this there is a serious danger of alienating the supporters from the people who used to be their idols.'

Despite the increasing number of foreign players in the Scottish game, a marked decline in outstanding talent, and a ludicrously demanding domestic programme which frequently decimates squad selections, Scotland has performed against expectations in recent years. Under Andy Roxburgh, the national coach, the Scots qualified for the 1990 World Cup finals, the fifth in succession to feature Scotland, and in 1991 the finals of the European championship for the first time. Roxburgh, a 48-year-old former teacher, took charge of the national team without having moved up through the conventional route of club management. He played with Falkirk, Partick Thistle and Clydebank, with whom he was also a coach, before joining the SFA as youth coach. In August 1986 he was appointed national coach and chose as his deputy, Craig Brown, who had been manager of Clyde and, like Roxburgh, a former headmaster, a circumstance which gave rise to jibes from others in the game who referred to the SFA offices as 'the staffroom'. But by 1992 Roxburgh's record in charge of the national side was unsurpassed and the sneers had ceased.

The senior side's performance, although the most visible aspect of his work, is only one aspect of a complex job. Roxburgh is the head of coaching for Scottish football and working with three assistants, he is responsible for every level from the international team to the Playball schemes for primary school children. A heavy load compared with the situation in The Netherlands, where the Dutch FA employs 27 full-time coaches, 20 in the regions and seven at their headquarters. In the development of young talent Scotland is far behind other European countries. In France, each first division league club runs its own school where pupils are coached in football in the morning and receive private education in the afternoon. The Scottish education system will not tolerate this. Instead, as in other sports, football training for the mass of youngsters is left to the school system, and the consequences of the teachers' strike were shocking, according to Bob Docherty of the Scottish Schools Football Association: 'In 1983–4 we had 45 000 pupils playing schools football each Saturday morning. The following year, after the strike, we had 4 600. We are now back to around 39 000 which, allowing for lower school rolls, represents a fairly full recovery. But football is the only sport which has come back as strongly and some others never recovered at all.'

Andy Roxburgh's view of the prospects for Scottish football are mixed. 'Other countries laugh at our methods or are amazed that we get so far with them. Our clubs are our centres of excellence and some have coaching schools across Scotland, but the game is so widespread here that far too little is properly structured. At least we recognize the need to spend money. Our coaching courses used to be like a travelling circus which came to a town and then disappeared. Professional coaching is beginning to develop here but we are way, way behind. Karl Hedergott, who was the West German national coach for more than 20 years, said to me: "You in Scotland have to be at least as efficient as us. Instead, you are light years behind." Part of the problem is that the old street environment has gone—the streets are busier and there are other sports and distractions. Part of it is that we encounter, to put it bluntly, an attitude of "OK, you entertain us" amongst kids, part of it is lack of finance and part stems from a bloody-minded attitude to coaching in some quarters, the feeling that we have some natural right to beat the rest of the world. It's not that we don't know what has to be done and it's not that we don't have the raw material. But you try finding a good indoor facility on a wet November night. We make our kids run around the gym—there's no football training in most cases—then they're overplayed with schools, youth clubs, junior teams, Sunday leagues. For me, it's tragic to see that our children are wasted when, if they were born in continental Europe they would be encouraged and developed. That's the way it has always been, though, and the one positive aspect is that it is, believe it or not, a lot better than it was a decade ago.'

Sport is a vital contributor to the welfare, economy and international image of Scotland. For many Scots it means personal fitness and private fulfilment. For tens of thousands it sustains employment and for most of the population at some time or another it provides a pleasant diversion or an antidote to bleak living or working conditions. Sport probably acts as a pressure gauge of national sentiment. Strong parallels can be suggested between the bombastic and insubstantial nationalism of the 1970s which withered in the anticlimax of the devolution referendum, and the footballing chronicle of Scotland under Ally McLeod, when a national fantasy was ruthlessly exposed in the Argentina World Cup campaign in 1978. Again, just as Scotland's traditional measure of football status—the annual international with England—was abandoned in the 1980s, English clubs were barred from European competition because of hooliganism culminating in the Heysel disaster. Scottish clubs were not affected by this ban and provided a practical example of the separate existence of Scotland in Europe at the same time as the SNP employed the slogan to notable effect in the political arena. In 1980, too, it seemed almost inconceivable that the Scottish Rugby Union would sanction the abandonment of 'God Save the Queen' as the anthem for the Scottish team. Yet at the 1990 Grand Slam match with England the emotional rendering of 'Flower of Scotland' suggested that the traditionally conservative rugby constituency had shifted its ground.

Sport resonates at every level of Scottish life. Yet it is a resource which is developed and exploited in a laughably haphazard fashion. To employ an apt image, Scottish sportsmen and sportswomen somehow continue to be front runners for a country which does not expend the energy required to keep up with the pack.

14

The Scottish Office

Peter Jones

On the side of Edinburgh's Calton Hill, overlooking the main railway to London, sits an imposing 1930s building looking not unlike the power stations of that vintage. It is an excellent visual symbol, for it opened in 1939 as the headquarters of the Scottish Office. Apart from when ministers decamped to the neo-brutalist surroundings of New St Andrew's House beside Edinburgh's main bus station, Old St Andrew's House has been the location for the office suites of the Secretary of State for Scotland and his ministers, also the leading civil servants, including the Permanent Under-Secretary of State (usually known as the Permanent Secretary). From these corridors of Scottish power, the instructions flow out to 10 500 civil servants employed directly by the Scottish Office to implement government policy and supervise the spending of the Scottish Office budget, which in 1991–2 reached just over £11 billion. Its London offices are housed in Dover House, whose cavernous state rooms overlook Horseguards Parade. There ministers conduct their business during the week when parliament is sitting.

A curious feature of the Scottish Office today is that although its work reaches into most parts of Scottish life, it remains a private world. An opinion poll carried out for *The Scotsman* in 1985 found that only 36 per cent of the sample of voters polled knew that there was a special government office responsible for Scotland, and even fewer, 28 per cent, correctly named it as the Scottish Office.

Yet, in its upper echelons are some of the sharpest and ablest minds in Scotland. Sir William Kerr Fraser, who held the top post of Permanent Secretary (1978–88), left an indelible mark on the shape of Scottish public administration today. Strongly in favour of devolution of power from London to Edinburgh, he gave what one official described as 'a craggy leadership', and aided many ministerial battles over the rights of the Scottish Office to pursue distinctive courses of action. A middle-class Glaswegian, educated at Eastwood School and Glasgow University, he brought an unstuffy approach to the job, insisting, for example, on making the Scottish Office rather more accessible to the media and academic researchers than many Whitehall ministries. During and since Fraser's time, much was published on the

Scottish Office. Without this, public ignorance of its workings would have been even greater.

Although the Permanent Secretary is officially described as the Secretary of State's principal policy advisor, one former Scottish Secretary said: 'Ninety per cent of my discussions with the Permanent Secretary were about the administration of the office: whether a department should be reorganized to do this or that, whether x or y should be appointed under-secretary, whether money should be spent on buildings, the honours lists, and so on.' He added, perhaps revealingly, that he 'suspected' the Permanent Secretary had a strong influence on policy within the department, but he never saw it.

Of course, if a Scottish Secretary asks for policy advice, it will be given, but it is not generally volunteered. Fraser, in a retirement interview, explained that when interviewed in 1955 for civil-service entry, he was asked: 'You are advising a minister that there are four courses of action and you suggest course B. He opts instead for course C. In a matter of weeks it becomes obvious that course B was correct. What do you do?' Fraser answered: 'Nothing—that was the right reply and that is why I have survived until today.'

Even though the picture of a Permanent Secretary as the chief administrator sounds dull, it is a powerful job. Sir Russell Hillhouse followed Fraser as Permanent Secretary in 1988. He was a surprise appointment, the junior of the departmental heads, who had been secretary of the education department for only a year before he got the top job at the relatively young age of 49. The decision over his appointment was made by Margaret Thatcher. Hillhouse was thought to have a reputation for radical thinking on policy, whereas the expected successor, William K Reid, who had been secretary of the home and health department since 1984, was more of a traditionalist. Hillhouse by comparison is described as 'excitable' or 'short-fused'. Reid left the Scottish Office and became the Parliamentary Ombudsman.

One of Hillhouse's management initiatives was to examine closely the Scottish Office's growth in dealings with the European Community. It was a common complaint amongst the few Scottish Office civil servants who went to Brussels, either on temporary attachment or to work permanently for the Commission, that they rarely saw the senior Scottish Office officials in Brussels. Hillhouse's review found that most of the management units in the Scottish Office devoted more time than anyone realized to EC affairs. In 1990 Ian Lang replaced Malcolm Rifkind as Scottish Secretary, and Lang's enthusiasm for the Scottish Office handling more of its own EC business instead of through the Foreign Office together with Hillhouse's groundwork, meant that the European dimension could be rapidly lifted up the Scottish Office priority list with the establishment of a European Coordination Unit to supervise staff-training in languages and in the workings of the Commission.

This example highlights how the crucial job of the Permanent Secretary is not to act as a policy advisor, but as policy implementor. Meeting ministerial priorities, Hillhouse said, 'means trying very hard to get resources from where they are not needed to where they are needed. And it's the successes in getting them where they are needed that makes the thing work.' Hillhouse has an additional attribute—excellent knowledge of the Treasury, both as an insider who worked there and as an outsider, having been the Scottish Office's principal finance officer (1980–5). Since the Treasury grudges every penny which leaves its coffers, and all cabinet ministers have to do annual battle with it, having a Permanent Secretary who knows its workings is of great value.

Unlike any other Whitehall ministry, the Scottish Office is a federal ministry. Each of its five departments retains a degree of autonomy as each departmental head is an accounting officer, responsible directly to the Secretary of State and to parliament for expenditure under their control. In Whitehall, only the Permanent Secretary is an accounting officer, and thereby entitled to tell a minister that he cannot support a proposed expenditure. The federal arrangement is necessary because of the vast spread of Scottish Office responsibilities.

The Permanent Secretary chairs and sets the agenda for the management group of departmental heads plus senior finance and personnel officials which meets fortnightly under Sir Russell Hillhouse, rather than weekly as under Sir William Fraser. It exists mainly to liaise on policy and staffing matters which cut across departmental structures.

The departmental heads are powerful civil servants, and collectively have a greater role in policy-making than the Permanent Secretary. Each is well known to the particular interest groups with whom they come into contact, an intimacy possible in a country of five million people and which most civil servants believe makes for swifter and better decisions. Perhaps the most influential department head in modern times has been Dr Gavin McCrone, who had established a formidable reputation as an economist before he joined the Scottish Office as senior economic advisor in 1970, an unusual example of entry into the civil service at a high level from another career, in McCrone's case, as an academic. As under-secretary for regional development (1972–80), and secretary of the Industry Department (1980–7), he played a vital role in regional development and inward investment policy. In 1987 he became secretary of the Scottish Development Department, since renamed the Scottish Office Environment Department. He retired finally in 1992 resuming academic life.

Most Scottish Office department heads come up through the Scottish Office ranks and only have brief spells working in other parts of the civil service. Loudon Hamilton, secretary of the Agriculture and Fisheries Department since 1984, is a good example. His career was spent almost exclusively in supporting agriculture. The Education Department has also been known for its exclusivity and refusal to admit outsiders to its mysteries.

But two appointments in the late 1980s demonstrate a very determined attempt to cross-fertilize in the Industry and Education Departments. The career of Peter Mackay, prior to his becoming secretary of the Industry Department, shows the changing political imperative for the department to become more interested in training and development. From 1983 to 1985 he was director for

Scotland of the Manpower Services Commission, in 1985–6 under-secretary in charge of manpower policy at the Department of Employment in London, and then in 1987–9 he was back at the Scottish Office as under-secretary in charge of further and higher education.

Similarly the appointment of Gerald Wilson as secretary of the Education Department in 1988 signalled the move to have industry more closely involved with education, as Wilson was for four years head of the Industry Department's Glasgow office. Regarded as one of the brightest talents in the Scottish Office, Wilson was also one of the first department heads to have significant experience of European affairs, having been a counsellor for social affairs and regional policy in the UK's diplomatic presence in Brussels (1977–82)—the UK Permanent Representation to the European Community.

Successive department heads have fought to retain the individuality and status of their departments (and hence their own jobs) and against losing departmental distinctiveness in a corporate Scottish Office identity which however was adopted in 1991. The reason for this compartmentalization lies in the rather piecemeal historical development of the Scottish Office. For example, until reorganization in 1939, the Scottish Education Department had a peculiar constitutional status as a creature of the Privy Council. It was only responsible to the Secretary of State by the device of the Scottish Secretary also being designated Vice-President of the Scottish Education Committee of the Privy Council, a committee which never met after 1913. The Home Department, which until 1939 was based in London, regarded itself as the senior department, steeped in the 'superior' Whitehall culture.

The Departments

The Scottish Office departmental structure parallels Whitehall structures, and indeed makes it a mini-Whitehall. The following summary of departments and their budgets for 1991–2 gives an idea of its organization: Agriculture and Fisheries, £282 million; Industry £1 088 million: Environment £961 million; Home and Health £3 887 million; Education £598 million; and Central Services £138 million. This last-named department provides personnel, finance, office management and other services to the other departments. The Environment Department is also the channel for the £4 598 million of Government grant to local authorities, 62 per cent of council spending. A further £18 million was spent by the various public records offices – the General Register Office for Scotland (population records), and Registers of Scotland (land and other legal registers). The Scottish Courts Administration cost £80 million. The range of each department's work is vast, and is covered in more detail in other chapters. But it is worth looking at some noteworthy aspects here.

Much of the Agriculture and Fisheries Department's work is surrounded by the complications of the European Community's Common Agricultural Policy and Common Fisheries Policy. Under the CAP, the department implements schemes for supporting farmers such as the Sheep Annual Premium, whereby in 1990–1 nearly £40 million was spent bridging the gap between the market price for sheepmeat and a basic price set by the EC. There are also the Hill Livestock Compensatory Allowances, payments for hill sheep and cattle breeding which totalled £47 million in 1990–1. These measures provide a vital life-support system to remoter rural areas. Were it to stop, much hill farming would cease to exist. The department also provides assistance to crofters, and launched in 1991 a Rural Enterprise Programme to help Highland farmers diversify.

It also has an increasing role in conservation and landscape management. It manages the Farm Woodland Scheme, begun in 1988 to encourage farmers to grow trees instead of crops, the scheme of Environmentally Sensitive Areas which by 1989 covered Breadalbane; Loch Lomond; the Machair of the Uists, Benbecula, Barra and Vatersay; and Whitlaw and Eildon. By 1990 around 800 farms covering over 100 000 hectares had joined the voluntary scheme and around £1 million was being paid out annually for conservation measures, such as stone-dyke and hedge restoration. Grants for farm improvements are also increasingly orientated towards conservation and anti-pollution measures.

The department has one other noteworthy resource—a small fleet of seven ships and two aircraft to enforce the EC's fisheries rules. These ships and planes have enabled successive Scottish Secretaries to boast that they have their own private navy and air force, which is perhaps why it was announced in 1991 that the 250 staff members including the shore-based Sea Fisheries Inspectorate were to become an executive agency, the Sea Fisheries Protection Agency.

Quite separate from the department has been the Forestry Commission, whose work has become one of the most familiar, but not always best-loved, features of the Scottish landscape, 13 per cent of which is now covered by woodlands. The economic demand for timber led to serried rows of Sitka Spruce blanketing Lowland and Highland hillsides. Modern forestry has to deal with the demand for more aesthetically-pleasing woodlands, which safeguard rather then extinguish wildlife, and encourage rather then deter public access. The commission is headquartered in Edinburgh rather than London, and in a curious administrative anomaly, the Scottish Secretary is responsible for all UK forestry, not just Scottish forestry. Private woodlands in Scotland (558 000 hectares in 1988) now cover more land than state forests (529 000 hectares in 1988), with the Commission having been selling 5 000 hectares of land a year and planting less than a quarter of the hectarage of private planting. The Commission is to be split into a Forest Authority, responsible for statutory functions such as grant aid, and Forest Enterprise, responsible for commercial timber operations. The whole tenor of the move to a private sector style of operations was under-lined when in 1989, the experienced Scots financier Raymond Johnstone was appointed chairman of the Commission. A year earlier, the Government signalled that it wanted fresh ideas when it plucked from New Zealand's Ministry of Forestry the north-east Scotland born and educated Robin Cutler to be the Commission's director-general.

The Scottish Office Industry Department is a relatively recent creation, formed in 1973 as the Scottish Economic Planning Department, for which the forerunner was the Scottish Economic Planning Board, set up in 1964 with officials from various UK departments in response to the then Labour Government's economic planning ideas. From 1964 there was a Scottish Office regional development division headed until 1972 by an outstanding civil servant, James McGuinness. His influence was vital in guiding the policy response to the milestone Toothill report on the Scottish Economy, compiled under the auspices of the Scottish Council Development and Industry, but with a strong Scottish Office input.

The response included the creation of the new towns of Livingston (1962) and Irvine (1966), the Highlands and Islands Development Board (HIDB) (1966), bridges over the Forth, Tay and Clyde estuaries, a start to the motorway system, the construction of a new Glasgow airport, and electrification of the Glasgow–London railway line. McGuinness's successor as the Scottish Office's lead economic planner, Gavin McCrone, in an essay collection *The Economic Development of Modern Scotland 1950–1980* wrote: 'Without these developments the economy could never have hoped to benefit from the inflow of overseas developments which has come to play such a major role.' In 1973 the Scottish Economic Planning Department took over sponsorship of the HIDB, the five new towns, the two electricity boards, and in 1975 gained administration of regional selective assistance, absorbing the Department of Industry's office for Scotland. The same year, the Scottish Development Agency (SDA) was founded.

The department supervises the successor bodies to the SDA, the HIDB, and the Training Agency—Scottish Enterprise and Highlands and Islands Enterprise. Its pivotal role throughout the 1970s and 80s in combatting economic decline, where its great success was the attraction of overseas investment, is no less pivotal in the 1990s, though the challenge is now to make the most of the advantages, and avoid the worst of the disadvantages, of the European Single Market.

With workforce skills and innovative ability increasingly being the key to competitive advantage among developed countries, much could depend on the degree of coordination achieved between the Industry and Education Departments. The Industry Department was responsible, for example, for spending in 1991–2 £14 million on boosting the work experience and technical skills content of education courses for 14–18 year olds, the Technical and Vocational Education Initiative, a responsibility gained from the Department of Employment. The Education Department itself has new challenges, having gained in the 1990s responsibility for administering the Scottish universities, finally making the department responsible for all aspects of primary, secondary and tertiary education in Scotland. The tools available to both departments for the key task of the next few decades, investment in people and their skills, have never been greater. Indeed it is arguable that given the massive expansion of post-school education envisaged by the end of the 1990s, the Education Department may have a more important role in economic development than in the Industry Department.

The Scottish Office Environment Department is the instrument through which the government maintains tight controls over local government taxation. In 1991–2, 24 per cent of councils' spending came from business rates and 15 per cent from the poll tax.

As the department is also the authorizing agent for borrowings by local authorities for their capital (construction) spending, which in 1991–2 were planned at £1 billion, it controls directly and indirectly around £10 billion of public spending. And control is the right word to use where local-authority spending is concerned. 'Local authorities can't even sneeze without our permission,' an official commented, going on to make it clear that he regretted the loss of local autonomy that has taken place.

A key area is housing. Ever since the right of council tenants to buy was granted in 1980, the department has cracked the whip over local authorities, so that, by 1991, 210000 houses and flats had been sold, increasing the proportion of property in Scotland which is owner-occupied from 35 per cent in 1979 to 50 per cent by June 1990. After the 1987 election that Scottish Office ministers decided to increase the pace. Two public bodies, the Scottish Special Housing Association, which used public funds to build low-rent housing in economic-growth areas, and the Housing Corporation in Scotland, which financed Housing Association construction of low-cost homes, were merged to form in 1989 the new body of Scottish Homes. Though it was set up to reduce the proportion of public-sector housing, it has become a powerful weapon of central-government intervention in housing.

Choosing the right chairman for an organization that was inevitably going to meet with a lot of hostility from the mainly Labour-controlled district housing authorities was obviously crucial. The agile mind of the chosen man, Sir James Mellon, a Scottish civil servant who went to the Foreign Office and became ambassador to Denmark and Consul-General in New York, has proven to be a major asset. Under his chairmanship, Scottish Homes has become innovative in its task of boosting the private rented sector, introducing pump-priming grants to encourage private developers, giving a boost to long-neglected cooperative housing ideas, as well as continuing to grant aid to the housing associations, with, in 1990–1, £204 million.

The department supervises another agency which is just as much in the public eye—Scottish Natural Heritage. The story of how this body came into being in April 1992 is related later. But the continual friction between the many conservation interest groups meant that the agency was always going to be in the eye of the storm. Fortunately, the author and broadcaster Magnus Magnusson agreed to chair it, leaving no room for doubting that it was going to be independent both of the competing interest groups and the Scottish Office. An official commented that Magnusson had the clout to be able to say 'no' to ministers without having to threaten resignation. The initial annual budget was set at £34.6 million, compared to the combined budgets of £26 million available to the predecessor bodies of the Nature Conservancy Council of Scotland and the Countryside Commission for Scotland.

In April 1991 the Historic Buildings and Monuments division became the Historic Scotland executive agency, an arm's length part of the Scottish Office with more freedom of action to spend the 1991–2 budget of £30 million looking after the ancient castles and other buildings in its care.

The Scottish Office Home and Health Department is certainly the biggest spending department, and perhaps therefore the senior department. Home affairs encompasses the police and fire services, policy on Scottish law, and the prison service. It also handles health service policy and management, and social work policy, including community and child care, and social work in the criminal justice system.

One aspect should be singled out here—the Scottish Prisons Service. From having had a foul reputation with some of the most over-crowded and toughest prisons in Europe, Scottish prisons have moved forward rapidly and are now regarded as innovative. Much is usually, and rightly, made of the Special Unit set up in 1973 at Barlinnie prison in Glasgow, where some of the worst trouble-makers and hardest men in the system were rehabilitated by being given a degree of freedom and responsibility hitherto unknown in the system. The best known example is that of the Glasgow gangland killer Jimmy Boyle who turned into a creative sculptor. But in the early 1980s, the prison system became heavily over-crowded, tensions rose, and between 1986–8 there were unprecedented riots throughout the system with rooftop protests, and prison officers being taken hostage. A riot at the brand new Shotts prison, where another special unit has been set up, demonstrated it was not necessarily the buildings and facilities that were the problem.

In 1988, a 48-year-old career civil servant who had been running industrial aid, Peter McKinlay, took over as chief executive of the prisons service, and turned out to be a brilliant manager. Assisted partly by a fall in the prison population, down from a daily average of 5 566 in 1986 to 4 724 in 1990, he turned the prisons' ethos round from containment to rehabilitation. He massively increased the training given to officers who previously often had only the basic five-week induction course. McKinlay gave the officers a pride in man-management skills and a dramatic fall in prison violence resulted. He also introduced fast-track promotion for promising officers, an outstanding success being the rise of Dr Andrew Coyle. As governor at Peterhead, Coyle oversaw its transition from a notorious university of hard men into an institution specializing in the rehabilitation of sex offenders. Reform in prisons is continuing, with an end to the degrading practice of slopping out promised and ideas like installation of TVs in cells being examined. But McKinlay moved on in 1991 to become director of Scottish Homes, where it was evidently hoped that his managerial skills and public relations flair would be applied to Scotland's housing problems.

This move draws atttention to a relatively new phenomenon in the public or quasi-public sector in Scotland—the high-flying civil servant who becomes a high-profile executive manager. McKinlay was followed at the Prison Service, for example, by Eddie Frizzell, a 45 year old who had emerged from the depths of the Scottish Office finance division some two years earlier to become director of Locate in Scotland. Another is Tom Band, who came out of the Scottish Office Industry and Finance Departments to become in 1984 director of Historic Buildings and Monuments, and from 1987, the chief executive of the Scottish Tourist Board.

The Ministers

During the 1980s the Scottish Secretary normally had four ministers in his team—one a Minister of State and the three others parliamentary under-secretaries of state. The difference between the two titles reflects the political pecking order, Minister of State being one rung under cabinet membership. Under the Labour governments of the 1970s, the Scottish Office had two Ministers of State, one from the House of Commons and one from the House of Lords, which gave the Scottish Office a slightly higher status in the invisible Whitehall rankings.

While under the Conservatives the Scottish Office had to make do with one less minister, the new Scottish Secretary in 1979, George Younger, made an innovation which was more significant than it sounded. Previously, ministers had just been known as 'the parliamentary under-secretary of state responsible for Scottish Education Department matters' etc. Younger announced that they would be known as the 'Minister for Education', and in that first allocation of portfolios, attempted to create ministerial bridges across the departments. Alex Fletcher was made Industry and Education Minister.

Younger's move also signalled that he intended to delegate much more to his junior ministers who now carry a heavy burden. They deal with the majority of the individual departmental questions raised by MPs and others. They also take legislation through its committee stages when it gets clause-by-clause consideration. But since Younger's move, junior ministers have become more autonomous in their own policy areas. Crucial to this relationship is trust between ministers and a recognition by the civil servants in a department that their minister does make the crucial decisions. Thus a Scottish Secretary, although a cabinet minister and a powerful politician, has to be careful when he overrules a junior minister.

What is peculiar to the Scottish Secretary's job is his wider area of responsibility. He has to have knowledge in width, rather than depth, of issues which are strictly speaking not his responsibility. The classic example is that of the Ravenscraig steelworks, the future of which technically is only a matter for the Department of Trade and Industry. But Scottish MPs and public opinion expect the Scottish Secretary to be heavily involved in such a matter.

Crucial to the Scottish Secretary is his private office, which sifts through all his correspondence, organizes his diary, gets him to official functions on time. The private secretary, normally a young civil servant expected to rise far, in particular is a vital gatekeeper controlling access to the minister. A former Scottish Secretary commented: 'The private office saw all the correspondence and it was up to their judgement as to what I saw.' One retired senior civil servant said: 'If a department head thought his minister was making odd decisions, then he would pick up the phone and tell the private secretary to make sure that the Secretary of State saw the relevant set of papers. That usually made sure the odd decisions were fixed.' Thus, private secretaries can be extremely valuable to a minister.

Also vital to the Scottish Secretary is the Wednesday morning meetings of ministers in Dover House every week that parliament is sitting. The Permanent Secretary and some of the senior officials attend as well, as does the Lord Advocate. Another important attender is the director of the information directorate, who is effectively the Scottish Secretary's chief public-relations officer. It is the job of the director, since 1992 the vivacious Liz Drummond from Ayrshire and an LSE graduate, to know what interests the parliamentary journalists covering the Scottish Office, and, through the network of Whitehall information officers, what is happening elsewhere in the Government. The Scottish Office comes under intense scrutiny from the media. Junior ministers, whose counterparts in Whitehall departments almost never see their name in the press, can expect to see their activities covered by the Scottish media on almost a daily basis.

When ministers work to each other's strengths, a formidable team can result. But relations can turn sour, as they did latterly in Malcolm Rifkind's 1986–90 period as Scottish Secretary. As something of a liberal, and with historic pro-devolution credentials, Rifkind was never part of the Thatcherite coterie. Nevertheless, Mrs Thatcher respected his intellect and, for a long period, his political judgement. During one visit to Scotland in 1987, she referred approvingly to 'Rifkindism', implying that while Rifkind might be pursuing his own policies in Scotland, they were policies which had her support. But in the winter of 1989–90, over various issues such as the future of Prestwick Airport, Mrs Thatcher grew to doubt Rifkind's judgement and rely instead on the views of Michael Forsyth. The rise and fall of Forsyth as party chairman in Scotland is another story, but the special relationship which developed between Forsyth and Thatcher, bypassing Rifkind, was disastrous for the Scottish Office. Ministers became a disunited team, with policy the football in a struggle for supremacy.

Sources of policy

The power of the Scottish Office is best measured by its policy output. Tracing that output back to its source displays exactly where that power is located. The civil service is extremely good at ensuring the public believes ministers are responsible for all policy, but it is not the case that ministers are the originators of all policy. Just like any business, the civil service takes in a raw material (policy), and converts it into a finished product (legislation). In the Scottish Office, as in any other part of the civil service, the political agenda drawn up by ministers from their party's manifesto has become a significant source of policy in recent decades: 'Manifestos used not to matter too much, but now they are increasingly important,' one old Scottish Office hand said. A manifesto commitment which had profound effects was the sale of council houses implemented by the new Conservative Government in 1979. A decade later, the proportion of public sector homes in Scotland had been reduced from 55 per cent to 45 per cent.

From the 1987 Scottish Conservative manifesto eventually came legislation setting up Scottish Homes (responsible for financing housing associations), schools boards and the extension of compulsory competitive tendering in local government. No objective was set out with any great precision; civil servants have to take the general idea and convert it into workable and cost-effective legislation. The machine will grind away at these policies, chipping bits off and adding other bits on until the finished product can bear little resemblance to the original idea. Much ministerial determination is often needed if the initial concept is to survive. An example was the creation in the 1987–92 parliament of school boards, where Education Minister Michael Forsyth wrote most of the initial consultation paper himself and resisted pressure from inside and outside the Scottish Office to water down the scheme, though he did accept some amendments.

But policy has also to be derived in response to events, the most dramatic example of which is the poll tax. A political crisis broke in 1984 when property was revalued for rating purposes and the bills, particularly of small businessmen, soared. The Secretary of State George Younger's initial reaction was that with suitable explanations, the row would subside. The Scottish Conservative party chairman James (later Lord) Goold thought otherwise, as did William (later Lord) Whitelaw, who was shocked when a Conservative meeting in the west of Scotland heckled him. Both told Margaret Thatcher that something had to be done. A free market think-tank, the Adam Smith Institute, set up in the early 1980s by two St Andrews University graduates, Madsen Pirie and Eamon Butler, had in 1983 published a paper written by a friend, Douglas Mason, also a St Andrews alumnus and then a Kirkcaldy District Councillor. It advocated a poll tax, as did another pamphlet written by Michael Forsyth then the new MP for Stirling, who had been part of the same student politician circle at St Andrews. In the winter of 1984, the scheme was fed into the group assembled by junior Environment Minister William Waldegrave who had been instructed by Margaret Thatcher to examine alternatives to the rates. Poll tax became its main opinion. In March 1985, with the affluent Tory suburbs of Scotland's cities in full revolt, Thatcher resolved at a Chequers meeting to introduce the poll tax. As is recounted by journalist Hugo Young in his epic biography of

Thatcher, *One of Us*, from then until the Cabinet meeting of 9 January 1986, only Chancellor Nigel Lawson and his chief secretary John McGregor fought against it, with serious reservations being expressed by Trade and Industry Secretary Leon Brittan. As fate would have it, just before the Cabinet decision was taken, Michael Heseltine resigned as Defence Secretary in mid-meeting, George Younger achieved his lifetime ambition of the defence portfolio, and Malcolm Rifkind, nursing a heavy cold at home in Edinburgh, was telephoned and told he was promoted to the Cabinet as Scottish Secretary. While Rifkind and Younger knew that the poll tax was going to present political difficulties, they feared losing seats in Scotland even more. Thus both pressed ahead with fervent poll tax advocacy and secured a major anomaly in the legislative process, getting the legislation in place in Scotland a year ahead of England and Wales. In retrospect, this proved to be almost as big a mistake as the poll tax itself.

The poll tax was to become one of the great political disasters of all time. Its introduction in Scotland led to accusations that the country was being used as a 'test-bed' for unpopular legislation, and its inherent unfairness roused demonstrations and non-payment protests, led by the SNP, which made a Glasgow Militant Tendency member, Tommy Sheridan, into a national figure. Overall, though Scottish Office officials burned much midnight oil trying to make the poll-tax plans work, they failed, as they always suspected they would. From the start, the civil service assessment was that the poll tax was 'unstable', a damning term meaning that the policy was unlikely to survive for long, and certainly would not survive a change of government. In the event, the poll tax did not even survive the change of Conservative party leader from Margaret Thatcher to John Major.

The civil service itself can be a major source of policy, though ministers tend to be suspicious of the machine which serves them having ideas of its own. George Pottinger, who served three Scottish Secretaries as principal private secretary, headed the agriculture department and might have become permanent secretary had he not been involved in the John Poulson corruption scandal in the early 1970s, wrote in his book *The Secretaries of State for Scotland 1926–76* : 'On a change of government, incoming Conservatives are convinced that they have landed in a bed of New Statesman addicts, left-wing sociologists, theoretical planners or worse. New Labour ministers have no doubt they are surrounded by classicists and reactionary élites. The bureaucrats in turn remember how recently the Minister, when in Opposition, denounced their activities.'

However, policy which has been in the departmental pipeline can survive such suspicions. An example is the replacement of the O-Grade examination by the Standard Grade, as proposed by the Munn and Dunning Committee reports of 1977. Although the proposal was conceptually egalitarian, involving the idea of certification for all pupils rather than a few, Labour ministers did nothing about it. One of the first things that the new Conservative Scottish Education Minister Alex Fletcher did was to have lunch with the Scottish Examination Board, whose then chairman Farquhar Macintosh was extremely keen on Standard Grade. He told Fletcher: 'Minister, if you implement Standard Grade, you will go down in history.' Fletcher replied: 'Farquhar, I don't want to go down in history, I want to go up in history.' Standard Grade was duly implemented.

The Scottish Office and Downing Street

The story of the poll tax is a reminder that while the Scottish Secretary is sometimes referred to as 'Scotland's Prime Minister', it is the Prime Minister in Downing Street who wields the ultimate power. Margaret Thatcher was unusual among prime ministers in her close scrutiny of, some would say interference in, the workings of every department, not just the Scottish Office. For example, during and after the general election campaign of 1987, the Scottish Secretary Malcolm Rifkind stated that he had no intention, in the short term at least, of moving to permit parents to take their childrens' school out of local authority control, to give opt-out powers as they were known. But after Eastwood MP Allan Stewart challenged Strathclyde Regional Council's plans to close the popular Paisley Grammar School, Thatcher took great interest in Scottish education policy. Rifkind later maintained that so manifestly unfair was Strathclyde's attempts to close Paisley, that he became convinced that giving parents opt-out powers was the only way to prevent such unfairnesses. However, Thatcher's influence was evident. In March 1988, her office wrote to Rifkind's office: 'The Prime Minister is glad that your Secretary of State is now going to develop, for inclusion in next session's Scottish Education Bill, a scheme whereby schools in Scotland can opt out of local authority control.' Thatcher also took a keen interest in public appointments. Delays of two or three months in announcing appointments to public posts occurred while notes whirled out from Downing Street inquiring into the suitability of appointees, and particularly into their political views. Once an appointment proposed by the Scottish Secretary was vetoed.

However, the Scottish Secretary represents a part of the UK the politics of which are generally a mystery to non-Scots, and therefore he has more clout in the Cabinet than the junior status which is normally ascribed to him. Successive prime ministers have come to understand that the political authority in Scotland of the Scottish Secretary depended on him being perceived as Scotland's man in the Cabinet, and not the Cabinet's man in Scotland. Malcolm Rifkind, although he was a non-Thatcherite, was more likely to win a policy discussion with Margaret Thatcher than was, for example an Education Secretary. Thatcher, as she acknowledged privately, did not understand Scotland, but as a former Education Secretary, she knew all about education. The sense of mystery in London about Scotland is accentuated by the different local government, education and legal systems. This gives the Scottish Secretary ample opportunity to argue for the right to apply a policy differently in Scotland, or even not to apply it at all. During Malcolm Rifkind's period as Scottish Secretary, he refused to privatize the Scottish water supply industry, as it was part of local government in Scotland and not run by free-standing boards as in England. Conversely, during discussions on electricity privatization, Thatcher assumed that Rifkind would not want to privatize the North of Scotland Hydro Electric Board, because of the social obligations written into its founding charter giving it a development role in the Highlands beyond a remit just to supply electricity. Much to her surprise, Rifkind declared he saw no reason why it should not be privatized, and it was. This rather ill-defined but important power wielded by the Scottish Secretary—essentially successive Labour and Conservative Scottish Secretaries threaten their Cabinet colleagues with tides of nationalism and other uncontrollable political forces—is one reason why public spending in Scotland on services like health, education, housing etc, was in 1990 some 23 per cent higher on a per capita basis. But despite the opportunity for different policy and practices the Scottish Office is a part of the UK government, and normality, as far as Whitehall is concerned, is when everything operates on the same basis thoughout the UK. As a general rule, so long as the policy objective is the same, the delivery mechanisms can be quite different north and south of the border. However, as another general rule, the Scottish Office, when viewed from Whitehall, looks like an anomaly. Sir William Kerr Fraser, former permanent under secretary and now Principal of Glasgow University, described what happens if the Scottish Office objects to an idea proposed by a Whitehall department, because, for example, it might have a bad effect on sparsely populated areas: 'Sitting in Whitehall, you may go to your minister and urge him not to let the Scottish tail wag the English dog. In nearly three decades at the Scottish Office, I have never heard this phrase used, but I have seen the argument deployed quite often.' The converse, according to Fraser, would be Whitehall objecting to proposals by the Scottish Office, as it might cause their minister to be embarrassed by questions in the House of Commons as to why he was not following the Scottish course of action. Annoyance rather than embarrassment is sometimes felt with some other Scottish Office stances. Considerable irritation is often felt in the Ministry of Defence, for example, when they propose shutting a military installation in Scotland. Instead of having just a few MPs and a couple of local councils lobbying them as in England, they can find another government department complete with a fully-armed Cabinet minister being brought to bear on them.

More sustained pressure for conformity comes from the Treasury, which takes every opportunity it can to try and eat into the Scottish Office spending block. This block is 95 per cent determined by the fixed Barnett formula, named after the Labour chief secretary to the Treasury, Joel Barnett, who introduced it in 1978 in preparation for a Scottish Assembly. The division of public spending on Government functions managed on a territorial basis by the Scottish, Welsh and comparable Whitehall departments, for example, health, education and housing, is done on the basis that England receives 85 per cent, Scotland 10 per cent, and Wales 5 per cent of the budgets ear-marked for these functions. The formula is based on 1977 population estimates. The Scottish Secretary has the autonomy of being able to switch spending around within the block. For example, during the 1980s the proportion of Scottish Office budget spent on housing fell, and that spent on health rose, but these were Scottish decisions, and not dictated by changes in spending implemented in England.

Different Scottish practices can cause difficulty. For example, water and sewerage services in England and Wales are provided by private companies. But in Scotland, water and sewerage is a local authority service, and publicly financed. Treasury ministers, reflecting a constant view of their officials that the Scottish Office is grossly over-funded, will argue against any cross-border policy differential that might create new anomalies. Equally Scottish Office ministers are reluctant to embark on any new policy that might cause them further difficulties with the Treasury. An example was the proposal in 1985 by the Scottish Tertiary Education Advisory Committee, that the control of Scottish universities finance should be shifted from Department of Education and Science to the Scottish Office. One of the reasons ministers did not act on that recommendation was that the Scottish four-year degree was a more expensive proposition than the English-style three-year degree, and the Treasury might not provide adequate funding through the Scottish Office.

A hidden power in Scotland?

This account of the Scottish Office as slightly removed from the rest of Whitehall provides a focus on an interesting question: Do Scottish civil servants have their own objectives regardless of whichever party is in government? The answer is almost certainly 'yes'. The objective is, however, not political but structural: to secure the transfer of more functions from Whitehall to Scotland. The pattern for this objective was set during the wartime administration of Tom Johnston, a fascinatingly strong character whose influence in securing more powers for the Scottish Office can still be felt. For instance, the Emergency Hospital Service run in Scotland during the war ensured that when the National Health Service was set up, the Scottish Office was responsible for services in Scotland. These were important decisions, demonstrating firstly Johnston's own strength, and secondly, the confidence of the Scottish Office that it could handle these functions. Since then, securing the administrative devolution from London to Edinburgh of government functions has become a Scottish Office corporate objective. In Scotland, such moves may make perfect sense, but in Whitehall, they look like predatory moves to be resisted. During the abortive efforts of the 1974–79 Labour Government to set up a Scottish Assembly, parallel attempts to move functions north were being made. To the men from the Edinburgh ministry, the battles with Whitehall were great fun. 'We had punch-ups all over the place,' recalled one ministry man. But to the men from Whitehall, this was an extremely serious business. A civil servant recalled that there had been a meeting at the Ministry of Agriculture, Fisheries and Food where a discussion on the Scottish Office becoming responsible for animal health matters dragged on. Eventually a weary Scottish Office official remarked that as the Scottish Secretary was responsible for human health, perhaps he could be trusted with animal health. 'Oh no, this is much more important,' said an MAFF official.

As a general rule, a policy objective is most likely to be swiftly achieved and be 'stable' if three conditions are met. One is that the political objective should meet administrative objectives of efficiency, which in the case of a function transfer to Scotland carries the implication that Scottish administration is more efficient than administration from London. A second is that it should have a degree of backing from what is broadly termed the Scottish lobby, ie the affected interest groups. A third is that it must meet with agreement in Whitehall. Occasionally, this third condition can become the tail which wags the dog. A good example of how political and administrative priorities, when matched with the views of interest groups, can come together and find a window of opportunity is the process whereby the Scottish Natural Heritage agency came to fruition in 1992. Scottish Office officials had long held the view that Scottish nature conservation ought to be handled in Scotland. Administratively, Scotland had two sides of a triangle: the Scottish Secretary as the Planning Minister, and the Countryside Commission for Scotland based in Perth and charged with countryside development responsibilities. The third side was the Nature Conservancy Council (NCC) charged with the scientific conservation of wildlife, but based in Peterborough and responsible to the Secretary of State for the Environment.

After the 1987 general election, the Scottish Secretary Malcolm Rifkind sounded out opinion on the creation of a new countryside agency that would bring everything under one roof, consulting informally both existing members of the Countryside Commission, and previous members such as Sir David Nickson, who had been Countryside Commission chairman 1983–85. Opinion, Rifkind decided, was favourable. So also was Lord Sanderson of Bowden, a Borders businessman and a senior Conservative party office-bearer who was ennobled and appointed Scottish Office Minister for the Highlands and Islands in 1987. He became aware of seething discontent over the actions of the NCC. One particular event that enraged him was a peremptory order from the NCC cutting the number of rooks that could be shot in the Western Isles. NCC staff were viewed by farmers, according to a report in *The Scotsman*, to be 'girls with science degrees straight out of English universities determined to show us peasants how to look after the land.' Lord Sanderson shared an office at Westminster with the Earl of Caithness, a minister at the Department of the Environment, and his support for breaking up the NCC along territorial lines was secured. With Rifkind's backing, Sanderson and Scottish Office officials trudged round Whitehall securing agreement from other departments such as the Agriculture Ministry. Sanderson's clinching argument with other ministers was that the move had close to unanimous support in Scotland at a time when green issues were well to the fore and that 'even *The Scotsman* will be in favour of this, because it is devolution'.

The NCC soon heard all about the proposal, and fought what Scottish Office officials consider was probably the most biased campaign ever put on by a public body. Even the Royal Society for the Protection of Birds was enlisted in the NCC propaganda war. But the decisive move came when Nicholas Ridley, Environment Secretary from 1986 until July 1989, discovered his department's sole responsibility north of the border was for nature conservation and that his budget was going to have to fork out large sums to conserve the Flow Country in Caithness from blanket afforestation. He thought the Scottish Office ought to be paying. Ridley, as is made plain in his book *My Style of Government*, detested the NCC. Seizing the opportunity, the Scottish Office said it would pay, but only if it got control of nature conservation.

For the civil servants, it was a classic window of opportunity to achieve something that they had had on the back burner for more than a decade. Time, chance and circumstance played its part: if the proposal had come in front of non-Thatcherite conservation-minded Chris Patten, Ridley's successor as Environment Secretary, instead of the Thatcherite, supposedly anti-conservation and anti-Scotland Ridley, then the most significant step forward for conservation in Scotland for many a year might not have happened. But for the politicians, it was a political victory, Ridley getting rid of an expense on his department, Sanderson solving something irritating the voters, and Rifkind having a new achievement to his credit. The day after the plans for the Scottish Natural Heritage agency were announced, Rifkind sat on the Edinburgh to London shuttle and read an editorial in *The Scotsman* attacking the proposals as liable to give landowners too much power over conservation. He burst out laughing.

The Scottish Secretary and his ministers have more policy autonomy, and hence power than is commonly believed. That power is circumscribed by the strategic authority over Scottish affairs exercised by the Prime Minister and Cabinet ministers acting either individually or collectively. But Scottish Office civil servants also have considerable influence, by virtue of being the permanent administration of Scotland and an administration which retains a continuity of objectives from one government to the next. A major objective is to increase the responsibilities of the Scottish Office, thereby increasing the power of the Scottish Secretary and making his department all the more interesting a place in which to work. Memories of the battles waged to win more functions are firmly embedded in Scottish Office thinking. Thus it is intriguing to note that during the 1987–92 Conservative Government, when opposition to political devolution became staunchest, the Scottish Office won some of its biggest devolution prizes. In the same way as powers over nature conservation was won with the creation of a new agency, so the creation of Scottish Homes moved responsibility for financing housing associations and their low-rent housing from the UK-wide Housing Corporation to Scotland. The creation of Scottish Enterprise wrested control of industrial training away from the Sheffield-based Training Agency.

The Scottish Office also gained control of the universities, the biggest prize of the lot though this was largely the incidental by-product of decisions to reorganize higher education finance in England and Wales. That the amount of administrative devolution increased markedly during this period, of anti-devolution, allegedly centralizing Government, makes a persuasive case for the proposition that Scottish Office civil servants are a hidden power in Scotland.

Permanent Under-Secretaries of State since 1885
(Permanent Under-Secretaries before 1926)

1885	Sir Francis R Sandford (later Lord Sandford)
1888	R W Cochhran-Patrick
1892	Col Sir Colin Scott Moncrieff
1902	Sir Reginald Macleod
1909	Sir James M Dodds
1921	Sir John Lamb
1933	Sir John Jeffrey
1937	John E Highton
1937	Sir Horace P Hamilton
1946	Sir David Milne
1959	Sir William Murrie
1964	Sir Douglas Haddow
1973	Sir Nicholas Morrison
1978	Sir William Kerr Fraser
1988	Sir Russell Hillhouse

Secretaries for Scotland, and Secretaries of State for Scotland, since 1885

Secretary for Scotland

1885 The Duke of Richmond and Gordon (Conservative)
1886 George Trevelyan (later Sir George Trevelyan) (Liberal)
1886 The Earl of Dalhousie (Liberal)
1886 Arthur J Balfour (later the Earl of Balfour) (Conservative)
1887 The Marquess of Lothian (Conservative)
1892 Sir George Trevelyan (again) (Liberal)
1895 Lord Balfour of Burleigh (Conservative)
1903 A Graham Murray (later Lord Dunedin) (Conservative)
1905 The Marquess of Linlithgow (Conservative)
1905 John Sinclair (later Lord Pentland) (Liberal)
1912 T Mackinnon Wood (Liberal)
1916 H Tennant (Coalition)
1916 R Munro (later Lord Alness) (Coalition)
1922 Viscount Novar (Conservative)
1924 William Adamson (Labour)
1924 Sir John Gilmour (Conservative)

Secretary of State for Scotland

1926 Sir John Gilmour (Conservative)
1929 William Adamson (again) (Labour)
1931 Sir Archibald Sinclair (later Lord Thurso) (National Government)
1932 Sir Godfrey Collins (National Government)
1936 Walter Elliot (National Government)
1938 John Colville (later Lord Clydesmuir) (National Government)
1940 Ernest Brown (Coalition)
1941 Tom Johnston (Coalition)
1945 The Earl of Rosebery (Caretaker Government)
1945 Joseph Westwood (Labour)
1947 Arthur Woodburn (Labour)
1950 Hector McNeil (Labour)
1951 James Stuart (later Viscount Stuart of Findhorn) (Conservative)
1957 John Maclay (later Viscount Muirshiel)
1962 Michael Noble (later Lord Glenkinglass (Conservative)
1964 William Ross (Labour)
1970 Gordon Campbell (later Lord Campbell of Croy) (Conservative)
1974 William Ross (later Lord Ross of Marnock) (Labour)
1976 Bruce Millan (Labour)
1979 George Younger (Conservative)
1986 Malcolm Rifkind (Conservative)
1990 Ian Lang (Conservative)

15

Politics

Peter Jones

Part 1   Introduction

The account so far given of the distinctively Scottish form of government administration, the peculiarities of the policy-making process, and the different party structure, is still inadequate in explaining what gives Scottish politics its distinctive flavour. Neither does it explain why in the post-war period there have been two periods when it seemed possible that Scotland could break away from the rest of the UK. This possibility, surely, is a remarkable thing. After all, there has been neither totalitarian oppression, nor the visible prosperity gulf which are the classic preconditions for such a revolutionary upheaval. If anything mystifies visitors to Scotland, it is this apparent desire for separation. The blunt truth is that despite the longevity of the Union of 1707 between Scotland and England, there is still a border running from Carlisle to Berwick. Signs indicating it may be glimpsed only briefly from a speeding car or train, but it is there nonetheless, and it has as real an effect as, say, the 49th parallel between the USA and Canada. The big problem has been that the British electoral system pretends that the border does not exist.

This pretence creates a massive anomaly. The opponents of a devolved Scottish Assembly, or a home rule Scottish parliament, within the UK, have claimed that such an institution would create intolerable anomalies and pressures that would eventually tear the Union apart. But there was an anomaly already putting tremendous strain on the Union. It is this: that the administration of all the government functions which have a major impact on people's lives are defined by the Scottish–English border; that much political rhetoric by which people are persuaded to vote for this or that political party is defined by the same border; but the mechanism by which control of those government institutions is gained fails to recognize it. Thus if the different political rhetoric deployed in Scotland inspires voters to vote for one political party, that party gains no prizes unless it has secured victory elsewhere in the UK.

This matters not at all if the party system is able to transcend the border, by and large since 1707, the party system has done so. Apart from periods such as during the rise of the Labour Party and eclipse of the Liberal Party in the 1920s, the history of British politics has been that of two parties, under a variety of names, competing for electoral support throughout the UK. Two conditions have produced constitutional stability: first that the party winning power has always enjoyed support throughout the UK, and secondly that both parties have had broadly equal chances of gaining power.

On this analysis, it is the party system which underwrites the constitution. It follows that if the party system is threatened with breakdown or indeed does break down in some way, then constitutional stability is undermined. This is exactly what happened in the late 1970s and again in the late 1980s. After the second 1974 general election, the SNP had surged to 30 per cent of the vote, winning a quite unprecedented 11 parliamentary seats. The Conservatives were reduced to a post-war low of 16 seats, and the SNP were second in 35 of Labour's 41 seats, a clear threat to the two-party hegemony. Politicians in both of the two major parties, ranging from the young Conservative MP for Edinburgh Pentlands, Malcolm Rifkind, to a rising star of Labour's Scottish executive, Gordon Brown, concluded that the Union between Scotland and England was under threat. So was born the series of events leading up to the 1979 devolution referendum as both parties struggled to find a halfway-house solution that would head off the nationalist threat. The referendum itself was an anticlimax. On 1 March, 1979, just under two-thirds of the Scottish electorate turned out to vote yes or no to the Scottish Assembly offered in the Scotland Act which James Callaghan's Government had struggled to get through Parliament. A total of 1 230 937 people voted 'Yes', 51.6 per cent, 1 153 502 voted 'No', 48.4 per cent. A majority surely? Yes, but a peculiar rule had been imposed by parliamentary devolution opponents, led by George Cunningham, the Labour MP for Islington South, that 40 per cent of the total electorate had to vote 'Yes' before the legislation could be implemented. Under this rule, once an 'adjustment' had been made to the electoral roll so that those who had died since the roll was compiled were not included, 32.9 per cent voted 'Yes', 30.8 per cent 'No', and 36.3 per cent did not vote. Opinion polls, incidentally, throughout 1978 had shown that 70 per cent of Scottish voters backed devolution.

After the 1987 election, a different problem occurred. There was no great nationalist surge, the SNP share of the vote rose only marginally from 12 to 14 per cent. But the Conservatives fell to a new post-war record low, losing 11 seats and retaining only 10. Never in modern times had the governing party so few seats in Scotland. The beneficiary was the Labour Party. Although it had previously achieved more than the 42 per cent of the vote it did in the 1987 election, the 50 seats produced by that vote was a modern record for any party. However Labour's problem was that in the UK it was as far away from achieving power as ever, facing a Conservative Government with a majority of 101. That third defeat in a row meant that Labour stood exposed as increasingly unlikely to win power and have a chance of translating Scottish aspirations into realities. Equally the Conservatives were exposed as having a narrow political base, bringing into question their right and ability to govern Scotland. These wounds in the constitutional body fabric caused seeping doubt and confusion throughout the 1987–92 parliament. Outwardly, much seemed to be normal, only the spasmodic shaking as in the November 1987 SNP Govan by-election victory, or the November 1991 Liberal Democrat Kincardine and Deeside by-election, sounded the alert that something was wrong underneath.

Nationalism

It is generally assumed that nationalism only appears at these periods of stress and that the 1970s brought the nationalist element into Scottish politics in a big way for the first time. It is true only if you define nationalism with a capital 'N', equating nationalism with the SNP and the political aim of achieving a nation state with all the trappings that go with such a status. But as the writer Tom Nairn has pointed out, there is a small 'n' nationalism. In political terms that means a recognition that Scotland is a nation within the UK, but does not require separate nation status, only different and appropriate treatment within the UK. Small 'n' nationalism has existed since, and to an arguable degree before, the agitation which led to the foundation of the Scottish Office in 1885. It has gradually permeated Scottish politics more and more deeply ever since. The founder of the Labour Party, Keir Hardie, wrote of his support for Home Rule for Scotland in his election address for the Mid Lanark by-election of 1888, when, as the first Labour candidate at any election in Britain, he got 617 votes. His views, like those of many others at the time, were largely formed by the more pressing problem of Irish Home Rule. William Gladstone, in his famous Midlothian campaign of 1879, produced the idea of 'Home Rule all round' for Ireland, Scotland, Wales and England, the basis of the present-day Liberal Democrat aim of a federal UK. Scottish Home Rule motions and bills were introduced nine times in the House of Commons between 1894 and 1914.

The creation of the Irish Republic after the 1918 general election, though it represented a massive failure of the UK, revealingly removed most of the political impetus behind 'Home Rule all round'. Despite the political agitation, the reality of pre-1914 Scotland was more of an enthusiastic participant in the great enterprise of the British Empire. Scottish capital poured into cattle-ranching and railway-building in North America. As capitalism and socialism became the twin poles around which politics in Scotland, as elsewhere, revolved, nationalism became a fringe activity. Though in 1928 the National Party of Scotland was formed, and the Scottish Party in 1932, both to amalgamate in 1934 into the Scottish National Party, nationalism then had a cultural emphasis. It was heavily linked with the literary renaissance of the time. The founding membership of the National Party included the poet Hugh MacDiarmid, and novelists Compton Mackenzie and Eric Linklater. But by that time the politics of class was dominant, and the radical route to emancipation of people was seen in terms of international solidarity of the working classes rather than rebirth of an ancient nation state.

Unionism

Rather more significant was the formation of the Unionist Party. During the Liberal schism over Irish Home Rule, the Conservatives in Scotland benefited greatly from their alliance with the Liberal Unionists. The two parties merged in 1912 to become the Scottish Unionist Association. Although modern political reference books give the Scottish Conservatives an unbroken lineage stretching back into the 19th century, they campaigned as Unionists in Scotland from 1912 until the 1966 election.

By and large, Unionism was a successful ideology, and its abandonment, it can be argued with hindsight, a major mistake which has contributed to the decline of Conservatism in Scotland. It was interesting that in its hour of greatest crisis just before the 1992 election, the Conservatives attempted to reclaim the Unionist title and present it as their major raison d'être. But such a move was never going to succeed as it did in the 1955 election when the Unionists secured 50.1 per cent of the popular vote, the only party to get over half the votes, winning 36 out of 71 seats. Labour won 34 seats and the nearly extinct Liberal Party clung on with one seat thanks to a future leader, Jo Grimond, retaining the Orkney and Shetland seat he won in 1950. In the 1950s, the Unionists managed what from the vantage point of the 1990s seems an impossible trick. They combined Unionism with nationalism. It was achieved by campaigning against nationalization of steel and other major companies on the grounds that this was removing control of Scottish industry from Scotland into the hands of faceless bureaucrats in Whitehall. A speech by Winston Churchill in Edinburgh in 1950 encapsulated the appeal: 'The principle of centralization of government in Whitehall and Westminster is emphasised in a manner not hitherto experienced or contemplated in the Act of Union. The supervision, interference and control in the ordinary details of Scottish life and business by the Parliament at Westminster has not hitherto been foreseen, and I frankly admit that it raises new issues between the two nations. I do not therefore wonder that the question of Scottish home rule and all this movement of Scottish nationalism has gained in step with the growth of socialist authority and ambitions in England.'

The movement of nationalism Churchill was referring to was that led by the charismatic ('King') John MacCormick, a lawyer who had broken with the SNP after he lost control of it in 1942 to the pacifist lecturer Douglas Young. MacCormick believed in the SNP as a movement rather than a party, a tool by which a consensus for home rule could be made. He formed an organization with just such an aim, the Scottish Convention, which in 1947 succeeded in gathering in a 'national assembly' some 600 representatives of churches, local authorities, trade unions, chambers of commerce, and others. It emphatically endorsed home rule, but its assaults on London government made the Labour Party, then in government, hostile. A third meeting of the Assembly in 1949 commenced the gathering of what eventually amounted to 2 million signatures on a National Covenant for Home Rule, an exciting event but which made no impact on the political system.

Unionism, however, having captured the small 'n' nationalist agenda went from strength to strength. The Unionist message chimed well with the broader 'One Nation' message of the Conservative Party under Churchill, Eden and Macmillan. The 1955 *Yearbook* of the Scottish Unionist Association, wherein one searches in vain for the word Conservative, emphasized: 'It is therefore wrong to describe the Unionist Party as being on the Right in the political scale. It is not "reactionary". It is not out to "exploit". Rather it is on the Middle Road, between the two extremes—the extremes of laissez-faire and Socialism.' Unionism also recognized Scottish sensitivities by keeping the constitutional question under constant review. In 1953, a Royal Commission chaired by the Earl of Balfour was set up to examine the system of administrative devolution. It proposed moving responsibility for roads and bridges to the Scottish Office, a move which was accepted and resulted in the go-ahead for the Forth Road Bridge. It also proposed that the Scottish Secretary should take over from the Lord Chancellor responsibility for appointing justices of the peace, and unsuccessfully proposed transfer of responsibility for animal health. Unionism clearly did not have the integrationist meaning it was to take on in later decades.

The Scottish political establishment learned an important lesson in the 1940s and 1950s; that by asserting a powerful Scottish identity and coupling it with express requirements, major concessions and benefits could be wrung from the UK political system. The results have been spectacular. They have included major 'one-offs' such as campaigns by Scottish Secretaries to prevent industrial closures: Willie Ross was instrumental in persuading the Labour Government to save the Chrysler car factory at Linwood in 1975, just as George Younger's wielding of a resignation threat in 1984 kept the Ravenscraig steel works open. Though analysts argue about it, there is at least a good case for saying that Scottish political muscle in the system is responsible for the greater per capita public spending on services like education and health in Scotland compared to England and Wales. The perceived need for Scotland to be represented at all levels of the political system often overrode party politics. An anecdote which makes the point neatly, concerns the senior Strathclyde Labour councillor, Dr Malcolm Green. He was summoned to the Scottish Office in 1983 by the Conservative Education and Industry Minister Alex Fletcher. Fletcher pressed a reluctant Green to take up one of two local authority positions on the UK board of the Manpower Services Commission. Fletcher made it clear to him that Scotland, on a population basis, was going to be over-represented on the board and therefore someone with Green's qualifications in educational matters was needed. 'If we don't have somebody of suitable stature, questions will be asked by No. 10 as to whether Scotland ought to have this seat,' Fletcher told him.

Part 2   Parties and their People

Since the 1970s, politics in Scotland has been a bruising four-party struggle within an electoral system made for two parties. There has been, as a result, much carnage. Government ministers, after years of toil at the dispatch box, have been unceremoniously slung out by voters such as those of Moray and Nairn who in February 1974 decided they did not want the services of the Tory Scottish Secretary Gordon Campbell any more and hired themselves a Glasgow lawyer instead, Nationalist Winnie Ewing. This tough environment means that the party, either as a supportive network for a vulnerable MP, or as the muscle behind an attacking campaign, is a key political organ. Outside election times, its members are the nerve endings from which flow the signals telling the leaders whether they are up or down in the public estimation.

The Scottish Conservative Party

Commentators are customarily scathing about the Scottish Conservatives as a political party. After all, the ordinary Tory member has no say in policy, the debates at its conferences are by and large meaningless, and as Douglas Hurd once remarked when accompanying Edward Heath to the Scottish conference, the party does not seem to have politicians, it has office-bearers instead. But the Scottish Conservatives are very much a political party, and unashamedly a leadership-driven party. For example, the Scottish Secretary Ian Lang, speaking at the 1991 Scottish conference, praised Prime Minister John Major as 'putting his stamp upon our party'. It expects to be led from the top. As long as there is a strong lead, the membership is content to applaud. The only real crime that a leader can commit is to fail to lead, and that is why the Conservatives dispose of leaders with complete ruthlessness. It is also a social organization. Again it is customary for commentators to be scornful of the ladies in hats at the daffodil teas. In reality these social units form foundations of a social network that stretches up to the leader of the party. Through that social network runs gossip, occasionally intelligence from the grass-roots, sometimes also the route to promotion in the party. Being a social organization means that personal relationships are usually much more important than political relationships. The ability to sit down at dinner with someone and converse amicably is usually more important in the long term than being on the same political wavelength. This background explains how some appointments to the party's rather curious structures come to be made. The political leadership of the party in Scotland rests with the Scottish Secretary (shadow if in opposition). But there is another leading post, that of party chairman, also appointed by the UK party leader. The party chairman supervises the professional staff working at headquarters and as constituency agents, attends many dinners and other functions in the constituencies, and keeps the party leader informed of party opinion. Margaret Thatcher's appointments from 1975 when she became leader provide an interesting insight. Her first chairman was the West Aberdeenshire MP Russell Fairgrieve (later Sir Russell). In 1977 when the Tories split over devolution, she accepted the resignation from the front benches of MPs Alick Buchanan-Smith and Malcolm Rifkind, but refused Fairgrieve's resignation though he was, like the two MPs, pro-devolution. She had come to trust Fairgrieve's reporting of party opinion, and wanted him as a counter-balance to the anti-devolutionary Teddy Taylor, the shadow Scottish Secretary. In 1980, when she came to replace Fairgrieve, she inquired among the party hierarchy about the idea of appointing one James Goold. Some had difficulty placing him, or knowing why Thatcher had alighted on him, until it was recalled that Thatcher was very friendly with Betty Harvie Anderson, the East Renfrewshire MP, and that Goold was her constituency chairman. The grandees advised that Goold was far too inexperienced, so she insisted he be given a post where he could get experience of the party at higher altitudes. Edinburgh South MP Michael Ancram got the chairmanship, but three years later Thatcher replaced him with Goold, knighting and then ennobling him during his six years tenure. Interestingly, Mrs Harvie Anderson's successor as MP, Allan Stewart, was the first of the 1979 intake of Scottish MPs to be promoted to ministerial office.

One of Lord Goold's administrative innovations after the 1987 general election, apart from making defeated minister John (now Lord) MacKay a high profile chief executive to replace the low-profile director Bill Henderson and increasing the research and campaign staff at headquarters, was to bring back the businessmen. Up to the early 1980s, businessmen had been part and parcel of the party structures, one towering example being the Glasgow industrialist Hugh Stenhouse, party treasurer in the 1960s. According to those involved at that time, business finance was never crucial to Conservative operations in Scotland, until Goold decided to end the subsidy arrangements from party headquarters in Smith Square, London. In a dose of internal Thatcherism, the Scottish Tories were made financially free-standing. Business finance became crucial, and to secure it, Goold set up a Scottish Business Group, whose policy advice function was viewed as less important than fund-raising. It was chaired by James Gulliver, then chairman of the foodstore-based Argyll Group. It included some of the new entrepreneurs of the Thatcherite years, such as property developer and Hearts Football Club chairman Wallace Mercer, and some business establishment elements, like the Edinburgh financier Angus Grossart. By 1991, it was much the most important source of party finance.

Strangely paradoxical though it may seem, the Conservatives are probably numerically strongest of all the parties; a 1990 survey of magazine readers estimated there to be 43 000 members, almost certainly an exaggeration as a number of members complained of receiving multiple copies, and 35 000 may be more realistic. However, the membership is often inactive: more than half were over the age of 65 according to the same survey, and half of the constituency associations were similarly said to be moribund. The grass-roots, or, in Conservative terminology, voluntary side of the party, is called the Scottish Conservative and Unionist Association (SCUA), the body densely populated with all the office-bearers at which Douglas Hurd marvelled. The constituency associations are grouped into three areas—Northern, Central and Southern, and West of Scotland—each having an area council. All the associations also send their chairmen and secretaries to the quarterly meetings of the SCUA executive council, as do the other SCUA bodies like the Young Conservatives, or Conservative Women, or the Society of Conservative Lawyers. The office-bearers of all these bodies, and there must be about 500 in total, and more particularly the 150 office-bearers or so who attend the SCUA executive council are, effectively, the party. For it is these people, plus the parliamentary candidates, who are consulted at moments of crisis like leadership elections. Heading this organization is the SCUA president, two vice-presidents, two secretaries, and one treasurer, who are, in a brave outbreak of internal Conservative democracy, all elected. For years, elections to the SCUA presidency operated on a Buggins' turn principle of area council chairmen becoming vice-presidents, and then president, until something of a revolution occurred in 1989. In the previous year's district council elections, the Conservatives hit another record low, winning only three councils out of 53, or 162 seats out of 1 154. When the then SCUA president, the amiable solicitor James Highgate, came to retire, a wave of party energy bore the popular Glasgow lawyer-entrepreneur Ross Harper past the Buggins' turn candidates and into the presidency. But in the accident-prone fashion which characterized the Scottish Tories after 1987, Harper found his private life the subject of tabloid newspaper headlines just six months later, and he was forced to quit his political career in September 1989. Again eschewing the Buggins' turn rule, SCUA elected former Strathkelvin and Bearsden MP Michael Hirst in his place.

Despite its tendency to demand leadership, SCUA is jealous of its autonomy. Paid officials from party headquarters occasionally tell ruefully of being asked to leave SCUA meetings. In 1990, the party chairman called the press conference to announce the agenda for the party conference, causing no end of internal fuss, as it is the conference of the SCUA to which the party chairman is invited. The relationship between SCUA president, chairman, and the (shadow) Scottish Secretary is usually harmonious, though it became seriously disrupted when Margaret Thatcher made another of her favourites, Michael Forsyth, chairman in 1988, again using his Thatcherite zeal to balance, even to invigilate, the liberalish tendencies of Scottish Secretary Malcolm Rifkind. Aware that was the public impression, Rifkind instructed his closest colleagues to emphasize both in public and in private, the warmth of his regard for Forsyth, who did much the same. The unwritten concordat was broken, mostly by Forsyth's over-zealous supporters. After news broke at the 1990 Scottish conference in Aberdeen that right-wing MPs, principally Tayside North MP Bill Walker, had considered the merits of plotting to replace Rifkind as Scottish Secretary by Michael Forsyth, and then as Walker and two other right-wing MPs, Sir Nicholas Fairbairn and Allan Stewart, threatened a few months later to destroy in committee a Law Reform Bill, Rifkind reluctantly decided he was being undermined by Forsyth. Although Forsyth took the view it was his job as party chairman to mediate between the MPs and the Scottish Secretary, Rifkind believed Forsyth's job was to support him and the Government's legislation. During a dark moment, Rifkind called in his closest political friends, ministers Ian Lang and Lord Sanderson. That Forsyth had to go from the chairmanship was their succinct advice. Rifkind concurred, particularly alarmed at the sundering of the Scottish party as people took up pro and anti positions on both men. Three months later, though she hated doing it, and raged privately at Rifkind for it, Thatcher accepted Forsyth's resignation from the chairmanship, thus demonstrating just how powerful a Tory Scottish Secretary can be.

The Labour Party in Scotland

Labour's parliamentary team has always enjoyed a better relationship with the party's elected Scottish executive committee than their counterparts have done at UK national level. In government, Scottish Secretaries Willie Ross and Bruce Millan regularly attended the monthly meetings, as Donald Dewar has done since he became shadow Scottish Secretary in 1983. Ross particularly dominated the executive. Dewar, though often excoriated by radicals for his caution, achieved respect for his hard work in leading the development of Labour's policy from the Scottish Assembly plans as they were abandoned in 1979 to the more radical and stronger Scottish parliament proposals in the 1992 manifesto.

Labour's Scottish executive is much more influenced by the constituency activists than is the national executive committee at UK level. The MPs have only two votes on the executive, one being that of the parliamentary spokesman, the official title of the (shadow) Scottish Secretary, as Dewar was always careful to point out to journalists who accused him of being Labour's Scottish leader. The trade unions have 12 seats, and tend to be unsympathetic to radicalism. Constituency parties have 10 seats and elect to fill them, not MPs, but the more energetic and radical activists who have managed to make a mark outside their own constituencies. Internal Labour factional organization is essential in determining who wins election to the executive. In the early 1980s the soft-left Labour Co-ordinating Committee (LCC) was so well organized that unless an activist had manoeuvered on to the LCC 'slate' there was little chance of election. By the 1990s, LCC strength had waned, and that of a new pressure group, Scottish Labour Action, had waxed. Scottish Labour Action, however, brandishes a form of nationalism which is not wholly acceptable to much of the Labour Party, and it has failed to reach the commanding position which the LCC held. The women's section of the executive, with five seats, provides another focus for grass-roots activism, and a much-needed route into the higher levels of the party for women. For all that the rhetoric of feminism permeated Labour's policies in the 1980s, the plums of political life such as parliamentary nominations in safe seats stayed out of reach to most Labour women as Labour's culture remained muscular and male-orientated.

Membership of Labour's constituency parties was estimated by Labour officials in 1989 at 25 000, probably a fairly realistic estimate as most constituency party memberships fall into the 200–700 range. Irrespective of size, there will usually be only about 50 active members who turn up to meetings and for work at elections. It made Labour constituency parties vulnerable to influence and takeover by entryist groups like the Militant Tendency, but though Militant came close to securing the parliamentary nominations in Glasgow Pollok and Glasgow Provan before the 1987 election, the local Labour establishments managed to beat them off. Militant's influence waned as Keir Hardie House directed a sustained effort to purge known Militants from Labour membership. Militant believed that their organization of people into Anti-Poll Tax groups aimed at non-payment of the tax would boost their membership. Indeed it did, especially in the housing schemes of Glasgow, but it also made Militant members easier to identify.

The powerbase of the Labour Party has always been the trade unions. Their membership provides not just an important source of party revenue, but a resource of people invaluable at election times, and of course, the block vote at party conferences. In the 1960s and 1970s the Transport and General Workers Union (TGWU), the General and Municipal Workers Union (GMWU), and the Amalgamated Engineering Union (AEU) under their top officials, Raymond MacDonald, Alec Donnet (who exercised such tight control the GMWU was often referred to as Donnet's union) and Alec Ferry, formed a crucial troika. The pivotal link with the Labour Party was through the party's Scottish organizer, a post held by Peter Allison 1971–5, Jimmy McGrandle 1975–7 and Jimmy Allison (no relation to Peter) 1977–91, the last being undoubtedly the most formidable and powerful manager Labour has had in Scotland. From Paisley where he was briefly a councillor, he became Glasgow party organizer in 1971 and assistant Scottish organizer in 1974. A small wiry man with a sharp mind and sharper tongue, he generated mixed emotions but always respect, particularly after he master-minded Donald Dewar's by-election victory in Glasgow Garscadden in 1978, a win which reversed the 1970s Nationalist tide. Though he maintained a large network of party contacts, through which he was in close contact with the party's mood, none were more important than the trade union barons. With the big three controlling about half the votes, when their support was secured, particularly that of the TGWU and the GMWU (now GMB), the rest would fall into line. In September 1974, when the National Executive Committee in London pressurized the Scottish executive into reversing the Scottish party's anti-devolution line, a special conference of a reluctant, grudging party convened in the Co-op Halls, Dalintober Street,

Glasgow. It was an all-day affair but by 11 am, after the TGWU and GMWU had spoken in favour of devolution, Jimmy Allison recalls: 'When I heard Gavin Laird of the engineers speak in favour, I turned to an MP and said—well that's it, we might as well chuck it now.' Allison, and his assistants Joe Hill and Gerald O'Brien were still adeptly fixing things in 1989. At the Scottish conference in Inverness, the activist-dominated Scottish executive put up four policy statements all of which were embarrassing to the leadership. All got voted down.

The unions remain important, but the focus of power has shifted since the 1970s, and will shift again in the 1990s with union mergers, and also if the Labour Party moves to reduce the size of the block vote. At the TGWU Raymond MacDonald was followed by Hugh Wyper, who, despite the fact that he was a member of the Communist Party, exercised firm and pragmatic control over how his delegation voted at conference. He was followed as regional secretary by David Shoat, whose control of the block vote on behalf of the 120 000 members was less sure as a degree of factionalism entered the workings of the regional committee. The GMB has remained steadfastly reliable as far as Labour has been concerned under both Jimmy Morrell, Scottish secretary 1978–89, and after him, Robert Thomson. He forged a political relationship with another Robert Thomson who became Scottish national officer of NUPE (National Union of Public Employees) in 1990, having been chairman of Labour's Scottish executive committee the previous year. The 110 000 member GMB and 65 000 member NUPE became an important axis of power. But the AEU, with 80 000 members remains a critical force. It is a relatively centralized union with many of the power lines from Scotland running back to the office of Gavin Laird, general secretary since 1982 and whose union career began as a shop steward in the long-vanished Clydebank Singers factory. Since a union reorganization in the late 1980s, the AEU's Scottish political officer, Bill Tynan, who has also sat on the Scottish executive, has been an important figure. A much-discussed merger between the AEU and the electricians' union EEPTU would create a significant force, but even that would be outweighed by a bigger proposal for NUPE to merge with the local government union NALGO (National and Local Government Officers' Association) and the health workers' union COHSE (Confederation of Health Service Employees).

Important though the Labour Party is to the unions, their own focus of activity is the Scottish Trades Union Congress (STUC), a body which has autonomy and a quite different character from the TUC. The STUC, which has in its membership unions not affiliated to the Labour Party such as NALGO and the teachers unions the EIS (Educational Institute of Scotland) and SSTA (Scottish Secondary Teachers Association), is no Labour Party poodle, although the very wide range of policies it adopts at its annual congresses are fairly closely aligned to that of the Labour Party. In general, the STUC proved more reluctant than the Labour Party in the late 1980s to abandon ideas of state intervention, but more enthusiastic about a Scottish parliament, and would certainly grant a Scottish parliament more powers than perhaps would delight a Labour Chancellor of the Exchequer.

In many ways that mixture of statism and devolution forms the core of Scottish socialism, and is typified by the old Communist Party (CP) and its influence on the Labour Party. The CP adopted support for the right of self-determination in 1964 and never budged from it. Through its activity among the engineers and shipworkers on the Clyde, and among the miners particularly in Fife where Willie Gallacher was MP for West Fife 1935–50, the CP drew great strength and some very talented individuals. Perhaps the most talented was James Milne, general secretary of the STUC 1975–84, but who had been influential long before that. Labour and the CP always accorded each other respect, summed up by Neil Kinnock's tribute to Mick McGahey when the miners' leader retired in 1987: 'We may have our differences, but divisions—never.' Milne and his STUC predecessor, James Jack, set a pattern of activity for the STUC which cemented it into the brickwork of Scottish society and is partly the reason the STUC managed, unlike the TUC, to survive the 1980s as a cohesive body. They saw the STUC as having a role wider than that of the Labour movement, as being a bridge to other sections of society for the Labour movement. Hence in 1972, the STUC organized a Scottish Assembly on unemployment, attended by 1 500 people from the Churches, business, all kinds of areas, and was then followed up by a Standing Commission chaired by the TGWU's Raymond MacDonald. It produced a report advocating various ideas for assisting the economy. The STUC general secretary since 1984, Campbell Christie, highly competent and from a public sector rather than industrial background, has worked hard in that tradition. He has been an energetic participant in the Constitutional Convention and was instrumental in the STUC organization in the late 1980s of a Standing Commission on the Scottish economy, chaired by the former Highlands and Island Development Board chairman Sir Kenneth Alexander.

The Labour movement is normally thought of as comprising the party and the trade unions, but in Scotland it has a large local authority component which grew enormously in the 1980s. In 1978, Labour had 176 regional, and 299 district, councillors. By 1990, the corresponding figures were 233 and 554, and Labour controlled 26 of the 53 districts, and also the big populous regions. In 1987, the party set up a Campaign Coordinating Committee, to link the many arms of the Labour movement together. Although it technically has no power in the constitutional structures, it brings together powerful people, and so has a shadowy influence on the direction and style of policy-making and campaigning. A typical meeting in 1991 would have been chaired by the chairman of the party's executive committee, engineering union official John Carty. Also from the executive would have been Anne McGuire, a long-standing constituency representative. Labour local authorities would have been represented by the former leader of Strathclyde Regional Council, Charles Gray, and Rosemary McKenna, Provost of Cumbernauld and Kilsyth. From the STUC there would have been Campbell Christie, his deputy Bill Spiers (also a former Labour executive chairman) and one member of the STUC general council. MPs would have been represented by Donald Dewar and his deputy, John Maxton. There would also have been a representative of the Co-operative Party, which is often overlooked, but probably has only slightly fewer members than the Scottish Liberal Democrats and is separately organized, although it attends Labour conferences as an affiliated organization.

At the centre of this web is the Scottish headquarters staff, particularly the Scottish party secretary, who since 1988 has been Murray Elder. Although his predecessor, Helen Liddell, was much admired by other party politicians for the disciplined appearance she gave the Scottish party, Elder is more respected, and wields more power, within the party. His dominance was asserted in 1991, when Jimmy Allison unexpectedly took early retirement. It was seen as a clash of personalities, and a victory for new-style politics over the old guard. It certainly confirmed Elder's supremacy, for Allison's successor as organizer, his assistant Gerald O'Brien, was very definitely junior in status. Elder's power was based on the very close relationship he formed with Donald Dewar, and also retained from his days as a parliamentary researcher to shadow cabinet members John Smith and Gordon Brown. He shared a flat in Edinburgh with the latter for a number of years. His strength, apart from his personal courage in coping with a heart transplant operation shortly after taking up the post, lay in his cool intellect, which helped convince Dewar to take Labour into the Constitutional Convention. One leading soft-left party figure commented: 'We all thought Murray was a clone of John Smith but he turned out to be quite radical.'

Neither the Scottish Liberal Democrats not the Scottish National Party have the financial resources of the Conservatives or the manpower of the Labour Party. But they have the enthusiasm of the small party with a committed goal, which when conditions are favourable, means they can make an impact beyond their size, as the SNP did in winning the Glasgow Govan by-election in November 1988 and the Liberal Democrats did in winning the Kincardine and Deeside by-election in November 1991.

The Scottish Liberal Democrat Party

The modern Liberal Democrat Party is a product of the old Liberal Party, which came close to expiring in the 1950s, and the Social Democratic Party (SDP), which came close to rupturing terminally the Labour Party in the 1980s. From 1950 until 1964, the Orkney and Shetland MP Jo Grimond was the party's only Scottish MP, becoming the UK party leader in 1956. Revival came throughout the UK with disenchantment at the end of the decade of Tory rule, a signal event in Scotland being Grimond's election in 1960 as rector of

Edinburgh University, a campaign run by two students, David Steel and Russell Johnston. Though the Social Democratic Party was derided in Scotland as a 'quiche and claret' party of the London suburbs, after the 1983 general election it drew half its parliamentary strength from Scotland. The founder, the former Labour Home Secretary Roy Jenkins, held the Glasgow Hillhead seat won in the 1982 by-election, Robert Maclennan's majority in Caithness and Sutherland was greatly improved by his defection from Labour to the SDP, and Charles Kennedy at the age of 23 came from nowhere (actually from post-graduate studies in the USA) to defeat Conservative Energy Minister Hamish Gray in Ross, Cromarty and Skye.

Though the Liberals and the SDP fought the 1987 election as the Alliance, they were chalk and cheese. The Liberals were grass-roots orientated and based on local campaigning, whereas the SDP were highly centralized and leader-orientated. The 1988 merger to create the Liberal Democrats was only partially successful in Scotland; some high profile SDP members like the former teaching union official turned public relations executive Denis Sullivan joined, but the SDP's hard-working Scottish organizer Arthur Adair did not. The resulting party is decidedly more Liberal than it is Social Democrat, particularly in the autonomy it has within the UK party structures, which are federal. The federal leader, strictly speaking, has no say over what the Scottish party does. Though Paddy Ashdown, and Sir David Steel as UK leader before him, enjoyed perfectly amicable relationships and did not interfere with the Scottish party, the potential for a schism, should interests diverge, is there. The Scottish party is passionately committed to Scottish home rule (a domestic affairs Scottish parliament in the UK), whereas the party in England has been rather more concerned with civil rights issues than with regional government for England.

From 1988 to 1992, the Scottish party was led by Malcolm Bruce, who was elected MP for Gordon in 1983. Bruce, an energetic former journalist, had to devote much time to internal reorganization and it was perhaps not until late 1991, when the Liberal Democrats won the Kincardine and Deeside by-election, that he merged with any kind of public profile. The difference between the sometimes impatient Bruce and the last leader of the Scottish Liberal Party, Russell (later Sir Russell) Johnston, who cultivated a friendly father-figure image and enjoyed eloquent oratory rather than committee meetings, perhaps sums up the difference between the old and the new parties.

There are two important central organs of the party. One is the 36-member Scottish executive, for which the party constituency associations elect 16 members and the conference delegates elect a further 13, including the chairman, the other is the 12-seat policy committee, for which four seats are elected by the conference, four by the executive, and the remaining four by the MPs. Thus the party leader is restrained from rising too high above the party. If power can be said to reside anywhere, it is probably mostly with the MPs. The nine MPs elected in 1987 were, remarkably, the most the party has had since the 1930s. When the number rose to 10 MPs with the Kincardine and

Deeside victory, it put the Liberal Democrats into second place in Scotland in terms of parliamentary representation. The Liberals were last in second place in the 1923 election. In the 1990s party, the MPs with most influence have tended to be Archy Kirkwood, David Steel's former research assistant who won Roxburgh and Berwick in 1983, the lawyer Menzies Campbell who became North-East Fife MP in 1987, and another lawyer, Jim Wallace, who inherited Jo Grimond's Orkney and Shetland fiefdom in 1983. All, but particularly Kirkwood, earned credit in the party for regular attendance at meetings of the Scottish executive.

The Scottish National Party

Although the Liberal Democrats had nine, then 10, MPs in the 1987–92 parliament, they regularly drew less media attention than did the SNP, a cause of much Liberal Democrat anger. This is partly because the Liberal Democrat MPs have to behave like a UK party intent on government and therefore must shadow the Government with a tenth of the manpower which Labour has available. The SNP, by contrast, treat the House of Commons merely as a soapbox which can be used periodically to gain attention for, and within, Scotland. The SNP also benefit from their history; in the 1970s they experienced explosive growth as no other political party in the UK, save Sinn Fein pre-Irish secession, has done. Watching for signs that the SNP could be about to repeat that trick is part of the media's undoubted fascination with the party.

But media commentators find the SNP difficult to understand. It is resolutely resistant to the usual analysis by division into left and right. There are left-wingers in the SNP, such as the former Labour MP Jim Sillars, and there are right-wingers, such as the former Conservative Party parliamentary candidate Iain Lawson. But within the party in the 1987–92 period they were close political allies and fervent advocates of the virtues of nationalization as a means of preventing the closure of the Ravenscraig steel works. As political scientist James Mitchell has pointed out, there are two other major divisions in the SNP. One is the movement–party division. The movement thesis would have an SNP bereft of policies other than those which are directed at achieving independence, and would envisage the SNP acting in an umbrella or catalytic role trying to persuade other parties to move down the independence road. Such was the position of the SNP in the early 1960s, until the conviction grew that it had to be a party with a political stance on the left of centre, as that seemed to be where the Scottish political centre of gravity lay. The other divide is the gradualist–fundamentalist division. In general terms, the gradualist believes that independence is achievable in a number of steps including devolution. But the fundamentalist sees devolution as a device to prevent independence and therefore to be resisted. The changing balance of opinion within the SNP on either sides of these divides is most clearly seen in the characters of its leaders, of whom there have been remarkably few.

William Wolfe, an accountant who became leader in 1969 in the wake of Winnie Ewing's dramatic Hamilton by-election victory in 1967, began the shift away from the movement ideal towards having a more thoroughgoing political platform. Though the SNP remained gradualist, and campaigned for devolution in 1979, the immediate backwash of the referendum and general election that year was to convert the party to fundamentalism, and to elect as leader one of its two remaining MPs, the hard-liner Gordon Wilson, MP for Dundee East 1974–87. The SNP discarded its support for devolution in favour of 'Independence, nothing less' but plunged into factional warfare. A grouping, called the 79 Group, argued that the party should have a sharper left-wing image and was critical of the fundamentalist position. It included some of the party's most able people: new recruit Jim Sillars and his wife-to-be Margo MacDonald, intellectuals Stephen Maxwell and Andrew Currie, and the future leaders such as Alex Salmond. But when they organized Labour-style 'slates' of candidates, the fundamentalists, led by Winnie Ewing, fought back. Salmond was among seven members expelled for a few months before the 1983 election.

From 1983, the SNP began to rebuild. Wilson, whose cheery, folksy manner belied his hard-line nationalism, was the first real politician to have been produced by the SNP. His achievement was mostly internal; he managed to steer the party towards a policy stance which bridged all the divides. His legal training made him more cautious than some of his colleagues would have liked. He was reluctant to take the party down the route of civil disobedience and into non-payment of the poll tax, a campaign which, however much it disrupted local authority finances, substantially boosted the SNP's profile after 1987. But his desire to maintain a broad church allowed Jim Sillars the room to put his case for the SNP to move to a new form of gradualism, that independence for Scotland should be sought within the context of the EC. The policy was adopted in 1988, and ironically, Europe, through the appointment of former Scottish Secretary Bruce Millan as a European commissioner, created the by-election which put Sillars back in parliament.

Sillars' political career has been a roller-coaster ride. He was picked out as a rising star by Labour and won the South Ayrshire by-election in 1970. In the mid-1970s, he split with Labour believing that much stronger devolution than was contemplated by the Labour Government was necessary. Searing in his excoriation of the SNP, he formed his own party, the Scottish Labour Party in 1976. It attracted only one other MP, Paisley's John Robertson, and far-left elements, particularly the International Marxist Group. The entryists destroyed the Scottish Labour Party and both Sillars and Robertson lost their seats in 1979. But Sillars remained one of the most effective platform orators in the UK, and when Gordon Wilson announced in 1989 that he was standing down, there was speculation that Sillars would bid for the leadership. He backed instead the Moray MP Margaret Ewing, who as Margaret Bain was MP for East Dumbartonshire 1974–79. She stood against Wilson's deputy, the hugely ambitious Alex Salmond, MP for Banff and Buchan. Salmond's hunger for the job, his disciplined campaign, and some suspicion about the motives of Mrs Ewing's backers, won him a comfortable victory.

Salmond was attracted into the SNP by William Wolfe's campaigns in his native West Lothian. He trained as an economist at St Andrews University, working successively for the Scottish Office and the Royal Bank of Scotland. His election as SNP leader at the age of 36 is testament enough to his political abilities, though his first year of office produced doubts about his facility for working with other people. Being a factional party, a leader's success lies in his ability to bridge divides and command allegiance from various groupings, particularly those represented on the national executive, elected annually by delegate votes at the conference. Within the executive, the party's senior office-bearers, the deputy leader, treasurer, secretary, and five vice-conveners for organization, local government, policy, publicity and administration (fund-raising) are especially important. Three groupings could be identified in the early 1990s, one of a socialist and European outlook around Jim Sillars, a second of a more traditionalist hue around Margaret Ewing, and the third around Mr Salmond himself. None was dominant, and all suffered set-backs in the 1992 general election, particularly the Sillars grouping when Sillars lost his Govan seat.

The 1992 Election

These differences were, however, swept aside in the pre-1992 election tide of nationalism which began when Sillars, and a close friend from Scottish Labour Party days, Alex Neil, then the party's publicity vice-convener, secured the services of film star Sean Connery. Connery did the voice-over for a party political broadcast in September 1991, which helped re-kindle public interest in the SNP. The flames were fanned by the Government's disaster in the Kincardine and Deeside by-election caused by the death of Tory liberal MP Alick Buchanan-Smith. Won by the Liberal Democrats, its novelty lay in the reduction in Scottish Tory MPs to nine, third place in terms of Scottish parliamentary strength, a position of unprecedented weakness for the governing party, and the new interest in the constitutional issue that the by-election provoked was evident by the time *The Scotsman* held a debate between the four party leaders in Edinburgh's Usher Hall in January. Some 5 000 applications for tickets were received, well beyond expectations. A few weeks earlier, news that the furnaces at the Ravenscraig steel works in Motherwell, the last living symbol of Scotland's heavy industrial past, were to be doused forever, pumped up the nationalist fire. At the end of January, the Scottish edition of *The Sun*, blazed from its front page 'Rise now and be a nation again'. Though it then sold 300 000 copies a day compared to the 750 000 copies of the Labour-supporting *Daily Record*, it was the first newspaper to back explicitly the cause of Scottish independence. A week later, an opinion poll for *The Scotsman* and Independent Television News found that support for independence had hit a historic high of 50 per cent among the Scottish electorate. With Scotland ablaze with constitutional ferment as it had not been since 1979, the scene was set for a showdown at the 1992 general election.

The election in Scotland was expected by politicians and pundits alike to produce another Conservative rout and a decisive step towards home rule. On polling day, the Conservative campaign team at the Leith party HQ bet each other on the number of seats the party would have. The most optimistic forecast was six, most thought three or four. The Scottish Secretary, Ian Lang, arrived in his Galloway and Upper Nithsdale constituency count looking like a beaten man. But he won, indeed all nine MPs held their seats, and moreover, Tories Raymond Robertson won Aberdeen South back from Labour, and George Kynoch took Kincardine & Deeside to end Liberal Democrat Nicol Stephen's brief parliamentary career.

The Conservatives' small gain of two seats and a 1.7 per cent increase in the share of the vote to 25.7 per cent was not enough to proclaim the death of the constitutional debate, but enough to win a breathing space for the Government, and certainly enough to demonstrate the residual appeal of Unionism. Mr Lang, in his first days back as Scottish Secretary, called for a new mood of tolerance in Scottish politics. He and the Prime Minister signalled that intention by moving their most abrasive minister, Michael Forsyth, to the obscurity of the Department of Employment, and bringing back the elderly and genial Dumfries MP Sir Hector Monro to the Scottish Office to join the courtly and courteous Lord James Douglas-Hamilton and the relaxed right-winger Allan Stewart. They also declared the constitutional dimension to be on their agenda by moving the Lord Advocate, Lord Fraser of Carmyllie, to the Scottish Office as Minister of State and, in an innovation, giving him specific responsibility for constitutional matters. To the left of the Conservative Party, and a most sociable and good-humoured man, he made it clear that the Government intended to move slowly and carefully on this matter.

Opposition parties were thrown into disarray, symptomized by the rapidity with which Labour's Donald Dewar took up the SNP's policy of seeking to demand a multi-option constitutional referendum between the Unionist status quo, a devolutionary Scottish parliament in the United Kingdom, and independence in Europe. The call was also backed by the Liberal Democrats, despite a feeling that they had suffered in their rural heartlands from being overly associated with Labour. Just as interesting was the sprouting of groups all with the same broad theme—that there should be unity amongst the parties seeking self-government, expressed in the appeal for a referendum. There was Common Cause, formed by writers such as Tom Nairn and William McIlvanney, prior to the election, at the Edinburgh home of Liberal Democrat vice-chairman Bob McCreadie, and intended to act as a fount of new ideas. There was Democracy for Scotland, formed hours after the election result by telephone calls between anti-nuclear, peace and environment campaigners mainly, and which initially resolved to maintain a vigil outside the would-be Parliament building in Edinburgh. But the noisiest and biggest was Scotland United, again formed within hours of the election, and which by Sunday 12 April had managed to mount a speech-and-music demonstration attended by 4 000–5 000 people in Glasgow's George Square. It was an interesting amalgam of the more nationalist leaning elements of the Labour Party, such as MPs George Galloway and John McAllion, and the nationalist elements of the music industry, such as popstars Pat Kane of Hue and Cry and Ricky Ross of Deacon Blue. Common to all groups was the notion that the Scottish self-government cause had been set back by internal divisions, rather than defeated by the Unionist case advanced by the Conservatives. Hence the argument was that 75 per cent of Scots had voted for parties espousing some form of self-government, and that the Conservatives with only 25 per cent of the vote had no mandate to govern Scotland. Therefore, the claim ran, Scots had the right to determine their own form of government, in this case, through a referendum. As such, the claim was essentially nationalist, a claim of self-determination for the Scottish nation, and, that it had an attraction beyond the ranks of the SNP, indicated there was a certain force in it.

But it was essentially following the route which after the 1987 election had led to the formation of the Constitutional Convention, itself the brainchild of a cross-party grouping which came together after the 1979 referendum and general election—the Campaign for a Scottish Assembly. They were determined to resolve the problem they believed had bedevilled the referendum—political division. The CSA's active membership was later to include James Ross, the Scottish Office civil servant who had been responsible for devolution in the 1970s. Largely through his influence, the CSA had produce a report *A Claim of Right* which was instrumental in persuading Donald Dewar, prior to the Govan by-election, to commit Labour to participation in a gathering of all those main forces in Scottish life who sought self-government. The SNP and the Conservatives did not take part, but the Liberal Democrats did, as did the trade unions, all the leading church denominations, and nearly all of the local authorities. In its initial membership of 49 Labour and 9 Liberal Democrat MPs plus the bodies mentioned above, the Convention claimed to be widely representative. Its public face came to be an eloquent Episcopalian churchman, Canon Kenyon Wright. Essentially it represented those elements of Scottish society which had been shut out of power (trade unions), or felt themselves threatened (local authorities), or believed their values were under assault (churches) by the Conservative government. It was also founded on a nationalist perspective, its participants signing a declaration acknowledging 'the sovereign right of the Scottish people to determine the form of Government best suited to their needs'. That turned out to be its great weakness, for although the Convention's three years of work in drafting a scheme for a Scottish Parliament served to drag Labour unexpectedly quickly towards electoral reform in general and proportional representation in particular, it failed to address the question of how the links with the rest of the United Kingdom would be affected. These questions—the role and number of MPs at Westminster, the role of the Scottish Secretary, and the financial relationship between the London and Edinburgh exchequers – were relentlessly probed by the Conservatives. Labour's and the Liberal Democrats' plans were also portrayed by the Conservatives as separatism by another name, a line of attack which proved highly effective, especially in north-east Scotland, where claims of central belt domination (the Red Clydeside card) were deployed effectively.

Divisions within Scottish society are certainly part of the reason why a Scottish Assembly or Scottish Parliament has not yet emerged from the restless ferment since the 1970s. It is not simply because the pro self-government lobby is divided, it is also the case that there is a substantial body of opinion which does not want Scottish home rule. But more fundamentally, the 1992 election proved the truth of a verdict passed by the distinguished politician and academic John P Mackintosh in his 1976 pamphlet *A Parliament for Scotland*: 'In practice, the Scots have developed a dual nationality; they are both Scottish and British. Some of the institutions that matter are peculiar to Scotland and create a sense of identity, while others – such as the tradition of Parliamentary democracy – are purely British.' As yet, no-one seems to have come up with proposals which satisfy voters' Scottish and British identities. The debate will go on.

Results by region of the March 1, 1979, Referendum on the question: 'Do you want the provisions of the Scotland Act 1978 to be put into effect?'

Region	Yes			No			Turnout
	Total Votes	% of those voting	% of total electorate	Total Votes	% of those voting	% of total electorate	
Borders	20 746	40.3	26.7	30 780	59.7	39.7	66.4
Central	71 296	54.7	36.1	59 105	45.3	29.9	65.9
Dumfries and Galloway	27 162	40.3	25.8	40 239	59.7	38.3	64.1
Fife	86 252	53.7	35.1	74 436	46.3	30.3	65.3
Grampian	94 944	48.3	27.6	101 485	51.6	29.5	57.2
Highland	44 973	51.0	33.0	43 274	49.0	31.7	64.7
Lothian	187 221	50.1	33.0	186 421	49.9	32.9	65.9
Strathclyde	596 519	54.0	33.7	508 599	46.0	28.7	62.5
Tayside	91 482	49.5	31.2	93 325	50.5	31.8	63.0
Orkney	2 104	27.9	15.1	5 639	72.1	39.0	54.1
Shetland	2 020	27.0	13.6	5 466	73.0	36.7	49.7
Western Isles	6 218	55.8	27.8	4 933	44.2	22.1	50.1
Scotland	1 230 937	51.6	32.5	1 153 502	.48.4	30.4	62.9

Source: H M Drucker and N Drucker (eds), *Scottish Government Yearbook 1980*, Paul Harris, Edinburgh, 1979

General Elections 1945–92 Summary of Results

	Labour		Conservative		Lib/All/Dem		Scot Nat		
	MPs	% Scottish (English)	MPs	% Scottish (English)	MPs	% Scottish (English)	MPs	%	Government
1945	40	48 (48)	27	41 (40)	0	5 (9)	0	1	Labour
1950	37	46 (46)	31	45 (44)	2	7 (9)	0	0.4	Labour
1951	35	48 (49)	35	48 (49)	1	3 (2)	0	0.3	Conservative
1955	35	47 (47)	36	50 (50)	1	2 (3)	0	0.5	Conservative
1959	38	47 (44)	31	47 (50)	1	4 (6)	0	0.8	Conservative
1964	43	49 (44)	24	41 (44)	4	7 (12)	0	2	Labour
1966	46	50 (48)	20	38 (43)	5	7 (9)	0	5	Labour
1970	44	44 (43)	23	38 (48)	3	5 (8)	1	11	Conservative
1974 Feb	40	37 (38)	21	33 (40)	3	8 (21)	7	22	Labour
1974 Oct	41	36 (40)	16	25 (39)	3	8 (20)	11	30	Labour
1979	44	42 (37)	22	31 (47)	3	9 (15)	2	17	Conservative
1983	41	35 (27)	21	28 (46)	8	25 (26)	2	12	Conservative
1987	50	42 (30)	10	24 (46)	9	19 (23)	3	14	Conservative
1992	49	39 (35)	11	26 (46)	9	13 (19)	3	21	Conservative

Note: Numerals refer to results in Scotland, both in share of the vote and seats won, italics to party vote shares in England.
The final column headed Government indicates which party formed the Government after the election, and the lines indicated in bold show where the result in Scotland was in broad agreement with the overall outcome of the General Election.

Source: James Kellar, *The Scottish Political System*, 4th edn, Cambridge University Press, 1989 and *The Scotsman* General Election Results, 11 April 1992.

Index

Index

Index

401

Index

Index

417

Index